Understanding Art

Teacher's Wraparound Edition

Glencoe
McGraw-Hill

New York, New York   Columbus, Ohio   Woodland Hills, California   Peoria, Illinois

About the Authors

Gene Mittler

Gene Mittler is one of the authors of Glencoe's middle school/junior high art series, *Introducing Art, Exploring Art,* and *Understanding Art*. He is also author of *Art in Focus*, a chronological approach to art for Glencoe's senior high program, and *Creating and Understanding Drawings*. He has taught at both the elementary and secondary levels and at Indiana University. He received an M.F.A. in sculpture from Bowling Green State University and a Ph.D. in art education from Ohio State University. He has authored grants and published numerous articles in professional journals and has lectured in the United States and abroad. Dr. Mittler is currently Professor Emeritus at Texas Tech University.

Rosalind Ragans

Rosalind Ragans is one of the authors of Glencoe's middle school/junior high art series, *Introducing Art, Exploring Art,* and *Understanding Art*. She served as senior author on the elementary program *Art Connections* for the SRA division of McGraw-Hill, and wrote the multi-level, comprehensive *ArtTalk* text for Glencoe's senior high program. She received a B.F.A. at Hunter College, CUNY, New York, and earned a M.Ed. in Elementary Education at Georgia Southern College and a Ph.D. in Art Education at the University of Georgia. Dr. Ragans has taught art in grades K-12, and has earned several honors including National Art Educator of the Year for 1992. She is currently Associate Professor of Art Education Emerita at Georgia Southern University.

Glencoe/McGraw-Hill

A Division of The **McGraw·Hill** *Companies*

Send all inquiries to:
Glencoe/McGraw-Hill
21600 Oxnard Street, Suite 500
Woodland Hills, CA 91367

ISBN 0-02-662359-5 (Student Text)
ISBN 0-02-662361-7 (Teacher's Wraparound Edition)

Printed in the United States of America.

3 4 5 6 7 8 9   004/043   03 02 01 00 99

Table of Contents

New Directions in the Visual and Performing Arts

Teaching art goes well beyond the excitement of watching students analyze works of master artists or produce their own creations. You know that every child who identifies a work of a master artist, picks up a paint brush, or molds a lump of clay will do more. Students involved in a quality, comprehensive arts program will learn to convey ideas, feelings, and emotions. They will sharpen their ability to analyze, critique, and make informed judgments. Through a quality arts experience, all students benefit as they are encouraged to ask questions, to think, to learn, and to CREATE!

A quality, comprehensive art program enriches student's lives and allows for discovery and creative problem solving. It provides students with a broader perception of their environment and a greater understanding of historical and cultural perspectives. In the process, a quality art program cultivates learners who are able to make positive contributions to society.

Glencoe Addresses the New Directions

Glencoe addresses the new directions by providing three programs designed specifically for the middle school student. These comprehensive programs are structured around the belief that students learn best in a classroom that is engaging, meaningful, and focused on art as a core curriculum subject, one that is built on their everyday experiences and enriches their learning in all areas.

Providing a Comprehensive Art Program

▶ Each book in the series allows teachers to customize their lesson plans around a specific emphasis—the study of themes in art, art media and techniques, or the chronology and history of art.

▶ All programs in the series are similar in their presentation of historical and cultural boundaries particular to the study of art.

▶ Each text is sequentially developed in order that art can be taught as a core subject.

▶ Regular features throughout each text provide students the opportunity to see how art is integrated with other disciplines.

▶ All programs cover a wide range of media, techniques, processes, and artistic styles.

Integrating the Four Components

▶ **Artistic Perception** At the very center of arts instruction is the process of being able to talk about works of art and learning the basic skills and knowledge necessary to communicate in each art form. By learning the elements and principles of art, working with various media, and evaluating master artists' works, students develop an awareness of and appreciation for the presence of art both within the classroom and in their everyday experiences.

▶ **Creative Expression** Studio lessons and studio activities give students the opportunity to create works of art and use various media and techniques, including computers.

▶ **Historical and Cultural Context** Throughout the programs, works of art from various periods, styles, and cultural groups develop a broad base for students to celebrate cultural diversity and understand various global views.

▶ **Aesthetic Valuing** As students explore, theorize, and apply the principles of aesthetics and art criticism to their own art work and the art work of others, they formulate a lifelong appreciation and satisfying experience in the arts.

Linking the Performing Arts and Other Curriculum Areas

▶ **Music, Dance, Theatre** The visual and performing arts are mutually reinforcing. Glencoe's art programs are designed to underscore that unity by presenting the exploration of art as it correlates to the performing arts. Students experience how the foundation of all areas of art are built upon corresponding concepts, whether those concepts are basic skills or cultural and historical contexts.

▶ **Cross-Curriclum Connections** The art classroom provides an exciting opportunity to make connections between visual arts and other curriculum areas. Students learn how concepts in one subject area, in this case art, can enhance and increase their interest in and knowledge of other subject areas. Throughout Glencoe's middle school art programs, students make connections that translate across a wide range of curriculum areas—math, science, social studies, and language arts.

Addressing The National Standards for Arts Education

The National Standards for Arts Education provide guidelines that set benchmark stardards for grade-appropriate competency in the performing and visual arts. The Glencoe art programs are correlated to the National Standards (see Scope and Sequence on pages TM 8-14), and can help teachers design their lessons around the National Standards.

Expanding the Arts Through Technology

Advances in technology offer exciting opportunities to art teachers and students. Through videodiscs, CD-ROMs, and the Internet, students can sharpen their visual perception. With computer art programs, student push the limits of their creative expression beyond their expectations. New activities and resource components provided with the Glencoe art programs provide a range of technology options that encourage exploration of new possibilities both in art education and production.

Including Assessment Strategies

Throughout the Glencoe art programs, students are encouraged to keep sketchbooks and to develop a portfolio featuring their selected works of art. In addition, the frequent self-examination of completed art works provides ongoing evaluation of each student's progress, fostering a sense of accomplishment and a commitment to high standards of art production, and preparing them for the transition to excellence in the work place.

Meeting the Needs of All Students

Believing that art is for all students, the Glencoe middle school art programs include activities and teaching strategies that help teachers adapt the art classroom to the specific needs of students. This inclusive approach reinforces the universal value of art education.

Glencoe answers the challenge to the new directions in art education with a 3-text middle school art series. This Series at a Glance displays a complete listing of chapters in the series.

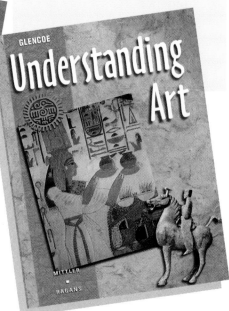

National Standards for the Visual Arts

The National Standards for Art Education represents, in part, the results of a 2-year effort by the Consortium of National Arts Education Associations to set standards for arts education in the United States. These six standards listed below are designed specifically for students in grades 5-8.

1. **Content Standard:** Understanding and applying media, techniques, and processes
   Achievement Standard:
   Students
   a. select media, techniques, and processes; analyze what makes them effective or not effective in communicating ideas; and reflect upon the effectiveness of their choices
   b. intentionally take advantage of the qualities and characteristics of art media, techniques, and processes to enhance communication of their experiences and ideas

2. **Content Standard:** Using knowledge of structures and functions
   Achievement Standard:
   Students
   a. generalize about the effects of visual structures and functions and reflect upon these effects in their own work
   b. employ organizational structures and analyze what makes them effective or not effective in the communication of ideas
   c. select and use the qualities of structures and functions of art to improve communication of their ideas

3. **Content Standard:** Choosing and evaluating a range of subject matter, symbols and ideas
   Achievement Standard:
   Students
   a. integrate visual, spatial, and temporal concepts with content to communicate intended meaning in their artworks
   b. use subjects, themes, and symbols that demonstrate knowledge of contexts, values, and aesthetics that communicate intended meaning in artworks

4. **Content Standard:** Understanding the visual arts in relation to history and cultures
   Achievement Standard:
   Students
   a. know and compare the characteristics of artworks in various eras and cultures
   b. describe and place a variety of art objects in historical and cultural contexts
   c. analyze, describe, and demonstrate how factors of time and place (such as climate, resources, ideas, and technology) influence visual characteristics that give meaning and value to a work of art

5. **Content Standard:** Reflecting upon and assessing the characteristics and merits of their work and the work of others
   Achievement Standard:
   Students
   a. compare multiple purposes for creating works of art
   b. analyze contemporary and historic meanings in specific artworks through cultural and aesthetic inquiry
   c. describe and compare a variety of individual responses to their own artworks and to artworks from various eras and cultures

6. **Content Standard:** Making connections between visual arts and other disciplines
   Achievement Standard:
   Students
   a. compare the characteristics of works in two or more art forms that share similar subject matter, historical periods, or cultural context
   b. describe ways in which the principles and subject matter of other disciplines taught in the school are interrelated with the visual arts

Reprinted by permission.

To identify how the lessons and activities in each chapter of *Understanding Art* meet these national standards, the Scope and Sequence on pages TM8–14 and each chapter opening page of the Teacher's Wraparound Edition displays the following abbreviated form for quick reference.

NATIONAL STANDARDS

This chapter addresses the following National Standards for the Visual Arts:

1.	(a, b)	**4.**	(a, b, c)
2.	(a, b, c)	**5.**	(a, b, c)
3.	(a, b)	**6.**	(a, b)

(R) = Chapter Review (CC) = Connections Feature (1), (2), (3) etc. = Lessons	Chapter 1 The Language of Art	Chapter 2 The Media of Art
NATIONAL STANDARDS FOR THE VISUAL ARTS	1. (a,b) 3. (a,b) 5. (a,b) 2. (a,b) 4. (c) 6. (b)	1. (a,b,c) 3. (a) 5. (a,b,c) 2. (a,b) 4. (a,b,c) 6. (a,b)
ARTISTIC PERCEPTION	Recognize elements of art (1) Analyzing non-objective art (2) Interpreting Lindner's *Rock-Rock* (3) Capturing ideas in images (4)	Define medium of art (1) Describe drawing (1) Describe painting (1) Evaluating computer art (2) Recognizing crafts as applied art (3)
CREATIVE EXPRESSION	Using elements of art (2) Using principles of art (4) Computer options (2,4)	Creating mixed media design (2) Computer option (2) Drawing computer landscape (4)
HISTORICAL/CULTURAL CONTEXT	Realism, Harnett (1) Use of color, Chagall (1) Non-objective art (2) Creating mood (3) Movement in art (3) Simple images (4)	Sketching (1) Chinese printmaking (1) Relief sculpture (3) Early crafts (3)
AESTHETIC VALUING	Effect of lines (1) Examining Your Work (2,4)	Seeing difference in media (1) Examining Your Work (2,4)
ELEMENTS AND PRINCIPLES OF ART	Introducing elements (1) Defining elements (1) Using elements (2) Introducing principles (3) Defining principles (3) Using principles (4)	Line in printmaking (1) Blending values in lithography (1) In mixed media design (2) Movement in sculptural design (3) In computer art (1,4)
ART FORMS	Paintings (1,2,3,4) Drawings (2,4)	Drawing (1) Mixed-media (2) Painting (1) Sculpture (3) Printmaking (1) Architecture (3) Computer art (1) Crafts (3)
MEDIA, TOOLS, TECHNIQUES, AND PROCESSES	Drawing media (2) Painting media (4) Use of color (1)	Pastels (1) Pencil (1) Paint media: watercolor, Acrylic, oils, tempera (1) Mixed media (2) Electronic media (2,4,CC) Pottery, weaving, glassblowing (3)
CURRICULUM AND PERFORMING ARTS CONNECTIONS	Language arts (R) Science (R,CC)	Social studies (R) Science (R) Technology (CC)
CAREERS/PORTFOLIOS	Portfolio Ideas (1)	Portfolio ideas (1)
SAFETY	Reviewing paint safety labels (4)	

Chapter 3 Aesthetics, Art Criticism, and Art History	Chapter 4 Art of Earliest Times	Chapter 5 Art of the Far East
1. (a,b) 3. (a,b) 5. (b,c) 2. (a,c) 4. (a,b,c) 6. (b)	1. (a,b) 3. (a,b) 5. (b,c) 2. (a,b,c) 4. (a,b,c) 6. (b)	1. (a,b) 3. (a,b) 5. (b,c) 2. (a,b,c) 4. (a,b,c) 6. (b)
Art criticism (1) Subject, composition, and content views (1) Art historian views (3)	Perceiving images (1) Understanding Stone Age life (1) Interpreting Egyptian painting (3) Explaining hieroglyphics (3) Understanding Mesopotamian culture (4)	Perceive defined (1)
Extending an expressive painting (2) Creating a Cubist painting (4)	Finding an image in natural form (1) Creating earth pigment painting (2) Designing hieroglyphic system (3) Creating a picture story (4) Computer options (2,5)	Making a scroll (2) Creating clay time capsule (4)
Defining art history (3) Steps art historians use (3) Cubism (4)	Culture defined (1) Old Stone Age, New Stone Age (1) Cave paintings (1) Stonehenge (1) Ancient Egyptian life (3) Hieroglyphics (3) Chinese history (3) Ancient Indian culture (4) Mesopotamian culture (4) Mohenjo-Daro (4) Sumerian writing system (4) Prehistoric art (1) Egyptian art style (3)	Chinese inventions (1) Chinese dynasties (1) Buddhist influences (1) Scroll defined (1) Buddhism (1) Japanese culture (3) Korean influence (3) Ukiyo-e and Yamato-e (3)
Defining art criticism (1) Steps in art criticism (1) Aesthetic view defined (1) Steps of art historians (3) Examining Your Work (2,4)	Culture defined (1) Crafts and architecture (1) Examining Your Work (2,5)	Recognizing cultural influences (1) Understanding role of religions (3) Preserving culture in art (4) Examining Your Work (2,4)
Describing the elements in a work (1) Using in Cubist style painting (4)	Balance, harmony in ancient vase (1) Shapes in hieroglyphics (3) Egyptian style, no depth of space (5) Proportion in Egyptian art (5)	Observing line, form, texture (1) Blue pigment vases (1) Use of space (2) Strong lines, flat areas (3)
Painting	Painting Cave paintings (1) Architecture (1,3,4) Hieroglyphic system (3)	Painting (1,2,3) Printmaking (3) Sculpture (1,3,4) Architecture (3)
Sketching (2, 4) Tempera paints (2, 4) Non-objective style (1) Realistic style (2,3)	Natural objects (1) Natural pigments (2) Pencil, paper (3) Watercolors (5)	Natural object, brush, ink (1) Paper, pencil, watercolor (2) Acrylics (3) Clay supplies, fabric, scissors (4) Drawing with brush and ink (1) Designing patterns (3) Clay slab (4)
Social studies (R) Language arts (R) Social studies (CC)	Math (R) Social studies (R) Science (CC)	Language Arts (R, CC) Social Studies (R) Nō Drama defined (3) Kabuki theater defined (3)
Portfolio ideas (1)	Portfolio ideas (1,3)	Portfolio ideas (1,3)
		Using markers (2)

(R) = Chapter Review (CC) = Connections Feature (1), (2), (3) etc. = Lessons	Chapter 6 Art of Pre-Columbian America	Chapter 7 Art of Greece and Rome
NATIONAL STANDARDS FOR THE VISUAL ARTS	1. (a,b) 3. (a,b) 5. (b,c) 2. (a,b,c) 4. (b,c) 6. (a,b)	1. (a,b) 3. (a) 5. (b,c) 2. (a,b,c) 4. (a,b,c) 6. (a,b)
ARTISTIC PERCEPTION	Genre defined (1) Recognizing Pre-Columbian contributions (1,3) Using stylized designs (4)	Interpret and judge architecture (4) Contributions of Greek artists (1) Contributions of Roman art, artists (3)
CREATIVE EXPRESSION	Making a clay urn (2) Making stylized motif (4) Computer option (4)	Symmetrical vase (1) Painting a vase design (2) Designing triumphal arch (3) Model for an arch (4) Computer option (2)
HISTORICAL/CULTURAL CONTEXT	Pre-Columbian defined (1) Early Mexican cultures (1) Olmec artifacts (1) West Mexican effigy (1) Mayan culture (1) Aztec culture (1) Art in the Andes (3) Chavin culture (3) Tiahuanaco culture (3) Incan culture (3)	Greek culture (1) Athens influence (1) Roman culture (3) Intention of concrete (3) Rounded arches (3) Roman aqueducts, arches (3)
AESTHETIC VALUING	Comparing pottery (3) Examining Your Work (2,4)	Aesthetics of Greek amphora (1) Lifelike sculpture (2,3) Examining Your Work (2,4)
ELEMENTS AND PRINCIPLES OF ART	Balance in headdress (1) Balance in Mayan architecture (1) Formal balance, repeating patterns (2) Shapes in weaving (3) Elements and principles in designing motif (4) Unity and harmony (4)	Shapes in Greek vases (1) Movement (2) Pantheon light source (3) Balance of the arch (4) Elements in architecture (4)
ART FORMS	Genre painting (1) Artifacts (1) Architecture (1) Motifs (2) Crafts (3) Monolith defined (3)	Sculpture (1,3) Architecture (1,3,4)
MEDIA, TOOLS, TECHNIQUES, AND PROCESSES	Clay and modeling (2) Joining with slip (2) Sketch paper, construction paper (4) Glue, scissors (4)	Paper, scissors (1,3) Painting (2) Black tempera (2) Realistic figure sculpture (2,3) Sketching design (3) Cereal box, construction paper (4)
CURRICULUM AND PERFORMING ARTS CONNECTIONS	Language Arts (R) Social Studies (R, CC)	Health (CC) Social Studies (R) Language Arts (R)
CAREERS/PORTFOLIOS	Portfolio ideas (1)	Portfolio ideas (1,3)
SAFETY	Glazing (optional) (2)	Using safe paints (2) Handling cutting tools (4)

Chapter 8 Art of India and Islam	Chapter 9 Art of Africa	Chapter 10 Art of the Middle Ages
1. (a,b) 3. (a,b) 5. (b,c) 2. (a,b,c) 4. (c) 6. (a,b)	1. (a,b) 4. (a,b,c) 6. (a,b) 3. (a,b) 5. (b,c)	1. (a,b) 3. (a,b) 5. (a,b,c) 2. (b) 4. (a,b,c) 6. (a,b)
Recognizing influences of Hinduism, Buddhism (1) Hindu sculpture design (2) Islamic cultural influences on art (3)	Interpreting sculpture (1) Abstract work defined (1) Spiritual meaning of sculptures (2) Interpreting face masks (3)	Understanding stained glass art (3) Lifelike painting by Giotto (3) Imaginary proportion of Gargoyles (4)
Creating a tree of life (1) Making dancing figure cutouts (2) Persian weaving (3) Islamic collage (4) Computer option (4)	Drawing a self-image (1) Making abstract cutout (2) Designing a mask (3) Making papier-mâché mask (4) Computer option (4)	Creating illuminations (1) Designing a castle (2) Rose window design (3) Making Gothic Gargoyle (4)
Hinduism described (1) Buddha sculpture (1) Book illustration (1,3) Shiva introduced (2) Islamic culture (3) Muhammad historical influence (3) Mosques, mihrabs, minarets defined (3)	African cultures (1) Tribal traditions (1,3) African face mask, headpieces, shoulder masks (3) Tyi Wara legend (3) Kente cloth tradition (CC)	Middle Ages (1) Fall of Roman Empire (1) Christianity in Middle Ages (1) Illuminations defined (1) Castle design (2) Cathedrals (3) Pointed arch, flying buttress (3) Gothic painting and crafts (3)
Interpreting Indian sculpture (1) Interpreting Hindu sculpture (2) Reasons for Islamic design (3) Examining Your Work (2,4)	Defining abstract (1) Examining Your Work (2,4)	Interpreting church sculpture, art (1) Romanesque times affected art (1) Examining Your Work (2,4)
Balance in Hindu sculpture (1) Movement in drawing figures (2) Elements of Islamic painting (4) Balance and harmony (4)	Mood with texture and composition (1) Texture and pattern in bronze (1) Movement in masks (3) Line in masks (3) Shape and form in sculpture (2) Elements used in headpiece (3) Line and shape in masks (4)	Line in Church architecture (1) Elements in illuminations (1) Elements of art in castle design (2) Radial balance in rose window (3) Emphasis in Giotto's work (3) Texture in gargoyles (4)
Arabesques (3) Architecture and sculpture (1,3) Painting (1,3) Calligraphy (3) Weaving (3)	Abstract sculptures (1) Bronze sculpture (1) Figure sculptures (2) Masks (3,4)	Romanesque architecture (1,2) Sculpture (1) Illumination (1) Gothic architecture (3) Stained glass (3) Sculpture (4)
Stone carving (1) Fine-tipped markers (1) Sketching, tempera paints (2) Yarn, Persian carpet weaving (3) Islamic miniatures (4) Collage (4)	Sketch paper (1) Wood carving (1) Bronze casting (1) Paper cutout (2) Scissors, tempera, brushes, gloss (2) Cardboard sculpture (3) Papier-mâché (4)	Oil pastels, drawing (1) Cardboard, assembling (2) Construction paper, chalk, tissue paper, glue (3) Clay supplies, modeling (4)
Dancing position (2) Social Studies (R) Language Arts (R) Math (CC)	Social Studies (R,CC) Science (R)	Language arts (R) Social Studies (R,CC)
Portfolio ideas (1,3)	Portfolio ideas (1,3)	Portfolio ideas (1,3)
	Avoiding unsafe paste (4)	

(R) = Chapter Review (CC) = Connections Feature (1), (2), (3) etc. = Lessons	Chapter 11 Art of the Renaissance	Chapter 12 European Art of the 1600s and 1700s
NATIONAL STANDARDS FOR THE VISUAL ARTS	1. (a,b) 3. (b) 5. (b,c) 2. (a,b) 4. (b,c) 6. (a,b)	1. (a,b) 3. (a,b) 5. (b) 2. (a,b,c) 4. (a,b) 6. (a,b)
ARTISTIC PERCEPTION	Vanishing point, linear perspective (1) Describing the Mona Lisa (1) Madonna defined (1) Describing Pietà (1) Illusion of space (2) Understanding symbolism (3)	Realism of Caravaggio (1) Expressive painting, Rembrandt (2) Imaginary sound, Watteau (3) Painting with affection, Chardin (3) Shocking war scenes, Goya (3)
CREATIVE EXPRESSION	Making triangular design (1) Pencil drawing (2) Precise detail drawing (3) Designing visual symbol (4) Computer options (2,4)	Drawing expressive hands (2) Painting common object (3) Constructing Rococo shoe (4) Computer option (2)
HISTORICAL/CULTURAL CONTEXT	Renaissance (1) Florence during Renaissance (1) Art of Northern Renaissance (3) Flanders (3) Oil paint defined (3) Precision in van Eyck's work (3) Emotion in art by van der Weyden (3)	Protestant Reformation (1) Counter-Reformation (1) Baroque defined (1) Dutch Genre painting (1) Portrait defined (1) Paris as center of art (3) Louis XIV and art (3) Versailles (3) Rococo art, Watteau (3,4) Domestic scenes (3) Etching defined (3)
AESTHETIC VALUING	Interpreting church sculpture, art (1) Romanesque times affected art (1) Examining Your Work (2,4)	Expressing mood in drawing (3) Make-believe world of Rococo (3) Expressing mood (3) Examining Your Work (2,4)
ELEMENTS AND PRINCIPLES OF ART	Balance in Renaissance sculpture (1) Values of complementary hues (1) Linear perspective (1) Value in da Vinci's work (1) Balance in triangle or pyramid plan (1) Proportion in Michelangelo sculpture (1) Line and texture in drawing (2) Overlapping to show space (2) Shape in visual symbol (4)	Church design (1) Movement, Rubens (1) Line to create mood (1) Flowing movement of Baroque (1) Light, Caravaggio (1) Shading for three dimensions (2) Color, form, texture in drawing (3) Color, shape, texture in design (4)
ART FORMS	Portraits (1) Sculpture (1) Still life (2) Symbolism (4)	Architecture (1,3) Portraits (1,3) Etching (3) Art in fashion design (4)
MEDIA, TOOLS, TECHNIQUES, AND PROCESSES	Pencil, paper, ruler, paint 1,2) Detail drawing (3) Oil paint discovered (3) Paint, design tools (4)	Paper, construction paper, crayon (2) Found object, pencil, paper, tempera (3) Cardboard, scissors, glue, scraps (4)
CURRICULUM AND PERFORMING ARTS CONNECTIONS	Math (CC) Language arts (R) Social Studies (R)	Music (R,CC) Social Studies (R)
CAREERS/PORTFOLIOS	Portfolio ideas (1,3)	Portfolio ideas (1,3)
SAFETY		

Chapter 13 Native American Art	Chapter 14 European Art of the Early 1800s	Chapter 15 Art of the Late Nineteenth Century
1. (a,b) 3. (a,b) 5. (a,b) 2. (a) 4. (a,b,c) 6. (a,b)	1. (a,b) 3. (a,b) 5. (b,c) 2. (a,b,c) 4. (c) 6. (a,b)	1. (a,b) 3. (b) 6. (a,b) 2. (a,b,c) 5. (a,b,c)
Natural resources () Symbols of nature (1)	Dramatic and exotic expression(1) Landscape (1) Communicating mood (1) Importance of the Salon (3) Understanding Impressionism (3) Center of interest (3)	Creating mood, Degas (1) Realism, Eakins (3) Storytelling in art, Homer (3) Dreamlike images, Ryder (3) Impressionism, Cassatt (3)
Painting a story (1) Round weaving (2) Inuit-style print (4) Computer option (4)	Sketching a mood (1) Designing stage set (2) Drawing point of interest (3) Painting a landscape (4) Computer option (4)	Drawing with color patches (1) Post-Impressionist painting (2) Using texture in drawing (3) Expressive watercolor (4) Computer option (2,4)

Native American cultures (1)
 Pueblo, Northwest Coast, Plains,
  Woodlands Petroglyphs (1)
Totem pole defined (1)
Contemporary American art (3)
Kachina traditions (3
Polychrome pots (3)
Sand painting (3)
Culture in contemporary sculpture,
  painting (3)
	French Revolution (1)
	Neoclassic art (1)
	Romantic Art (1)
	Landscapes, Turner (1)
	Salon (3)
	Art Movement defined (3)
	Impressionist painting (3)
	Use of light, Monet (3)
	Portraits, Renoir (3)
	Capturing mood, Morisot (3)
	Uneven surface sculpture, Rodin (3)
		Post-Impressionism defined (1)
		Color patches, Cézanne (1)
		Capturing feeling, van Gogh 1)
		Unusual color, Gauguin (1)
		Pointillism, Seurat (1)
		American art introduced (3)
		Realism defined (3)

Aesthetics, traditional and contemporary (3) Abstract sand painting (3) Traditions in crafts (3) Examining Your Work (2,4)	Exotic subjects, Romanticism (1) Impressionism view (3) Examining Your Work (2,4)	Aesthetics of Post-Impressionism (1) Feelings in art (3) Examining Your Work (2,4)
Shape in design (1) Color and pattern in weaving (2) Color and pattern in painting (2) Balance in Kenojuak print (4) Line, shape, and color, Howe (3,4)	Use of line, Delacroix (1) Elements in a stage set (2) Texture, Rodin (3) Color for emphasis (3) Use of color, Monet (4) Color, value, intensity (4) Warm and cool colors (4)	Brush strokes to show form (1) Arbitrary and optical color (1) Texture in drawing (3) Elements, principles in painting (4) Harmony with colors, Cézanne (1) Texture and color, van Gogh (1) Light source, Ryder (1) Light and mood, Cassatt (3) Hue, value, shape, Tanner (4)
Petroglyphs (1) Totems (1) Hide paintings (1) Pottery (3)	Painting (1,2,3,4) Sketch (1) Stage set design (2) Impressionist painting (3,4)	Painting (1,2,3,4) Composition and content (1) Rubbing (3)
Weaving techniques (2) Molding and carving (3) Pencil, eraser, cardboard, brayer, knife (4)	Watercolors, paper, drawing (1) Tempera, shoe box, mat board, glue (2) Found object, paper, pencil (3) Tempera, paper, pencil (4)	Bottle, pencil (1) Tempera (2) Watercolors, brushes, tempera (4) Pen, India ink (4)
Language arts (CC) Science (R) Social Studies (R)	Science (CC) Social studies (R) Language arts (R)	Social studies (R,CC) Language arts (R)
Portfolio ideas (1)	Portfolio ideas (1,3)	Portfolio ideas (1,3)
		Using safe paints (2)

(R) = Chapter Review (CC) = Connections Feature (1), (2), (3) etc. = Lessons	Chapter 16 Art of the Early Twentieth Century	Chapter 17 Art of Today
NATIONAL STANDARDS FOR THE VISUAL ARTS	1. (a,b) 3. (a,b) 5. (b,c) 2. (a,b,c) 4. (c) 6. (a,b)	1. (a,b) 3. (a,b) 5. (b,c) 2. (a,b,c) 4. (c) 6. (a,b)
ARTISTIC PERCEPTION	European art movements (1) Artistic views of The Eight (3) Twentieth-century artistic trends (3)	Dreamlike picture, de Chirico (1) Realistic dream style, Magritte (2) Interpreting Hanson's work (3)
CREATIVE EXPRESSION	Creating a photo collage (1) Cubist chalk drawing (2) Expressive abstract design (3) Action print (4) Computer option (4)	Drawing Surrealist scene (1) Painting in Surrealist style (2) Experiment with action painting (3) Hard-Edge and Op art (4) Computer options (2,4)
HISTORICAL/CULTURAL CONTEXT	Fauvism (1) Use of color, Matisse (1) Expressionism introduced (1) Cubism introduced (1) Picasso, Braque, Lipchitz and Cubism (1) Ashcan school (3) Photography as art form (3) Regionalism introduced (3) Mexican art (3) Muralist defined (3)	Dada introduced (1) Surrealism defined (1) Abstract Expressionism (3) Hard-Edge defined (3) Social protest painting (3) New Realism (3) Op Art (4) Technology (5) Multi-media art (5) Kinetic art (5) Laser art (CC)
AESTHETIC VALUING	Expressing mood in collage (1) Innermost feelings, Expressionism (1) Non-objective art (1) Examining Your Work (2,4)	Abstract view (3) Social protest (3) Examining Your Work (2,4)
ELEMENTS AND PRINCIPLES OF ART	Elements and principles in Non-objective art (1) Unity (1) Light and dark values (1) Bold color, Fauvism (1) Form in nature (1) Texture and harmony, Lipchitz (1) Color, shape, line, Kandinsky (1) Texture and unity, Braque (2) Emphasis, Sloan (3) Creating movement, Bellows (3) Emphasis, Curry (3)	Harmony (1) Line to create tension (1) Texture in sculpture (1) Unity and variety in sculpture (1) Positive and negative shapes (3) Line and shapes of optical illusion (4)
ART FORMS	Painting (1,3) Still-life drawing (2) Printmaking (1) Sculpture (1) Chalk (2) Photography (3) Printmaking (4)	Painting (1,2,3,4) Sculpture (1,3) Assemblage (3) Mobiles (3) Kinetic art (3,5) Multi-media (5) Photography (5)
MEDIA, TOOLS, TECHNIQUES, AND PROCESSES	Collage (1) Chalk and drawing (2) Magazines, Tracing paper, India ink (3) Pencil, tray, brayer, printing ink (4)	Pencil, crayons, chalk (1) Sketch paper, tempera (3) Construction paper, watercolor, swabs (3) Illustration board, India ink, pen (4)
CURRICULUM AND PERFORMING ARTS CONNECTIONS	Social studies (CC) Language arts (R,R)	Technology (CC) Language arts (R) Social studies (R)
CAREERS/PORTFOLIOS	Portfolio ideas (1,3)	Portfolio ideas (1,3,5)
SAFETY	Using chalk safely (2) Using fixative safely (2)	

(R) = Chapter Review (CC) = Connections Feature (1), (2), (3) etc. = Lessons	Handbook
NATIONAL STANDARDS FOR THE VISUAL ARTS	1. (a,b) 3. (a,b) 5. (a,b,c) 2. (a,b) 4. (a,b,c) 6. (a,b)
ARTISTIC PERCEPTION	Computers in art (1,4,5) In performing arts (pp. 316–333)
CREATIVE EXPRESSION	Computer quilt design (1) Coil pot (2) Silk screen print (3) Computer cartoon (4) Computer advertisement (5)
HISTORICAL/CULTURAL CONTEXT	Native American pottery (2) American art, Warhol (3) Computers in design (1,4,5) Profiles: Cézanne, Giotto, Goya, Lewis, Leyster, Michelangelo, Miró, Monet, Morisot, Nevelson, Ryder, Rivera, Stieglitz, Tanner
AESTHETIC VALUING	Examining Your Work (1,2,3,4,5)
ELEMENTS AND PRINCIPLES OF ART	Line in design (1,3,4,5) Color in design (1,3,4,5) Balance, harmony (1,3,5) Proportion (2,3,4) Rhythm (1,3,5)
ART FORMS	Drawing (1,3,4,5) Printmaking (3) Sculpting (2) Electronic media (1,4,5)
MEDIA, TOOLS, TECHNIQUES, AND PROCESSES	Drawing (1,3,4,5) Computer software (1,4,5) Paint programs (1,4,5) Printmaking tools (3) Clay, sculpting tools (2) Drawing tips Painting tips Printmaking tips Sculpting tips Measuring, mounting, scoring paper Making a mat Mounting two-dimensional work
CURRICULUM AND PERFORMING ARTS CONNECTIONS	Dance (pp. 317, 322, 324, 325, 329–332) Language arts (pp. 317, 318, 320, 321, 322, 323, 324, 327, 328, 329, 333) Music (pp. 318, 319, 320, 321, 324, 326, 328) Physical education (pp. 323) Social studies (pp. 318, 321, 325, 326, 332, 333) Theatre (pp. 318, 323, 327, 333)
CAREERS/PORTFOLIOS	Art Director · Interior Designer Art Teacher · Magazine Designer Computer Graphics Specialist · Medical Illustrator Editorial Cartoonist · Museum Curator Exhibit and Display Designer · Photojournalist Graphic Designer · Special Effects Designer Industrial Designer · Urban Planner
SAFETY	

The Work Students Do

The *Understanding Art* student text introduces students to a chronological, art-history based program, laying the foundation for lifelong art appreciation and art production skills. Art works and art styles of various cultures and times in history are showcased. The 17 chapters interweave studio production with narrative lessons on the elements and principles of art, reinforcing the concepts of aesthetics, art criticism, and art history.

CHAPTER OPENING Each chapter opens with a full-color motivational reproduction of a work of art related to the chapter's content. A brief introduction helps students focus on the chapter. Chapter objectives are listed as well as vocabulary terms that will be in the chapter.

CHAPTER 1

The Language of Art

To learn how a watch works, you might take it apart and study the pieces. While the parts are spread out before you, however, the watch cannot run. Only when the parts are in place will the familiar ticking tell you that the watch is working.

Like watches, works of art are made up of parts. When an artist skillfully puts the pieces of an art work together, it succeeds as art. You can see how the parts work together to make a unified whole. In this chapter you will learn about these parts and how they can be organized, as in the painting at the left, to make a pleasing whole.

OBJECTIVES

After completing this chapter, you will be able to:
- Define and recognize the elements of art.
- Make an abstract design, experimenting with the elements of art.
- Identify the principles of art.
- Use the elements of art and principles of art in a studio experience.

WORDS YOU WILL LEARN

balance
color
emphasis
form
harmony
line
movement
non-objective art
proportion
rhythm
shape
space
texture
unity
variety

PORTFOLIO IDEAS

Keep your art work in a portfolio. A **portfolio** is a carefully selected collection of art work kept by students and professional artists. Make sure each entry includes:
- Your name and the date you completed the art work.
- A summary or self-reflection of the assignment.
- Any additional information requested by your teacher.

Throughout the book, watch for other "Portfolio Ideas." Professional artists do similar types of exercises for their own portfolios.

Henri Rousseau has skillfully used the language of art to create a colorful, intriguing painting. Can you name the colors he used? Can you point to curved and straight lines? Does he use both large and small shapes?
Henri Rousseau. *The Equatorial Jungle.* 1909. Oil on canvas. 1.406 x 1.295 m (55¼ x 51"). The National Gallery of Art, Washington, D.C. Chester Dale Collection.

XVIII

PORTFOLIO IDEAS With the increasing attention given to art portfolios as both a presentation and an assessment tool, each chapter begins with a suggestion of how students can use or adapt the activities within the chapter for their art portfolios.

NARRATIVE LESSONS Art concepts are presented and reinforced in accessible, easy-to-understand language, using relevant examples from art, from students' daily lives, or from history. Check Your Understanding provides a short review for each lesson.

STUDIO ACTIVITY Hands-on activities found in narrative lessons explore ways for students to quickly grasp ideas presented in the lessons. They are specifically designed to require minimal time and resources.

LESSON 1

The Art of China

The Chinese have a long history of being highly creative. Two thousand years before the invention of the seismograph, they were recording earthquakes. Long before the first Texas oil wells were drilled, they were drilling holes 2000 feet deep. The compass and kite are two other early Chinese inventions.

Added proof of the Chinese gift for creating can be found in their art. In this lesson you will learn about the important contributions they have made.

MODERN CHINESE CULTURE

The "modern" period of Chinese civilization is thought to have begun with the Han dynasty. This dynasty lasted from 206 B.C. to A.D. 220. To this day, the Chinese still refer to themselves as the "Han people."

During this period a new religion came to China, called Buddhism (boo-diz-uhm), which stressed the oneness of humans with nature. An important part of Buddhism is meditation, focusing one's thoughts on a single object or idea. This experience allows the person to know the inner beauty of the object or idea. Chinese art of the last 2000 years has been greatly influenced by Buddhism and meditation.

Scroll Painting

The Chinese were the first people to think of "picture painting" as honorable work. This was because many artists were also scholars. They wrote with brushes that could make thick and thin lines. They used the same brush and line technique to paint pictures. They painted fans, pages of books, and scrolls. A **scroll** is a long roll of illustrated parchment or silk. Some scrolls were meant to hang on walls. Other scrolls were made of long rolls of silk or paper. They were meant to be unrolled a little at a time and read like a book.

Like other Chinese artists, scroll painters began a work only after a long period of meditation. The work itself was an attempt to capture a feeling, not an image. Shapes and figures were limited to the barest essentials. The artist included only those lines and shapes needed to capture the mood of the scene. (See Figure 5–3 on page 70.)

Landscape Painting

The earliest Chinese paintings were filled with images of people illustrating the beliefs that people should live together peacefully and be respectful of their elders. With the influence of a new religion, the focus of painting began shifting away from humans and toward nature. By around A.D. 1100, the landscape was the main theme of Chinese painting.

The work that opened this chapter on page 66 is a landscape painting. Look closely at the work. Can you find a covered deck, or pavilion (puh-vil-yuhn), nestled within the hills? Studying the painting more closely still, do you see two small shapes inside the pavilion? These are meant to be seen as the heads of people. What statement is the artist making about the place of humans in nature?

Sculpture

For many centuries important people in China were buried in tombs with objects they could use in the afterworld. These figures were made from clay. Many, like the horses in Figure 5–1, were of animals. Notice how the artist creates a sense of movement in the clay sculptures of horses and riders.

After the collapse of the Han Dynasty, China fell into chaos. It remained this way until the mighty T'ang (tahng) dynasty rose to power some 400 years later. It was during this new dynasty that Chinese sculpture flourished.

▲ Figure 5–1   Notice how these figures show action. Centuries ago they played games similar to those we play today. What kind of game do you think they are playing?

Four Ladies of the Court Playing Polo, T'ang Dynasty, A.D. 618–906. Painted terra cotta. Nelson-Atkins Museum of Art, Kansas City, Missouri.

Crafts

The T'ang dynasty was followed in A.D. 960 by another powerful dynasty, the Sung (soong). Landscape painting soared to new heights during the Sung dynasty. So did the making of **porcelain** (pore-suh-luhn), a fine-grained, high-quality form of pottery. Porcelain is made from a fine and fairly hard-to-find white clay called kaolin (kay-uh-luhn).

Work in porcelain reached its highest point ever during the Ming dynasty (1368–1644).

▲ Figure 5–2   The blue pigment came from Persia. Unless the firing was precise, the blue could turn black or brown during the firing.

Pair of Vases, Meiping. Reign of Xuande. Ming Dynasty, 1426–1435. Porcelain with underglaze blue decoration. Nelson-Atkins Museum of Art, Kansas City, Missouri.

STUDIO ACTIVITY

Perceiving an Object

Chinese artists, you have learned, began a work only after long meditation on an object. This helped the artist capture the mood he wanted to show. Many artists train themselves to **perceive**, or to become aware of objects through the senses. Artists think about and study the properties of the subject that might otherwise go unnoticed.

Bring a natural object, such as a leaf, rock, or pine cone, to class. Sit silently for five minutes and study the object from every angle. Notice the object's lines, form, and textures. Do the lines curve around the form? Is the object rough or smooth? Are there shiny highlights? Now place the object out of sight. Using brush and ink, draw what you perceived on a sheet of paper.

PORTFOLIO

Write a short paragraph describing how you used the elements and principles of art to draw the object. Keep the paragraph and the drawing together in your portfolio.

The remarkable matched vases shown in Figure 5–2 date from this period. The painted dragon designs are protected by a glass-like finish, or **glaze**, on these Ming porcelains. What kind of balance does each of the vases have? What kind of balance do they have as a matched set?

✓ CHECK YOUR UNDERSTANDING

1. Name two inventions credited to the early Chinese.
2. What religion was introduced to China during the Han dynasty?
3. What is meditation? What has been its role in Chinese art of the last 2000 years?
4. What are scrolls?
5. What art form flourished during the T'ang and Sung dynasties?
6. What art form reached its highest point during the Ming dynasty?

68   Lesson 1   The Art of China

Lesson 1   The Art of China   69

Other Features of the Student Text:

Handbook includes Technique Tips, Artist Profiles, Career Spotlights, and Additional Studios.

Artsource®: Performing Arts Handbook highlights contemporary performing artists in music, dance, and theatre.

Artists and Their Works lists all artists and titles of their art works and page references.

Glossary/Glosario defines each vocabulary term in English format, then separately in the Spanish Glosario.

Bibliography lists print and media resources for both the student and the teacher.

Index serves as a study aid and assists students in finding particular topics.

STUDIO LESSONS Within each chapter, Studio Lessons are provided that build on previous narrative lessons and studio exercises. Each one gives students the opportunity to use various media and techniques. The lessons are illustrated by examples of fine art and include exemplary student art work.

EXAMINING YOUR WORK This section guides students in applying the process of art criticism to their own works of art.

LESSON 4

Making a Collage in the Islamic Style

Look at the Islamic miniature painting in Figure 8–15. Everything seems to be flat on the picture plane. The colors are intensely bright. How many different scenes or images do you see? Notice how the artist presents many points of view in the same work of art. A variety of patterns are used to fill the background spaces. Shapes, colors, and patterns are emphasized. By doing so, the illusion of depth is not felt.

WHAT YOU WILL LEARN

In this lesson you will create a collage, *an art work made up of bits and pieces of two-dimensional materials pasted to a surface.* Your collage will focus on several scenes related to a current event or activity. The work will be organized, however, in the manner of a flat, patterned Islamic miniature painting. You will use bright colors, decorative patterns, and flat shapes as in Figure 8–15. You will create the background shapes using patterned fabrics and papers. People and other objects can be made by drawing and painting them on white paper. See Figure 8–16.

WHAT YOU WILL NEED

- Pencil, sketch paper, ruler, scissors
- Sheet of white paper or poster board, 22 x 28 inches (56 x 71 cm)
- A variety of patterned fabrics and papers
- White glue, colored pencils
- Small pieces of white drawing paper

◄ Figure 8–15 This is a page of a book meant to be held in the hand and studied closely. Notice the patterns, rhythmic designs, and bright colors. Some of the pigments for the work were made by grinding precious metals such as gold and silver.

'Abd Allah Musawwir. *The Meeting of the Theologians.* c. 1540–1549 Colors on paper. Bokhara. Nelson-Atkins Museum of Fine Arts, Kansas City, Missouri.

WHAT YOU WILL DO

1. Brainstorm with classmates for ideas that could best be explained by showing several different scenes. For example, to show a football game you might have one scene of a huddle, one of a tackle, and one of the ball being kicked. Pick an event, such as a school dance, a parade, or a wedding. Make pencil sketches of different objects and scenes from the event you picked.
2. Make a plan to arrange your best ideas within rectangles of different sizes. Using the ruler and pencil, lightly draw these rectangles on the poster board.
3. Measure each shape and cut out patterned fabric or paper to fit each shape. As you select each pattern for the background, consider how one will look next to another. Look for contrast in the fabric so that you can see the distinction between each shape. If you wish, you may draw and color patterns in some of the spaces. Glue the pieces of fabric and paper to the poster board.
4. Draw and color figures and objects to place in each scene. Measure first to be sure that the figure will fit inside its area. Cut out the drawn objects and glue them onto the design.
5. When the glue is dry display your work. See whether classmates can guess what event your collage celebrates.

EXAMINING YOUR WORK

- Describe   Identify the different scenes and objects related to your events. Explain why you placed each scene or object where you did.
- Analyze   Show where you used contrast in your design. Identify how you used the element of space. Explain how the many different patterned areas made your work look different from other art works you have created.
- Interpret   State what feeling or mood your work communicates to viewers.
- Judge   Tell whether you feel your work succeeds. Explain your answer.

► Figure 8–16   Student art. Collage in the Islamic style.

Try This! COMPUTER OPTION

■ Make patterned papers on the computer to use in your collage. Cover the page with patterns and textures using tools, menus, and special effects provided in your software. If available, scan and import fabrics, pictures, or photos. Use a digital camera to capture people or objects you want to add. Once imported, these images can be resized for your collage. Print. Follow directions in the Studio Lesson.

124   Lesson 4   *Making a Collage in the Islamic Style*

Lesson 4   *Making a Collage in the Islamic Style*   125

COMPUTER OPTIONS Where appropriate, technology alternatives for Studio Lessons are offered. They give students an opportunity to learn how to use the computer as an art tool, and how it can be used with traditional media and methods of creating art.

STUDENT ART Exemplary student art work of middle school/junior high students is displayed within the text to motivate your students.

Integrating the Performing Arts

The Artsource®: Performing Arts Handbook is an exciting new addition to the *Understanding Art* Student Text. It features 17 artists or groups from the three fields of performing arts—dance, music, and theatre. The artists and groups are specifically chosen to correlate to the chapters in the book. *Understanding Art* provides this handbook as an opportunity for students to recognize and appreciate the connections that exist between the four arts disciplines. You are invited to use them as supplements to your lessons, or to have students work independently with the features as extension activities.

DANCE

Cross-Curriculum Links

Your visual arts classroom comes to life with a **Connections** feature, new to this edition of *Understanding Art*. These self-contained pages weave the study of art with that of science, math, literature, social studies, health, and so on.

You will find the Connections feature at the end of each chapter, just before the chapter review page. Use it as a culminating activity that will deepen students' understanding of the links between what they learn in the art classroom with lessons and concepts from other curriculum areas. If your school encourages cross-disciplinary teaching, this feature is a worthwhile place to invite a teacher from the featured curriculum area to team teach with you.

MATH

SCIENCE

Support for the Art Teacher

The Teacher's Wraparound Edition provides complete lesson plans, teaching suggestions, supplemental information, cross-references, and more—all conveniently "wrapped" around every page of the reduced student text. Teachers will discover that the consistent, easy-to-follow lesson plan format gives a variety of teaching strategies to motivate students; to introduce, teach, and reinforce concepts; and alternative teaching strategies for adapting the program to your own teaching style and to the learning styles of your students.

CHAPTER OPENER

- Chapter Scan
- Resource cross-reference
- Artsource®: Performing Arts Handbook reference
- National Standards for the Visual Arts correlation
- Featured Artists
- Developing a Portfolio
- Strategies for introducing the Chapter
- National Museum of Women in the Arts reference

Organized with the Teacher in Mind

LESSON PLANS The teaching material follows a consistent, easy-to-use pattern. The complete lesson cycle—Focus, Teach, Assess, and Close—makes it easy for you to plan a lesson. As the core of the Teacher's Wraparound Edition, this lesson cycle provides you with complete suggestions for introducing each chapter and lesson and allows you to tailor the lesson to your own style and to the specific needs of your students.

FOCUS

- Suggested class time for each Studio Lesson
- A list of student objectives
- A convenient list of Supplies needed for the lesson
- Cross-references to supplemental blackline masters in the Teacher's Classroom Resources

TEACH

- A Motivator activity to involve students in the lesson
- A Vocabulary activity to help students build vocabulary skills
- Various activities related to the lesson's content, including Art Criticism, Art History, Cultural Diversity, Studio Skills, Cooperative Learning, and Aesthetics

ASSESS

- Assessment techniques, including strategies for reteaching students who have difficulty mastering the important lesson concepts
- Extension activities designed for students who are able and willing to explore the content further

CLOSE

- An activity that brings closure to the lesson and recaps important concepts from the lesson

BOTTOM COLUMN ANNOTATIONS Boxes at the bottom of the page give you additional information related to the content of the Student Text. This information supplements the core lesson plan by focusing on various areas of interest. The categories include:

More About. . .	Safety Tips
Resources Beyond the Classroom	Developing a Portfolio
Curriculum Connections	Technology Options
Meeting Special Needs	Internet Activities
Meeting Student Diversity	Answers to Check
Technique Tips	Your Understanding

MAKING ART AVAILABLE FOR ALL STUDENTS

Teaching strategies in the Meeting Special Needs and Meeting Student Diversity boxes incorporate cultural perspectives, strategies for the physically and mentally disabled, and strategies for addressing different learning styles.

SPECIAL BOXED FEATURES
Stimulating and creative ideas to help you manage your classroom and help students recognize the presence of art all around them are available in three types of boxes set off from the lesson cycle.

Art in Everyday Life

Have students look around the classroom and notice how many different types of lines they see. Have them write on a sheet of paper examples of horizontal, vertical, diagonal, zigzag, and curved lines. Have them examine the lines around pictures hanging on the walls, lines in doors and windows, lines in clothing or objects on their desks. Have students take turns reading their lists aloud while volunteers write the various types of lines under appropriate headings on the board.

Art on a Shoestring

Foam meat trays make excellent paint mixing trays. Sometimes store meat managers will sell some to you at a low cost if they know they are for school use.

Sparking Creativity

Give students a sense of rhythm and movement in a creative way. Tell them: Rhythm in dance is found in the movements of the dancers. Try to see it and give it visual form. Ask one or two students to dance and have the class draw their movements rather than their bodies. Try a slow, graceful dance and then a rock rhythm. Compare students' drawings. Experiment with various tools and media and see how it will affect the rhythm of the designs.

STUDIO ACTIVITY Each activity in the Student Text has a corresponding box in the Teacher's Wraparound Edition that provides alternative ways for students to address the hands-on activity.

STUDIO ACTIVITY

Finding Natural Forms
Encourage students to bring in their own found natural objects for this activity. If your school is in an area where it is possible to take a nature walk to locate objects, talk with your administrator and arrange to go as a class on a nature hunt to prepare for this exercise.

INTERNET ACTIVITY

Art on the Web You and your students are invited to take a trip through Glencoe's Fine Arts Site on the World Wide Web. Your class can explore *Studio Cyberspace*, full of art activities; *Glencoe Student Galleria*, a changing showcase of student art works; links to lots of adventures through art museums, worldwide cultural treasures, and contact with other art teachers. You simply need a computer with a modem, an Internet hook-up, and curious minds. To reach the Glencoe Fine Arts page, type in the URL address exactly as shown:

http://www.glencoe.com/sec/art

Check the *Internet Activity Booklet* included with the *Understanding Art* program for more information.

INTERNET ACTIVITY Each Internet Activity box, found at the bottom of the Connections feature, offers ways for teachers to access and make use of Glencoe's new Fine Arts web site. Additionally, the feature offers strategies for implementing safe, educational Internet exploration in the classroom.

The Teacher's Resource Binder

A separate *Understanding Art* Teacher's Resource Binder provides you with a correlated supplemental resource for *Understanding Art*. It contains a wealth of additional handouts, teaching strategies, and resource material designed for more effective teaching. You can choose the materials that complement the skill level, time framework, and interest level of your class. The Teacher's Resource Binder is organized into chapters. In addition to chapter specific sections, the binder includes a section for resources and another that helps you integrate technology into your art classroom. The following types of teaching materials have been provided for each chapter.

- Reproducible Master
- Cooperative Learning Activities
- Aesthetics/Art Criticism
- Art History
- Studios
- Appreciating Cultural Diversity
- Chapter Test

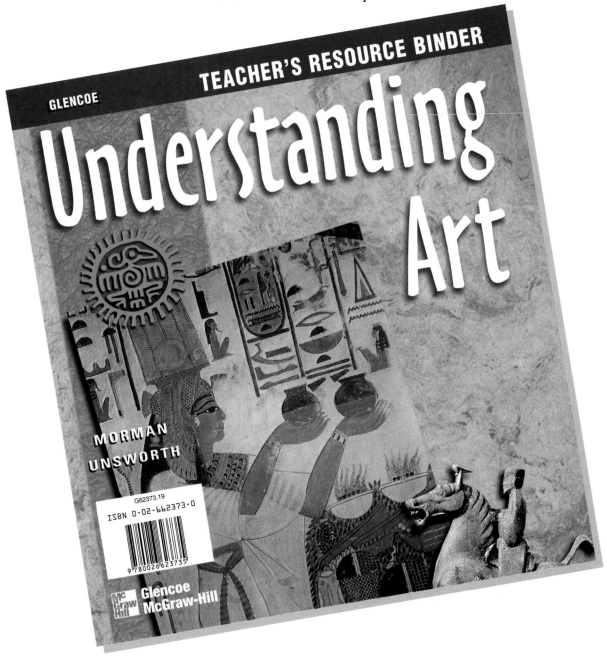

Assessment

All subject areas recognize the importance of measuring individual student performance in attaining specified goals and objectives. A booklet titled *Portfolio and Assessment Techniques* is designed to address basic information used in portfolio assessment for visual art. Why is portfolio assessment important to use? Portfolio assessment provides

- Tangible evidence of anticipated student outcomes.
- Contextual information on student growth as an artist.
- An opportunity for students to reflect on their work, acknowledge their accomplishments, and evaluate personal artistic goals.
- Consistency and objectivity in the evaluation process for the instructor.

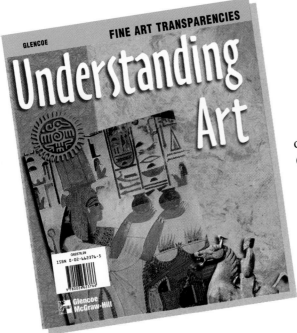

Fine Art Transparency Package

The ready-to-use overhead color transparency package contains 17 full-color Fine Art Transparencies, 17 Cross-Curriculum Transparencies, and 10 transparencies of student art work. Accompanying the transparencies is an Instructor's Guide with background information and student activity sheets to assist the teacher in guiding discussion, all in a convenient 3-ring binder.

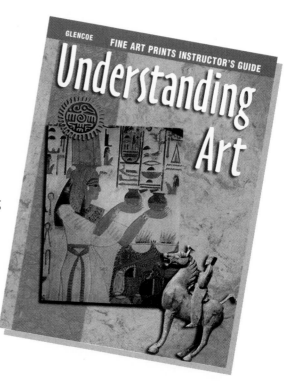

Fine Art Print Package

Twenty quality art masterpieces are printed on sturdy self-supporting stock to supplement the art work appearing in the student text. The laminated prints are resistant to wear and are presented in a durable portfolio for convenient classroom use and storage. This package includes an Instructor's Guide with a page for teaching strategies and a student worksheet.

Media and Technology Support

National Gallery of Art Videodisc

This full-length video features 1,645 art works from the National Gallery of Art collection, along with a tour of the gallery. Glencoe has published a separate *National Gallery of Art Correlation Bar Code Guide* for your convenience, including 300 art works from the entire videodisc collection. Selected bar codes are reprinted in the Teacher's Wraparound Edition that correlate to lesson contents. The videodisc is available on loan free of charge by contacting:

Department of Education Resources
Extension Programs Section, Education Division
National Gallery of Art
Washington, D.C. 20565
202-842-6231   www.nga.gov

Artsource®: Performing Arts Package 3

This new performing arts package provides a multi-media resource for further exploration of artists and groups within the three performing arts areas—dance, music, and theatre. The units within the package supplement the *Artsource®: Performing Arts Handbook* in the Student Text, and include an Instructor's Guide that provides additional information about each artist and group and their performances. The media package includes both video and audiocassettes.

National Museum of Women in the Arts CD-ROM and Videodisc

This videodisc of 200 art works from the collection of the National Museum of Women in the Arts includes a video introduction to the museum itself. The videodisc includes a 24-page bar code guide for all images. The CD-ROM provides multi-media access and activities for the 200 works, including an assessment tool to test students' knowledge of artist, time, location, media, and subject.

To assist with the planning and development of your individual course, this Pacing Chart is included in this section. These are only intended as suggested guidelines. Individual teachers will need to make necessary adjustments and modifications as required by their local, state, and national curriculum guidelines, and by the ability level and learning styles of their students.

		6 wk 30 days	9 wk 45 days	18 wk 90 days	36 wk 180 days
	Total Days				
Chapter 1 The Language of Art					
Lesson 1 The Elements of Art		1 day	1 day	1 day	2 days
Lesson 2 Using the Elements of Art		1 day	1 day	1 day	2 days
Lesson 3 The Principles of Art		1 day	1 day	1 day	2 days
Lesson 4 Using the Principles of Art		1 day	1 day	1 day	2 days
	Total	4 days	4 days	4 days	8 days
Chapter 2 The Media of Art					
Lesson 1 Drawing, Painting, Printmaking, and Computer Art		1 day	1 day	1 day	2 days
Lesson 2 Creating Mixed-Media Art		1 day	1 day	1 day	2 days
Lesson 3 Sculpture, Architecture, and Crafts Media		1 day	1 day	1 day	2 days
Lesson 4 Computer Landscape Drawing			1 day	1 day	2 days
	Total	3 days	4 days	4 days	8 days
Chapter 3 Art Criticism, Aesthetics, and Art History					
Lesson 1 Art Criticism and Aesthetics		1 day	1 day	1 day	3 days
Lesson 2 Painting an Expressive Scene		1 day	1 day	1 day	2 days
Lesson 3 Art History		1 day	1 day	1 day	3 days
Lesson 4 Painting in the Cubist Style		1 day	1 day	1 day	2 days
	Total	4 days	4 days	4 days	11 days
Chapter 4 Art of Earliest Times					
Lesson 1 Prehistoric Art		1 day	1 day	1 day	2 days
Lesson 2 Painting Using Earth Pigments				1 day	2 days
Lesson 3 Art of Ancient Egypt		1 day	1 day	1 day	2 days
Lesson 4 Ancient China, India, and Mesopotamia			1 day	1 day	2 days
Lesson 5 Creating a Picture Story		1 day	1 day	1 day	2 days
	Total	3 days	4 days	5 days	10 days
Chapter 5 Art of the Far East					
Lesson 1 The Art of China		1 day	1 day	1 day	2 days
Lesson 2 Making a Scroll			1 day	1 day	2 days
Lesson 3 The Art of Japan		1 day	1 day	1 day	2 days
Lesson 4 Creating a Time Capsule				2 days	3 days
	Total	2 days	3 days	5 days	9 days
Chapter 6 The Art of Pre-Columbian America					
Lesson 1 The Art of Mesoamerica		1 day	1 day	1 day	2 days
Lesson 2 Making a Clay Urn				2 days	3 days
Lesson 3 Art of the Andes			1 day	1 day	2 days
Lesson 4 Making a Stylized Motif		1 day	1 day	1 day	2 days
	Total	2 days	3 days	5 days	9 days
Chapter 7 Art of Greece and Rome					
Lesson 1 Art of Ancient Greece		1 day	1 day	1 day	2 days
Lesson 2 Making a Painting for a Greek Vase			1 day	1 day	2 days
Lesson 3 Art of Ancient Rome		1 day	1 day	1 day	2 days
Lesson 4 Making a Model of a Roman Triumphal Arch				2 days	3 days
	Total	2 days	3 days	5 days	9 days
Chapter 8 Art of India and Islam					
Lesson 1 Art of India		½ day	½ day	1 day	2 days
Lesson 2 Making a Life-Size Dancing Figure			1 day	2 days	2 days
Lesson 3 Art of Islam		½ day	½ day	1 day	2 days
Lesson 4 Making a Collage in the Islamic Style				1 day	2 days
	Total	1 day	2 days	5 days	8 days

		6 wk 30 days	9 wk 45 days	18 wk 90 days	36 wk 180 days
	Total Days				
Chapter 9 Art of Africa					
Lesson 1 The Figure Sculptures of Africa		1 day	1 day	1 day	2 days
Lesson 2 Abstract Self-Portrait Cutout			1 day	1 day	2 days
Lesson 3 The Masks of Africa				1 day	2 days
Lesson 4 Making a Mood Mask Relief				2 days	2 days
	Total	1 day	2 days	5 days	8 days
Chapter 10 Art of the Middle Ages					
Lesson 1 Art of the Romanesque Period		1 day	1 day	1 day	2 days
Lesson 2 Romanesque Castle Relief				2 days	2 days
Lesson 3 Art of the Gothic Period		1 day	1 day	1 day	2 days
Lesson 4 Making a Gothic Gargoyle				1 day	2 days
	Total	2 days	2 days	5 days	8 days
Chapter 11 Art of the Renaissance					
Lesson 1 Art of Italian Renaissance		1 day	1 day	1 day	3 days
Lesson 2 Drawing a Still Life			1 day	1 day	2 days
Lesson 3 Art of the Northern Renaissance			1 day	1 day	3 days
Lesson 4 Designing a Visual Symbol				2 days	2 days
	Total	1 day	3 days	5 days	10 days
Chapter 12 European Art of the 1600s and 1700s					
Lesson 1 Art of the 1600s		1 day	1 day	1 day	3 days
Lesson 2 Drawing Expressive Hands				1 day	2 days
Lesson 3 Art of the 1700s			1 day	1 day	3 days
Lesson 4 Constructing a Rococo Shoe				2 days	2 days
	Total	1 day	2 days	5 days	10 days
Chapter 13 Native American Art					
Lesson 1 Native American Art of the Past		1 day	1 day	1 day	3 days
Lesson 2 Making a Round Weaving				3 days	3 days
Lesson 3 Native American Art Today				1 day	3 days
Lesson 4 Inuit-Style Print				1 day	2 days
	Total	1 day	1 day	6 days	11 days
Chapter 14 European Art of the Early 1800s					
Lesson 1 Neoclassic and Romantic Art			1 day	1 day	3 days
Lesson 2 Designing a Neoclassic Stage Set				1 day	2 days
Lesson 3 European Art—Late 1800s		1 day	1 day	1 day	3 days
Lesson 4 Painting an Impressionist Landscape				1 day	1 day
	Total	1 day	2 days	4 days	9 days
Chapter 15 European Art of the Late Nineteenth Century					
Lesson 1 Art of the Post-Impressionists		1 day	1 day	1 day	3 days
Lesson 2 Painting in the Style of Post-Impressionists				1 day	2 days
Lesson 3 American Painting in the Late 1800s		1 day	1 day	1 day	3 days
Lesson 4 Making an Expressive Watercolor Painting				1 day	2 days
	Total	2 days	2 days	4 days	10 days
Chapter 16 Art of the Early Twentieth Century					
Lesson 1 Art of the Early Twentieth Century in Europe		1 day	1 day	1 day	3 days
Lesson 2 Making a Cubist Chalk Drawing				1 day	2 days
Lesson 3 Art of the Early Twentieth Century in America		1 day	1 day	1 day	3 days
Lesson 4 Making a Print of a Figure in Action				1 day	2 days
	Total	2 days	2 days	4 days	10 days
Chapter 17 Art of Today					
Lesson 1 European Art Today		1 day	1 day	1 day	3 days
Lesson 2 Painting in the Surrealist Style		1 day	1 day	1 day	2 days
Lesson 3 American Art Today				1 day	3 days
Lesson 4 Making a Hard-Edge Op Art Work				1 day	2 days
Lesson 5 Art of the Next Frontier				1 day	2 days
	Total	2 days	2 days	5 days	12 days
Handbook					
				10 days	22 days

Safety in the Art Classroom

Art teachers and their students are often in contact with potentially harmful materials, although many may be totally unaware of the danger. Lead poisoning, cancer, nervous system disorders, anemia, silicosis, chemical pneumonia, asthma, dermatitis—all of these as well as others are recognized as industrial diseases caused by hazardous chemicals. However, many fail to recognize that these same diseases are found among artists, craftspeople, theater technicians, teachers, and students using art and craft materials without adequate precautions.

Although studies have been conducted and the findings published, many teachers remain unaware that toxic substances may be in some of the art materials they use routinely in their teaching. Other teachers, aware of the problem, feel that they are exercising adequate precautions by referring to the labels on the art products they use.

Labeling of Art Materials

The labeling of art materials continues to be limited in many ways. Ingredients that caused laboratory animals to perish within two weeks after a single dose was administered were identified as "acutely toxic" and must bear a warning label. However, if fewer than half the animals die, the product may be labeled "nontoxic." In addition, when products are imported or repackaged, the hazards may not be listed or properly described on the label.

Teachers should be aware of the fact that the Federal Hazardous Substances Act and other legislation introduced at the federal level, have not been entirely successful at rectifying problems of this kind. Some worrisome inadequacies persist.

Industry Safety Standards

Not to be overlooked is the fact that the art-materials industry has, for many years, supported voluntary safety standards. These standards have been developed with the cooperation and input of various manufacturers. The Arts and Crafts Materials Institute (ACMI) has for some time adhered to a voluntary program designed to ensure the safety of younger students working with art materials. Most art teachers are familiar with the two ACMI safety labels—AP indicating Approved Product, and CP specifying Certified Product. These labels certify that the products on which they are placed have been found to contain no ingredients in sufficient quantities to be toxic or harmful to users. In addition, products bearing a CP seal abide by certain quality standards pertaining to workmanship, working qualities, and color.

While the AP/CP seal applies to art products intended for use by younger students, a Certified Label (CL) is used to identify products considered to be more appropriate for older students and adults. The CL seal on a label indicates that the product's ingredients have been examined by toxicologists. The label lists any safety precautions required by law and by labeling standards developed by the American Society of Testing and Materials. Teachers are advised to read and adhere to the safety precautions listed on these labels.

Material Safety Data Sheets and Their Use

Teachers should realize that they may request a Material Safety Data Sheet (MSDS) from manufacturers pertaining to any art products they are unsure of. Among the items included on the MSDS are a listing of all the ingredients for which industrial standards exist, health-hazard information, fire-hazard data, and the chemicals with which the product might react dangerously.

In most school systems, central ordering procedures are—or should be—developed as a means of ensuring that all art materials entering the school are approved by appropriate authorities (for example, the Health Department or Board of Education). Requiring Material Safety Data Sheets from suppliers as a condition of purchase should eliminate many of the toxic materials that might otherwise be brought into the classrooms by unsuspecting teachers.

Protection from Exposure

Considerable protection from exposure to toxic materials can be achieved by promoting good hygiene in the classroom. Safe storage and proper labeling of art and craft supplies, keeping dust to a minimum by damp mopping rather than sweeping, and thorough cleanup after use of art and craft materials will help prevent toxic exposures. Personal hygiene also plays a role in the prevention of potentially harmful exposures. Students should refrain from eating or drinking while engaged in art projects, and they should wash their hands thoroughly when finished. Another general safety practice is to ensure proper ventilation in the art classroom so that contaminants may be diluted and eventually removed from the air. Exposure to hazardous dusts and fumes will be minimized if the instructor premixes dry materials with water (for example, tempera, wheat paste, and so forth) and fires ceramic products when students are away from the kiln area. If an art material has been transferred to an unlabeled container and its identity is unknown, it should be disposed of. For specific information on the proper disposal of art and craft materials, please contact your local county health department. (From the California Department of Education Program Advisory # CIL: 94[95-01].)

Safety Precautions for Students

In order for a chemical in an art material to harm a student, it must first come into contact with or enter the body. Teachers should be aware of the following three ways in which this can occur.

Skin Contact. Some chemicals such as those used in etching, or solvents like lacquer and paint thinners, can irritate the skin on contact and result in a variety of skin problems. Other chemicals, known as sensitizers, can cause skin allergies. Examples of these sensitizers include formaldehyde found in some color photography solutions, turpentine, epoxy glues and resins, nickel and chromium compounds, and many tropical woods.

However, the danger with regard to skin contact does not end here. Many toxic chemicals do not just damage the skin itself. They can also be absorbed through the skin into the bloodstream where they can affect other organs. Examples include methyl alcohol found in some shellacs, toluene found in lacquer thinners and silk screen inks, and glycol ethers found in photo etching materials.

Inhalation. Dusts, powders, vapors, gases, aerosols, and other airborne substances may be readily inhaled and, therefore, represent a health hazard. Examples include solvent vapors from paints, inks, and thinners; spray mists from air brush or aerosol spray cans; gases from photographic baths; pottery kiln firing; metal fumes from soldering, welding, and metal casting; and dusts from dyes and pigments, pottery glazes, and woodworking. Some of the chemicals in these materials can result in lung damage from inhalation while others can be absorbed into the bloodstream, where they can lead to a variety of problems including lead poisoning, nerve damage, and kidney damage.

Ingestion. Ingestion is of particular concern with younger students who are inclined to experiment and put things in their mouths. However, ingestion of hazardous substances can occur in the case of older students as well. These students can be affected if they eat, drink, or apply make-up in a classroom where art materials can contaminate these items.

Precautions in Selecting and Using Art Materials

Although some products on the market are labeled as "nontoxic," they should not be purchased for use by students in grades K-6 unless assurance is obtained from the manufacturer. A major reason for this is that the product may have been tested for acute toxicity only. Chronic hazards, cancer-causing potential, and other sensitivities are not included in acute toxicity testing. The "nontoxic" label can thus be misleading, and products identified with such labels should not always be regarded as safe for use by children.

There are certain safety precautions that all teachers should take when selecting art materials for use in their classrooms. Included in these precautions are the following:

- Make certain that the materials obtained for younger students (age 12 or under) have an AP or CP seal of approval; materials secured for use by older students should have a CL seal.

- Incorporate into the art curriculum written information on the potential hazards of art materials and techniques; students should be tested on this information just as they are tested with regard to other aspects of curriculum content. Documentation of this type of instruction should be made and filed.

- Carefully supervise students in the classroom, making certain that safety rules are understood and observed. Teachers must also remember to obey these safety rules themselves in order to impress upon their students the seriousness of these regulations. Students should never be allowed to work in the classroom, during or after school hours, without direct teacher supervision.

- Avoid using solvents or products containing solvents in the art room. These include turpentine, lacquer, shellac, paint thinner, rubber cement and rubber cement thinner, permanent markers, and solvent-based inks such as silkscreen printing ink.

- Do not use acids, alkalies, or bleaches.

- Do not use aerosol spray cans in the classroom, since the inhalation of the spray mist can cause injury to lung tissue.

- Use dust-causing products with care in a well-ventilated area. This precaution applies to the use of pastels, chalks, plaster and clays in dry form, copper enamels, glazes, papier-mâché mixtures, and powdered tempera paints.

- Place kilns in a separate room, outdoors, or if this is not possible, in an out-of-the-way part of the room where students are not likely to come into contact with them when they are in operation. In addition, all kilns should have local exhaust ventilation.

- Remember that good ventilation is an absolute necessity whenever using any art or craft material.

- Be prepared for emergencies by having written emergency procedures prepared, posted, and explained to students. This includes fire drill procedures and the use of fire extinguishers.

- Report all accidents, even minor ones such as a small cut. Illnesses suspected of being related to art materials should be reported in writing to the school principal or other designated authority at once so that an investigation can be conducted and corrective action determined.

A 1992 bulletin from the Consumer Product Safety Commission stated that art materials with any warning labels whatever are not suitable for use by students in grade 6 and under. These students cannot be expected to understand the hazards of toxic substances or to carry out precautions effectively or consistently. A teacher must "childproof" the art room to prevent either intentional or unintentional access to toxic materials or dangerous machinery.

At the beginning of each school year or new term, teachers are urged to determine if any of their students are asthmatic, visually impaired, hearing impaired, or on prescribed medication. If asthmatic students are enrolled in the art class, they should not be exposed to dusts, fumes, or vapors because of their breathing difficulties. Visually impaired students understandably operate very close to their art work and, as a consequence, are more likely to inhale harmful dusts, vapors, and fumes. Students with hearing impairments should not be exposed to activities requiring loud hammering or noisy machinery, because this can aggravate their condition. If students are found to be on medication, the teacher should seek their physician's advice regarding the potentially harmful interaction between their prescribed medicine and the art materials they might use in class.

Similar precautions are recommended in situations involving students who are physically handicapped in other ways or who may be learning disabled or emotionally disturbed. These students are at an even greater risk from toxic materials and require special care and attention. In some instances, they might not be able to use the same materials and processes as other students. Careful evaluation is needed in each case to determine what special precautions might be necessary.

Clearly, the need to direct time and effort to safeguarding the health and safety of students in the art classroom is essential. Art teachers, aware of their responsibilities in this regard, recognize that assistance may be needed. In order to properly inform and train their students, teachers need specially tailored hazard communication (HAZCOM) training. The curriculum must include formal health and safety training at levels far above the basic information required by the law. This is not only proper, it provides an opportunity for the school to develop training materials for which there is a demand.

Steps to Incorporate Training into Your Program

First find out which law applies to you. There are state and federal HAZCOM laws and they differ somewhat in their requirements. Ask your employer, but do not stop there! Call your Department of Labor's Occupational Safety and Health Department to be absolutely sure whose jurisdiction you are under. Ask for a copy of the law and any additional free materials they may have.

Learning the Rules

1. Spend a few moments looking at the HAZCOM file. If you do not know where this file is kept, ask your school administrator. OSHA requires employers to include the file's location in HAZCOM training.

2. Look at the condition of the file. OSHA requires that it is organized and easy to read. Included in the file should be:
   a. A written program telling how the school will comply (including names of parties responsible for each compliance activity).
   b. A survey of all the potentially toxic substances in the school and their locations.
   c. An organized collection of material safety data sheets (MSDSs) on these substances.
   d. A record of training sessions, which usually includes dates of training, lists of participants, qualifications of trainers, results of quizzes given, and so on.

3. Check your classroom/shop.
   a. Are there any containers that do not have the following information:
      - identity of the substance (must be the same as on the MSDS)
      - hazard warnings, if needed
      - name and address of the manufacturer (required for transport)
   b. If children grade 6 and under ever have access to your classroom/shop, be sure there are no materials with warnings on them of any kind, no sharp tools, and no hazardous equipment. Look under sinks, in drawers, and so on. Children's classrooms, like homes, must be childproofed.
   c. Be sure you have a dilution ventilation system separate from the ventilation in the rest of the school if you work with solvents or solvent-containing products, black-and-white photo developing, resin casting, or any other process requiring it.
   d. Be sure you have local ventilation systems (e.g. spray booth and flexible ducts) for any process that puts substances into the air, such as spraying, air brushing, machine sawing, sanding, soldering, welding, mixing clay or glazes, and so on.

REMEMBER: No amount of training will make up for teaching without the proper safety equipment. **If you cannot demonstrate a process with all proper precautions, safety equipment, and ventilation, eliminate the project from the curriculum.** Don't ever let students see you violate safety rules or the law.

More information on safety in the art environment is available from:

Arts, Crafts, and Theater Safety (ACTS)
181 Thompson Street #23
New York, New York 10012–2586
(212) 777-0062
http://www.caseweb.com/acts/

Understanding Art

ABOUT THE PROGRAM

Understanding Art takes a chronological approach to art, focusing on art works from ancient to contemporary times. The text blends art history with cultural and social traditions, emphasizing the role of art in everyday life. The images and content present art as historical evidence of the creative process.

ABOUT THE COVER ILLUSTRATION

Queen Nefertari Presenting Her Offerings. 19th Dynasty. Egyptian wall painting, Tomb of Nefertari, Valley of the Queens, West Thebes, Egypt. Giraudon/Art Resource, New York.

***Chinese Horseman.* Chinese.** Later Han Dynasty. Bronze, from Lei-t'a, China. Giraudon/Art Resource, New York.

Mexican Bird Motif. Culhuacan. Flat stamp. *Design Motifs of Ancient Mexico,* Dover Publications, New York.

The wall painting of Queen Nefertari is an example of the unique Egyptian art style and also provides a glimpse into the traditions and practices of an ancient lifestyle. The Chinese tomb figure and the medallion from a Mesoamerican relief carving represent more art of advanced civilizations that existed hundreds of years ago.

Understanding Art

Gene Mittler, Ph.D.
Professor Emeritus
Texas Tech University

Rosalind Ragans, Ph.D.
Associate Professor Emerita
Georgia Southern University

Glencoe
McGraw-Hill

New York, New York   Columbus, Ohio   Woodland Hills, California   Peoria, Illinois

ABOUT THE AUTHORS

Gene Mittler

Gene Mittler is one of the authors of Glencoe's middle school/junior high art series, *Introducing Art, Exploring Art,* and *Understanding Art.* He is also author of *Art in Focus,* a chronological approach to art for Glencoe's senior high program, and *Creating and Understanding Drawings.* He has taught at both the elementary and secondary levels and at Indiana University. He received an M.F.A. in sculpture from Bowling Green State University and a Ph.D. in art education from the Ohio State University. He has authored grants and published numerous articles in professional journals and has lectured in the United States and abroad. Dr. Mittler is currently Professor Emeritus at Texas Tech University.

Rosalind Ragans

Rosalind Ragans is one of the authors of Glencoe's middle school/junior high art series, *Introducing Art, Exploring Art,* and *Understanding Art.* She served as senior author on the elementary program *Art Connections* for the SRA division of McGraw-Hill, and wrote the multi-level, comprehensive *ArtTalk* text for Glencoe's senior high program. She received a B.F.A. at Hunter College, CUNY, New York, and earned a M.Ed. in Elementary Education at Georgia Southern College and Ph.D. in Art Education at the University of Georgia. Dr. Ragans has taught art in grades K–12, and has earned several honors including National Art Educator of the Year for 1992. She is currently Associate Professor of Art Education Emerita at Georgia Southern University.

ABOUT ARTSOURCE®

The materials provided in the Performing Arts Handbook are excerpted from *Artsource®: The Music Center Study Guide to the Performing Arts,* a project of the Music Center Education Division. The Music Center of Los Angeles County, the largest performing arts center in the western United States, established the Music Center Education Division in 1979 to provide opportunities for lifelong learning in the arts, and especially to bring the performing and visual arts into the classroom. The Education Division believes the arts enhance the quality of life for all people, but are crucial to the development of every child.

Glencoe/McGraw-Hill

A Division of The **McGraw·Hill** Companies

Send all inquiries to:
Glencoe/McGraw-Hill
21600 Oxnard Street
Woodland Hills, CA 91367

ISBN 0-02-662359-5 (Student Text)
ISBN 0-02-662361-7 (Teacher's Wraparound Edition)

Printed in the United States of America.

3 4 5 6 7 8 9   004/043   03 02 01 00 99

EDITORIAL CONSULTANTS

Claire B. Clements, Ph.D.
Specialist, Special Needs
Associate Professor and Community Education
   Director at the Program on Human Development
   and Disability
The University of Georgia
Athens, Georgia

Robert D. Clements, Ph.D.
Specialist, Special Needs
Professor Emeritus of Art
The University of Georgia
Athens, Georgia

Cris Guenter, Ed.D.
Specialist, Portfolio and Assessment
Professor, Fine Arts/Curriculum and Instruction
California State University, Chico
Chico, California

Nancy C. Miller
Booker T. Washington High School for the
   Performing and Visual Arts
Dallas, Texas

Faye Scannell, M.A.
Specialist, Technology
Bellevue Public Schools
Bellevue, Washington

Dede Tisone-Bartels, M.A.
Specialist, Curriculum Connections
Crittenden Middle School
Mountain View, California

Jean Morman Unsworth
Art Consultant to Chicago
Archdiocese Schools
Chicago, Illinois

CONTRIBUTORS/REVIEWERS

Jill Ciccone-Corey
Art Teacher
Monmouth Regional High School
Tenton Falls, New Jersey

Pat Gullett
Art Teacher
Morton East Intermediate School
Highland Park, Illinois

Jennifer Lawler
Art Consultant
Lenexa, Kansas

Pam Layman
Art Teacher
Bardstown Middle School
Bardstown, Kentucky

Diane Mark-Walker
Art Consultant
Los Angeles, California

Barbara Perez
Art Teacher
St. Athanasius School
Evanston, Illinois

Jan Stephens, M.A.
Art Specialist
Birmingham Museum of Art Liaison
Jefferson County Board of Education
Birmingham, Alabama

Johanna Stout
Art Teacher
New Caney High School
New Caney, Texas

PERFORMING ARTS HANDBOOK CONTRIBUTORS

Joan Boyett
Executive Director
Music Center Education Division
The Music Center of Los Angeles County

Melinda Williams
Concept Originator and Project Director

Susan Cambigue-Tracey
Project Coordinator

Arts Discipline Writers:
   Dance—Susan Cambigue-Tracey
   Music—Rosemarie Cook-Glover
   Theatre—Barbara Leonard

STUDIO LESSON CONSULTANTS

Acknowledgements: The authors wish to express their gratitude to the following art coordinators and specialists who participated in the field test of the studio lessons.

Donna Banning, El Modena High School, Orange, CA; Thomas Beacham, Telfair County High School, McRae, GA; Lydia Bee, Junction Middle School, Palo Cedro, CA; Kellene Champlain, Fulton County Schools, Fulton, GA; Jane Dixon, Highlands Junior High School, Jacksonville, FL; Karen Roach Ford, Tecumseh Middle School, Lafayette, IN; Nadine Gordon, Scarsdale High School, Scarsdale, NY; Margie Ellen Greer, Ridgeway Junior/Senior High School, Memphis, TN; Barbara Grimm, Taylor Road Middle School, Alpharetta, GA; Wanda Hanna, South Florence High School, Florence, SC; Ken Hatcher, Douglas Anderson School of the Arts, Jacksonville, FL; Annette Jones, Fletcher Junior High School, Jacksonville Beach, FL; Audrey Komroy, Akron Central School, Akron, NY; Frances Kovacheff, Charles N. Scott Middle School, Hammond, IN; Geri Leigh, Stanton College Preparatory School, Jacksonville, FL; Nellie Lynch, Duval County Schools, Jacksonville, FL; Mary McDermott, Valleywood School, Kentwood, MI; Sandra Moore, John Sevier Middle School, Kingsport, TN; Bunyon Morris, Marvin Pittman Laboratory School, Statesboro, GA; Barbara Perez, St. Athanasius School, Evanston, IL; Virginia Marshall Ramsey, Mabry Middle School, Marietta, GA; Joanne Rempell, Bradwell Institute High School, Hinesville, GA; Lahwana Reynolds, Glen Hills High School, Augusta, GA; Jane Rhoades, Georgia Southern College, Statesboro, GA; Julia Russell, Memphis City Schools, Memphis, TN; Faye Scannell, Medina Elementary, Bothell, WA; Barbara Shaw, Cobb County Schools, Cobb County, GA; Linda Smith, Millen Middle School, Millen, GA; Carolyn Sollman, Eminence School, Eminence, IN; Catherine Stalk, North Augusta High School, North Augusta, SC; Nancy Walker, Colonial Junior High, Creative & Performing Arts School, Memphis, TN; Betty Womack, William James Middle School, Statesboro, GA; Shirley Yokley, Tennessee Department of Education, Nashville, TN

Table of Contents Illustration:
Lisa Pomerantz/Deborah Wolfe, Ltd.

CONTENTS

Credit line, page 254.

Credit line, page 78.

Credit line, page 84, bottom.

Credit line, page 142.

Credit line, page 145.

Credit line, page 206.

Credit line, page 218.

Credit line, page 34.

Credit line, page 42.

LISTING OF STUDIO LESSONS BY MEDIA/TECHNIQUE

Understanding Art

The Language of Art

(pages xviii–15)

Resources

- 1-10 Chapter Test, TRB page 39
- 1-1 Gabriele Münter, TRB page 25 (artist profile)
- Transparency CC-1, *Microcosm and Macrocosm* by Helen Lundeberg
- Transparency 1, *Family Group* by William Glackens
- Fine Art Print 1, *Staffelsee in Autumn* by Gabriele Münter

 Dance
While studying this chapter, use Performing Arts Handbook page 317. Tell students that every art form has a language. The Alvin Ailey American Dance Theater uses the language of dance to create a work of art.

NATIONAL STANDARDS

This chapter addresses the following National Standards for the Visual Arts:

1. (a, b) 4. (c)
2. (a, b) 5. (a, b)
3. (a, b) 6. (b)

▲ Henri Rousseau has skillfully used the language of art to create a colorful, intriguing painting. Can you name the colors he used? Can you point to curved and straight lines? Does he use both large and small shapes?

Henri Rousseau. *The Equatorial Jungle*. 1909. Oil on canvas. 1.406 x 1.295 m (55¼ x 51″). The National Gallery of Art, Washington, D.C. Chester Dale Collection.

FEATURED ARTISTS

Giacomo Balla
Marc Chagall
Charles Demuth
William Harnett
Grace Hartigan

Richard Lindner
Pierre Auguste Renoir
Henri Rousseau
Vincent van Gogh

CHAPTER 1

The Language of Art

To learn how a watch works, you might take it apart and study the pieces. While the parts are spread out before you, however, the watch cannot run. Only when the parts are in place will the familiar ticking tell you that the watch is working.

Like watches, works of art are made up of parts. When an artist skillfully puts the pieces of an art work together, it succeeds as art. You can see how the parts work together to make a unified whole. In this chapter you will learn about these parts and how they can be organized, as in the painting at the left, to make a pleasing whole.

PORTFOLIO IDEAS

Keep your art work in a portfolio. A **portfolio** is *a carefully selected collection of art work kept by students and professional artists.* Make sure each entry includes:

- Your name and the date you completed the art work.
- A summary or self-reflection of the assignment.
- Any additional information requested by your teacher.

Throughout the book, watch for other "Portfolio Ideas." Professional artists do similar types of exercises for their own portfolios.

OBJECTIVES

After completing this chapter, you will be able to:
- Define and recognize the elements of art.
- Make an abstract design, experimenting with the elements of art.
- Identify the principles of art.
- Use the elements of art and principles of art in a studio experience.

WORDS YOU WILL LEARN

balance
color
emphasis
form
harmony
line
movement
non-objective art
proportion
rhythm
shape
space
texture
unity
variety

1

The Elements of Art

✓ OBJECTIVES

After completing this lesson, students will be able to:

- Recognize and define the elements of art.
- Work with the art elements using various methods and materials.
- Make abstract designs by experimenting with the art elements.

✓ SUPPLIES

- Patches of colored paper.
- Reproductions of art work of various types and periods.
- White glue.
- Sketch paper.
- Watercolors.
- A variety of brushes.
- Colored pencils, markers, crayons.

Resources

- 1-2 *The Elements of Art*, TRB page 27 (reproducible master)
- 1-3 *Space in Painting*, TRB page 28 (reproducible master)
- 1-4 *A Dozen Right Answers*, TRB page 30 (art history)
- 1-5 *Feel the Space of a Japanese Home*, TRB page 31 (appreciating cultural diversity)

Art is a powerful language. Through it, artists communicate thoughts, ideas, and feelings. Like most languages, the language of art has its own special vocabulary. Unlike other vocabularies, however, the vocabulary of art is not made up of words. Rather, it is made up of visual elements. The visual elements include color, line, shape, form, space, and texture.

COLOR

Have you ever noticed it is harder to see colors when the light is dim? Color relies on light. In fact, **color** is *what the eyes see when light is reflected off an object*.

Color has three properties, or traits. These are:

- **Hue**. Hue is the name of a color, such as red, blue, or yellow. Hues are arranged in a circular format on a color wheel. Red, yellow, and blue are the primary hues. They are equally spaced on the color wheel. (See Figure 1–1.) Look at the picture in Figure 1–2. How many different hues, or colors, can you find in this work? Which ones can you name?
- **Value**. Value is the lightness or darkness of a hue. The value of a hue can be changed by adding white or black. Can you point out different values of any one color in the picture in Figure 1–2?

▶ **Figure 1–1 Color Wheel.**

TECHNOLOGY OPTIONS

National Gallery of Art Videodisc   Use the following images to show additional works by artists presented in this lesson.

Henri Rousseau
Tropical Forest with Monkeys

Search Frame 1588

William M. Harnett
My Gems

Search Frame 1972

Use Glencoe's *Correlation Bar Code Guide to the National Gallery of Art* to locate more art works.

- **Intensity**. Intensity is the brightness or dullness of a hue. Pure hues are high-intensity colors. Dull hues are low-intensity colors. Which objects in Figure 1–2 would you describe as high in intensity? Which would you describe as low in intensity?

Colors can be combined to produce many interesting and striking results. Artists make use of different types of color schemes to create different effects. Following are some of the color schemes that trained artists use:

- **Monochromatic** (mahn-uh-kroh-**mat**-ik) **color scheme**. This scheme uses different values of a single hue. For example, dark green, medium green, and light green make a monochromatic scheme.
- **Analogous** (uh-**nal**-uh-gus) **color scheme**. This scheme uses colors that are side by side on the color wheel and share a hue. Look at the color wheel in Figure 1–1. What colors share the hue red?
- **Warm or cool color scheme**. Warm color schemes—with red, yellow, and orange colors—remind us of the sun and warmth. Artists use blue, green, and violet—cool color schemes—to make us think of cool items such as ice or grass.

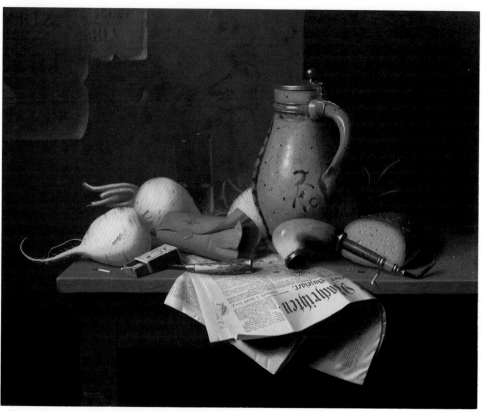

▲ Figure 1–2   Can you point to places where the value changes are gradual? How do these gradual changes of value help to suggest round, three-dimensional form? Can you find places where the value changes are sudden?

William Michael Harnett. *Munich Still Life.* 1882. Oil on canvas. 62.5 x 76.8 cm (24⅝ x 30¼").
Dallas Museum of Art, Dallas, Texas.

Lesson 1   *The Elements of Art*   **3**

■ **Motivator**

Give students different colored paper patches of primary, secondary, or intermediate colors in various values and intensities. Have students place the patches against their clothing and arrange themselves in a color circle. Explain the relationships of the colors in monochromatic, analogous, warm, and cool color schemes. Ask students to group themselves in these relationships. Have each group identify which color scheme it represents.

■ **Vocabulary**

Have students make a vocabulary chart that includes all of the terms and definitions as they are learned. Have students keep a copy of the chart in their portfolios for reference and review.

■ **Art Criticism**

Have students choose an illustration from the text and write a short description of the work, the elements that they see, and the effect that those elements create. Encourage them to point out how artists use the elements of art in different ways to create a variety of art works.

■ **Studio Skills**

Have students collect examples of colors in all hues, values, and intensities. They may use fabric samples, colored paper, or cutouts from magazines. Instruct them to glue small patches of the colors to sketch paper. Then have them try to match the colors with watercolor paints. Demonstrate the process of mixing colors to get light and dark color values and bright and dull hues. Refer to the Technique Tip on how to mix paint to change the value of color in the Handbook, page 280.

CURRICULUM ▸ *CONNECTIONS*

Language Arts   Remind students that poets often write about the visual arts, and that poetry is like painting pictures with words. You may wish to read aloud excerpts from the works of Robert Frost, e.e. cummings, or William Carlos Williams. Pay special attention to the images created through the descriptions in these poems. Tell students to listen for sounds of words. Help them to recognize metaphor, simile, personification, and the other figures of speech that color poetry and prose. Students can apply the same kind of careful analysis to reading as they apply to the study of visual art forms.

■ Aesthetics

Help students understand how the elements of art can be pieced together to make a successful art work. Play a game called "Pass the Paper." Divide the class into groups of five. Give each group a blank sheet of paper and provide pencils, markers, or crayons. Read to students the following steps, giving them 20 seconds to complete one step before passing the paper to the next student.

1. Draw three shapes.
2. Fill one shape with a pattern to show texture.
3. Add three different types of lines to the work.
4. Draw an organic shape.
5. Place something small in background or something large in foreground to create depth.

After all the elements have been tested, have students pass the paper back to the first student. Discuss whether the work is successful in using all the art elements.

LINE

An element of art that can be used to send different messages to viewers is a line. **Line** is defined as *the path of a moving point through space.* You can draw lines on paper or scratch a line in wet clay with a tool. Lines can be seen in your environment, such as the web of a spider or the railing on a stair.

There are five main kinds of lines:

- Horizontal lines, which run parallel to the ground, appear to be at rest.

- Vertical lines—lines that run up and down—seem to show dignity, formality, and strength.
- Diagonal, or slanting, lines signal action and excitement.
- Zigzag lines, which are made from combined diagonal lines, can create a feeling of confusion or suggest action.
- Curved lines express movement in a graceful, flowing way.

▶ **Figure 1–3   How is color used to help emphasize the figure in this painting? Do you think the artist's use of both large and small shapes makes this picture more pleasing to look at?**

Marc Chagall. *Green Violinist.* 1923–1924. Oil on canvas. 198 x 108.6 cm (78 x 42¾"). Solomon R. Guggenheim Museum, New York, New York. Gift of Solomon R. Guggenheim.

4   Lesson 1   *The Elements of Art*

─ *more about* ● ● ●

Marc Chagall   Marc Chagall was born in Russia in 1889 and was able to draw from a rich background of Jewish folktales and traditions as subjects for his paintings. He attended art schools in St. Petersburg and maintained a sense of fantasy expressed in his poetic works. During his studies in Russia, he was influenced by artists such as van Gogh, Gauguin, and Matisse. Later, in Paris, he was influenced more by the innovations of Cubist artists. His style developed further when, after the Russian revolution, he worked in Moscow painting murals and designing sets and costumes for the Yiddish theater. Working on a large scale in this setting inspired some of his most exciting paintings, like the one shown in Figure 1-3.

Look again at Figure 1–2 on page **3**. How many different lines can you find? In what directions do these lines go?

In art, line quality and line variation influence the viewer's reaction to a work of art. Line quality is the unique character of the line. It can be affected by the tool or medium used to produce the mark or by the particular motion of the artist's hand. Line variation describes the thickness or thinness, lightness or darkness of a line.

SHAPE AND FORM

Every object — a cloud, a house, a pebble — has a shape. **Shape** is *an element of art that refers to an area clearly set off by one or more of the other elements of art*. Shapes are limited to two dimensions — length and width.

All shapes belong to one of two classes:

- **Geometric** (jee-uh-**meh**-trik). Geometric shapes look as though they were made with a ruler or drawing tool. The square, the circle, the triangle, the rectangle, and the oval are the five basic geometric shapes. Look at the painting in Figure 1–3. Can you find any geometric shapes?
- **Organic**. Also called free-form, organic shapes are not regular or even. Their outlines may be curved or angular, or they may be a combination of both, to make free-form shapes. Organic shapes, such as clouds and pebbles, are usually found in nature. Can you find any organic shapes in Figure 1–3?

Like shapes, forms have length and width. Forms also have a third dimension, depth. **Form** is *an element of art that refers to an object with three dimensions*. With the forms found in works of art, such as sculpture and architecture, you can actually experience the three dimensions by walking around or into the works.

SPACE

All objects take up space. **Space** is *an element of art that refers to the distance between, around, above, below, and within things*. Which objects in Figure 1–3 appear closest to you? Which seem to be farther back in space?

In both two- and three-dimensional works of art, the shapes or forms are called the positive area. The empty spaces between the shapes are called negative spaces. The relationship between the positive and negative space will affect how the art work is interpreted.

TEXTURE

Run your fingers over the top of your desk or work table. You are feeling the surface's texture. **Texture** is *an element of art that refers to the way things feel, or look as though they might feel, if touched*.

Imagine you could touch the objects in the picture in Figure 1–2 on page **3**. Which of them do you think would feel smooth? Do any look rough or uneven?

✔ CHECK YOUR UNDERSTANDING

1. What are the three properties of color?
2. What message do vertical lines send to a viewer? What message do diagonal lines send?
3. What is the difference between shape and form?
4. What is the difference between the positive area and the negative area in a work of art?
5. Define *texture*.

Answers to ✔ CHECK YOUR UNDERSTANDING

1. Hue, the name of the color; value, the lightness or darkness of the hue; and intensity, the brightness or dullness of the hue.
2. Vertical lines convey dignity, formality and strength to the viewer. Diagonal lines signal action or excitement.
3. Shapes are limited to two dimensions; length and width. Form refers to an object with three dimensions: length, width, and depth.
4. Positive areas are occupied by objects in a work of art; negative areas are the empty spaces between the objects.
5. The element of art that shows how the surface of an object might feel if it were touched.

☑ OBJECTIVES

After completing this lesson, students will be able to:
- Create a non-objective design using the elements of art.
- Analyze a non-objective design and recognize the various elements of art.

☑ SUPPLIES

- Small, textured objects.
- Pencils, rulers.
- Sheets of white drawing paper, 18 x 24 inches (45 x 60 cm).
- Colored markers.
- Colored pencils, crayons.
- Yarn.
- Strips of construction paper.
- Black and white photos.

Resource

- ■ 1-6 *The Elements in Your Life*, TRB page 33 (studio)

TEACH

■ Motivator

Help students understand the concept of *non-objective art*. Have them examine the work by Grace Hartigan in Figure 1-4. Ask what recognizable objects they can find. Ask them to point out which elements of art they can find. Explain that a work of art can be successful without showing any recognizable objects. Tell them that artists accomplish this by carefully combining the elements of art.

LESSON 2

Using the Elements of Art

Sometimes artists create **non-objective art**. These are *works in which no objects or subjects can be readily identified*. Figure 1–4 is such a work. This one is by Grace Hartigan. She has combined several elements of art in this work to create unusual effects.

WHAT YOU WILL LEARN

This is the first of many studio lessons. In these lessons you will use your creative skills and experiment with different media. You will create many works of art that may be displayed.

For this first studio experiment, you will create a non-objective design using all the elements of art. You will use pencil, felt-tip markers, colored pencils, and crayons. (See Figure 1–5.)

WHAT YOU WILL NEED

- Pencil and ruler
- Sheet of white drawing paper, 18 x 24 inches (46 x 61 cm)
- Colored markers, colored pencils, and crayons

WHAT YOU WILL DO

1. Using one continuous pencil line, make a design that fills the sheet of drawing paper. Allow your pencil to drift off the edge of the paper and return. Try to create a design that has both large and small shapes.
2. Using the ruler, divide your paper into eight equal rectangles. Each should measure 6 x 9 inches (15 x 23 cm). Number the eight boxed areas lightly in pencil. You may order the numbers any way you like (Figure 1–6).

▲ Figure 1–4 Hartigan has painted a non-objective work that shows several elements of art combined to make a pleasing whole. What elements can you identify in this painting?

Grace Hartigan. *The Faraway Places*. 1974. Oil on canvas. 228.6 x 166.4 cm (90 x 65½"). McNay Art Museum, San Antonio, Texas. Purchase made possible by a grant from the National Endowment for the Arts with matching funds, Marion Koogler.

3. Using primary *hues* of crayons, color the shapes in Area 1. (See the color wheel on page **2**.)
4. Using light and dark *values* of colored pencils, color in the shapes in Area 2. Using bright and dull *intensities* of colored pencils, color in the shapes in Area 3.
5. Using the pencil, go over the *lines* in Area 4. Make some of the lines straight and others curved. Try pressing down on the pencil for some of the lines. This will give a thicker, darker result.

6   Lesson 2   *Using the Elements of Art*

MEETING SPECIAL NEEDS

Peer Assistance   To help students with mental, visual, or neurological disabilities, you may wish to pair them with a partner. In the studio lesson above, the partner can assist the student in measuring, dividing his or her paper into eight sections, and explaining the specific step-by-step directions. You may also want to write the directions on the board or prepare a handout with printed instructions of the steps to help students who have difficulty following a sequence of steps, or for those who have hearing problems. To include students who are blind, try using a medium that creates a raised line to follow, such as dried white glue, and let them fill in shapes with scented markers.

6. Using pencil, crayons, colored pencils, or markers, create three different *textures* in Area 5.
7. Using the markers, draw outlines around *shapes* in Area 6. Fill in some of the shapes with the markers. Leave the others white.
8. Use pencil to add a new shape that overlaps the existing shapes in Area 7 to show *space*. Add to this feeling of space by using colored pencil to color this shape in a bright hue. Color the other shapes in dull hues.
9. Using the pencil, shade the shapes in Area 8 little by little. Try to make these shapes look like rounded, three-dimensional *forms*. (For information on shading, see Technique Tip **6**, *Handbook* page **278**.)
10. Display your design. See if other members of your class can identify the different art elements found in each area.

▲ Figure 1–5 Student work. Non-objective design.

EXAMINING YOUR WORK

- **Describe** Tell which element each area of your design highlights. Identify the media you used to create the different areas.
- **Judge** State whether your design clearly highlights each element of art. Tell which section of your design you think is the most successful. Explain your answer.

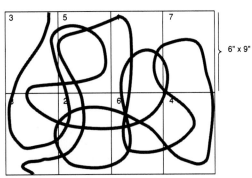

▲ Figure 1–6 Drawing the elements of art.

Try This! ## COMPUTER OPTION

■ Use a medium Brush tool. Draw a continuous line that drifts off the edges of the screen and fills the page. Draw an open box around your line design, 8 x 10 inches (20 x 25 cm). Use the Grids and Rulers option to guide you. Select the Straight Line tool and hold down the Shift Key. Click and drag straight lines to divide the large box into eight small sections 2½ x 5 inches (6.4 x 12.7 cm). Follow directions in the Studio Lesson. Choose colors and Drawing tools on the computer to create texture and value.

Lesson 2 *Using the Elements of Art* **7**

■ **Studio Skills**
Help students understand how to add texture to an art work. Bring several small objects with different textures to class. Examples might include sandpaper, fabric samples such as silk or wool, corkboard, aluminum foil, rough rocks, leather, and beaded cloth. Assemble the collection of objects and shine a light source on the objects. Have students draw what they see, trying to reproduce the look of each surface using drawing pencils and markers.

· · · · · · · · · · · · · · ·
ASSESS

■ **Self-Assessment**
Have students use Examining Your Work to evaluate their non-objective designs created in this Studio Lesson. Responses may be written or oral.

■ **Reteaching**
Review with students the visual elements used in Figure 1-4. Ask them to describe the feeling they get when viewing the work.

■ **Enrichment**
Have groups of students research the work of various artists, such as Wassily Kandinsky, who created non-objective works. Ask them to report back to the class why their artist chose to work non-objectively and which visual elements were most important to that artist.

· · · · · · · · · · · · · · ·
CLOSE

Ask students to explain how a non-objective work of art can be successful even though it does not depict any recognizable objects.

MEETING STUDENT DIVERSITY

Learning Styles For a further challenge, offer independent learners an extension to the studio lesson. Have them draw a simple still life using *lines* to create each of the *shapes*. Tell them to try overlapping some of the *shapes* to add a feeling of *space*. Then have them choose three hues to add *color* to the picture. Tell students that gradual and sudden changes in value should be used to make some shapes look like three-dimensional *forms*. They may create different rough and smooth *textures*. Then have students identify and discuss each of the elements of art they included in their works.

The Principles of Art

☑ **OBJECTIVES**

After completing this lesson, students will be able to:
• Recognize and define the principles of art.
• Use the principles of art to organize the elements of art.

☑ **SUPPLIES**

• Black squares of paper for an overhead projector layout; or black squares of felt and a white feltboard.
• Yarn, round objects such as buttons and washers, thin sticks.
• Cut paper shapes from magazines and newspapers.
• White drawing paper, 18 x 24 inches (45 x 60 cm).
• Scissors, white glue.
• Construction paper.

Resources

■ 1-7 *How a Work of Art "Works,"* TRB page 34 (reproducible master)
■ 1-8 *The Language of Art in Your Home,* TRB page 35 (aesthetics/art criticism)

• • • • • • • • • • • • • •

TEACH

■ **Motivator**

Show students an evenly spaced arrangement of black squares on the overhead projector. Ask them to move, change, or add shapes and lines and try to arrange the items to create the various kinds of balance: formal, informal, and radial.

If you want to use a language, knowing the vocabulary is not enough. You must also know how the words go together. You must know the rules of grammar for that language.

The same is true of art. Instead of rules of grammar, the language of art has art princi-ples. These principles, or guidelines, govern how artists organize the visual elements to create a work of art.

The principles of art include balance, vari-ety, harmony, emphasis, proportion, move-ment, and rhythm.

▶ **Figure 1–7** This picture combines familiar images from our modern rock culture. Do you think the artist has succeeded in organizing the elements of art to create a visually pleasing whole?

Richard Lindner. *Rock-Rock.* 1966. Oil on canvas. 177.8 x 152.4 cm (70 x 60"). Dallas Museum of Art, Dallas, Texas. Gift of Mr. & Mrs. James H. Clark.

TECHNOLOGY OPTIONS

National Gallery of Art Videodisc   Use the following images to demonstrate the use of balance, harmony, and movement.

Auguste Renoir *A Girl with a Watering Can*	Auguste Renoir *Pont Neuf, Paris*	Vincent van Gogh *Farmhouse in Provence, Arles*
Search Frame 1300	Search Frame 1288	Search Frame 1524

Use Glencoe's *Correlation Bar Code Guide to the National Gallery of Art* to locate more art works.

BALANCE

If you have ever carried a stack of dishes or books, you know the importance of balance. In art, balance is also important. **Balance** is *a principle of art concerned with arranging elements so no one part of a work overpowers, or seems heavier than, any other part.* In art, balance is seen or felt by the viewer.

In works of art, three kinds of balance are possible. They are formal balance, informal balance, and radial balance. In works of art with formal, or symmetrical (suh-**meh**-trih-kuhl), balance the two halves are mirror im-

ages. In works with informal, or asymmetrical (ay-suh-**meh**-trih-kuhl), balance two unlike elements seem to carry equal weight. For example, a small shape painted bright red will balance several larger items painted in duller reds.

Radial balance occurs when elements or objects in an art work are positioned around a central point. Study the art works in Figures 1–7, 1–8, and 1–9. Which uses formal balance? Which uses informal balance? Which uses radial balance?

▲ **Figure 1–8** Compare this painting with the one in Figure 1–7. How are they similar? Do the different elements in these paintings help suggest a certain kind of music? Would the mood of this painting change if the artist used the same colors as those in Figure 1–7?

Auguste Renoir. *Young Spanish Woman with a Guitar.* 1898. Canvas. 55.6 x 65.2 cm (21⅞ x 25⅝″). National Gallery of Art, Washington, D.C. Ailsa Mellon Bruce Collection.

■ Studio Skills

Divide the class into groups of two or three students. Ask each group to develop a composition that illustrates the art principles of variety, harmony, emphasis, or proportion. Have the groups make their compositions on sheets of paper using yarn, thin sticks, found objects, and squares and circles cut from magazines. Students also may want to cut various shapes of their own.

Encourage groups to experiment with a number of arrangements to find one that uses the space effectively and best illustrates the principle or principles they wish to achieve. When students have determined the best layout, have them glue the pieces into place.

■ Art Criticism

Ask students to examine the fabric sections shown on pages 90 and 92. Have them compare the effects of movement and rhythm shown in the Peruvian shirt section in Figure 6-15 and the textile fragment shown in Figure 6-18. Ask volunteers to explain which one shows movement and which shows alternating rhythm.

■ Cultural Diversity

Explain to students that the styles of art vary from culture to culture and change throughout time. Nevertheless, they all follow the same principles of design and can be analyzed according to the organization of their visual elements. Point out that radial balance is frequently found in folk art traditions and in Asian decorative art. Have students look for examples of radial design and report on how it was used in each culture where it is found. (Examples may be found on textbook pages 105, 117, and 118.)

▲ **Figure 1–9** How many different art elements did Vincent van Gogh use in this painting? What has he done to create the illusion of movement? What images in this painting do not appear to move?

Vincent van Gogh. *The Starry Night.* 1889. Oil on canvas. 73.7 x 92.1 cm (29 x 36¼"). Collection, The Museum of Modern Art, New York, New York. Acquired through the Lillie P. Bliss bequest.

VARIETY

The same routine day after day can become dull. The same color or shape repeated over and over in an art work can become equally dull. To avoid dullness, artists use the principle of variety in their works. **Variety** is *a principle of art concerned with combining one or more elements to create interest by adding slight changes.* By giving a work variety, the artist heightens the visual appeal of the work.

Look again at the picture in Figure 1–7. How does the artist's use of color add variety to the work? Which other elements are used to add variety?

HARMONY

If too little variety can become boring, too much variety can create chaos. Artists avoid chaos in their works by using the principle of harmony. **Harmony** is *a principle of art concerned with blending elements to create a more calm, restful appearance.*

Of the two paintings in Figures 1–7 and 1–8, which has greater harmony? Which elements does the artist use to introduce harmony to the work?

10   Lesson 3   *The Principles of Art*

— *more about* ● ● ●

Vincent van Gogh   The artistic career of Vincent van Gogh (Netherlands, 1853–1890) was filled with frustration, misfortune, religious torment, and depression. Early in his life, van Gogh sought to become a preacher, but was dismissed when he was deemed overly zealous. He lived in extreme poverty, and turned to art in 1880. He once wrote, "To try to understand the real significance of what the great artists, the serious masters, tell us in their masterpieces, that leads to God." Van Gogh produced hundreds of canvases that reflect his intense emotional nature. He never sold one painting during his lifetime.

EMPHASIS

To attract a viewer's attention to important parts of a work, artists use the principle of emphasis. **Emphasis** is *making an element in a work stand out*. Emphasis can be created by contrast or by extreme changes in an element.

Look once more at Figure 1–8. What has been done to emphasize the face of the young woman?

PROPORTION

Have you ever tasted a food that was so salty you couldn't eat it? The problem was one of proportion. **Proportion** is *the principle of art concerned with the relationship of one part to another and to the whole*.

The principle of proportion is not limited to size. Elements such as color can be used in differing proportions to create emphasis. It is used this way in Figure 1–7. Which color is used in greatest proportion?

MOVEMENT

You may not have realized it, but when you look at a work of art your eye moves from part to part. Artists use the principle of movement to lead the viewer's eyes throughout the work. **Movement** is *the principle of art used to create the look and feeling of action and to guide a viewer's eye throughout the work of art*.

Study yet again the paintings in Figures 1–7, 1–8, and 1–9. How have the artists used line and shape to move your eyes throughout the works?

RHYTHM

Often artists seek to make their works seem active. When they do, they call upon the principle of rhythm. **Rhythm** is *the principle of art concerned with repeating an element to make a work seem active or to suggest vibration*. Sometimes to create rhythm, an artist will repeat not just elements but also the same exact objects over and over. When this is done, a pattern is formed.

Compare the works in Figures 1–7, 1–8, and 1–9. Which uses the principle of rhythm? What element is repeated?

UNITY IN ART

When you look at works of art, it may be difficult to determine where one part ends and the other begins. Instead, the piece of art works together as a whole. It has unity. **Unity** is *the arrangement of elements and principles with media to create a feeling of completeness or wholeness*. You will sense this unity as you look at works of art in which artists use the elements and principles with skill, imagination, and sensitivity.

✔CHECK YOUR UNDERSTANDING

1. What are principles of art?
2. Name three kinds of balance. Describe each kind.
3. What principles do artists use to prevent works from being static?
4. How can emphasis be created in a work of art?
5. Define *movement*.

Sparking Creativity

Give students a sense of rhythm and movement in a creative way. Tell them: Rhythm in dance is found in the movements of the dancers. Try to see it and give it visual form. Ask one or two students to dance and have the class draw their movements rather than their bodies. Try a slow, graceful dance and then a rock rhythm. Compare students' drawings. Experiment with various tools and media and see how it will affect the rhythm of the designs.

ASSESS

■ **Self-Assessment**

Have students complete the review questions on this page. Answers are provided below.

■ **Reteaching**

Review with students the various steps they made in the classroom composition Motivator exercise that illustrated the different design principles. Ask the following: Where did the creative process begin? What were the steps in that process? Which of the arrangements would you call art? Must art necessarily be done on purpose to qualify as art? Can something be aesthetically stimulating and not be art?

■ **Enrichment**

Have students investigate and explain the geometrical principles used to create formal and radial balance.

CLOSE

Review with students art principle terms and definitions.

Answers to ✔CHECK YOUR UNDERSTANDING

1. The seven principles artists use to organize the visual elements of a work are balance, variety, harmony, emphasis, proportion, movement, and rhythm.
2. The three kinds of balance are formal or mirror-image; informal or asymmetrical, where two unlike elements seem to carry equal weight; and radial, where objects are arranged around a central point.
3. Artists can use movement and rhythm to prevent an art work from looking static.
4. Emphasis can be created by using contrast or extreme change in an element.
5. Movement is the principle used to create a feeling of action and to lead the viewer's eye throughout the art work.

Using the Principles of Art

(pages 12–13)

LESSON TIME: 45 minutes

• • • • • • • • • • • • • •
FOCUS

☑ OBJECTIVES

After completing this lesson, students will be able to:
• Create a design that imaginatively illustrates their name and includes all the principles of art.

☑ SUPPLIES

• Sheets of scrap paper.
• Pencils.
• Rulers.
• Erasers.
• White drawing paper, 18 x 24 inches (46 x 61 cm).
• Watercolor paints.
• A variety of brushes.
• Tempera paints.
• Paint mixing trays.
• Construction paper.
• Scissors.

Resource

■ 1-9 *Be an Interior Designer*, TRB page 37 (cooperative learning)

• • • • • • • • • • • • • •
TEACH

■ Motivator

Have students write the letters of their name or nickname horizontally on a sheet of paper. Have them brainstorm to think of one descriptive word for each letter, and write that word. Ask them to describe what they think of when they hear the words they have written.

12

Using the Principles of Art

Artists use the language of art in different and often highly imaginative ways. Figure 1–10 gives us painter Charles Demuth's (duh-**mooth**) view of a fire engine racing through a rain-swept city at night.

Notice that the artist has not attempted to create a true-to-life picture. There are no clear images of trucks, wet streets, or darkened buildings. Rather, Demuth has captured the *idea* of those images. Look closely and you can almost hear the screaming of Engine Company 5's siren. You can almost see the red truck's lights flashing.

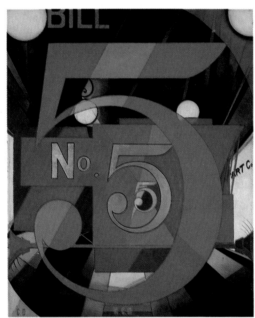

▲ **Figure 1–10** How is the principle of proportion demonstrated in this work? Explain how repetition is used to suggest movement and rhythm. Do you think this painting demonstrates unity?

Charles Henry Demuth. *I Saw the Figure 5 in Gold*. 1928. Oil on composition board. 91.4 x 75.6 cm (36 x 29¾"). The Metropolitan Museum of Art, New York, New York. The Alfred Stieglitz Collection.

WHAT YOU WILL LEARN

You will create the "idea of your name." You will do this through a design made up of the letters of your name or nickname. All the principles of art will be used in your design. You will use watercolor paint and tempera paint in your work. (See Figure 1–11.)

WHAT YOU WILL NEED

• Sheets of scrap paper
• Pencil, ruler, and eraser
• Sheet of white drawing paper, 18 x 24 inches (46 x 61 cm)
• Watercolor paint and several brushes
• Tempera paint and mixing tray

WHAT YOU WILL DO

1. On scrap paper, practice making block letters of different sizes and shapes. Focus only on the letters in your name or nickname.
2. Working lightly in pencil, create a design with the letters on the sheet of drawing paper. Arrange for some of the letters to overlap and some to go off the page. Fill the entire sheet of paper.
3. Using the ruler, divide your paper into eight equal rectangles. Each should measure 6 x 9 inches (15 x 23 cm). Number the eight boxed areas lightly in pencil in any order you like.
4. Using the pencil and eraser, draw in or erase lines to rearrange the shapes in Area 1 so they have formal *balance*. Fill in some of the shapes with pencil.
5. Using a *variety* of hues of tempera, paint the shapes in Area 2.
6. Using no more than three hues, paint the shapes in Area 3. Repeat one of these colors over and over to add *harmony*.

more about • • •

Charles Demuth   Charles Demuth's painting *I Saw the Figure 5 in Gold* demonstrates the influence of several twentieth-century art movements. Demuth was friendly with Marcel Duchamp and other Cubists who lived in New York during World War I, and his relationship with them is reflected in the faceted and geometric forms. Demuth's later development of a style known as Precisionism, strongly influenced by the clean lines and architectural emphasis of Futurism, can also be seen in Figure 1-10. Demuth's canvas ultimately became part of the heritage of Pop artists.

7. Identify the most interesting shape in Area 4. Using the brightest hue, paint this area to give *emphasis* to this shape. Paint other shapes with dull hues.

8. Using the pencil and eraser, rearrange the shapes in Area 5 to create *rhythm*. Use watercolors to paint the shapes.

9. Using watercolors, paint the shapes in Area 6. Increase the *proportion* of one of the colors you use. Notice how doing this *emphasizes* that color.

10. Using the pencil and eraser, rearrange the shapes in Area 7 to create a sense of *movement* in any direction. Use watercolors to paint the shapes. Pick colors that will add to the feeling of movement.

11. Rearrange similar shapes in Area 8 to create a pattern. Pick one color of tempera to paint the shapes in Area 8. Paint the nearest shapes. Paint the other shapes, adding white to lighten the value of the hue. (For information on mixing paint to change value, see Technique Tip **12**, *Handbook* page **280**.) In this way the shapes will appear to create rhythm.

12. Display your design and identify the different principles of art found in each area.

balance	variety	rhythm	proportion
emphasis	harmony	movement	unity

▲ Figure 1–11   Grid showing principles of art in Figure 1–12.

Try This! **STUDIO OPTION**

■ On a sheet of white paper, create a second design. This work should be based on your initials. Focus on the part of your first design that you found most interesting. Complete your work using techniques from the Studio Lesson.

EXAMINING YOUR WORK

- **Describe**   Tell where the different letters of your name or nickname are found in your design. Identify the art media you used to create the different areas.
- **Analyze**   Name the principle of art highlighted in each area of your design.
- **Judge**   Tell whether your design clearly highlights each principle of art. Tell which section of your design you think is the most successful. Explain your answer.

▲ Figure 1–12   Student work. Design using the principles of art.

Lesson 4   *Using the Principles of Art*   **13**

Have students examine Figure 1-10 and identify the principles of art in Demuth's painting. Discuss how variety and proportion are shown in the various sizes and placement of the number five. List the principles on the board until all are named and discussed.

Art on a Shoestring

Foam meat trays make excellent paint mixing trays. Sometimes store meat managers will sell some to you at a low cost if they know they are for school use.

• • • • • • • • • • • • •
ASSESS

■ **Self-Assessment**

Have students use Examining Your Work to evaluate their own work. Responses may be written or oral.

■ **Reteaching**

Have students choose another art work in the chapter and examine it in terms of the art principles. Ask them to identify which principles make this a successful painting.

■ **Enrichment**

Point out to students the red "Bill," the "Carlo" in gold light, and the "W.C.W." that appear in Figure 1-10. Explain that the poet William Carlos Williams was an old friend of Demuth. Have volunteers locate the Williams poem that inspired Demuth's painting and share it with the class.

• • • • • • • • • • • • •
CLOSE

Have students discuss whether they find conceptual art works, such as Figure 1-10, as satisfying as a more straightforward illustration of a subject. Ask them to discuss why or why not.

▽ TECHNIQUE TIP

Studio Lesson   Although Figure 1-12 does not show the grid lines, students will be dividing the page into eight rectangles as they did for the Studio Lesson on pages 6–7. Remind students that they have already learned to divide their 18- x 24-inch (46 x 61 cm) paper into eight equal rectangles. Figure 1-6 shows how to divide the long sides into four six-inch segments and the short sides into two. These will give them eight 6- x 9-inch (15 x 23 cm) rectangles which they can number in any order they desire.

CONNECTIONS *Science*

Giacomo Balla. *Dynamism of a Dog on a Leash.* 1912. Oil on canvas. 89.8 x 109.9 cm (35⅜ x 43¼"). Albright Knox Art Gallery, Buffalo, New York. Bequest of A. Conger Goodyear and Gift of George F. Goodyear. 1964.

How Does the Eye Perceive Movement?

Our eyes and brain work together to help us make sense of what we see. Human eyes provide an amazingly detailed, three-dimensional view of the world. How do the eyes accomplish this work?

Everything we see depends on rays of light. Light rays pass into the eye through the cornea. A thin layer of cells called the retina picks up these rays of light, detecting the image created by the light. Some of the light-sensitive cells of the retina detect shapes and shades of light but not color. Other cells are sensitive to details, colors, and movement.

The eye then sends a pattern of signals to the brain. The brain decodes the signals and makes sense of the shapes, colors, and movements transmitted through the rays of light. Thus it is the brain that really interprets colors, shape and form, and movement. Sometimes what we see can play tricks on the brain, as with Giacomo Balla's painting shown here. Balla tried to create the illusion of movement using brush strokes that imitate the process of animation. In this technique, a series of images is repeated quickly, one right after another. The eye and brain blend the images together to give the impression that the image is moving.

┌─ **MAKING THE CONNECTION**

- ☑ In Giacomo Balla's *Dynamism of a Dog on a Leash,* what technique has the artist used to imitate actual movement?
- ☑ Find some examples of multiple-exposure photographs. How is Balla's painting similar to the photographs?
- ☑ Find other examples of art that simulate, or imitate, movement. Explain the technique the artist has used and why you think the technique was or was not successful.

INTERNET ACTIVITY

Visit Glencoe's Fine Arts Web Site for students at:

http://www.glencoe.com/sec/art/students

INTERNET ACTIVITY

Art on the Web You and your students are invited to take a trip through Glencoe's Fine Arts Site on the World Wide Web. Your class can explore *Studio Cyberspace,* full of art activities; *Glencoe Student Galleria,* a changing showcase of student art works; links to lots of adventures through art museums, worldwide cultural treasures, and contact with other art teachers. You simply need a computer with a modem, an Internet hook-up, and curious minds. To reach the Glencoe Fine Arts page, type in the URL address exactly as shown:

http://www.glencoe.com/sec/art

Check the *Internet Activity Booklet* included with the *Understanding Art* program for more information.

CHAPTER 1 REVIEW

 BUILDING VOCABULARY

Number a sheet of paper from 1 to 15. After each number, write the term from the box that best matches each description below.

balance	proportion
color	rhythm
emphasis	shape
form	space
harmony	texture
line	unity
movement	variety
non-objective art	

1. What the eyes see when light is reflected off an object.
2. Path of a moving point through space.
3. The way things feel, or look as though they might feel, if touched.
4. An area clearly set off by one or more of the other elements of art.
5. An object with three dimensions.
6. Arranging elements so no one part of a work overpowers, or seems heavier than, any other part.
7. Combining one or more elements to create interest by adding slight changes.
8. Blending elements to create a more calm, restful appearance.
9. Making an element in a work stand out.
10. The repeating of an element to make a work seem active or to suggest vibration.
11. The relationship of one part to another and to the whole.
12. The arrangement of elements and principles with media to create a feeling of completeness or wholeness.
13. The principle of art used to create the look and feeling of action and to guide a viewer's eye throughout the work.
14. Art works in which no objects or subjects can be readily identified.
15. The distance between, around, above, below, and within things.

 REVIEWING ART FACTS

Number a sheet of paper from 16 to 20. Answer each question in a complete sentence.

16. What are the elements of art?
17. Which of the three properties of color refers to a color's name and place on a color wheel?
18. What are the two different kinds of shapes?
19. What is non-objective art?
20. What is symmetrical balance? What is asymmetrical balance?

THINKING ABOUT ART

On a sheet of paper, answer each question in a sentence or two.

1. **Extend.** What kind of lines would you use in creating a picture of an action-packed horse race? What kind of lines would you use in creating a calm, peaceful picture of a lake and trees? Explain your answers.
2. **Compare and contrast.** What do the elements of shape and form have in common? In what ways are the two different?

MAKING ART CONNECTIONS

1. **Science.** Make a list of the elements of art. Choose an object from nature that shows examples of these elements. Beside each art element listed, write a one- or two-word description of the natural object you chose.

2. **Language Arts.** Think about a career in art. Read a book with interviews of people working in the art field, *Careers for Artistic Types*, by Andrew Kaplan. Make a poster that shows some of the art careers you read about.

Chapter 1 Review **15**

The Media of Art

(pages 16–31)

Resources

- 2-8 Chapter Test, TRB page 61
- Transparency CC-2, *Model of Super Power Plant* by Howard Finster
- Transparency 2, *High Steppin' Strutter 1* by Miriam Schapiro
- Fine Art Print 2, *The Carpet Merchant* by Jean-Léon Gérôme

Theatre

While studying this chapter use Performing Arts Handbook page 318 to help students recognize how performers from In the Heart of the Beast Puppet and Mask Theatre use a variety of media to create plays and pageants.

NATIONAL STANDARDS

This chapter addresses the following National Standards for the Visual Arts:

1. (a, b)	4. (a, b, c)
2. (a, b)	5. (a, b, c)
3. (a)	6. (a, b)

▲ What art media did the artist choose to create this sculpture? What method of sculpting was used?

Luis Jiménez. *Vaquero*. Modeled 1980/ cast 1990. Acrylic urethane, fiberglass, steel armature. 505.5 x 289.6 x 170.2 cm (199 x 114 x 67"). National Museum of American Art, Smithsonian Institution, Washington, D.C. Gift of Judith and Wilbur L. Ross, Jr., Anne and Ronald Abramson, Thelma and Melvin Lenkin. Art Resource, New York. ©1980 Luis Jiménez.

16

FEATURED ARTISTS

Barbara Aubin	Helen Frankenthaler	John Marin
Isabel Bishop	Antonio Gaudi	Joan Miró
Mary Cassatt	Edward Harvey	Gertrud and Otto Natzler
Paul Cézanne	Vinnie Ream Hoxie	Philip Nicholson
Abastenia St. Leger Eberle	Luis Jiménez	

The Media of Art

You may think of an artist as someone who paints. While it is true that many artists are painters, paint is just one material artists use. Some artists prefer to work with the tools and materials of printmaking. Others prefer to work with the tools and materials of architecture. Still others would rather work with the tools used to create the sculpture at the left.

In this chapter you will learn about the many different materials of the artist's profession.

PORTFOLIO IDEAS

Often, you will begin an art work in a sketchbook. A **sketchbook** is *a pad of drawing paper on which artists sketch, write notes, and refine ideas for their work.* Think about a work of art you know and like. In your sketchbook describe the art work using the elements and principles of art.

What media was used to create it? What do you like about the art work? Date this entry. Refer to this written entry in the future and use it as a source of inspiration for one of your art works.

OBJECTIVES

After completing this chapter, you will be able to:
- Identify drawing, painting, and printmaking media.
- Discover the ways electronic media and computers can be used to create art works.
- Explain the basic methods of printmaking and sculpting.
- Explain the basic uses of architecture and crafts.
- Create art work using different art media.

WORDS YOU WILL LEARN

architecture
binder
crafts
edition
freestanding sculpture
medium of art
mixed media
menus
pigment
pixels
printmaking
relief sculpture
solvent

17

Drawing, Painting, Printmaking, and Computer Art

● ● ● ● ● ● ● ● ● ● ● ● ●
FOCUS

☑ **OBJECTIVES**

After completing this lesson, students will be able to:

• Define the term *medium of art.*
• Name four different kinds of painting media.
• Explain the use of electronic media in art.
• Name four methods of making prints.

☑ **SUPPLIES**

• Variety of drawing media.
• Sketch paper.
• Index cards.
• Painting tools such as brushes, palette knives, sponges, drawing paper.

Resource

■ 2-1 *The Medium is the Message*, TRB page 43 (Aesthetics/Art Criticism)

● ● ● ● ● ● ● ● ● ● ● ● ●
TEACH

■ **Motivator**

Distribute different kinds of drawing media to students. Have them experiment with the media. Have students work with partners to discuss what they have discovered about the different media. Ask students which media they prefer and why.

One of the most important decisions for an artist is which medium to use. A **medium of art** is *a material used to create a work of art.* Paint is one medium. Pencil and crayon, which you have used, are two others. The computer has also become an important medium for artists. When we speak of more than one medium at a time, we use the plural *media.*

When artists use several different media, such as pen and ink and watercolor, they create a mixed media work of art. **Mixed media** means *the use of more than one medium in a work of art.*

In this lesson you will learn about the media used in drawing, painting, printmaking, and computer art.

DRAWING

Pen, pencil, charcoal, and chalk are some of the media used to draw. The picture in Figure 2–1 was made using another medium, pastels. This is a soft, chalky medium. Notice how delicately the artist has used this medium to capture her subject.

The Purpose of Drawing

Artists use drawing for different purposes. One is to create finished works of art. Another use is to help plan projects. Artists often make studies, or sketches, for their works. Look at the drawing in Figure 2–2. This was done by French artist Paul Cézanne (say-**zahn**) as a study for the painting in Figure 2–3.

PAINTING

Like other artists, painters use a wide variety of media. Before a painter begins a work, he or she chooses a type of paint and an appropriate surface on which to work. Canvas, paper, or fabric are three surface materials that painters use.

Regardless of the type of paint, all paint has three basic parts:

• **Pigment** (**pig**-muhnt) is *a finely ground, colored powder that gives every paint its color.*
• **Binder** is *a liquid that holds together the grains of pigment.* The binder is what makes the pigment stick to a surface.
• **Solvent** is *a material used to thin a paint's binder.* The thickness or thinness of a paint depends on the amount of solvent used.

▲ **Figure 2–1** Works created with pastels sometimes seem like paintings. What does this work have in common with a painting? How is it different?

Mary Cassatt. *Sleepy Baby.* c. 1910. Pastel on paper. 64.7 x 52.0 cm (25½ x 20½"). Dallas Museum of Art, Dallas, Texas. Munger Fund.

TECHNOLOGY OPTIONS

National Gallery of Art Videodisc   Use the following images to show examples of additional works by artists presented in this lesson.

Mary Cassatt
The Boating Party

Search Frame 2016

Paul Cézanne
Still Life with Apples and Peaches

Search Frame 1460

Mary Cassatt
The Loge

Search Frame 2004

Use Glencoe's *Correlation Bar Code Guide to the National Gallery of Art* to locate more art works.

▲ Figure 2–2 Cézanne used pencil and watercolors for his study of a card player. Did he use all the detail captured in this sketch for his painted version?

Paul Cézanne. *The Card Player.* 1892. Pencil and watercolor. 53.4 x 36.4 cm (20¼ x 14⁹⁄₁₆"). Museum of Art, Rhode Island School of Design, Providence, Rhode Island. Gift of Mrs. Murray S. Danforth.

Turpentine is the solvent in oil paints. Water is the solvent in watercolors. Solvents are also used to clean brushes.

Painting Media

Every medium of painting has its own unmistakable look. Some of the most commonly used media are the following:

- **Oil paint.** Oil paint takes its name from its binder, linseed oil. Turpentine is its solvent. Because oil paint dries slowly, the artist is able to blend colors right on the canvas. The painting in Figure 2–3 was done with oils.
- **Tempera** (**tem**-puh-ruh). Some of the earliest paintings on record were made with tempera. A mixture of pigment, egg yolk, and water, tempera is very hard to use. The school tempera you use is a different type. It is also called poster paint.
- **Watercolor.** Watercolor is named for its solvent. Its binder, gum arabic, is a gummy plant matter. Watercolor gives paintings a light, misty quality. In Figure 2–4, notice how the sun rays seem to "melt" into the sky and water.

◄ Figure 2–3 Did the medium make a difference in how Cézanne painted the figures in his oil painting? Compare the man in the sketch with the one in the final version.

Paul Cézanne. *The Card Players.* Oil on canvas. 65.4 x 81.9 cm (25¾ x 32¼"). The Metropolitan Museum of Art, New York, New York. Bequest of Stephen C. Clark.

■ **Vocabulary**

Have students make note-cards with the names of different painting media on one side and the definition on the reverse. Divide into groups and have them quiz each other. Then have them write a sentence using each of the vocabulary words.

Sparking Creativity

Want students to form the habit of sketching art all the time? Encourage students to carry their sketchpad and pencils with them wherever they go. Show them how Cézanne's study for *The Card Players* was a starting point for his finished oil painting. Explain that it was during the Renaissance that artists began planning and drawing sketches before producing large art works. This is where the widespread use of drawing media began.

■ **Studio Skills**

Let students experiment with painting media. Allow them to choose their own tools. Have them divide their paper into quarters and use a different kind of paint in each quarter. Encourage them to discuss the differences in the paint media. Have students share their work with the class and discuss the different painting tools. Have them make notes about the results and keep their experiments in their portfolios.

Lesson 1 *Drawing, Painting, Printmaking, and Computer Art* **19**

more about • • •

Mary Cassatt Like many of America's finest eighteenth- and nineteenth-century artists, Mary Cassatt spent the majority of her life in Europe. The lightness of her palette, her brush strokes, and the intimate, contemporary nature of her subject matter all constitute Cassatt's exploration of the Impressionist style. As the Impressionist movement declined in popularity, Cassatt began to develop a more monumental style, relying less on the perception of spontaneity and more on elegant drawing and stable picture arrangements. In her search for a more timeless subject, Cassatt began to focus on the traditional mother and child theme.

■ **Aesthetics**

Ask students to raise their hands if they have used computers to type reports for school. Then ask whether any of them have used computers to create art works. Have volunteers identify places they have seen computer art. *(Possibilities include: in print advertisements, film special effects, computer games.)* Tell them that throughout this book they will have opportunities to experiment with art on the computer.

■ **Studio Skills**

The elements and principles of art can be taught using tools and menus on the computer. Encourage students to experiment with the Computer Options provided at the end of some of the Studio Lessons in this program. They can use the computer as any other medium to practice using the principles of art to combine the elements in different ways.

■ **Cultural Diversity**

Block printmaking was practiced in Japan beginning around A.D. 700. Other countries and cultures have also used various printmaking methods. Have students divide into groups and assign each group one of the printmaking techniques shown in the art works on the following pages: Aquatint on page 21, Japanese woodblock on page 75, intaglio print, page 187, and Inuit print, 204.

▶ **Figure 2–4   Study the painting on the right. Can you find spots in the picture where the artist seems to have used a lot of solvent? Do you remember what the solvent for watercolor is?**

John Marin. *Sunset, Casco Bay.* 1936. Watercolor on paper. Wichita Art Museum, Wichita, Kansas. Ronald P. Murdock Collection.

- **Acrylic** (uh-**kril**-ik). A quick-drying water-based paint, acrylic is a very popular medium among painters today. Acrylics are synthetic, or manufactured, paints that were introduced in the 1950s. Because its solvent is water, acrylic is easy to use. It offers the artist a wide range of pure, bold colors. Notice the lively splashes of color in the work in Figure 2–5.

COMPUTER ART

Artists use the computer like any other medium to create images. Art work produced on the computer can look computer-made or it can imitate other media. Computer art is still judged by the same criteria as other fine art, by the ability to communicate an idea effectively.

Painting and Drawing Programs

Two types of art applications for a computer are Paint or Draw programs. Some programs combine the advantages of both.

- **Paint programs** simulate other creative art media such as watercolors, oils, or chalks.

Working in a Paint program is like sketching with a pencil or painting with a brush. With a Paint program you can create custom shapes and textures and edit *individual squares on the computer screen,* called **pixels.**

- **Draw programs** are based on mathematical formulas. Graphics and text are object-oriented. Working in a Draw program is similar to cutting out shapes and making a collage. You can use a Draw program to create smooth, crisp graphics and quickly select and move objects.

PRINTMAKING BASICS

Another form of art is called **printmaking.** This is *a technique in which an inked image from a prepared surface is transferred onto another surface,* such as paper or fabric.

There are three basic steps in printmaking. First, the printmaker creates a printing plate by altering a surface to create an image. Next, ink is applied to the plate. Finally, the printmaker transfers the ink to the paper or cloth by pressing the plate against the surface to be printed and then pulling the paper or cloth off the plate.

20   Lesson 1   *Drawing, Painting, Printmaking, and Computer Art*

more about • • •

Helen Frankenthaler   Color Field painter Helen Frankenthaler inherited the large scale and abstract, gestural strokes of the Abstract Expressionists. Her work is composed of floating fields of color, scattered fountains of color on bare canvas, and sometimes areas of pulsating, warm earth tones. To create her compositions of light and color, Frankenthaler pours her paint directly onto a canvas laid out on the floor. The pools of paint flow outward, but she channels the paint with sponges, wipers, and other tools. Frankenthaler insists that the artist should know how to work with the accidental and not rely on an accident to create the art by itself.

▲ Figure 2–5 What is the name used to identify art works like this one? Since the artist was clearly not interested in painting realistic subjects, what was she interested in showing?

Helen Frankenthaler. *Interior Landscape*. 1964. Acrylic on canvas. 266.4 x 235.3 cm (104⅞ x 92⅝"). San Francisco Museum of Modern Art, San Francisco, California. Gift of The Women's Board.

These steps may be repeated many times for a given plate. *A series of identical prints made from a single plate* is called an **edition.**

Printmaking Methods

Printmakers may choose from one of four main methods to create a print.

- **Relief printing.** In relief printing, the image to be printed is raised from a background. A medium used often in relief printing is wood.
- **Intaglio** (in-**tal**-yoh). Intaglio may be thought of as the reverse of relief printing. In this method, the image to be printed is scratched or etched into a surface. (See Figure 2–6.) The plates for intaglio prints are often made of metal.
- **Lithography** (lith-**ahg**-ruh-fee). To make a lithograph, the artist draws the image to be printed on a limestone, zinc, or aluminum slab with a special greasy crayon. Lithography lets the artist blend, little by little, light and dark values of a hue.
- **Screen printing.** To make a screen print, the artist transfers the design through various processes on a silk screen. The areas not to be printed are blocked off so that a kind of stencil remains. Screen prints that are handmade by an artist are also known as serigraphs (**ser**-uh-grafs).

✔ CHECK YOUR UNDERSTANDING

1. Define *medium of art.*
2. Name three media used in drawing.
3. Name three media used in painting.
4. How is computer art judged?
5. Describe two printmaking methods.

◀ Figure 2–6 How are the figures emphasized in this intaglio print? Do all the figures seem to be moving? Explain how the principles of harmony and variety are demonstrated.

Isabel Bishop. *Men and Girls Walking*. 1969. Aquatint on paper. 21.3 x 29.2 cm (8⅜ x 11½"). National Museum of Women in the Arts, Washington, D.C. Gift of Mr. and Mrs. Edward P. Levy.

Lesson 1 *Drawing, Painting, Printmaking, and Computer Art* **21**

Creating Mixed-Media Art

(pages 22–23)

LESSON TIME: 90 minutes

• • • • • • • • • • • • •
FOCUS

☑ **OBJECTIVES**

After completing this lesson, students will be able to:

• Define the term mixed media.
• Explain harmony and rhythm.
• Plan and create a mixed-media design.

☑ **SUPPLIES**

• Examples of mixed-media designs.
• Pencils and scratch paper.
• Found materials; magazines; envelopes; scissors; white glue.
• Construction paper or lightweight posterboard of various colors, cut into sheets of 12 x 18 inches (30 x 46 cm).
• Watercolor markers, thick and thin-tipped.
• Crayons, colored pencils, and watercolor paints.
• Examples of graphic art.

Resource

◼ 2-2 *Mixed-Media Studio,* TRB page 48 (studio)

• • • • • • • • • • • • •
TEACH

◼ **Motivator**

Show students examples of various mixed-media designs. Ask them to identify the different media in each design. Have them name the elements used to create unity, including harmony, balance and rhythm. Ask: How do artists use the different media? What effects are created? How does a mixed-media work differ from one made with just one medium?

22

LESSON 2

Creating Mixed-Media Art

Study the mixed-media work of art in Figure 2–7. Notice how the artist has united visual and verbal symbols. The letters are woven into the design so that their shapes are as important as their meanings. They are not written in neat rows that are easy to read, but are integrated into the surface of the work.

Some of the visual symbols are directly related to the words, while other symbols just fit the design. Some visual symbols have been drawn and painted by the artist, or have been printed with rubber stamps. Others are made with decals, lace, and stamps. Notice that some of the letters are written and printed by the artist. Stick-on letters or those cut from magazines and glued on are also used.

WHAT YOU WILL LEARN

You will create a mixed-media design uniting visual and verbal symbols in the manner of Aubin. Weave the letters into the design so that their shapes are as important as their meanings. Use the principle of rhythm to create a sense of visual movement in the work. Use harmony of shape, color, and texture to unify your work.

▲ **Figure 2–7** The artist, Barbara Aubin, created a dream-like mood in this work. What other sources of inspiration do artists use in getting ideas for their art?

Barbara Aubin. *I Dreamed I Saw a Pink Flamingo in the Salle de Bain.* 1981. Mixed media on paper. (Detail.) 45.7 x 61 cm (18 x 24").

MEETING SPECIAL NEEDS

Mixed Media The process of gluing down various kinds of design materials may appeal to and be enjoyed by students with special needs. Build peer partnerships with higher and lower cognitively functioning students to help interpret and discuss the poem or story lines used for this Studio Lesson. Students can search magazines for images that express the poem's meaning. To avoid distraction while students look through magazines, provide an assortment of pre-selected pictures for students who have difficulty in concentrating. Stencil letters or stick-on letters may be helpful for some students with visual impairments.

WHAT YOU WILL NEED

- Pencil and sketch paper
- Found materials
- Magazines, scissors, and white glue
- Envelope
- Construction paper or lightweight poster board, 12 x 18 inches (30 x 46 cm), in a color of your choice
- Watercolor markers, thick and thin-tipped
- Crayons, colored pencils, and watercolor paints

WHAT YOU WILL DO

1. Select some lines from a favorite poem, song, story, or saying. The words may be your own or something you have read. Write the words on your sketch paper.
2. Make sketches of objects and scenes to go with your words.
3. Look through magazines and cut out interesting shapes, letters, or printed words for your work. Collect found materials that fit your ideas. Keep all the small cutouts in an envelope. Select a color for your background.
4. Notice how Aubin has used the letters as design elements. They are not written in neat rows that are easy to read, but are woven into the composition as shapes. Make some rough sketches to plan your design on your sketch paper. Repeat shapes to create movement that makes the viewer's eyes move through the work. Plan for harmony by using monochromatic or analogous colors as well as related shapes and textures. Select your best idea, and sketch it lightly on your construction paper or poster board.

EXAMINING YOUR WORK

- **Describe**   Identify the media you used. Read the phrase you chose, and explain why you chose it. Describe the visual images you chose to go with the words.
- **Analyze**   What shapes did you repeat to create rhythmic movement? How did you use color, shape, and texture to create harmony?
- **Judge**   Did you create a unified design? Are the verbal symbols and visual images equally important? If not, how could the unity of the work be improved?

5. Place the found objects and cutouts on your design. Do not glue them down. Take time to arrange and rearrange your words and images until you are satisfied. Then glue them down.
6. Use a variety of media to draw and paint the remaining images and words. For example, use paints to fill large spaces, and use fine-line markers to draw thin lines.
7. Place your work on display with that of your classmates. Look for works in which the words and pictures are unified.

Try This! COMPUTER OPTION

■ Choose the Text tool and large Font to write favorite words or phrases. Use Selection tool or Transformation tools to move and Flip or Rotate letters. Use clip art files or scanned images to make a collage. Follow the Studio Lesson directions to organize the elements. Save and title your work.

MEETING STUDENT DIVERSITY

Kinesthetic Learners   The art classroom offers the perfect opportunity for students to learn by manipulating objects and making art works with their hands. As students work with the mixed-media design project, allow plenty of time for them to cut out letters, words, and symbols and to organize their found materials and cut-outs. Give them the opportunity to choose textured objects, as well as varied shapes and sizes of found materials. Encourage students to try moving and organizing the objects into many different positions before deciding on a final design for their art work.

■ Vocabulary

Have students look around the room and find examples of where *rhythm* and *harmony* appear. Have them discuss the concepts of rhythm and harmony in the music world and to name examples of musical works that demonstrate rhythm and harmony. Ask if they can apply the same ideas to art. Point out the visual and verbal elements in Aubin's work. Ask how the relationship of the words and pictures create harmony and rhythm.

• • • • • • • • • • • • • • •
ASSESS

■ Self-Assessment

Have students use Examining Your Work to evaluate their art work created in this Studio Lesson. Responses may be written or oral.

■ Reteaching

Have students browse through books that have photographs of art work. Have them choose two or more reproductions and let them share their reproductions with the class. Ask students to identify the work as single-medium or mixed-media art.

■ Enrichment

Bring in examples of graphic art and have students discuss the use of color and shape in the design. Ask them to identify how the words and pictures together create a coherent message. Then have them design posters on a theme such as bicycle safety or environmental concerns. Have them be sure their designs allow the words and the art work together.

• • • • • • • • • • • • • • •
CLOSE

Display students' mixed-media works and have volunteers explain how they used the principles of art in their designs.

Sculpture, Architecture, and Crafts Media

Drawings, paintings, and prints created as two-dimensional works often appear to have roundness and depth. Some works of art have *real* roundness and depth. These works, which have height, width, and depth, are known as three-dimensional works.

In this lesson you will learn about three areas of art—sculpture, architecture, and crafts—in which three-dimensional works are created. You will learn about the media used in making such works.

SCULPTURE

Sculpture is art that is made to stand out in space. All sculpture is of one of two types, freestanding or relief. Also called sculpture "in the round," **freestanding sculpture** is *sculpture surrounded on all sides by space*. It is meant to be seen from all sides. The work in Figure 2–8 is an example of freestanding sculpture.

Relief sculpture, on the other hand, is *sculpture only partly enclosed by space*. It is flat along the back and is meant to be viewed only from the front. The work in Figure 2–9 is an example of relief sculpture.

Sculpting Methods

Sculptors use four basic methods or techniques in their work. These are:

• **Carving.** Carving is cutting or chipping a shape from a mass. Often stone and other hard materials are used in carving. The sculpture in Figure 2–8 was carved from a block of marble.

▲ Figure 2–8　Do you think a work like this is meant to be viewed from a fixed position or from all sides? When talking about this work, would you refer to its shape or its form?

Vinnie Ream Hoxie. *Abraham Lincoln.* 1870. Marble. 210.8 cm (6′11″) high. United States Capitol Art Collection.

TECHNOLOGY OPTIONS

National Gallery of Art Videodisc　Use the following images to compare examples of simple and detailed sculptural form.

Constantin Brancusi
Maiastra

Search Frame 2561

XV century, Florentine School
Madonna and Child

Search Frame 2352

Use Glencoe's *Correlation Bar Code Guide to the National Gallery of Art* to locate more art works.

▲ Figure 2–9 Notice how the horses seem to be galloping in this relief sculpture. This frieze circles the top of a famous Greek temple known as the Parthenon.

Horsemen Riding at a Gallop. Parthenon. British Museum.

If some students insist that it is three-dimensional, have them turn the paper over to show you the back of the cube they drew.

■ **Cultural Diversity**

Explain that sculptors choose low relief over freestanding sculptures for many reasons. Discuss how low relief has been used as narrative art—that is, art that tells a story. Have students break into three groups and have each group look through this book to locate one of the following examples of low relief:

- Mayan architecture (page 84),
- Roman arches (pages 106, 107),
- African art (page 132).

Then have them explain the similarities and differences in the use of low relief styles.

- **Casting**. In casting, a melted-down metal or other liquid substance is poured into a mold to harden. Bronze is a material often used in casting. (See Figure 2–10.)
- **Modeling**. In modeling, a soft or workable material is built up and shaped. Clay is the material used most often in this sculpting method.
- **Assembling**. Assembling is gathering and joining different kinds of materials. Wood, wire, glue, and nails are a few of the materials used in assembling. The sculpture in Figure 17–14 on page **267** is an example of assembling.

■ **Studio Skills**

Have students create a three-dimensional object in clay, fashioned after an example they find from one of the cultures mentioned in the textbook. They may use any technique they wish—carving, slab building, or coil. Encourage students to discuss the differences between creating the object in two-dimensions and in three-dimensions.

► Figure 2–10 How did the sculptor show movement in this figure? Would you have needed the title to tell you the wind was blowing?

Abastenia St. Leger Eberle. *The Windy Doorstep.* 1910. Bronze. 34.5 x 24.4 x 16 cm (13⅝ x 9⅝ x 6⅜"). Worcester Art Museum, Worcester, Massachusetts.

Art in
Everyday Life

Ask students to consider the various forms of three-dimensional art they experience in their daily lives. Help them to identify the difference between fine art and applied art. Point out various three-dimensional objects around the classroom such as a vase, a pot, or the chairs they are sitting on, and discuss which category it should be in—applied art or fine art.

Lesson 3 *Sculpture, Architecture, and Crafts Media* **25**

CURRICULUM ⟩ CONNECTIONS

Social Studies The friezes of the Parthenon once ran continuously around the center block of the building. They tell the story of the preparations for a procession in honor of the goddess Athena. The friezes illustrate town activities such as officials and attendants leading animals for sacrifice, and they culminate in a ceremony attended by a group of Olympian gods. The features are modeled in the calm, thoughtful style that is characteristic of Classical sculptors who had little interest in expressing emotion in the facial features of their subjects. According to the prevailing philosophy, idealized mortals are almost divine and are certainly not subject to ordinary passions.

■ Cooperative Learning
Tell students that the architecture of Antonio Gaudi represents an original approach for the period. Have students work in groups to discover more innovative architectural styles that have developed since Gaudi's time. Each group should choose a geographic area in the United States or Europe. Have them locate structures that demonstrate unique design ideas. Groups should find facts about the buildings and their designers. Have them bring illustrations or photos to share with the class.

■ Art History
Pottery is an ancient craft that has been practiced in every part of the world in which clay deposits are found. Point out to students that through the art we find from these ancient peoples we learn about the people who made it. We can answer questions such as: How did they design their pottery? Does this decoration vary according to what the pottery will be used for? Have students investigate some civilizations that made large amounts of pottery, including the Chinese (Chapter 5), the Aztecs (Chapter 6), the Greeks (Chapter 7), and Native Americans (Chapter 13).

Art on a Shoestring
You can enhance students' ability to appreciate art works by displaying the works as slides. A good, inexpensive source of materials is vacation slides or negatives that can be processed into slides at a nominal cost. Museum gift shops often sell high-quality slides of their major works.

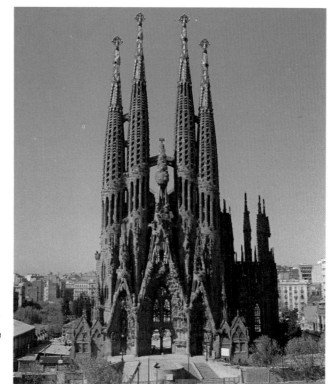

▶ **Figure 2–11** This is a unique example of architecture. Notice how the architect repeated the pointed arch shape in the towers, emphasizing the height of the structure.

Antonio Gaudi. *Church of the Sacred Family.* Barcelona, Spain.

ARCHITECTURE

All art is made to be seen. Some art is made to be used as well as seen. Works of art known as architecture fit into this second category. **Architecture** is *the planning and creating of buildings.* The success of a work of architecture is measured partly by how well it does the job it was meant to do and partly by its appearance.

The Uses of Architecture

Since earliest times, a chief form of architecture has been the creation of dwelling places. This has by no means been the only type, however. Two other examples have been the artistic creation of the following kinds of buildings:

- **Structures for prayer.** The building of temples, churches, and other houses of worship dates to the dawn of history. The unusual house of prayer shown in Figure

2–11 was begun in the late 1800s. It is still under construction. Notice how this unique building seems almost to be reaching toward the sky.

- **Structures for business.** With the spread of civilization in ancient times came the need for places to carry on business. In our own time that need is often met by vertical creations such as skyscrapers.

CRAFTS

In ages past, artists worked not only out of a desire to create but also out of a need to provide items required for everyday use. Clothing, cooking pots, and whatever other goods people needed were handmade.

Artistic craftspeople still make functional items that are often considered aesthetically pleasing works of art. The useful and decorative goods these artists make, and *the different areas of applied art in which craftspeople work* are called **crafts**.

more about ●●●

Tapestry Although the Miró tapestry illustrated in Figure 2-13 is a beautiful example of weaving, it may confuse some students who are trying to determine a clear boundary between fine art and functional objects that are aesthetically produced. If you prefer, discuss more functional examples of the needlecrafts, such as medieval tapestry cloths, colonial American bed quilts, and the woven paisley shawls that were popular in Europe during the middle of the nineteenth century.

Craft Areas

Craftspeople today, like those long ago, work in a number of special areas. Some of these are:

- **Pottery.** This is the making of objects from clay. Before objects of pottery can be used, they must be hardened by heat, or fired. This takes place in a special oven called a kiln. Ceramics is the name of objects made in this fashion. The vase shown in Figure 2–12 is an example of modern American ceramics.
- **Weaving.** This is the interlocking of fiber strands to create objects. Fibers such as wool, cotton, plant materials, and synthetic materials are used in weaving. Weaving is done on a special machine called a loom, which holds the threads in place as they are woven together. The weaving in Figure 2–13 was done by twentieth-century Spanish artist Joan Miró (zhoh-**ahn** mee-**roh**).
- **Glassblowing.** This is the shaping of melted glass into objects. Glassblowers work by forcing air through a tube into globs of melted glass.

▲ **Figure 2–13** This weaving shows large areas of color against a textured background. Can you see a woman in the tapestry?

Joan Miró, Josep Royo. *Woman*. 1977. Dyed New Zealand Wool. 105.3 x 604.3 cm (415 x 238"). National Gallery of Art, Washington, D.C. Gift of the Collectors Committee and George L. Erion.

▲ **Figure 2–12** The Natzlers are famous for their glazes. They called this a crater glaze.

Gertrud Natzler/Otto Natzler. *Pilgrim Bottle*. c. 1956. Earthenware. 43 x 33 cm (17x 13"). Los Angeles County Museum of Art, Los Angeles, California. Gift of Howard and Gwen Laurie Smits.

✔ CHECK YOUR UNDERSTANDING

1. What are the two main types of sculpture?
2. What are the four basic sculpting methods?
3. Define *architecture*. How is the success of a work of architecture measured?
4. Define *crafts*. Name three areas in which craftspeople work.

■ Art Criticism

Point out that some artists think the distinction between fine art and applied art is unnecessary. Some artists say that paintings are done for mere decoration and are therefore applied art. Discuss: Should the works of an architect be considered art? Is the work of a potter of equal value to the work of a painter? Why or why not? Why is the work of a sculptor, who might use clay, considered a fine art and the work of a potter, who also uses clay, considered an applied art?

• • • • • • • • • • • • •

ASSESS

■ Self-Assessment

Have students complete the review questions on this page. Answers are provided below.

■ Reteaching

Have each student choose a category—architecture, sculpture, or crafts—and research a contemporary artist who works in that area. Ask students what the artist has to say about his or her work, and why he or she creates art. Have students share their results with the class. Guide a class discussion about different points of view.

■ Enrichment

Have students bring in an example of their own hobbies. Ask: Are any of these hobbies fine art? Are any applied art? Ask students to describe why they enjoy the hobbies they do. Ask a local craft club to demonstrate a simple craft for students.

• • • • • • • • • • • • •

CLOSE

Ask students to identify one example each of freestanding sculpture, relief sculpture, architecture, and crafts from the illustrations in their textbooks.

Answers to ✔ CHECK YOUR UNDERSTANDING

1. The two main types of sculpture are freestanding and relief.
2. The four methods used by sculptors are carving, casting, molding, and assembling.
3. Architecture is the planning and creating of buildings. The success of a work of architecture is measured partly by how well it does the job it was meant to do and partly by its appearance.
4. The term crafts refers to the different kinds of applied arts techniques used by artisans and the functional and decorative products they make. Three areas crafts-people work in are pottery, weaving, and glassblowing.

Computer Landscape Drawing
(pages 28–29)

LESSON TIME: 90 minutes

☑ OBJECTIVES

After completing this lesson, students will be able to:

- Create a landscape design using computer software.
- Define the term *menu* as it applies to computer software programs.
- Use various colors, textures, and tools to create an interesting landscape.

☑ SUPPLIES

- Computer with art application.
- Mouse or graphics tablet.
- Stylus or drawing pen.
- Floppy disk to save work.
- Color printer if possible.

• • • • • • • • • • • • • • • •

TEACH

■ Motivator

Have students work with partners to become familiar with the toolbar and menus on the computer screen. Tell them to find the Shape tool. Then have them choose one primary color (red, blue, or yellow), and draw a closed shape outline in that color. Next ask them to find the Flood-fill tool and to fill the shape with a contrasting color. Refer them to the Color Wheel on page 2 if necessary.

■ Vocabulary

Remind students to check the Help menu of the computer Draw or Paint program they are using to find explanations of words they may not be familiar with.

Computer Landscape Drawing

The computer is a new medium or art tool for students and artists. While not intended to replace paint, pens, chalk, pastels, or other drawing and painting media, computer software makes ordinary drawing tasks easier. Artists use tools and **menus,** *drop-down boxes on the computer screen that list selections available in the software program.* The artist can then manipulate lines, shapes, and forms as well as add colors and textures. The artist still makes all the choices and decisions.

Your classroom computer may have either a Paint or Draw program for you to work with. You will use a mouse or a stylus or drawing pen to create your drawing. The best way to learn how to manipulate the computer

tools is to experiment with them. In this lesson you will be able to work with several of the tools available on your computer.

WHAT YOU WILL LEARN

Working individually or with a partner, you will explore the computer's tools and menus to discover the many effects and texture combinations available. Using the tools you like best, you will create a landscape. You will determine landforms and objects you want to include such as mountains, plants, people, or animals. The scene can be a real or imaginary subject. You will select colors, textures, and special effects that emphasize the mood of the landscape.

▲ Figure 2–14   Notice how the artist included the elements of line, color, and texture in his work by using computer software tools.

Philip Nicholson. *Landscape.* Philip Nicholson Illustrations AB. Träslövsläge, Sweden.

─ *more about* • • • ─

Media   Have students research how new techniques allow artists to make new kinds of art. For example, a process for making multicolored prints was developed in the eighteenth century, which allowed inexpensive color prints to be made for the first time. Another possible topic of investigation is the nineteenth-century invention of the

paint tube, which permitted artist to work outdoors for long periods of time and encouraged a whole new generation of landscape artists to paint directly from their subjects instead of working only from sketches and memory. Ask students to discuss the impact of computers as an art medium.

WHAT YOU WILL NEED

- Computer with an art application
- Mouse or graphics tablet with a stylus or drawing pen
- Floppy disk to save your work
- Color printer to make a hard copy of your work

WHAT YOU WILL DO

1. Begin by exploring the Brush tools: chalk, pastels, pens, spray paint, and so on. Change the Brush sizes, shapes, and types, as well as colors and textures, to discover effects made by different combinations. Try drawing or painting on rough or smooth paper textures, if available. Change the opacity of the paint: make some hues transparent. Record combinations that you like so you can remember them later.
2. Use the Pencil or Brush tools to sketch a landscape. Draw important objects, plants, or animals, and the background with the Shape or Brush tools. Add colors and textures directly with the Brush tool or use the Bucket tool to Flood-fill spaces.
3. Title and save your work. This will enable you to return to this point and begin again to try other tools, menus, and solutions.
4. Continue to save the work by using the "Save As" command, retitling and saving often as you work. If the original title is "Landscape," subsequent saved files can be numbered: "Landscape 1," "Landscape 2," "Landscape 3," and so on. Not only does this allow you to redo the landscape from any saved point, it also records the history of its production.
5. Save, print, and display your final landscape.

Try This!

STUDIO OPTION

■ If you don't have a computer, combine a variety of art materials to create a landscape. Choose from oil pastels, crayons, colored pencils, chalks, pens, watercolors, and tempera. Explore textures with soft and hard brushes, thick and thin, wet and dry brush, spattering and layering colors. Work directly on one sheet of paper, combining several media. Make several texture papers. Cut and arrange shapes to make a landscape collage.

EXAMINING YOUR WORK

- **Describe** Describe the hues, objects, and textures in your landscape. Explain how to title and save your work to a file or disk.
- **Analyze** Identify the colors and textures and the tools or menus used to create these effects. Explain how your work is organized and the sequence you followed—which part was drawn first, last, and so on.
- **Interpret** Tell what is happening in the landscape. Does the scene remind you of a time, event, or place you know? What mood or feeling is created by the objects, colors, and textures? What title did you choose?
- **Judge** Did you explore the computer's tools and menus to discover colors and textures to make an interesting landscape? What worked best? What would you change?

▲ Figure 2–15   Student work. Computer landscape.

Lesson 4   *Computer Landscape Drawing*   **29**

Studio Skills

Help students plan their landscape designs by offering the following suggestions: Use the Pencil or Brush tool to draw overlapping lines that represent mountains, hills, and fields. Use the foreground, middle ground, and background spaces on your screen. Add winding roads, streams, or fences and change size and direction as objects are placed higher on the picture plane. Use Copy and Paste commands and Scale or Resizing tool to repeat details and overlap shapes.

ASSESS

■ Self-Assessment

Have students use Examining Your Work to evaluate their art work created in this Studio Lesson. Responses may be written or oral.

■ Reteaching

Have students use a word processor to write a paragraph about their experience making the computer landscape, noting how they would change their art work or improve it.

■ Enrichment

Have students scan a photo of a landscape scene. You may provide a previously scanned image that you have prepared. Using the appropriate Paint or Draw program, have them open the scanned image. Then have them make changes to the colors, textures, or objects in the photo to create their own new picture.

CLOSE

Display student computer art works and ask them to discuss various computer techniques used in creating the landscape designs.

RESOURCES BEYOND THE CLASSROOM

Media Supply Houses Students rarely need to obtain art supplies beyond the minimum—acrylic paints, inexpensive brushes. By introducing them to media supply houses, you can help them feel more confident in understanding and using various media, in analyzing cost, and understanding the care of materials and supplies. Visits to media supply houses can also provide them with stimuli for their creative imaginations. The more obvious examples are places such as crafts stores and hobby shops, small boutiques such as bead shops, and the like. Fabric stores can be equally interesting, as can architectural supply stores, print shops, school specialty supply houses, photo shops, and even hardware stores and sheet metal suppliers.

CONNECTIONS *Technology*

How is 3-D Computer Art Created?

Edward Harvey. *Mantis and Fly.* 1996. Three-dimensional ray-traced image.

1.

2.

3.

Scientists understand how light travels. It originates from a source such as the sun or a light bulb and bounces off objects. It is the light that is bounced off of objects that allows us to see them as three-dimensional (3-D) objects. Formulas for how light bounces off different types of objects are used by scientists when designing mirrors and lenses (for example, those used in microscopes).

With the invention of modern computers and software, a tool became available to create images of objects that look three-dimensional. Recreating an image requires tracing many rays of light from their source to their destinations. This process is known as *ray tracing*. Only a computer can make the millions of calculations necessary to trace the path of all the rays of light in a scene.

Today low-cost desktop computers are powerful enough to do ray tracing. Many artists have begun to use these formulas in their art work. First, they use 3-D graphics design software to create "wire frames" of objects (see Step 1). Next, they create "skins" for the wire frames, identifying textures and the reflective qualities of the covering material (see Step 2). Then they set up the lights that they will use in the scene. Finally, they "render" the picture by directing the computer to compute the ray tracing. This provides a final picture that is photo-realistic (see Step 3).

MAKING THE CONNECTION

✔ What does ray tracing mean and how does it help us see objects as three-dimensional?
✔ Look at the illustration and use it to explain the steps involved in rendering three-dimensional images.
✔ There are other types of animation used by artists, such as cell frame animation (painting one frame at a time), or clay animation. Find out more about these techniques and how they are used.

INTERNET ACTIVITY

Visit Glencoe's Fine Arts Web Site for students at:

http://www.glencoe.com/sec/art/students

OBJECTIVES

After completing this feature, students will be able to:
- Explain ray tracing as used to create a three-dimensional image.
- Identify the steps in rendering three-dimensional images.

Teaching the Connection

- Have students read the feature on this page and study the illustrations.
- Ask volunteers to share what they know about computers and three-dimensional drawing. What kinds of software is used to create three-dimensional figures? *(Architects use CAD programs to render architectural drawings. The art on this page was done using 3-D Studio.)* What educational or entertainment computer games use three-dimensional images? *(Answers will vary.)* Why do the images in the illustrations appear to be 3-D? *(They appear to have form: height, width, and depth.)*
- Tell students that creating 3-D images is also used to solve problems. Computers using X-ray data can create 3-D images of body parts such as the brain or spine, helping doctors identify disorders.

Answers to Making the Connection

✔ Ray tracing is the tracing of light from its source to its destination.
✔ First "wire frames" are created; artists create "skins" for the wire frames; then the computer figures the ray tracing.
✔ Responses will vary.

30

INTERNET ACTIVITY

Curriculum Links Explore World Wide Web links related to the content of each chapter in this book. These pre-selected links can be found under *Curriculum Links* in the *Teacher Resources* section of Glencoe's Fine Arts Site. Find the chapter you are studying in the Table of Contents and click on one of the highlighted or underlined "hot links" that will transport you to an appropriate, previewed site guaranteed to expand your students' experience. Many of these sites offer views of extensive art collections from museums and art galleries. Cultural connections will link students to Internet sites around the world. They can learn first-hand about art, artists, and art history. Find us at **http://www.glencoe.com/sec/art**

REVIEW

 BUILDING VOCABULARY

Number a sheet of paper from 1 to 13. After each number, write the term from the list that best matches each description below.

architecture	mixed media
binder	menus
crafts	pigment
edition	pixels
freestanding sculpture	printmaking
	relief sculpture
medium of art	solvent

1. A material used to create a work of art.
2. A finely ground powder that gives every paint its color.
3. A liquid that holds together the grains of pigment in paint.
4. A material used to thin a paint's binder.
5. Drop-down boxes that list selections available in the software program.
6. A technique in which an inked image from a prepared surface is transferred onto another surface.
7. A series of identical prints made from a single plate.
8. Sculpture surrounded on all sides by space.
9. Sculpture partly enclosed by space.
10. The planning and creating of buildings.
11. The different areas of applied art in which craftspeople work.
12. The use of more than one medium in a work of art.
13. Individual squares on the computer screen.

 REVIEWING ART FACTS

Number a sheet of paper from 14 to 20. Answer each question in a complete sentence.

14. What are the two main ways in which artists use drawing?
15. Working with computer Paint programs is similar to sketching with what familiar media?
16. Describe the steps in printmaking.
17. What is a lithograph? What is a serigraph? What is a woodcut?
18. What is "in the round" a substitute term for?
19. In what method of sculpting is a melted-down metal poured into a mold?
20. What are three types of architecture?

 THINKING ABOUT ART

On a sheet of paper, answer each question in a sentence or two.

1. **Compare and contrast.** Some paints, as you learned, dry slowly and others dry quickly. What would be some of the advantages and disadvantages of each type?
2. **Extend.** In attempting to define *art* over the centuries, scholars have often noted that an art work is a one-of-a-kind creation. Does accepting this view rule out prints or computer drawings as forms of art? Explain your answer.
3. **Analyze.** Which of the methods of sculpting you learned about would be best for making a sand castle? Explain your choice.

MAKING ART CONNECTIONS

1. **Social Studies.** Many people today create crafts as a leisure activity. Try to find an individual you know who is interested in a craft. Interview him or her and make a report for your class. Tell how the craft affects the life of the person you interviewed.

2. **Science.** Find out how the study of anatomy contributes to the work of a sculptor. Compare an anatomical drawing from a science book to a freestanding sculpture of the same subject. What similarities and differences do you see?

Chapter 2 Review **31**

Building Vocabulary

1. medium of art
2. pigment
3. binder
4. solvent
5. menus
6. printmaking
7. edition
8. freestanding sculpture
9. relief sculpture
10. architecture
11. crafts
12. mixed media
13. pixels

Reviewing Art Facts

14. Artists use drawing for sketches during the planning stage and for finished works.
15. Pencil or brush.
16. Making the plate by altering the surface to create an image; applying ink to the plate's surface; transferring ink to the paper or cloth.
17. Lithograph: a print made from a metal or stone plate that has been drawn on with a greasy crayon. Serigraph: a print made by forcing ink through unmasked areas of a silk screen. A woodcut is a relief print made from the raised surfaces of a wood block.
18. Freestanding sculpture is a substitute term for "in the round."
19. The casting method.
20. Three types of architecture are dwellings, churches, and business structures.

THINKING ABOUT ART

1. Responses will vary. Students should consider the time element and how the artist wants to blend the paints.
2. No, the original work of art, whether it is a plate for a print or a computer image, is one of a kind. Duplicates of the original have the same criteria.
3. Modeling and carving could be used at different stages—modeling to build the basic shape, carving for details.

Art Criticism, Aesthetics, and Art History

(pages 32–45)

Resources

- 3-9 Chapter Test, TRB page 77
- Transparency CC-3, *Retroactive I* by Robert Rauschenberg
- Transparency 3, *Saint George and the Dragon* by Raphael
- Fine Art Print 3, *Poor Man's Cotton,* by Hale Woodruff

 Music
While studying this chapter, use Performing Arts Handbook page 319 to show students how they can apply art criticism and aesthetic views to the captivating music of Duke Ellington.

NATIONAL STANDARDS

This chapter addresses the following National Standards for the Visual Arts:

1. (a, b)   **4.** (a, b, c)
2. (a, b, c)   **5.** (b, c)
3. (a, b)   **6.** (b)

▲ What do you notice first when you view this work? How has the artist emphasized color in his work? How many different kinds of line do you see?

Juan Gris. *Breakfast.* 1914. Cut and pasted paper, crayon, and oil over canvas. 80.9 x 59.7 cm (31⅞ x 23½"). The Museum of Modern Art, New York, New York. Acquired through the Lillie P. Bliss Bequest.

32

FEATURED ARTISTS

George Caleb Bingham   Jan Steen
Willem de Kooning   Beatrice Whitney van Ness
Juan Gris
Edward Hopper
Pablo Picasso

Art Criticism, Aesthetics, and Art History

Imagine you were visiting the museum where the painting on the left is hung. What questions might you ask as you look at the painting? You might ask:

- With what media and how was the painting made?
- What elements and principles of art are used?
- How does the painting make me feel?
- Who is the artist, and when and where was the art work made?

What other questions might you ask? In this chapter you will learn how to find your own answers to the questions about works of art.

PORTFOLIO IDEAS

Find an art work in your book that catches your eye, that interests you. What do you see? What is the subject matter? How does the art work make you feel? What was it that caught your eye in the first place? Who created the art work? When was it created? After you have answered these questions, answer this one. Do you think this is a successful work of art? Explain why. Date your written responses and put them in your portfolio.

OBJECTIVES

After completing this chapter, you will be able to:

- Describe the four steps used in art criticism.
- Identify three aesthetic views.
- Explain the four steps used by art historians.
- Create paintings based on art criticism and art history.

WORDS YOU WILL LEARN

aesthetic view
art criticism
art history
composition
content
style
subject

33

Art Criticism and Aesthetics

FOCUS

☑ OBJECTIVES

After completing this lesson, students will be able to:
• Define art criticism.
• Describe three aesthetic views.
• Identify four steps of art criticism.

☑ SUPPLIES

• Sketch paper; pencils.
• White drawing paper.
• Watercolor markers.
• Erasable colored pencils.
• Charcoal pencils.
• Kneaded rubber erasers.
• White glue.
• Assortment of magazines.

Resources

■ 3-1 *Art and Plenty of It,* TRB page 65 (reproducible master)
■ 3-2 *Aesthetics: Another Side,* TRB page 66 (appreciating cultural diversity)
■ 3-3 *Invent Your Own Chair,* TRB page 67 (studio)

. . . .

TEACH

■ **Motivator**

Display reproductions of several paintings. Have students choose one and list what they notice in the selection. Then have them sketch the painting. Ask them to list at the bottom of their sketches things that they notice only after sketching the work. Discuss the importance of careful observation of art criticism.

34

You have heard the saying "Don't judge a book by its cover." What this saying means is that to judge something fairly, you need to have all the facts. It is not enough to look at the surface of the object. You need to dig beneath the surface — to understand as much as you can about the object.

In this lesson you will learn ways of looking at art that will help increase your understanding and appreciation of it.

ART CRITICISM

Have you ever looked at a work of art and wondered if there was more to the painting than you understood? You may have asked yourself this question when you looked at Figure 3–1. Works of art are sometimes like mysteries. Solving art mysteries is one of the jobs of people in the field called art criticism. **Art criticism** is *studying, understanding, and judging works of art.*

In carrying out their work, art critics often use a four-step system. The four steps are describing, analyzing, interpreting, and judging.

 Figure 3–1   In describing this art work, what element would you choose to discuss first? What do you think the artist was most interested in as he created this oil painting?

Willem de Kooning. *Merritt Parkway.* 1959. Oil on canvas. 203.2 x 179.1 cm (80 x 70½"). The Detroit Institute of Arts, Detroit, Michigan.

TECHNOLOGY OPTIONS

National Gallery of Art Videodisc   Use the following images to discuss art criticism and aesthetics.

Jan Steen	Jan Steen	Arshile Gorky
The Dancing Couple	*The Dancing Couple*	*One Year the Milkweed*
Search Frame 924	Search Frame 926	Search Frame 2311

Use Glencoe's *Correlation Bar Code Guide to the National Gallery of Art* to locate more art works.

Describing an Art Work

In describing an art work, the critic notes certain key facts. These include the following:

- **The size of the work, the medium, and the process used.** The credit line gives the viewer information about the size of the work and the medium used. It also lists the process, such as serigraph or woodcut.
- **The subject, object, and details.** The **subject** is *the image viewers can easily identify in an art work.* The subject answers the question "What do I see when I look at this work?" The subject in Figure 3–2 is a group of people, probably a family, at a holiday gathering. What other objects and details might the art critic mention? What subject, object, and details would be described in Figure 3–3 on page **36**?

- **The elements used in the work.** Look again at Figure 3–2. Line and color are two of the elements of art that play an important part in this work. Can you identify the other art elements? What elements can you point out in Figure 3–3?

Notice that while every work of art uses elements, not all have subjects. Figure 3–1 is a painting without a recognized subject. Because such works are not "about" something, some viewers are uncertain how to describe them. These viewers should learn to focus attention on the elements of art. This is what the critic—or anyone else—will see in this work. This is called describing the formal aspects of the work.

■ Vocabulary

Discuss what the word *criticism* means in every day usage. How is the meaning of *art criticism* different? Point out that art criticism does not necessarily entail a negative evaluation.

Sparking Creativity

Get students to think creatively about aesthetics. Tell them: We use a critical eye and aesthetic judgment in many aspects of our lives. Have students test their own aesthetic sense. Have them cut from catalogs some furnishings and decorations they would consider for a well-designed room. Have students arrange the cutouts on sheets of paper representing the room, and share their designs with classmates.

■ Cultural Diversity

Explain to students that it is easy for someone to misinterpret or dislike art from another culture until he or she has learned the aesthetic views held by that culture. Have students view a Japanese flower arrangement and have them discuss their reactions and how the simplicity demonstrates the culture that created it.

■ Studio Skills

Have students use watercolor markers, torn magazine illustrations, and glue to create a composition that expresses a single message or emotion. Instruct students to glue the torn shapes on plain drawing paper and use the markers to enhance or obscure parts of the composition as needed. Have each student display his or her own work and see whether classmates can determine its intended message.

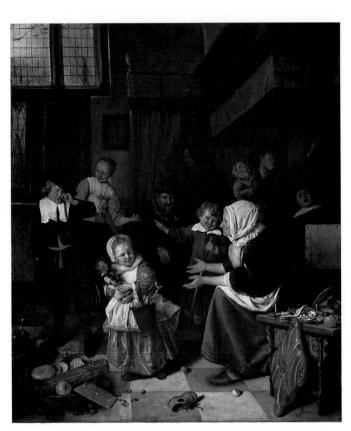

◀ **Figure 3–2** Notice the title of the work. What American holiday is similar to the one being celebrated in this picture? What do you think the man at the right is pointing to?

Jan Steen. *Eve of St. Nicholas.* c. 1667. Canvas. 81.9 x 70.5 cm (32¼ x 27¾"). Rijksmuseum, Amsterdam.

Lesson 1   *Art Criticism and Aesthetics*   **35**

RESOURCES BEYOND THE CLASSROOM

Art Museums   Art museums have much more to offer than just guided tours. In addition to providing brochures, maps, and newsletters about the collection, museums often have gift shops where postcards and slides, featuring reproductions of art works, can be purchased inexpensively. Museums also offer high quality reproductions of museums pieces that can be purchased or borrowed. Major museums such as The Metropolitan Museum of Art in New York City and the National Gallery of Art in Washington, D.C., provide catalogs that describe and depict all or part of their collections for educational purposes. Other resources include museum "lending libraries," where film, video, and multimedia presentations of art are made available to schools.

■ **Aesthetics**

Discuss why art critics may not always interpret an art work in the same way the artist had in mind. Ask students whether they think that different interpretations of a particular art work are necessarily wrong. Have students examine the compositions they created in the Studio Skills activity on page 35. Begin a dialog, encourage students to ask one another: why did they place objects where they did, why did they choose certain colors; what do they want the viewer to see when viewing this work? Then ask the class: Is it all right for an art work to mean different things to different people?

Art in **Everyday Life**

Help students develop a sense of how light affects their surroundings at different times of the day or night. Have them select a site to observe, either indoors or outdoors, making certain that the illumination changes during a 24-hour period. Have them observe the area several times over the period of a week. Students should record in their sketchbooks: the times that they make their observations; the quality of light present at each time; and how it altered the mood or character of the scene. Students may sketch the scene at different times, and present their findings to the class.

▲ **Figure 3–3**   Is this work successful because it looks lifelike or because it expresses an idea or mood? Why is it necessary to use more than one aesthetic view when judging works of art?

Beatrice Whitney van Ness. *Summer Sunlight.* c. 1936. Oil on canvas. 99.1 x 124.5 cm (39 x 49"). National Museum of Women in the Arts, Washington, D.C. Gift of Wallace and Wilhelmina Holladay.

Analyzing an Art Work

In analyzing an art work, the critic focuses on the work's composition. **Composition** is *the way the art principles are used to organize the art elements of color, line, shape, form, space, and texture.* Look once again at the painting in Figure 3–2 on page **35**. Find the long loaf of bread in the lower left and the chair in the lower right. Notice how the diagonal lines of these and other objects lead your eye to the center of the picture. There you find a small child grinning and looking out at you. The child is one of the most important figures in the work. How are the elements organized in the painting in Figure 3–3?

Interpreting an Art Work

In interpreting an art work, the critic focuses on the work's **content**. This is *the message, idea, or feeling expressed by an art work.* Each art critic may interpret an art work differently, according to individual feelings. Your interpretation of an art work will be based on your personal opinions and experiences.

Look once more at Figure 3–2. Notice that the grinning child is pointing at another child, who is crying. It appears that this second boy has received no presents. His smiling sister holds his wooden shoe in which his gifts were to be placed. But the shoe holds

---

MEETING STUDENT DIVERSITY

Language Proficiency   If you have students who experience language difficulties, try the following strategies: Permit students to use a buddy system. Pair these students with native speakers of English and allow students' individual strengths to complement each other as they complete the lessons. Have students focus on the section headings first. The headings in each section are designed to help students understand what ideas will be presented and tell them what to focus on as they read. Such information may prove invaluable to students with a limited grasp of the language.

only a hickory stick instead of presents. Maybe the artist's message to children of all ages is that gifts come only to those who behave. What mood or feeling does the painting in Figure 3–3 communicate to you?

Judging an Art Work

In judging an art work, the critic tells whether the work succeeds. He or she answers the question "Is this a successful work of art?"

How, exactly, the critic answers this question depends on his or her particular aesthetic (ess-**thet**-ik) view. An **aesthetic view** is *an idea, or school of thought, on what is important in a work of art*. Such views help critics better understand and explain the meaning of art to others.

AESTHETICS AND ART

Through the ages, scholars have put forth many different aesthetic views. The following are three common ones:

- **The subject view.** In this aesthetic view, a successful work of art is one with a lifelike subject. Look yet again at the picture in Figure 3–2. The members of the family are painted to look like real people. Critics holding this aesthetic view would praise this work for being true to life. How do you think these same critics would react to the painting in Figure 3–3? How would they judge the painting in Figure 3–1?
- **The composition view.** In this view, what is most important in an art work is its composition. Notice how light and dark

values of hue in Figure 3–2 create a feeling of depth. Critics taking this view would praise the artist's use of the elements and principles of art to create a visually pleasing design. How do you suppose these same critics would respond to the work in Figure 3–3? How might they react to the picture in Figure 3–1?
- **The content view.** In this view, what counts most is the content, or the mood or feeling, an art work communicates. Critics supporting this view would praise the work in Figure 3–2 for the joyous holiday mood it captures. What do you imagine these critics would have to say about the painting in Figure 3–3? What might their response be to the painting in Figure 3–1?

Keep in mind that few critics limit themselves to a single aesthetic view. Most feel that learning as much as possible from an art work requires keeping an open mind. How might a critic accepting all three views above react to the painting that opened this chapter on page **32**?

✔ CHECK YOUR UNDERSTANDING

1. What is art criticism? Name the four steps used by art critics.
2. What are subject, composition, and content?
3. What is an aesthetic view?
4. Describe the three commonly held aesthetic views detailed in this lesson.

Answers to ✔ CHECK YOUR UNDERSTANDING

1. Studying, understanding, and judging art works. The four steps art critics use are describing, analyzing, interpreting, and judging.
2. The subject of an art work is the image viewers can identify. Composition is the way the art principles are used to organize the art elements of color, line, shape, form, space, and texture. Content is the message, idea, or feeling expressed.
3. An idea on what is important in a work of art.
4. Subject, composition, and content. Subject view: a successful work of art has a realistic or lifelike subject. Composition view: values most the artist's use of composition. Content view: what counts most is the content or mood conveyed to the viewer.

■ **Art Criticism**

Have students choose an art work from this lesson and imagine they are professional art critics. Direct them to use the four steps of art criticism to write short reviews of the works. Read aloud the different critical evaluations of each picture. Discuss how critics may legitimately arrive at different opinions of a given artwork.

• • • • • • • • • • • • • •
ASSESS

■ **Self-Assessment**

Have students complete the review questions on this page. Answers are provided below.

■ **Reteaching**

Have students select a studio project that they completed in this class and write a short critical review of it. Have them clearly label the four steps of art criticism in their review. These reviews may later be added to student portfolios.

■ **Enrichment**

Have students read short art reviews that you have gathered from local news papers or national magazines such as *Art in America, ArtNews, New Art Examiner, Arts,* and *Artforum.* Select the simplest and most clearly written examples and, if possible, choose reviews that are accompanied by an illustration of the art under discussion. Have students try to identify the four steps of art criticism in each review.

• • • • • • • • • • • • • •
CLOSE

Have each student briefly explain to the class what he or she thinks is most important in a work of art. Ask: Is there one aesthetic view that best expresses your outlook on art?

Painting an Expressive Scene

(pages 38–39)

LESSON TIME: 90 minutes

• • • • • • • • • • • • •
FOCUS

☑ OBJECTIVES

After completing this lesson, students will be able to:

• Describe how the formal elements of an art work contribute to its expressive qualities.
• Appreciate and express stylistic features similar to Edward Hopper's art.

☑ SUPPLIES

• Pencils and erasers.
• White drawing paper, 8 x 13 inches (20 x 33cm).
• Tempera paints.
• Variety of brushes.
• Mixing trays.
• Still life or simple diorama.
• Several hand-held light sources, such as a flashlight.

Resource

☐ 3-4 *Edward Hopper*, TRB page 69 (artist profile)

• • • • • • • • • • • • •
TEACH

■ Motivator

Have students describe their neighborhood on an early Sunday morning. Encourage them to identify every possible detail of the scene. Discuss which details would best convey the atmosphere of this scene if it were painted.

38

Painting an Expressive Scene

Study the painting in Figure 3–4. The work is by American painter Edward Hopper. How do you think an art critic would react to this painting? What is the work's subject? What elements are emphasized? What principles are used to organize the elements? What mood or feeling does the work express? Does the work succeed? Why, or why not? One last question: How do you think the painting would look if the artist had extended its left boundary?

WHAT YOU WILL LEARN

You will create a painting that continues the row of empty shops in Figure 3–4. You will use the same hues, values, and intensities in your work. You will create harmony by repeating the same vertical and horizontal lines. You will add variety by placing a circular shape somewhere in your work. Finally, you will try to capture the same feeling of loneliness. (See Figure 3–5.)

WHAT YOU WILL NEED

• Pencil, sketch paper, and eraser
• Sheet of white drawing paper, 8 x 13 inches (20 x 33 cm)
• Tempera paint and several brushes
• Mixing tray

WHAT YOU WILL DO

1. Imagine the scene in Figure 3–4 as it might appear if the artist had continued it on the left side. Make several pencil sketches of possibilities you imagine. Use horizontal and vertical lines like the ones in the painting to outline shapes. For variety, include somewhere in each sketch an object with a circular shape. (Did you discover the circular shape in Hopper's painting when you examined its elements?) Let your imagination guide you.

▶ **Figure 3–4** Do you think the mood of this painting would have been different if the artist had added people? Can you find the circular shape? How does this shape add variety to the work? What has the artist done to give the painting harmony?

Edward Hopper. *Early Sunday Morning*. 1930. Oil on canvas. 88.9 x 152.4 cm (35 x 60"). Whitney Museum of American Art, New York, New York. Gertrude Vanderbilt Whitney Funds.

MEETING SPECIAL NEEDS

Mixing Paints   Pre-mixed paints can help facilitate success for students with some kinds of disabilities. Use limited amounts of paint in unbreakable jars, and provide holders for paint and water containers. This will make it easier for students with neurological or orthopedic disabilities to control the paint as they work. To facilitate cleanup, provide newspapers for tables and smocks for students. Cakes of paint in paper holders can also help prevent paint spills. Consider using water-based magic markers instead of paints for increased control in adding details.

2. Place the sheet of drawing paper along-side the photograph of Figure 3–4. Line up the paper so that it touches the left edge of the photograph. Starting at the edge of the paper, carefully continue the horizontal lines of the buildings and side-walk. Working lightly in pencil, draw de-tails from the best of your sketches.
3. Mix tempera colors to match the hues, values, and intensities of Figure 3–4. Use a brush to fill in the shapes of your draw-ing with color. (For information on using a brush see Technique Tip **4**, *Handbook* page **277**.)
4. Allow time for your painting to dry. Dis-play the finished work alongside those created by other members of your class. Discuss your works using the steps in art criticism.

▲ Figure 3–5   Student work. Expressive scene.

 Try This!

 COMPUTER OPTION

■ Pretend you live in an apartment above the barber shop. Change the Page Setup to Horizontal, and draw the view of the opposite side of the street with the Pencil or Brush tool. Draw long, low buildings. Repeat window and door shapes by using Select, Copy, and Paste. Choose dark color values to depict mood and time of day. Add a circular shape for variety. Save and title your work.

EXAMINING YOUR WORK

- **Describe**   Point out the row of build-ings and empty streets in your picture. Explain how they resemble the buildings and streets in Figure 3–4. Identify the hues, values, and intensities in your work. Show where these same elements are found in Figure 3–4.
- **Analyze**   Explain how you used the principles of harmony and variety. Point to places in Figure 3–4 where these same principles have been used.
- **Interpret**   Ask other students to de-scribe the mood expressed by your pic-ture. See if they are able to identify a mood of loneliness.
- **Judge**   Tell whether your picture looks like the one in Figure 3–4. State whether it uses many of the same elements and prin-ciples. Tell whether your work is success-ful in expressing the same mood of loneliness.

TECHNOLOGY OPTIONS

National Gallery of Art Videodisc   Use the following images to show how mood is affected by colors and perpective.

Edward Hopper *Cape Cod Evening*	Paul Cézanne *Houses in Provence*	Maurice Utrillo *Street at Corté, Corsica*
Search Frame 2106	Search Frame 1436	Search Frame 2163

Use Glencoe's *Correlation Bar Code Guide to the National Gallery of Art* to locate more art works.

■ **Aesthetics**

Ask students to identify the source of lighting in Figure 3-4. Explain that Hopper often took ad-vantage of striking or unusual lighting. Set up a still life or sim-ple diorama. Darken the room, if possible, and use a flashlight to demonstrate how different de-grees and angles of illumination can dramatically change the mood of the subject.

• • • • • • • • • • • • • • • •

ASSESS

■ **Self-Assessment**

Have students use Examining Your Work on this page to evalu-ate their own expressive scenes. Responses may be written or oral.

■ **Reteaching**

Have students bring in maga-zine and newspaper pictures that convey the feeling of loneliness as shown in the work by Hopper. Have students share their find-ings. Discuss the many different ways in which an artist might ex-press a single mood.

■ **Enrichment**

Explain to students that Hop-per was one of a number of early twentieth-century artists who painted distinctively American subjects. Have groups of students find resources on other members of this group, such as Georgia O'Keeffe, Thomas Hart Benton, Charles Burchfield, Grant Wood, and Marsden Hartley. Have groups role play these artists and describe or express the mood each artist emphasized in his or her art works. Have students share and compare their results.

• • • • • • • • • • • • • • • •

CLOSE

Have students make a list of words describing the feelings they tried to express in their scenes.

Art History

Art History

Look briefly again at the painting in Figure 3–4 on page **38**. Having created an "extension" to the work, you now have a better understanding of its composition and content. What do you know about its artist, Edward Hopper? When and where did he live? Did

his other paintings look like the one in Figure 3–6? Is he thought to be an important artist?

Answering these and similar questions is the goal of art history. In this lesson you will learn ways of answering these questions.

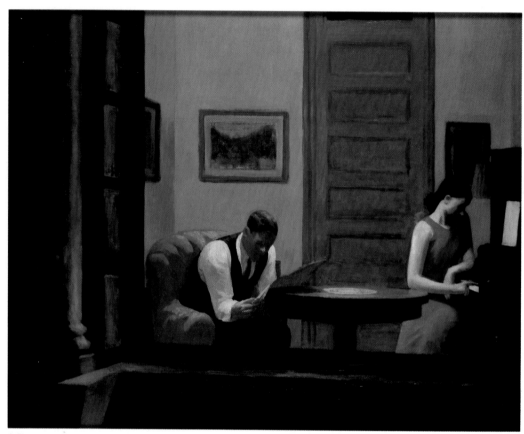

▲ **Figure 3–6** **What makes this work more than just a realistic picture of two people in a room? How do these people behave toward each other? How do their actions make you feel?**

Edward Hopper. *Room in New York*. 1932. Oil on canvas. 71.1 x 91.4 cm (28 x 36"). Sheldon Memorial Art Gallery, University of Nebraska, Lincoln, Nebraska. F. M. Hall Collection.

40 Lesson 3 *Art History*

FOCUS

☑ OBJECTIVES

After completing this lesson, students will be able to:
- Understand the difference between art criticism and art history.
- Define *style*.
- Describe the kinds of information that an art historian discovers.

☑ SUPPLIES

- Several prints of paintings from a variety of art historical periods, including works by twentieth-century realists.

Resources

- 3-5 *Rhythms of the Ages*, TRB page 71 (reproducible master)
- 3-6 *Art Through the Ages*, TRB page 72 (art history)

TEACH

■ Motivator

Have students bring in photos of themselves before beginning this lesson. Discuss what someone might think about a person if a photo were all the information available about the subject. Ask students how someone would go about collecting more information about a subject of a photo. Draw a parallel between their responses and an art historian's use of interviews, letters, diaries, and knowledge of the culture in which an art work was produced.

40

ART HISTORY AND YOU

To understand an art work completely, you need to do more than just look at it. You need to look beyond it. You need to know when and where the work was done. You need to know something about the artist who created it. Searching of this sort is the job of people in the field of art history. **Art history** is *the study of art from past to present*.

When they study art, art historians often use the same four steps art critics use: they describe, analyze, interpret, and judge. Unlike art critics, however, art historians do not use these steps to learn *from* art. They use them to learn *about* art.

Describing an Art Work

In describing an art work, art historians answer the questions "Who?" "Where?" and "When?" In other words, "Who painted the work, and when and where was it painted?" Look at the painting in Figure 3–6. Acting as an art historian, you can answer the first two of these questions by reading the credit line. The "who" is, again, Edward Hopper. The "when" is 1932. A visit to your school or local library will give you more information about the artist. There you will find that Hopper was an American painter who lived from 1882 to 1967.

Analyzing an Art Work

In analyzing an art work, the historian focuses on questions of style. **Style** is *an artist's personal way of using the elements and principles of art and expressing feelings and ideas in art*. Two typical questions the historian asks when analyzing a work are the following:

- What style did the artist use?
- Did the artist use the same style in other works?

Look again at the painting in Figure 3–6. An art historian would describe the style of this work as realistic. Compare this work with Figure 3–4 on page **38**. Would you say that both are done in a realistic style? Do you sense the same feeling of quiet loneliness in each?

Interpreting an Art Work

In interpreting an art work, the historian tries to determine how time and place may have affected the artist's style. Usually, this requires some research on the art historian's part. A trip to the library would reveal that:

- The painting in Figure 3–6 was completed during a period called the Great Depression.
- The Depression was a time during the 1930s when many people were out of work and money was scarce.
- To many people living through the Depression, the future looked hopeless.

In this work, Hopper captures the loneliness many people felt during that bleak time. The painting shows two people in a room. Notice that they do not face one another. Each, in fact, seems to be ignoring the other. A large door seems further to separate them. The people share the room but little else. Each is neglected and alone.

Judging an Art Work

In judging an art work, the historian notes its place in all art history. The historian decides whether the work and its artist make an important contribution to art. One way in which an artist can make a contribution is by introducing new materials or perfecting a style. Hopper is noted for developing a style that captured the mood of the times more effectively than most artists of that period.

✔ CHECK YOUR UNDERSTANDING

1. What is art history?
2. Explain *describing, analyzing, interpreting,* and *judging* as the terms are used by art historians.
3. Define *style*.

Answers to ✔ CHECK YOUR UNDERSTANDING

1. Art history is the recorded study of art from past to present.
2. When art historians *describe* an art work, they answer the questions, "who," "where," and "when." In *analyzing* a work, they focus on style, the artist's way of presenting the elements and ideas. Interpreting consists of determining how time and place may have affected the artist's subject and style. In *judging* a work, the art historian notes its place in all art history and tries to determine whether the work and the artist have made an important contribution.
3. Style is an artist's personal way of using the elements and principles of art and expressing feelings and ideas.

LESSON TIME: 90 minutes

• • • • • • • • • • • • •

FOCUS

☑OBJECTIVES

After completing this lesson, students will be able to:
• Evaluate the art principles and elements in a Picasso work.
• Produce a composition based on the Cubist style.

☑SUPPLIES

• Tracing paper, pencils, and rulers.
• White drawing paper, 8 x 24 inches (20 x 61 cm).
• Tempera paints and a variety of brushes, mixing trays.

Resources

▪ 3-7 *Where Do Ideas Come From?* TRB page 74 (aesthetics/art criticism)

▪ 3-8 *Practice Creative Thinking*, TRB page 76 (cooperative learning)

• • • • • • • • • • • • •

TEACH

▪ Motivator

Referring to Figure 3-7, discuss with students the following quote by Picasso: "Cubism is no different from any other school of painting. The same principles and the same elements are common to all. The fact that for a long time Cubism has not been understood and that even today there are people that cannot see anything in it, means nothing. I do not read English, an English book is a blank book to me. This does not mean that the English language does not exist..." (1923)

42

Painting in the Cubist Style

Study the painting in Figure 3–7 using the four art history questions to learn about the work and the artist who created it. The painting is an example of Cubism. The subject appears to be broken into different shapes and then put back together in new ways. The development of Cubism had an important effect on the course of art history.

WHAT YOU WILL LEARN

Using tempera, you will enlarge and re-create a section of the painting in Figure 3–7 or of another Cubist painting. You will use the same colors, lines, shapes, and textures in your work that were used in the original. You will use the principles of variety and harmony to organize these elements. Your section will be added to those completed by your classmates to form a large version of the work. (See Figure 3–8.)

WHAT YOU WILL NEED

• Tracing paper, pencil, and ruler
• Sheet of white drawing paper, 8 x 24 inches (20 x 61 cm)
• Tempera paint and several brushes
• Mixing tray

▲ **Figure 3–7** Pablo Picasso was one of the leading artists of the Cubist movement. Can you find the three primary colors in this painting? Notice how using hues widely separated on the color wheel results in a contrasting and lively composition. Which aesthetic view would you use when judging this work of art?

Pablo Picasso. *Mandolin and Guitar.* 1924. Oil with sand on canvas. 140.6 x 200.4 cm (55⅜ x 78⅞"). Solomon R. Guggenheim Museum, New York, New York. Photograph by David Heald, © The Solomon R. Guggenheim Foundation, New York. FN53.1358

42   Lesson 4   *Painting in the Cubist Style*

---

more about • • •

Cubism   Cubism is the first truly twentieth-century artistic style. Heralded by Picasso's 1907 work *Demoiselles d'Avignon*, Cubism involved entirely new approaches to the treatment of pictorial space and to the representation of emotions and states of mind. Picasso's familiarity with sculpture from the Ivory Coast and other French colonies helped him treat the human form in a more radically conceptual fashion than was possible within the confines of the Renaissance paradigm. The result was not only the reduction of body parts to geometrical forms and the loss of a normal scale of human proportion, but also the suggestion of three-dimensional relationships that would not hinge on the convention of illusionistic, one-point perspective.

WHAT YOU WILL DO

1. Lay a sheet of tracing paper over the painting in Figure 3-7. Using pencil, lightly and carefully trace the lines and shapes of the picture.
2. Using a ruler, divide your drawing into sections measuring 3 x 1 inches (8 x 2.5 cm). Your teacher will assign you one of the sections. Enlarge and draw freehand the lines and shapes of your section onto the sheet of drawing paper. Stay as close as you can to the original work.
3. Mix tempera colors to match the hues used in Figure 3-7. (For information on mixing paints, see Technique Tip **12**, *Handbook* page **280**). As you work, try also to use the same lines, textures, and shapes found in the original painting.
4. When your section is dry, add it to those completed by other members of your class. Compare your class effort with the original work. Decide whether it is made up of the same features as the original.

EXAMINING YOUR WORK

- **Describe**   Identify the objects in your section of the class painting. Show where these same objects are found in the matching section of the original art. Point out the colors, lines, textures, and shapes in your section. Show where these same elements are found in the matching section of the original.
- **Analyze**   Did your use of the principles of harmony and variety match the way they were used in the original painting? What could you have done to add *more* harmony? *More* variety?
- **Judge**   Tell whether your section of the painting blends in with those completed by classmates. If it does not, explain why. Tell whether the class effort as a whole succeeds. Explain your answer.

▶ **Figure 3–8** Student work. Cubist style painting using another Cubist work.

STUDIO OPTIONS

Try This!

■ Make another painting of your section. This time limit yourself to different values of a single hue. Be prepared to discuss in what ways this new version is different from the original.

■ Pick another painting from this chapter. Using tracing paper, copy a section of the work measuring 2 x 2 inches (5 x 5 cm). Enlarge the drawing to fit a larger square sheet of drawing paper. Paint the section using tempera. See if classmates can identify the original work of art and the section of the work you used.

Lesson 4   *Painting in the Cubist Style*   **43**

CONNECTIONS *Social Studies*

CONNECTIONS *Social Studies*

☑ OBJECTIVES

After completing this feature, students will be able to:

- Describe the feeling of nationalism in the U.S. in the early 1800s.
- Identify the spirit of national pride in Bingham's painting.

Teaching the Connection

- Have students read the feature on this page.
- Ask students to share what they know about the early exploration and settlement of the American frontier. What did Lewis and Clark set out to do in 1803? *(President Jefferson sent them to survey the land and major waterways west of the Mississippi.)* How did fur traders and settlers help the nation prosper? *(They created trade and markets for products and crops.)* What is the importance of the waterway in Bingham's painting? *(It is a means of transporting people and goods.)*
- Explain that George Caleb Bingham (1811–1879) was very patriotic. He is best known for his paintings of frontier river life and political scenes. He felt optimistic about the prosperity and political future of the new nation. His works reflect that proud optimism.

Answers to Making the Connection

- ☛ A feeling of good times.
- ☛ The people working along the river helped move goods to market. Such trade made the country more prosperous.
- ☛ Manifest Destiny was a belief that the U.S. was meant to acquire more and more land. Bingham's work shows he favored Westward expansion.

George Caleb Bingham. *The Jolly Flatboatmen.* 1846. Oil on canvas. .969 x 1.232 m (38⅛ x 48½"). Private collection on loan to the National Gallery of Art, Washington, D.C.

How Do Time and Place Affect an Artist's Work?

In 1806, Lewis and Clark completed their successful expedition west along the Missouri River. After this, thousands of adventurous fur traders, mountaineers, and settlers made their way along the Missouri River, the Oregon Trail, and the Santa Fe Trail to seek their fortunes on the great Western frontier. The push west brought prosperity to the growing nation, but it also triggered many wars with the Native Americans. St. Louis, along the Mississippi River, became the gateway to the expansion westward.

George Caleb Bingham was born in 1811. While he was growing up in Missouri, a strong wave of nationalism was spreading across the United States. The country was expanding by leaps and bounds. Farmers, traders, and trappers of the western territories contributed to the economy. The rivers played an important part in expedition and trade for settlers of these new lands. Bingham and other artists of the time tried to capture this spirit of national pride and adventure in their realistic paintings of life along the Missouri and Mississippi rivers.

┌ MAKING THE CONNECTION

- ☛ What feeling do you think Bingham was trying to communicate in *The Jolly Flatboatmen?*
- ☛ How did the lives and work of people along the river affect the growing nation?
- ☛ Find out about the doctrine of Manifest Destiny. Do you think Bingham's work shows how this idea affected the spirit of the times?

INTERNET ACTIVITY

Visit Glencoe's Fine Arts Web Site for students at:

http://www.glencoe.com/ sec/art/students

INTERNET ACTIVITY

Glencoe Student Galleria This very special on-line gallery showcases the work of student artists who have produced exemplary models of art. Each entry in the *Glencoe Student Galleria* displays an image of the art work and includes comments and reflections from the student artist. Introduce your students to this site and let them examine the art of other students. You might ask them to examine these works using the steps of art criticism from the student text. Don't forget to check the *Galleria Archives* for a glimpse of past featured art. Find out how you can submit art works made by your students for possible inclusion on these pages in the *Teacher Resources* area of Glencoe's Fine Arts Site. Find us at **http://www.glencoe.com/sec/art**

BUILDING VOCABULARY

Number a sheet of paper from 1 to 7. After each number, write the term from the list that best matches each description below.

aesthetic view   content
art criticism   style
art history   subject
composition

1. Studying, understanding, and judging works of art.
2. The image viewers can easily identify in an art work.
3. The way art principles are used to organize the elements of art in an art work.
4. The idea, feeling, mood, or message expressed by an art work.
5. An idea, or school of thought, on what is important in a work of art.
6. The study of art from past to present.
7. An artist's personal way of using the elements and principles of art and expressing feelings and ideas in art.

 REVIEWING ART FACTS

Number a sheet of paper from 8 to 17. Answer each question in a complete sentence.

8. What is *describing*, as the term is defined by art critics? What are two key facts a critic would note when describing a work?
9. What is *analyzing*, as the term is defined by art critics?
10. What is *interpreting*, as the term is defined by art critics?

MAKING ART CONNECTIONS

1. **Social Studies.** Visit the library and learn what you can about the artist of the sculpture in Figure 2–8 on page **24**. How would an art historian say that time and place affected the artist's work?

2. **Language Arts.** Pretend you are an art critic. Write an article you could submit to a magazine judging the work in Figure 3–4 by Edward Hopper.

11. What question is asked by art critics when judging a work?
12. Summarize the three aesthetic views discussed in the chapter.
13. What are three questions an art historian would answer when describing a work?
14. What are two typical questions an art historian would ask when analyzing a work?
15. What is *interpreting*, as the term is defined by art historians?
16. What questions do art historians ask when interpreting an art work?
17. What do art historians decide during the judging stage?

 THINKING ABOUT ART

On a sheet of paper, answer each question in a sentence or two.

1. **Interpret.** Could two art critics using the four-step system of art criticism come up with different judgments of a work? Explain your answer.
2. **Interpret.** Is any one step in art criticism more or less important than any other step? Which step? Explain your answer.
3. **Extend.** Art, it is often said, is not created in a vacuum. To which lesson in this chapter does this statement apply? Explain your answer.
4. **Analyze.** Give an example of events taking place in the world right now that could affect an artist's style.
5. **Compare and contrast.** In what ways is the judging of art similar for art critics and art historians? In what ways is the task different?

Chapter 3 Review   **45**

Art of Earliest Times

(pages 46–65)

Resources

- 4-10 Chapter Test, TRB page 97
- Transparency CC-4, *Aïda* by Leo and Diane Dillon
- Transparency 4, *Tutankhamen's Throne*
- Fine Art Print 4, *Dragon of Marduk*, Mesopotamia

Music

While studying this chapter, use Performing Arts Handbook page 320 to help students enjoy the combination of ancient and modern sounds from the musical group called Bali and Beyond.

NATIONAL STANDARDS

This chapter addresses the following National Standards for the Visual Arts:

1. (a, b)   4. (a, b, c)
2. (a, b, c)   5. (b, c)
3. (a, b)   6. (b)

▲ Aafenmut, a scribe or secretary in the Pharaoh's treasury, is seen making a food offering to the falcon-headed lord of heaven. How does the artist show the sun making its daily journey across the sky?

Funerary Stela of Aafenmut. *Aafenmut Offering before Horus, above Sun's Barque.* Thebes, Khokha, Third Intermediate Period, Dynasty 22, ca 924–715 B.C. Painted wood. 23 x 18.2 x 3.5 cm (9 x 7¼ x 1⅜"). The Metropolitan Museum of Art, New York. Rogers Fund, 1928.

46

FEATURED ART

Bear-tooth Necklace
Cave Paintings
Chinese Wine Vessel
Clay Bison
Egyptian Wall Paintings
Neolithic Pottery

Soapstone Seal
Sphinx and Pyramid of Khafre
Stela of Aafenmet
Stonehenge
Sumerian Sculpture

Temple of Luxor
Tutankhamun's Sarcophagus
Ziggurat

Art of Earliest Times

Before they could write or fashion a metal knife, our earliest ancestors were seeking ways to express their ideas and feelings in visual form. Paintings on the walls of prehistoric caves and ancient Egyptian tombs like the one at the left are like windows through which we can peer into the distant past. Art is the oldest form of human record and, throughout history, one of the highest achievements of human beings.

In the pages that follow you will learn about the artistic achievements of the past, beginning, in this chapter, with the art of earliest times.

PORTFOLIO IDEAS

Look at the art works in this chapter. Find one that you like. Do a quick sketch of it. Then describe how it uses the elements of color, line, space, shape, form, and texture. Find another that you like and sketch it. Compare how it uses one or more of the elements of art. Date your sketches and written entries and place them in your portfolio. Refer to these later and note how the use of elements and principles changes in different cultures.

OBJECTIVES

After completing this chapter, you will be able to:
- Define the term *culture.*
- Describe life during ancient times.
- Tell what kinds of art were created during ancient times.
- Create art works with media in the art styles of early civilizations.

WORDS YOU WILL LEARN

culture
hieroglyphic
megaliths
post and lintel system
stele
urban planning
ziggurat

Prehistoric Art

• • • • • • • • • • • • • •
FOCUS

☑ **OBJECTIVES**

After completing this lesson, students will be able to:
• Define *culture.*
• Describe life in ancient times.
• Tell what kinds of art were created in early times.
• Describe the difference between Paleolithic and Neolithic societies.

☑ **SUPPLIES**

• Found natural objects (such as stones, shells, pieces of wood, chunks of clay).
• Sharp tools.
• Crayons, markers, and chalk.

Resource

◗ ■ *Ceramic Brick Relief,*
◗   TRB page 81, (cooperative
◗   learning)

• • • • • • • • • • • • • •
TEACH

■ **Motivator**

Call on students to spell the word *artifact*. Tell them that archaeologists use artifacts to gain information about early civilizations that kept no written records. Point out that the first three letters of artifact are ART. The art of prehistoric people is an important source of information about their daily lives.

As long as there have been people, there has been art. The need to create has always been a driving force among people. In this lesson you will look at prehistoric art. This is art dating back to the time before people kept written records. By studying this art, you will find out about the civilizations of early times. You will learn about their **culture**, or *ideas, beliefs, and living customs.*

ART OF THE OLD STONE AGE

The earliest art works modern experts have uncovered date back to the Old Stone Age. Also known as the Paleolithic (pay-lee-uh-**lith**-ik) period, the Old Stone Age lasted from around 30,000 until about 10,000 B.C.

The lives of people during the Old Stone Age were filled with danger, hunger, and fear. Each day meant a new struggle just to survive. In the winter they searched for shelter against the snow and cold. In the summer they battled the heat and the sudden rains that flooded their caves. Those lucky enough to survive were old by age 40. Few lived past their fiftieth year.

Painting

Many of the Old Stone age art works that have lasted into recent times are paintings. The animal painting in Figure 4–1 is one such work. It was discovered on the wall of a cave in France. Others like it have been found in Spain and elsewhere in western Europe. Examples of cave art have been found on every continent, from the Sahara desert to the Arctic. Notice also how lifelike the animals look.

No one knows the real reason behind the creation of paintings like this one. Such works have always been found deep within caves, far from entrances and daylight. Their

▲ **Figure 4–1   The cave which houses this painting was discovered by two boys playing ball. What do you suppose was their first reaction to this painting?**

Cave painting. c. 15,000–10,000 B.C. Lascaux, Dordogne, France.

location has led experts to think they were not created merely as decoration. Some think the paintings played a part in hunting rituals. Many have imagined scenes like the following . . .

> *The evening meal over, the men of the tribe stood. The boy — now a man — stood with them. One by one, they moved away from the warm cooking fires and into the cool, shadowy depths of the cave. Suddenly the boy felt himself being shoved to his knees. As he groped forward, he found himself crawling through a narrow passageway.*
>
> *By and by, the path widened again. In the distance ahead, the boy could see the glow of a fire. Soon he found himself in a great hall lighted by torches. On one wall was a huge bison. In the flickering light, the beast seemed to be charging toward him. The boy's heart raced.*
>
> *As the boy watched with wide eyes, an artist began creating a second bison. With a sharp-ended stick, the artist scratched the outlines of the animal into the wall. Using clumps of fur and moss, he filled in the body with a variety of reds and browns. Using a bit of coal, he added a single fierce eye.*

48   Lesson 1   *Prehistoric Art*

■■■ *CURRICULUM* ▶ *CONNECTIONS*

Social Studies   The cave paintings found in France are remarkably similar to prehistoric paintings from many other parts of the world, including Spain and North America. For example, the stenciled hand is one of the most common prehistoric images, and it appears worldwide. Some symbols found in French caves, such as the symbol of bear paw marks, have remained unintelligible until a very similar mark elsewhere has provided a clue. Bulls and other commonly painted animals also bear a strikingly universal resemblance. Careful attention is invariably given to depicting the horns, antlers, and feet.

▲ Figure 4–2   These figures were found in a chamber one mile underground. In what ways did their location help preserve them?

Clay Bison from Le Tuc d'Audoubert Cave, France. c. 17,000 B.C. Archeological Museum, Madrid, Spain.

At last the second beast was finished. The men, now excited about the promise of tomorrow's hunt, began to chant. The boy chanted with them. He picked up the spear his father had carved for him. With his fellow hunters, he attacked the "spirit" of the bison up on the wall, just as he would attack the real bison during the hunt.

Sculpture and Crafts

Old Stone Age artists were skilled not only at painting, but equally talented at sculpture and crafts. Notice the attention to detail in the bison shown in Figure 4–2. These remarkable sculptures, which are thought to date to around 17,000 B.C., were modeled out of clay.

The necklace in Figure 4–3 was found in an ancient grave. It is made of animal teeth and shells. Stone, ivory, and bone were some other media used by early sculptors and craftspeople.

▲ Figure 4–3   During prehistoric times, there were many animals to hunt. Bear and lion teeth such as those in this necklace were easy to find.

Bear-tooth necklace. c. 13,000 B.C. Private collection.

Show students slides, prints, or photographs of the animals painted in the caves of Lascaux or other recent discoveries. Describe the qualities of each animal and list them on the board, for example, quick, powerful, strong. Ask: How did the artist represent these attributes? Was he or she successful?

Art in
Everyday Life

Have students look at the necklace in Figure 4-3 on page 49. Explain that people make ornaments out of material they consider beautiful or valuable. Ask students if this is a necklace that people would enjoy wearing today? Why or why not? Ask them to note how each culture chose natural resources and made use of all parts of animals, including creating decorative jewelry. Discuss parallels in our society that could benefit from this approach to use of available resources.

■ **Cultural Diversity**

Explain to students that the same symbols and colors sometimes mean very different things in different cultures. For example, in prehistoric art the snake was a symbol of life, energy, and rebirth and was a benevolent creature. It later took on the symbolism of evil. Ask students to list on the board what they associate with the color red, or the different meanings of black and white, in their own culture and in various other cultures.

50

ART OF THE NEW STONE AGE

People gradually began to change as civilizations moved into the New Stone Age. Prehistoric peoples stopped wandering and formed villages. They learned to raise livestock and started growing their own food. Ways of making art changed, too.

Crafts

In the area of crafts, people learned to spin fibers, weave, and make pottery. Figure 4–4 shows a vase made about 6000 B.C. Note the potter's use of formal balance in this piece. Notice how the geometric design and balance combine to give the work a sense of unity.

▲ Figure 4–4   What steps did the maker of this work take to obtain harmony? How was variety achieved?

Neolithic pottery. Vase with flat base. Ceramique armoricaine. St. Germainen Lays.

▲ Figure 4–5   Some scholars believe this circle of stone was built as an accurate calendar. What other purpose might it have served?

Stonehenge. Salisbury Plain, Wiltshire, England.

50   Lesson 1   *Prehistoric Art*

Local Art Museums   Although major art museums usually serve only large metropolitan areas, smaller cities and towns are often home to more specialized museums. Make use of local art museums by arranging for guided tours. Children's museums, historical museums, and even natural history museums can illuminate concepts learned in class. Children's museums house exhibits that appeal to school-age children and often specialize in collectibles, hand-crafted toys, and mechanical objects. Historical museums generally highlight local arts and crafts, as well as give a sense of local history. Natural history museums are a source of natural forms for inspiration. Just looking at the exhibits can stimulate the imagination and spark a creative urge!

Architecture

The New Stone Age, or Neolithic (nee-uh-**lith**-ik) period, also saw the first attempts at architecture. One kind of early building took the form of *large stone monuments* called **megaliths** (**meg**-uh-liths). The most famous of these is Stonehenge in England (Figure 4–5). This style of construction demonstrated the **post and lintel system**. This is *an approach to building in which a crossbeam is placed above two uprights*. As with the early cave paintings, the reason behind the creation of Stonehenge is unknown. As much a mystery is how the stones, many of which weigh 50 tons, were set in place. To this day, we can only guess and wonder.

▲ **Figure 4–6** Student work. Image on natural object.

STUDIO ACTIVITY

Finding Natural Forms

Bring a rounded stone about the size of your fist to class. Look at it carefully from every angle until the natural form suggests a simplified real or imaginary animal to you. Use a black marker or pencil to lightly draw the animal on the stone. Add color by using tempera or acrylic paints. Details can be added with a black marker. For a durable finish, paint your piece with varnish or acrylic medium after the tempera has dried.

PORTFOLIO

Exchange art works with a classmate. Use what you see in the art work to write a short paragraph describing the animal your classmate created. Review your classmate's written description of your imaginary animal. Does it match the feeling or idea you wanted to convey? Write one or two sentences explaining how your art work was successful and what you might do differently next time. Include your classmate's description, your written statement, and a drawing or photograph of your art work in your portfolio.

✔ CHECK YOUR UNDERSTANDING

1. Define the term *culture.*
2. Describe life during the Old Stone Age.
3. What is a possible explanation for the creation of the cave paintings?
4. What changes in the way people lived took place in the New Stone Age?
5. What is a megalith? What is the name of the most famous megalith? Where is it found?

STUDIO ACTIVITY

Finding Natural Forms

Encourage students to bring in their own found natural objects for this activity. If your school is in an area where it is possible to take a nature walk to locate objects, talk with your administrator and arrange to go as a class on a nature hunt to prepare for this exercise.

ASSESS

■ Self-Assessment

Have students complete the review questions on this page. Answers are provided below.

■ Reteaching

Have students make a cartoon illustration that compares and contrasts the life of a young person of 20,000 years ago with one who lives today. Have them include information on how each person spends their time, how each one's diet differs, and what is required by each person for survival.

■ Enrichment

Many students are fascinated with Stonehenge. Have students research facts about the size and proportions of the stone monument. Then have them brainstorm how the post and lintels of Stonehenge might have been built. Have interested students research legends associated with the stone megalith.

CLOSE

Go around the room and ask students to name one medium or tool used by ancient artists that they have read about.

Answers to ✔ CHECK YOUR UNDERSTANDING

1. Ideas, beliefs, and living customs.
2. The lives of humans during the Old Stone Age were filled with danger, hunger, fear, and a struggle simply to survive.
3. The cave paintings may have been created to play a part in hunting rituals.
4. Answers should include the following: hunters became herders as they learned to raise livestock; food gatherers became food producers; wanderers formed villages; art forms became more abstract and geometric.
5. A large stone monument. Stonehenge in England.

Painting Using Earth Pigments

(pages 52–53)

LESSON TIME: 90 minutes

• • • • • • • • • • • • • •
FOCUS

☑ OBJECTIVES

After completing this lesson, students will be able to:

- Name earth pigments and the color each one represents.
- Create unusual effects with different tools.
- Design and complete a scene representing their daily life.

☑ SUPPLIES

- Pencils and sketch paper.
- Yellow chalk.
- White paper, 12 x 18 inches (30 x 46 cm).
- Mortar and pestle.
- Natural pigments.
- School acrylic paint.
- A variety of brushes and palettes.
- Diluted white glue.
- Several small jars, palette knives.
- Water and paper towels.
- Bark, twigs, cloth, and the like for applying paint.

• • • • • • • • • • • • • •
TEACH

■ Motivator

Explain to students that artists of prehistoric times used natural pigments such as ground rocks and minerals. Have students gather around you as you demonstrate grinding the pigments. Ask them to speculate about the resulting colors. Explain the purpose of the glue and what a binder does. Ancient artists used animal fat and blood for binders. Demonstrate how to add the binder.

Painting Using Earth Pigments

When prehistoric artists created their cave paintings, they weren't able simply to open paint jars. They made use of natural sources of pigment around them. For reds, browns, and golds, they mixed ground-up earth minerals in animal fat, vegetable juices, and egg whites. For black they used charcoal from burned firewood. Minerals like these do not fade over time as other materials do. Notice how the painting in Figure 4–7 has kept its brilliant color for 15,000 years.

WHAT YOU WILL LEARN

You will create a painting about your environment using earth pigment paints that you have made from local earth minerals. At least half the paint you use in your work will be made from natural earth pigments. Use thin and built-up layers of this paint to obtain different textures that will add variety to your painting. For the remaining paint, you will use two hues of school acrylics plus black and white. (See Figure 4–8.)

WHAT YOU WILL NEED

- Pencil and sheets of sketch paper
- Yellow chalk
- Sheet of white paper, 12 x 18 inches (30 x 46 cm)
- Natural pigments
- School acrylic paint, several brushes, and palette
- Diluted white glue and a small jar
- Painting knife
- Water and paper towels

▶ **Figure 4–7 Can you identify the main features of this animal? Does it appear to be standing still or moving? How do you know?**

Horse from Cave Painting. c. 15,000–10,000 B.C. Lascaux, Dordogne, France.

MEETING SPECIAL NEEDS

Prehistoric Culture Digging in the earth to collect different earth colors and mixing the earth pigments will facilitate involvement and enjoyment for many students with special needs. Provide each student with a small plastic bag to collect soil from where they live for use in this lesson. Depicting animals and pets showing characteristics which they have or would like to have can be especially beneficial for students with low self esteem. During discussion, students who are shy and especially those who have difficulty expressing themselves can discuss these characteristics and cite their value in prehistoric culture and in the present day.

WHAT YOU WILL DO

1. Collect and grind your own earth pigment. (See Technique Tip **11**, *Handbook* page **280**.)
2. Make several sketches of scenes from your environment that would make good use of these colors. White sand would be good for a beach scene. Gray dirt could be used to show city sidewalks. Reddish-brown colors would work well for brick walls. Look at the colors you have, and let the colors give you ideas.
3. Select your best sketch. Using yellow chalk, draw the outline shapes of your sketch on the sheet of white paper.
4. Choose the colors of paint you will use. Remember to limit yourself to two hues of school acrylic, plus black and white. Prepare the earth pigment paints. Take care to mix no more than what you will use in a single day.
5. Paint your scene. Experiment with different ways of using the earth pigments. For a thin smooth area, use only the liquid part of the paint. For a built-up, textured area, make a thick binder using extra glue and add plenty of powder. Apply the thick paint with the painting knife.
6. Display your work when it is dry. Look for ways in which your work is similar to and different from those of your classmates. Take note of any unusual effects created using the earth pigments.

EXAMINING YOUR WORK

- **Describe**   Tell what scene from your environment you chose to make. Identify the different earth colors you used. Name the hues of school acrylic paint you used.
- **Analyze**   Point out areas in which you used thick and thin layers of paint to create different textures. Explain how these different textures add variety to your picture.
- **Interpret**   Explain why this scene represents your environment.
- **Judge**   Tell whether you feel your work succeeds. Explain your answer.

▲ **Figure 4–8   Student work. Earth pigments.**

 Try This!

COMPUTER OPTION

- Explore the Air Brush tool and settings. Choose earth colors. Use small width of Air Brush and dense setting to draw animal shapes. Experiment with other settings. Build up layers of paint to simulate an uneven rock surface. Make notes of what settings you use and record the effects for future use. Save and title your work.

SAFETY TIP ⚠

Grinding Pigments   Avoid grinding highly toxic pigments such as lead, manganese, and cadmium. Accidental poisoning may occur by getting pigments in cuts or sores or by contacting a paintbrush to lips, eating while painting, and failing to wash hands after working in the studio. See *Artist Beware* by Michael McCann (New York: Watson-Guptill Publications, 1979) for a discussion of pigments and their respective toxicity levels. You might want to have students experiment with painting on a light color of construction paper to determine whether the results are more interesting than those obtained on white paper.

■ **Vocabulary**

Show students tubes of yellow ochre or burnt umber oil or watercolor paints. Explain that earth pigments are still used by artists today. Many potters use pigments called oxides to glaze their bowls and pots.

■ **Studio Skills**

Explain that prehistoric artists used their hands, fur, bark, twigs, moss, and leather to achieve subtle colors and textures. Encourage students to use a variety of tools and keep a technique chart listing the different materials used and the results.

• • • • • • • • • • • • •
ASSESS

■ **Self-Assessment**

Have students use Examining Your Work to evaluate their own painting with earth pigments. Responses may be written or oral.

■ **Reteaching**

Have students role-play an ancient artist who is being interviewed by a local television station. Have them think of questions that explore how and why ancient people created art.

■ **Enrichment**

Have students investigate how archaeologists date cave paintings and other artifacts. The best artifact dates come from combining data from carbon-14 analysis with information from ancient calendars, rock layers, geological activity, and annual growth rings in trees.

• • • • • • • • • • • • •
CLOSE

In their portfolios, have students write a short paragraph that describes which technique they enjoyed the most and why.

Art of Ancient Egypt

• • • • • • • • • • • • • •
FOCUS

☑ OBJECTIVES

After completing this lesson, student will be able to:
- Discuss the importance of religion and the afterlife to ancient Egyptians.
- Discuss the purpose of the pyramid.
- Describe the difference of relief sculpture and a tomb painting.

☑ SUPPLIES

- Clay and rolling pins.
- Tools for modeling clay.
- Pencils and strips of white paper, 12 x 8 inches (30 x 20 cm).

Resource

- ■ 4-2 *Artists of Ancient Times,* TRB page 83 (artist profile)

• • • • • • • • • • • • • •
TEACH

■ Motivator

Ask students to look at the pyramid in Figure 4-10. Ask them to tell why they think these great stone monuments were built. Ask them to speculate how a pharaoh might plan a tomb to be constructed using today's technology.

During prehistoric times the chief enemy of the human race was nature. Unfriendly weather and fierce beasts of prey kept early humans always on their guard. By the time people began keeping written records, they had a new enemy. That enemy was other people.

As tribes learned to herd animals and grow crops, they also learned to live in harmony with their surroundings. This peaceful balance was upset by population growth. Small tribes began to fight over grazing land and soil suitable for growing crops. They were forced to band together into more organized groups for protection and also to be able to produce more food. By around 3000 B.C. four major civilizations had developed at different points on the globe. The ancient civilizations of Egypt, China, India, and Mesopotamia (mes-uh-puh-**tay**-mee-uh) emerged at this time.

In this lesson you will learn about the culture and art of ancient Egypt.

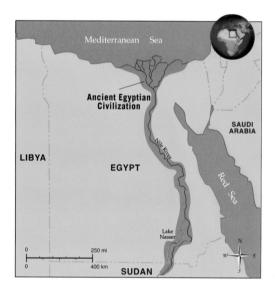

Figure 4–9   Ancient Egypt.

ANCIENT EGYPTIAN CULTURE

Ancient Egypt developed along the banks of the Nile before 3000 B.C. Find this area on the map in Figure 4–9. This civilization lasted for almost 3000 years. The arts of ancient Egypt reflect the endurance and solid foundation of that culture.

Egypt was ruled by a leader called a pharaoh (**fehr**-oh). The pharaoh was not merely a king in the eyes of the Egyptian people, he was also a god. After death he was believed to join other gods, whom the Egyptians identified with forces of nature. The afterlife of the pharaoh and other important people is a theme running through much of ancient Egyptian art.

Architecture

There can be little doubt that ancient Egypt's greatest achievement in art was in architecture. Figure 4–10 shows the civilization's most remarkable achievement of all, the great pyramids. These magnificent structures were built as tombs for the pharaohs. Thousands upon thousands of workers toiled for decades to build a single pyramid. Today the pyramids remain among the true wonders of the world.

Proof of the genius of later Egyptian architects is found in temples like the one in Figure 4–11. This temple is named in honor of the Egyptian sun god, Re (**Ray**). Apart from their beauty, temples like this were among the first buildings ever to use the post and lintel system. What structure of the New Stone Age that you studied also used posts and lintels?

◀ **Figure 4–9   Ancient Egypt.**

CURRICULUM > CONNECTIONS

Geography   Throughout the art history lessons in this text you will find maps to help students recognize locations important to art of various cultures. Have students look at the map of Egypt on this page and locate the Nile River valley. Help students understand the importance of the Nile River in the life of ancient Egyptians. Point out that the Nile River valley is met by vast expanses of desert on both the eastern and western sides. Ask students to imagine what kinds of hardships a scarcity of fertile farm land and space for homes might impose on a culture. Point out that Egyptians placed tombs for the dead in the desert and cliffs. Discuss how the land conditions might have influenced this decision.

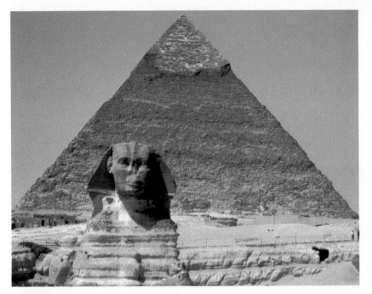

◀ **Figure 4–10** In ancient times, these pyramids were each covered with a layer of polished white limestone. What do you suppose happened to this outer layer?

Sphinx and Pyramid of Khafre. c. 2600 B.C. Giza.

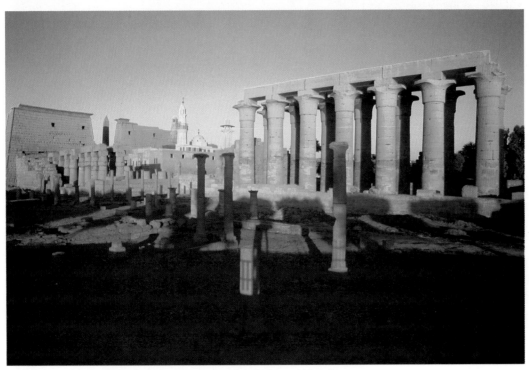

▲ **Figure 4–11** It is thought that the post and lintel system dates back to prehistoric times. Trees and bundles of stalks may have served as the first posts and lintels.

Built by Amenophis III. *Temple of Luxor.* Pylon and Hypostyle Hall. Egypt.

■ Vocabulary

Have students consult a large dictionary to look up the root words of *hieroglyphics*. Discuss why Egyptian writing was called "sacred" by the Greeks. Note that hieroglyphics were used only on monuments, tomb and temple walls, statues, and funerary stelae. A cursive script known as hieratic writing was used for everyday purposes.

■ Art History

Lead a discussion on the pyramids of Giza, possibly the most familiar architectural forms in the world. Tell students that the Great Pyramid of Cheops *(key*-ops) is almost 500 feet high and is a maze of passageways and a few small rooms. This maze was intended to confuse and trap looters that wanted the jewels and precious art objects that were buried with the king. Nevertheless, the tombs at Giza were plundered.

■ Cultural Diversity

Discuss with students the team nature of Egyptian artistic production. Point out that Egyptian artists worked as members of a team of professional craftspeople that usually include an "outline scribe" who marked out the preliminary drawing, a person who chiseled the relief, and a third artist who added the paint. Artists in many other cultures have also worked in teams. Have students work in teams of three to plan and create a simple clay relief carving in the manner described. Discuss the advantages and the drawbacks of teamwork in creating art.

TECHNOLOGY OPTIONS

Transparencies An overhead projector is a valuable teaching aid. The overhead enlarges images to make materials easily visible to a large group while leaving the teacher free to observe and interact with the class. Printed illustrations can be lifted from clay-coated magazine pages by adhering the printed side to a sheet of clear, adhesive-backed acetate and soaking off the paper from the back. The overhead provides a good way to illustrate the visual elements and to experiment with composition. Glencoe's *Fine Art Transparencies* package that accompanies *Understanding Art* provides a variety of fine art works and technique tips that can be used with this textbook.

■ Aesthetics

Have students examine the art work illustrated in Figure 4-12. Then have them find another reproduction of a life-sized figural sculpture. (See pages 24, 100, 116, 134, and 267.) Have them create a chart or diagram to compare how the two artists depicted the facial features and other forms of the body.

■ Studio Skills

Have students examine the stele that appears in the opening pages of this chapter. Have students roll out thin clay slabs in the shape of a stele and draw out several frames. In each frame, have students depict an activity or an event in their lives. Invite students to present their life histories to the rest of the class.

■ Art History

As students examine the wall painting in Figure 4-12, remind them that this painting is from an Egyptian tomb, buried for centuries. Explain that while much Egyptian art was buried, this does not mean that it was not intended to be seen and appreciated. Visitors were encouraged to offer prayers and present offerings in the tomb. Have students find examples of funerary art in other sections of this book and develop a chart listing whether they are in the form of carvings, paintings, vessels, or statuary.

■ Art Criticism

Review the four steps of art criticism, and discuss how they might be applied to architecture. Have students examine Figure 4-10 again and together complete the four steps, listing the results on the board.

▲ Figure 4–12   Much of the information we have about daily life in Egypt comes from paintings on walls and coffins found in tombs.

Egyptian. *Fishing Scene: Attendants with harpoons and string of fish*. 1436–1411 B.C. Wall painting from the Tomb of Kenamun. 43.5 x 53 cm (17 x 21″). Egyptian Expedition of The Metropolitan Museum of Art, New York, New York. Rogers Fund.

 CURRICULUM *CONNECTIONS*

Language Arts   Egyptian hieroglyphics, some of which derive from representations of objects, are an art form in themselves. Ideograms were generally placed at the ends of words composed of several phonetic symbols. In art, however, large scale figures might themselves stand in for the final ideogram. For example, the written names of men and women were terminated by a male or female figure. In a funerary relief where the deceased is depicted, the final ideogram of the deceased's name would be omitted because the picture was considered to have completed the name.

Sculpture

In Egypt it became customary to decorate the tombs of rich or important people. Often this was done with painted relief sculptures. An example of this type of art appears in the relief that opened this chapter (page **46**). This is a **stele** (**stee**-lee), *a carved upright stone slab used as a monument.* Each frame shows a different part of a person's life or preoccupation for the afterlife. The frame closest to the top shows the subject seated at his own funeral banquet.

Painting

The wall paintings found in the tombs of royalty and the wealthy tell us about the daily life of the Egyptians. Figure 4–12 shows a typical Egyptian painting. Scenes from the buried person's life were painted on the walls. Notice that some body parts are painted as they would appear from the side. The head, arms, and legs are three such parts. Other parts appear as they would if we were seeing the people head-on. The single eye and shoulders demonstrate this. These views show the strict rules that artists of ancient Egypt followed. One of these was to show every body part from its most visible angle.

STUDIO ACTIVITY

Creating a Writing System

Look once again at the stele on page **46.** Notice the rows and columns of small birds and other shapes. These are examples of **hieroglyphic** (hy-ruh-**glif**-ik), *an early form of picture writing.* In this writing system, shapes stand not for sounds, as in our modern alphabet, but for ideas. (A heart shape, for instance, might be used to mean "love.") Here the symbols provide a written record of the achievements of the stele's subject.

Imagine that you are a citizen of a future civilization who has been called upon to create a new writing system. As you begin to work on this task, remember that you know nothing of modern alphabets. Think about what ideas you will need to express in your culture. Create a shape for each idea. When your system is complete, create a sentence and see if anyone in your class can read the message.

PORTFOLIO

Copy your new writing system and your sentence or message and keep them in your portfolio. As a self-reflection, explain what you learned about how writing helps in communication.

✔ CHECK YOUR UNDERSTANDING

1. When did ancient Egypt come into being? How long did the civilization survive?
2. Who were the pharaohs? What part did they play in the art of ancient Egypt?
3. Name two achievements in ancient Egyptian architecture.
4. What is a stele?
5. How did Egyptian artists show the human figure in their work? What was their reason for doing this?

STUDIO ACTIVITY

Creating a Writing System

To prepare for this activity, display pictorial symbols or icons that occur in today's society. You might ask students ahead of time to bring examples to class.

ASSESS

■ Self-Assessment

Have students complete the review questions on this page. Answers are provided.

■ Reteaching

Ask students to think of a popular saying, perhaps from a television show or commercial. Have them draw a bumper sticker that communicates the saying in hieroglyphics.

■ Enrichment

Have students find out what articles were discovered in the tomb of King Tutankhamun. The enormous quantity of treasures found include belongings that he might be expected to enjoy in the afterlife, amulets to protect him in his journey in the underworld, and tools to perform any labors that the gods might request.

CLOSE

Call on students to name one recognizable feature that is typical of Egyptian art styles.

Answers to ✔ CHECK YOUR UNDERSTANDING

1. Ancient Egypt came into being before 3000 B.C. It lasted for almost 3000 years.
2. A pharaoh was a leader who ruled with absolute power. The afterlife of the pharaohs and others is a theme in ancient Egyptian art.
3. The creation of the great pyramids and the development of the post and lintel system.
4. A stele is a carved upright stone slab used as a monument.
5. The human figure was depicted with some body parts shown head on and some viewed from the side. The reason for this was that artists were bound by strict rules, one of which was to show every body part from the most familiar angle.

Ancient China, India, and Mesopotamia

LESSON 4

Ancient China, India, and Mesopotamia

(pages 58–61)

• • • • • • • • • • • • • • •

FOCUS

☑ **OBJECTIVES**

After completing this lesson, students will be able to:

• Name the four ancient civilizations that developed simultaneously.

• Discuss the artistic achievements of early Chinese civilization.

• Describe a ziggurat.

☑ **SUPPLIES**

• Erasers and utility knives.

• Stamp pads.

• Poster paint and brushes.

• Milk carton.

Resources

⊃ ■ 4-3 *The King Tut Discovery,* TRB page 84 (appreciating cultural diversity).

⊃ ■ 4-4 *The Silk Road,* TRB page 86 (art history)

⊃ ■ 4-5 *China Today,* TRB page 87 (appreciating cultural diversity)

⊃ ■ 4-6 *Uncovering Ancient Life,* TRB page 88 (aesthetics/art criticism)

⊃ ■ 4-7 *Time Line,* TRB page 90 (reproducible master)

Like Egypt, the ancient civilizations of China, India, and Mesopotamia each developed in a river valley. Like Egypt, each had a king and a religion that was based on nature.

Yet, despite some similarities, each civilization had its own separate culture and ways of making art. In this lesson you will learn about the culture and art of these civilizations.

ANCIENT CHINESE CULTURE

The first Egyptian pyramids were built around 2600 B.C. Around that time another new civilization was emerging a continent away, in the Yellow River valley. Can you find the Yellow River on the map in Figure 4–13? This civilization, China, is still alive today. It boasts the oldest continuous culture in the history of the world.

The history of China, until modern times, is divided into periods known as dynasties. Dynasties are named for ruling families of emperors. The first of these, the Shang dynasty, began around 1766 B.C. The last of them, the Ch'ing, ended in fairly recent times. Like the history of China itself, the art of China is grouped by dynasties.

ANCIENT CHINESE ART

The ancient Chinese were skilled in all areas of art. Legends show that Chinese artists were creating pictures as early as 2200 B.C. The works we have today were made in bronze and on stone and pottery instead of silk or paper, which has not survived. The architecture of this early period has also vanished, though large building foundations have been unearthed.

Sculpture and Crafts

The single greatest achievement of early Chinese artists was their work in bronze. A bronze pitcher dating from the Shang Dynasty is shown in Figure 4–14. Like most art of the time, the work is covered with motifs and squared spirals. Experts today believe the spirals to stand for clouds, rain, or water. What do these images seem to say about the ancient Chinese view of nature?

◄ **Figure 4–13** Ancient China, India, and Mesopotamia.

— *more about* • • • —

Motifs Shang dynasty bronzes were embellished with a number of characteristic motifs, some of which were placed in a horizontal band, as shown on the vessel in Figure 4-14. Others covered the entire surface. Among the most common decorative features were dragons, birds, the thunder scroll, the cloud scroll, a bowstring ornament, small circles, vertical ridges, and a variety of animals including the ox, the sheep, the goat, and the cock. Remind students as they create art works in this class that there are many subjects that can be used as motifs, and they may wish to look back at these ancient works for examples.

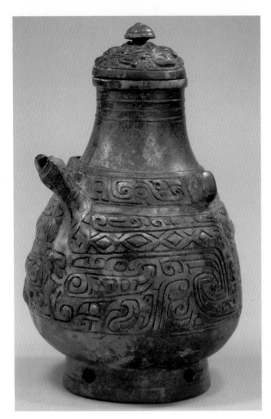

ANCIENT INDIAN CULTURE

Like that of the Shang dynasty, the culture of ancient India remained a legend until modern times. In 1856 railroad workers laying track in the Indus River valley made a discovery. Near the city of Harappa (huh-**rap**-uh), they found a hill of crumbling fired clay bricks. These bricks date to between 2500 and 1500 B.C. Can you find the city of Harappa on the map in Figure 4–13? In what modern country is it located?

In addition to bricks, the railroad workers found a number of small relief carvings in soapstone. One of these is shown in Figure 4–15. These carvings are the oldest examples of Indian art.

Did you notice the odd lines and shapes above the animal form? These are known to be letters from an ancient system of writing. Scholars have yet to decipher the Harappan language.

◀ **Figure 4–14** Would you describe the images shown on this pitcher as realistic? If not, how would you describe them?

Chinese. Ritual Wine Vessel, with Spout. Shang Dynasty, 14th Century B.C. Bronze. 21.6 cm (8½"). The Metropolitan Museum of Art, New York, New York. Gift of Ernest Erickson Foundation, Inc.

◀ **Figure 4–15** Soapstone seals may have been used as personal adornment. Could the symbols have identified the owner?

Soapstone seal from Mohenjo-daro showing a Brahmani bull. Harappan culture. c. 2300–1750 B.C. 3.5 cm (18½"). British Museum, London, England.

Lesson 4 *Ancient China, India and Mesopotamia* **59**

CURRICULUM *CONNECTIONS*

Language Arts The Sumerians constructed ziggurats in the belief that mountaintops were the dwelling places of their gods. Lacking real mountains on the Mesopotamian plain, the Sumerians had to create their own artificial ones to provide a suitable home for their gods. The cult statues placed inside the ziggurat temple were believed to embody the deities that they depicted. Sumerians also made statues of worshippers to send prayers and messages to the gods in their place.

■ **Studio Skills**

Have students examine Figure 4-15. Ancient Indians used chiseled and drilled seals as amulets to stamp their agreements. Have students use utility knives to carve personal seals out of their rubber erasers. Than have them print the seals with ink or paint on plain paper to make "official" stationery.

Art in ▰▰▰
Everyday Life

The images on the vessel in Figure 4-14 provide a kind of information about what was important to the ancient Chinese. Display a milk carton. Compare the vessel decoration with the kind of information printed on a modern-day milk carton. Ask: What appears to be important to each culture? Do North Americans think about natural and spiritual forces when they pour their milk? Were the ancient Chinese concerned about having exact nutrition information on a vessel?

■ **Cultural Diversity**

The ziggurats were the Sumerians' most distinctive and monumental form of architecture, and they reflect the importance of religion in Mesopotamia. Explain to students that the larger and more developed buildings of other cultures also suggest the values of the people. Have students work in small groups to brainstorm the different concerns that are reflected when a society spends large sums of money to construct a pyramid, a cathedral, a grand opera house, a skyscraper, and a sports stadium. Have them present their findings to the class.

60

▲ **Figure 4–16** Perhaps the most famous ziggurat of all is the one recorded in the Bible. It is the tower of Babylon.

Ziggurat at Ur, Iraq.

Architecture

In 1922 a second ancient city was found in the area of Harappa. Its name is Mohenjo-Daro (moh-hen-joh-**dahr**-oh), which means "Hill of the Dead." The city is believed to have had a population of 35,000.

Mohenjo-Daro is an early example of the art of **urban planning**. This is *arranging the construction and services of a city to best meet its people's needs*. The ancient city had wide, open streets dividing it into large blocks about the size of four football fields. There were homes, shops, and large buildings thought to be houses of worship.

MESOPOTAMIAN CULTURE

The culture of Mesopotamia was more the culture of a region than of a people. The region was the fertile crescent of land between the Tigris (**ty**-gruhs) and Euphrates (yoo-**frayt**-eez) Rivers. This land is shared today by Syria and Iraq. (See Figure 4–13.) The people of Mesopotamia lived in city states that each had their own king. Sometimes these city states fought with each other and one would become more powerful.

60   Lesson 4   *Ancient China, India and Mesopotamia*

— *more about* • • • —

Egyptian Style   Artistic balance and a sense of realism were not prized by Egyptian artists who painted tomb walls. The goal was to render the most complete possible cycle of events so that the spirit of the deceased person could watch them. In most cases, people are not shown in a particular moment of action, but in a posture that typifies that task. Have students compare the drawings of Nahkt and his wife with the other people in Figure 4-18 on page 62. Why is the couple shown larger? Are all of the figures equally stiff and formal? Why might underlings be drawn with less dignity than royal persons? Also point out how all the space is used. Discuss the advantages of filling all the space in a painting.

The first important group to live in Mesopotamia was the Sumerians (soo-**mehr**-ee-uhns). Where the Sumerians came from is unclear. There is evidence that they learned to control the floods that were common in the fertile crescent. They also built strong walled cities, each with its own king.

The Sumerians were the first people to have a system of writing. Called cuneiform (kyoo-**nee**-uh-form), the system was made up of wedge-shaped characters. The Sumerians did not have paper so they wrote the cuneiform upon clay tablets.

Other city states that later became important were Babylon and Assyria.

Architecture

At the center of the Sumerian city, and of their form of art, was the **ziggurat** (**zig**-uh-rat). This was *a stepped mountain made of brick-covered earth.* A temple honoring the god of the city was placed at the top of the ziggurat. Figure 4–16 shows a ziggurat dating from 2100 B.C. What other ancient building does the ziggurat resemble?

Sculpture

As with other ancient cultures, the tribes of Mesopotamia often expressed their religious beliefs in their art. Study the sculpture in Figure 4–17. This marble figure stands for a Sumerian goddess or worshipper. This work has been dated from between 2700 and 2600 B.C. What other art that you studied in this chapter was completed around the same time? How does the style of that work compare with this?

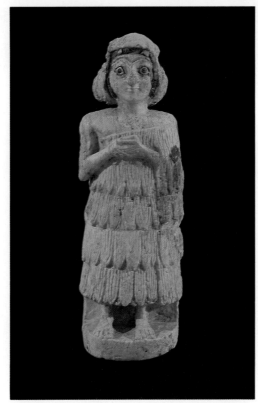

▲ **Figure 4–17** What type of balance is used in this figure? Can you point to places where different textures are used? How does this figure make you feel?

Statua di Donna. c. 2700–2600 B.C. Marble. The Iraq Museum, Baghdad, Iraq.

✔CHECK YOUR UNDERSTANDING

1. What are dynasties? How do they relate to the art of China?
2. How was the Harappan culture of ancient India discovered?
3. Why is the ancient city of Mohenjo-Daro important?
4. What is a ziggurat? In what culture were ziggurats built?

ASSESS

■ **Self-Assessment**

Have students complete the review questions on this page. Answers are provided below.

■ **Reteaching**

Mohenjo-Daro was carefully planned to meet the needs of those that dwelled there. Have students draw a map of their neighborhood on the board. Ask whether the layout reflects any principles of urban planning and whether the ideas of Mohenjo-Daro still seem relevant today.

■ **Enrichment**

Invite an urban planner, an archaeologist, or an art historian who specializes in ancient art to explain his or her work. If such professionals are not available, have students investigate the phenomenon of desertification. Ask them to identify areas of the world today that, like the Indus Valley, are being lost to the encroaching desert.

CLOSE

Hold up an object from your classroom and ask students to imagine what art historians could determine about our culture by studying the markings on it.

Answers to ✔CHECK YOUR UNDERSTANDING

1. Dynasties are periods of history in China. The art of China is grouped by dynasty.
2. The Harappan culture of ancient India was discovered by railroad workers who uncovered a hill of crumbling clay bricks.
3. The ancient city of Mohenjo-Daro is important because it was one of the first examples of urban planning.
4. A ziggurat was a stepped mountain made of brick-covered earth. Ziggurats were built by the Sumerians, the first group to live in Mesopotamia.

LESSON TIME: 45 minutes

. . . .
FOCUS

☑ OBJECTIVES

After completing this lesson, students will be able to:

- Draw and paint in the style of the ancient Egyptians.
- Explain characteristics of Egyptian tomb art.

☑ SUPPLIES

- Comic strips from a Sunday newspaper.
- Pencils, erasers, and sketch paper.
- Watercolor paints and brushes (suggested sizes are #2, #3, and #8).
- Sheets of white paper, 18 x 24 inches (46 x 61 cm).
- Containers for water.
- Paper towels.
- Candle (optional).
- Prints of images from all cultures studied so far.

Resources

- 4-8 *Making Papyrus*, TRB page 93 (reproducible master)
- 4-9 *Media of Earliest Times*, TRB page 94 (studio)

. . . .
TEACH

■ Motivator

Display comic strips from a Sunday newspaper. Have students discuss the ways in which Figure 4-18 is like the comics and how the two are different.

LESSON 5

Creating a Picture Story

Egyptian artists, as you have read, followed strict rules when they worked. One rule required that they show human body parts from their most familiar angle. Another required artists to make the most important people in a work the largest. Both these rules are followed in the wall painting in Figure 4–18. The important man and woman at the left are observing a hunting and fishing scene. The smaller figures are the servants. The painting tells a story.

WHAT YOU WILL LEARN

You will paint a picture story about the important events in your life. You will use the rules of Egyptian art shown in Figure 4–18. (For example, make your proportions larger to emphasize your importance.) Select lines and shapes to look stiff and dignified. Use contrasting colors to draw attention to the center of interest. Do *not* show depth of space in your painting. Instead, give it the same flat look as an Egyptian work. (See Figure 4–19.)

▲ Figure 4–18   Can you identify any of the activities represented in this painting? Which figures do you think are meant to be the Pharaoh and his queen? Did you notice that little shading is used? The images look flat, as though they are cut from paper.

Wall painting from the Tomb of Nakht. *Nakht and his Wife.* Egypt. c. 1425 B.C. The Metropolitan Museum of Art, New York, New York.

CURRICULUM ✕ CONNECTIONS

Social Studies   Explain to students that Egyptian artists followed strictly established rules that had religious significance. For example, because the sculptures, paintings, and relief sculptures are of the dead and are intended to act as substitutes for the body in the afterlife, the artist was careful to render all parts of the body. Have students research other rules that guided Egyptian artists and report their findings to the class. Discuss whether socially and religiously imposed rules held the Egyptians to create more powerful art or whether the rules inhibited creative expression.

WHAT YOU WILL NEED

- Pencil, sheets of sketch paper, and an eraser
- Watercolor paints and several watercolor brushes, some thick and some thin
- Sheet of white paper, 18 x 24 inches (46 x 61 cm)
- Paper towels

WHAT YOU WILL DO

1. Brainstorm with your class about ideas for your story painting. Some possibilities might be a birthday party, a school dance, a ride on your bike, a family get-together, passing an important test, and taking part in a class play or athletic event. You may want to pick more than one event for your work.
2. Study the figures in Figure 4–18. Make some rough pencil sketches that show figures in the same way. These should help you plan not only the story but also the size, location, and proportion of figures. The pictures do not have to read across the paper like the lines in a story. Rather, you may, if you like, place the most important scene in the center. Let your imagination guide you.
3. Choose your best plan. Working lightly in pencil, sketch it on the sheet of white paper.
4. Use your watercolors to paint the scene. Using your brushes, paint the areas. Take care not to smear any areas of paint. (For information on using watercolors, see Technique Tip **14**, *Handbook* page **281**.)
5. When your work has dried, display it. See if any of your classmates can "read" your picture story.

EXAMINING YOUR WORK

- **Describe** Describe the events in your painting. Tell how you used size to emphasize the most important person—you.
- **Analyze** Tell whether your lines and shapes give a feeling of stiffness. Explain how you used contrasting color to create a center of interest. Tell how you used proportion to emphasize yourself.
- **Interpret** State whether a viewer will be able to "read" your picture story and identify the important events in your life. Give your work a title.
- **Judge** Tell whether you feel your work succeeds. Explain your answer.

▲ Figure 4–19   Student work. Picture story.

Lesson 5   *Creating a Picture Story*   **63**

Try This! COMPUTER OPTION

■ Change Page Setup to Horizontal. Use your own story idea. Use Selection and Transformation tools to Copy and Paste duplicate figures in varying sizes from large to small. Choose a variety of Brush, Chalk, Marker tools and patterns, textures, and special effects to fill in objects and background. Save and title your work.

• • • • • • • • • • • •
ASSESS

■ **Self-Assessment**

Have students use Examining Your Work to evaluate their own picture stories. Responses may be written or oral.

■ **Reteaching**

Present prints of images from all the cultures studied so far. Have students identify where each work was produced and explain their reasons.

■ **Enrichment**

Have students find several good color photographs of Egyptian painting. Discuss the pigments that produced the brilliant colors that have survived in much ancient Egyptian painting. Almost all the pigments were made from natural mineral substances. The white came from chalk, the black was soot that was scraped from the bottom of cooking pots, the red is from iron oxides, the green is from copper, and the blue is a compound of silica, copper, and calcium.

• • • • • • • • • • • •
CLOSE

Ask students to consider whether their work looks Egyptian. Why or why not? You may want to crumple the work and carefully burn the edges with a candle to make it resemble ancient papyrus.

TECHNIQUE TIP ▼

Aging Art Works   The picture story created for this Studio Lesson, as well as the earth pigment lesson on page 52, can be enhanced by creating an aged look to the paper by slightly burning the edges of the paper. Be careful when using a candle to burn the edges of art work. Hot wax can spill out of a tipped candle and cause a burn. Do not let students "age" their own art work. Plan a time when you can supervise and do several pieces at once. Work in an area where the work surface has been cleared of any flammable materials.

CONNECTIONS *Science*

How Did the Egyptians Make Mummies?

Mummification was the process of preserving the dead for an anticipated afterlife. For thousands of years it was a major part of Egyptian culture. How was a body "mummified"?

Mummification could take up to 70 days. Embalmers first drained the blood from the body and removed all internal organs, including the brain. Any moisture left would be a breeding ground for bacteria, causing decay. After cleaning the body out, the embalmers packed it with *natron*, a salt found in the Egyptian desert. The body was then left to dry for about 40 days, and then cleansed with water, wine, and sweet spices.

Next the embalmers stuffed the body with sawdust or wads of linen

and covered the body with molten resin. Then they painted the body, using red ocher for men, yellow for women.

The last step was the wrapping. The body was covered in layer after layer of linen, head to foot. The embalmers used as much as 3,850 square feet (375 sq m) of linen in this process. Then resin was poured on each layer for waterproofing. Finally, a red shroud was wound around the mummy and a painted portrait mask was attached.

Over time, more decorative masks, ornate coffins, and elaborate tombs became more important to the Egyptian death ritual than the actual mummification.

Inner coffin of Tutankhamun's sarcophagus. From the tomb of Tutankhamun, Valley of the Kings. Dynasty 18, 1336–1327 B.C.E. Gold inlaid with glass and semiprecious stones. Egyptian Museum, Cairo, Egypt.

> **The inner coffin of Tutankhamun's sarcophagus is made of several hundred pounds of solid gold. It is decorated with colored enamel, gemstones, and hieroglyphic inscriptions.**

MAKING THE CONNECTION

↙ The photograph on this page is the inner coffin of King Tutankhamun's sarcophagus. His mummy was inside. Read the credit line. How old is this mummy?

↙ Why do you think it is so important to remove the blood and internal organs from the body?

↙ Find out more about natron. Why did it make a good preservative?

INTERNET ACTIVITY

Visit Glencoe's Fine Arts Web Site for students at:

http://www.glencoe.com/sec/art/students

INTERNET ACTIVITY

Safe Passage on the Net   You may have concerns about how to supervise students while on-line to keep them on track and in safe areas as they explore the resources provided on Glencoe's Fine Arts Site. Guide students' first experiences by directing them to the *Glencoe Student Galleria* or to the activities in *Studio Cyberspace*. The information contained here is confined to materials and activities designed or reviewed by Glencoe's Internet Development Staff. Check the *Teacher Resources* area for more on teaching with the Internet. You will find additional guidelines for Internet use in the *Internet Activity Booklet* included in the *Understanding Art* program. Find us at **http://www.glencoe.com/sec/art**

BUILDING VOCABULARY

Number a sheet of paper from 1 to 7. After each number, write the term from the box that best matches each description below.

culture	stele
hieroglyphic	urban planning
megaliths	ziggurat
post and lintel system	

1. The ideas, beliefs, and living customs of a people.
2. Large stone monuments, such as Stonehenge in England.
3. Approach to building in which a cross-beam is placed above two uprights.
4. Carved upright stone slab used as a monument.
5. An early form of picture writing.
6. Arranging the construction and services of a city to best meet its people's needs.
7. Stepped mountain made of brick-covered earth.

 REVIEWING ART FACTS

Number a sheet of paper from 8 to 15. Answer each question in a complete sentence.

8. What is another term for the Paleolithic period, and when did it begin?
9. What fact about the cave paintings has led experts to suspect they were not created for decoration alone?
10. Name three media used by sculptors and craftspeople during the Old Stone Age.
11. How did the style of art change by the time of the Neolithic period?
12. What are two mysteries surrounding Stonehenge?
13. How did ancient Egyptian artists show the human body in their works? Why?
14. Name two ways in which ancient China, India, and Mesopotamia were like ancient Egypt.
15. What was the greatest achievement of early China?

 THINKING ABOUT ART

On a sheet of paper, answer each question in a sentence or two.

1. **Summarize.** From a historical standpoint, why are the soapstone carvings of the Harappan culture important?
2. **Extend.** Suppose you learned of the discovery of a new civilization dating to 3000 B.C. Based on your reading of this chapter, what themes might you expect to find running through its art?
3. **Compare and contrast.** Some art scholars, you will recall, believe a successful art work is one with a realistic subject. Which of the ancient periods and civilizations you studied would appeal most to such a person? Which would appeal least? Explain your answers.

MAKING ART CONNECTIONS

1. **Mathematics.** Construction of the ancient pyramids was based on specific mathematical formulas. This is one reason why they have existed so long. Look up *pyramid* in an encyclopedia. What math facts and principles were used in designing these architectural structures?

2. **Language Arts.** Find out how pottery was made and used in ancient times by reading *Fired Up! Making Pottery in Ancient Times* by Rirka Gonen. Then research and compare the methods used by ancient artists with how pottery is made today.

Chapter 4 Review **65**

Art of the Far East

(pages 66–79)

Resources

- 5-10 Chapter Test, TRB page 115
- Transparency CC-5, Tomb Figure, T'ang Dynasty
- Transparency 5 *View of Mt. Fugi from Seven-Ri Beach* by Katsushika Hokusai
- Fine Art Print 5, *Drying Clothes* by Suzuki Harunobu

Music
While studying this chapter, use Performing Arts Handbook page 321 to help students discover how the Taiko drum music of John Y. Mori represents a traditional Asian art form blended with the modern Japanese style.

NATIONAL STANDARDS

This chapter addresses the following National Standards for the Visual Arts:

1. (a, b)
2. (a, b, c)
3. (a, b)
4. (a, b, c)
5. (b, c)
6. (b)

▲ **Can you find any evidence of people in this landscape? Why do you think the artist made the figures so small?**

Artist unknown. *Gazing at a Waterfall.* 1127–1279. Album leaf, ink and color on silk. 23.8 x 25.2 cm (9⅜ x 9⅞"). The Nelson-Atkins Museum of Art, Kansas City, Missouri. Gift of Robert H. Ellsworth.

66

FEATURED ART

Bronze Buddha sculpture
Chinese sculpture
Zhu Derun scroll
Torii Kiyotada print
Ishiwata Kōitsu print

Japanese headbands
Japanese temples
Ming vases
Fakaya Roshu screen
T'ang Dynasty sculpture

CHAPTER 5

Art of the Far East

At roughly the same time the seeds of civilization were being planted along the banks of the Nile in Egypt, others were taking root half a world away in China. The art of early China was natural and gentle. Later, Japanese artists adopted and built upon the achievements of the Chinese to create works of art in their own unique style. In this chapter you will learn about the remarkable artistic achievements that took place in these far-off countries.

PORTFOLIO IDEAS

Select one of the art works that you make in this chapter as a portfolio entry. On a sheet of paper answer the following questions: Is the art work a drawing, painting, or sculpture? How does it show an influence of the art of the Far East? How did you make the art work? What materials did you use? What elements and principles did you use? Do you think this is a successful work of art? Explain why. Date your written responses and put them in your portfolio.

OBJECTIVES

After completing this chapter, you will be able to:
- Describe the role of religion in the art of China and Japan.
- Identify key developments in Chinese painting, sculpture, and crafts.
- Identify key developments in Japanese architecture, sculpture, painting, and printmaking.
- Create art objects that record experiences or events in your world.

WORDS YOU WILL LEARN

glaze
pagoda
perceive
porcelain
screen
scroll
Ukiyo-e
woodblock printing
Yamato-e

67

■ Chapter Overview

Explain that the goal of Chinese painters was to capture the spirit, as well as the form, of their subject. Tell students that in this chapter they will learn about the role of religion in the art of the Far East and become familiar with important works created by Chinese and Japanese artists and architects. They will also create their own art works inspired by the art of China and Japan.

■ Chapter Motivator

Tell students to focus their attention on the figure in the pavilion in the work on page 66. Ask students to use their imaginations to project themselves into the work. Have them describe what they *see, hear,* and *feel.* Explain that Chinese and Japanese landscapes *were not done* to tell a dramatic story, teach an important lesson, or decorate a wall of a house. They were meant to stimulate the same deep thoughts in the viewer that passed through the mind of the artist while the work was being created.

■ Examining the Art Work

Direct student attention to *Gazing at a Waterfall* on the facing page. Inform students that this painting was done by brushing ink and watercolors on silk. Explain that line is the basic structural element of all Chinese painting as opposed to light and shadow which is used more in Western art. Point out the fine lines used to create the tall, slab-like cliff on the right and the way the feathery foliage of the distant trees contrasts with the precise outlines of trees in the foreground. Direct student attention to the use of space in this work. Explain that Chinese artists paid special attention to creating this sensation of deep space.

DEVELOPING A PORTFOLIO

Parental Review Periodically throughout the course, you may wish to have the student portfolio entries reviewed by parents. This not only gives the student additional feedback, but it helps communicate the purpose and scope of the art class. To assist with the review process, send a handout with points of discussion that can be used to facilitate the parent review.

Some discussion questions could include: (1) What was the goal of the work you reviewed? (2) What was the student trying to do or say with his or her art work? (3) Why did the student make the decision(s) he or she made? (4) Why did the student choose to include this entry in his or her portfolio? Also, include space for additional comments, ideas, and thoughts.

The Art of China

LESSON 1

The Art of China

(pages 68–69)

● ● ● ● ● ● ● ● ● ● ● ●

FOCUS

☑ OBJECTIVES

After completing this lesson, students will be able to:

- Describe the role of religion in the art of China.
- Identify key developments in Chinese painting, sculpture, and crafts.
- Take time to perceive natural objects and make pen-and-ink drawings.

☑ SUPPLIES

- Slide or display-size photograph of a Chinese sculpture of Buddha.
- Two pieces of pottery: earthenware or stoneware, and porcelain.
- Found objects. White drawing paper; ink; brushes.
- Objects of various shapes and sizes: mugs, rulers, vases.

Resources

- 5-1 *Chinese Dynasties and Art Forms*, TRB page 101 (art history)
- 5-2 *Oriental Views in Design*, TRB page 103 (reproducible master)

● ● ● ● ● ● ● ● ● ● ● ● ● ●

TEACH

■ Motivator

Display an image of a Chinese sculpture of Buddha. Explain that Buddhism is a religion that emphasizes the oneness of humans with nature and that meditation is a practice of focusing thoughts on a single idea. Tell students that in this lesson they will learn about Chinese art and how it has been influenced by this religion.

68

The Chinese have a long history of being highly creative. Two thousand years before the invention of the seismograph, they were recording earthquakes. Long before the first Texas oil wells were drilled, they were drilling holes 2000 feet deep. The compass and kite are two other early Chinese inventions.

Added proof of the Chinese gift for creating can be found in their art. In this lesson you will learn about the important contributions they have made.

MODERN CHINESE CULTURE

The "modern" period of Chinese civilization is thought to have begun with the Han dynasty. This dynasty lasted from 206 B.C. to A.D. 220. To this day, the Chinese still refer to themselves as the "Han people."

During this period a new religion came to China, called Buddhism (**boo**-diz-uhm), which stressed the oneness of humans with nature. An important part of Buddhism is meditation, focusing one's thoughts on a single object or idea. This experience allows the person to know the inner beauty of the object or idea. Chinese art of the last 2000 years has been greatly influenced by Buddhism and meditation.

Scroll Painting

The Chinese were the first people to think of "picture painting" as honorable work. This was because many artists were also scholars. They wrote with brushes that could make thick and thin lines. They used the same brush and line technique to paint pictures. They painted fans, pages of books, and scrolls. A **scroll** is *a long roll of illustrated parchment or silk*. Some scrolls were meant to hang on walls. Other scrolls were made of long rolls of silk or paper. They were meant to be unrolled a little at a time and read like a book.

Like other Chinese artists, scroll painters began a work only after a long period of meditation. The work itself was an attempt to capture a feeling, not an image. Shapes and figures were limited to the barest essentials. The artist included only those lines and shapes needed to capture the mood of the scene. (See Figure 5–3 on page **70**.)

Landscape Painting

The earliest Chinese paintings were filled with images of people illustrating the beliefs that people should live together peacefully and be respectful of their elders. With the influence of a new religion, the focus of painting began shifting away from humans and toward nature. By around A.D. 1100, the landscape was the main theme of Chinese painting.

The work that opened this chapter on page **66** is a landscape painting. Look closely at the work. Can you find a covered deck, or pavilion (puh-**vil**-yuhn), nestled within the hills? Studying the painting more closely still, do you see a small shape inside the pavilion? This is meant to be seen as the head of a person. What statement is the artist making about the place of humans in nature?

Sculpture

For many centuries important people in China were buried in tombs with objects they could use in the afterworld. These figures were made from clay. Many, like the horses in Figure 5–1, were of animals. Notice how the artist creates a sense of movement in the clay sculptures of horses and riders.

After the collapse of the Han Dynasty, China fell into chaos. It remained this way until the mighty T'ang (**tahng**) dynasty rose to power some 400 years later. It was during this new dynasty that Chinese sculpture flourished.

68   Lesson 1   *The Art of China*

---

more about ● ● ●

Perception   Relate to students the following story. Two artists, one from Eastern and one Western cultures, attended an advanced class in landscape art. They were assigned one week to complete a landscape of the sea. Every day the Western artist sketched and drew furiously for hours at a time. Each day the Eastern artist sat, looked, and watched, and perceived his view of the landscape—painting only on the last day—in his room. Both paintings were accurate, but were achieved through different methods: the Western artist used sketches and multiple studies. The Eastern artist used all of his senses and observations and painted what he knew.

▲ Figure 5–1 Notice how these figures show action. Centuries ago they played games similar to those we play today. What kind of game do you think they are playing?

Four Ladies of the Court Playing Polo. T'ang Dynasty. A.D. 618–906. Painted terra cotta. Nelson-Atkins Museum of Art, Kansas City, Missouri.

Crafts

The T'ang dynasty was followed in A.D. 960 by another powerful dynasty, the Sung (**soong**). Landscape painting soared to new heights during the Sung dynasty. So did the making of **porcelain** (**pore**-suh-luhn), *a fine-grained, high-quality form of pottery.* Porcelain is made from a fine and fairly hard-to-find white clay called kaolin (**kay**-uh-luhn).

Work in porcelain reached its highest point ever during the Ming dynasty (1368–1644).

▲ Figure 5–2 The blue pigment came from Persia. Unless the timing was precise, the blue could turn black or brown during the firing.

Pair of Vases, Meiping. Reign of Xuande. Ming Dynasty. 1426–1435. Porcelain with underglaze blue decoration. Nelson-Atkins Museum of Art, Kansas City, Missouri.

The remarkable matched vases shown in Figure 5–2 date from this period. The painted dragon designs are protected by a *glass-like finish,* or **glaze,** on these Ming porcelains. What kind of balance does each of the vases have? What kind of balance do they have as a matched set?

✔ CHECK YOUR UNDERSTANDING

1. Name two inventions credited to the early Chinese.
2. What religion was introduced to China during the Han dynasty?
3. What is meditation? What has been its role in Chinese art of the last 2000 years?
4. What are scrolls?
5. What art form flourished during the T'ang and Sung dynasties?
6. What art form reached its highest point during the Ming dynasty?

Lesson 1   *The Art of China*   **69**

. . . .
FOCUS

☑ OBJECTIVES

After completing this lesson, students will be able to:
- Plan and create original scroll paintings in the style of Chinese painters.
- Describe, analyze, interpret, and judge their own scrolls.

☑ SUPPLIES

- Sheets of drawing paper, colored pencils.
- Small pieces of drawing paper, markers, string.
- Sheets of white paper, 1 x 6 feet (30 cm x 2 m); pencils; watercolor markers.
- Transparent tape; dowels, 14 inches (36 cm); ribbon, 24 inches (61 cm).

Resource

- ■ 5-3 Hokusai Sketch, TRB page 104 (reproducible master)

. . . .
TEACH

■ Motivator

Have students work in small groups to select a specific location such as the school grounds or a local park. What mood or feeling do they have when they recall that location? Have group members work together to draw a picture of the scene, emphasizing the feeling or peaceful mood it creates. Then have each group share its work with the class.

70

Look at the Chinese scroll painting in Figure 5–3. The work is by Zhu Derun, and shows a man and his servant approaching a bridge. It presents a popular theme in the art of this time, the artist-scholar retreating from the distractions of the world to enjoy the peace and quiet of the countryside. Though the artist trained himself to paint quickly, this work was meant to be viewed slowly. Viewing it slowly from right to left, a person was meant to meditate on each scene just as the artist did before painting it.

WHAT YOU WILL LEARN

You will create a scroll recording the events of a nature walk in the manner of the Chinese painter. Record scenes of your walk on a long strip of paper, using pencils and markers. Leave large areas of negative space around the shapes. Shapes to be emphasized will be filled with color. (See Figure 5–4.)

WHAT YOU WILL NEED

- Sheet of white paper, 1 x 6 feet (30 cm x 2 m)
- Pencil, watercolor markers, and transparent tape
- 2 dowels, 14 inches (36 cm)
- Piece of ribbon, 24 inches (61 cm)

WHAT YOU WILL DO

1. Set aside time to walk slowly through your school and around the school grounds. Gaze at objects and scenes as though you are seeing them for the first time. Stop as necessary to perceive the visual impression of the texture of a bush or the color of a flower. Try to focus on the feeling or mood each scene communicates. This feeling may come to you in a small detail, such as the texture of a wall or the line of the path you walk.

▲ **Figure 5–3** Did you notice how you are invited into this scene from the right foreground? What does this painting have in common with the one on page 66? Of course, both have pavilions from which one can view and marvel at the beauty of nature.

Zhu Derun (Chu Te-Jen). *Returning from a Visit.* Yuan Dynasty. 1270–1368. Ink on paper. 28.2 x 119.3 cm (11¼ x 47″). Kimbell Art Museum, Fort Worth, Texas.

70   Lesson 2   *Making a Scroll*

---

more about • • •

Scrolls Chinese artists intended scrolls to be viewed in portions. Unlike Western painters, who rely primarily on composition and subject matter to affect audiences, the Chinese scroll artists force viewers to study their works actively. As the scroll is slowly revealed to the viewer, the relationships of height, depth, and direction draw the audience's interaction. The scroll provides the artist with an excellent medium for presenting a panoramic view of nature. If any human elements are included, they are overwhelmed by the natural elements. Villages and boats are portrayed in a miniature scale to emphasize their insignificance in comparison to the huge landscapes.

2. Roll the large sheet of paper into a scroll. Close your eyes and try to picture one of the scenes and the mood attached to it. Keep the lines, shapes, colors, and textures uppermost in your mind. Unroll 10 inches (25 cm) of your scroll and, using pencil, very lightly draw the scene. The scene should not fill the section of paper. You should, in other words, have plenty of negative space around shapes and objects.

3. Using markers, trace over the pencil lines. Make sure no pencil marks are left showing. Fill in the shapes you want to emphasize with color. Do not color everything in the scene.

4. When you are satisfied with your work, unroll another 10 inches (25 cm) of scroll. Close your eyes again and try to picture another scene. Again record the scene in pencil and trace over the lines with markers. Continue to work in this fashion until you have used up all your paper.

5. Using tape, fasten each end of your scroll to a dowel. Roll up the scroll and tie it with the ribbon.

6. Exchange scrolls with a friend. Study the works slowly and silently. See if you can identify the scenes in the other person's work.

SAFETY TIP

When a project calls for the use of markers, always make sure to use the water-based kind. Permanent markers have chemicals in them that can be harmful when inhaled.

Try This! ## STUDIO OPTIONS

■ Using a brush and one hue of watercolor, paint the scenes in your scroll. (For information on working with watercolors, see Technique Tip **14**, *Handbook* page **281**.)

■ Create a vertical scroll. Start with the scene at ground level in front of your feet. Shift your eyes upward little by little. The last scene in your scroll should be the sky. At each level, search for and include details that capture the mood of the scene.

EXAMINING YOUR WORK

● **Describe**   Tell what scenes you chose to show. State whether your work has any pencil lines showing.

● **Analyze**   Point to the places where you used negative space in your scroll. Point to places where you used color for emphasis. Identify other elements you used.

● **Interpret**   Show features in your work that would help a viewer understand how it captures a mood. Identify the different moods of the scenes.

● **Judge**   Tell whether you feel your work succeeds. Explain your answer.

▲ **Figure 5–4   Student work. Scroll painting.**

71

Vocabulary

Ask students to recall the definitions of a scroll. (Refer them to page 68 if necessary.) Then have them write the definition on small pieces of drawing paper, roll the paper to form scroll shapes, and tie their scrolls with string.

• • • • • • • • • • • • • • •
ASSESS

Self-Assessment

Have students use Examining Your Work to evaluate their scrolls. Responses may be written or oral.

Reteaching

Have students form groups, and have each group sit silently and study a natural object, such as a small branch or a small houseplant. Then have them draw the object as they perceive it. Then lead students in comparing their drawings and discuss how working in groups influenced their perception.

Enrichment

Ask volunteers to find and share reproductions of Chinese calligraphy. Help students discuss this form of writing and compare it to drawing or painting. Are some examples of calligraphy works of art? Is all calligraphy art? Why or why not? Encourage students to express and support various points of view.

• • • • • • • • • • • • • • •
CLOSE

Go around the room and have individuals unroll their scrolls slowly and tell about what they have included.

MEETING SPECIAL NEEDS

Working in Groups   For a group project, disperse students with disabilities evenly throughout the class groups. Help the groups to divide the studio into tasks that all students can accomplish (sponge-painting trees and clouds, drawing grass, bricks or stones, using a spray bottle with watercolors for tinted skies). On the walk around the school, you may need to help some students to select objects with clear details. Try a "Blind Walk," wherein a student is blindfolded and a responsible peer safely guides the blindfolded student. This is a good exercise for students to become aware of the kind of sensitivities in other sense areas that are used by students with visual difficulties.

The Art of Japan

• • • • • • • • • • • • • •

FOCUS

☑ OBJECTIVES

After completing this lesson, students will be able to:

• Describe the role of religion in the art of Japan.

• Identify key developments in Japanese architecture, sculpture, painting, and printmaking.

• Make a headband with a painted decorative design.

☑ SUPPLIES

• Slides or photographs of Japanese architecture, including interiors and gardens.

• Long pieces of white paper or cloth (for headbands), pencils, school acrylic paints, and brushes.

• Sheets of drawing paper, colored pencils.

Resources

5-4 *Aesthetics and Japanese Art,* TRB page 105 (aesthetics)

5-5 *Opening Japan to the World,* TRB page 107 (art criticism)

5-6 *Plan a Nō Performance,* TRB page 108 (cooperative learning)

5-7 *Oriental Customs,* page 109 (appreciating cultural diversity)

5-8 *Hokusai,* TRB page 111 (artist profile)

The history of Japanese art began around 5000 B.C. In the years that followed, art influenced every aspect of Japanese life. In this lesson you will learn about the one-of-a-kind culture and art of the "floating world" called Japan.

JAPANESE CULTURE

Japan makes its home on an island group in the North Pacific. Find Japan on the map in Figure 5–5.

In most civilizations, art follows culture. In a sense, the reverse is true of Japan. In A.D. 552 the ruler of a kingdom in nearby Korea sent the Emperor of Japan a gift. The gift was a piece of art. More specifically, it was a bronze figure of Buddha (**bood**-uh), the founder of Buddhism. Along with the sculpture came priests to spread Buddhist teachings. Eventually the people of Japan came to accept this new religion. They also learned

◀ **Figure 5–5** Japan.

about different ways of making art. For the next 250 years Japanese art would show strong traces of Korean, Chinese, and other Asian styles.

Architecture

Before the arrival of the bronze Buddha, the only Japanese art worth noting was prehistoric. Clay objects created by artists of the ancient Jomon (**joh**-muhn) culture are thought to date as early as 3000 B.C.

The first important Japanese art of "modern" times began being created in A.D. 594. These were magnificent Buddhist temples like the one shown in Figure 5–6. These temples were designed by Chinese or Chinese-trained architects and show a strong Chinese influence. Since the islands have little usable rock, wood was the main building material, except for the roofs which were made from tile. One of the most interesting features of early Japanese temples was the **pagoda** (puh-**gohd**-uh). This is *a tower several stories high with roofs curving slightly upward at the edges.* Figure 5–7 shows a pagoda from one of the greatest temples of the day. It is exactly like the first pagoda built at this temple. What does this fact reveal about the design of the building and how the Japanese feel about the past?

72   Lesson 3   *The Art of Japan*

RESOURCES BEYOND THE CLASSROOM

Local Manufacturers Tour a local manufacturer of art supplies where students might learn how paint or ink is made and mixed, or how fabric is woven, or how wood is milled. Such tours can alert students to the potential hazards of the art materials they may use, so that they will be more likely to follow the appropriate procedures and wear the appropriate safety equipment. If no paint factory or textile mill operates nearby, use your imagination and consider how other manufacturers contribute to art—perhaps a foundry to show how metal, used in sculpture, is forged, or a paper manufacturer to show how sketch paper is made.

▲ Figure 5–6   At least 10,000 pieces of the art of the period have been stored at this temple for over a thousand years.

Nara Todai-Ji Temple. c. A.D. 600. Japan.

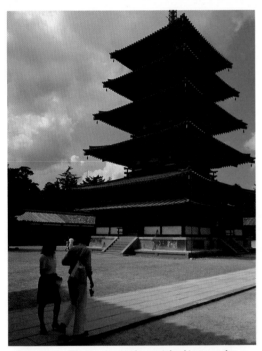

▲ Figure 5–7   This temple complex contained two pagodas, a main hall containing a sculpture of the Buddha, a lecture hall, a library, and a bell tower. It is considered to be among the greatest architectural achievements in Japan's history.

Nara Horyu-Ji Temple Pagoda. A.D. 700. Japan.

Sculpture

The Japanese of this early period modeled small sculptures out of clay. They also carved images of wood and cast them in bronze. Most, like the one in Figure 5–8, featured the figure of the Buddha. As a new emperor came into power he would order a new Buddha to be cast. Each emperor would order his Buddha to be made larger than before to emphasize the emperor's own importance.

▲ Figure 5–8   Huge images of the Buddha sometimes were 70 feet (21 m) tall. What does the Buddha appear to be doing?

Bronze Buddha of Todai-Ji. Japan.

Lesson 3   *The Art of Japan*   **73**

■ Art History

Write the following statement on the board: "In general, Japanese artists have represented the figure of Buddha in their works, while Chinese artists have represented the teachings of Buddhism in their works." Have students find art works in the text and other sources to support this statement. Then have student groups display these works and discuss how they represent differences between Japanese and Chinese Buddhism, and the cultures of the two lands.

■ Studio Skills

Let students plan and make their own small Japanese-style screens. Have them use colored pencils to draw on sheets of white paper. Encourage them to select a subject related to the Japanese art works they have been studying and to try drawing in a style that reflects either the Yamato-e or the Ukiyo-e style. Have students fold their completed papers, accordion-style, to create small screens.

Art in Everyday Life

Remind students that houses of worship in many cultures are considered art works. Ask volunteers to find photographs of several of the following: Buddhist temples in Japan, Romanesque churches of Western Europe, Renaissance churches of Western Europe, modern churches of Western Europe and the United States.

Have groups prepare a display of these structures, clearly labeling similarities and most important differences among these structures.

Painting

In 784 Japan entered its golden age of art. During this period, which lasted some 400 years, countless new temples were built. The period also witnessed, around 898, the birth of a new painting style. Its name, **Yamato-e** (yah-**mah**-toh-ay), means *pictures in the Japanese manner*. Paintings done in this style were the first true examples of pure Japanese art.

Figure 5–9 shows a Yamato-e screen painting. A **screen** is *a partition used as a wall to divide a room*. Painted screens like this were often made in sections and were used to brighten the dimly lit interiors of temples and homes as a temporary wall to divide a room. Screens made it easy to rearrange a house and use space more efficiently. Once in place they were meant to be viewed from right to left in the same manner as scrolls.

The Ivy Lane shows travelers on a golden-colored road that winds magically through a rocky landscape. Do you think it is painted in a realistic way? Do the rocks look solid and three-dimensional, or flat like stage props? Do you think the artist did this intentionally?

Printmaking

The outbreak of civil war brought the golden age to an end in 1185. Japan remained in a state of political unrest for the next 430 years. The art of these stormy times focused both on the harsh realities of war and on escaping those realities. When peace came at last, another new style of art came with it. This style was called **Ukiyo-e** (oo-**kee**-yoh-ay), meaning *pictures of the floating world*. These pictures show different ways the Japanese enjoyed life.

The demand for art works in the new style was great. To meet this demand, artists turned to a new technique, **woodblock printing**. This is *making prints by carving images in blocks of wood*. The prints, or woodcuts, were made by a team of artists and craftspeople. Figure 5–10 shows a woodcut in the Ukiyo-e style. Notice the artist's use of strong lines and flat areas of color. Both were typical of such works. Equally typical was the balance shown here. What kind of balance has the artist of this print used?

▲ **Figure 5–9   Can you find something repeated throughout this work that helps give it unity?**

Fakaya Roshu. *Tsuta-no-hosomichi (The Ivy Lane)*. Edo period, 1699–1755. Six-fold screen, opaque color on gold ground. 133 x 271.8 cm (52⅜ x 107″). Cleveland Museum of Art, Cleveland, Ohio. John L. Severance Fund.

CURRICULUM CONNECTIONS

Social Studies   The interesting and elegant dress often represented in Japanese art is called the *kimono*. This traditional dress is worn by both men and women. Kimonos are still made and worn for special occasions, for praying at a shrine, for the tea ceremony, and for marriages and other special family events. For funerals, black kimonos with the family crest are worn. The shape of the kimono and its dimensions are carefully prescribed. The fabric is silk or cotton, decorated with embroidery or intricate batik designs. Lengths of fabric are sewn together to make long, straight panels in front and back, and include deep sleeves. Kimonos are often passed along as family treasures.

▲**Figure 5–10** What does this figure appear to be doing? Why do you think such dramatic, violent action by an actor is sometimes necessary?

Torii Kiyotada. *An Actor of the Ichikawa Clan.* Woodcut, hand colored. 28.6 x 15.2 cm (11¼ x 6"). The Metropolitan Museum of Art, New York, New York. Harris Brisbane Dick Fund.

STUDIO ACTIVITY

Decorate a Headband

The print in Figure 5–10 is of a Kabuki (kuh-**boo**-kee) actor. Kabuki is a form of popular Japanese theater. Notice the richly decorated costume. Another Japanese stage tradition with even more spectacular costumes is the Nō (**noh**) drama. Figure 5–11 shows the type of headbands worn by a Nō actor. Notice the highly decorative pattern in the headband. Design a decorative pattern using symbols of an activity you enjoy. Using school acrylic paint, transfer the pattern to a headband made of paper or cloth.

PORTFOLIO

Mount your headband following the instructions in the Technique Tips section of the *Handbook*. Keep the mounted art work in your portfolio.

✔ CHECK YOUR UNDERSTANDING

1. What important event in the history of Japanese art happened in A.D. 552?
2. What is a pagoda?
3. When did the golden age of Japanese art begin? What painting style came into being during that period?
4. What is Ukiyo-e? What technique was most commonly used for Ukiyo-e art?

◄**Figure 5–11** What do you think the purpose of these headbands might have been? What is the purpose of headbands today?

Headbands for Nō costumes. Japanese. Edo Period. 1615–1867. Embroidered in silk on satin., 40 x 3.2 cm (15¾ x 1¾"). The Metropolitan Museum of Art, New York, New York. Gift of Mr. and Mrs. Teigi Ito.

Lesson 3   *The Art of Japan*   **75**

STUDIO ACTIVITY

Decorate a Headband

When students have completed their headbands for the Studio Activity, create a display by hanging them end-to-end along the walls of the classroom, or above the windows and bulletin boards, for a colorful decoration on parents' night or another occasion.

• • • • • • • • • • • • • • •

ASSESS

■ **Self-Assessment**

Have students complete the review questions on this page. Answers are provided below.

■ **Reteaching**

Help small groups of students discuss their work in the Studio Activity. What symbols have group members used on their headbands? What do those symbols represent? How are the headbands similar to that of the Nō actor shown in Figure 5-11? How are they different? Is that headband a work of art? Why or why not? Are students' headbands works of art? Why or why not?

■ **Enrichment**

Have students work in three groups to research the important events in Japanese history and culture during these periods: around 5000 B.C.; A.D. 522; A.D. 898. Let the members of each group share their findings with the rest of the class. Then guide the class in discussing how the events and culture influenced the art of each period.

• • • • • • • • • • • • • • •

CLOSE

Ask students to name and describe Japanese styles of painting and printmaking.

Answers to ✔ CHECK YOUR UNDERSTANDING

1. The rulers of a kingdom in Korea sent the Emperor of Japan a bronze figure of a the Buddha.
2. A pagoda is a Japanese temple several stories high with its roof curving slightly upward at the edges.
3. Japan entered its golden age of art in A.D. 784. The new style of painting depicted scenes from everyday life and was called Yamato-e, meaning "pictures in the Japanese manner."
4. Ukiyo-e style meant "Pictures of the floating world," and artists used the new technique of woodblock printing to supply the increased demand for this art.

LESSON 4

Creating a Time Capsule

In 1974 well diggers in central China accidentally uncovered part of the tomb of the first emperor of China. Guarding the tomb was an army of life-size clay soldiers, horses, and attendants—at least 7000 of them (Figure 5–12).

Imagine that students of your school have been asked by community leaders to create clay objects. These are to be buried in a time capsule to tell future cultures about our own. Working in small groups, you will create a clay model of a teenager's room. You may use your own room at home or you may invent the room of your dreams. In the room you will include objects that represent the lifestyle of your group.

WHAT YOU WILL LEARN

You will make and join together clay slabs to create a teen's room. Your model will have a floor and three walls. Furniture and other details will be modeled from clay. In designing your room you must consider the elements of space, shape, form, and texture. Use

the principles of proportion and variety to organize the elements. (See Figure 5–13.)

WHAT YOU WILL NEED

- Pencil, notepad, and sheets of sketch paper
- 2 guide sticks, each about ½ inch (13 mm) thick
- Newspaper
- Clay
- Rolling pin, needle tool, modeling tools, and ruler
- Sheet of plastic
- Slip (a mixture of water and clay used for joining clay pieces) and container of water
- Scissors and scrap of fabric

WHAT YOU WILL DO

1. On the notepad, list the furniture, objects, and details your room will have. Note also the different shapes, forms, and textures you will use. Make pencil sketches of the room and its contents.

▶ **Figure 5–12** Does the soldier look relaxed or is he at attention? Why would figures like these have been placed in the tomb of the emperor? These lifelike clay figures, buried since 210 B.C., offer us a wealth of clues about early Chinese civilization.

Cavalryman and Saddle Horse from Earthenware Army of First Emperor of Qin. c. 210 B.C. Terra cotta. Cultural Relics Bureau, Beijing, and The Metropolitan Museum of Art, New York, New York.

---

more about • • •

Time Capsules   Explain to the class that as they study objects from ancient times, they can consider how to create art objects that record experiences or events in their own world. Ask whether the class knows what a time capsule is and what kinds of objects are placed in time capsules today. What do the choices we make in the areas of music, art, and extra-curricular activities say about us? If a time capsule were opened in the year 2500, what conclusions might be drawn about teen lifestyles of the twenty-first century? Ask what items they would like to include in a time capsule to tell other generations about themselves.

• • • • • • • • • • • • • •
FOCUS

☑ OBJECTIVES

After completing this lesson, students will be able to:
- Make clay models of a teen's room, include furniture and other details.
- Describe, analyze, interpret, and judge their own clay models.

☑ SUPPLIES

- Sheets of sketch paper, pencils.
- Pencils; notepads; sheets of sketch paper; guide sticks; each about ½ inch (13 mm) thick; newspaper; clay; rolling pins, needle tools; modeling tools; rulers; sheets of plastic; slip; scissors; scraps of fabric.

Resource

■ 5-9 *Woodblock Print*, TRB page 112 (studio)

• • • • • • • • • • • • • •
TEACH

■ Motivator

Have each student sketch a room that communicates who American teens are and what they are interested in. Let students work in small groups to compare and discuss their sketches. Then ask: What do you think the average American teenager's room says about American teenagers? Encourage students to share and discuss their ideas.

2. Set up the guide sticks 10 inches (25 cm) apart on the sheet of newspaper. Using the slab method, place the clay between these two guide sticks. Flatten the lump with the heel of your hand. Resting a rolling pin on the guide sticks, roll out the clay. This will help keep the thickness of the slab even. Using a ruler and knife or other sharp object, make four rectangles, each measuring 10 x 10 inches (25 x 25 cm). Cover the slabs loosely with the sheet of plastic. Leave them out overnight to firm up to the leather hard stage. This is the stage where clay is still damp but too hard to model.

3. The next day, score one of the slabs along three of its edges. This slab is to be the floor. Working a slab at a time, score each of the other slabs along its bottom. Use slip to join the walls to the floor. (For information on joining clay slabs and pieces, see Technique Tip **17**, *Handbook* page **281**.)

4. Model the furniture and other objects and details. Use proper joining methods for such tasks as adding legs to chairs. Using slip, attach the furniture and other objects to the floor.

5. When the clay is totally dry, fire the work. Complete your room by adding details — window coverings and a bedspread, for example — cut from the fabric.

6. Display your finished work. Look for similarities and differences between your work and that of other students.

EXAMINING YOUR WORK

- **Describe**   Point to the floor and walls of your room. Describe the furniture and details you chose to include. Tell whether you followed the rules for making clay slabs and joining pieces.
- **Analyze**   Show where you used the elements of space, shape, form, and texture. Explain how you used the principles of proportion and variety. Point out examples of each.
- **Interpret**   Show what features in your work would help a viewer of the future understand this to be a teenager's room.
- **Judge**   Tell whether you feel your work succeeds. Explain your answer.

▲ Figure 5–13   **Student work. Model of classroom.**

Lesson 4   *Creating a Time Capsule*   **77**

Try This!   ## STUDIO OPTIONS

■ Choose a room in your school. Some possibilities are the gym, the cafeteria, or the art room. Think about what furniture and other objects you find in that room. Make a clay model of the room.

■ Make a clay model of a whole single-story building. You might base your work on an actual building in your town or city, or you might invent your own. Think about what furniture and other objects you would find in each of the rooms. Add these details to your work.

TECHNIQUE TIP

Clay Techniques   As students work on this Studio Lesson, you may wish to review with them the following stages of clay: *Plastic clay*—clay wet enough to hold its shape. *Slip*—clay with water added to make it runny. Slip is used to glue together shaped pieces of damp clay. *Leather hard clay*—clay which is still damp but too hard to model. Pieces of leather hard clay can be joined with slip. *Greenware*—very dry clay that will break easily. An object at the greenware stage is ready to be fired. *Bisqueware*—fired pottery that is hard but still not ready to use. *Glazeware*—pottery coated with powdered chemicals that melt during firing into a hard, glass-like finish.

■ Vocabulary
Review with students the definitions of *proportion* and *variety* as principles of art. Point out that artists often communicate messages by consciously not using one of these principles in an art work.

■ Art Criticism
Remind students that clay has been used for thousands of years as a medium for both arts and crafts—for sculpture, which is considered a form of fine art, and for pottery, which is considered a form of applied art. Are your own clay models examples of sculpture or pottery? Why? What do you think distinguishes sculptures from pottery?

ASSESS

■ Self-Assessment
Have students use Examining Your Work to evaluate their art work created in this Studio Lesson.

■ Reteaching
Ask students to find out about any local time capsules: Where are they? Why were they created? What do they include? What would students think about your culture if your art works were found 200 years from now?

■ Enrichment
Let small groups plan what they would include in their own time capsule. For whom would they create the time capsule? What specific objects would they put in it? Let group members make oral and visual presentations to the rest of the class.

CLOSE
Let students in each group present their model to the rest of the class and explain what they like best about their work.

CONNECTIONS *Language Arts*

How is Culture Preserved in Art Forms?

OBJECTIVES

After completing this feature, students will be able to:

- Define haiku, a Japanese poetic form.
- Describe how haiku and Kōitsu's woodblock print both reflect Japanese culture.

Teaching the Connection

- Have students read the feature on this page.
- Ask volunteers to share what they may know about Japanese art and culture. What are some traditional Japanese values? *(Some possible responses: close family structure; respect of elders; respect for nature and serenity.)* What are Japanese haiku often about? *(Nature: animals, plants, the beauty of the sky, the sea, the land.)* How is Kōitsu's artwork similar to haiku? *(Simple, orderly, precise.)*
- Tell students that artists like Kōitsu believe in preserving the traditions and values of their Japanese culture. As Japan became more Westernized, art traditions like woodblock printing declined. In the 1920s Kōitsu and others helped revive an interest in this traditional art form. Encourage students to discuss how literature and art can both be used to preserve any culture.

Answers to Making the Connection

- Possible answers: a peaceful, rural market, unhurried and simple.
- Students' haiku should fit the prescribed format.
- Responses will vary. The most famous haiku poet is Basho.

Ishiwata Kōitsu. *View of Koyasuchō in Kanagawa Prefecture (Vegetable Shop)*. 1931. Color woodblock print. Paper. 39.2 x 26.6 cm (15⅟₁₆ x 10¼"). Los Angeles County Museum of Art, Los Angeles, California. Anonymous gift.

This colorful woodblock print by Ishiwata Kōitsu is a reflection of traditional Japanese values and customs. It shows in delicate detail the everyday routine of the marketplace. Modern artists and writers alike try to preserve timeless Japanese images. They include rural landscapes, twilight lake scenes, majestic mountains, and simple village life in their works of art.

For centuries Japanese writers have used unique poetry forms to express their simple yet intricate view of nature and cultural values. These poems follow a special format of syllables and lines. Each word is carefully chosen, and the grammar must be precise. The poems express deep personal feelings and experiences.

In the seventeenth century, the *haiku* became popular in Japan. This poetic form is written in 17 syllables, with three lines of 5, 7, and 5 syllables each. Haiku combines images of nature with personal insights. Haiku poetry is similar to Japanese painting. Like a delicate Japanese ink drawing, haiku uses clean outlines to depict an image, mood, or sensation.

Modern haiku, like modern Japanese art, reflects strong Japanese traditions, yet its appeal crosses many cultures.

MAKING THE CONNECTION

- How would you describe the scene in the print? What do the details tell you about Japanese culture?
- Write a haiku of your own, describing something in your neighborhood. Remember to use the precise form and include an image from nature.
- Learn more about haiku. Discover a well-known Japanese poet and read some of his or her poetry.

INTERNET ACTIVITY

Visit Glencoe's Fine Arts Web Site for students at:

http://www.glencoe.com/sec/art/students

INTERNET ACTIVITY

Virtual Field Trips Your students can experience and appreciate the fine art collections of countless museums and art galleries in every part of the world represented on the World Wide Web. Have your students spend a class period roaming through the collections of the de Young Museum in San Francisco, or check the current exhibits at the Solomon R. Guggenheim in New York. Work on a longer-term project as students discover art of the masters at the National Gallery in Washington, D.C. Give students a close-up view of folk art and ethnic works at regional and indigenous galleries. Locations of some sites are in the *Curriculum Links* or the *On-Line and Multimedia Resources* areas of the *Teacher Resources*. Find us at **http://www.glencoe.com/sec/art**

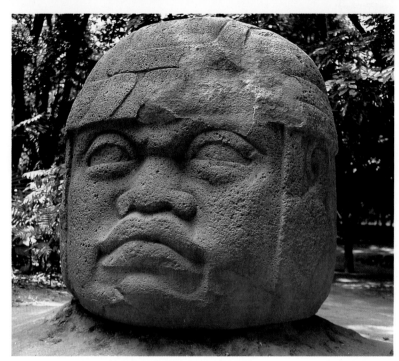

◀Figure 6–2   Records show that this 40-ton (40,000-kg) stone head was moved 60 miles (96 km), through swampland. What does this tell you about the Olmecs?

Olmec Head. 1500–800 B.C. Basalt. La Venta Archeology Museum, Mexico.

■ **Vocabulary**

Help students examine the prefixes in the terms *Pre-Columbian* and *Mesoamerica.* Ask volunteers to explain the meaning of *pre-* and to suggest a few other words in which a prefix is used. Ask: Based on the definition of the prefix, how would you define term *Pre-Columbian?* Then have a volunteer use a dictionary to look up the meaning of the prefix *meso-* or *mes-.* Ask: Based on this definition, how would you define *Mesoamerica?* Which modern countries do you think are included in Mesoamerica? You may want to have students refer to a wall map as they respond to this question.

At one time these sculptures were thought to be **genre** (**zhahn**-ruh) **pieces**. These are *art works that focus on a subject or scene from everyday life.* It is now known that ancient Mexicans viewed dogs as having special powers. Specifically, the animals were believed to serve the dead. A sculpture of this type is called an **effigy** (**eff**-uh-jee), *an image that stands for ideas or beliefs.*

MAYAN CULTURE

The first great Pre-Columbian civilization was that of the Mayas (**my**-uhs). By around A.D. 800 their empire covered the Yucatán (yoo-kuh-**tahn**) peninsula, modern Belize (buh-**leez**), Guatemala, and Honduras. Find these places on the map in Figure 6–1. The Mayas were gifted mathematicians. They had the most accurate calendar of any people in history. They were also great builders. The Mayas erected huge temples and cities with tools of wood, stone, and bone.

▲ Figure 6–3   This is a hollow clay form. The swollen lower body is typical of Colima figures.

Effigy Vessel. c. A.D. 250. Ceramic. Fowler Museum of Cultural History, UCLA, Los Angeles, California.

■ **Art Criticism**

Let students work in small groups to describe, analyze, and interpret one of the works reproduced in this lesson. Have group members begin by selecting either the West Mexican sculpture in Figure 6-3 or the Mayan sculpture in Figure 6-5. Have them describe the work (What elements of art do you see in the work?), analyze it (how are the principles of art used to organize elements in the work?), and then interpret it (What idea or mood does the work suggest?). Then have students work independently to judge the work, writing paragraphs in response to these questions: Is this a successful work of art? Consider how and where the art works were used.

Lesson 1   *Art of Mesoamerica*   **83**

more about • • •

The Olmec   Little is known about the Olmec culture that carved the series of gigantic heads resting in La Venta, Mexico. The Olmec pantheon included gods with human and animal elements. The widespread appearances of half-human, half-jaguar figures indicates that religion played a big role in the arts as well as other aspects of Olmec life. Because they flourished early, from about 1200 B.C. to 300 B.C., and shared many practices with future cultures, the Olmecs are considered to be a "mother culture" to the area.

■ **Cooperative Learning**

Have students form six groups, and ask each group to learn more about one of these topics: the Mayan writing system, the Mayan calendar, the Mayan religion, the Aztec writing system, the Aztec calendar, the Aztec religion. Have members of each group research their assigned topic; then have them discuss the effect on the works of art in that culture. Ask each group to prepare and present a visual display or video summarizing what they have learned.

Sparking Creativity

Let students explore working with clay to create small animal figures like the dog sculpture shown in Figure 6-3 on page 83. Ask students to think of favorite or fanciful animals to create small sculptures in a similar style. Encourage students to discuss and sketch their ideas. Have them roll clay into a ball, then use thumbs to dig into the ball and pinch the clay to about ¼ inch (6.5 mm) on all sides. Turn and shape the clay to create the head and body of an animal of their choice.

■ **Cultural Diversity**

Ask the class: What other cultures and religions have represented various gods and goddesses in the art of the culture? Ask volunteers to work in small groups to find out about the art of these cultures. Have groups look for examples in the text of art works depicting these entities (see Chapters 4, 5, 8, 9, 11, 13, for some examples).

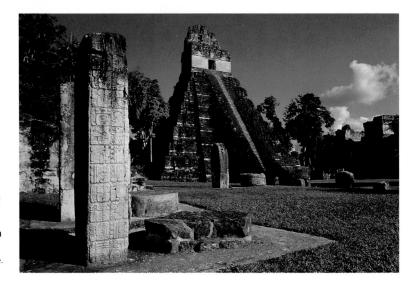

▶ **Figure 6–4   The project to dig up this ancient city is one of the biggest in history. Why do you think scientists spend so much time and effort digging up lost civilizations?**

Mayan-Tikal Site. Jaguar Temple. c. A.D. 800. Peten, Guatemala.

Architecture

In the late 1800s scientists digging in northern Guatemala found traces of an ancient city. This Mayan city, Tikal (tih-**kahl**), is known to have covered an area of 50 square miles (130 sq km). The city is thought to have been home to some 55,000 people. Figure 6–4 shows a view of the site.

Mayan architects not only built outward but they also built upward. Look again at Figure 6–4. The pyramid in the background has a temple on top of it. It is typical of many temples built throughout the Mayan civilization. Two others have been discovered at Tikal alone. Amazing structures like these rose at times to heights of 175 feet (53 m). What kind of balance did Mayan architects use in designing these impressive temples?

Sculpture

Most of the Mayan sculpture that has lasted is relief carvings on buildings and monuments. In the early stages of the Mayan civilization, these carvings were mostly simple and realistic. In some later temples a more complex, geometric style came to be the rule.

The surviving works of Mayan civilization range from the smallest objects to great temples covered with relief carvings. Among the smallest art works of the Maya are many beautifully designed clay figures only a few inches high.

The one illustrated in Figure 6–5 represents a Maya ruler dressed to look like a mythical king of the past. His complex costume identifies his rank, his association with the gods, and his own important position in the universe.

▲ **Figure 6–5   Can you see the god represented in the elaborate headdress worn by this Maya ruler? He is Chac-Xib-Chac, a god associated with war, sacrifice, dancing, and fishing.**

Ruler Dressed as Chac-Xib-Chac and the Holmul Dancer. Maya, c. A.D. 600–800. Ceramic with traces of paint. 23.8 cm (9⅜″) high. Kimbell Art Museum, Fort Worth, Texas.

84   Lesson 1   *Art of Mesoamerica*

more about • • •

Calendar Stone   The Aztecs founded Tenochtitlán, which is now Mexico City, in about 1325. One sculpture that remains is the Aztec Calendar Stone. Arranged around *Tonatiuh*, the sun god, the twelve-foot-diameter stone lists the days and months and indicates occasions for sacrifice or celebration. Because their religion states that the sun god had died to create man, the Aztecs believed that they had to repay the god in human blood. While the circular calendar stone was possibly used as a receptacle for human hearts sacrificed to Tonatiuh, the Aztecs never used the circle shape in wheel form as a tool or method of transportation.

▲ **Figure 6–6** This sculpture and its base are decorated with a number of designs. Can you see any that look like flowers?

Xochipilli, Lord of the Flowers. Aztec. National Museum of Anthropology, Mexico City, Mexico.

▲ **Figure 6–7** The stone was more than a calendar. It told the story of the universe. It stated when the Aztec world began and predicted when it would end.

Stone of the Sun. Aztec Calendar Stone. c. 1500. National Museum of Anthropology, Mexico City, Mexico. Photograph by Michael Zabe. Art Resource, New York.

The largest of the cultures of ancient Mexico and Central America was the Aztec. This civilization emerged sometime between A.D. 1200 and 1325. The Aztecs were a warlike tribe. Like other Pre-Columbian peoples, they were very religious. When their god told them to leave their comfortable homeland and settle where they saw an eagle perched on a cactus, they did. A swampy island, which they called Tenochtitlán (tay-noch-tee-**tlahn**), became the center of their great empire. By the time Spanish conquerors arrived in 1519, their island city covered over 25 square miles (66 sq km). Today we know the city, which is no longer on an island, as Mexico City. Find Mexico City on the map in Figure 6–1.

Sculpture

The Aztecs adopted many of the ways of making art used by the people they conquered. They carved huge ceremonial sculptures like the one shown in Figure 6–6. This sculpture is one of 1600 gods and goddesses in the Aztec religion.

One unusual piece of Aztec art is the calendar stone, shown in Figure 6–7. The work is so called because its rim is decorated with signs for the 20 days of the Aztec month. The stone measures 12 feet (3.6 m) in diameter and weighs over 24 tons (22,000 kg).

✔CHECK YOUR UNDERSTANDING

1. Which culture is the mother culture of Mexico?
2. What is a genre piece? What is an effigy?
3. What was the first great Pre-Columbian civilization? What huge structures did the people of this civilization build?
4. What is the calendar stone? What Pre-Columbian civilization created the calendar stone?

Lesson 1   *Art of Mesoamerica*   **85**

Then let them give a presentation to the class highlighting the role of gods and goddesses in the art of these cultures.

• • • • • • • • • • • • • •
ASSESS

■ Self-Assessment

Have students complete the review questions on this page. Answers are provided below.

■ Reteaching

Have students work with partners to make charts summarizing what they have learned about the Olmec, West Mexican, Mayan, and Aztec cultures. The charts should include this information for each culture: Place, Time, Kind of Sculpture. Then let students compare, discuss, and—if necessary—revise their charts.

■ Enrichment

Guide students in discussing what modern people have learned by studying the art of the Pre-Columbian peoples. Then ask: What do you think people centuries from now might conclude about our lives by studying our works of art? Let students discuss their ideas; then have each student write at least one paragraph explaining his or her own responses to the questions.

• • • • • • • • • • • • • •
CLOSE

Go around the room and ask students to describe characteristics of one of the Pre-Columbian cultures in this lesson.

Answers to ✔CHECK YOUR UNDERSTANDING

1. The Olmec culture is often called the "mother culture" of Mexico.
2. A genre piece is an art work that focuses on a subject or scene from everyday life. An effigy is an image that stands for an idea or belief.
3. The Mayan culture was the first great Pre-Columbian civilization. Mayan architects constructed pyramids, some rising to heights of 175 feet.
4. An unusual piece of Aztec art. The rim of the calendar stone depicted signs for the 20 days of the Aztec month. Some stones measured 12 feet in diameter and weighed as much as 24 tons. The Aztecs created the calendar stone.

Making a Clay Urn

(pages 86–87)

LESSON TIME: 5 hours

. . . .

FOCUS

☑ OBJECTIVES

After completing this lesson, students will be able to:

- Make cylinder-shaped clay containers that exhibit formal balance and repeating patterns.
- Describe, analyze, interpret, and judge their own clay containers.

☑ SUPPLIES

- Pencils; sheets of sketch paper; guide sticks; each about ½ inch (13 mm) thick.
- Newspaper; clay; rolling pins; rulers; needle tools.
- Paper towels; modeling tools; slip; containers of water; plastic bags; glaze or school acrylics (optional).

Resource

- 6-4 *Mexican Primitive Sculptors*, TRB page 123 (appreciating cultural diversity)

. . . .

TEACH

■ Motivator

Ask students: Which of your interests and activities are most important to you? What shapes and objects symbolize your interests and activities? Then explain that students will use these ideas in creating their own art works.

 LESSON 2

Making a Clay Urn

Look again at the work that opened this chapter on page **80**. It is a **funerary** (fyoo-nuh-rehr-ee) **urn,** *a decorative vase or vessel found at burial sites.* Compare it with the clay vessel in Figure 6–8. The works were created by different Pre-Columbian cultures, but they have much in common. Both use formal balance and are covered with a repeated motif (moh-**teef**). A **motif** is *part of a design that is repeated over and over in a pattern or visual rhythm.* Finally, both works are rich with symbols that had special meaning for members of their cultures.

WHAT YOU WILL LEARN

You will make a cylinder-shaped container at least 6 inches (15 cm) high using the clay slab method. You will decorate your container with a figure wearing symbols that represent your life. You will use formal balance and repeating patterns in your work. The pattern will be in the style of an ancient Mexican culture. You may paint your figure using school acrylics, or you may glaze it. (See Figure 6–9.)

WHAT YOU WILL NEED

- Pencil and sheets of sketch paper
- 2 guide sticks, each about 1/2 inch (13 mm) thick
- Newspaper
- Clay
- Rolling pin, ruler, needle tool, paper towel, and modeling tools
- Slip (a mixture of water and clay used for joining clay pieces), and container of water
- Plastic bag
- *Optional:* Glaze or school acrylics

WHAT YOU WILL DO

1. Brainstorm with your classmates for ideas for personal symbols to be used to decorate your figure. For example, if you play football, the figure could be wearing a helmet. You could decorate the helmet with a pattern of footballs for a headdress. If your major interest is math, the headdress might be covered with numbers. The hands might hold pencils and a notebook to symbolize the student. Make pencil sketches of the figure and the different decorations you will use.

▲ **Figure 6–8** **What relationship do you suppose existed between the figure of the clay vessel and what it was used for?**

Pottery jar with removable head. Teotihuacan, Mexico. American Museum of Natural History, New York, New York.

■ ■ **MEETING STUDENT DIVERSITY** ■

Visual/Spatial Learners Have students prepare a visual display of several of the ruins of ancient Pre-Columbian civilizations. Have them locate photographs in magazines or books to photocopy and organize in a display. Students should include short captions describing each picture.

2. Set up the guide sticks 6 inches (15 cm) apart on the sheet of newspaper. Using the slab method, make a rectangle, 6 x 12 inches (15 x 30 cm). Keep the unused clay damp by covering it with a lightly moistened towel. Score the short edges of your rectangle. Carefully bend your slab into a cylinder. Apply slip to the scored surfaces and press them together. Smooth both the inside and outside surfaces of the cylinder along the seams.

3. Using a portion of the remaining clay, roll out a slab measuring 10 inches square (625 sq cm). Stand the cylinder on top of the square. Using the needle tool, lightly trace around the cylinder. Score the surface of the circle you have created and the edges of the cylinder. Apply slip, and press the two surfaces together. Add a thin coil of clay inside your cylinder along the bottom. Press it gently into the seam to make the cylinder stronger. Cut off the excess clay from around the base of the cylinder.

4. Model the head, arms, legs, and headdress for your figure. Attach them using scoring and slip. With modeling tools add patterned markings to create rhythm to your work. Note that you may need to support the head and headdress as the work dries. Prop these in place using an object of the right height.

5. When your clay container is bone dry, fire it in a kiln.

6. *Optional*: Glaze or paint the fired container using acrylics.

7. Place the finished work on display. See if your friends can guess what the decorations on your work stand for.

Try This! STUDIO OPTIONS

■ Make a second container, this time using the medium of paper. (For information on making paper sculptures, see Technique Tip **21**, *Handbook* page **284.**)

■ Using construction paper or poster board, design and make a piece of jewelry in the style of the Mesoamerican cultures.

EXAMINING YOUR WORK

● Describe   Show that your container is at least 6 inches (15 cm) high. Show that the parts are properly joined. Describe the figure and symbols you used to decorate your container. Identify the hues used to color your figure.

● Analyze   Describe the kind of balance you used. Identify the repeating rhythmic pattern in your work.

● Interpret   Identify the features of your work that are similar to those of the ancient Mexican culture you used as a model. Explain how the symbols represent your life.

● Judge   Tell whether you feel your work succeeds. Explain your answer.

▲ Figure 6–9   Student work. Clay urn.

MEETING SPECIAL NEEDS

Clay as Therapy   Working with clay can be especially therapeutic for students with visual difficulties, behavioral disorders, and neurological and orthopedic difficulties. Rolling clay into balls, snakes, and coils provides important tactile expression. Balls of clay can be patted into flattened slabs and features can be inscribed and clay decorations can be added. Be certain to supervise students when working with the needle tool to avoid danger for some students with physical or behavior disorders. The expression of emotions is especially beneficial for students with behavioral disorders. You might encourage students to express the emotions or expressions depicted in their figures as they show their completed projects.

Art of the Andes

• • • • • • • • • • • • • • • • •

FOCUS

☑ OBJECTIVES

After completing this lesson, students will be able to:

• Name and describe four Pre-Columbian cultures of the Andes.

• Identify the contributions made by those four Pre-Columbian cultures to the art world.

☑ SUPPLIES

• Slides or display-sized photographs of Machu Picchu (if available); wall map of South America or of Peru (if available).

• Sheets of white drawing paper, pieces of sturdy cardboard (such as corrugated cardboard), tape, scissors, yarn in various colors.

Resources

⤷ ▪ 6-5 *Peruvian Cloth Factory*,
⤷ TRB page 125
⤷ (reproducible master)
⤷ ▪ 6-6 *The Inca Gold Culture*,
⤷ TRB page 127
⤷ (aesthetics/art criticism)
⤷ ▪ 6-7 *Latin American Artists*,
⤷ TRB page 128
⤷ (appreciating cultural
⤷ diversity)

Taken together, the four major cultures of Mesoamerica spanned a period of several thousand years. While these civilizations were developing, parallel developments were taking place in the Andes (**an**-deez) Mountains of South America.

In this lesson you will read about the culture and art of the Chavín, Moche, Tiahuanaco, and Inca Tribes.

CHAVÍN CULTURE

The earliest of the Andes civilizations, the Chavín (chuh-**veen**), made their home in the highlands of present-day Peru. The discovery of artifacts places the beginning of Chavín civilization at around 1000 B.C. Their name is taken from their ceremonial center, Chavín de Huántar (**hwahn**-tahr). Today stone pyramids and stone sculpture can still be found at that site. Find this place on the map in Figure 6–10.

▲ Figure 6–10   Andean Cultures.

Crafts

Like other Andean cultures, the Chavín held the jaguar to be sacred. Images of the cat turn up in much of their art.

One area of art in which the Chavín were especially skilled was crafts. The clay jaguar pitcher in Figure 6–11 is an example of one of their works. Notice the unusual stirrup-shaped spout. This design feature, used by later Andean cultures, was typical of Chavín pottery.

▲ Figure 6–11   This hollow vase is decorated with relief designs. Why do you think the Chavín developed the stirrup spout? What motif is used to help identify the animal as a jaguar?

Peru. Stirrup-Spout Vessel, Feline. 700–500 B.C. Ceramic. 23.5 x 14.1 x 20.9 cm (9⅜ x 5⅝ x 8⅛"). The Metropolitan Museum of Art, New York, New York. Michael C. Rockefeller Memorial Collection.

TECHNOLOGY OPTIONS

Cameras   A collection of simple cameras can be very useful in the classroom. With a little instruction, students can use them to explore subject matter, record images, and illustrate reports. Some students who are hesitant about their artistic talents in other media find the medium of photography considerably less intimidating. By carrying a camera, students may become more aware of the visual details of their environment and more apt to record them. Students may also use cameras to record images that will be used later in a studio project, or to record art works for their portfolios.

▲ Figure 6–12 The figure is the size of a thumb. It wears a movable nosepiece and carries a movable war club.

Earring. National Geographic Society, Washington, D.C.

Another way in which this object is typical is in the stylized look of its subject. **Stylized** means *simplified or exaggerated to fit a specific set of rules of design*. Did you notice the circles on the head and body? These were meant to stand for the jaguar's spots.

MOCHE CULTURE

West Mexican culture developed roughly between A.D. 100 and 700. Approximately these same years, interestingly, mark the rise and fall of Moche (**moh**-chay) culture. The Mochica (moh-**cheek**-uh), as these people were called, lived on the northern coast of what is now Peru. Find this area on the map in Figure 6–10.

The Mochica were farmers who irrigated the strips of desert between the Andes and the Pacific Coast. They grew corn, beans, squash, and peanuts. They built great pyramids and platforms with **adobe** (uh-**doh**-bee), or *sun-dried clay*. Here they buried their nobles.

▲ Figure 6–13 This stirrup-spout vessel represents a deer. It shows two figures having a conversation. One has the head of a frog.

Peru, Moche. Stirrup-Spout Vessel in the Form of a Seated Deer. A.D. 200–500. Ceramic. 27.9 cm (11″). The Metropolitan Museum of Art, New York, New York. Gift of Nathan Cummings.

Crafts

The Mochica buried fine works of gold and pottery with their dead. One of these, a gold and turquoise earring, is shown in Figure 6–12. The object was found in 1987 in a tomb near Sipan (see-**pahn**), Peru. The tomb is one of few untouched by thieves that scientists have located. In it, they discovered the remains of a warrior-priest, several servants, and a dog. Did you notice the headdress and necklace worn by the human figure on the earring? One of the skeletons in the tomb was dressed in much the same way.

In the design of their pottery, the Mochica borrowed from the Chavín. A Mochica stirrup-spout pitcher is shown in Figure 6–13. Compare this object with the jaguar pitcher in Figure 6–11. Which spout do you find more graceful? Which of the two ways of showing figures do you find the more stylized?

Lesson 3 *Art of the Andes* **89**

more about • • •

The Incan Empire Two aspects of the Incan Empire should be noted when considering current ideas of civilization. First, the cities were not the usual settlement type, and second, the people had no written language. Their primary form of religion was a form of ancestor worship centering on the perpetual care of the mummies of their dead, which were brought to participate in major ceremonies. Contrary to the Aztecs, the Inca practiced little in the way of human sacrifice and, even then, primarily sacrificed animals. Because the Incan Empire was designed to be ruled by a small, elite group, Francisco Pizarro was able to overtake them with only 168 soldiers.

TEACH

■ **Motivator**

Have students look at Figure 6-16. Explain that Machu Picchu was built by members of another Pre-Columbian culture, the Incas, who lived in and around the area that is now Peru. Have volunteers point out Peru and the city Cuzco on a wall map; Machu Picchu is about 50 miles (80 km) northwest of Cuzco. Machu Picchu was not discovered by the Spaniards, and the city remained hidden until 1911.

■ **Vocabulary**

Ask: From what shorter English word is *stylized* formed? How does the word *style* help you understand the word *stylized?* Then ask volunteers to look up *adobe* in a dictionary. Ask: From what language does the word adobe come? Why do you think we use a Spanish word for this kind of building material? Finally, ask students about *monolith:* What prefix do you recognize at he beginning of this word? In what other words is the same prefix used? What does the prefix mean? How can understanding this prefix help you understand the word *monolith?*

■ **Aesthetics**

Have students compare the Chavín stirrup-spout pitcher shown in Figure 6-11 and the Moche stirrup-spout pitcher shown in Figure 6-13. How are the two works similar—and different—in subject? How is the use of visual elements similar in the two works? How is it different? Which principles of art are used to organize the elements in each work? Do the two works communicate the same idea or feeling to you? If so, what is the idea or feeling? If not, how are the messages of the messages of the two works different?

■ Studio Skills

Let students create their own weaving in the style of the Andean artists. Have them begin by using colored pencils to draw simple designs in two or three colors. Then let students tape their drawings onto pieces of sturdy cardboard slightly larger than the sheets of drawing paper.

Have students cut small notches, about ¼ inch (6.5 mm) apart, along the top and bottom of their cardboard pieces. Then have each student choose a piece of yarn in a neutral color to wrap as the warp on this cardboard loom; using the notches to secure the yarn The two ends of this warp yarn should be tucked under nearby strands.

Have students cut small pieces of cardboard to use as shuttles. Have them wind their weft yarn on their shuttles and then use the shuttles to weave over and under the yarn on the loom. Remind students to follow their drawn designs, taped under the wrapped yarns. When their designs require color changes, students should make new shuttles with yarn in different colors. Monitor students' work. Encourage students to work together as they weave, asking one another for suggestions and help as necessary.

90

TIAHUANACO CULTURE

The Tiahuanaco (tee-uh-wahn-**ahk**-oh) civilization developed around the time the Mayas were coming to power. The Tiahuanaco made their home in the Andes highlands of modern Bolivia, just below Lake Titicaca (tee-tee-**kahk**-uh). Find Lake Titicaca on the map in Figure 6–10.

Architecture

Like the Mayas, the Tiahuanaco were master builders. The gateway to their great ceremonial center is a **monolith,** *a structure created from a single stone slab.* A doorway was cut through and a large, richly carved stone laid across the top. See Figure 6–14. Carved in the center of this stone is the image of the sky god, a short figure standing on a carved pedestal holding staffs in both hands. On either side are running figures with weapons, ready to answer the sun god's commands.

Crafts

The unusually dry climate of the Andes highlands has helped preserve another side of Tiahuanaco art. That is the civilization's work in weaving. Figure 6–15 shows a detail from a shirt of the culture. Notice how many colors the weaver used. Would you describe the shapes in this design as organic or geometric?

▲ Figure 6–14   What two techniques has the carver used to emphasize the importance of the sun god carved in the center of this gateway?

Gate of Sun Creator. Tiahuanaco. A.D. 600. Virachocha, Aymara Culture, Bolivia. Photo © by Robert Frerk.

INCAN CULTURE

About 1450 the Incas conquered the other Andean tribes. The Incan empire stretched more than 2500 miles (4023 km) from north to south. It included present-day Peru plus parts of Ecuador, Chile, Argentina, and Bolivia. Find these countries on the map in Figure 6–10. Each tribe the Incas conquered was forced to learn their language, Quechuan (**kech**-wahn). Today 6 million people speak this language.

▲ Figure 6–15   Can you find the repeated figure of a crowned cat carrying a staff in its paw? Notice how the details change in each figure. In what way is this design similar to the designs used in relief carvings such as those seen in Figure 6–14?

Peru, Coastal Huari-Tiahuanaco. Shirt Section. A.D. 600–1000. Wool, cotton. 53.5 cm (21″). The Metropolitan Museum of Art, New York, New York. Michael C. Rockefeller Memorial Collection.

─ *more about* • • • ─

Tiahuanaco   Welcoming people to commercial or religious centers, portrayals of gods were often carved above Tiahuanaco gateways in a combination of art and architecture. Artists could convey the relative importance of the depicted gods by scaling them appropriately, making the lesser deities shallower, centering or raising the placement of the important figures, or assigning numbers of attending characters. The Tiahuanaco sculptors prevent potentially cluttered scenes by composing the figures geometrically or arranging them around a greater god. The successful blending of aesthetics and religion is noteworthy.

▲ Figure 6–16 This town was built quickly. Yet it stood up to all invaders. What does this reveal about the skill of its builders?

Machu-Picchu, Peru.

▲ Figure 6–17 Some of the feathers in this work are from tropical birds that lived far from the Incan capital of Cuzco. Some experts believe that this demonstrates that the Inca may have carried on trade with other civilizations.

Peru, South Coast. Pre-Inca period. A.D. 800–1300. Tunic. Feathers on canvas. 75.9 x 59.1 cm (29⅞ x 23¼"). The Metropolitan Museum of Art, New York, New York. Fletcher Fund.

The Incas never developed a true writing system. They did, however, develop a method for counting called quipu (**kee**-poo). In quipu, knotted strings were used to stand for numbers. These knots were also used as memory aids in reciting Incan history. The Incas' abilities with numbers is reflected in their art. Incan artifacts were made with great mathematical precision.

Architecture

The Incas were masters of shaping and fitting stone. They were also highly skilled urban planners. Proof of both talents can be found in the walled city of Machu Picchu (**mahch**-oo **peek**-choo). Figure 6–16 provides a view of this ancient city. Built on a mountainside to discourage would-be attackers, the city has withstood five centuries of earthquakes. The stones of its buildings were so carefully matched a knife blade cannot be slipped between any two.

Crafts

Like the Tiahuanaco, the Incas were also gifted weavers. Figure 6–17 shows a woven panel covered with feathers. The colors in the work are the natural ones found in the feathers. Why do you think the Incas chose feathers to decorate their works?

✔CHECK YOUR UNDERSTANDING

1. Which Andean tribe was the earliest? When did it come into being?
2. What is the meaning of *stylized*? What art works did you study in this lesson that were stylized?
3. For what types of art work are the Tiahuanaco best known?
4. The Incas were masters of what type of skills?

Lesson 3   *Art of the Andes*   **91**

LESSON 4

Making a Stylized Motif

(pages 92–93)

LESSON TIME: 45 minutes

Making a Stylized Motif

FOCUS

☑ OBJECTIVES

After completing this lesson, students will be able to:

- Create stylized motifs that could be used for fabric or wallpaper.
- Describe, analyze, interpret, and judge their own motif designs.

☑ SUPPLIES

- Pencils; sheets of sketch paper; sheets of white paper, 6 x 9 inches (15 x 23 cm); sheets of construction paper in assorted colors, 12 x 18 inches (30 x 46 cm); rulers; scissors; white glue.
- Long sheets of butcher paper, pencils, tempera paints, brushes.

Resources

- 6-8 *Figure Wall Hanging*, TRB page 129 (studio)
- 6-9 *Frida Kahlo*, TRB page 131 (artist profile)

TEACH

■ Motivator

Refer students to the student art works in Figure 6-19 and 6-20. Ask them to identify the motifs that are used in the works and discuss how the art works were created.

92

Animals, as you have seen, play an important role in Pre-Columbian art. Look at Figure 6–18. The artist has used a stylized pairing of a man and animal as a motif. Notice how the man in the motif is holding a torch. Notice also how the motif is repeated through the use of shapes and colors.

WHAT YOU WILL LEARN

You will pick two related objects that are important in modern life. You will stylize and combine these into a motif that could be used in a design for fabric or wallpaper. Pick colors that add harmony to your design and carry over shapes from one object to the other to create a feeling of unity in your design. (See Figure 6–19.)

▲ **Figure 6–18** Motifs may be simple or complex. Which word would you use to describe the motif in this shirt? Can you find motifs in any of the items of clothing you are wearing right now?

Peru. Textile fragments. Late Chimu. c. A.D. 1000. Cotton, wool. The Metropolitan Museum of Art, New York, New York. Gift of Henry G. Marquand.

WHAT YOU WILL NEED

- Pencil and sketch paper
- Sheet of white paper, 6 x 9 inches (15 x 23 cm)
- Sheets of construction paper in assorted colors, 12 x 18 inches (30 x 46 cm)
- Ruler, scissors, and white glue

WHAT YOU WILL DO

1. Brainstorm with members of your class to identify objects associated with late twentieth-century living. Some possibilities are cars, telephones, computers, and radios. Pick one object that holds particular importance for you. Then think of a second object that in some way is related to it. A car, for example, might be paired with a gasoline pump; a telephone might be paired with a teenager.
2. Make rough pencil sketches for a motif that combines the objects you picked. Connect the two in some manner. The curly wire of a telephone, for instance, could become the hair of a teenager. Draw one of the objects larger than the other. If possible, simplify some of the larger shapes or forms to geometric ones. Carry one or more shapes from one object over to the other. (Notice how the diamond shapes appearing as eyes on the animal in Figure 6–18 also appear on the man.) This will help lend a feeling of unity to your design.
3. Pick your best motif. Transfer it to the sheet of white paper. Draw the design large enough to fill most of the paper. Cut it out. This is your motif pattern.
4. Pick hues of construction paper that suit the mood of your design. Use one of these colors to serve as a background for

92   Lesson 4   *Making a Stylized Motif*

---

more about • • •

Maya Animal Symbolism   While animals are attractive artistic subjects, the Mayas primarily treated animals as equals and not just as patterns. Mayas avoided offending or mistreating other creatures because, like humans, animals maintained varying relationships with magic. Mayans gave extra respect to dogs, which they kept as pets. The serpent was especially significant according to Mayan beliefs. As a magical creature, the dragon provided shamans with the ability to perceive and interpret revelations during religious ceremonies. Snakes were common in the depictions of a ruler, where they symbolized a governor's rightfulness, and a feathered and bearded serpent represented the Mayan god Kikulcan (Quetzalcoatl to other Pre-Columbian cultures).

your work. Using the ruler and working lightly in pencil, divide a sheet in this color into four equal boxes.

5. Trace your motif pattern onto your remaining sheets of construction paper. You will need four copies in all. You may use the same color for each motif or use a different color for each. (See Figure 6–20.) Using scissors, carefully cut out the motifs you have drawn.

6. Experiment with arranging your motifs in the four boxes on your background sheet. Try turning two of the motifs upside down. When you have found an arrangement that satisfies you, glue the motifs in place.

7. Use leftover scraps of construction paper to make designs for your motif. Whatever designs you add to one must appear on all others.

8. Place your work on display. Can you identify the stylized objects in your classmates' works?

EXAMINING YOUR WORK

- **Describe**   Tell what objects you chose for your motif. Tell how you connected them. State whether you stylized your objects. Identify the hues you selected.
- **Analyze**   Tell how the colors you picked add harmony to your design. Point out the shape or shapes you carried from one object to the other to create unity.
- **Interpret**   Name one or more ways in which your design might be used. Tell whether your design is similar in style to the one in Figure 6–18.
- **Judge**   Tell whether you feel your motif succeeds. Explain why you feel it does or does not.

▲ **Figure 6–20** Student work. Stylized motif.

▲ **Figure 6–19** Student work. Stylized motif.

Try This! **COMPUTER OPTION**

■ Use Paint or Shape tools. Make a line drawing of two objects for your motif. Use Selection tool and Transformation menu to Flip, Turn, and Rotate design.

Choose an analogous or complementary color scheme, use earth tones, or tints and shades. Flood-fill shapes in your motif with Bucket tool. Save and title your work.

RESOURCES BEYOND THE CLASSROOM

Community Patrons   Community groups sponsor art education in many ways. Some groups specifically promote the arts, such as the Texas Visual Arts Association. These groups can identify local resources, and may even have films, slides, and other media available for loan. They can provide guest speakers in such diverse areas as art careers, art history and criticism. Other groups, such as

quilters' clubs, are a resource of information and talent about a specific area of art. Such groups often compile histories of their particular art, which they are willing to share. Community groups can sponsor question-and-answer sessions, exhibit art work—both student and professional—and otherwise support and encourage the appreciation of art outside the classroom.

OBJECTIVES

After completing this feature , students will be able to:

- Identify aspects of Aztec culture.
- Describe the two calendars used by the Aztecs.

Teaching the Connection

- Have students read the feature on this page.
- Ask volunteers to share what they know about Aztec culture. Where and when did the Aztec civilization flourish? *(The Aztecs lived in what is now Mexico in about the twelfth to fifteenth centuries.)* What was life like in Aztec cities? *(There were markets, schools, parks, and temples. Most people lived in adobe houses.)* What were some Aztec beliefs? *(They worshipped many gods with ceremonies and sacrifices.)* How does the calendar stone reflect some of their religious beliefs? *(The stone shows the sun god and other important gods.)*
- Point out that the painting depicts a large stone monument that was designed to honor the sun. Aztec worship centered on nature and aspects of their agricultural life.

ANSWERS TO MAKING THE CONNECTION

- Possibilities include: vulture, eagle, jaguar, dog, snake, lizard. They were all part of the Aztec life.
- The compass directions refer to concepts important to farmers: the sun rising in the east, setting in the west, warm southerly breezes, cool air from the north.
- Answers will vary.

94

How Do You Read the Aztec Calendar?

The Aztecs actually used two calendars. One was based on the sun and was tied to the agricultural cycle. The other was a sacred calendar, used by astrologers for making predictions and planning ceremonies. The two were used in combination like two interlocking cog wheels. Every 52 years the first days of the two calendars coincided. Great ceremonies were planned to please the gods because the Aztecs feared that the world might come to an end on this date.

Twenty day signs are represented on the inner ring. Each day sign had an animal symbol and also was associated with a god.

The face of Tonatiuh, the Sun God, is represented in the center of the stone.

Quetzalcoatl was the god of wind and air, represented by a feathered serpent.

The twenty day-signs were divided into four sections that coincided with the four compass directions, North, South, East, and West.

Tomas Filsinger. *Aztec Cosmos*. 1984. Colored paper. 90 x 90 cm (36 x 36"). Celestial Arts, Berkeley, California. Excerpted from Aztec Cosmos ©1984 by Tomas Filsinger. Reprinted by permission of Celestial Arts.

MAKING THE CONNECTION

- What figures are shown on the painting of the calendar stone? What do they tell you about Aztec life?
- Why do you think the compass directions would be important to an agricultural calendar?
- Find out more about the Aztec rituals and sacrifices that took place at the end of each 52-year cycle.

INTERNET ACTIVITY

Visit Glencoe's Fine Arts Web Site for students at:

http://www.glencoe.com/sec/art/students

INTERNET ACTIVITY

Teacher Resources In this section designed just for teachers, you can access resources to help you with your teaching needs. You will find *Curriculum Links* filled with content-related web sites matched to each chapter of this text. Linking to *Classrooms On-Line* allows you to visit other sites that have been created by teachers and by art classrooms to share their explorations and experiences. Listings of national organizations and schedules of conferences will help you keep abreast of new teaching strategies and art-related information. This is also the place to submit student works for consideration in the Glencoe Student Galleria. Find us at **http://www.glencoe.com/sec/art**

94

BUILDING VOCABULARY

Number a sheet of paper from 1 to 8. After each number, write the term from the list that best matches each description below.

adobe   genre pieces
artifacts   monolith
effigy   motif
funerary urn   stylized

1. Simple handmade tools or objects.
2. Art works that focus on a subject or scene from everyday life.
3. An image that stands for ideas or beliefs.
4. A decorative vase or vessel found at burial sites.
5. Simplified or exaggerated to fit a specific set of rules of design.
6. Sun-dried clay.
7. A structure created from a single stone slab.
8. Part of a design that is repeated over and over in a pattern or visual rhythm.

 ## REVIEWING ART FACTS

Number a sheet of paper from 9 to 17. Answer each question in a complete sentence.

9. What does the term *Pre-Columbian* mean? How do art historians use the term?
10. What is an artifact?
11. Why is the Olmec culture often called the "mother culture" of Mexico?
12. What city was the center of West Mexican culture?

13. What ancient city did scientists discover in northern Guatemala in the late 1800s? To what culture did this city belong?
14. What was the largest civilization of ancient Mexico and Central America?
15. What animal did the Chavín hold to be sacred?
16. What design feature did the Chavín create in their works that was later used by other cultures?
17. Why was Machu Picchu built on a mountainside? What evidence can be used to support the claim that the builders were talented architects?

 ## THINKING ABOUT ART

On a sheet of paper, answer each question in a sentence or two.

1. **Summarize.** Tell how developments taking place throughout Pre-Columbian America were expressed through the art of the following time periods: 1000 B.C. to A.D. 100; A.D. 300 to 1000; A.D. 1000 to 1500.
2. **Compare and contrast.** Which of the two cultures of Mesoamerica that you read about were most alike? Which were the least alike? Support your answers with information from the chapter.
3. **Compare and contrast.** Review what you learned about the great Egyptian pyramids in Chapter 4. Which of the Pre-Columbian cultures built pyramids for the same reason? Which built pyramids for other reasons?

MAKING ART CONNECTIONS

1. **Language Arts.** Imagine you are touring the parts of present-day South America you studied in this chapter. Write a letter to a friend back home expressing your reactions to the art of ancient peoples of the region. Use the descriptions and pictures from this chapter as a starting point.
2. **Social Studies.** Research cultural and religious traditions of the Incan or Aztec cultures. Report your findings to the class.

Chapter 6 Review **95**

■ Building Vocabulary

1. artifacts
2. genre pieces
3. effigy
4. funerary urn
5. stylized
6. adobe
7. monolith
8. motif

■ Reviewing Art Facts

9. Pre-Columbian means before Columbus. Historians use the term to refer to art made before the time of Columbus.
10. An artifact is a simple tool or object found in the region of an old civilization.
11. The Olmec culture is often called the "mother culture" of Mexico because the artifacts found in the region are the most ancient.
12. The center of West Mexican culture was the city of Colima.
13. Scientists discovered the city of Tikal in northern Guatemala. This city was part of the Mayan culture.
14. The Aztec culture was the largest civilization of ancient Mexico and Central America.
15. The Chavín held the jaguar sacred.
16. The stirrup-shaped spout design was later used by other cultures.
17. Machu Picchu was built on a mountainside to discourage attackers. The city has withstood five centuries of earthquakes.

? THINKING ABOUT ART

1. 1000 B.C.–A.D. 100: Art by the Olmec included an accurate calendar and large carved stone heads; the West Mexican culture left small clay dog effigies. A.D. 300–1000: Mayans left buildings with relief sculpture, pyramids, and the most accurate calendar. A.D. 1000–1500: Aztecs created huge ceremonial sculptures of gods and goddesses and created a calendar stone.

2. Mayan and Aztec civilizations were alike because they were large and advanced. The Olmec and West Mexican were alike because they were older and less advanced.
3. The Egyptians built their pyramids as tombs for pharaohs; the Moche culture built theirs to bury their nobles. The Mayan pyramids were built as temples.

Art of Greece and Rome

(pages 96–111)

Resources

- 7-11 Chapter Test, TRB page 157
- Transparency CC-7, *Bellerophon Riding Pegasus*
- Transparency 7, *Bedroom from the Villa of P. Fannius Synistor at Boscoreale*
- Fine Art Print 7, *Nike of Samothrace*

 Theatre
While studying this chapter, use Performing Arts Handbook page 323 to help students recognize how masks, used originally in Greek theatre, represent human emotion in the work by Robert Faust and Faustwork Mask Theater.

NATIONAL STANDARDS

This chapter addresses the following National Standards for the Visual Arts:

1. (a,b)   4. (a, b, c)
2. (a, b, c)   5. (b, c)
3. (a)   6. (a, b)

▲ This temple was once used as a Christian church and then as a mosque. Later it was used to store ammunition. It was partly destroyed when an artillery shell exploded in its center.

Parthenon. Temple of Athena. 5th Century B.C. Acropolis, Athens, Greece.

96

FEATURED ART

Acropolis	Discus Thrower
Arch of Constantine	Pantheon
Arch of Septimus	Parthenon
Bust of Philip the Arab	Pont du Gard
Greek Amphoras	Olympics Poster

Art of Greece and Rome

What did you think of when you read the title for this chapter—grand buildings like the Greek Parthenon and the Roman Colosseum? Perhaps your thoughts turned to splendid sculptures of winged goddesses or powerful emperors. Chances are that you *did not* think of Greek vase paintings or Roman triumphal arches. You may be familiar with more famous works by Greek and Roman artists and architects.

In this chapter you will discover that there is a great deal to see in *all* forms of ancient art. You may even find that some of your most rewarding discoveries are made while viewing Greek vases or Roman triumphal arches.

PORTFOLIO IDEAS

Create an art work for your portfolio that represents the influence of Greek or Roman art. Exchange your finished art work with a classmate and ask for a peer evaluation. This helps you get different viewpoints and opinions about your art work. Peers can tell you what they like about your art work and offer suggestions for revising the work. Decide whether you want to revise or change your art work based on the peer review. Then store the peer evaluation, your preliminary sketches, and the final art work in your portfolio.

OBJECTIVES

After completing this chapter, you will be able to:
● Identify the contributions of the ancient Greeks and Romans to the history of art.
● Name some important works by ancient Greek and Roman artists.
● Paint in the style of Greek and Roman artists.
● Model in the architectural style of ancient Greece and Rome.

WORDS YOU WILL LEARN

amphora
aqueduct
concrete
frieze
round arch
triumphal arch

■ **Chapter Overview**
Tell students that in this chapter they will learn about important art works and contributions of the ancient Greeks and Romans to the history of art. They will also create their own paintings and architectural models in the style of ancient Greece and Rome.

■ **Chapter Motivator**
Ask students to look at a wall map of the Mediterranean countries. Have volunteers point out the areas they think of when they study ancient Greece and the Roman Empire. Ask students if they can identify contributions made by these two great ancient civilizations. Explain that much of what we know of these cultures is derived from the art and architecture they left behind.

■ **Examining the Art Work**
Direct students' attention to the Parthenon, Temple of Athena, shown on the previous page. Explain that the Parthenon is the largest structure of several built on the Acropolis, or "high hill," in Athens, Greece, in 447 B.C. Point out the sense of unity and harmony which gives it a graceful appearance. Suggest that its placement on the highest point on the Acropolis, along with its tall, vertical columns gives the viewer the impression of strength and grandeur. Explain that the columns and other reliefs were hand carved with extreme precision. Ask students to consider the strength of commitment these people had to their city and the goddess Athena, for whom the temple was built.

97

DEVELOPING A PORTFOLIO

Long-term Projects Long-term projects are generally more complex and involve self discipline on the part of the student and trust on the part of the teacher. Building in written reflection over the length of the assignment helps both student and teacher see the progress being made. Rubrics provide a common point of reference for the students in completing the assignment and a clear understanding of what is expected. A long-term assignment allows for comparison from beginning to end. Discussion of student reflection helps both student and teacher assess the results of the long-term project. For more information on the value of long-term projects, refer to the separate booklet, *Portfolio and Assessment Techniques* that accompanies the *Understanding Art* program.

Art of Ancient Greece

☑ OBJECTIVES

After completing this lesson, students will be able to:

- Identify the art contributions of the ancient Greeks.
- Name some important works by ancient Greek artists.
- Make symmetrical cutouts of Greek vases.

☑ SUPPLIES

- Pencils, colored pencils, sheets of drawing paper.
- Large sheets of white paper, pencils, scissors.
- Square sheets of construction paper, pencils, rulers, colored markers, compass.

Resources

- ■ 7-1 *Time Line,* TRB page 137 (reproducible master)
- ■ 7-2 *Capital Sisters,* TRB page 140 (reproducible master)
- ■ 7-3 *Greek Capitals,* TRB page 141 (art history)
- ■ 7-4 *The Three Periods of Greek Art,* TRB page 142 (art history)
- ■ 7-5 *The Elgin Marbles,* TRB page 144 (art criticism)
- ■ 7-6 *Phidias,* TRB page 146 (artist profile)

Why study events that happened over 3000 years ago in a country the size of Arizona? Why bother learning the names of artists whose works no longer exist? The reason in both cases is that the country — Greece — was the birthplace of Western civilization. The influences of ancient Greek culture and art can still be felt and seen today.

In this lesson you will learn about that culture and art.

THE BEGINNING OF GREEK CULTURE

The story of ancient Greece begins around 1500 B.C. It was around this time that different groups from the north settled in the region bordering the Aegean (ih-**jee**-uhn) Sea. Find the Aegean on the map in Figure 7–1.

▲ **Figure 7–1** Aegean Civilization.

Greece never became a nation. Instead, the tribes that formed it remained small, separately ruled powers called city-states.

Part of the reason for this was geography. High, rocky mountains and miles of sea divided the different city-states. Two other, and more important, factors were self-pride and jealousy. It was loyalty to their own and distrust of others that prevented the city-states from banding together to form a nation.

One of the largest and most powerful of the city-states was Athens. Athens was also the most important in the history of art.

Architecture

The artists of Greece valued above all else grace, harmony, and precision. These qualities are present in the work that opened this chapter on page **96**. This famous building is the Parthenon. The Parthenon was a temple built in honor of the Greek goddess Athena (uh-**thee**-nuh). It stood along with other temples on a sacred hill known as the Acropolis (uh-**krop**-uh-luhs). (See Figure 7–2.) The word *acropolis* means "high city."

The Parthenon is thought to be the most perfect building ever created. Take a moment to study this art treasure. Like other works of Greek architecture, it uses the post and lintel system. Do you remember learning about this system of building in Chapter 4? Can you find the posts in the Parthenon? Can you find the lintels?

more about • • •

The Acropolis Acropolis is a term used to name the highest and most easily defended part of any ancient Greek city. The most famous acropolis, of course, is the Athenian Acropolis (shown in Figure 7-2). The four major monuments still to be seen on the Athenian Acropolis were erected during a major building project initiated by Pericles during the fifth century B.C. The largest and best-known monument on the Athenian Acropolis is the temple of Athena Parthenos, usually called the Parthenon. The temple was designed by two architects, Iktinos and Callicrates, and constructed between 447 and 432 B.C.

▲ Figure 7–2   The Acropolis rises 500 feet (150 m) above Athens. It was once filled with magnificent buildings. The Parthenon is the large building in the center.

Acropolis, Athens, Greece.

Sculpture

Sculpture was another of the outstanding achievements of ancient Greek art. At first sculptures were stiff and awkward. In time, however, as Greek sculptors gained skill and confidence, they began creating works that were remarkably lifelike and natural. Figure 7–3 shows one such work. Notice the attention to detail. Even the veins in the arm have been made to stand out in sharp relief. Carved in marble, sculptures like this looked even more realistic because sometimes their surfaces were painted.

Another example of Greek sculpture can be found in Figure 2–9 on page **25**. This long horizontal relief carving is a frieze (**freez**) from the Parthenon. A **frieze** is *a decorative band running across the upper part of a wall.* See how the horses almost seem to gallop across the work. The carving of this frieze was over-

seen by a sculptor named Phidias (**fid-ee-uhs**). Art historians agree that Phidias was among the greatest of all Greek sculptors. One of his most famous works was a magnificent statue of the goddess Athena created for the Parthenon. Made of gold and ivory, the statue rose 40 feet (12 m) to the ceiling. Sadly, this statue and almost all of Phidias's other individual works have been lost. The only knowledge we have of them comes through ancient written descriptions.

Painting and Crafts

Even more famous than the sculptors of ancient Greece were its painters. Like the sculptors, the painters sought to make their pictures as realistic as possible. None of the works of the great Greek painters have survived, however. As with the sculpture of Phidias, these works exist for us only in the words of ancient writers.

99

TEACH

■ Motivator

Ask students if they know what subjects are depicted on many Greek sculptures. How do they think the elements of color, line, form, shape, space, and texture were used in ancient Greek sculpture? Have partners work together to sketch sections of a frieze from ancient Greece. Have students share their drawings and display them along the walls.

■ Vocabulary

Have volunteers use dictionaries to check the derivations of *amphora*. Ask: What is the meaning of the Greek word from which the English word *amphora* is derived? What connection can you see between the meaning of the modern English word?

■ Art Criticism

Ask students to examine the two amphoras shown in Figure 7-4 and 7-5. Let students describe what they see in both works, noting the shapes of the vases themselves and the paintings on the vases: How are the two works alike? What are the most important differences between them? What functions do you think these amphoras were created to serve? Do you think they were originally works of fine art or applied art? Which do you think they are now? Why? After the class discussion, have each student choose one of the amphoras and write a paragraph about it, responding to these questions: What is the meaning, mood, or idea of this work of art? Is the work successful? Explain.

CURRICULUM CONNECTIONS

Social Studies   The first Olympic Games were held in Greece on the Olympia plain around 776 B.C. They lasted five days and were held every four years. The prize given to winners was a garland of wild olive branches, and as in today's Olympic games, victorious athletes earned great honor and esteem. The games deteriorated when Rome succeeded Greece as a military power and were finally banned by decree of Roman Emperor Theodosius in A.D. 394, after having been celebrated for over one thousand years. Mention that many Greek sculptors depicted athletes and athletic events.

■ Art History

Remind students that artists do not work in isolation; they always build on—or react to—the works of artists around them. What were the works of art from which the ancient Greeks learned and developed? Have groups of volunteers research Minoan and Mycenaean art. Then have the groups present their findings to the rest of the class, sharing photographs of Minoan and Mycenaean art works.

■ Studio Skills

Ask one or two volunteers to read and then tell the rest of the class about ancient Grecian labyrinth. Explain that labyrinth (or maze) designs have been found on ancient Greek pottery and in mosaics made to decorate Greek pavements and homes. Have students use square sheets of paper to draw their own labyrinth designs. They should begin by folding their paper in half. If students want to create circular maze designs, they should cut their folding papers in half circles and then unfold the papers to make full circles. Ask students to use the folds in their papers as guidelines to plan and draw symmetrical maze designs. Suggest that students use dark blue or black markers to draw the lines that form their mazes and that they use brighter colors to decorate the labyrinth pathways. This use of color will make their designs resemble the mosaic work used by ancient Greeks.

Some examples of ancient Greek painting do exist, however, in the pictures found on surviving pottery. The earliest Greek vases were decorated with bands of geometric patterns. One of these objects is shown in Figure 7–4. Found in a cemetery in Athens, this **amphora** (**am**-fuh-ruh), or *twin-handled vase*, was used as a grave marker. The small scene toward the center shows a burial ceremony.

▲ Figure 7–3   The original statue by Myron is known only through descriptions and reconstructed copies. Notice how the sculptor used balance and rhythm to show harmonious form.

Myron. *The Discus Thrower.* Roman copy of a bronze original of c. 450 B.C. Life-size. Museo Nazionale Romano, Rome, Italy.

Human figures were later added to the decorations on vases. At first these were little more than stick figures. Later they became more realistic and lively. Often the subjects were gods and goddesses or popular heroes. Scenes from sports and battles were also popular. The amphora in Figure 7–5 shows runners in a race. Notice how the repeated pattern of running figures adds a sense of movement. The curved surface of the vase adds to this feeling. Vases like this were sometimes used as prizes at the games held each summer in Athens. They were filled with olive oil from sacred groves and presented to victorious athletes.

▲ Figure 7–4   Notice the geometric patterning. Does this design remind you of those created by any cultures you have read about? If so, which ones? This vase was used as a grave marker in much the same way tombstones are used today.

Amphora. Geometric Style. Athens National Museum, Athens, Greece.

CURRICULUM CONNECTIONS

Math   Use vase reconstruction to reinforce math concepts and puzzle problem-solving. Make a photocopy of several Greek vases that depict various scenes. Glue each copy on a separate color of construction paper and then cut the copy into sixteen shapes to create a puzzle. Give each student one or more of the puzzle pieces. Ask students to sketch how they think the remainder of the picture might look. After they have completed their sketch, have them get together with their classmates to put the puzzles together. Did any of the students' sketches closely resemble the actual piece? Compare this to the tasks that archaeologists encounter when they attempt to visualize their discoveries of broken pieces.

▲ Figure 7–5 Are all the figures on this vase alike? Notice how the curved surface of the vase makes it appear as if the runners are racing over a circular course.

Amphora. *Runners in a Race*. Etruscan. Vatican Museum.

▲ Figure 7–6 Examples of Greek vase shapes.

✔ CHECK YOUR UNDERSTANDING

1. Why did the city-states of ancient Greece never join together to form a nation?
2. What three qualities did the artists of Greece value most?
3. What was the Parthenon? On what sacred hill is it found?
4. What is a frieze? What famous artist oversaw the work on the Parthenon's frieze? What other contribution to the Parthenon did he make?
5. What sorts of designs were painted on early Greek vases? What was painted on later Greek vases?

Lesson 1   *Art of Ancient Greece*   **101**

Answers to ✔ CHECK YOUR UNDERSTANDING

1. Two reasons why the city-states of ancient Greece never formed a nation were: rugged geography separated areas; loyalty to their own and jealousy of others prevented the tribes from banding together.
2. The artists of Greece valued grace, harmony, and precision.
3. A temple built to honor the Greek goddess Athena; Parthenon is on the Acropolis.
4. A frieze is a decorative band running across the upper part of a wall. Phidias oversaw the work on the Parthenon frieze. His other major contribution was a 40-foot gold and ivory statue of the goddess Athena.
5. Geometric designs were painted on early Greek vases. Later, human figures were added.

LESSON 2

Making a
Painting for a
Greek Vase

(pages 102–103)

LESSON TIME: 150 minutes

Making a Painting for a Greek Vase

Art critics, you will recall, judge works in terms of different aesthetic views. Look carefully at the Greek amphora pictured in Figure 7–7. How might a critic stressing the importance of the subject of a work react to this vase? Do the figures on the vase look real? Are their actions lifelike?

Think next about how a critic emphasizing composition might respond to the work. Can you find the X made of real and imaginary lines? Do you notice how these lines link the warriors to each other and to the amphora's handles? Note, finally, how a critic stressing content might react to this vase. Did you notice the two women at either side of the work? Could these be the mothers of the two warriors? Could it be they are weeping and pleading for their sons to stop fighting?

A measure of this amphora's greatness is that it succeeds in terms of all three aesthetic views.

WHAT YOU WILL LEARN

You will use tempera to paint one of the following: a scene of warriors in battle, a wedding, an athletic event. Your picture will have at least two figures. Make these figures as realistic as you can. Use the principle of movement to organize the lines and shapes. Finally, your scene will communicate a meaning, mood, or feeling. Paint your scene on a vase cutout like the one you made for the Studio Experience in Lesson 1. (See Figure 7–8.)

WHAT YOU WILL NEED

• Pencil and sheets of sketch paper
• Scissors
• Sheet of white paper, 18 x 24 inches (45 x 61 cm)
• Black tempera paint, several brushes, and mixing tray

▲ **Figure 7–7   This is one of two scenes of combat painted on this vase. Both show warriors of the Trojan war. Have you ever heard of that war? Do you know which sides fought in it?**

Black Figured Panel Amphora. Painter of the Medea Group, Greek. 520–510 B.C. Terra cotta, glazed. Lip 19.7 x Base 16.4 x Height 46.4 x Diameter 27.9 cm (Lip 7¾ x Base 6⁷⁄₁₆ x Height 18¼ x Diameter 11".) Dallas Art Museum, Dallas, Texas. Munger Fund.

SAFETY TIP

When a project calls for paints, use watercolors, liquid tempera, or school acrylics. If you must use powdered tempera, wear a dust mask. Try also to work away from other class members.

☑ OBJECTIVES

After completing this lesson, students will be able to:
• Plan and paint scenes that might appear on amphoras.
• Describe, analyze, interpret, and judge their own paintings.

☑ SUPPLIES

• Cutouts of vase shapes (made by students for the Studio Activity in previous lessons).
• Pencils; sheets of sketch paper; scissors; sheets of white paper, 18 x 24 inches (45 x 61 cm); black tempera paint; brushes in several sizes; mixing trays.
• Clay, slip.

Resource

■ 7-7 *The Golden Rectangle,* TRB page 147 (cooperative learning)

TEACH

■ Motivator

Display the cutouts of vase shapes created by students during the previous lesson. (See Studio Activity, page 101.) Let students identify the shapes and then discuss and compare them.

■ Vocabulary

Help students review the terms *aesthetics* and *aesthetic views:* What does the study of aesthetics involve?

MEETING SPECIAL NEEDS

Hands-on Techniques   Provide examples from the prehistoric period that clearly show the beauty of stick-figure representations for students who may not be able to easily visualize the figures they will paint on their vase shapes. For students with visual difficulties or those who do not draw representational figures, encourage them to feel the cut-out shape of the paper vase. Rather than painting their vases, have these students try gluing on designs made of yarn, toothpicks, and bands of cut-out geometric shapes. As an alternate to this Studio Lesson, you may wish to have some students decorate red clay flower pots, brought from home, using marking pens.

WHAT YOU WILL DO

1. Pick one of the three themes for your painting. Make several pencil sketches of scenes that have this theme. Use the vase painting in Figure 7–7 as a model. In your design, create real and imaginary lines that add a sense of movement to it. Keep your design simple. Make sure to emphasize the figures in it. Choose your best sketch.
2. Review the vase shapes in Figure 7–6 on page **101**. Decide which of the shapes would be best suited to your sketch. Using scissors, create this shape out of the large sheet of white paper. Follow the instructions given in the Studio Experience on page **101**.
3. Transfer your sketch to the cutout. Using a fine-pointed brush and black tempera, trace over the outlines of your figures. Carefully paint around lines that are to appear within figures. These lines will appear white in the finished painting.
4. Decorate and paint the rest of your vase using black only. (*Hint*: The neck, handles, and foot of the vase are well suited to decorations.)
5. When your vase painting is dry, display it. Note ways in which it is similar to and different from those created by your classmates.

EXAMINING YOUR WORK

- **Describe** Tell which of the three scenes you picked for your work. Describe the shape of amphora you chose. Tell whether the figures in your work look lifelike.
- **Analyze** Tell whether you used the principle of movement to organize the lines and shapes in your picture. Tell whether the shape of the vase is well suited to the picture you created.
- **Interpret** State whether your picture communicates a meaning, mood, or feeling. Note whether your classmates are able to identify this mood or feeling.
- **Judge** Tell whether you feel your work succeeds. Explain your answer.

▶ **Figure 7–8** Student work. Greek vase painting.

Try This! COMPUTER OPTION

■ Begin with the Symmetry tool or menu. Choose Mirrors or Bilateral Symmetry. Draw a vase using ideas shown on page 101. Save. Design an active figure in profile.

Select, Move, Copy, and Repeat figure. Add a small border to frame the figures. Use the Bucket Flood-fill tool or a Brush to color the figures and vase with contrasting black and earth tones.

Lesson 2 *Making a Painting for a Greek Vase* **103**

MEETING STUDENT DIVERSITY

Logical/Math Learners Have students prepare a chart of Arabic numerals (1–15, then 20, 30, 40, 50 by tens to 100, 500, and 1,000). Then ask them to write the corresponding Roman numerals and the Latin names for the numerals. Have students research how Romans performed mathematical calculations using their numerals, and write a few simple examples.

Verbal/Linguistic Learners Have students create a bulletin board showing "The Legacy of Ancient Greece and Rome." Ask each student to write on some aspect of architecture, art, history, literature, science, math, or philosophy from one of these civilizations. Have students illustrate their subjects and explain why each is an important contribution to Western civilization.

■ Aesthetics

Let students work in groups to discuss the content of the art on the amphora shown in Figure 7-7. What message or feeling do you think the painting on this vase is intended to communicate?

■ Cultural Diversity

Let students examine the amphora shown in Figure 7-7 and the funerary urns shown on page 80 and in Figure 6-8 on page 86. Have students compare the vessels from ancient Greece and from Pre-Columbian America. Ask them: What are the most important differences? What do these works tell about the two different cultures? What influences on our own culture and art can you identify?

ASSESS

■ Self-Assessment

Have students use Examining Your Work to evaluate their Greek Vase paintings. Responses may be written or oral.

■ Reteaching

Ask students to write paragraphs explaining what they like best about Greek art or culture. Then have students work in groups to compare and discuss their responses.

■ Enrichment

Ask groups of students to research ancient Greek plays. Ask each group to select an interesting method of presentation (such as a short play or a mural) and use that presentation to share its information with the rest of the class.

CLOSE

Ask students to describe basic shapes and uses of Greek vases.

Art of Ancient Rome

(pages 104–107)

Art of Ancient Rome

• • • • • • • • • • • • • • • •

FOCUS

☑ OBJECTIVES

After completing this lesson, students will be able to:

• Identify the contributions of the ancient Romans to the history of art.

• Name some important works by ancient Roman artists.

• Draw triumphal arches that include freestanding sculpture and relief carvings.

☑ SUPPLIES

• Slides or large photographs of the city of Rome.

• Sheets of drawing paper, pencils.

• Sheets of white paper, 6 x 6 inches (15 x 15 cm); pencils; scraps or pieces of construction paper in various colors; scissors; glue.

Resources

◗ ■ 7-8 *Roman vs. Greek Aesthetics*, TRB page 150 (aesthetics)
◗
◗ ■ 7-9 *Pompeii—A Buried City*, TRB page 152 (appreciating cultural diversity)
◗
◗ ■ 7-10 *Draw in Perspective*, TRB page 154 (studio)
◗

• • • • • OBJECTIVES • • • • •

TEACH

■ Motivator

Show slides or photographs of today's Rome, showing ancient structures next to modern buildings and traffic. Discuss Rome as a city, Rome as an ancient culture and civilization, and Rome as the center of an empire.

104

The Greek city-states were not only unable to band together to form a nation, they were also unable to keep the peace among themselves for long. Frequent outbreaks of fighting over a 1300–year period weakened the country. It made Greece helpless against attack from outside forces. Finally in 197 B.C., Greece fell to the Romans.

Although the Greek empire was defeated, Greek influence continued. The Romans were influenced by Greek ideas about art and used them in their own works.

In this lesson you will learn about some of those works.

ANCIENT ROMAN CULTURE

By the time of its takeover of Greece, Rome was the greatest power in the civilized world. At its peak, the city had a population of over one million people. Find this city on the map in Figure 7–9.

◀ **Figure 7–9   Ancient Rome.**

Rome was a city of contrasts. There were magnificent public buildings, baths, and parks, but there were also narrow streets crammed with shabby dwellings.

The Romans were a practical-minded people. They were more interested in such things as engineering, law, and government than in art. Romans did, however, make some very important contributions to the world of art.

Architecture

Rome's greatest contributions were in the field of architecture. Among its accomplishments were:

• **Concrete.** This *mixture of powdered minerals and small stones* was used to create buildings with great domes and ceilings. One such building is shown in Figures 7–10 and 7–11. This is the Pantheon. It was a temple built to honor all the Roman gods. Concrete made it possible for Roman architects to build a huge dome over this temple. The Pantheon is the largest domed building from ancient times still standing.

• **The round arch.** This *curved arrangement of stones over an open space* opened up new building possibilities. A series of round arches could be used to build bridges and other structures.

104   Lesson 3   *Art of Ancient Rome*

---

more about • • •

Roman Architecture   The Roman arch improved upon the post-and-lintel system favored by the Greeks. The post and lintel limited builders in terms of the space it could bridge. A stone lintel could not be used to span a wide space because it would break. Unlike a lintel, an arch is made of a number of bricks or cut stones. These are held in place by a wooden form until the top stone, called a keystone, is fit into place. The space that can be spanned in this manner is much greater than the space bridged by a lintel. However, an arch needs the support of another arch or wall. For this reason, the Romans created a series of smaller arches to replace the single large arch.

◀ **Figure 7–10** Greek temples were built to be "used" only by their gods. Roman temples like this one were built to be used by the people for prayer. The building is large enough to hold 3000 people.

Restored by Hadrian. Pantheon Facade and Piazza della Rotunda. A.D. 118–125. Rome, Italy.

◀ **Figure 7–11** The dome of the Pantheon soars to a height of 144 feet (44 m). The hole at its center is the building's only source of light. Though the hole looks small, it is actually 30 feet (9 m) across.

Restored by Hadrian. Pantheon Interior. A.D. 118–125. Rome, Italy.

Lesson 3   *Art of Ancient Rome*   **105**

■ **Vocabulary**

Have students use dictionaries to find the meanings of these words: *arch, aqueduct, concrete*. What is the meaning of the Latin words from which these English words came?

Sparking Creativity

Help students imagine how a design for a classical building originates. Have them view the Pantheon shown on this page as you read aloud the following quotation attributed to the Emperor Hadrian at whose direction the Pantheon was completed:

"My intention had been that this sanctuary of All Gods should produce the likeness of the terrestrial globe and of the stellar spheres."

Then ask: How do you imagine you would feel walking toward this building? What kind of space can you see inside the Pantheon? How do you think that space would make you feel once you were in the building? What message or feeling does this work of art communicate? Ask students whether Hadrian's intentions are fulfilled in the structure of the Pantheon.

CURRICULUM CONNECTIONS

Math   The Pantheon, constructed under the rule of Hadrian and completed about A.D. 125, was built to honor all the Roman gods. The proportions of the Pantheon's space have been widely praised for their harmony. The diameter of the rotunda is equal to the height of the building, measured from the floor to the top of the dome. The height of the walls is equal to the height of the dome above them. The Pantheon was constructed primarily from concrete and bricks. The walls of the rotunda are 20 feet (6.1 m) thick, and the dome was formed by rotating a series of rounded arches above the circular walls. The oculus, or circular window, helped reduce the weight of the dome to decrease pressure on the Pantheon's walls.

Ask students if they can imagine an event that might preserve all art works, architecture, and artifacts that exist in their homes and classrooms at this moment. Have students work in groups to find out what happened to Pompeii and Herculaneum in A.D. 79. Then discuss these questions: What kinds of homes did the people of Pompeii and Herculaneum live in? How were their homes decorated? What different kinds of statues have been found? What can we learn about ancient Roman art and ancient Roman life from the ruins of Pompeii and Herculaneum?

■ Studio Skills

Display pictures of mosaics used to decorate ancient Roman homes. Then have students create their own mosaic-style works. They should lightly draw either common household objects or simple natural objects—a seashell, a flower, a leaf. Then lightly draw decorative borders around the edges of their papers. Have students cut colored construction paper into confetti-size pieces to use as mosaic tiles. Have them apply a small line of white glue to a section of their drawings and then carefully place the pieces of colored paper onto the glue, allowing very small amounts of white background to show. Students should use this technique to complete their central drawings and their decorative borders. Display the completed mosaic-style works in the classroom where students can compare and discuss them.

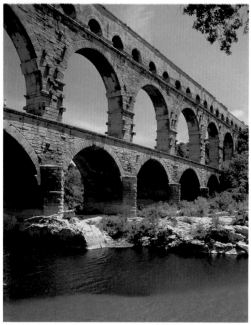

▲ **Figure 7–12** Aqueducts sloped ever so slightly. This allowed gravity to carry the water on its way. This aqueduct was part of a system 25 miles long that carried water to the city of Nimes.

Pont du Gard. 20–16 B.C. Near Nimes, France.

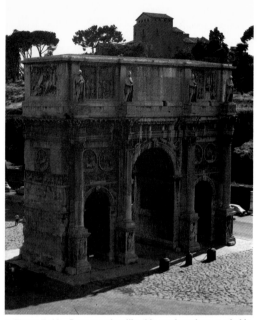

▲ **Figure 7–13** Roman arches like this one have been copied in later periods all over Europe. This arch was the largest and most elaborate of those erected by the Romans.

Arch of Constantine. A.D. 312–15. Rome, Italy.

- **The aqueduct** (**ak**-wuh-duhkt). This *network of channels, meant to carry water to a city*, was another type of structure that used round arches. The aqueduct in Figure 7–12 was built to carry water over a valley 600 yards (548 m) wide. This impressive structure is 160 feet (48 m) high. Note how the arches are placed side by side. This allowed them to support each other and carry the weight to the ground.
- **The triumphal** (try-**uhm**-fuhl) **arch**. This was *a monument built to celebrate great army victories*. The largest ever built was the Arch of Constantine, shown in Figure 7–13. The round arch was used here by the ancient Romans for purely decorative reasons. Notice how the structure uses three round arches. The emperor and his officers would ride chariots or horses through the large center one. Foot soldiers would march through the smaller side arches as the people of Rome cheered.

Sculpture

Like the Greeks before them, the Romans aimed for realism in their sculpture. A number of the works that remain are portrait sculptures. One of these is pictured in Figure 7–14. Study this work. Notice the care the sculptor has taken to capture not just lifelike detail but also the features of a specific individual. The eyes look as though they might blink at any moment. What mood or feeling does this sculpture communicate?

The Romans also excelled at relief sculpture. The ones shown in Figure 7–15 are from the Arch of Constantine. These reliefs tell of the deeds of the emperor in battle. What events seem to be taking place in the section of the story shown?

RESOURCES BEYOND THE CLASSROOM

Shadowing   Students can learn about art careers by "shadowing" adults who work in art-related fields. The students follow—shadow—these adults in the workplace for a few hours. Students can actually participate in work activities, for instance, by arranging the background for a display case. An alternative is a "lunch-buddy" program, where students are paired up with adults in art-related fields. At lunchtime, the adults eat with their assigned student in the school cafeteria. Students get a chance for one-on-one discussions of art careers, and adults have the opportunity to mentor a young person. Lunch buddy programs work best when "buddies" meet several times throughout the year.

▲ Figure 7–14   What is there about this face that makes it look like someone you might see on the street?

Bust of Philip the Arab dressed in a toga. A.D. 244–249. Marble. Vatican Museum, Rome, Italy.

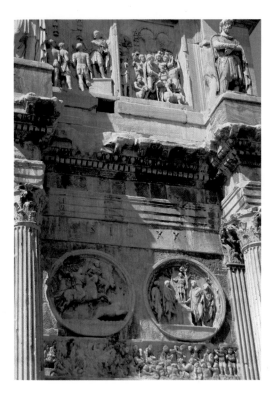

◄ Figure 7–15   Many of the relief carvings on this arch were taken from earlier monuments. Some of the figures on them were changed so they would look more like the emperor Constantine.

Arch of Constantine. A.D. 312–15. (Detail.) Rome, Italy.

✔ CHECK YOUR UNDERSTANDING

1. What led to the downfall of Greece? When was Greece finally conquered?
2. What were Rome's three main contributions to the history of architecture?
3. What was the Pantheon?
4. What is an aqueduct? What is a triumphal arch? What was the triumphal arch used for?
5. What was a key aim of Roman sculpture?

Answers to ✔ CHECK YOUR UNDERSTANDING

1. Frequent outbreaks of fighting over a 1300-year period weakened Greece and led to its downfall in 197 B.C.
2. The use of concrete, the development of the rounded arch, and the creation of aqueducts.
3. The largest domed building from ancient times, built to honor the Roman gods.
4. Aqueduct: network of channels used to carry water to a city. Triumphal arch: a round-arched monument built to celebrate great army victories. The emperor and his officers would ride chariots through the arch as the people cheered the victors.
5. The Romans aimed for realism in their sculpture.

LESSON 4

Making a Model of a Roman Triumphal Arch

(pages 108–109)

LESSON TIME: 90 minutes

FOCUS

☑ OBJECTIVES

After completing this lesson, students will be able to:

• Build models of triumphal arches.

• Describe, analyze, interpret, and judge their own models.

☑ SUPPLIES

• Drawings of triumphal arches (made by students for Studio Activity in previous lesson).

• Empty cardboard boxes, as for soap or cereal; tape; large sheets of construction paper in various colors, including gray and black; pencils; scissors; white glue; old magazines featuring sports illustrations; scraps of heavy cardboard.

• Clay, modeling tools.

TEACH

■ Motivator

Let each student present, the triumphal arch he or she drew for the Studio Activity in the previous lesson. Encourage students to discuss and compare their designs, noting the subjects depicted, the lines and the shapes shown, the kinds of balance used, and the moods or messages communicated.

Making a Model of a Roman Triumphal Arch

Art critics often approach their study of architecture just as they do the study of paintings or sculptures. They begin by describing what they see, and then they analyze the ways the principles have been used to organize the elements. After that they interpret the meanings, moods, and feelings the work communicates. Finally, they judge whether the work succeeds and explain why. Doing this helps the critic understand and appreciate a work of architecture.

Look at the triumphal arch pictured in Figure 7–16. What do you think an art critic would say about this arch during each of the four steps of art criticism? How would you, as an art critic, describe, analyze, interpret, and judge it?

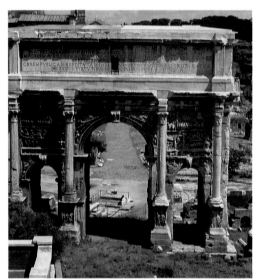

▲ Figure 7–16 Describe how the light creates different values on the surface of this monument. How does repetition of shapes add to the harmony of the arch?

Arch of Septimus. Roman Forum.

WHAT YOU WILL LEARN

You will build a model of a triumphal arch out of cardboard and construction paper. Your arch will have all the features outlined in the Studio Experience in Lesson 3. You will use a variety of different shapes and forms. Some of these will be repeated to add harmony. Your work will have formal balance. (See Figure 7–17.)

WHAT YOU WILL NEED

• Empty cardboard soap or cereal box, taped shut
• Large sheets of colored construction paper, including gray and black
• Pencil, scissors, and white glue
• Assortment of magazines featuring sports illustrations
• Scraps of heavy cardboard

WHAT YOU WILL DO

1. Place the cardboard box down flat on a sheet of gray construction paper. With the pencil, trace around the box. Hold a second sheet of gray construction paper firmly against the first. Using scissors, carefully cut through both sheets along the line you drew. Glue the sheets to the front and back of the box. Cover the top and side panels of the box with gray construction paper.

2. Look back at the drawing you made for the Studio Experience in Lesson 3. Doubling two sheets of black construction paper, cut out two large rounded arches and four smaller ones. Glue these arches in place on the front and back of the box. Use your drawing as a guide.

more about • • •

Roman Society The people of ancient Rome did not barter; they purchased goods and services and paid their taxes with coins. Many of these Roman coins were intricate works of art created in gold, in silver, or even in copper covered with silver. To make the coins official, highly trained artisans imprinted them with images of Roman emperors, temples and other buildings, altars, gates, aqueducts, tombs, fountains, harbors, and lighthouses. The Roman coins provide one source of information about the appearance of ancient buildings that have been altered or lost completely. The public currency of ancient Rome includes images of more than 200 buildings; the coins of provincial cities record 800 more structures.

3. Use construction paper to create columns and other decorations. Glue these in place.
4. Look through the sports magazines. Locate black-and-white photographs showing scenes of the sport you chose for your design drawing. Look for action shots that focus on athletes. Cut these out and trim them to fit on your arch. Glue those that are to work as reliefs directly to the arch. Glue those that are to work as free-standing sculpture to small scraps of heavy cardboard before gluing them in place on the arch. This will make them seem to project outward in space.
5. When the glue has dried, display your arch. Compare your work with that of your classmates.

SAFETY TIP

Be very careful when using cutting tools such as scissors and knives. Pick these up only by the handle, never by the blade. Make sure also to offer the handle when you are handing the tool to another person.

EXAMINING YOUR WORK

- **Describe** Point out the round arches on the front and back of your arch. Point out the columns. Point out the two different types of sculpture.
- **Analyze** Tell whether your arch has formal balance. Identify the variety of shapes and forms you used. Tell whether these add harmony to the work.
- **Interpret** State whether your arch tells the story of an important team win. Tell whether it communicates pride in this victory.
- **Judge** Tell whether you feel your work succeeds. Explain your answer.

▲ Figure 7–17 Student work. Triumphal arch.

Try This! STUDIO OPTIONS

■ On a large sheet of poster board, draw the outline of a triumphal arch using a black felt-tipped marker. Decorate the arch with magazine cutouts standing for a personal victory. Possibilities include learning to play a musical instrument, making one of the school's athletic teams, or joining a school club.

■ Create another triumphal arch, this time out of clay. Use the clay slab method. Be sure to use proper joining techniques. Use a clay tool to carve decorations and relief sculptures on your arch.

■ Vocabulary
Help students review the term *triumphal arch*. What were triumphal arches built to celebrate? How many arches did they include? How were those arches used?

■ Studio Skills
Let students experiment with modeling clay to create relief sculpture that might be used to decorate their triumphal arches.

• • • • • • • • • • • • • •
ASSESS

■ Self-Assessment
Have students use Examining Your Work to evaluate their models of a Roman arch created in this studio lesson. Responses may be written or oral.

■ Reteaching
Work with small groups of students to review the structure and purpose of Roman triumphal arches: What new development in Roman architecture made the construction of these arches possible? For whom were the triumphal arches built? What do the triumphal arches tell us about the art and culture of ancient Rome?

■ Enrichment
Encourage students to find photographs and read about the world's largest triumphal arch, the Arc de Triomphe de l'Etoile in Paris. How is it similar to the Roman triumphal arches shown in Figures 7-13 and 7-16? How is it different?

• • • • • • • • • • • • •
CLOSE
Ask students what it would mean to their community if a structure like a triumphal arch were constructed today and how they think it might be decorated.

CURRICULUM CONNECTIONS

Social Studies Among the many leisure activities practiced by ancient Romans were playing games, going to the baths, or listening to music. Board games played with counters or dice were popular with adults. The most popular activity for Romans was chariot racing. Large numbers of people gathered to cheer their favorite teams, and even the champion horses had their own fans.

The stadium was always filled, and it was a good place to meet people and enjoy a day's outing with friends and family. Children of ancient Rome had their own games. Toys ranged from dolls, model soldiers, and toy animals. Children's games were often played using hoops, sticks, and marbles.

OBJECTIVES

After completing this feature, students will be able to:

- Explain the ancient Greek ideal of a healthy mind and body.
- Describe the origin of the Olympic games.

Teaching the Connection

- Have students read the feature on this page.
- Ask volunteers to share what they know about ancient Greece. How did the ancient Greeks view education? *(Greek intellectuals and teachers like Socrates sought knowledge for its own sake. They encouraged students to ask questions.)* How did the Greeks keep fit? *(They worked out at gyms; they competed in games.)* How does the poster reflect the ancient Greek ideal of health as well as the modern ideal of world peace? *(The figure is strong and athletic; the background symbols represent global cooperation.)*
- Explain that the diet of the ancient Greeks contributed to their overall health. They ate lots of fresh vegetables and fruit, plenty of grains, yogurt and cheese, and fish. Meat was served at special events.

Answers to Making the Connection

- The athlete looks graceful as he is about to release the javelin; he is in harmony with the world; he is muscular and healthy looking.
- Answers will vary. Students should give reasons for their views.
- Responses will vary. The modern games are much bigger; the competitive spirit is similar, though.

How Did the Olympics Originate?

The people of ancient Greece valued grace, harmony, and precision not only in their art and architecture but also in their minds and bodies. A keen mind in a healthy, strong body was the ideal. The ancient Greeks described a backward person as someone who could "neither swim nor spell."

Education and athletic training were part of daily life. Physical exercise was just as important as intellectual development. Individual and team sports were offered at local gymnasiums, and libraries and reading rooms were also available there.

The Greeks' love of athletic competition was an important part of most religious festivals. The most famous of these was the festival in honor of the god Zeus. It was held every four years at Olympia, beginning in 776 B.C. Athletes from all over Greece competed in such events as foot races, wrestling, boxing, and the pentathlon. Though the Olympics were open to only men and boys, women had their own games held in honor of the goddess Hera.

In 1896, the first modern Olympic games were held in Athens, Greece, to promote individual character and world peace. Women competitors were included beginning in 1900.

Orsi. *Games of the VIIIth Olympiad, Paris.* 1924. Lithograph. 120.5 x 81.5 cm (47½ x 32″). Collection. Amateur Athletic Foundation of Los Angeles.

MAKING THE CONNECTION

- How does the Olympic athlete pictured here reflect the Greek ideals of grace, harmony, and physical development?
- In what ways are attitudes toward sports and education in today's society similar to or different from the Greeks' views?
- Find out more about the Olympic games of long ago as well as the modern games. How are they alike? How are they different?

INTERNET ACTIVITY

Visit Glencoe's Fine Arts Web Site for students at:

http://www.glencoe.com/sec/art/students

INTERNET ACTIVITY

Group Participation   Guide students in sharing computers and working cooperatively to enhance their Internet experiences and make lessons more enjoyable. Arrange students in groups of 2, 3, or 4 at each computer terminal so that everyone can view the monitor. Assign responsibilities among group members for use of the keyboard and the mouse. Have one member of the group read aloud from the computer screen. Have one student take notes as needed. Encourage students with experience to demonstrate for others. Be sure to provide each student an opportunity to practice using computer skills. Find us at **http://www.glencoe.com/sec/art**

BUILDING VOCABULARY

Number a sheet of paper from 1 to 6. After each number, write the term from the list that best matches each description below.

amphora   frieze
aqueduct   round arch
concrete   triumphal arch

1. A decorative band running across the upper part of a wall.
2. A twin-handled vase.
3. A mixture of powdered minerals and small stones used in building.
4. A curved arrangement of stones over an open space.
5. A network of channels meant to carry water to a city.
6. A monument built to celebrate great army victories.

 REVIEWING ART FACTS

Number a sheet of paper from 7 to 15. Answer each question in a complete sentence.

7. What are two reasons why the Greek city-states never banded together?
8. Which was the largest and most powerful of the Greek city-states?
9. What is the Acropolis? What does the word *acropolis* mean?
10. What goddess was the Parthenon built to honor?
11. To make their sculptures appear even more realistic, what did the Greeks do?

12. Who was Phidias? Name two contributions he made to the Parthenon.
13. In what area of art did the Romans make their greatest contribution?
14. What made possible the building of the dome on the Pantheon?
15. Name two structures in which the Romans used the round arch.

 THINKING ABOUT ART

On a sheet of paper, answer each question in a sentence or two.

1. **Interpret.** Look again at the sculpture in Figure 7–3 on page **100**. Tell what you think this figure is doing. Decide what word you would use to describe his feelings at this moment. Explain your answer.
2. **Compare and contrast.** Using the Parthenon and Pantheon as models, list the similarities and differences between Greek and Roman temples.
3. **Analyze.** Examine the aqueduct shown in Figure 7–12 on page **106**. What art elements can you identify in this structure? What principles of art have been used to organize the elements?
4. **Extend.** As you have read, the Romans were influenced by Greek ideas about art and used them in their own works. In which area of art do you find this influence to be most evident? Support your answer with facts and examples of specific works from the chapter.

MAKING ART CONNECTIONS

1. **Social Studies.** In this chapter you learned that the Romans were very interested in law and government. In an encyclopedia or other library resource, read about these areas. Search for ties between Rome's system of government and its architecture. Write a short report on your findings.

2. **Language Arts.** The early Greeks and Romans created beautiful mosaic works, some of which have lasted for centuries. Read *Piece by Piece! Mosaics of the Ancient World,* by Michael Avi-Yonah, to learn about ancient and modern mosaic techniques.

Chapter 7 Review **111**

■ **Building Vocabulary**

1. frieze
2. amphora
3. concrete
4. round arch
5. aqueduct
6. triumphal arch

■ **Reviewing Art Facts**

7. Loyalty to their own and jealousy of others as well as rugged geography were two reasons why the Greek city-states never banded together.
8. Athens was the largest and most powerful city-state.
9. The Acropolis was a sacred hill. The word acropolis means "high city."
10. The Parthenon was built to honor the goddess Athena.
11. Sometimes the Greeks painted the surfaces of their sculptures.
12. Phidias was one of the greatest Greek sculptors. He worked on the frieze and the statue of Athena.
13. Romans made their greatest art contributions in the area of architecture.
14. Concrete made it possible to build the dome of the Pantheon.
15. The round arch appeared in aqueducts, bridges, and triumphal arches.

 THINKING ABOUT ART

1. The figure is preparing to throw the discus. His state is one of intense concentration.
2. Similarities can include such items as: both were built as temples and were considered outstanding examples of architecture. Differences include post-and-lintel system vs. dome, being built to honor one Greek goddess vs. to honor all Roman gods, and only

one still stands in its entirety.
3. Elements include line, form, space, and texture. Principles include balance, proportion, and harmony.
4. Answers will vary. Students can mention architecture; Greeks and Romans both valued grace, harmony, and precision as shown in the Parthenon and the Pantheon. They can also mention realism in their sculpture.

Art of India and Islam

(pages 112–127)

Chapter Scan

Lessons

1 Art of India
2 Making a Life-Size Dancing Figure
3 Art of Islam
4 Making a Collage in the Islamic Style

Resources

- 8-10 Chapter Test, TRB page 179
- Transparency CC-8, *Prayer Rugs at Saifudden Mosque*
- Transparency 8, *Advantages Derived from Animals: A Doe and a Deer*
- Fine Art Print 8, *The Feast of Sadeh* by Sultan Muhammad

Dance/Music
While studying this chapter, use Performing Arts Handbook page 324 to help students learn about an ancient culture through the performances of the Ranganiketan Manipuri Cultural Arts Troupe of India.

NATIONAL STANDARDS

This chapter addresses the following National Standards for the Visual Arts:

1. (a, b)   4. (c)
2. (a, b, c)   5. (b, c)
3. (a, b)   6. (a, b)

▲ This miniature painting was part of a collection noted for elaborate margins and brilliant coloration. Notice how the entire space is filled with objects and patterns.

A Pair of Lovers. Manuscript page from the Vignier Album, Iran. c. 1590–1610. Opaque watercolor, ink, and gold on paper, mounted on board. 40.2 x 27.8 cm (15⅞ x 10⅞″). Smithsonian Institution, Washington, D.C. Arthur M. Sachler Gallery.

FEATURED ART

Ardabil carpet
Ceramic tile panel
Leaf from the Koran
Manuscript page, Iran
Mosques
Musawwir collage

Nadu Shiva sculpture
Rock Cut Temple, India
Seated Buddha
Stupas
Taj Mahal
Tree of Life and Knowledge

CHAPTER 8

Art of India and Islam

In a way, the frame around a work of art is like a window. The miniature painting on the left contains a scene within a scene. The couple within the smaller window is separated from the scenes of hunting and feasting that surround them. The panels surrounding them are filled with patterns of arabesque decoration as if to set them apart.

This miniature is from an album of paintings that illustrate the legends of Iran and its leaders. The artist used intricate details and rich colors to enhance this story.

You will learn to interpret images like this one in the pages that follow.

PORTFOLIO IDEAS

Select one of your art works from this chapter for a portfolio entry. Explain how the art work represents the influence of Indian or Islamic art. Is the art work a drawing, painting, or sculpture? Explain how you made the art work. What elements or principles of art did you emphasize? Date and store your written entry along with the art work in your portfolio.

OBJECTIVES

After completing this chapter, you will be able to:
- Identify the major Indian contributions to architecture and sculpture.
- Explain how Islamic culture began.
- Identify the major Islamic contributions to painting, architecture, and crafts.
- Create a design in the Hindu style.
- Make an art work in the Islamic style.

WORDS YOU WILL LEARN

arabesques
calligraphy
collage
mihrab
minaret
mosque
stupas

Art of India

FOCUS

☑OBJECTIVES

After completing this lesson, students will be able to:

- Identify the major Indian contributions to architecture and sculpture.
- Explain how the religions of Hinduism and Buddhism have influenced the art of India.
- Draw personal designs inspired by the *Tree of Life and Knowledge.*

☑SUPPLIES

- Wall map of the world (if available).
- Sheets of drawing paper, pencils, fine-tipped markers.
- Pieces of Indian embroidered fabric (if available), small pieces of plain dark fabric, yellow chalk, needles, embroidery thread in bright colors.

Resource

- 8-1 *Religion and Aesthetics,* TRB page 161 (aesthetics/art criticism)

TEACH

■ Motivator

Write on the board the names of two religions: *Hinduism; Buddhism.* Ask students to recall from their study of the Far East in Chapter 5 some statements that describe Buddhism. Write these statements under the term. Then have them read the first page of this lesson. Ask students to add statements under the term *Hinduism.*

114

Art of India

India is a land of opposites. It is a country of snow-capped peaks and tropical lowlands, of parched deserts and rain-soaked valleys.

Yet, for all its differences, India is a land joined by the strong religious beliefs of its people. These beliefs have in large measure shaped Indian art since the dawn of civilization. In this lesson you will learn about the religion and art of India.

THE RELIGIONS OF INDIA

Indian culture has long been guided by two religions. One of these, Buddhism, you read about in Chapter 5. The other, and older, of India's religions, Hinduism (**hin**-doo-iz-uhm), has its roots in prehistoric times. It was as an outgrowth of Hinduism that Buddhism emerged around 500 B.C.

Unlike Buddhism, Hinduism is not based on the teachings of a single leader. Rather, it is the collected ideas and beliefs of many peoples and cultures over thousands of years. A key belief of Hinduism is that the individual can come to know the powers of the universe through worship. Another is that the soul never dies. Instead, it is reincarnated (ree-uhn-**kahr**-nayt-uhd), or reborn, into a lower or higher life form depending on a person's behavior during his or her previous life.

Hinduism and Buddhism—sometimes together, sometimes separately—have influenced Indian art over the last 2500 years.

Architecture

Among the earliest, and most important, examples of modern Indian architecture are **stupas** (**stoop**-uhs), which are *beehive-shaped domed places of worship.* These were built by Buddhist architects to honor their religion's founder and other important leaders. Each stupa was reached through four gates covered with relief sculptures. Figure 8–1 shows the Great Stupa at Sanchi (san-**chee**). Find Sanchi on the map in Figure 8–2. Completed before A.D. 1, this impressive structure rises to 50 feet (15 m) at its highest point. Notice the contrast between the dome's smooth surface and the detailed carvings of the gate.

▶ **Figure 8–1   Believers would pass through one of the gates, then slowly walk around the dome. All the while they would meditate. Do you recall what meditation is?**

The Great Stupa. c. A.D. 1. Sanchi, India.

MEETING STUDENT DIVERSITY

Logical/Math Learners   Have students use a Venn diagram to compare and contrast the religions of India—Hinduism and Buddhism. Venn diagrams are constructed by using two or more overlapping geometrical figures, such as a circle, that share an area in common. Have students list characteristics and beliefs unique to each religion in the areas of the circle not shared, and elements that are common to both religions in the commonly shared area of the circle. This will give students an opportunity to focus on the contrasts and comparisons between the two religions.

Kinesthetic Learners   Have students draw poster-size pictures of calligraphy, arabesques, or a combination of the two for a bulletin board display.

▲ Figure 8–2 India.

No less impressive were the great temples Hindu architects created some 600 years later. One of the most striking facts about these temples is how some of them were built. They were cut directly into solid natural rock formations.

Figure 8–3 shows an important achievement of Hindu temple building. This amazing structure was cut from a hilltop by many craftspeople. Its hall, almost 100 feet (30 m) square, is decorated with deeply carved religious panels. Yet, like other early Hindu temples, it was made to be viewed mainly from the outside. To the Hindus, a temple was as much sculpture as it was architecture.

▲ Figure 8–3 Temples like these were cut from solid rock and needed no structural support. However, they were made to look like earlier wooden buildings.

Rock Cut Temple, India.

■ **Vocabulary**

Have volunteers look up the word *stupa* in a dictionary and read the entry to the rest of the class. Have them explain the language the word *stupa* comes from and which religion stupas are associated with.

■ **Aesthetics**

Guide students in discussing the Great Stupa at Sanchi shown in Figure 8-1 and the Hindu temple building shown in Figure 8-3. How do you respond to each work? What similarities between the two works can you identify? What are the most important differences? Explain that stupas were not houses of worship. Instead they housed a statue of the god, and worshipers gathered around the outside to offer prayers.

■ **Cooperative Learning**

Have students form four groups in which to report on the Gupta period in Indian history. Have members of one group find out who the Gupta kings were, and when and where they ruled. A second group should read about the political development of India under the Gupta kings. Have the third group research visual arts created during the period. The fourth group can research other Gupta arts, such as literature and dance. Then have all students share and discuss what they have learned.

more about • • •

Hindu Temples One of the great works of Hindu art in India is the Kailasa temple at Ellora. The temple was created in a single piece from a hillside; the hill itself was cut away, from the top down. The temple was probably built during the reign of Rashtrakutan King Krishna I, who ruled from about 756 to 773. Ellora is the site of more than 30 other sanctuaries, carved into rock formations or within caves. Ellora, a village about 270 miles (435 km) northeast of Bombay, is built on a lava plateau. The temples were carved into the lava, most between the fourth and ninth centuries.

Sparking Creativity

To help them connect with the finely woven fabric artists of India, have students imagine that they are going to do a project in which they will draw with thread. Let students create their own embroidered designs in the Indian style. Have students use chalk to outline very simple designs on small pieces of dark cloth. Suggest that students draw designs with symmetrical balance. Then have students choose the brightest colors of thread and use simple stitches to embroider their chalked designs. Cross-stitching (forming a series of small X's) is rather easy and is often used by Indian craftspeople. Let them work together, asking questions and making suggestions for one another.

■ Cultural Diversity

Ask a group of volunteers to read about the development and spread of Buddhism: Where and when did Buddhism begin? In what other countries did Buddhism become an important religion? In what countries is Buddhism an important religion today? How important is this religion in the lives of modern Indians? How can the spread of Buddhism be tracked in sculptures of the Buddha and in other works of art? Ask these volunteers to plan an oral and visual presentation, and let them give the presentation for the rest of the class.

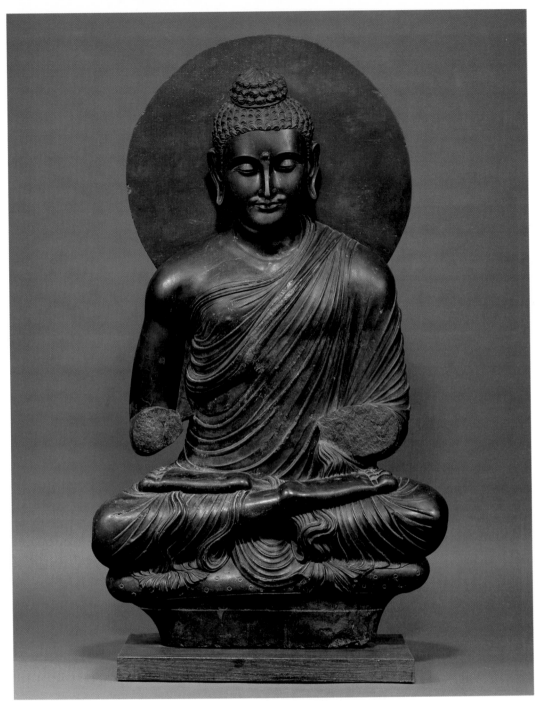

▲ **Figure 8–4 Born around 563 B.C., a rich Indian prince named Siddhartha Gautama went out in search of knowledge. His search eventually led the prince to reform the Hindu religion. He became known as Buddha, or "The Enlightened One," and he preached a simple message of salvation, which was to meditate, give up worldly possessions, and do good works.**

Seated Buddha. Indian, Gandhara region. Kushan Period. First half of 3rd Century A.D. Gray schist. 100 x 29.5 cm (39⅜ x 11⅝"). The Cleveland Museum of Art, Cleveland, Ohio. Leonard C. Hanna, Jr. Fund.

116   Lesson 1   *Art of India*

 CURRICULUM *CONNECTIONS*

Music   Remind students of the philosophical view that great art, literature, and music share a universal language. Exotic sounds and specialized instruments from the Indian culture speak to listeners in the same way that all art reaches out to communicate an idea or feeling. Test this theory by playing a recording of Indian folk music. Ask students to listen to the music for several minutes with their eyes closed. Then discuss the message or mood communicated by the music. Have volunteers find out about the interest in Eastern music and culture that developed during the 1960s when Westerners were introduced to the richness of Eastern culture through the music of the British rock group known as the Beatles.

Sculpture

Many sculptures, such as the work in Figure 8–4, show the Buddha seated in meditation. Look closely at this sculpture. Notice the dot on the forehead, the seated pose, and the unusually long earlobes of the figure. All are standard features of the Buddha image, each having its own special meaning. The earlobes, for instance, are a reminder of the heavy earrings the Buddha, who was born an Indian prince, wore before he gave up worldly possessions.

In sharp contrast to the weighty stone Buddha figures are the light, open sculptures of cast metal created later by Hindu sculptors. One of these works, the *Tree of Life and Knowledge*, is pictured in Figure 8–5. This sculpture expresses the Hindu belief in the creative force of the universe. Many animals were sacred to the Hindus, especially the cow. Can you find the cows in this work? What other creatures and birds do you notice? What kind of balance has the sculptor used?

◄ **Figure 8–5** The "tree of life" ties in with the Hindu belief in reincarnation. Since Hinduism teaches that animals have souls, they too can be reborn into higher or lower forms.

Tree of Life and Knowledge. Southern India, Late 1500–1600 A.D. Bronze. Nelson-Atkins Museum of Art, Kansas City, Missouri. Given anonymously.

STUDIO ACTIVITY

Decorating Your Tree of Life

Look again at Figure 8–5. Each animal in the work plays a special part in the Hindu view of life. The goose at the end of each branch stands for the soul's ability to "take flight." The five-headed serpent at the center is a sign of evil and danger.

With a pencil and fine-tipped markers, create your own tree of life. Use the same kind of balance noted in the *Tree of Life and Knowledge*. Fill the branches of your tree with objects that play a part in your personal happiness: pets, symbols of favorite pastimes, or good luck charms. Create decorative patterns of repeated objects similar to the patterns in Figure 8–5. Indicate the importance of objects based upon where they appear on your tree.

P O R T F O L I O

Mount your tree of life on poster board to keep it in your portfolio. In your sketchbook, tell why you included the items that you did. Review your tree of life in a month, to see if you would add or delete any of the items you included.

✔ CHECK YOUR UNDERSTANDING

1. What are two key beliefs of Hinduism?
2. What is a stupa?
3. How was the temple shown in Figure 8–3 created?
4. Name three standard features of early Indian Buddhist sculptures.

Help students focus on choosing areas of interest: sports, hobbies, nature, special friends or family members. Then remind students about choosing symbols to represent these choices. After students have made their selections and completed their personal tree of life, they will have a memento showing symbols of their values.

A S S E S S

■ Self-Assessment

Have students complete the review questions on this page. Answers are provided below.

■ Reteaching

Let students work with partners or in small groups to discuss their own Studio Activity drawings and compare them to the *Tree of Life and Knowledge* shown in Figure 8-5. What does your own drawing reflect about your interests and your life? How does it reflect the style of the *Tree of Life and Knowledge*? What are the most important differences between the *Tree of Life and Knowledge* in Figure 8-5 and the drawings made by all students?

■ Enrichment

Ask volunteers to find out more about the gods of Hinduism and how they are represented in sculpture and other art forms. Have them prepare a presentation of slides or photographs for the class.

C L O S E

Have students write a brief description stating the basic beliefs of Hinduism.

Answers to ✔ CHECK YOUR UNDERSTANDING

1. Two key beliefs of Hinduism are reincarnation and that an individual can come to know the powers of the universe through worship.
2. A stupa is a beehive-shaped domed temple.
3. The temple was cut from a hilltop by many craftspeople.

4. Three standard features of early Indian Buddhist sculpture included a dot on the forehead, a hand motion, and unusually long earlobes.

Making a Life-Size Dancing Figure

(pages 118–119)

LESSON TIME: 90 minutes

• • • • • • • • • • • • • • •
FOCUS

☑ OBJECTIVES

After completing this lesson, students will be able to:

• Recognize the contrast of stillness and movement in a Hindu sculpture.

• Create a life-size paper dancing figure based on the Hindu style.

☑ SUPPLIES

• Audio tapes of music in various tempos.

• Butcher paper and scissors.

• Pencils, black markers.

• Tempera paint, brushes, mixing trays, paint cloth.

Resource

■ 8-2 *Batik Print*, TRB page 164 (reproducible master)

• • • • • • • • • • • • • • •
TEACH

■ Motivator

Bring to class and play several audio tapes of music in different tempos. Ask students to describe the kind of dance one might do with each type of music. Have individuals demonstrate dance positions by dancing while you play music for a minute, then turn it off and ask students to hold positions when the sound stops.

118

 LESSON 2

Making a Life-Size Dancing Figure

Hindu art is full of contrasts. Study the sculpture in Figure 8–6. This is Shiva (**shee-vuh**), one of three main gods of the Hindu religion. Notice the contrast between the vertical calm of Shiva's head and the diagonal movement of his arms, legs, and body. His pose captures the feeling of Hindu dance.

WHAT YOU WILL LEARN

You will create a life-size dancing figure based on the style of the Hindu sculpture. You will contrast the vertical calm of the head with the diagonal movements of the arms, legs, and body. Tempera paint in two contrasting hues will be used to paint the figure. You and your classmates will work together to create the shapes of your figures. When completed, the dancing figures may be combined to create a dramatic display.

WHAT YOU WILL NEED

• Section of butcher paper large enough to accommodate your entire body
• Pencil
• Scissors
• Tempera paint, large and small brushes, mixing tray, and paint cloth
• Black marker with a medium point

WHAT YOU WILL DO

1. Study carefully the sculpture of Shiva. Notice the position of the head, arms, and legs.
2. Place the butcher paper on the floor and lie down on it. Keep your head in a vertical position but adjust your arms and legs to look as if you are dancing.
3. Have another student use a pencil to trace a line completely around your body. Then trace around the other student's body.

◀ **Figure 8–6** Every part of this sculpture has a meaning. The arch and its three-tongued flames stand for the universe and its destruction by fire. The drum in the figure's "upper right" hand stands for the sound of the bang beginning the universe.

Tamil Nadu. *Shiva, King of the Dancers* (Nataraja). Chole Dynasty, 10th Century. Bronze. 76.2 x 57.1 x 17.8 cm (30 x 22½ x 7"). Los Angeles County Museum of Art, Los Angeles, California. Given anonymously.

118   Lesson 2   *Making a Life-Size Dancing Figure*

MEETING SPECIAL NEEDS

Dance   Physically enacting dancing positions is a good way especially for students with disabilities to kinesthetically experience how the body feels in different positions. Students in wheelchairs will also like to make dancing gestures. After providing a time of actively experiencing dancing gestures, be sure to calm the class down, especially if there are students with behavior disorders. Have students be seated and begin a discussion about the positions they just experienced. Students are fascinated with brass fasteners, and students with certain disabilities especially like to use them to make figures with arms and legs that swing and dance.

4. Use scissors to cut out the figure.
5. Select two *complementary colors* of tempera with which to paint a decorative costume. Use a black marker to add details and simplified facial features.
6. Arrange all the cut-out figures in your class along a wall to suggest a ceremonial dance.

EXAMINING YOUR WORK

● **Describe** Can you easily identify the arms, legs, body and head of your figure? Does it look as if it is dancing?
● **Analyze** How does your figure show movement? Does the vertical calm of the head contrast with the diagonal movements suggested by the arms, legs, and body?
● **Interpret** What kind of dance does your figure suggest—slow and graceful, or fast and lively?
● **Judge** Using subject and content as the basis for judgment, do you think your work is successful? What could have been done to make it even better?

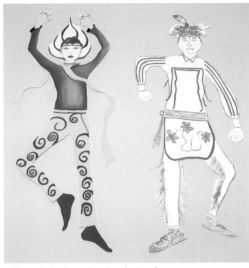

▲ Figure 8–7 Examples of student work.

■ Studio Skills

Pair students, boys with boys and girls with girls. Have one member of each pair lie on the paper and assume a dancing pose. Remind students to make certain the head is kept in a vertical position, to imitate the style of the dancing Shiva figure. Demonstrate with one student how to draw a line carefully around the body. Painting can be done most easily on the floor.

ASSESS

■ Self-Assessment

Have students use Examining Your Work to evaluate their dancing figures. Responses may be written or oral.

■ Reteaching

Have students notice the position of the dancer in Figure 8-6. Ask them to explain the use of balance and rhythm that gives this figure the appearance that it is dancing.

■ Enrichment

Have students find out about special fabrics created in India made in the batik method of using wax and dyes to make designs directly on the fabric. Have them find examples of this fabric design and make a display to share with other students.

Try This! STUDIO OPTIONS

■ Do a second version of your dancing figure, this time using a monochromatic color scheme with tempera paint. Describe in what ways this design differs from your original.

■ Draw the figure and cover it with a chalk line pattern. Paint between the lines and paint the negative space.

CLOSE

Ask students to decide on an exciting way to display their dancing figure art works in the classroom or the school for a special event.

more about • • •

Buddhism Followers of the Hindu religion usually accept a multitude of gods; the most important deities, however, are Shiva, Vishnu, and Brahma. The god Shiva has many aspects and many forms. Shiva is the god of death; he is also the god of dance and love. Every portion of the sculpture is rich with symbolism. One left hand holds the flame of spiritual light that burns away the veils of illusion. The other left hand points with the "teaching" gesture to the raised left foot, which represents release. One right hand shows the fear-dissolving pose, while the other holds the drum that beats eternity's rhythms. Under Shiva's right foot lies forgetfulness, which takes away the memory of past lives.

Art of Islam

•••••••••••••••
FOCUS

☑ **OBJECTIVES**

After completing this lesson, students will be able to:

- Explain how Islamic culture began.
- Identify the major Islamic contributions to painting, architecture, and crafts.
- Define the terms *calligraphy, arabesque, mosque, mihrab,* and *minaret.*
- Create their own small samples of knotted-pile rugs.

☑ **SUPPLIES**

- Small Persian rug or photographs of Persian rugs.
- Strips of lightweight cardboard, scissors, glue, tapestry, needles, yarn.
- Sheets of drawing paper, pencils, black ink, small brushes.

Resources

- 8-3 *Adapting Styles*, TRB page 165 (appreciating cultural diversity)
- 8-4 *The Prayer Rug*, TRB page 167 (appreciating cultural diversity)
- 8-5 *Persian Miniatures,* TRB page 169 (art history)
- 8-6 *Bringing the East to the West*, TRB page 171 (cooperative learning)
- 8-7 *Make Your Own Miniature*, TRB page 173 (studio)

Hinduism, which had lost favor in India with the rise of Buddhism, began making a comeback around A.D. 600. During this same period another religion was taking shape 2000 miles (3220 km) to the west. This new religion would grow into one of the world's largest, with some half billion followers. Its name is Islam (**iz**-lam).

THE GROWTH OF ISLAM

The birthplace of Islam is the city of Mecca (**mek**-uh), located on the Arabian peninsula. Find Mecca on the map in Figure 8–8. There in A.D. 613 a merchant named Muhammad (moh-**ham**-uhd) began preaching a faith centering on one god. This god, called Allah, had revealed himself to Muhammad during meditation. People who came to share Muhammad's beliefs recognized him as Allah's holy messenger. The followers of Muhammad are called Muslims (**muhz**-luhms).

▲ Figure 8–8   The lands of Islam.

Muhammad's lifelong dream was a world united under Islam. By the early 700s, his followers had spread his message to the Middle East, North Africa, Europe, and Asia.

Painting

The Koran (kuh-**ran**) is a collection of sacred writings of Islam. It is a record of the beliefs of Muhammad. A page from the Koran is shown in Figure 8–9. Some of the finest examples of early calligraphy (kuh-**lig**-ruh-fee) are found in this book. **Calligraphy** is *a method of beautiful handwriting sometimes using a brush.* Notice the circular gold decorations among the flowing letters. **Arabesques** (ar-uh-**besks**) are the *swirling geometric patterns of plant life used as decorations.* These became a popular decoration because the early Muslim teachings forbade picturing humans or animals.

Architecture

Muhammad taught that dying in battle for the faith guaranteed Muslims entrance into Paradise. As a result, Islam was often spread through force rather than preaching. Each new conquest was celebrated by the building of a **mosque,** a *Muslim house of worship.* By the 800s the Muslim capital of Córdoba (**kord**-uh-vuh), Spain, alone was reported to have 300 mosques.

Social Studies   Have students use the map on this page to locate the city of Mecca where the Islamic faith began. Have them trace the spread of Islam through the Middle East, on to North Africa and Spain, and into parts of France. Help students understand the scope of this spread of faith. Much of the Islamic arts found in Europe, including pins, rings, and Islamic pendants, were carried to these countries during this expansion. Remind students that for hundreds of years the Muslims remained in Spain, where they were called Moors. Point out that there are few Muslims in Spain now, but they remain today in large areas of North Africa and the Middle East.

▲ **Figure 8–9** **Calligraphy means "beautiful writing." The work that opened this chapter on page 112 also makes use of calligraphy. Can you find it in among the figures?**

Leaf from Qur'an (Koran), in Maghribi Script. Islamic, North African. c. 1300. Ink, colors and gold on parchment. 53.3 x 55.8 cm (21 x 22"). The Metropolitan Museum of Art, New York, New York. Rogers Fund.

Figures 8–10 and 8–11 show two views of a Spanish mosque begun in the 700s. In Figure 8–10 you can see a **mihrab** (**mee**-ruhb), which is *a highly decorated nook found in a mosque.* Covered with calligraphic inscriptions from the Koran, the mihrab is found on the wall closest to the holy city of Mecca. The origin and purpose of the mihrab is still a mystery. Some scholars feel it may honor the place where Muhammad stood in his own house when he led his followers in prayer. It became a standard feature of all mosques. Rising above the outside of such mosques are found one or more minarets (min-uh-**rets**). A **minaret** is a *slender tower from which Muslims are called to prayer* five times a day. Can you

Lesson 3   *Art of Islam*   **121**

more about • • •

Mosques   The main religious building of Islam is the mosque. The word comes from the Arabic *masjid,* meaning "a place to kneel or prostrate oneself." Every mosque must be oriented toward Mecca, the birthplace of Muhammad. In addition, a mosque must have a courtyard, a mihrab, a gate, and at least one minaret. Statues or other visual depictions of human and animal forms are not found within mosques. Most decoration takes the form of geometric and floral motifs on the walls of the mosque. The floor is usually covered with carpets or matting on which worshipers kneel and touch their foreheads to the ground in prayer.

TEACH

■ **Motivator**

Display a small Persian carpet where students can examine it closely. Ask students: What kinds of patterns are woven into the rug? What colors are used? How would you describe the texture of the rug? Explain that Persian rugs are one of the outstanding contributions of Islamic art; students will learn about other contributions as they study this lesson.

■ **Vocabulary**

Have volunteers use dictionaries to look up the words *calligraphy* and *arabesque.* From what two ancient Greek words does our word calligraphy come? What is the meaning of those two Greek words? What is the meaning of the word from which *arabesque* is derived? Which definition of *arabesque* relates to the art of ballet? What connection can you see between those two meanings?

■ **Aesthetics**

Have students work in groups to examine and discuss the page from the Koran shown in Figure 8-9: What do you see in this work? How does it make you feel? What purpose was this page intended to serve when it was created? What feeling or message does it communicate to you now? What distinguishes this page as a work of art?

■ **Art Criticism**

Guide students in discussing the Spanish mosque shown in Figures 8-10 and 8-11. Remind students that works of architecture are usually considered examples both of fine art and of applied art. Let students describe, analyze, and interpret the mosque as shown in these two photographs. Then ask students to judge the work both as fine art and as applied art.

■ Studio Skills

Have students plan and draw their own arabesque designs. They should begin by drawing very light pencil lines down the middle of the papers; they can use these lines to show the center, from which symmetrical balance can be established. Then have students use pencils to draw an organic shape—a leaf or flower, for example—on one side of their center lines; have them repeat that shape on the other side of the lines. Next have students draw surrounding shapes of vines or curls that connect with each other; these designs should also start at the center and be repeated as exactly as possible on the other side. Encourage students to fill their pages with balanced, controlled, intricate designs. When students have completed their drawings in pencil, have them dip small brushes in ink and redraw the lines.

■ Cultural Diversity

Ask a group of volunteers to research Moorish art: What is Moorish art? When and where was it created? How is it related to Islamic art? In what respects is it different? How can the Moorish heritage be seen in the architecture and decorative arts of Spain today? Let the volunteers plan and present a summary of their findings, using slides or photographs of Moorish art works if possible.

▲ Figure 8–10   Muslims always turn toward Mecca while praying. An arched dome in the mosque frames the mihrab, which is visible at the bottom of the picture.

The Great Mosque of Abd-ar-Rahman. 8–12th Century. Moorish. Mihrab with arched dome. Córdoba, Spain.

▲ Figure 8–11   The exterior of the Great Mosque in Córdoba offers little hint of the glories inside. The interior is filled with a forest of columns creating aisles that guide the visitor to the mihrab, the most important part of the mosque.

The Great Mosque and Roman Bridge. Córdoba, Spain.

► Figure 8–12   This work was built by a Muslim leader as a memorial to his wife. Notice the perfect symmetry of the building and all that surrounds it.

Taj Mahal, garden and pools. c. 1650. Agra, India.

RESOURCES BEYOND THE CLASSROOM

Home Tours   Many communities sponsor tours of private homes in the spring, fall, or holiday season in connection with real estate agents, architects, builders, and interior designers. Certain homes, designated "show homes," are carefully built and decorated to show off the talents of the people and companies involved, and to encourage community members to think about refurbishing their homes or buying new ones. Such home tours are an excellent opportunity for students to study architecture more closely, and to observe architectural forms and building construction techniques. These tours can also give students a clearer understanding of several art-related careers.

find the minarets in the famous structure in Figure 8–12? Do you know the name and location of this famous building?

Crafts

One of the great contributions of Islamic art is the knotted-pile, or Persian, carpet. The knots in this type of carpet are so close together that when the pile (raised loops of yarn) is worn away the colors of the design are still visible. The shimmering surface of the carpet in Figure 8–13 is filled with a delicate pattern of vines and blossoms, some in full bloom and others emerging from buds.

▲ Figure 8–13 This carpet is considered to be among the world's great works of art. In sixteenth-century Iran the arts, particularly textiles and book arts, flourished.

The Ardabil Carpet. Maqsud of Kashan, Persia, Tabriz. Safavid Dynasty. 1540. Silk and wool. 8.7 x 4.9 m (23'11" x 13'5"). Los Angeles County Museum of Art, Los Angeles, California. Gift of J. Paul Getty.

STUDIO ACTIVITY

Making Persian Knots

Look again at Figure 8–13. A feature common to carpets like this is the Persian knot, illustrated in Figure 8–14. Using knots like these, the weaver was able to create an unusually tight weave.

Make a very small cardboard loom and make a warp. (See Chapter 13, Lesson 2, for a description of how to make a warp.) Using a tapestry needle and yarn, alternate rows of Persian knots with rows of tabby (simple over, under, over, under) weave.

PORTFOLIO

You can keep your weaving in your portfolio. If you prefer to display your sample, photograph it for portfolio use.

▲ Figure 8–14 Persian knot diagram.

✔CHECK YOUR UNDERSTANDING

1. Who was Muhammad? When and where did he begin preaching his new faith?
2. What are his followers called?
3. What is the Koran? What is calligraphy?
4. What is an arabesque? Why did arabesques become popular?
5. What is a mosque? What are two standard features of mosques?
6. What kind of carpets are Islamic artists famous for?

Lesson 3   *Art of Islam*   **123**

STUDIO ACTIVITY

Making Persian Knots

Try another medium for this weaving activity. Paper ropes can be created by twisting lengths of discarded computer paper. Glue the paper ropes onto poster board in a weaving pattern. When dry, the weaving may be painted with acrylic or tempera.

ASSESS

■ Self-Assessment

Have students complete the review questions on this page. Answers are provided below.

■ Reteaching

Review with students the most important features of Islamic architecture. Have them browse through books that include photographs of Islamic structures and identify photographs of mosques, minarets, and mihrabs. What makes each unique?

■ Enrichment

Have students form research teams in which to learn about the Islamic religion and culture. Let students in each team choose four or five questions that interest them and then organize themselves to find answers to those questions. Ask the members of each research team to summarize what they have learned in written or oral reports.

CLOSE

Go around the room and ask individuals to define the vocabulary terms learned in this lesson.

Answers to ✔CHECK YOUR UNDERSTANDING

1. Muhammad was a merchant. He began preaching his faith about A.D. 613 in Mecca.
2. Followers of Muhammad are called Muslims.
3. The Koran is the sacred book of Islam. Calligraphy is a method of decorative handwriting using a brush.
4. Arabesques are swirling geometric patterns of plant life used as decoration. These became popular

because Muslim teachings forbade picturing animals or humans.
5. A mosque is a Muslim house of worship. Two standard features of mosques are mihrabs and minarets.
6. Islamic artists are famous for knotted-pile, or Persian, carpets.

LESSON 4

Making a
Collage in the
Islamic Style

(pages 124–125)

LESSON TIME: 90 minutes

Making a Collage in the Islamic Style

FOCUS

☑OBJECTIVES

After completing this lesson, students will be able to:

- Create collages in the manner of Islamic miniatures.
- Describe, analyze, interpret, and judge their own collages.

☑SUPPLIES

- Several collages, including student works or reproductions of collages.
- Pencils; sheets of sketch paper; rulers; scissors; sheets of white paper or poster board, 22 x 28 inches (56 x 71 cm); variety of patterned fabrics and papers; white glue; colored pencils; white drawing paper.
- Magazines, tracing paper, pencils.

Resources

- 8-8 *Islamic Geometric Designs*, TRB page 175 (reproducible master)
- 8-9 *Creating an Islamic Design*, TRB page 176 (studio)

TEACH

■ Motivator

Display several collages. Ask: What makes collages different from other kinds of art works? Tell students they will make collages in the style of ancient Islamic paintings.

124

Look at the Islamic miniature painting in Figure 8–15. Everything seems to be flat on the picture plane. The colors are intensely bright. How many different scenes or images do you see? Notice how the artist presents many points of view in the same work of art. A variety of patterns are used to fill the background spaces. Shapes, colors, and patterns are emphasized. By doing so, the illusion of depth is not felt.

◄ **Figure 8–15   This is a page of a book meant to be held in the hand and studied closely. Notice the patterns, rhythmic designs, and bright colors. Some of the pigments for the work were made by grinding precious metals such as gold and silver.**

'Abd Allah Musawwir. *The Meeting of the Theologians.* c. 1540–1549. Colors on paper. Bokhara. Nelson-Atkins Museum of Fine Arts, Kansas City, Missouri.

WHAT YOU WILL LEARN

In this lesson you will create a **collage**, *an art work made up of bits and pieces of two-dimensional materials pasted to a surface.* Your collage will focus on several scenes related to a current event or activity. The work will be organized, however, in the manner of a flat, patterned Islamic miniature painting. You will use bright colors, decorative patterns, and flat shapes as in Figure 8–15. You will create the background shapes using patterned fabrics and papers. People and other objects can be made by drawing and painting them on white paper. See Figure 8–16.

WHAT YOU WILL NEED

- Pencil, sketch paper, ruler, scissors
- Sheet of white paper or poster board, 22 x 28 inches (56 x 71 cm)
- A variety of patterned fabrics and papers
- White glue, colored pencils
- Small pieces of white drawing paper

---

more about • • •

Arabesques   Because early Islamic artists could not depict the figures of humans or animals, they developed a style of flat, abstract designs to be used in a variety of works. Best known is the arabesque, which comes from the Italian word meaning "Arab-like." These swirling, interlaced designs are apparently based on plant shapes, but the forms of leaves, branches, and vines have been transformed into scrolls, spirals, and curves. Such arabesque designs were first used during the 900s in all Muslim countries. Arabesques and other geometric designs have been used to decorate the walls of buildings, tiles, miniature paintings, rugs, metalware, and other craft objects.

WHAT YOU WILL DO

1. Brainstorm with classmates for ideas that could best be explained by showing several different scenes. For example, to show a football game you might have one scene of a huddle, one of a tackle, and one of the ball being kicked. Pick an event, such as a school dance, a parade, or a wedding. Make pencil sketches of different objects and scenes from the event you picked.
2. Make a plan to arrange your best ideas within rectangles of different sizes. Using the ruler and pencil, lightly draw these rectangles on the poster board.
3. Measure each shape and cut out patterned fabric or paper to fit each shape. As you select each pattern for the background, consider how one will look next to another. Look for contrast in the fabric so that you can see the distinction between each shape. If you wish, you may draw and color patterns in some of the spaces. Glue the pieces of fabric and paper to the poster board.
4. Draw and color figures and objects to place in each scene. Measure first to be sure that the figure will fit inside its area. Cut out the drawn objects and glue them onto the design.
5. When the glue is dry display your work. See whether classmates can guess what event your collage celebrates.

▶ **Figure 8–16 Student art. Collage in the Islamic style.**

EXAMINING YOUR WORK

- **Describe**   Identify the different scenes and objects related to your events. Explain why you placed each scene or object where you did.
- **Analyze**   Show where you used contrast in your design. Identify how you used the element of space. Explain how the many different patterned areas made your work look different from other art works you have created.
- **Interpret**   State what feeling or mood your work communicates to viewers.
- **Judge**   Tell whether you feel your work succeeds. Explain your answer.

Try This!

COMPUTER OPTION 🖥

■ Make patterned papers on the computer to use in your collage. Cover the page with patterns and textures using tools, menus, and special effects provided in your software. If available, scan and import fabrics, pictures, or photos. Use a digital camera to capture people or objects you want to add. Once imported, these images can be resized for your collage. Print. Follow directions in the Studio Lesson.

Lesson 4   *Making a Collage in the Islamic Style*   **125**

■ **Vocabulary**

Ask students to find the derivations of the words *miniature* and *collage:* What is the meaning of the Latin word from which our English word miniature comes? How does that meaning help explain the technique of making a collage?

■ **Studio Skills**

To prepare for drawing small figures to use in their collages, let students trace small photographs or drawings from magazines.

⋯⋯⋯⋯⋯⋯

ASSESS

■ **Self-Assessment**

Have students use Examining Your Work to evaluate their collages. Responses may be written or oral.

■ **Reteaching**

Ask students: Why is collage a good art form for creating works that echo the style of miniature painting? Which of the collages made in this lesson best captures the feeling of Islamic miniature paintings? Would you have found it harder—or easier—to imitate this style in a painting? Why?

■ **Enrichment**

Let students try creating original drawings or paintings in the style of Islamic miniature paintings.

⋯⋯⋯⋯⋯⋯

CLOSE

Have students explain the differences between Islamic miniature paintings and Western styles of painting.

TECHNIQUE TIP ▼

Collecting Materials   In preparation for this lesson, ask for volunteers to collect and bring materials for classroom use. One group could bring fabric remnants, another might be in charge of clipping magazine pages, a third could donate patterned wrapping paper. The class can then share materials and benefit from a greater variety. Each student can also bring a personal supply to supplement and trade. After the projects have been completed, those with related background materials can be displayed together.

125

CONNECTIONS *Math*

How Is Geometry Used in Art?

OBJECTIVES

After completing this feature, students will be able to:

- Identify geometric shapes used in art.
- Understand the importance of geometry in art.

Teaching the Connection

- Have students read the feature on this page.
- Ask volunteers to share what they know about geometry. What are some of the geometric shapes you are familiar with? *(Square, circle, rectangle, triangle, hexagon, octagon, parallelogram.)* Where else besides wall panels and floor tiles might you see geometry used artistically? *(In many primitive and modern cultures: woven rugs and blankets, scarves, vases, architecture.)* How do the geometric shapes in the tiles relate to each other? *(They fit together in a balanced, fluid pattern.)*
- Tell students that strict Islamic religion prohibited artists from making lifelike images; it was disrespectful of Allah, whom they believed was the only creator of life. Instead, floral motifs and geometric patterns became common in Muslim countries, though occasionally animals and human figures were used.

Answers to Making the Connection

- Hexagons and six-pointed stars.
- Floral and abstract images; probably to balance out the geometric patterns.
- Responses will vary.

Living creatures have always depended on geometry for survival. Spider webs, beehives, and nests are all examples of geometry at work in nature. Everything around us reflects the balance, order, and symmetry of geometry.

The use of geometry developed from practical human needs. In the fourteenth century B.C., for example, King Sesostris of Egypt divided the land equally among his subjects. Each received a rectangle of the same size of land and it was taxed accordingly. If a person lost land due to the annual flooding of the Nile River, the king sent someone to measure, and the owner's taxes were reduced. In ancient Greece, the study of geometry was the cornerstone of one's education. It still is.

Geometry is used to solve everyday problems, but it is also used to create beautiful designs. The designs found in Islamic art often use geometric shapes like the circle, triangle, square, hexagon, and six-pointed star. Such designs were based on the belief that art should embellish rather than imitate real life. Working with geometric shapes gives an artist an infinite variety of combinations, limited only by the artist's imagination.

Molded Tile Panel. Kashan, Iran, 13th–14th Century. Design of six-pointed star and hexagonal tiles. Ceramic, turquoise, and cobalt glaze. 60.9 x 105 cm (24 x 41½"). Excavations of The Metropolitan Museum of Art, 1936, and Rogers Fund, 1937.

MAKING THE CONNECTION

- Identify the geometric shapes used in the Islamic wall panel shown here.
- What other images did the artist use in the wall panel besides geometric shapes? Why do you think the artist chose these images?
- Find additional examples of Islamic wall panels and tiles. Compare the artists' use of geometric shapes and images.

INTERNET ACTIVITY

Visit Glencoe's Fine Arts Web Site for students at:

http://www.glencoe.com/sec/art/students

INTERNET ACTIVITY

Studio Cyberspace You and your students will want to visit this area of Glencoe's Fine Arts World Wide Web Site often. It is the place where creative adventures begin. You will find well-planned, outcome-based activities designed to motivate students to find their way around cyberspace. They will answer questions, accomplish tasks, complete projects, and increase their knowledge about art and artists of the world. Students will find easy-to-follow instructions and clearly marked pathways to help them through their web experiences. Many choices await them in activities such as virtual field trips, studio tours, collages and crafts, applied arts experiences, and gallery-hopping adventures. Find us at **http://www.glencoe.com/sec/art**

REVIEW

 ## BUILDING VOCABULARY

Number a sheet of paper from 1 to 7. After each number, write the term from the list that best matches each description below.

arabesques   minaret
calligraphy   mosque
collage   stupas
mihrab

1. Beehive-shaped domed places of worship.
2. A method of beautiful handwriting sometimes using a brush.
3. Swirling geometric patterns of plant life used as decorations.
4. A Muslim house of worship.
5. A highly decorated nook found in a mosque.
6. A slender tower from which Muslims are called to prayer.
7. An art work made up of bits and pieces of two-dimensional materials pasted to a surface.

 ## REVIEWING ART FACTS

Number a sheet of paper from 8 to 15. Answer each question in a complete sentence.

8. What two religions have played a major role in the art of India over the last 2500 years?
9. How were Hindu temples like the one shown in Figure 8–3 created?

10. What is the explanation for the unusually long earlobes found on Buddha sculptures?
11. What Hindu belief is revealed in the *Tree of Life and Knowledge* sculpture?
12. What is the name of the god of Islam? How did Muhammad come to know this god?
13. In what book central to the Islam faith was calligraphy used?
14. What buildings did Muslim conquerors raise after each new conquest?
15. What can you see in Persian carpets that reveals the special weaving method with which they were made?

? THINKING ABOUT ART

On a sheet of paper, answer each question in a sentence or two.

1. **Interpret.** Read the following statement: "To appreciate fully a work of religious art, you must be a member of the religion." Tell whether you agree or disagree. Defend your position with information and examples from this and other chapters.
2. **Compare and contrast.** What common features can you find between Buddhist and Hindu temples? What differences between the two can you note?
3. **Analyze.** Pick one art work from the chapter. Note how the elements of art and principles of art were used in the work. Identify the way they were used.

MAKING ART CONNECTIONS

1. **Social Studies.** Like Islam, Buddhism spread far from its birthplace. Compare the Japanese sculpture of Buddha you studied in Chapter 5 on page **73** with Figure 8–4. List the ways the two works are alike and different. Note the style features of each sculpture.

2. **Language Arts.** Create a verse for a greeting card. Write your poem using a calligraphy style. Illustrate your card with arabesque decorations. Add small details and fill your illustrations with color.

■ Building Vocabulary

1. stupas
2. calligraphy
3. arabesques
4. mosque
5. mihrab
6. minaret
7. collage

■ Reviewing Art Facts

8. Buddhism and Hinduism have played a major role in the art of India.
9. Hindu temples like the one in Figure 8-3 were sometimes cut from a hilltop.
10. The long earlobes on the Buddha sculptures were a reminder of the heavy earrings he wore before giving up worldly possessions.
11. *The Tree of Life and Knowledge* expresses the Hindu belief that many animals are sacred, especially the cow.
12. The god of Islam is called Allah. He revealed himself to Muhammad during meditation.
13. Calligraphy was used in the Koran.
14. Muslims built a mosque to celebrate each new conquest.
15. Persian knots are so close together that when the pile has worn away the colors of the design remain visible.

? THINKING ABOUT ART

1. Students may disagree with the statement. They should cite the steps an art critic and an art historian would use to judge a work of art in order to understand it.
2. Buddhist stupas were domed and beehive-shaped; Hindu temples were cut from solid rock formations. Both could contain relief sculpture.
3. Answers will vary. Students should show they know the elements and the principles and can accurately identify them in a work of art.

Chapter Scan

Lessons

1 The Figure Sculptures of Africa
🎨 2 Abstract Self-Portrait Cutout
3 The Masks of Africa
🎨 4 Making a Mood Mask Relief

Resources

- 9–10 Chapter Test, TRB page 199
- Transparency CC-9, *Gold Pendant*, Baule
- Transparency 9, *Dahomey Appliqué* (African)
- Fine Art Print 9, *Throne with Shells* (African)

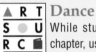 **Dance** While studying this chapter, use Performing Arts Handbook page 325 to help students recognize the influence of African culture in dance throughout the world with Chuck Davis and the African American Dance Ensemble.

NATIONAL STANDARDS

This chapter addresses the following National Standards for the Visual Arts:

1. (a, b)   5. (b, c)
3. (a, b)   6. (a, b)
4. (a, b, c)

▲ Headdresses like this were made to be worn during ceremonies as a sign of magical power. This one celebrates the power of Orangun, a mythic warrior-king. Note the importance placed on the central figure.

Bamgboye of Odo-Owa. *Epa Cult Mask.* c. 1920–1930. Wood. 121.9 cm (48") high. Detroit Institute of Arts, Detroit, Michigan. Founders Society Purchase, Friends of African Art Fund.

128

FEATURED ART

Antelope Headpiece (Bumana)
Chibinda Ilunga Katele (Chokwe)
Epa Cult Mask (Yoruba)
Equestrian Figure (Senufo)
Face Masks (Buluba)
Head Sculpture (Bini)

Headdress (Baga)
Helmet Mask (Senufo)
Kente Cloth (Ashanti)
Mounted King and Attendants (Benin)
Wood Figure (Buye)

CHAPTER 9

Art of Africa

The art of Africa gives us a glimpse into the traditions, ideas, and beliefs of the many cultures from across this vast continent. African artists use materials from the natural environment to create art works that serve a practical function in the day-to-day activities of peoples from each geographic region.

Much of the African art you see in museums today was created for decoration or display. Works like the one pictured at the left are a tribute to the imagination and skill of recent African artists. They honor the tradition of generations of artists who came before. In this chapter you will learn about figure sculptures, masks, headpieces, and Kente cloth.

PORTFOLIO IDEAS

Create an entry for your portfolio that shows the influence of African art. Think of something you *really like*—an animal, object or place. Using the art works in this chapter as sources of inspiration, create an art work using the media of your choice. Provide a brief explanation of how the African art work influenced your final product. Put your name and date on it, and place it in your portfolio. If it is a three-dimensional art work, take a picture of it and mount the photo on tagboard with the date and title. Store it in your portfolio.

OBJECTIVES

After completing this chapter, you will be able to:
- Describe the figures in wood and bronze made by African tribal sculptors.
- Name the three kinds of masks made by African tribal sculptors.
- Work with different media to create abstract and imaginative art objects.

WORDS YOU WILL LEARN

abstract work
face mask
headpieces
papier-mâché
shoulder masks

■ Chapter Overview
Tell students that in this chapter they will learn about wood and bronze figures as well as the different kinds of masks produced by African artists. They will also work with different media to create their own art objects inspired by the art of Africa.

■ Chapter Motivator
Have students refer to the Epa Cult Mask and tell them that it is actually made to be worn as a ceremonial headdress. Ask students to think about how this sculpture would make them feel if they saw it moving above a crowd of onlookers. Do they think it would be moving rapidly or slowly? What kind of music would accompany it's appearance?

■ Examining the Art Work
Ask students how the figure of the warrior-king has been emphasized. Explain that he is the only mounted figure, that he is larger than the figures surrounding him, and that he is placed in the center of the composition. Write the following words on the board *powerful, delicate, dignified, uncertain, confident, tense.* Ask students to select the ones that best describe the king: Can they identify a circular pattern in the way the carving is organized? Point out how the soldiers and musicians accompanying the king encircle him and face outward in every direction—protecting and entertaining him. They are smaller to show that they are less important than their leader.

129

DEVELOPING A PORTFOLIO

Peer Critiques Providing key points for review helps students see the range and differences in portfolio development and assignment interpretation. Reviewing portfolios in pairs allows students to develop skills in sharing, talking about their art and applying rationales to assignments in a situation that is less threatening than a whole group critique setting. Peer critiques often provide more individual time for direct, active engagement in portfolio discussion and reflection. In successful peer critiques, students can learn to listen and appreciate and take ownership for their opinions. For more information on peer critiquing, refer to the separate booklet, *Portfolio and Assessment Techniques* that accompanies the *Understanding Art* program.

LESSON 1

The Figure Sculptures of Africa

(pages 130–133)

The Figure Sculptures of Africa

African art works represent centuries of history and culture. Africa is the second largest continent in the world, and the population is divided into almost a thousand different cultural groups. Figure sculptures and carvings of humans and animals were created for traditions and events that relate to everyday lives of the artists. For this reason, the sculpture of Africa is an important contribution to the world's cultural heritage.

THE CULTURES OF AFRICA

The peoples of Africa below the Sahara live in many different nations and kingdoms. (See the map in Figure 9–1.) Each culture has made its own unique contribution to the world of art. Rock carvings and etchings in the south were created 27,000 years ago. The Mombasu and Lamu create ornate wood carvings influenced by trade with India. From the Kongo in central Africa come examples of masks, textiles, carvings, and funerary figures. In this lesson, you will read about the human figure sculptures created by African artists of the Western regions.

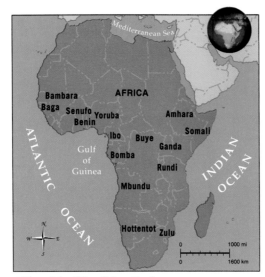

▲ Figure 9–1   Africa. Major cultural groups.

130   Lesson 1   *The Figure Sculptures of Africa*

Carved Wood Figures

A favored medium of the early African sculptor was wood. Carvings were usually made from a single log. This technique is found in art from many different areas, including headrests from Ethiopia and Konso grave figures. The original shape of the log was often suggested in the finished works.

Figure 9–2 shows a carving by an artist from northeastern Angola. Like all African wood figures, the work is boldly carved. It is also typically abstract. An **abstract work** is *a work in which the artist uses a recognizable subject but portrays it in an unrealistic manner.*

▲ Figure 9–2   African carvings were not done to please people living in the real world. They were done to satisfy spirits living in the next world.

Chibinda (The Hunter) Ilunga Katele. Chokwe, from northeastern Angola. Middle 19th Century. Wood, hair, hide. 40.6 cm (16″) high. Kimbell Art Museum, Fort Worth, Texas.

FOCUS

☑ OBJECTIVES

After completing this lesson, students will be able to:
- Describe the wood and bronze figures made by African tribal sculptors.
- Define the term *abstract work.*
- Draw themselves, creating figures that reveal their personalities rather than their appearances.

☑ SUPPLIES

- Map of Africa.
- Pencils, sheets of drawing paper.
- Photographs of animals, sheets of drawing paper, sheets of tracing paper, markers.
- An adz, or photograph of an adz.

Resources

- ■ 9-1 *Beauty in Pattern,* (aesthetics/art criticism), TRB page 183
- ■ 9-2 *Yoruba Twin Sculptures,* (aesthetics/art criticism), TRB page 185

CURRICULUM CONNECTIONS

Geography   Point out to students that the continent of Africa is very large—three times the size of the United States. Refer them to the world map on pages 314–315. Ask them to compare the size of the African continent with North and South America. Ask if any students have traveled across the United States by plane or car. Let them share their experience of how great the distance seems when driving. Then remind them that most African tribes traveled by foot from one location to another, therefore they were not apt to go very far from their tribal location. This contributed to the isolation of tribes and the fact that they each maintained their own language, religious beliefs, and customs.

Figure 9–3 shows a Senufo carving. This one appears to be a man on a horse. Actually, it is much more than that. Legend has it that the rider is a magician. His powers allow him to travel between the spirit world and the real world. Notice how this carving seems almost to reveal the artist at work. You can almost picture the artist's knife slashing the forms of horse and rider from the log. The finished work captures the dignity and pride of the rider with his shoulders back and his chest and chin thrust forward.

◄ **Figure 9–3   In creating figures like this, the artist would perform certain rituals. One was making an offering to the tree the wood was taken from.**

Equestrian Figure. Africa, Ivory Coast, Senufo Tribe. 19th-20th Century. Wood, patination. 32.08 x 7.3 x 22.23 cm (12⅝ x 2⅞ x 8¾"). Dallas Museum of Art, Dallas, Texas. Gustave and Franyo Schindler Collection of African Sculpture. Gift of the McDermott Foundation in honor of Eugene McDermott.

Lesson 1   *The Figure Sculptures of Africa*   **131**

■ Studio Skills

Let students experiment with drawing abstract figures. First display photographs of various animals. Have each student choose a specific animal and make a clear contour drawing of it. Be sure students recognize that these drawings are to be realistic. When students are satisfied with their initial work, have them place sheets of tracing paper over the realistic drawings. Then, using the drawing underneath as a guide, have students make abstract drawings of their chosen animals. Encourage students to simplify lines and forms and to use straight lines and angles in place of curves whenever possible. Finally, have students work in small groups to compare and discuss their realistic and abstract drawings.

■ Cultural Diversity

African sculpture had an important impact on the works of Western European artists, particularly during the early years of the twentieth century. Have volunteers read about the works of Amedeo Modigliani, Henri Matisse, Georges Braque, and Pablo Picasso: What and how did each artist learn about African sculpture? How can the influence of African sculpture be seen in the artists' works? Ask the volunteers to make short presentations to the rest of the class, displaying reproductions of African and European art works if possible.

▲ **Figure 9–4**   In addition to his size, what other clues are provided to emphasize the importance of the Benin king? Note the rich textures and patterns created on this high relief sculpture.

Africa. Nigeria. Court of Benin, Bini Tribe. *Mounted King and Attendants.* c. 1550–1680. Bronze. 49.5 x 41.9 x 11.3 cm (19½ x 16½ x 4½"). The Metropolitan Museum of Art, New York, New York. The Michael C. Rockefeller Memorial Collection. Gift of Nelson A. Rockefeller.

132   Lesson 1   *The Figure Sculptures of Africa*

— *more about* • • • —

Benin   Explain to students that the sculptures of the Benin Empire (such as the one shown in Figure 9-4) are among the most famous examples of African art. The sculptors of Benin, most of whose work was created between the sixteenth and nineteenth centuries, probably learned the techniques of casting from the sculptors of Ife. Ife is in southwestern Nigeria. From about the eleventh century until the seventeenth century, Ife was the seat of the Yoruba kingdom. Many art historians think that the sculptures of both Benin and Ife can be traced back to the Nok culture, centered in what is now northern Nigeria. Examples of Nok sculpture have been dated between the fifth century B.C and second century A.D

Cast Bronze Figures

The art of Africa first came to the attention of Western Europe in the late 1400s when the Portuguese explored the continent. Archaeological research continues to uncover the rich diversity and skill of African sculptors.

During the 1800s, bronze sculptures were first brought to Europe. These sculptures were made by artists of the Benin (buh-**neen**) Empire. Among the most remarkable of the works were reliefs used to decorate the wooden pillars of the palace. One of these appears in Figure 9–4. It shows the powerful king of the tribe on horseback. Two servants protect him from the sun with their shields. Two others support him with their hands, while still another supports the king's feet with his head. Notice the sculptor has made the figure of the king larger than those of the servants. This was done to emphasize the king's importance. What ancient culture that you read about had a similar practice?

Not all bronze castings by African artists are reliefs. Some, like the sculpture in Figure 9–5, are freestanding. Bronze heads like this one were placed on an altar as memorials to the king's ancestors. Notice the lifelike quality of this sculpture. What kind of balance has the artist used?

◀ **Figure 9–5** Bronze sculptures like this one demonstrate the skill of Benin artists. Notice how the different textures add to this work's visual appeal.

Africa, Nigeria. Court of Benin, Bini Tribe. Head. c. 1550. Bronze. 23.5 x 22 x 22.9 cm (9¼ x 8⅝ x 9"). The Metropolitan Museum of Art, New York, New York. Bequest of Nelson A. Rockefeller.

STUDIO ACTIVITY

Drawing Your Personality

Study Figures 9–2 and 9–3 again. Works like these were created to honor family ancestors. Suppose you lived in a place where images of past relatives were kept in every home. Think of how you would like future generations of your family to remember you. Then complete a pencil drawing of yourself as seen from the front. Show yourself in an activity that reveals your personality. The figure does not need to be a perfect likeness. It must, however, tell viewers about the kind of person you were. Try to use facial expression and stance as the artists in Figures 9–2 and 9–3 have done. Your personality, not your appearance, should be shown.

PORTFOLIO

Ask two or three classmates to describe your work in one word. List their words in your sketchbook, and compare them to the image you wanted to show. Then tell what, if anything, you might do differently if you drew yourself again.

✔ CHECK YOUR UNDERSTANDING

1. Explain why the art of each African tribe has been an important contribution to the art world.
2. What is the meaning of *abstract work?*
3. How was the bronze relief casting in Figure 9–4 used? Explain how the details in the work help us understand the traditions of the Benin Empire.

Answers to ✔ CHECK YOUR UNDERSTANDING

1. The art of each African tribe has been an important contribution to the art world because each tribe has its own language, customs, and religion.
2. An abstract work is art with a recognizable subject portrayed in an unrealistic manner.
3. Reliefs were used to decorate the palace. The king appears larger than the servants and shows his importance in the tribal culture.

STUDIO ACTIVITY

Drawing Your Personality

After students have completed their pencil drawings, you may wish to have them develop the drawings into masks to be worn or displayed around the classroom.

• • • • • • • • • • • • • • •
ASSESS

■ **Self-Assessment**

Have students complete the review questions on this page. Answers are provided below.

■ **Reteaching**

Help students learn about and discuss the tools and techniques used by African sculptors. Show students an adz (or a photograph of an adz), the tool most commonly used by African carvers. Let students imagine how it might feel to carve figures from wood with this tool: What might the advantages and disadvantages be?

■ **Enrichment**

Explain to the class that, when the bronze sculptures from Benin were first shown in Europe in 1897, many people assumed that the works had been influenced—or even created by—Portuguese artists. Help students understand the impact of this idea: Why do you think this theory was accepted? What does it show about European attitudes? What can you as a student of art today learn from this theory?

• • • • • • • • • • • • • • •
CLOSE

Let students browse through the sculptures in the text. Then ask: How is African sculpture similar to the sculpture created by artists in other cultures?

LESSON TIME: 90 minutes

• • • • • • • • • • • • • •
FOCUS

☑ OBJECTIVES

After completing this lesson, students will be able to:

• Create abstract cardboard self-portrait cutouts.
• Describe, analyze, interpret, and judge their own self-portraits.

☑ SUPPLIES

• Sheets of drawing paper pencils.
• Pencils; sheets of sketch paper; cardboard or tagboard, 6 x 12 inches, (15 x 30 cm); rulers; scissors; tempera paints in black and white; brushes; polymer gloss medium; heavy cardboard scraps; transparent tape.
• Sheets of drawing paper, watercolors, brushes.

Resource

■ 9-4 *Contemporary Totems*, TRB page 188, (studio)

• • • • • • • • • • • • • •
TEACH

■ Motivator

Have students draw several views of a human face, practicing ways to divide it into geometrical planes. Suggest that they begin by sketching an oval and then use corners and angles to replace the curves. Discuss different geometric shapes that might be drawn to represent parts of a face.

134

LESSON 2

Abstract Self-Portrait Cutout

The African figure sculptures you studied in Lesson 1 were made to honor past tribe members. They were also made to hold the spirits of past tribe members. Figure 9–6 shows another of these figure sculptures. Notice that, like other African standing figures, it is highly abstract. This work goes a step further, however. The artist here has simplified the human figure into a series of flat shapes and simple forms. You may be able to see how this abstract style had an effect on the later development of cubism in European art.

▲ **Figure 9–6   Did you notice how the features have been stylized? What has been done to simplify the figure?**

Africa, Zaire. Buye style. 19th-20th Century. Wood, kaolin. (Detail.) 77.5 x 28.9 x 21.6 (30½ x 11⅜ x 8½″). The Metropolitan Museum of Art, New York, New York. The Michael C. Rockefeller Memorial Collection. Gift of Nelson A. Rockefeller.

WHAT YOU WILL LEARN

You will create an abstract cardboard cutout self-portrait as seen from the front. Show yourself in a posture or activity that tells something about your personality. You will use flat shapes and simple forms for body parts and features. You will give the work a three-dimensional look by painting certain parts of the figure in black and white. You will add harmony by using only sharp-angled shapes and forms. (See Figure 9–7.)

WHAT YOU WILL NEED

• Pencil and sheets of sketch paper
• Piece of cardboard, 6 x 12 inches (15 x 30 cm)
• Ruler and scissors
• Black and white tempera paint
• Brushes and polymer gloss medium
• Scrap of heavy cardboard and transparent tape

WHAT YOU WILL DO

1. Look back at the drawing you made for the Studio Experience in Lesson 1. Do another drawing, this time replacing all curved lines with straight ones. Simplify the facial expression, but make sure your new version still shows a pose or expression that tells viewers about the kind of person you are. Make several sketches.
2. Draw the best of your sketches on the piece of cardboard. Use the ruler to make sure all the lines in your drawing are straight. Take care also to create shapes that are flat and angled.

MEETING STUDENT DIVERSITY

Auditory/Musical Learners   Play short excerpts of recorded African music and ask students to listen to the music and identify the use of percussion instruments and repeated rhythms. Have them use both hands and play the rhythm patterns on their laps in time with the music to set a mood for the Studio Lesson.

Kinesthetic Learners   Challenge students to create a dance through which they can teach classmates about some aspect of African culture. Dancing groups may have a narrator who helps interpret the symbolic meaning of their dance steps. Encourage students to bring rhythm instruments such as hand drums, bells, rattles, or maracas to play during the dance.

3. Using the scissors, cut out your shape. Add more straight lines *within* the shapes on your cutout. These should suggest flat surfaces at different angles to each other. This will make the shapes seem more like three-dimensional forms.

4. Study the carving in Figure 9–6. Decide which shapes in your work could be painted either black or white to give it a sense of depth. Paint the cutout with black and white tempera.

5. When the paint has dried, apply a coat of polymer gloss to your cutout. Cut a wedge shape from the scrap of heavy cardboard. Using tape, attach the wedge to the back of your cutout. This will allow you to stand the cutout for display.

▲ Figure 9–7   Student work. Abstract self-portrait.

EXAMINING YOUR WORK

- **Describe**   Tell how you created your cutout to be a standing figure as seen from the front. Tell whether your work is abstract. Explain why your work is considered an abstract piece.
- **Analyze**   Point out the flat shapes and simple forms in your work. Identify the places where you used black or white paint to add a three-dimensional look to the work. Explain why the use of angled shapes and forms throughout adds harmony to the work.
- **Interpret**   Show what features in your work would help a viewer understand what kind of person you are.
- **Judge**   Identify what is most successful about your cutout. Explain whether the work succeeds because of its abstract look. Tell whether its success arises out of your use of art elements and principles. State, finally, whether its most successful feature is the message it communicates about you as a person.

STUDIO OPTIONS

Try This!

■ On a sheet of white paper, make a pencil drawing of another standing figure. The subject this time should be a friend or relative you admire. Decide what qualities you admire most in the person. Decide how best to show these qualities in your work.

■ Make another cardboard cutout, this time of a figure on horseback. Your figure should exhibit an emotion or feeling, such as pride, humility, or anger. Use the sculpture in Figure 9–3 on page **131** as your model. Again, simplify each of the figures into a series of flat shapes and forms. Paint your cutout with two complementary colors.

Lesson 2   *Abstract Self-Portrait Cutout*   **135**

■ **Studio Skills**

Have students plan and paint realistic watercolor portraits of themselves that show the same activity portrayed in their cutouts. Display portraits beside the cutouts and compare them.

Art on a Shoestring

Students will not be making real bronze sculptures, but you can give them an understanding of the warmth of wood or bronze by by letting them add orange or brown to the color palette as they paint their figures and give them a richer look.

ASSESS

■ **Self-Assessment**

Have students use Examining Your Work on this page to evaluate their self-portrait cutouts. Responses may be written or oral.

■ **Reteaching**

Have small groups of students discuss their abstract cutouts: How is the principle of harmony evidenced in each work? Then have students review the African sculptures shown in Figures 9-2, 9-3, 9-4, and 9-5 in Lesson 1. Has harmony been used to organize the visual elements in each work?

■ **Enrichment**

Have students write stories or essays to go along with their cutouts, explaining how they would like future generations of their families to remember them.

CLOSE

Have students display the cardboard cutouts and discuss the abstract appearance.

135

The Masks of Africa

• • • • • • • • • • • • • •
FOCUS

☑ OBJECTIVES

After completing this lesson, students will be able to:

• Name the three kinds of masks made by African tribal sculptors.

• Make simple masks and describe the experience of wearing them.

☑ SUPPLIES

• African masks or photographs of African masks, recording of traditional African music (if available).

• Pieces of tagboard, scissors, staplers, construction paper, tempera paints, brushes, found objects, glue.

• Large brown paper bags, cardboard boxes, scissors, tempera paints, brushes, scraps of fabric and/or construction paper, found objects, glue.

Resources

- ◼ 9-5 *Geometry of African Masks*, TRB page 190, (reproducible master)
- ◼ 9-6 *Picasso and the African Mask*, TRB page 191, (art history)
- ◼ 9-8 *Contemporary African Art*, TRB page 195, (appreciating cultural diversity)

136

African tribespeople had several ways of relating to the spirit world through art. One, which you read about in Lesson 1, was through figure sculptures. Another was through masks. Like the figure sculptures, the masks made by African tribal artists were richly carved. They are among the finest and most remarkable art forms of Africa. The masks also held great supernatural importance.

The artists of Africa created three different types of masks. These were the face mask; the headpiece, or headdress; and the shoulder mask.

▲ Figure 9–8 **What do you think is the most impressive feature of this face mask? How do you think a dancer wearing this mask would appear to those watching?**

Africa. Chumbanndu, Buluba. Face Mask. American Museum of Natural History, New York, New York.

136   Lesson 3   *The Masks of Africa*

THE FACE MASK

The **face mask** was *a mask worn to hide the identity of the wearer.* The wearer even changed his or her voice so as not to be recognized. An example of a face mask is shown in Figure 9–8. Animal furs, feathers, and shells are included in its decoration. The decorations were chosen according to the resources available in each region.

The face mask was used in a number of different tribal ceremonies. These ceremonies were held to protect the tribe from unknown forces of nature, or to ensure a good harvest. Yoruba masks honored gods of warfare. The Bundu masks were made to celebrate female beauty and power. Creation of face masks continues today in celebration of African tradition and culture.

THE HEADPIECE

Not all African masks were made to hide the wearer's identity. The headpieces created by artists of the Bambara tribe of west Africa were made with an abstract animal design. **Headpieces** were *masks carved of wood and worn on the head like a cap.* In Bambara culture the antelope is a symbol for a rich harvest and appeared as the model for their headpieces. Figure 9–9 shows examples of these headpieces.

Bambara headpieces were used in a ritual performed when a new field was readied for planting. This ritual honored Tyi Wara, a mythical being who was credited with having taught the Bambara how to plant and grow crops. The design of the headpiece was meant to blend the speed and grace of the antelope with the powerful spirit of Tyi Wara. Study the headpiece in Figure 9–9. What element in the work is used to capture a feeling of grace? What art element is used to capture a feeling of power?

CURRICULUM ⟩ CONNECTIONS

Social Studies   Most often worn with a full costume and accessories, the African mask is used for social or religious purposes. In the Dan tribe in West Africa, the wearer of a policeman mask, for example, would serve as a policeman. The Dan also used masks in religious activities to represent spirits and gods. Because they are worn by performers, African masks require extra care in their construction. The wearers must be able to stand, dance, and perform acrobatics while wearing the traditional garb. Even the most graceful, athletic performers require masks that provide adequate ventilation, allow freedom of motion, and preserve stability. When considering the many demands on the mask maker, artistic notions such as atmosphere, movement, and balance are important.

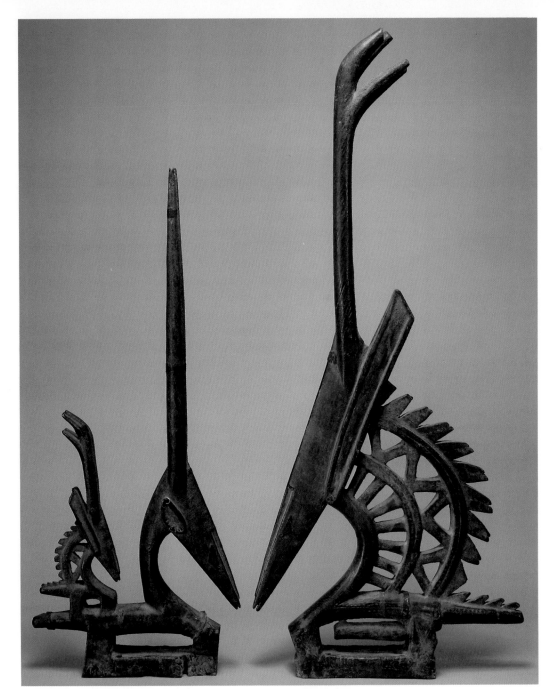

▲ **Figure 9–9** The antelope on the right is male. Notice its beautiful, flowing mane. The female carries a baby on her back.

Africa, Mali, Bamana Tribe. Two Antelope Headpieces. 19th-20th Century. Wood, metal bands. Left: 71.2 x 30.9 x 5.4 cm (28 x 12⅛ x 2⅛"). Right: 90.7 x 40 x 8.5 cm (35¾ x 15¾ x 3⅜"). The Metropolitan Museum of Art, New York, New York. The Michael C. Rockefeller Memorial Collection. Gift of Nelson A. Rockefeller.

■ **Motivator**

Introduce the lesson by displaying African masks (or reproductions or photographs of masks). Explain that masks were used as part of various tribal ceremonies; often these ceremonies included music, dancing, and chanting or singing. As students examine the masks, play recordings of traditional African music and/or read the following "Drum Call" from Zaire:

> All of you, all of you
> come, come, come, come
> let us dance
> in the evening
> when the sky has gone
> down river
> down to the ground

Ask students to imagine the feelings these ceremonies might evoke in participants and observers: How would the masks affect the people who wore them? How would they affect the people who were watching? Encourage students to share and discuss their responses. Explain that students will learn more about different kinds of African masks as they study this lesson.

■ **Vocabulary**

Introduce the names of the three different kinds of masks presented in this lesson: *face masks, headpieces,* and *shoulder masks.* Let students suggest the likely meaning of each term. Then have them check the definitions and look at the photographs in the text.

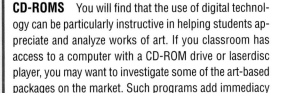

TECHNOLOGY OPTIONS

CD-ROMS   You will find that the use of digital technology can be particularly instructive in helping students appreciate and analyze works of art. If you classroom has access to a computer with a CD-ROM drive or laserdisc player, you may want to investigate some of the art-based packages on the market. Such programs add immediacy to the study of art by displaying works as they were meant to be seen—from various angles and, in the case of outdoor sculptures and works of architecture, in the context of their natural surroundings. See the Bibliography for some titles that are available for use in the art classroom.

■ **Cooperative
Learning**

Have students work in small
groups to discuss their ideas for
making headpieces and shoulder
masks. Make available materials
such as large paper bags, cardboard boxes in various sizes,
paints, and found objects such as
buttons, beads, feathers, and so
on. Ask group members to work
together in planning what kind of
mask to make, what construction
techniques to use, and what decorations to include. Then have them
carry out their plans together. Let
the members of each group share
their headpiece or shoulder mask
with the rest of the class.

■ **Cultural Diversity**

Have students investigate the
masks made by various Native
American groups and by Polyne-
sian, Micronesian, and Australian
peoples. Ask all volunteers to
share with the class how the
masks are made and used, and to
display photographs or drawings.
Then guide the class in discussing
similarities and differences among
the various kinds of masks.

THE SHOULDER MASK

Face masks were meant to cover the face of the wearer. Headpieces were meant to cover the wearer's head. The third kind of African mask, shoulder masks, were meant to do both. **Shoulder masks** were *large, carved masks made to rest on the shoulders of the wearer.*

They are sometimes called helmet masks. A shoulder mask of the Baga tribe is shown in Figure 9–10. It was used during a dance performed as part of a ceremony to guarantee a successful harvest. Notice how the face in this work is highly stylized.

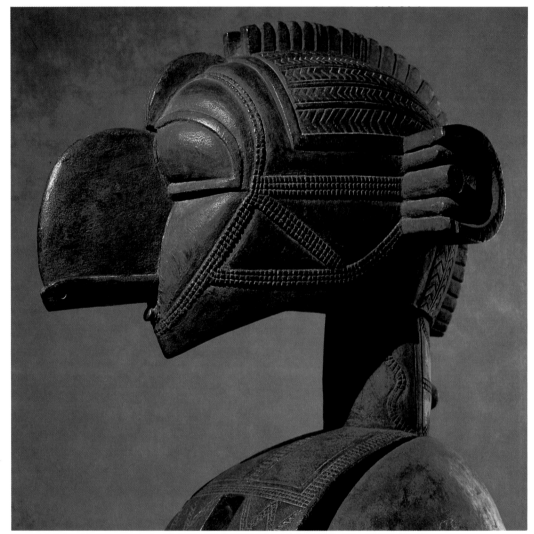

▲ **Figure 9–10   Masks are meant to be seen in motion. They were thought to have great
magical powers.**

Africa, Guinea, Baga Tribe. Headdress. 19th-20th Century. Wood. 122.6 x 40.9 x 70.3 cm (48¼ x
16⅛ x 27⅝"). Dallas Museum of Art, Dallas, Texas. The Gustave and Franyo Schindler
Collection. Gift of the McDermott Foundation in honor of Eugene McDermott.

CURRICULUM   CONNECTIONS

Social Studies   Inform students that this work comes from the Baga people who live in the area of Guinea in West Africa. Explain that most African art works were created for use in various ceremonies or rituals. These typically combined visual works of art with music, danc-ing, and poetry. Masks and headdresses were made to be worn by dancers performing at these ceremonies and rituals and were thought to have great supernatural pow-ers. They were intended to aid efforts to communicate with the mysterious world of spirits. The dancers who wore them believed that they either became or served as mediums to various spirits. For this reason, these masks and headdresses are regarded by many Africans as very powerful and are to be treated with great respect.

The wearer of a shoulder mask peered out through holes cut in the chest. Like face masks and headpieces, shoulder masks were part of a complete costume. Long strips of fiber were used to cover the body of the wearer. Unlike the other masks, shoulder masks were quite heavy, often weighing 75 pounds (34 kg) or more. When the mask was in place, the wearer stood over 8 feet (243 cm) tall. Wearing such a mask called for very strong performers. Even so, they could perform in rituals for only a short time.

▲ **Figure 9–11 Student work. Cardboard mask.**

STUDIO ACTIVITY

Constructing a Mask

What happens when you cover your face with a mask? Do you feel and act differently? Can you hide your identity from others when the mask is in place?

Design a mask using thin cardboard. Cut strips of the material and staple them into cones and cylinders large enough to fit over your head. (See Figure 9–11). Cut holes or slits to see through. Use construction paper, tempera paint, and found objects to create facial features and decorations. Compare your mask with those created by classmates.

PORTFOLIO

If your mask will not fit in your portfolio, take a photograph, make a drawing or diagram, or write a detailed description of your art work. In your sketchbook, discuss how you feel when you are wearing your mask.

✔ CHECK YOUR UNDERSTANDING

1. What are face masks? What were face masks used for?
2. What role did the antelope play in Bambara culture? Who or what was Tyi Wara?
3. In what way were shoulder masks different from face masks and headpieces?

Lesson 3   *The Masks of Africa*   **139**

STUDIO ACTIVITY

Constructing a Mask

Instead of constructing masks out of paper, you may find your students would like to use papier mâché or plaster gauze to design and create masks molded to their own faces. Make this an after-school or extra-credit project.

• • • • • • • • • • • • •
ASSESS

■ Self-Assessment
Have students complete the review questions on this page. Answers are provided below.

■ Reteaching
Have small groups work together to create a story to go with one of the masks they have studied. Once they have planned their story, let them decide on a method for presenting it to the rest of the class. Possible methods include skits, pantomimes, murals, written story. Let groups choose one method and plan and present their stories.

■ Enrichment
Some of the richest gold mines in the world are located on the African continent. Have students find out about a topic related to gold in Africa: history of gold mining techniques; specific tribes that have mined and used gold; African gold figures; African gold jewelry.

• • • • • • • • • • • • •
CLOSE

Go around the room and call on students to describe one type of African mask and tell how it is used.

Answers to ✔ CHECK YOUR UNDERSTANDING

1. The face mask was worn to hide the identity of the wearer. The masks were used during various tribal ceremonies.
2. In Bambara culture, the antelope is a symbol for a rich harvest. Tyi Wara was a mysterious being credited with having taught the Bambara how to grow crops.
3. Shoulder masks covered the head and face, could weight up to 75 pounds, and made the wearer appear to be 8 feet tall.

LESSON TIME: 90 minutes

• • • • • • • • • • • • •
FOCUS

☑ OBJECTIVES

After completing this lesson, students will be able to:
• Create papier-mâché mask reliefs.
• Describe, analyze, interpret, and judge their own mask reliefs.

☑ SUPPLIES

• Sheets of drawing paper, colored pencils.
• Pencils; sheets of sketch paper; heavy-duty aluminum foil; newspaper, masking tape; large sheets of cardboard.
• Non-toxic commercially prepared papier-mâché paste or white glue; plastic mixing bowls; water; torn strips of newspaper, about ½ inch x 1½ inches (1.3 x 3.9 cm).
• Fine-grain sandpaper; scissors or other sharp cutting tools; tempera paints; brushes; yarn, cloth, and cotton for decoration; polymer gloss medium.

Resource

■ 9-9 *Appliqué Class Quilt*, TRB page 196, (studio)

Making a Mood Mask Relief

The goal of African artists was to make expressive art. Masks were meant to communicate a mood or feeling to the viewer. Study the helmet mask shown in Figure 9–12. It is known as the "Firespitter." What mood does this half-animal, half-human mask communicate?

WHAT YOU WILL LEARN

You will create a mask relief that communicates a particular feeling or mood. You will model your mask out of papier-mâché (pap-yay-muh-**shay**). **Papier-mâché** is *a sculpting technique using newspaper and liquid paste*. You will use a variety of different shapes, forms, and textures. You will exaggerate the proportions of the shapes and forms used for the face features. Your shapes and forms will be organized into patterns to decorate the whole mask. (See Figure 9–13.)

WHAT YOU WILL NEED

• Pencil and sheets of sketch paper
• Heavy-duty aluminum foil and newspaper
• Masking tape and a large sheet of cardboard
• Non-toxic commercially prepared papier-mâché paste or white glue
• Plastic mixing bowl and water
• Newspaper torn into strips about 1/2 inch x 1 1/2 inches (13 x 39 mm)
• Fine-grain sandpaper
• Scissors or other sharp cutting tool
• Tempera paint and brushes
• Yarn, cloth, and cotton for decoration
• Polymer gloss medium

WHAT YOU WILL DO

1. Pretend that you belong to a tribe that has been having a series of misfortunes. The crops are dying and the water supply is low. Create a mask to be used in a ceremony your tribe might perform to restore your tribe's good fortune.
2. Do sketches for a mood mask expressing joy and happiness to attract the spirit of good fortune. Exaggerate the proportions of the features of the face. Use lines and shapes to create decorative patterns.

◄ **Figure 9–12** Notice the care with which this work was designed. Real and imaginary lines of the horns, tusks, and mouth are used to unify the work.

Helmet Mask. African, Ivory Coast, Senufo. 19th–20th Century. Wood. 96.5 cm (38"). The Detroit Institute of Arts, Detroit, Michigan. Gift of Governor and Mrs. G. Mennen Williams.

140   Lesson 4   *Making a Mood Mask Relief*

⌐ *more about* • • •

Spirit Masks Each face mask worn in a tribal ritual stood for a different spirit. Although it combines animal and human features, the Firespitter looks neither animal nor human. When it was worn, a burning coal was placed in its open jaws. The wearer blew on this to produce smoke and sparks that came out through the mouth and nose. This, along with its half-animal, half-human appearance, made the Firespitter a frightening sight. The Firespitter's awesome appearance should not keep the students from noticing how well it is designed. Have them notice how effectively the elements and principles have been used to create a visually appealing work of art.

3. Cut a sheet of heavy-duty aluminum foil large enough to cover your face. Using your fingers, gently press the foil around your eyes, nose, and mouth.

4. Place the foil mask on the cardboard and stuff wads of newspaper under it. This will help it keep its shape when the papier-mâché is applied. Using masking tape, fasten the stuffed foil to the cardboard.

5. Follow the instructions for applying papier mâché in Technique Tip **20,** *Handbook* page **283.** As you work, take care not to press too hard on the foil. If you do, the raised areas may collapse. Set the mask aside overnight to dry.

6. The next day sand your mask lightly with the fine-grain sandpaper. Trim the edges with scissors and carefully cut holes or slits for eyes. If you do not wish to wear your mask you might want to paint the eyes on your mask instead.

7. Look back at your sketches. Working in pencil, transfer the other face features and decorative patterns from your best sketch.

8. Pick colors of tempera paint for your mask. Your color choices should emphasize the joyous mood of the work. Paint your mask and add yarn, cloth, or cotton to create texture. Apply a coat of polymer gloss to add sheen to the mask.

SAFETY TIP

Avoid using wallpaper paste and similar glues for your work in papier-mâché. These glues have poisons in them that can enter the body through the skin.

 Try This! COMPUTER OPTION 🖥

■ Decide on the mood and purpose of your mask. Use the Symmetry tool or menu. Exaggerate and fill page with mask shape, or, if your program allows, draw the image to cover several pages. Print and mount on light cardboard. Slit and overlap the top edge to make a three-dimensional mask. Glue on grasses, yarns, and other objects to create texture and mood.

EXAMINING YOUR WORK

● **Describe**   Point to the different face features of your mask.
● **Analyze**   Identify where your mask has a variety of different shapes, forms, and textures. Explain how shapes and forms are organized into decorative patterns. Point out the exaggerated proportions of shapes and forms in the face features of your mask.
● **Interpret**   Point to the features in your work that would help a viewer understand its joyous mood. Explain how exaggeration helped communicate this mood.
● **Judge**   Tell whether you feel your work succeeds. Identify the best features of your mask.

▲ **Figure 9–13   Student work. Mood mask.**

■ **Motivator**

Explain that, in this lesson, students will create masks that express specific moods. Have each student use colored pencils to sketch at least three different masks expressing three different moods. You may use sketches from the Studio Activities in previous lessons.

■ **Studio Skills**

Encourage students to experiment with other ways to create masks from papier mâché. One possibility is to build masks over balloons.

ASSESS

■ **Self-Assessment**

Have students use Examining Your Work to evaluate their mood masks created in this Studio Lesson. Responses may be written or oral.

■ **Reteaching**

Work with small groups of students to review relief sculpture. What distinguishes relief sculpture from freestanding sculpture? Which bronze casting in Lesson 1 of this chapter is an example of relief sculpture? What makes the masks created in this lesson reliefs?

■ **Enrichment**

Ask students to explore the uses of masks in both traditional and modern theater forms. Encourage interested students to make their own masks for theatrical presentations.

CLOSE

Ask students to consider the mood the class experienced when sharing their mood masks.

---

more about • • •

Papier-Mâché   When students work with papier-maché for this Studio Lesson, have them wear old clothes. The paste can be messy, and the acrylic paints can stain clothing. Assist students in mixing the papier-maché paste so that it is not too thick or too runny. If students elect to use plaster and cloth or gauze instead of the prepared paste, be sure to show them how it is used before allowing them to start work. Have students collect found objects to decorate their masks. Objects like bird feathers, interesting leaves, and seeds can be used to express the spirit's personality. Let students arrange a display of the masks in a way that enhances each individual mask as well as making a harmonious group.

CONNECTIONS   *Social Studies*

Kente Cloth. Wrapper. Ashanti culture, Ghana. 20th Century. Silk. 209.6 x 130.8 cm (82⁵⁄₁₆ x 51⁵⁄₁₆"). National Museum of African Art and National Museum of Natural History, Washington, D.C. Purchased with funds provided by the Smithsonian Collections Acquisition Program.

What Is Ashanti Kente Cloth?

The Kente cloth pictured here represents another example of traditional African art. As in other African art forms, this piece is created for a purpose: to be used on special occasions and religious ceremonies, or to honor ancestors, a king, or queen.

The famous Kente fabrics of Ghana were originally worn by Ashanti royalty. Although both Ashanti men and women were accomplished weavers, they produced different kinds of fabric. Women wove wide strips of colorful cotton fabric for everyday use. The male weaver, however, was considered a master of his craft, creating Kente cloth for tribal leaders. On a special loom, he wove long, thin strips of dazzling silk or cotton that were then sewn together. Master weavers of Kente were highly respected and favored by members of the royal court and high officials in the Ashanti tribe.

Each pattern, color, and design used in Kente cloth has its own special meaning. One pattern, for example, is called "wise old woman." It symbolizes old age and wisdom. Blue represents love; ivory stands for joy. Today, traditional Kente cloth is the national costume of Ghana, worn on special occasions, and the fine art of weaving Kente cloth is still passed down from one generation to the next.

MAKING THE CONNECTION

- In the example of Kente cloth shown here, how has the weaver achieved balance? How would you describe the pattern the artist used?
- If you could design a unique cloth pattern for yourself, what special meaning would you want it to have? When would you want to wear it?

INTERNET ACTIVITY

Visit Glencoe's Fine Arts Web Site for students at:

http://www.glencoe.com/sec/art/students

INTERNET ACTIVITY

On-Line and Multimedia Resources   Visit the *Teacher Resources* area to find lists of helpful *On-Line and Multimedia Art Resources.* Here you can click on World Wide Web links to find out about art media and reference materials, image libraries, and art history resources. Locate distributors of computer art software, art-related CD-ROMS, and art media and supplies you can use in your art classroom. You may even have your own favorite resources that you would like to add to our listings. Simply click on the *Contact Us* button to send us information about resources you think would be useful to other art teachers. We welcome your feedback on this sand other resources of our site. Find us at **http://www.glencoe. com/sec/art**

OBJECTIVES

After completing the feature, students will be able to:
- Describe the characteristics of Kente cloth.
- Understand the cultural importance of Kente cloth and its weavers.

Teaching the Connection

- Have students read the feature on this page.
- Ask volunteers to share what they know about Ghana and the Ashanti weavers of Kente cloth. Why were the weavers of Kente so highly regarded? *(The cloth was worn for special events and so was highly valued. As a result, the weavers were well respected.)* What looms did the weavers use? *(The Kente weavers used a loom that could be folded up and carried. That way the weavers could move around and serve many members of the ruling class.)* How would you describe the Kente cloth shown here? *(Answers will vary. It is colorful, unified, detailed, calm.)*
- Tell students that the Ashanti are the largest and most powerful ethnic group in Ghana. Today, Ashanti weavers are famous for their art and craft in producing Kente cloth.

Answers to Making the Connection

- Possible answer: Balance is achieved through the pattern of vertical rows and the borders at the edges. The pattern is simple and repetitive, yet intricate in its detail.
- Responses will vary.

REVIEW

 BUILDING VOCABULARY

Number a sheet of paper from 1 to 5. After each number, write the term from the list that best matches each description below.

abstract work	papier-mâché
face mask	shoulder masks
headpieces	

1. A work in which the artist uses a recognizable subject but portrays it in an unrealistic manner.
2. A mask worn to hide the identity of the wearer.
3. Masks carved of wood and worn on the head like a cap.
4. Large, carved masks made to rest on the shoulders of the wearer.
5. A sculpting technique using newspaper and liquid paste.

 REVIEWING ART FACTS

Number a sheet of paper from 6 to 13. Answer each question in a complete sentence.

6. When did Portuguese explorers first come to Africa?
7. What is the favored medium among African tribal sculptors?
8. As a result of choosing this medium, what form did the art work often take?

9. Which African tribe created the remarkable bronze sculptures that arrived in Europe in the 1800s?
10. What three kinds of masks were created by African artists?
11. Name two ceremonies in which face masks were used. In what ceremonies were Bambara headpieces used?
12. What mysterious being did the Bambara credit with having taught them about planting?
13. Why did rituals calling for shoulder masks require strong tribe members?

 THINKING ABOUT ART

On a sheet of paper, answer each question in a sentence or two.

1. **Extend.** You read in this chapter that the antelope has a special meaning among the Bambara of Africa. In what other cultures that you read about were animals important?
2. **Analyze.** Which of the works in this chapter do you find the most stylized? The least stylized? Explain your answers.
3. **Compare and contrast.** Look back at the works in Figures 9–3 and 9–12. Both were created by artists of the Senufo tribe. Make a list of the similarities and differences between the two objects.

MAKING ART CONNECTIONS

1. **Social Studies.** You read in this chapter that the African continent provides natural resources from varied geographic regions. Look up Africa in an encyclopedia or atlas. Learn what you can about the regions and what types of natural resources artists might use to create their works.

2. **Science.** Artists all over Africa were able to choose from a large variety of wildlife for inspiration. List some animal forms unique to the continent of Africa. Choose an animal that interests you and research its habitat and lifestyle. Write a one-page report on your animal. Comment on its traits and how those traits might be admired by an artist and represented in an art work.

■ **Building Vocabulary**
1. abstract work
2. face mask
3. headpieces
4. shoulder masks
5. papier-mâché

■ **Reviewing Art Facts**
6. Portuguese explorers came to Africa in the late 1400s.
7. Wood was the favorite medium of African tribal sculptors.
8. The form of the log from which the work of art was carved.
9. The Benin tribe created the bronze sculptures.
10. African artists created face masks, headpieces, and shoulder masks.
11. Face masks were used to ensure a good harvest and to protect the tribe from the unknown forces of nature. Bambara headpieces were used in a ritual when a new field was prepared for planting.
12. The Bambara credited a mysterious being Tyi Wara with having taught them about planting.
13. Shoulder masks weighed up to 75 pounds.

THINKING ABOUT ART

1. Answers can include the cultures in India, Egypt, Mesoamerica, Andes, and the prehistoric cave dwellers.
2. Answers will vary, but students can include chapter opening (Epa Cult Mask) and Figure 9-4 (Benin Bronze) as least stylized and Figure 9-9 (Mali wood headpieces) and Figure 9-10 (Baga headdress)

among the most stylized. Their answers should indicate they know what stylized and realistic mean.
3. Similarities: stylized figures, made of wood, and defined features. Differences: Figure 9-3 is a statue and Figure 9-12 is a helmet mask.

Art of the Middle Ages

(pages 144–159)

Resources

- 10-10 Chapter Test, TRB page 221
- Transparency CC-10, *Chasse of Saint Thomas Becket* (French)
- Transparency 10, *Enthroned Madonna and Child* (Byzantine)
- Fine Art Print 10, *Cover of the Lindau Gospels*

Music
While studying this chapter, use Performing Arts Handbook page 326 to help students experience the beauty of a musical form from the Middle Ages in traditional Gregorian Chant by Paul Salamunovich.

NATIONAL STANDARDS

This chapter addresses the following National Standards for the Visual Arts:

1. (a, b)   **4.** (a, b, c)
2. (b)   **5.** (a, b, c)
3. (a, b)   **6.** (a, b)

▲ This illumination is from a French book of Psalms, or sacred poems. The simple pictures teach a story from the Bible. Does the arrangement of scenes remind you of a stained glass panel?

Scenes from the Life of King David. Psalter, Paris. c. 1250–1260. Ink, tempera colors and gold leaf on vellum, bound between pasteboard covered with deep violet morocco. 19.2 x 13.4 cm (7⁹⁄₁₆ x 5¼"). J. Paul Getty Museum, Malibu, California. Ms. Ludwig VIII 4.

144

FEATURED ART

Scenes from the Life of King David	CASTLES	CATHEDRALS AND CHURCHES
Stained Glass Panel	La Calahorra	Anersall
The Flight Into Egypt, Giotto	Penafiel	Avila
The Tablets of the Law	Rio Elsa	Chartres
	Walled City of Carcassone	Santa Maria la Real
		Notre Dame

CHAPTER 10

Art of the Middle Ages

The period of history beginning about A.D. 500 is known by several names. One is the Middle Ages. Another is Medieval (mid-**ee**-vuhl) times. This period has been referred to as the Dark Ages but, in the world of art, these times were anything but dark. Sculpture and painting were used to express ideas of society and religion. Architecture found expression in magnificent churches. Stained glass and sculpture added splendor to these cathedrals. Illuminations like the one on the facing page decorated books of the period. In this chapter you will learn about the art of this period.

PORTFOLIO IDEAS

From time to time, you may want to review the contents of your portfolio. If you have been using it to hold all of your notes, sketches, and finished art works, you may decide to add or take out some of your entries. You may decide to keep an art work because it represents your best example of using the elements and principles of art. You may keep other entries because they show growth in a specific medium. You may want to keep your Gothic Gargoyle work (page **156**) because it demonstrates a process—working with clay.

OBJECTIVES

After completing this chapter, you will be able to:
- Tell how life in Romanesque times affected the art of the period.
- Identify the role of Romanesque sculpture and illuminations.
- Describe the contributions of Gothic artists to architecture and painting.
- Work with Romanesque and Gothic styles of architecture and sculpture.

WORDS YOU WILL LEARN

buttress
castles
cathedral
fresco
gargoyle
illuminations
pointed arch
stained glass

DEVELOPING A PORTFOLIO

Art of the Romanesque Period

• • • • • • • • • • • • • • •
FOCUS

☑ OBJECTIVES

After completing this lesson, students will be able to:

• Tell how life in Romanesque times affected the art.
• Identify the role of Romanesque architecture, sculpture, and illuminations.
• Draw illustrations in the style of illuminations.

☑ SUPPLIES

• Sheets of sketch paper, colored pencils.
• Sheets of drawing paper, pencils, oil pastels.
• Reproductions of illuminated manuscripts featuring decorated capital letters, sheets of white paper, pencils, tempera paint, brushes.

Resources

◼ 10-1 *Charlemagne and the Manuscript*, TRB page 203 (aesthetics)
◼ 10-2 *Tapestry Details*, TRB page 205 (reproducible master)
◼ 10-3 *Chart of Lettering*, TRB page 206 (reproducible master)
◼ 10-4 *Learn Calligraphy*, TRB page 207 (studio)

History teaches many meaningful lessons. One is that even the most powerful empires, in time, weaken and crumble. Rome was no exception. The Roman Empire fell to invading armies around A.D. 400. Both the style of life as well as the art of this period were affected by these historical changes. Temples and palaces were torn down and the stone was used to build fortresses to keep out the invaders.

Shortly before Rome fell, the practice of Christianity became widely accepted. The Catholic Church stood as the single most important influence in western Europe. Its influence on people and events was widespread throughout the span of history now called the Middle Ages. The art and architecture at the end of the Middle Ages is divided into two periods: the Romanesque (roh-muh-**nesk**), from around 1050 to around 1150, and the Gothic from around 1150 to about 1500. In this lesson you will learn about the art of the Romanesque period.

LIFE IN ROMANESQUE TIMES

Warfare was common during the Romanesque period. Since land was the main source of power and wealth, kings and rich landowners were forever fighting among themselves to protect or add to their holdings.

Architecture

To protect themselves, the rich lived in **castles**, or *fortlike dwellings with high walls and towers*. These castles were often protected further by a moat and drawbridge. One of these structures is pictured in Figure 10–1. Notice how sturdy the castle looks even now, some 600 to 700 years after it was built. The structure has few windows. Why do you suppose this is so? Do you think the builder was more interested in constructing a structure that was comfortable or well fortified?

▶ Figure 10–1 Early castles like this were massive and strong. They were also dark and drafty. Instead of windows, narrow slits were cut into the walls. These helped those inside detect, and attack, intruders.

La Calahorra Castle. Andalucia, Spain. 16th Century.

— *more about* • • • —

Post and Lintel   The post and lintel structure of windows and doors has been used since the earliest buildings were erected. The Egyptians used post and lintel structures in tombs; the ancient Greeks and Romans used them in temples; Europeans used them in churches. Today the post and lintel structure is still the most common way of building an opening without losing structural strength or stability. There is, however, a problem with post and lintel structures: the stress on the lintel can cause it to crack. This problem was solved by Roman and European architects, as well as Eastern architects, through the use of arches. The arch allows the weight of a building to be distributed differently, and so is inherently stronger. Arches have often survived in buildings after the walls have fallen down.

▲ Figure 10–2   High, thick walls and towers protected those living in this city. Only a few well-protected gates allowed people to enter or leave the city.

Walled City of Carcassone. c. 1100. Southern France.

The leaders and rulers lived in the castles during the Middle Ages. Communities of people living outside the castles were left open to attack. For this reason, whole towns and cities were surrounded by walls for protection. At first these walls were made of wood. In the 1100s and 1200s stone began to be used. One of the most impressive of these walled cities is shown in Figure 10–2. Today this city looks much as it did during the Middle Ages.

During this time the Catholic Church also had a great influence on the architecture. As early as A.D. 400 churches were springing up in towns and villages across Europe. All, like the one shown in Figures 10–3 and 10–4, were low and thick-walled. Windows, which might weaken the walls and bring the heavy stone roof crashing down, were avoided. As a result, these churches were dark and somber inside.

▲ Figure 10–3 (Left) and Figure 10–4 (Right)   Thick walls and lack of windows made these churches look like forts, or fortresses. This may be the origin of the phrase "fortresses of God," used to describe these churches.

Anersall-Romanesque Church.

■ **TEACH**

■ **Motivator**

Ask students to imagine what life in a castle might have been like: What would your castle have looked like from the outside? What kinds of achievements would have kept you busy if you had lived in a castle? Let students think about these questions and then make sketches to show their ideas about castles and the lives of the people who lived in them. Then have them compare their sketches to the castle shown in Figure 10-1: How do their sketches compare to the massive, strongly-built castle shown in the photograph?

■ **Art Criticism**

Guide students in discussing the sculptures on the churches and cathedrals shown in this lesson. Have them examine the pictures and then discuss these questions: What makes these sculptures part of the church building? What makes these sculptures stand out as individual works? How do you judge these works in terms of subject, composition, and content?

■ **Cultural Diversity**

In what other parts of the world did people build castles? Why did these people build castles? What did their castles look like? Ask volunteers to read about castles of other cultures, such as those built in Japan (during the Momoyama period) and those built in ancient Egypt. Let these volunteers give a brief presentation to the rest of the class.

CURRICULUM *CONNECTIONS*

Social Studies   Combat during the Middle Ages took great strength and endurance. Knights on horseback wore over 50 pounds of armor. Their helmets alone weighed up to 11 pounds. They wore all this while charging each other at full gallop holding a horizontal lance measuring half the length of a telephone pole! Have students work in small groups and research the different types of armor and weapons used during the Middle Ages and present their findings to the class. Encourage them to use photocopies of pictures or make their own drawings to illustrate their presentation.

Sparking
Creativity

Want students to think creatively about color and shape as they prepare to make illuminated designs? Suggest this: Put a spoonful of cooking oil and a few drops of food coloring in a shallow dish of water. Use a stick to move the oil and watch the shapes it takes. Try putting small quantities of oil, water, and color in a sealed plastic bag and place it on an overhead projector. Gently move the bag and watch the projected shapes change. Students may incorporate shapes and colors from this exercise into backgrounds of their illuminations.

■ Cooperative
Learning

Have students work in groups to investigate Hindu medieval art, which was created in India around the time of the Romanesque period in Europe. Encourage students to find photographs of the Hindu temples and bronze sculptures created by Indian artists. Then have students compare the art works of the period being created in India and in Europe. Have them prepare displays showing how the subjects of the works are alike and how they are different. What similarities can you find in the ideas or feelings these works are intended to create? What differences can you identify?

Sculpture

The Church was also responsible for the development of sculpture during this period. Since most people were unable to read, sculpture was used to teach religion. The exteriors of churches were covered with reliefs and statues like the ones in Figure 10–5. These sculptures portrayed the same Bible teachings that were taught verbally. Look closely at Figure 10–5. Notice the detailed figures shown in the half-round space above the doorway.

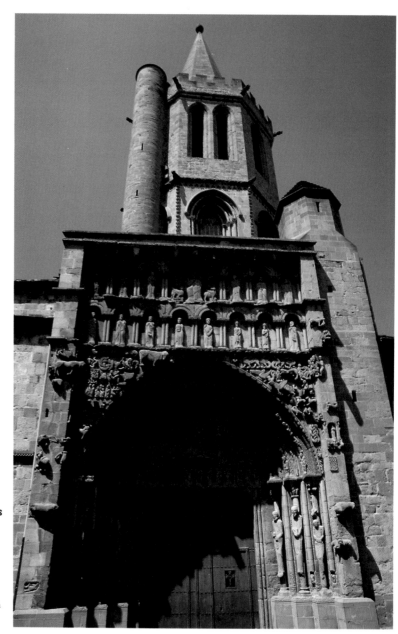

▶ Figure 10–5 Can you see from this example why churches built in the Middle Ages were called "bibles in stone?" The many sculptures on the outside of these churches were meant to teach people who could not read about the Christian faith.

Santa Maria la Real Church. 13th Century. Sanguesa, near Pamplona, Spain.

148   Lesson 1   *Art of the Romanesque Period*

Verbal/Linguistic Learners   As students study the art of the Middle Ages, read portraits from Chaucer's *Prologue to The Canterbury Tales* aloud to them. Discuss the details provided by Chaucer on the characters and the lifestyles of the period to help students visualize artists working during this time.

Interpersonal Experience   Have students work together to identify some of the many technological improvements that date from the Middle Ages. Some possibilities are: trousers, barrels, skis, horseshoes, the water mill. Have groups create advertisements for these innovations and display them in the classroom.

Painting

In addition to being portrayed in sculpture, the teachings of the Church were spread through hand-lettered books, which contained illuminations. **Illuminations** are *hand-painted book illustrations.* For nearly a thousand years, these illustrations were the most important paintings created in Europe. Figure 10–6 shows an illumination from a prayer book. The work shows a scene from the life of Moses. In the illustration, Moses is looking up to receive the word of the Lord. His upturned face and outstretched arms suggest his willingness to accept the teachings for his people. Would you describe the work as realistic? What do you suppose was the artist's main goal in creating this illumination? Which aesthetic view would you use if someone asked you to judge this work?

▲ Figure 10–6   The story in this work was told simply so it could be understood by anyone who knew the Bible. The picture does not look real because the story was more important to the artist than was a lifelike subject.

Illuminated Page of the Bible. *The Tablets of the Law.* 13th Century. Psalter of Ingeburg of Denmark. France.

Illustrating a Story

The story illustrated in Figure 10–6 is from the Old Testament. Notice how the artist in portraying this story includes only those details needed in its telling.

Working in pencil in your sketchbook, draw an illustration of a scene from a favorite story from literature or a movie. As in the illumination, leave out all unnecessary details. Keep your figures flat, and outline them with a variety of thick and thin black lines. Add bright colors to your picture with oil pastels. Share your finished work with classmates. See if anyone can identify the scene or story you have illustrated.

PORTFOLIO

Critique your illumination by explaining how you combined the elements and principles of art to create your painting. Include your critique with your painting in your portfolio.

✔ CHECK YOUR UNDERSTANDING

1. In what century did Rome fall? What became the single most important influence in western Europe after its collapse?
2. When did the Romanesque period begin? When did it end?
3. What fact of life in the Middle Ages led to the building of castles?
4. Why were Romanesque churches thick-walled and without windows?
5. What was the purpose of sculpture during the Romanesque period? What other art form had the same purpose?

Illustrating a Story

Encourage students to use their own initials as part of this activity. Develop a class project and paint the illumination on a larger scale, with everyone adding a section. Add touches of gold leaf paint to make the work resemble real illuminations.

• • • • • • • • • • • • • • •

ASSESS

■ **Self-Assessment**

Have students complete the review questions on this page. Answers are provided below.

■ **Reteaching**

Work with small groups of students to review the most important features of Romanesque architecture, sculpture, and painting. Then point out that the word *Romanesque* originally meant "in the Roman manner." Help group members discuss this meaning: Why might the word have been used? To what extent is it descriptive of Romanesque art and architecture?

■ **Enrichment**

Remind students that, in many parts of Europe, buildings from the Middle Ages are still standing—and in use. Ask students to work with partners or in small groups to explore European cities where Romanesque castles, churches, and walls can be seen. Suggest that they use travel books as well as art books and history books in their research. Then have each pair or group describe a short tour through Romanesque Europe.

• • • • • • • • • • • • • • •

CLOSE

Ask students to explain the reasons castles were constructed during the Middle Ages.

Answers to ✔ CHECK YOUR UNDERSTANDING

1. Rome fell around the fifth century. The church then became the governing force in Western Europe.
2. The Romanesque period began in 1050 and ended about 1150.
3. Warfare to gain land led kings and rich landowners to protect themselves by building fort-like dwellings with high walls and towers.
4. Roman churches were thick-walled and windowless because windows would have weakened the walls.
5. Since most people were unable to read, sculpture was used to teach religion. Hand-lettered books containing many illustrations served the same purpose.

• • • • • • • • • • • • • •

FOCUS

☑ OBJECTIVES

After completing this section students will be able to:

• Design their own Romanesque castles and create reliefs of them.

• Describe, analyze, interpret, and judge their own castle reliefs.

☑ SUPPLIES

• Pencils; notepads; sheets of sketch paper; sheets of cardboard, 12 x 18 inches (30 x 45 cm); scissors; tape; heavy wrapped cord; white glue; sheets of aluminum foil, 16 x 20 inches (41 x 50 cm).

• Cardboard tubes (such as those inside rolls of wrapping paper), self-hardening clay (no firing needed), white glue, scissors, sheets of aluminum foil.

Resource

- 10-5 *Sculpture—From Romanesque to Gothic,* TRB page 211 (art history)

• • • • • • • • • • • • • •

TEACH

■ Motivator

Let students begin by discussing what they know about Romanesque castles. Ask groups of students to discuss their ideas; together, group members should list at least eight adjectives that describe Romanesque castles. Also have them list at least eight specific features of castles.

150

 LESSON 2

Romanesque Castle Relief

Castles, as you have read, were common in Europe during the Romanesque period. Two more of these structures are shown in Figures 10–7 and 10–8. The ridged geometric pattern along the top of each is called a battlement. Can you guess what battlements were used for? Can you identify any other features in these castles?

WHAT YOU WILL LEARN

You will design a castle of your own. You will create a relief of your castle using heavy cord and aluminum foil. Focus on the use of line to highlight the different features of your castle. Use the element of line to add harmony to your design. (See Figure 10–9.) Your castle should look strong and safe.

WHAT YOU WILL NEED

• Pencil and notepad
• Sheets of sketch paper
• Sheet of cardboard, 12 x 18 inches (30 x 45 cm)
• Scissors, tape, and heavy wrapping cord
• White glue
• Sheet of aluminum foil, 16 x 20 inches (41 x 50 cm)

WHAT YOU WILL DO

1. Begin by studying the castles in Figures 10–1 (on page **146**), 10–7, and 10–8. On your notepad, list the features common to these buildings. One common feature

▲ **Figure 10–7** How many features can you find that helped make these castles safe?

Castle at Penafiel, Spain. c. 14th Century.

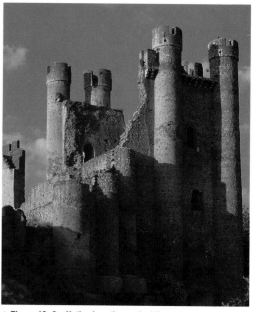

▲ **Figure 10–8** Notice how the vertical lines give a sense of strength to this structure.

Gothic Castle on Rio Esla, south of Leon, Spain. 15th Century.

---

more about • • •

Castles The first European castles were probably erected during the ninth century; the first stone castles were built during the eleventh century. The thick, sturdy walls served to keep the people within the castle safe— and to notify outsiders that here was the home of a wealthy, powerful noble. A castle was usually built on a hillside or an artificial mound and surrounded by high, turreted walls. These walls had to be thick enough to withstand attack and, at the top, wide enough to provide space for those defending the castle. Within the walls were residence and support buildings, providing housing for the noble family and all their retainers.

in the castles shown here, for example, is the battlement. On a sheet of sketch paper, make several drawings of an original castle. Show the building as it appears from the front. Draw all the features included on your list.

2. Choose your best design. Make a line drawing of this sketch on the sheet of cardboard. Fill the surface of the cardboard with your drawing.

3. Glue cord along the lines in your drawing. To do this, squeeze a thin band of glue along the line. Press the piece of cord into place. Repeat this process until all lines are covered.

4. Small pieces of cardboard can be glued to your castle design to give it more detail.

5. Cover your design with the sheet of aluminum foil. Wrap the foil around the ends and sides of the cardboard. Using tape, fasten the foil to the cardboard along the back.

6. Using the end of your pencil, carefully but firmly press down on the foil along the cord lines and around the cardboard shapes. Display your finished work to your class. Note ways in which your castle relief is similar to and different from those of other class artists.

EXAMINING YOUR WORK

● **Describe**   Point out the features of your castle listed on your notepad.
● **Analyze**   Tell whether the use of line adds harmony to your design.
● **Interpret**   State whether your castle communicates the ideas of strength and safety. Tell whether the castle shown would succeed in protecting those inside from attackers.
● **Judge**   Tell whether you feel your work succeeds. Explain your answer.

▲ **Figure 10–9   Student work. Castle relief.**

Try This! STUDIO OPTIONS

■ Spray your castle with black paint. When the paint is dry, lightly rub the relief with steel wool. This will remove the paint from the raised surfaces, creating an interesting effect.

■ Create another castle relief, this time out of a continuous piece of 14-gauge steel wire. Show each feature in your castle by bending and twisting the wire until it has the right shape.

Lesson 2   *Romanesque Castle Relief*   **151**

SAFETY TIP ⚠

Wire Frames   Before students begin to form a wire relief for the Studio Option, they should cover both ends of the wire with masking tape or electrician's tape. While working, they should wear protective goggles. Both of these tips will help prevent students from scratching or poking their eyes and skin while they work.

Spray Paints   If students choose to use spray paints on their finished castle reliefs, be sure to take safety precautions. Remember to paint in a well-ventilated space or have students spray their projects outdoors. Prior to using spray paints, determine whether any students suffer from asthma or other respiratory problems, and arrange for these students to use brushes when painting surfaces.

■ Vocabulary
Write the word *battlement* on the board. Then have students look at the castles shown in Figures 10-7 and 10-8 and identify the battlements.

■ Art Criticism
Guide students in discussing the two castles shown in Figures 10-7 and 10-8. Remind students that works of architecture are considered both fine art and applied (functional) art. Ask: Are these castles successful works of fine art? Why or why not? Are they successful works of applied art? Why or why not?

● ● ● ● ● ● ● ● ● ● ●
ASSESS

■ Self-Assessment
Have students use Examining Your Work on this page to evaluate their castle reliefs created in this Studio Lesson. Responses may be written or oral.

■ Reteaching
Work with small groups of students to examine and discuss their castles reliefs: Which aspect of each work is most important in suggesting a Romanesque sculpture? Next, guide members in discussing other media they might use in creating castle reliefs of models of castles. Encourage a variety of ideas. Ask: Which media would be best adapted to creating a Romanesque work? Why?

■ Enrichment
Let students work in groups to create stories set in castles. One group should begin the story by establishing a setting. Another group will create a main character. The next group will work on an event. Another group may illuminate or illustrate scenes. Arrange for the story to be acted out or presented.

● ● ● ● ● ● ● ● ● ● ●
CLOSE
Ask students to describe important features of castles.

☑ OBJECTIVES

After completing this lesson, students will be able to:

- Describe the contributions of Gothic artists to architecture and painting.
- Explain the importance of the pointed arch and the flying buttress.
- Make paper models of rose windows.

☑ SUPPLIES

- Slides or display-size photographs of a Romanesque church and a Gothic church.
- Sheets of sketch paper; pencils; black construction paper; tissue paper in various colors; white glue.
- Small cardboard boxes; scissors; tempera paints; brushes.

Resources

- 10-6 *Life of an Artist in the Middle Ages*, TRB page 214 (appreciating cultural diversity)
- 10-7 *Architectural Styles*, TRB page 216 (reproducible master)
- 10-8 *Giotto*, TRB page 217 (artist profile)
- 10-9 *Playing Card Designs*, TRB page 218 (cooperative learning)

152

LESSON 3

Art of the Gothic Period

Throughout history an important part of creating art has been solving problems. A key problem facing artists of the Romanesque period was mentioned in Lesson 1. This was figuring out how to build walls that could both contain windows and support a heavy roof.

Romanesque builders never solved this problem. Architects of the Gothic period did, however. In this lesson you will learn about this and other contributions of artists of the Gothic period.

▲ **Figure 10–10** The two towers seen from the front of this cathedral are from different periods. The one on the left was begun in 1135 and completed in the 16th century. The tower on the right dates from about 1145.

Facade, Chartres Cathedral. France. Vanni/Art Resource, New York.

152   Lesson 3   *Art of the Gothic Period*

LIFE IN GOTHIC TIMES

Toward the end of the Romanesque period, Europe began to change. With the growth of trade, money replaced land as the measure of wealth. Castles became unpopular as cities grew and thrived. Many of these cities developed into large population centers by the year 1200.

The Church continued to have a great effect on the people as well as on the art of these new European cities.

Architecture

One structure that exists as a great contribution of Gothic artists is the cathedral. A **cathedral** is *a large, complex church created as a seat of office for a bishop.* The bishop would have several parishes, or congregations, under his leadership. An example of one of these huge structures is shown in Figure 10–10. Notice the openness of this building. Note the rose window design. Notice how the two towers seem to soar upward. Magnificent works of architecture like these were possible thanks to two improvements made by Gothic French architects. These were:

- **The pointed arch.** The **pointed arch** is *a curved arrangement of stones reaching up to a central point.* Gothic architects found that the vertical shape of this design feature allowed it to carry weight downward. Examine the inside view of a cathedral in Figure 10–11 and find the pointed arches.
- **The flying buttress.** A **buttress** (buh-truhs) is *a brace or support placed on the outside of a building.* Such supports are said to "fly" when they arch out over other parts of a building. In Gothic cathedrals, flying buttresses took on some of the load of the heavy roof. Which structures in Figure 10–12 are flying buttresses?

◀ **Figure 10–11** The weight of the roof is carried by the pointed arches and transferred to columns inside the building. Can you find the pointed arches in this church?

Avila Cathedral. Avila, Spain.

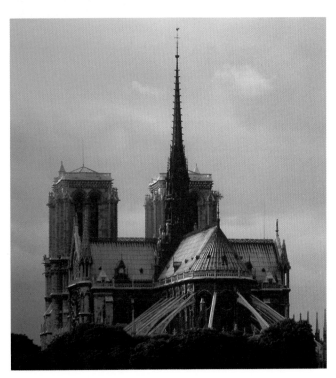

▶ **Figure 10–12** Flying buttresses like these helped make thick solid walls unnecessary in Gothic cathedrals. What replaced these walls?

Notre Dame Cathedral. Paris, France.

Lesson 3 *Art of the Gothic Period* **153**

■ **Motivator**

Begin by showing students a slide or large photograph of a Romanesque church. Ask students to brainstorm a list of words that describe the structure and the feelings it evokes. Record all their ideas on the board. Then show a slide or photograph of a Gothic church. Again, let students brainstorm a list of descriptive words, and record all their suggestions. After both lists are complete, let students identify the first church as an example of Romanesque architecture; identify the second as an example of Gothic architecture, about which they will learn more in this lesson. Then let students examine the two photographs and think about the two lists; help them discuss basic differences between the two styles of architecture.

■ **Aesthetics**

Have students examine and discuss Giotto's fresco shown in Figure 10-14: What is the subject of this painting? What do you think Giotto intended to communicate with this art work? What message or mood does the work communicate to you? How do you think the subject, composition, and content of this work might have been different if Giotto had used a different medium, such as stained glass or oil paints? Then ask students to compare this fresco with the illumination in Figure 10-6, page 149.

■ **Art Criticism**

Guide students in discussing the stained glass window shown in Figure 10-13: How do you imagine the colors in this work change in sunlight? What do the colors of glass contribute to the message of the work? What do you think the artist's purpose was in creating this work? When the stained glass window was designed and created, was it an object of fine or applied art? Why? Which do you think it is now? Why?

RESOURCES BEYOND THE CLASSROOM

Illustrated Books Children's books, such as picture books and certain editions of children's classics, provide good examples of the art of manuscript illumination. Just as a medieval scribe would decorate the pages of a manuscript with ornate letters and pictures that related to the text, children's book illustrators also capture scenes from the story in their paintings. Exemplary children's book illustrations convey a sense of character, setting, action, and time. Although their choice of subject matter, media, and other elements might be restricted, children's book artists often create masterpieces of art. Good places to start are editions of *Aesop's Fables* and *Grimm's Fairy Tales,* as well as the Caldecott Medal books. Children's libraries can assist you with appropriate titles.

■ Art History

Ask groups of volunteers to report on some of the literature written during this period of European history. For example, groups might choose to learn about a work such as the *Song of Roland* or the *Romance of the Rose* or about a writer such as Giovanni Boccaccio, Dante, Geoffery Chaucer, Sir Thomas Mallory, or Francis Villon. Have the members of each group summarize what they have learned for the rest of the class. Then help students discuss the relationship between the art and the literature of the Middle Ages.

■ Cooperative Learning

Have students work in groups to read about the various styles of round and pointed arches. Then have group members cut models of different arches into the sides of a small cardboard box. Ask students to paint the box a single color and then to paint on details that emphasize the unique features of each cut arch.

■ Cultural Diversity

What kinds of art and architecture were being created in Mesoamerica, in the Andes, in Japan, and in China, during the approximate period of Gothic art in Europe? Ask four groups of students to research these questions and to report their answers to the rest of the class. Then guide the class in discussing similarities and differences among the works of various cultures.

Crafts

The pointed arch and flying buttress did away with the need for solid walls. They also opened up the possibility of having many windows in churches and cathedrals. This created yet another outlet for expression by artists and craftspeople of the day. Brilliantly colored stained glass windows like those in Figure 10–13 began gracing the walls of cathedrals. **Stained glass** is made of *colored glass pieces held in place with lead strips*. These windows filled the cathedrals with softly tinted light. The pictures in these windows, focusing on religious figures and events, also helped teach the Bible. Do you recall which art forms of the Romanesque period showed Bible stories?

▲ Figure 10–13 The lead strips appear as dark lines in the finished design. Do you feel these lines add to or take away from the beauty of the work? Explain your answer.

Stained Glass from Cathedral of Leon — *Head of a Prophet.* Leon, Spain.

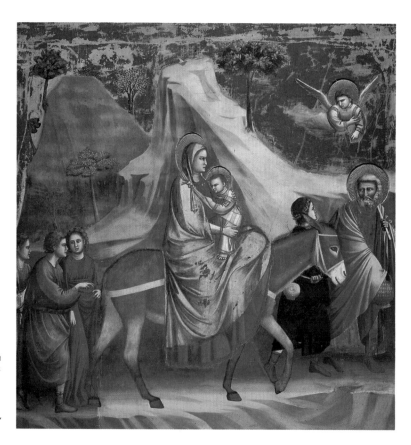

► Figure 10–14 What has the artist done to make the people in this work look lifelike? What has he done to emphasize the woman, child, and donkey?

Giotto. *The Flight Into Egypt.* c. 1305–06. Fresco. Arena Chapel, Padua, Italy.

CURRICULUM CONNECTIONS

Social Studies Tell students that in the Middle ages almost all skilled trades were represented by guilds, which are similar to the trade unions of today. These guilds were often quite wealthy and powerful. Individuals who were skilled in a craft, and those people who worked in many of the arts were often apprenticed with members of a guild and then required to join the guild once they perfected their skills. Discuss with students the details of apprenticeship. You might have interested students make a comparison by researching contemporary trade unions and finding the similarities and differences between the two types of organized labor.

Painting

The Gothic style of building cathedrals never fully caught on in Italy. There churches continued to be built in the Romanesque manner with large, unbroken walls. Instead of stained glass, religious decoration was added with a form of painting known as fresco. **Fresco** (fres-koh) is *a painting created when pigment is applied to a section of wall spread with fresh plaster. Fresco is the Italian word for* "fresh." This technique required the artist to work quickly before the plaster dried. The pigment was absorbed and the painting was permanently preserved.

The work in Figure 10–14 is a fresco. It is one of a series found on the walls of a chapel in Padua, Italy. All were done by a gifted artist named Giotto (**jah**-toh). Take a moment to study this work. In creating this and other frescoes, Giotto wished to do more than tell Bible stories. His goal was to make the people in his pictures come alive. His genius was such that a century would pass before an artist of equal skill would appear.

▲ Figure 10–15   Student work. Rose window design.

Rose Window Cutout

Make a pencil sketch in your sketchbook based on a rose window design. Rose windows sometimes appear on the front of a church or cathedral. They are round, so your design should have either symmetrical or radial balance. Leave out all unnecessary details in your work. Transfer your sketch to a sheet of black construction paper. Go over all the lines with white chalk. Make some of the lines thicker than others.

Using scissors, cut out all the spaces between the chalk lines. Cut out patches of tissue paper in the shape of the spaces, only slightly larger. Pick different colors of paper for different spaces. Using white glue, attach these patches to the construction paper along their edges. You may want to use two thicknesses of black construction paper and sandwich pieces of tissue paper between the outlined areas. Turn your work over to reveal your own stained glass window. (See Figure 10–15.)

 P O R T F O L I O

Write a short paragraph explaining how you chose colors, shapes, and use of space. Keep your description and your stained glass window together in your portfolio.

✔ CHECK YOUR UNDERSTANDING

1. What problem faced architects of the Romanesque period? What two improvements allowed Gothic architects to solve this problem?
2. What is a cathedral?
3. What is stained glass? For what purpose did Gothic artists use stained glass?
4. What is a fresco? How were frescoes created?
5. Who was Giotto? What was his goal?

Lesson 3   *Art of the Gothic Period*   **155**

Rose Window Cutout

Review with students the principle of balance and what they should do to achieve symmetrical or radial balance. Have them look back to page 9 for explanations.

A S S E S S

■ Self-Assessment

Have students complete the review questions on this page. Answers are provided below.

■ Reteaching

Display the rose windows created in the Studio Activity. Ask students: In what ways is the rose window an important feature of Gothic art? Were rose windows created in earlier periods? Why or why not? Are rose windows commonly created now?

■ Enrichment

Ask students to do further reading about life during the Gothic period. Have them work in small groups to read and then share and discuss information. After completing their research, have students assume specific identities—a merchant in a busy town or a student at one of the relatively new universities, for example. Have students hold an empty picture frame in front of their faces as they relate the story, posing behind the frame.

C L O S E

Have each student write responses to these questions: Which development in Gothic art and architecture do you find more interesting? What do you find interesting about the development?

Answers to ✔ CHECK YOUR UNDERSTANDING

1. The problem facing Romanesque architects was how to build walls that could both contain windows and support a heavy roof. Gothic French architects began to use the pointed arch and the flying buttress.
2. A cathedral is a large, complex church created as a seat of office for a bishop.
3. Stained glass art is colored pieces of glass held in place with lead strips. Stained glass windows illustrated with religious figures and events helped teach the Bible.
4. A fresco is a painting created when pigment is applied to a section of wall spread with fresh plaster.
5. Giotto was a gifted fresco artist. His goal was to create paintings that made the people look lifelike.

• • • • • • • • • • • • • • • •

FOCUS

☑ OBJECTIVES

After completing this lesson, students will be able to:

• Use clay to model and carve gargoyles that have imaginary proportions.

• Describe, analyze, interpret, and judge their own gargoyles.

☑ SUPPLIES

• Sheets of sketch paper, pencils.

• Pencils; sketchbooks, slips of paper; small boxes; clay; clay modeling tools; burlap or other cloth cut into squares, 14 x 14 inches (36 x 36 cm); glaze in several colors.

• • • • • • • • • • • • • • • •

TEACH

■ Motivator

Before students turn to the lesson, ask them to imagine and then sketch pictures of fantastic creatures. Encourage students to be as imaginative as possible. Let students share and discuss their work: Which creatures are most fantastic? What mood does each sketch create? Then have students look at the gargoyles in Figure 10-16: What distinguishes these gargoyles as fantastic creatures? What mood do they create? How are the creatures in their sketches similar to these gargoyles?

156

Making a Gothic Gargoyle

If you look up to the highest point of a Gothic cathedral, you will see creatures known as gargoyles. Look at Figure 10–16. A **gargoyle** is *a projecting ornament on a building carved in the shape of a fantastic animal or grotesque creature.* Gargoyles were made of carved stone and metal. They were meant to look like spirits fleeing, or being driven, from the holy building. However, these strange creations actually served a very practical purpose. They are really rain spouts that carried rainwater from the roof of the cathedral.

Creating these fascinating, sometimes frightening creatures required a great deal of imagination. In this lesson you will have an opportunity to design a gargoyle like the ones that appeared on Gothic cathedrals. (See Figure 10–17.)

WHAT YOU WILL LEARN

You will use clay to model and carve a gargoyle that will have imaginary rather than realistic proportions. Surface patterns will be created with a variety of textures to suggest fur, hair, scales, or feathers. Your model will be a freestanding sculpture.

WHAT YOU WILL NEED

• Pencil and sketchbook
• Slips of paper and small box
• Clay and clay modeling tools
• Burlap or cloth cut into sections, 14 x 14 inches, (36 x 36 cm)

▶ **Figure 10–16** How do you suppose someone of Gothic times would have felt to look up and find these odd-looking figures overhead?

Gargoyles at Narbonne, France.

156   Lesson 4   *Making a Gothic Gargoyle*

MEETING SPECIAL NEEDS

Visually Impaired   Working with clay can be a satisfying tactile experience for students who are blind. Provide these students with models of clay figures from previous classes, or three-dimensional figures of gargoyles, before the lesson so that they might touch the shapes and feel the proportions. Remind students to work carefully as they add texture and details to their sculptures. Be sure to give them a sufficiently large amount of clay so they are able to model the features and the open mouth. You may find that putting the clay into a plastic bag first will help students to keep the clay in one piece as they work.

WHAT YOU WILL DO

1. Find examples of gargoyles in books from the library. Make a list of the animals or parts of animals used in these gargoyles.
2. On three separate slips of paper, write the name of a different animal. Place these slips of paper, along with those completed by other students, in a box.
3. Pass the box around the room. Without looking, pick out two slips.
4. Complete several pencil sketches in which you combine the animals named on your slips of paper to create a gargoyle design. Use your imagination to draw a creature unlike anything seen in real life. Add details such as hair, fur, scales, and feathers.
5. Complete a three-dimensional version of your gargoyle in clay. Begin by modeling the basic form of the gargoyle. Add details using both modeling and carving techniques.
6. Add interesting textures and surface patterns with modeling tools. These can be made to look like hair, fur, scales, feathers, or a combination of these.
7. Hollow out your model so it will dry more quickly and thoroughly. Work from the back to create a channel through the sculpture that exits through the open mouth. This channel can represent the passage through which rainwater would flow in a real gargoyle.
8. Fire your sculpture.
9. *Optional:* You may wish to add color by glazing in one or several colors. After glazing, fire the gargoyle again.

- **Describe**   Show how your gargoyle combines more than one animal. Does it have fantastic proportions?
- **Analyze**   Did you use a variety of actual textures to create an interesting surface pattern?
- **Interpret**   Does your gargoyle resemble any animal seen in real life? How does it make you feel?
- **Judge**   Does your sculpture look as though it belongs as a decoration of a Gothic cathedral?

▲ **Figure 10–17   Student work. Gargoyle.**

Try This! STUDIO OPTIONS

■ If you choose not to glaze your gargoyle, shoe polish may be applied to the fired piece and rubbed to a shine with a soft cloth.

■ Make another gargoyle, this time as a relief sculpture. Use the slab method. Trace your design onto the soft clay with a pencil. Use modeling tools to carve your picture out of the clay. Add textures to the surface of your relief.

Lesson 4   *Making a Gothic Gargoyle*   **157**

■ Vocabulary

Explain that the derivation of *gargoyle* is related to the word *gargle*. Remind students of the practical purpose of gargoyles.

■ Cultural Diversity

In what other parts of the world have sculptors created figures of fantastic creatures? Ask each student to find and share with the class at least one photograph of the figure of a fantastic creature from another culture.

● ● ● ● ● ● ● ● ● ● ● ● ● ●
ASSESS

■ Self-Assessment

Have students use Examining Your Work to evaluate their gargoyle models. Responses may be written or oral.

■ Reteaching

Let students work in small groups to review the most important features of Gothic art and architecture: How are they similar to the art and architecture of the Romanesque period? What are some of the most important differences?

■ Enrichment

Ask students to find out more about the term *Middle Ages:* What are the middle ages "in the middle of"? Who first used the name for this period? What other terms have been used to name this period?

● ● ● ● ● ● ● ● ● ● ● ● ● ●
CLOSE

Ask students to tell one thing they learned about working with clay during this lesson.

more about • • • •

Gargoyles   Tell students that, originally, a gargoyle was a plain drain pipe. The pipe was important in protecting the walls of a building from rainwater that might accumulate on the roof. During the Middle Ages, stonemasons began creating grotesque figures—usually part human and part animal—around these pipes. Gargoyles are commonly found along the roof or eaves of Gothic buildings. They served an important purpose, because the cathedrals, palaces, and other structures of the time had no gutters. They were also a popular form of decoration. Some gargoyles projected as much as 3 feet (91 cm) from the side of a building. Sometimes grotesque figures are added to buildings simply as decorations, not drain pipes. These are called *chimera*.

CONNECTIONS   *Social Studies*

What Was the Purpose of a Coat of Arms?

In ancient civilizations, symbols on emblems and flags were often used to show loyalty. In the Middle Ages, the use of symbols expanded as feudal lords in Europe put unique images on their shields and banners. These images were meant to represent them and their kinsmen. The study of the symbols used in this way is called heraldry. Such symbolic emblems are called coats of arms.

Coats of arms were commonly displayed on the shields of knights during the early 1100s to identify the knights in tournaments and military campaigns. Christian knights who fought in the Crusades relied on their coats of arms to identify one another on the battlefield. As heraldry grew, rules were established for the design and use of coats of arms, not only for individuals, but also for towns, guilds, and other groups. Some coats of arms could be inherited, but others had to be officially granted. The elements of most coats of arms are often highly stylized and exclusive to that family or group.

The main element of a coat of arms is the **shield**.

The **motto** is shown below the coat of arms.

A **crest** appears above the helmet, and a **crown** below. The shield is supported by spears.

You can see the **helmet** above the shield at the top, flanked by red plumes.

Look for the symbols that appear on this shield: the quarter moon, a checkered field called *chequy,* a tower, and an animal or bird figure.

Heraldry Shield. Image from PhotoDisc Fine Art, Series 3. Antique Maps and Heraldic Images.

MAKING THE CONNECTION

☞ In the coat of arms pictured here, what animal figure is featured on the shield? Why do you think this symbol was chosen?

☞ The lines, colors, designs, and symbols used on shields became standardized. Certain combinations had standard meanings and placements. Do you think standardizing features could limit creativity?

☞ Find out more about coats of arms. How were shields designed? What was the purpose of the motto?

INTERNET ACTIVITY

Visit Glencoe's Fine Arts Web Site for students at:

http://www.glencoe.com/sec/art/students

INTERNET ACTIVITY

Community Outreach   Make use of the Information Superhighway to transport your students beyond the classroom door and into your community. Your own school or district may have its own World Wide Web site. Offer to have some of your students contribute studio or computer art to that Home Page. Use the on-line search capabilities to locate art societies, local galleries, or artists in your community. Many cities and counties maintain community calendars or events schedules on their Home Page. There you might find opportunities to stage exhibitions of your students' art works. Let members of the community know what your art classes are accomplishing, and what they can do to encourage growth in the arts. Find us at **http://www.glencoe.com/sec/art**

REVIEW

 BUILDING VOCABULARY

Number a sheet of paper from 1 to 8. After each number, write the term from the list that best matches each description below.

buttress   gargoyle
castles   illuminations
cathedral   pointed arch
fresco   stained glass

1. Fortlike dwellings with high walls and towers.
2. Hand-painted book illustrations.
3. A large, complex church created as a seat of office for a bishop.
4. A curved arrangement of stones reaching up to a central point.
5. A brace or support placed on the outside of a building.
6. Colored glass pieces held in place with lead strips.
7. A painting created when pigment is applied to a section of wall spread with fresh plaster.
8. A projecting ornament on a building carved in the shape of a fantastic animal or grotesque creature.

 REVIEWING ART FACTS

Number a sheet of paper from 9 to 13. Answer each question in a complete sentence.

9. Name three common features of a Romanesque castle.
10. What was the purpose of the sculptures found on the outside of Romanesque churches?
11. Where were illuminations found? What were they used for?
12. Under what circumstances can a buttress be said to "fly"?
13. What subjects appeared in the stained glass windows of Gothic cathedrals?

 THINKING ABOUT ART

On a sheet of paper, answer each question in a sentence or two.

1. **Analyze.**   Look back at the picture of a castle in Figure 10–1. What changes in society would have had to take place in order for this building's architects to add more windows?
2. **Compare and contrast.**   What are the most important differences between Romanesque churches and Gothic cathedrals?
3. **Extend.**   Imagine yourself walking through one of the Gothic cathedrals pictured in this chapter. What feature do you think would impress you most?

MAKING ART CONNECTIONS

1. **Language Arts.**   Acting as an art critic, describe, analyze, interpret, and judge the illumination in Figure 10–6 on page **149**. Use these questions to guide you: Do the people in the picture look lifelike? Why, or why not? Which elements of art are important in this picture? What clues tell you this is a religious work? In judging the work, tell whether your reaction is based on subject, composition, or content.

2. **History.**   Find the term *fresco* in an encyclopedia or art history book in your library. Learn as much as you can about how frescoes are made and what difficulties fresco painters experienced. If you can, make photocopies of several different frescoes showing the range of possibilities within the medium. Share your findings with your class in an audiovisual presentation.

■ Building Vocabulary

1. castles
2. illuminations
3. cathedral
4. pointed arch
5. buttress
6. stained glass
7. fresco
8. gargoyle

■ Reviewing Art Facts

9. Romanesque castles were protected by high walls and towers, few windows, and a moat and drawbridge.
10. Since most people were unable to read, sculptures portraying Bible teachings were used to teach religion.
11. Hand lettered books containing illuminations were also used to teach religion.
12. A buttress is said to "fly" when it arches out over other parts of the building.
13. Religious figures and events were found in stained glass windows.

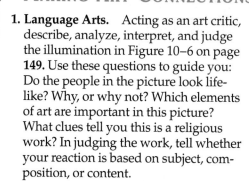 **THINKING ABOUT ART**

1. Society would have to become less warlike.
2. Romanesque churches were low, thick-walled and drab; they had few windows. Gothic cathedrals were tall, had many stained glass windows, and were light inside.
3. Answers might include the stained glass windows and the height of the interior.

Art of the Renaissance

(pages 160–175)

Resources

- 11-10 Chapter Test, TRB page 243
- Transparency CC-11, *The Artist's Treatise on Geometry* by Albrecht Dürer
- Transparency 11, *Doge Andrea Gritti* by Titian
- Fine Art Print 11, *The Hunt of the Unicorn II* Tapestry

Theatre
While studying this chapter, use Performing Arts Handbook page 327 to help students see how Jennifer Tipton's directing interpretation brings out the timeless human experience represented in Shakespeare's play, *The Tempest.*

NATIONAL STANDARDS

This chapter addresses the following National Standards for the Visual Arts:

1. (a, b)	**4.** (b, c)
2. (a, b)	**5.** (b, c)
3. (b)	**6.** (a, b)

▲ This artist's portraits were highly praised in her day. One writer stated that they were "so lifelike that they lack only speech."

Sofonisba Anguissola. *Portrait of the Artist's Sister, Minerva.* c. 1559. Oil on canvas. 85 x 66 cm (33½ x 26"). Milwaukee Art Museum, Milwaukee, Wisconsin. Gift of the Family of Mrs. Fred Vogel, Jr.

160

FEATURED ARTISTS

Sofonisba Anguissola	Masaccio
Filippo Brunelleschi	Raphael
Michelangelo Buonarroti	Jan van Eyck
Leonardo da Vinci	Rogier van der Weyden

Art of the Renaissance

The years following the Middle Ages in Europe were a time of great growth and discovery. Trade spread, and so did knowledge. New discoveries were made in every field, including science and geography. One of the most startling was the discovery of the New World by Christopher Columbus.

This period also saw great discoveries in art. Among the most important were ways of making art works look more lifelike. It was during this period too that women began to gain recognition as artists. The painting at the left is by Sofonisba Anguissola, the first of these women artists to gain an international reputation. In the chapters to follow, you will learn about many more.

PORTFOLIO IDEAS

Choose two art works from the Renaissance period. Compare and contrast the works of art. What is the subject matter? How do the artists use the elements of line, color, texture, space, and shape/form? How do they use the principles of art? What media were used to create the art works? Describe the mood or feeling of the art works. Date your written entries and place them in your portfolio. At a later date, compare these art works with ones created from a different time period.

OBJECTIVES

After completing this chapter, you will be able to:
- Identify artists of the Italian Renaissance and describe their contributions.
- Identify the contributions of artists working in northern Europe during the Renaissance.
- Use details and symbolism in studio experiences.

WORDS YOU WILL LEARN

linear perspective
Madonna
oil paint
Pietà
Renaissance
symbolism

161

■ **Chapter Overview**
Tell students that in this chapter they will learn about the artists of the Renaissance and their contributions. They will also incorporate details and symbolism into their own works of art.

■ **Chapter Motivator**
Point out to students that the painting on the facing page is by Sofonisba Anguissola, the first Italian woman to gain a worldwide reputation as an artist. Tell them that it was not until the Renaissance that women artists were recognized as serious artists. Encourage students to discuss why this may have been the case.

■ **Examining the Art Work**
The portrait by Sofonisba Anguissola is of her sister, dressed in black and wearing finely detailed jewelry. Point out how the lighting and color sets off her face and lovely complexion. The expressive eyes, warm colors, and crisp detail is typical of the style of the artist. Her skill is demonstrated in the way even the smallest coral beads are set off in a soft light. This skill is what makes her style very notable. Look closely at the medallion the woman is wearing. It depicts the Roman goddess of wisdom and arts, also known as "Minerva."

National Museum of Women in the Arts
You may wish to use the National Museum of Women in the Arts videodisc and/or CD-ROM. The videodisc features a bar code guide, and the interactive CD-ROM provides stimulating activities.

DEVELOPING A PORTFOLIO

Art Criticism Entries Whether students critique their own art work, the work of another student, or the work of a famous artist, art criticism entries kept in their portfolio provide excellent opportunities to demonstrate their knowledge of the elements and principles of art. It also allows them to share their personal interpretation of works of art in a non-threatening, written format. Remind students that interpretation and judgment may vary from person to person. There are no right or wrong answers. It's up to the students to provide facts and evidence to support their opinions. Encourage students to periodically review their art criticism entries to determine whether they have seen any growth in their art knowledge, since they evaluated the art work.

Art of the
Italian
Renaissance

(pages 162-165)

• • • • • • • • • • • • •

FOCUS

☑ OBJECTIVES

After completing this lesson, students will be able to:

• Describe the style of Italian Renaissance art.

• Name several Italian Renaissance artists.

• Explain the terms *Madonna, Pieta,* and *linear perspective.*

☑ SUPPLIES

• Pencils, rulers, and sheets of white paper.

• School acrylic paints or tempera; paint brushes.

• Paper for making simple scrapbooks.

• Magazines and markers.

Resources

■ 11-1 *Renaissance Costumes,* TRB page 225 (reproducible master)

■ 11-2 *Leonardo da Vinci,* TRB page 227 (artist profile)

■ 11-3 *Drawing the Human Figure,* TRB page 229 (reproducible master)

■ 11-4 *The Renaissance Artist and Anatomy,* TRB page 230 (studio)

• • • • • • • • • • • • •

TEACH

■ Motivator

Have students examine Figure 11-2. Tell them how this painting of the Trinity was so lifelike to fifteenth-century people that when they saw it for the first time they became frightened and ran from the church. Discuss how photography has changed people's views.

162

Art of the Italian Renaissance

During the Middle Ages the teachings of the Catholic Church were the focus of much of the art work. By the beginning of the 1400s, however, artists gradually began to change their style. After centuries of creating religious works, artists began to paint pictures to look as realistic as possible. The emphasis was not always on religious subjects. This time is known as the **Renaissance** (ren-uh-sahns), *a period of great awakening.* The word renaissance means "rebirth."

THE RENAISSANCE IN ITALY

The shift in interests that took place during the Renaissance was especially noticeable in Italy. There, a number of cities grew into trading and business centers. One of these, Florence, became the capital of Europe's cloth trade and home to its richest bank. Find Florence on the map in Figure 11–1.

◄ **Figure 11–1   Renaissance Italy.**

Florence also became a center for art during the Renaissance. In this lesson you will read about the contributions of its artists.

Painting

Among the people living in Florence during the early 1400s was a young artist named Masaccio (muh-**zahch**-ee-oh). Masaccio continued where Giotto had left off a century earlier. He made the figures in his works seem solid and real. (See Figure 11–2.)

Masaccio also sought to add a true-to-life, three-dimensional quality using a technique called linear perspective (puhr-**spek**-tiv). **Linear perspective** is *the use of slanted lines to make objects appear to extend back into space.* (See Figure 11–3.) The technique was discovered by an architect and friend of Masaccio named Filippo Brunelleschi (fi-**leep**-oh broon-uhl-**ess**-kee).

The artist adds to this realistic appearance by giving the subject an expression of genuine grief. This combination of three-dimensional form and emotion became a trademark of Renaissance art.

Masaccio died suddenly at the age of 27. Some believe he may have been poisoned by a jealous rival. Luckily, there were other artists with the talent to build upon Masaccio's discoveries. One of these was a man whose talents were not limited to art. He was also skilled in science, literature, and music. The name of this gifted man was Leonardo da Vinci (lee-uh-**nard**-oh duh **vin**-chee).

TECHNOLOGY OPTIONS

National Gallery of Art Videodisc   Use the following images to examine other art works by artists discussed in this lesson.

Masaccio
Profile Portrait of a Young Man

Leonardo da Vinci
Ginevra de´ Benci

Raphael
The Small Cowper Madonna

Search Frame 70

Search Frame 170

Search Frame 210

Use Glencoe's *Correlation Bar Code Guide to the National Gallery of Art* to locate more art works.

◀ **Figure 11–3** Diagram showing linear perspective. Linear perspective is based on a trick the eyes play on us. This trick causes the sides of a highway, for example, to seem to come together in the distance. The point at which such lines appear to meet at the horizon is called the vanishing point.

Eye level

Vanishing point

Lesson 1   *Art of the Italian Renaissance*   **163**

more about • • •

Masaccio Masaccio is regarded as the first important artist of the Italian Renaissance. Masaccio took the innovations of Giotto and developed them further to produce a style that became the trademark of the Italian Renaissance. It was a simple style that owed a great deal to the fresco painting technique that continued to be popular throughout Italy. The Gothic architectural style, with its walls of glass, did not appeal to Italians. They preferred the solid walls and cool, dark interiors of the Romanesque style. The walls of their churches were covered with bright mosaics and large frescoes. While painters in northern Europe were making intricate stained glass windows and manuscript illuminations, Italian artists such as Masaccio were doing huge wall paintings on the interiors of their churches.

■ **Studio Skills**

Demonstrate different techniques for achieving the chiaroscuro that was central to Renaissance illusionism. Explain how hatching, crosshatching, blending, and stippling can enhance the sense of three dimensions on a drawing or painting. Then draw the outlines of various geometric solids on the board and have students practice the shading techniques to make the forms appear three-dimensional.

Art in
Everyday Life

Ask students what having a portrait made means in today's society. They may only be familiar with the school yearbook photographs and family portrait photos. Have them think about how they might dress and pose differently if they were to have their portraits painted, rather than photographed. What would they wear, what facial expression would they pose in, what background would they choose? How would a painted portrait be displayed differently than a photograph of themselves?

■ **Cultural Diversity**

Discuss how one's cultural background helps a person interpret an art work produced in the same culture. For example, even without special training in art history most Westerners would know that Figure 11–5 depicts the mother of Christ. Ask students to write a paragraph that explains how a person whose background didn't include familiarity with Christianity might interpret this painting. Ask: Would it appear to be a picture of an ordinary woman and her baby?

164

Leonardo's most famous work is a portrait, the *Mona Lisa*. Figure 11–4 shows another of his haunting portraits. In this painting Leonardo uses light and dark values in the manner developed by Giotto and Masaccio. The blending is so precise, however, that it is impossible to tell where one value ends and the next begins. Notice how these gently changing values help make the sad face seem three-dimensional. Notice how the figure of the woman stands out dramatically against the dark background.

Leonardo was recognized as a great artist even in his own day. Artists from all over flocked to Florence in the hopes of learning from him. One of these was a young painter named Raphael (**raf**-ee-el). Figure 11–5 is one of over 300 Madonnas that Raphael painted. A **Madonna** is *a work showing the Virgin Mary with the Christ Child*. In this one, Leonardo's influence can be seen in the soft change from light to dark values. Notice the expressions of the faces of the different people. How would you describe each one?

Sculpture

Like Leonardo, Michelangelo Buonarroti (my-kuh-**lan**-juh-loh bwon-nar-**roe**-tee) excelled in many fields, including poetry, painting, and architecture. As an artist, however, he thought of himself as a sculptor first. One of Michelangelo's greatest and best-known works is his *Pietà* (pee-ay-**tah**), pictured in Figure 11–6. A **Pietà** is *a work showing Mary mourning over the body of Christ*. Michelangelo carved his *Pietà* when he was 24 years old.

Study this work. Can you find anything unusual about the proportion of the two figures? Did you notice that Mary is much larger than her son, a full-grown man? In fact, if the figure were to stand, she would be nearly 9 feet (3 m) tall! Michelangelo purposely planned the sculpture this way. He wanted the viewer to focus on the work's mood—not on Mary's struggle to support the weight of Jesus' body. How would you describe the mood of Michelangelo's *Pietà*?

▲ **Figure 11–4   Who is this woman, and why is she so sad? Some historians claim she was the daughter of a rich banker abandoned by the man she loved.**

Leonardo da Vinci. *Ginevra de' Benci*. c. 1474. Wood. 38.8 x 36.7 cm (15¼ x 14½"). National Gallery of Art, Washington, D.C. Ailsa Mellon Bruce Fund.

▲ **Figure 11–5   Where has the artist used linear perspective? How has the use of linear perspective added to this painting?**

Raphael. *Madonna and Child Enthroned with Saints*. Tempera on wood. 169.2 x 169.5 cm (66⅝ x 66¾"). The Metropolitan Museum of Art, New York, New York. Gift of J. Pierpont Morgan.

164   Lesson 1   *Art of the Italian Renaissance*

---

more about • • •

Frescoes   Italian Renaissance frescoes were created by the rapid application of a water-based paint to wet patches of wall plaster. The artist could only work on the amount of wall that would remain wet for that work day. (Because of this time restriction, viewers today can see ridges that define each day's painting.) A fresco painter began by making a drawing on the wall. These preliminary drawings were first discovered when conservators removed frescoes that were damaged in World War II. Once paper was invented in the mid-fifteenth century, artists could make life-size cartoons that helped artists efficiently plan frescoes. The cartoons were applied to the wall and pricked with colored dust to provide guide lines.

▲ **Figure 11–6** Notice that the two figures — one horizontal, the other vertical — seem almost to form a pyramid. Can you trace the lines of that pyramid with your finger?

Michelangelo. *Pietà*. c. 1501. Marble. St. Peter's Basilica, Rome, Italy.

▲ **Figure 11–7** Triangles and pyramids used for balance.

STUDIO ACTIVITY

Using the Triangle

Many Renaissance artists followed a triangular or pyramid plan to organize the main figures in their works. This can be seen in the *Pietà* (see Figure 11–7). Find a similar plan in other works in this lesson.

Using pencil and ruler, draw a large triangle on a sheet of white paper. Within this shape, fit one or more of the letters that make up your initials. Fill as much of the space inside the triangle as you can. Use only straight, ruled lines for your letters.

Now continue some of the lines beyond the triangle to the edge of the paper. This will divide the rest of your composition into various shapes. Paint the shapes within the triangle with different values of a single hue. Paint the outside shapes with different values of the complementary hue.

PORTFOLIO

For your portfolio, write what you learned by creating this painting. Does your work reflect the same balance and organization as that of the Renaissance painters? Explain.

✔ CHECK YOUR UNDERSTANDING

1. How did the art in Europe at the beginning of the 1400s differ from that of the Middle Ages?
2. What was the Renaissance? What city was its center in Italy?
3. What is linear perspective? Who discovered it? Who was one of the first artists to use it in a painting?
4. What is remarkable about the portraits painted by Leonardo da Vinci?
5. What is a Madonna? What Renaissance artist was influenced by Leonardo in his painting of Madonnas?
6. What is a Pietà? What is unusual about the use of proportion in Michelangelo's *Pietà*?

Lesson 1   *Art of the Italian Renaissance*   **165**

STUDIO ACTIVITY

Using the Triangle

As a warm-up to this activity, have students look through this book and other sources to identify more examples of the pyramid organizational style.

ASSESS

■ Self-Assessment

Have students complete the review questions on this page. Answers are provided below.

■ Reteaching

Have students make a shaded drawing of their own faces. They should sit so they can look into a mirror, place a lamp to light their faces from one side, and model the shadows and highlights using one of the shading techniques presented in class. Then have students compare their results with the portrait on page 160. Discuss whether their studio experience helps them to appreciate Anguissola's ability to render three-dimensional forms.

■ Enrichment

Explain to students that Italian Renaissance painters created numerous images of ancient Greek or Roman myths in addition to Christian themes. Have students research paintings such as Sandro Botticelli's *Birth of Venus*, Raphael's *Galatea*, Piero di Cosimo's *Mythological Scene*, Luca Signorelli's *School of Pan*, and Andrea Mantegna's *Parnassus*. Discuss why the classical period was of such interest to Italian Renaissance nobles.

CLOSE

Ask students to name the five Renaissance artists mentioned in this lesson and tell something about each one.

Answers to ✔ CHECK YOUR UNDERSTANDING

1. European artists began to change their focus from religious works to other subjects; they began to paint those subjects to look as realistic as possible.
2. The Renaissance was the "period of great awakening." Florence was its center in Italy.
3. The use of slanted lines to make objects appear to extend back in space. Brunelleschi. Masaccio.
4. Subtle blending of light and dark values.
5. A Madonna is a work showing the Virgin Mary with the Christ Child. Raphael was influenced by da Vinci.
6. A work showing Mary mourning over the body of Christ. Michelangelo distorted the proportion of the figure by making Mary much larger than Jesus in his Pietà to intensify the mood.

LESSON 2

Drawing a Still Life

(pages 166–167)

LESSON TIME: 90 minutes

● ● ● ● ● ● ● ● ● ● ● ●

FOCUS

☑ OBJECTIVES

After completing this lesson, students will be able to:

• Describe some of Leonardo da Vinci's many interests.
• Create a highly detailed drawing of a found object.
• Use overlapping objects and other means of creating the illusion of space in drawing.

☑ SUPPLIES

• Pencils and sketch paper.
• Sheets of white drawing paper, 12 x 18 inches (30 x 46 cm).
• Examples of da Vinci's sketches.
• Objects that possess a variety of textures, such as scraps of velvet or silk, ridged seashells, pieces of wood, and various plants.
• Wide variety of drawing materials suitable for rendering different textures.

● ● ● ● ● ● ● ● ● ● ● ●

TEACH

■ Motivator

Show students examples of pages from Leonardo da Vinci's notebooks. List on the board all the different subjects that interested him, including architecture, mathematics, botany, sculpture, painting, anatomy, poetry, literature, music, geology, and hydraulics. Have students look around the classroom and create a page of notes and sketches such as Leonardo might have made if he were sitting there.

166

Drawing a Still Life

Many artists use sketch pads to record sights and ideas that interest them. In his lifetime Leonardo da Vinci filled some 100 sketchbooks with drawings on many subjects. Some of these were of storm clouds. Some were of rock formations and the action of waves. Some—like the one in Figure 11–8—were of the human body. What sets Leonardo's drawings apart was how precisely he captured every detail of an object. Clearly, this Renaissance master had remarkable powers of concentration.

WHAT YOU WILL LEARN

You will make a pencil drawing of a still life, using your powers of concentration to make the drawing as accurate as possible. Gradual and sudden changes of value will be used to suggest rounded and angular forms. Space will be shown by overlapping these forms. Differences in texture will be emphasized. (See Figure 11–9.)

▶ **Figure 11–8   Leonardo was left handed. He wrote the notes you see backward to keep his ideas private. A mirror was needed to read them.**

Leonardo da Vinci. *Studies of Male Shoulder.* Royal Library, Windsor Castle, England.

— *more about* ● ● ● —

Leonardo da Vinci   Leonardo da Vinci was the first artist to systematically study the structure of the human body. One of his means of investigation was dissection, a practice that he developed to an unprecedented degree. He is said to have dissected bodies during a time when the practice was outlawed and subject to severe punishment. Dissection helped Leonardo to learn how arms and legs bend and how muscles shift as the body moves. He was especially interested in the head, particularly how the eye sees and the mind reasons. He searched for the part of the brain where the senses meet, believing that this was where the soul would be found.

WHAT YOU WILL NEED

- Pencil and sheets of sketch paper
- Sheet of white drawing paper, 12 x 18 inches (30 x 46 cm)

WHAT YOU WILL DO

1. Bring an unusual found object to class, something that is broken or in some other way altered. Possibilities are a crushed can, a broken toy, or an old hand tool.
2. Set your object on a table in front of you. Place the point of your pencil on a sheet of sketch paper. Without taking your eyes off the object, begin to draw it. Attempt to feel the lines of the object with your pencil as you draw. Concentrate on and draw each object in accurate detail. Make several more drawings on the same sheet until your work looks like your object.
3. Working with four other students, arrange your five objects in an interesting way. Some of the objects should overlap others. Make a drawing of the arrangement. Concentrate on overlapping objects to create an illusion of space. (See Technique Tip 2, *Handbook* page **277**.)
4. Carefully draw the key lines of your sketch onto the large sheet of drawing paper. Include in this finished version as many details as you can, including differences in texture. Use your pencil to add gradual and sudden changes of value to show rounded and angular forms.
5. Display your work along with those of your classmates. Discuss how this drawing has helped you to better see details.

EXAMINING YOUR WORK

- **Describe**   Tell what objects you sketched. Point to the features of your drawing that would help others identify the objects.
- **Analyze**   Point to the objects in your still life that overlap others. Explain whether this overlapping adds a feeling of space to the work. Tell how gradual and sudden changes of value suggest rounded and angular forms. Show the different textures you have emphasized.
- **Interpret**   Give a name to your work that reflects the feelings you experienced while doing it.
- **Judge**   Tell whether you feel your work as a whole succeeds as an accurate still life. Point to the most successful parts of your drawing. Explain why you think these parts are successful.

▲ Figure 11–9   Student work. Still life.

 Try This! ## COMPUTER OPTION

- Work in groups of 3 to 4 students at the computer. Each student should take a turn to draw and arrange a familiar object using a mouse or drawing pen (stylus). After each student has a turn, title and save the work as a Line Drawing. Determine the light source. Use a pressure-sensitive tool such as a drawing pen to create different values. Apply colors and shades with choice of Brushes (Chalk, Watercolor, or Markers) and paper textures. Retitle, save, and print the work.

Display items that possess distinctive textures and have students select one to draw or paint. Students should use whatever medium they think will help them render the texture most accurately. If they desire, they should experiment with several media.

ASSESS

■ **Self-Assessment**

Have students use Examining Your Work to evaluate their still-life drawings created in this lesson. Responses may be written or oral.

■ **Reteaching**

Have students draw their own bare leg or foot. Then have them study the underlying bone structure and musculature of those parts in an anatomy text and draw the leg or foot again. Discuss whether the scientific information increased the students powers of observation.

■ **Enrichment**

Have students carry a sketch pad everywhere they go for at least two days. During that time they should draw and take notes about everything that catches their interest. Be sure that students get permission before they sketch during classes. Discuss whether a companion sketchbook is a good tool for learning.

CLOSE

Ask: What would it be like to have Leonardo as a classmate or friend? If Leonardo were alive today, what kind of work would he be doing? Would he be more likely to be a scientist or an artist?

MEETING SPECIAL NEEDS

Working with Groups   In forming groups to arrange the objects, students with disabilities should be interspersed into each group. Have students bring in objects of their choice (perhaps stuffed animals and model airplanes) and arrange them to tell a story for a cathartic, normalizing experience in cooperative learning, especially for students with behavior disorders. When drawing overlapping objects, some students with retardation may demonstrate earlier stages of visual conception, draw separate objects, or even scribble. You should continue to offer praise in order that the student will feel a sense of accomplishment with the activity.

LESSON 3

Art of the Northern Renaissance

● ● ● ● ● ● ● ● ● ● ● ● ● ● ● ●

FOCUS

☑ OBJECTIVES

After completing this lesson, students will be able to:

• Describe the preparation and advantages of oil paint.
• Define symbolism.
• Characterize the style of Northern Renaissance art.
• Name two Northern Renaissance painters.

☑ SUPPLIES

• Drawing pencils and sheets of white drawing paper.
• Pigments, linseed oil, turpentine; jar and stick for mixing.
• Tempera and watercolor paints; paint brushes, markers.
• Magazines.
• Several garments in different styles.
• Magnifying glasses.

Resources

◼ 11-5 *Dürer's Perspective Technique*, TRB page 232 (reproducible master)
◼ 11-6 *Invention of the Modern Mind*, TRB page 233 (aesthetics)
◼ 11-7 *Renaissance and Exploration*, TRB page 236 (appreciating cultural diversity)
◼ 11-8 *A Classical Rebirth*, TRB page 238 (art history)

The shift from a Gothic to a Renaissance art style happened in northern Europe later than in Italy. The changes were also slower to develop and found different forms of expression.

In this lesson you will read about the contributions of Renaissance artists of northern Europe.

THE RENAISSANCE IN THE NORTH

The Northern Renaissance was concentrated in the area of Europe known as Flanders. It had as its center the modern Belgian capital of Brussels. Find Flanders and the city of Brussels on the map in Figure 11–10.

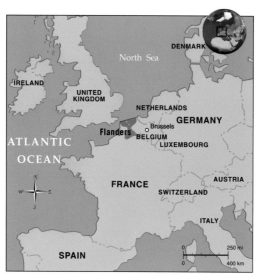

▲ Figure 11–10 Renaissance Europe.

The art of the Northern Renaissance continued to make use of several Gothic techniques and features. One of these was symbolism. **Symbolism** is *the use of an image to stand for a quality or an idea*. A dog, for example, was a symbol of loyalty; a lily could mean purity.

In other ways Northern Renaissance artists experimented with new ideas. This was especially true in the area of painting.

Painting

The most important contribution of the Northern Renaissance was a new painting technique. Artists discovered that **oil paint**, *a mixture of pigment, linseed oil, and turpentine*, gave them a slow-drying paint. This oil-based paint was far easier to use than tempera. It allowed the artist to work more slowly and add more details. Colors, moreover, could be mixed right on the canvas.

Jan van Eyck

The person often credited with discovering the oil painting technique was a Flemish artist named Jan van Eyck (**yahn** van **ike**). Like painters working in Italy, those in the North were fascinated with precision. Van Eyck was no exception. He would spend hours using the smallest brushes he could find to paint patterns of bark on a tree or the blades of grass in a meadow. Notice the attention to detail in the brilliantly colored work in Figure 11–11. Look especially at the textures of the cloak and the sparkling glass. The paint is applied so skillfully that not a single brush stroke can be seen. Can you tell from the painting that the man shown is a religious figure?

TECHNOLOGY OPTIONS

National Gallery of Art Videodisc   Use the following images to demonstrate the use of detail in Renaissance paintings.

| Jan van Eyck *The Annunciation* | Jan van Eyck *The Annunciation* | Jan van Eyck *The Annunciation* |
| Search Frame 576 | Search Frame 578 | Search Frame 580 |

Use Glencoe's *Correlation Bar Code Guide to the National Gallery of Art* to locate more art works.

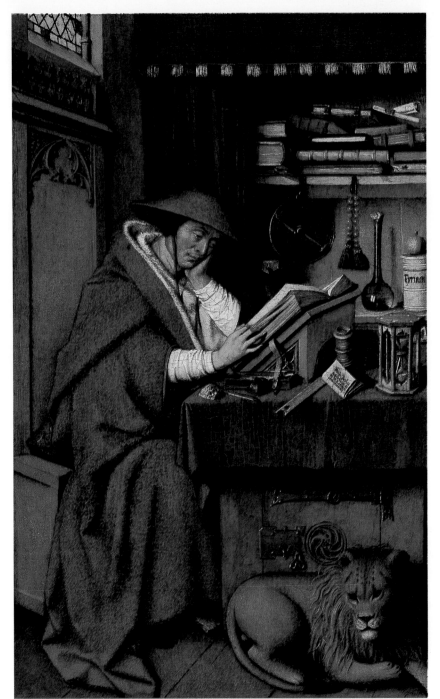

▲ Figure 11–11 This work is rich in details. The books and articles on the table seem to glow softly in the mellow light. Notice the deep colors of green in the tablecloth, the reds and blues of the cloak and drapery. Even the textures in the paper, wool, leather, and glass add to the precise detail of van Eyck's work, a style that has never been equaled.

Jan van Eyck. *Saint Gerome in His Study*. 1435. Oil on linen paper, mounted on oak panel. 20.6 x 13.3 cm (8⅛ x 5¼"). Detroit Institute of Arts, Detroit, Michigan. City of Detroit Purchase.

■ **Motivator**

Have students discuss or present objects that symbolize something important to them. They should explain what the item symbolizes and how it came to have that meaning for them. Present a symbolic object of your own.

■ **Vocabulary**

Demonstrate how to mix pigment, linseed oil, and turpentine to create *oil paint.* Point out that the pigment does not actually dissolve—it remains suspended in the vehicle, and when it is applied to a canvas or panel it stays on the surface instead of soaking in like a dye. Have students create small demonstration panels of oil paint, tempera, and watercolor swatches. Compare the different effects of each medium after the panels dry.

Art in Everyday Life

The human figure continues to be an important subject of art, but ideals change from day to day. Have students compare van Eyck's and van der Weyden's representations of the human figure with magazine photographs of people of our time. Discuss the differences between realism of highly detailed Northern Renaissance paintings and the realism of photographs that we see every day.

RESOURCES BEYOND THE CLASSROOM

Festivals and Fairs Festivals and fairs let budding artists explore the arts of other countries and different times. Ethnic and religious festivals, such as Greek Orthodox fairs, Native American powwows, and African-American festivals show how different cultures create and use art. Some cities may see the Chinese New Year celebrated, while others will emphasize a St. Patrick's Day parade. These events allow students to see artists and craftspeople at work. Other kinds of fairs are growing more common, in particular medieval or Renaissance festivals, which re-create societies from hundreds of years ago. Authentic foods, crafts, and leisure activities are all re-created and re-enacted at these events.

■ **Studio Skills**

Have students scrutinize Figure 11-11 with a magnifying glass and select a small square or detail to enlarge, such as items on the wall or desk, or the fabrics or the glass window. If possible, display a larger reproduction of this work than is presented in the students' text. Students should use drawing pencils, paint or markers to reproduce their section onto a sheet of white paper.

Sparking Creativity

Want students to experience a Renaissance sense of discovery? Challenge them to come up with new, innovative ways of using or looking at a familiar, everyday item. Provide resources from classroom supplies or from home. Choose items such as school supplies, kitchen utensils, or clothing accessories. Display the items and tell students to look at them as though they had never seen the items before. Have them choose one item or combine several. Then have them write a description and provide a sketch of the item and its new function.

■ **Cultural Diversity**

Have students investigate how religious figures are depicted in non-western cultures. Consider the lively Hindu statues of gods and goddesses, the sometimes terrifying representations of deities in Tibetan mandalas, and the enormous and placid stone Buddhas located in Ceylon. Have students share their findings in a brief oral presentation, and have the class compare these works and the religious figures depicted in this lesson.

170

▲ Figure 11–12   Who do you think the woman in blue might be? Study her pose closely. Can you find another figure in the painting with the same pose? Why do you think the artist did this?

Rogier van der Weyden. *Descent from the Cross.* c. 1435. Museo del Prado, Madrid, Spain.

Rogier van der Weyden

Another important Northern Renaissance painter is Rogier van der Weyden (roh-**jehr** van duhr **vyd**-uhn). Van der Weyden was greatly influenced by van Eyck. Like van Eyck, he was able to reproduce each hair, each stitch in his paintings. Unlike van Eyck, whose pictures are calm and quiet, van der Weyden painted powerful, emotional scenes.

One of these is shown in Figure 11–12. In this picture, 10 life-size figures are placed in a shallow nook. The nook is just wide enough to hold them. The wall behind pushes the figures forward, bringing them closer to the viewer. In this way the artist forces the viewer to look at and experience this emotional scene from the Bible. Notice how the different people are reacting to the death of Christ. What has just happened to the woman in the blue dress in the foreground?

Auditory/Musical Learners   Have students collect and present examples of court, church, and popular music that were common in Europe during the Renaissance period. Suggest they locate recordings by musicians such as Guillaume Dufay, Johannes Ockeghem, Jacob Obrecht, Heinrich Isaac, William Byrd, Thomas Morley, or Thomas Campion.

Visual/Spatial Learners   Have students design a bulletin board display that contains a time line and identifies important Renaissance paintings, sculptures, and buildings. Encourage students to use resources from history books and encyclopedias as well as information from this text.

▲ Figure 11–13   Student work. Detail drawing.

✔ CHECK YOUR UNDERSTANDING

1. What area became the center of the Northern Renaissance?
2. What Gothic feature continued to be used by Northern Renaissance artists?
3. What was a major contribution of artists of the Northern Renaissance? Who is credited with having discovered it?
4. In what ways were the religious paintings of Jan van Eyck and Rogier van der Weyden similar? In what ways were they different?

STUDIO ACTIVITY

Sketching Details

Look again at the paintings by van Eyck and van der Weyden in Figures 11–11 and 11–12. Notice how every detail in both pictures is captured in sharp focus, demonstrating the artists' powers of observation.

Exercise your own powers of observation by drawing two detailed, close-up views of a pencil on separate sheets of paper measuring 3 x 1½ inches (7 x 3.5 cm). Show the pencil point in one drawing and the eraser end in the other. Complete both drawings in sharp focus and use shading to suggest the three-dimensional form of the pencil. Mount both drawings on a sheet of black construction paper.

P O R T F O L I O

On a separate piece of paper, use descriptive words and phrases to list your observations as you drew the pencil. What do your results tell you about the powers of observation? Were you successful in capturing those observations in your drawings? How did you use the elements and principles of art to create sharp focus and three-dimensional form? What might you do differently if you drew the pencil again? Include your written observations with your drawings in your portfolio.

STUDIO ACTIVITY

Sketching Details

After students have successfully completed the detail of the pencil, have them choose another item that interests them. Be sure the object contains many small details to allow students to perfect their technique of drawing detail.

• • • • • • • • • • • • •

A S S E S S

■ Self-Assessment

Have students complete the review questions on this page. Answers are provided below.

■ Reteaching

Have students compare Figure 11-11 with a medieval and an Italian Renaissance painting of the same theme. List on the board the differences and similarities in the settings, gestures, garments, moods, and use of symbols. Ask: Do paintings from various times seem to express different ideas and feelings about religious themes?

■ Enrichment

Invite a professional art conservator from a local art museum or art restoration business to speak to the students. Have the speaker discuss the profession—the experience of transferring paintings to new surfaces and filling in decomposed or otherwise missing parts of an art work. If possible, the speaker should show slides or examples of his or her work.

• • • • • • • • • • • • •

C L O S E

Ask how much students feel they have in common with the people of van Eyck's and van der Weyden's time?

Answers to ✔ CHECK YOUR UNDERSTANDING

1. Brussels, in Flanders, became the center of the Northern Renaissance.
2. Northern Renaissance artists continued to use the Gothic feature of symbolism.
3. A major contribution was the use of oil paint. Flemish painter Jan van Eyck was credited with discovering the medium.
4. Jan van Eyck and Rogier van der Weyden's realistic styles were similar. Their choices of subject matter were different. Jan van Eyck's pictures are calm and quiet; van der Weyden painted powerful, emotional scenes.

Designing a Visual Symbol

☑ OBJECTIVES

After completing this lesson, students will be able to:

• Explain the meaning of symbols used by Jan van Eyck.

• Identify symbols found in modern life.

• Create a visual symbol for a shoe company.

☑ SUPPLIES

• Pencils and sheets of sketch paper.

• Rulers; scissors; and shoe box lids.

• Sheets of white paper, 12 x 18 inches (30 x 46 cm).

• Tempera paints and brushes; white glue.

• Variety of shoes to augment those supplied by students.

• Photos of couples at their wedding ceremonies, culled from bridal magazines.

Resource

■ 11-9 *Create Your Own Renaissance Society*, TRB page 240 (cooperative learning)

• • • • • • • • • • • • • •

TEACH

■ Motivator

Have students examine their belongings and clothing for evidence of a company's symbol or logo. Discuss how the design of each symbol enhances the quality of the item on which it is found.

172

Symbolism, as you have read, was an important feature of Northern Renaissance art. Its importance can be seen in the picture by Jan van Eyck in Figure 11–14. The painting, which shows a wedding ceremony, is heavy with symbols. The dog stands for the loyalty the marriage partners have promised each other. The single burning candle in the chandelier symbolizes the presence of God at the event. Even the shoes on the floor have

▲ Figure 11–14 The translation of the words above the mirror is: "Jan van Eyck was here." Experts have put forth the idea that this painting might have been an official wedding document. If it was, what importance would these words have?

Jan van Eyck. *Giovanni Arnolfini and His Bride.* 1434. National Gallery, London, England.

meaning. They have been removed to show that the couple is standing on ground made holy by the exchange of vows.

Symbolism is as popular today as it was over 500 years ago. Think of all the symbols you see every day for cars, fast-food chains, and brands of clothing. Can you think of other products in our culture that use symbols? What symbols do these products use?

Imagine you have been asked to design a symbol for a shoe company. The design is to be colorful, detailed, and easy to recognize. It is also to be strictly visual—without any lettering.

WHAT YOU WILL LEARN

You will create a visual symbol for a shoe company. You will use repeated flat shapes to give harmony to your design. Variety will be obtained by making the shapes in different sizes. Use color to emphasize the most important shoe in your design. (See Figure 11–15.)

WHAT YOU WILL NEED

• Pencil and sheets of sketch paper
• Ruler and scissors
• Shoe box lid
• Sheet of white paper, 12 x 18 inches (30 x 46 cm)
• Tempera paint and several brushes
• White glue

WHAT YOU WILL DO

1. Look at the table of shoes that your teacher has arranged.
2. Make several pencil sketches of the shoe pile. Use only lines in your sketches. Do not fill in any of the shapes with shading.

172   Lesson 4   *Designing a Visual Symbol*

---

more about • • •

Jan van Eyck's Painting The painting of *Giovanni Arnolfini and His Bride* is richly detailed. This is one of van Eyck's best-known works, and includes precision that is rarely equaled. The subdued light entering through an open window is one of the first examples of the dramatic effects of atmospheric diffusion of light. The painting depicts the marriage ceremony of a rich Italian merchant. He sought the best available artist to paint himself and his bride at their wedding. In the painting, both figures look real, yet frozen in their poses. Notice the detail in the faces: the bride's is white and smooth as a china doll, but Giovanni's is much more natural. The mirror on the far wall of the room shows even more detail. In it appears a reflection of the room, the wedding couple, and two others.

3. Choose the best of your sketches and study it. Using the ruler, draw a rectangle around the part of your sketch that seems most interesting. This is to be your design.
4. Using the ruler, measure the length and width of the shoe box lid. Rule off a rectangle with the same measurements on the sheet of white paper. With scissors, cut out the rectangle.
5. Draw your design sketch on the rectangle, filling the space. Keep the shapes flat to give your design harmony. Make some of the shapes larger than others to add variety. Pick out one shoe that you would like to emphasize. Add details to this shoe.
6. Paint your design using tempera. Paint the different shoes so they look flat. Use a contrasting hue for the shoe you want to emphasize.
7. When the paint is dry, glue your painting to the shoe box lid. Display your finished work along with those of your classmates. Include some professionally designed shoe box lids in the display. Discuss which of the designs works best as a symbol for a shoe company. Try to identify the reasons for your opinions.

EXAMINING YOUR WORK

- **Describe** Tell whether you can instantly identify your design as a symbol for shoes. Are the shoes in your design easily recognized?
- **Analyze** Tell whether you used only flat shapes in your design. State whether the repeated use of these flat shapes adds to the harmony of the design. Point out the different-sized shapes in your work. Explain how these add variety to the design. Point out the one shoe you emphasized. Tell what you did to emphasize this shoe.
- **Interpret** Tell whether your design is unique enough to be identified with a particular shoe company.
- **Judge** Tell whether you feel your work succeeds. Explain your answer. Tell what changes you would make if you had a chance to do the design over.

▲ **Figure 11–15** Student work. Design of a visual symbol.

Try This!

COMPUTER OPTION

■ Design an inventive shoe that has special features or attributes. Perhaps the shoe has wings, small wheels, batteries, or levers. Draw a large shoe, filling the computer page, with Pencil or Brush. Think of a brand name that symbolizes the shoe and emphasizes its special ability. Use the Text tool to add letters and Transform commands to Flip, Rotate, Distort, or change size of letters. Save and title your work. Choose solid colors or use patterns. Color shoe and letters in bright hues. Add lighter or contrasting background hues. Save, title, and print your work.

Lesson 4 *Designing a Visual Symbol* **173**

• • • • • • • • • • •
ASSESS

■ **Self-Assessment**
Have students use Examining Your Work to evaluate their shoes. Responses may be written or oral.

■ **Reteaching**
Discuss the visual symbols that are part of modern weddings. List them on the board. If necessary, refer again to the bridal magazine photos to remind students of the important rings, flowers, a white dress, and other accessories of a traditional American wedding.

■ **Enrichment**
Invite a graphic designer who has worked on corporate logos to speak to the class. Have him or her discuss the various stages a symbol goes through before it reaches its final form.

• • • • • • • • • • •
CLOSE

Ask: Do symbols make an art work more interesting or fun to look at? Do symbols make it harder to understand art from a different time and place?

CURRICULUM CONNECTIONS

Social Studies The Medici family was the ruling family of Florence during the fifteenth century, and had a lasting impact on the art and society of the times. Giovanni de' Medici, the founder of the family, was a wealthy merchant. He and his sons Cosimo and Lorenzo were devout patrons of the arts. Cosimo, a banker, established the Florence Academy. Lorenzo, known as "the Magnificent," was a man of varied ideas. He encouraged learning in the arts and sciences and patronized numerous artists of the Renaissance. The esteem enjoyed by the Medici family inspired other ambitious and wealthy Florentine families to also commission many works of art. Because of this attention by influential merchants, the arts in Florence enjoyed a lasting prosperity.

CONNECTIONS *Math*

How Is the Dome Supported?

Filippo Brunelleschi created the extraordinary dome on the Florence cathedral. Construction of this huge dome was revolutionary for architecture of the time.

As the construction of the cathedral in Florence neared completion, a competition was held to see who would design the dome. Brunelleschi won, but he knew it would be no easy task to build. The drum, or walls on which the dome was to rest, was a polygon. It spanned 138½ feet (42.2 m) across and was 180 feet (54.9 m) high. This was a problem, because the span was too wide for the temporary wooden scaffolds that workers typically needed. Also a dome of this size would be too heavy to use wood in such a way. Brunelleschi converted his octagonal dome into a circle at the base. Using precise measurements and detailed drawings, he built a ribbed inner dome that was connected to an outer dome. This approach helped distribute the enormous weight, estimated to be over 25,000 tons!

Brunelleschi was not just a brilliant architect. He also invented innovative machines and hoists. His creative construction techniques were less costly, more efficient, and safer than ever before.

Filippo Brunelleschi. View of Dome, Duomo. Florence, Italy.

MAKING THE CONNECTION

- Filippo Brunelleschi included passages and stairs between the two dome shells. How do you think such features would have been useful?
- Brunelleschi was educated as a sculptor and a goldsmith. How might such a background, combined with his discovery of linear perspective, have helped him as an architect?
- There are many different kinds of domes. Each kind depends on the shape of the base and the shape of the cross-section of the dome. Find out about some other kinds of domes. What are some famous ones you are familiar with?

INTERNET ACTIVITY

Visit Glencoe's Fine Arts Web Site for students at:

http://www.glencoe.com/ sec/art/students

INTERNET ACTIVITY

Meet the Masters Introduce students to the many-faceted world of great artists throughout history as they work with resources found in our Internet activities. Have small groups find out about an artist such as: Michelangelo, da Vinci, Monet, Renoir, or van Gogh. Students will experience the lifestyle, locale, influences, techniques, and art works of this artist. Locate the step-by-step guidelines and worksheets for this activity in Studio Cyberspace. You may print out the instructions, or use the scrolling frame on the monitor to follow each step. Each activity screen will provide students with highlighted hot links which will, with a click of the mouse, take them to information on the World Wide Web to complete the activity. Find us at **http://www.glencoe.com/sec/art**

BUILDING VOCABULARY

Number a sheet of paper from 1 to 6. After each number, write the term from the list that best matches each description below.

linear perspective   Pietà
Madonna   Renaissance
oil paint   symbolism

1. A period of great awakening.
2. The use of slanted lines to make objects appear to extend back into space.
3. A work showing the Virgin Mary with the Christ Child.
4. A work showing Mary mourning over the body of Christ.
5. The use of an image to stand for a quality or an idea.
6. A mixture of pigment, linseed oil, and turpentine.

 REVIEWING ART FACTS

Number a sheet of paper from 7 to 14. Answer each question in a complete sentence.

7. Name three things the city of Florence was noted for in the 1400s.
8. Who was Masaccio? What is he remembered for?
9. Name two areas besides art in which Leonardo da Vinci was skilled.
10. In what way can Leonardo's influence be seen in the works of Raphael?

11. What is unusual about the proportions of the two figures in Michelangelo's *Pietà*?
12. What geometric shape did Renaissance artists use as a way of planning their works?
13. What feature of Gothic art did Northern Renaissance artists continue to use in their works?
14. What Northern Renaissance painter is credited for discovering oil paint?

 THINKING ABOUT ART

On a sheet of paper, answer each question in a sentence or two.

1. **Interpret.** Read the following statement: "Art of the present would not be possible without art of the past." Describe three facts about artists or events of the Renaissance that you would use to support this statement.
2. **Analyze.** Look once again at the two paintings by Jan van Eyck (Figures 11–11 and 11–14). Which has the most lifelike details? Which particular details struck you as looking most like a photograph?
3. **Compare and contrast.** In what ways were the art styles of the Renaissance in Italy and in the North similar? In what ways were they different?

MAKING ART CONNECTIONS

1. **Language Arts.** Another artist of the Northern Renaissance, Hieronymus Bosch, painted imagery and symbolism into his works. Read *Pish, Posh, Said Hieronymus Bosch*, by Nancy Willard. Discover in this poem how creatures in his paintings come to life and upset the woman who cares for his household.
2. **Social Studies.** Michelangelo, as you read in this chapter, was gifted in many

fields. Two of these were painting and architecture. In an art history book or encyclopedia, read about his contributions in these two areas. Note names of specific projects and, if possible, make photocopies of pictures of the works. In addition, gather details of Michelangelo's life. Combine your findings with information on his sculpture into a book.

■ Building Vocabulary

1. Renaissance
2. linear perspective
3. Madonna
4. Pietà
5. symbolism
6. oil paint

■ Reviewing Art Facts

7. Florence in the 1400s was the capital of Europe's cloth trade, the home of its richest bank, and a center for art.
8. Masaccio was a painter. He was remembered for being the first painter to use linear perspective to give his paintings a three-dimensional quality.
9. Leonardo da Vinci was skilled in science, literature, and music as well as art. (Students may choose two.)
10. Leonardo influenced Raphael to use subtle blending of light and dark values.
11. Michelangelo made Mary much larger than Jesus in his Pietà to intensify the mood of mourning.
12. Many Renaissance artists used a triangle or pyramid plan to balance their work.
13. Northern Renaissance artists continued to use the Gothic feature of symbolism.
14. Jan van Eyck is credited with discovering oil paint.

THINKING ABOUT ART

1. Answers will vary but should include the shift to realism, introduction of three-dimensional form and emotion into painting (Masaccio), discovery of oil paint (van Eyck), and continued use of symbolism.
2. Answers will vary. Both paintings have many realistic details as well as many symbols. Students will list different items.

3. Similarities include the use of symbolism, love of accurate details, three-dimensionality, and emotion. Differences include media: fresco painting in Italy and oils in northern Europe.

European Art of the 1600s and 1700s

(pages 176–191)

Resources

- 12-10 Chapter Test, TRB page 259
- Transparency CC-12, *Dissertation in Insect Generations* by Maria Merian
- Transparency 12, *The Night Watch* by Rembrandt van Rijn
- Fine Art Print 12, *A Philosopher Giving a Lecture* by Joseph Wright
- Fine Art Print 13, *Head of Holofernes* by Artemisia Gentileschi

ART SOURCE

Music
While studying this chapter, use Performing Arts Handbook page 328 to help students discover the early period singing style of Diana Zaslove.

NATIONAL STANDARDS

This chapter addresses the following National Standards for the Visual Arts:

1. (a, b)	**4.** (a, b)
2. (a, b, c)	**5.** (b)
3. (a, b)	**6.** (a, b)

176

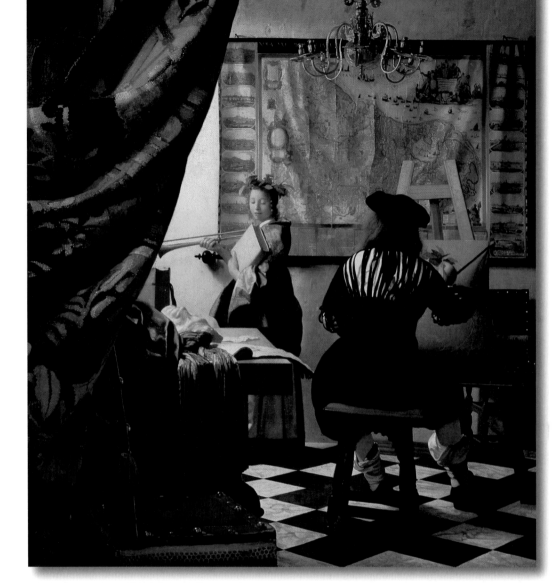

▲ Notice the careful use of light in this work. The viewer's eye is directed to the subject of the artist's attention, the model he is painting.

Jan Vermeer. *The Painter and his Model as Klio.* 1665–66. Oil on canvas. 120 x 100 cm (47¼ x 39⅜"). Kunsthistoriches Museum, Vienna.

176

FEATURED ARTISTS

Oliver Michel Barthelemy
Francesco Borromini
Michelangelo Merisi da Caravaggio
Jean-Baptiste Siméon Chardin

Francisco Goya
Louis Le Vau and Jules Hardoin-Mansart
Judith Leyster
Peter Paul Rubens
Rachel Ruysch

Rembrandt van Rijn
Diego Velázquez
Jan Vermeer
Élisabeth Vigée-Lebrun
Antoine Watteau

CHAPTER 12

European Art of the 1600s and 1700s

The mood of unrest in Europe following the Renaissance resulted in a religious revolution during the 1500s. This was followed a century later by yet another revolution.

This second revolution resulted in a new, peaceful atmosphere. It also resulted in a new wave of artists and new ways of making art. The picture at the left was done in a style of the age. Can you identify any of its features? You will soon be able to recognize them.

PORTFOLIO IDEAS

Find an art work in this chapter that has a dramatic feel. What elements of art did the artist use to create the expressive qualities? What principles of art were used? Create your own dramatic art work for your portfolio entry. Include your preliminary sketches and any notes you made to show the processes and techniques you used.

OBJECTIVES

After completing this chapter, you will be able to:

- Explain what new ways of creating art were brought about by the Counter-Reformation.
- Identify features of the Baroque style and name important artists who practiced it.
- Describe features of the Rococo style and identify important artists of the period.
- Create art works in the expressive style of Rembrandt.
- Experiment with art in the Rococo style.

WORDS YOU WILL LEARN

Baroque
etching
facade
portrait
Rococo

LESSON 1

Art of the 1600s

• • • • • • • • • • • • • • • •
FOCUS

✔OBJECTIVES

After completing this lesson, students will be able to:
• Describe the Protestant Reformation and Counter-Reformation movements.
• Characterize Baroque artists and architecture.
• Name Baroque artists from northern and southern Europe.

✔SUPPLIES

• Popular magazines.
• Objects for a naturally lit scene.
• Paints and brushes.
• Sheets of white paper, 18 x 24 inches (30 x 46 cm).

Resources

⊙ ■ 12-1 *Out of the Picture,*
⊙ TRB page 247
⊙ (reproducible master)
⊙ ■ 12-2 *The Art of Light and*
⊙ *Shadow,* TRB page 248
⊙ (reproducible master)
⊙ ■ 12-3 *Study Dutch Genre*
⊙ *Paintings,* TRB page 249
⊙ (cooperative learning)
⊙ ■ 12-4 *Baroque Sculpture,*
⊙ TRB page 251 (aesthetics/
⊙ art criticism)

When Rome collapsed, you will recall, the Catholic Church became more influential. It remained this way until the early 1500s, when the Church's power began to slip. A group of Christians led by a man named Martin Luther splintered off from the Church in revolt to form their own religion.

▲ **Figure 12–1** Study the changing light and dark values on the surface of this church. What principles are used to organize these different values?

Francesco Borromini. San Carlo alle Quattro Fontane. c. 1665–1676. Rome, Italy.

The Protestant Reformation, as this movement was called, drew many people away from the Catholic Church. In an effort to win them back, the Church started its own reform movement in the 1600s. This movement, which began in Italy, is known as the Counter-Reformation.

Art was an important part of the Counter-Reformation. Artists were called upon to create works that would renew religious spirit. A sense of flowing movement is one feature of a new art style of the day, **Baroque** (buh-**rohk**), or *an art style emphasizing movement, contrast, and variety.*

ARCHITECTURE AND PAINTING

In architecture the call to renew religious spirit was answered by, among others, an artist named Francesco Borromini (fran-**ches**-koh bor-uh-**meen**-ee). The church pictured in Figure 12–1 won Borromini great fame. He created the **facade** (fuh-**sahd**), *the outside front of a building,* to express his art. Do you notice how the surface seems to flow — first in, then out, then in again? Notice how the structure looks almost as though it were modeled from soft clay. This helps create a pattern of light and dark values across the whole facade. The Baroque emphasis on movement is also seen in painting of the period. Although the style originated in Italy, it spread to Spain and northern Europe.

Italy

The leader of the Baroque style in Italy was a young painter named Michelangelo Merisi da Caravaggio (kar-uh-**vahj**-yo). One of his key contributions was the use of light in a daring new way. This ability is combined with the artist's skill as a storyteller in the picture in Figure 12–2. Take a moment to study the work, which pictures the burial of

TECHNOLOGY OPTIONS

National Gallery of Art Videodisc   Use the following images to show more examples of art by artists introduced in this lesson.

Peter Paul Rubens
The Assumption of the Virgin

Search Frame 784

Judith Leyster
Self-Portrait

Search Frame 894

Diego Velázquez
The Needlewoman

Search Frame 533

Use Glencoe's *Correlation Bar Code Guide to the National Gallery of Art* to locate more art works.

Christ. It is as if a spotlight has been shone on real actors on a stage. Find the man holding Christ's legs. This man, whose eyes meet yours, draws you into the painting. Notice the puzzled expression on his face. He seems about to ask you to identify yourself. Perhaps he will also ask if you intend to merely watch or to help in laying Christ in his tomb. In this way, Caravaggio makes you feel that you are a part of the drama.

Spain

Not all Baroque paintings showed such tense, dramatic movement. Movement of another sort is found in the works of Spanish painter Diego Velázquez (dee-**ay**-goh vuh-**las**-kez). One of these, a simple painting of a woman sewing, is pictured in Figure 12–3.

Examine this painting. Note how the fingers of both hands are blurred. This helps show that her fingers are moving rapidly as she sews.

Northern Europe

The major talents in Northern Europe, you will remember, developed during the Renaissance. This trend continued into the 1600s, led by a Flemish painter named Peter Paul Rubens. No other Baroque artist came close to Rubens in capturing the action and feeling of the new style. Notice his use of line in the work in Figure 12–4 on page 180. The picture shows the Virgin Mary rising toward heaven. Can you find the line—partly real, partly imaginary—beginning in the raised arm of the figure at the left? Where does this line lead? What kind of line is it? Notice how the line pulls the viewer into the work, making him or her feel present.

▲ **Figure 12–2** Light is used to emphasize the most important details of this picture. These details are shown in shocking realism. Notice that even the soles of Christ's feet are painted to look dirty.

Caravaggio. *The Deposition*. 1604. Vatican Museum, Pinacoteca, Rome, Italy.

▲ **Figure 12–3** The young woman in this picture may be the artist's daughter. She is known to have married one of his pupils.

Diego Velázquez. *The Needlewoman*. c. 1640–1650. Oil on canvas. 74 x 60 cm (29⅛ x 23⅝"). National Gallery of Art, Washington, D.C. Andrew W. Mellon Collection.

Lesson 1   *Art of the 1600s*   **179**

■ Motivator

Ask students to think of a passionate, dramatic story they have told in order to persuade someone of something. Discuss when a cool and logical approach is most persuasive and when a dramatic story works best. Explain the Counter-Reformation church's belief that emotionally charged accounts of Biblical tales were necessary to persuade people to remain within the Catholic Church.

■ Vocabulary

Have students look up the definition of *Baroque* in a dictionary. Tell them how the term was once considered an insult. Discuss how people who were used to the orderliness and balance of Italian Renaissance art might see Baroque art and architecture as tortured, exaggerated, and grotesque. If possible, augment the discussion with a picture of Baroque-era furnishings.

■ Aesthetics

Have students examine Figure 12-3. Discuss how Velázquez used the art elements and principles to capture the sitter's character and to create an atmosphere of dignity and concentration. Ask: Does Velazquez provide a sense of his subject's inner self? Explain to students that an interest in the psychological aspects of portraiture was another feature of much Baroque art.

■ Art History

Remind students that art historians rely on a variety of documents to identify who made a particular art work. Have students fabricate a document that answers historians' questions for Figure 12-5a. Students can write a page in Judith Leyster's diary, a critic's review of the painting, or a letter from a fellow artist.

RESOURCES BEYOND THE CLASSROOM

City Tours   City tours are a fruitful way to discuss architecture; they help students understand that this form of art indeed surrounds them all the time. Each region has certain specialties that are common throughout the area: eastern cities often have excellent examples of colonial architecture; southern cities often have well-maintained examples of antebellum architecture. Many towns have Victorian or Victorian-type homes that are of interest to art students, and even more towns have examples of "classical" architecture—Greek and Roman-like buildings with stately columns and formal gardens. Guided tours of area architecture frequently are conducted by the local chamber of commerce or the local tourism office.

■ **Art History**

Have students study Figure 12-4. Point out Mary's hefty proportions. Ask students to hypothesize why Rubens painted her so large. Explain that large-bodied women were considered highly attractive in this era, and show other paintings by Rubens to illustrate this fact. Have students search through magazines and identify examples of what are considered ideal female bodies today. Emphasize how standards of attractiveness vary according to time and place.

■ **Studio Skills**

Set up a scene that is lit by a sunny window. Have the light fall diagonally from outside of the picture frame. If at all possible, include a person in the scene who is engaged in a focused activity. Have students paint the scene and attempt to render the shadows and dramatic lighting in the manner of Vermeer's painting in the chapter opener on page 176.

■ **Cultural Diversity**

Discuss the sculptural qualities of Borromini's facade shown in Figure 12-1 on page 178. Then have students research Hindu temples in Northern India, such as the Lingaraja temple in Bhubaneshwar and the Lakshmana temple in Khajuraho, and religious architecture in Cambodia, such as the Angkor Wat. These buildings also have highly sculptural exteriors. Help students characterize the ways in which the facades of these buildings embody some of the same elastic, rhythmic, and three-dimensional qualities as San Carlo alle Quattro Fontane in Rome.

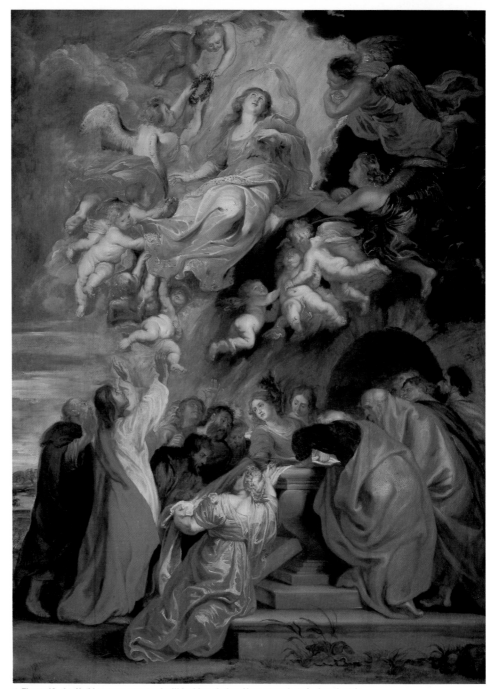

▲ **Figure 12—4** Nothing seems to stand still in this painting. You are made to feel as though you are witnessing a moment in time.

Sir Peter Paul Rubens. *The Assumption of the Virgin.* c. 1626. Wood. 125.4 x 94.2 cm (49⅜ x 37⅛"). National Gallery of Art, Washington, D.C. Samuel H. Kress Collection.

more about • • •

Peter Paul Rubens   Of all the European artists of the seventeenth century, Peter Paul Rubens most completely captured the exciting spirit and rich effects of the Baroque style. While still a young man, he spent eight years in Italy. There he came to know sixteenth-century Italian painting and the works of Caravaggio.

When he returned to his native Antwerp he set up a studio that soon became the busiest in Europe. Assisted by many helpers, Rubens turned out portraits, religious pictures, and mythical scenes. He also gained fame as a diplomat and as a man of learning.

In neighboring Holland, which remained a Protestant stronghold, a new subject matter for paintings was busily being explored. Genre pictures showing simple scenes from daily life were preferred over religious paintings. Other kinds of paintings that were popular were the **portrait,** *a painting of a person,* and the still life. A gifted young painter named Judith Leyster (**lye**-stuhr) specialized in portraits, using quick, dazzling brush strokes. This allowed her to catch the fleeting expressions on the faces of her subjects. Figure 12–5a shows a portrait she did of herself. Note how she seems to smile out of the picture at the viewer. Could she be eager for the viewer's reaction to the painting she is working on?

In seventeenth-century Holland, flowers were one of the most prized still-life subjects.

▲ **Figure 12–5a** By the time she was 17, the artist was already gaining fame as a painter. With her detailed style and careful brush work, Leyster created portraits that invite the viewer to interact with the subject.

Judith Leyster. *Self-Portrait.* c. 1635. Canvas. 72.3 x 65.3 cm (29⅜ x 25⅝"). National Gallery of Art, Washington, D.C. Gift of Mr. & Mrs. Robert Woods Bliss.

▲ **Figure 12–5b** Ruysch was interested in producing a faithful reproduction of nature, and she worked slowly and carefully toward that goal. She once spent seven years finishing three pictures as a wedding gift for her daughter.

Rachel Ruysch. *Roses, Bonvolvulus, Poppies, and Other Flowers in an Urn on a Stone Ledge.* c. 1745. Oil on canvas. 107.95 x 83.82 cm (42½ x 33"). The National Museum of Women in the Arts, Washington, D.C. Gift of Wallace and Wilhelmina Holladay.

One of the most highly respected flower painters of this century was Rachel Ruysch. Figure 12–5b is an excellent example of the realistic style. Notice how the flowers are arranged to form an S-curve. This was a technique Ruysch used in many of her paintings.

✔ CHECK YOUR UNDERSTANDING

1. What was the Protestant Reformation? Who was its leader?
2. What was the Counter-Reformation?
3. What new art style arose during the period of the Counter-Reformation? What are the main features of this style?
4. What was a main contribution of Caravaggio?
5. Name a major Baroque painter of northern Europe.
6. What is a portrait? What artist that you read about specialized in painting portraits?

Drawing Expressive Hands

(pages 182–183)

LESSON TIME: 90 minutes

Drawing Expressive Hands

FOCUS

☑ OBJECTIVES

After completing this lesson, students will be able to:

- Describe the expressive qualities of various hand positions.
- Create an expressive drawing of hands.
- Use three-dimensional shading techniques.

☑ SUPPLIES

- Pencils and sketch paper.
- Sheets of black construction paper, 9 x 12 inches (23 x 30 cm).
- White crayons.

Resources

- 12-5 *Rembrandt and The Night Watch,* TRB page 252 (art history)
- 12-6 *Chiaroscuro Ink Drawing,* TRB page 254 (studio)

TEACH

■ Motivator

Ask students to think of a body posture that reflects a particular feeling. Have each student assume their position in turn and see if the rest of the class can guess what emotion is being expressed. Discuss the phenomenon of body language and its importance to artists. Ask: Do you notice in daily life how people position their bodies? Is body language something that you respond to on a subconscious level?

182

The leading Dutch painter of the 1600s is a man named Rembrandt van Rijn (**ryn**). Figure 12–6 shows a portrait by this master. The artist uses a soft light to highlight the main parts of the picture. The subject, you will notice, is not beautiful. She seems, however, not to care about this. She is not bothered by the fact that others may be more attractive. If anything, she appears to be at peace with the world and her place in it. Notice how even her hands mirror this gentle calm. The artist has managed to make them look totally relaxed and at rest.

WHAT YOU WILL LEARN

You will make a drawing of your hand on black construction paper. Draw the hand to express a particular feeling. White crayon will be used to emphasize the three-dimensional form of the hand. (See Figure 12–7.)

WHAT YOU WILL NEED

- Pencil and sheets of sketch paper
- Sheet of black construction paper, 9 x 12 inches (23 x 30 cm)
- White crayon

▶ **Figure 12–6** The artist uses a straight horizontal line in the center of this picture. He separates the linen scarf from the lady's clothing. Do you remember what kind of mood a straight line like this calls to mind?

Rembrandt van Rijn. *Portrait of a Lady with an Ostrich-Feather Fan.* c. 1660. Canvas. 99.5 x 83 cm (39¼ x 32⅝"). National Gallery of Art, Washington, D.C. Widener Collection.

TECHNOLOGY OPTIONS

National Gallery of Art Videodisc   Use the following images to examine artists' treatment of hands in paintings.

Rembrandt van Rijn
Portrait of a Lady with an Ostrich-Feather Fan

Search Frame 876

Rembrandt van Rijn
Detail

Search Frame 878

Elisabeth Vigée-Lebrun
Portrait of a Lady

Search Frame 1091

Use Glencoe's *Correlation Bar Code Guide to the National Gallery of Art* to locate more art works.

WHAT YOU WILL DO

1. Brainstorm with your classmates on ways hands can show different moods and feelings. Some possibilities for discussion are surprise, anger, sadness, joy, and nervousness. Choose one of these moods or feelings. Do not tell anyone in your class which one you have picked.
2. Pose the hand you do not use to draw with in a way that shows the mood you have selected. It might be relaxed, clenched, or distorted in some way. With your drawing hand, make pencil sketches of the posed hand. Make your drawings as accurate as you can.
3. Still using pencil, draw the best of your sketches on the sheet of black paper. Make the drawing large enough to fill the sheet.
4. Switching to white crayon, add highlights to your drawing. Begin by coloring lightly. Gently blend the crayon around the fingers and other hand parts to make them look three-dimensional and lifelike. (For information on shading techniques, see Technique Tip **6**, *Handbook* page **278**.) Press lightly when coloring shadowed areas. Press harder on the crayon when coloring the most highly lighted areas.
5. Place your finished drawing on display with those of other students. Decide which of the drawings are most lifelike. Are your classmates able to guess the feeling or mood your hand drawing expresses?

EXAMINING YOUR WORK

- **Describe**   Tell whether your drawing looks like your hand. Identify its most realistic features.
- **Analyze**   Show where you used white crayon to highlight your drawing. State whether the light and dark values emphasize the three-dimensional form of the hand.
- **Interpret**   Tell whether your drawing expresses a particular mood or feeling. Tell whether viewers were able to identify this feeling.
- **Judge**   Identify the best feature of your drawing. Tell whether it is the realistic appearance of your work, the use of light and dark to give a sense of roundness, or the expressive content of your drawing.

▲ **Figure 12–7   Student work. Expressive hands.**

 Try This! COMPUTER OPTION

■ Select a hand position that expresses a mood. Flood-fill page or canvas with a dark color. Use light chalk or charcoal Brush to draw hand with a mouse or light pen. Choose a rough paper texture if available.

Show hand and finger contours by adding light areas with small strokes of Brush tool. Gradually blend strokes to slowly move from very dark to lightest areas. Title, save, and print your work.

Lesson 2   *Drawing Expressive Hands*   **183**

■ Art History

Display reproductions of a variety of Dutch Baroque paintings that include women. Some good choices are Frans Hals's *Isabella Coymans* and *Regentesses of the Old Men's Home* and genre scenes by Pieter de Hooch and Garard ter Borch. Then have students write a page out of the diary of a seventeenth-century Dutch woman. Have students read aloud their diary pages.

• • • • • • • • • • • • • • • • •
ASSESS

■ Self-Assessment

Have students use Examining Your Work to evaluate their expressive hands drawing created in this lesson. Responses may be written or oral.

■ Reteaching

Have students select magazine photos showing various body parts portrayed in different positions. Working in small groups, have them assemble composite human figures out of their clippings by pasting the components onto a sheet of paper. Have the groups present their work to the class.

■ Enrichment

Students may be interested in researching pictures by other artists who excelled at rendering expressive hands. These artists include the Northern Renaissance printmaker and painter Albrecht Dürer, the German Expressionist painter Oskar Kokoschka, and the twentieth-century American painter Alice Neel. Suggest that students also compare these images with the very different and formal expressiveness achieved in figural works by Egyptian and Byzantine artists.

• • • • • • • • • • • • • • • • •
CLOSE

Ask students to describe the most difficult and most rewarding parts of doing this Studio Lesson.

Art of the 1700s

Just as events of the 1500s brought in the Baroque style, so events of the 1600s brought about its end. The most important of these was the crowning of one of history's most colorful, pleasure-loving rulers. Because this king chose the sun as his emblem, he became known as the Sun King.

In this lesson you will learn about this king, the period in which he lived, and the new art style that he helped inspire.

EUROPE IN THE LATE 1600s

During the 1600s France emerged as Europe's strongest and wealthiest nation. Its capital, Paris, became the center of art. Find this city on the map shown in Figure 12–8.

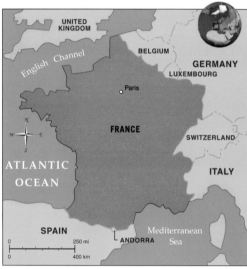

▲ **Figure 12–8   France.**

The force behind these changes was a powerful king with very rich tastes. He was Louis XIV, who ruled France for over 70 years. Louis' tastes were to help chart the course Western art would follow over the next 100 years.

Architecture

The beginnings of the new art style were put into motion in 1661. That year Louis ordered architects to build him the biggest, most elaborate palace in the world. It was built at Versailles (vuhr-**sye**), a short distance from Paris (Figure 12–9).

No photograph can begin to do the Palace of Versailles justice. The building covers 15 acres and contains enough rooms to house 10,000 people. The landscaped gardens around the palace cover another 250 acres. In Louis' time, 4 million flower bulbs were brought in each year from Holland to fill these gardens with the flowers the king loved.

Painting

Life for the king and his friends at Versailles was happy and carefree. This mood gave rise to a new style of art in the early 1700s. This style, which has come to be called **Rococo** (ruh-**koh**-koh), is *an art style stressing free, graceful movement; a playful use of line; and bright colors*.

The first artist to create works in the Rococo style was a painter named Antoine Watteau (an-**twahn** wah-**toh**). Watteau's pictures show a make-believe world peopled by untroubled members of France's ruling class. The painting in Figure 12–10 is one such picture. Like the figures in Watteau's other works, the people in this one appear to have not a care in the world. They are shown in a parklike garden listening to music. Notice

---

MEETING STUDENT DIVERSITY

Auditory/Kinesthetic Learners   To help students organize the artists and styles introduced in this chapter, divide the class into two teams. Have students plan a Who? What? When? Where? guessing game about the artists, art works, art forms, and art styles. Each team should write clues on cards and write the answers on the back.

One team can work on Who? and What? clues while the other team prepares Where? and When? cards. After each team has prepared about six cards, students can take turns guessing the answers. At the end of the game, teams should give answers to clues not guessed.

▲ Figure 12–9   The gardens at Versailles also included a small zoo with unusual animals and birds. Louis XIV spent nearly three-fourths of all taxes collected to pay for this and other luxuries of his palace.

Louis Le Vau and Jules Hardouin-Mansart. Palace at Versailles, France.

◀ Figure 12–10   This painting shows a group of aristocrats about to leave the legendary island of romance. Notice the delicate figures, rich costumes, and dreamlike setting. These, along with the soft colors, are typical of Watteau's Rococo style.

Antoine Watteau. *Embarkation from Cythera*. 1717–1719. Charlottemburg Museo, The Louvre, Paris, France.

Lesson 3   *Art of the 1700s*   **185**

more about • • •

Antoine Watteau   Watteau's fête galante painting *Embarkation from Cythera* was the work that he presented to obtain membership in the Academy. It represents an island dedicated to love and the worship of Venus. The goddess of love was said to have first stepped on firm ground at Cythera, which is a real island in the Mediterranean. All the protagonists in this painting are couples. The staff and little capes worn by the people show they have gone on a pilgrimage to Cythera to seek a land where romance lives forever. According to historian Stephen Jones, "The thrill for the aristocrats who saw such a picture may have lain in the implication that some high romantic aspiration inspired their own elegant but pointless existence."

■ Vocabulary

Invite a printmaker to speak to the class about various forms of printmaking, including *etching*. The speaker should present examples of prints executed in each printmaking technique so that students can appreciate their different qualities.

■ Aesthetics

Tell students that the great majority of eighteenth-century intellectuals strongly objected to Rococo art on the grounds that it was frivolous and lacking in serious moral purpose. Divide students into debating teams. One side should defend paintings such as those by Watteau and the other side should say why they are worthless, if not morally harmful. If possible, display reproductions of works but Rococo artists Francois Boucher and Jean-Honoré Fragonard as reference points during the debate.

■ Art Criticism

Have students examine Figure 12-11. Explain that commissioned portraits often represent the sitter as he or she ideally wants to be perceived. Have students find and study images of women in magazine ads. Help students see how the ads reflect modern notions of beauty and glamour, just as Vigée-Lebrun's society portraits show how women were supposed to look in the eighteenth-century.

■ Art History

Have students investigate other paintings by Watteau, especially ones that are set in a garden or park. Ask students to write a paragraph that characterizes the mood of these works and explains why such scenes were so popular with Rococo period dealers and collectors.

■ **Cultural Diversity**

Ask students to find information on a non-European building that is as lavish and extravagant in its own way as the palace at Versailles. Students should write a page that describes the style of the building and explains when, where, and for whom it was created. They should also complete a careful drawing of their chosen structure. You may wish to suggest the following buildings to students who are having difficulty selecting one: Santa Sophia in Constantinople (present day Istanbul), Madrasah on Registan in Samarkind, Persia (present day Iran), the Taj Mahal in India, and the Temple of Angkor Wat in Cambodia.

Art in
Everyday Life

Tell students to consider their own lifestyles and clothing as art works. Have students draw a very fanciful scene based on their own life. Their pictures should incorporate as many elements of the Rococo style as possible. Students should draw themselves in Rococo clothing and engaged in a carefree activity, but the drawing should also contain identifiable features of twentieth-century life.

▲ **Figure 12–11** The artist lived to be 87. When she died, her will called for a relief carving of a painter's palette and brush on her tombstone.

Élisabeth Vigée-Lebrun. *Portrait of a Lady.* 1789. Wood. 107 x 83 cm (42⅛ x 32¾"). National Gallery of Art, Washington, D.C. Samuel H. Kress Collection.

▲ **Figure 12–12** Chardin painted many scenes like the one in this work. Each treats familiar scenes and ordinary objects with respect and affection.

Jean-Baptiste-Siméon Chardin. *The Kitchen Maid.* 1738. Canvas. 46.2 x 37.5 cm (18⅛ x 14¾"). National Gallery of Art, Washington, D.C. Samuel H. Kress Collection.

that the viewer seems to be looking at this scene from far off. What reason might the artist have had for removing us—and himself—from the events in the painting?

The members of the French ruling class enjoyed having their portraits painted. An artist who met this demand was Élisabeth Vigée-Lebrun (ay-**lee**-zah-bet vee-**zhay**-luh-**bruhn**). Before she was 20, Vigée-Lebrun had painted many important nobles. By the time she was 25, she was named the queen's personal portrait painter. Vigée-Lebrun's portraits often put the subject in a very favorable light. She also reveals, in works like the one in Figure 12–11, how successful a simple pose can be. Notice how the young woman appears to be watching and listening *to you*. How flattering this is. No doubt this attention adds to a warm feeling about her.

Another side of French life was shown in the Rococo paintings done by Jean-Baptiste Siméon Chardin (**zhahn**-bah-**teest** see-may-**ohnh** shahr-**danh**). His genre pictures take the viewer into the simple homes of everyday people. One of these works, Figure 12–12, shows a woman preparing a meal. She seems to be lost in dreamy thought as she works. Everyone has had similar experiences when a sound or image sets the mind wandering for a few moments. Notice how the artist blends mellow colors and carefully painted still-life objects to communicate a quiet mood. The world of Chardin's art is one where time stands still and nothing disturbs the peacefulness. The viewer is able to observe simple domestic scenes treated with respect and affection.

186   Lesson 3   *Art of the 1700s*

---

more about • • •

Vigée-Lebrun Marie Louise Élisabeth Vigée-Lebrun is one of history's most celebrated women artists. Before she was twenty, she had studied in a convent, received private art lessons from colleagues of her artist father, and painted portraits of important members of the French aristocracy. By the age of twenty-five, she was employed by Queen Marie-Antoinette, whose portrait she painted often.

On the night the queen and king were arrested, Vigée-Lebrun escaped from Paris. The French Revolution did not stop her career, however. She continued to work in other European capitals. Vigée-Lebrun's easy, charming portraits present sitters at their best advantage. They also preserve for posterity a picture of the aristocratic way of life as it faded from history.

ROCOCO ART IN SPAIN

The Rococo style in painting was not limited to France. In Spain the style was picked up by a free-thinking artist named Francisco Goya (fran-**sis**-koh **goy**-uh). Through his early forties, Goya painted softly lighted portraits of people from Spanish high society. A glimpse of the horrors and suffering of war, however, changed all that.

In 1808 French troops attacked Spain. The bloody scenes Goya witnessed prompted a series of etchings. An **etching** is *an intaglio print made by scratching an image onto a specially treated copper plate*. The etching in Figure 12–13 shows a French firing squad taking aim at a captured war prisoner. The figures and weapons stand out against a darkened sky. Goya's view of war is stripped of brave warriors and glorious victories. It is a shocking vision of death and destruction.

▲ **Figure 12–13** How do you suppose viewers in the 1800s reacted to the manner in which Goya chose to express scenes like this in his work?

Francisco de Goya. *Cornered (From the Disasters of War).* Barbares, Paris, France. Bibliotheque Nationale.

STUDIO ACTIVITY

Make It Extraordinary

Look once again at the painting in Figure 12–12 by Jean-Baptiste Siméon Chardin. The artist, it might be said, changes the ordinary into the extraordinary. With a little imagination, you can do the same.

Find a small, ordinary object. Focus your search on something you would not usually think of in connection with a painting. Some examples are a clothespin, a nail, or a safety pin. Study the object carefully, and then draw it on a sheet of white paper. The drawing should totally fill the page. It should also be as accurate as you can make it. Use tempera to add color. Work at capturing the color, form, and texture of the object. Paint the background a dark color so the object will stand out boldly.

PORTFOLIO

When your painting is complete, assess your work. Write your responses to the questions on page **177**. Keep your self-assessment and your painting together in your portfolio.

✔ CHECK YOUR UNDERSTANDING

1. What country became the center of art in the late 1600s? What king helped bring about the change?
2. What new art style grew out of the carefree life of the ruling class at Versailles? What are the main features of works done in this style?
3. What kinds of paintings were created by Antoine Watteau? What kind of paintings were done by Élisabeth Vigée-Lebrun and by Jean-Baptiste Siméon Chardin?
4. What are etchings? What events prompted Goya's etchings of war-related scenes? What do these etchings tell about Goya's view of war?

Lesson 3   *Art of the 1700s*   **187**

STUDIO ACTIVITY

Make It Extraordinary

If students are hesitant to draw the object on a full page, let them begin by sketching the object in pencil to see where they should add lines and details.

ASSESS

■ Self-Assessment

Have students complete the review questions on this page. Answers are provided below.

■ Reteaching

Tell students that some art historians have found the roots of Rococo style in Rubens's paintings. Have students re-examine Figure 12-4 on page 180 and discuss the features that resemble elements of the Rococo art illustrated in this lesson.

■ Enrichment

Show students reproductions of the high society portraits that Goya created early in his career as an artist. Compare them with Figure 12-13 and characterize the mood of each. Then have students write a short story in which a dramatic event leads to a completely new outlook on life.

CLOSE

Ask students to name one artist from the Rococo period and describe one of his or her paintings.

Answers to ✔ CHECK YOUR UNDERSTANDING

1. France. Louis XIV helped bring about the change.
2. *Rococo* style. It was characterized by free, graceful movement, playful use of line, and bright colors.
3. Antoine Watteau painted pictures showing a make-believe world by untroubled members of France's ruling class. Élisabeth Vigée-Lebrun painted portraits of the ruling class and was named the queen's personal portrait painter. Jean-Baptiste Siméon Chardin focused on life in the simple homes of everyday people.
4. An etching is an intaglio print made by scratching an image onto a specially treated copper plate. Goya emphasized death and destruction.

• • • • • • • • • • • • • •
FOCUS

☑ OBJECTIVES

After completing this lesson, students will be able to:
- Describe clothing and hairstyles of the 1700s.
- Design a shoe that incorporates Rococo features.

☑ SUPPLIES

- Pencils and sketch paper; scissors.
- Heavy cardboard scraps; white glue, and staplers.
- Pieces of brightly colored, richly patterned cloth.
- Scrap materials, such as buckles, laces, bows, and sequins.
- Video of the film *Amadeus*.

• • • • • • • • • • • • • •
TEACH

■ Motivator

Have the students watch a scene from the film *Amadeus* that includes clear views of Rococo clothing and hairstyles. The ballroom scene near the beginning of the film is a good choice, and even includes a look at Mozart's shoes. Discuss the most prominent features of fashions from that era. Ask: In what ways do the costumes in *Amadeus* resemble the outfits shown in Watteau's painting?

 LESSON 4

Constructing a Rococo Shoe

The 1700s were, above all else, a period of high fashion. It was said that if a woman left Paris on a short vacation, she would return to find all her clothes outdated. Hairdos grew taller and taller, and so did the heels on shoes—men's as well as women's. Architects began raising doors higher so people could pass through. Paintings by Antoine Watteau, like the one in Figure 12–14, mirror this concern for fashion. The figures in this painting look almost like fashion dolls.

Imagine that the president of a modern-day shoe company has decided to stage a contest. Designers are to come up with ideas for a shoe. It is to be of a type that might be found on the foot of a figure in a Watteau painting.

WHAT YOU WILL LEARN

You will design and create a Rococo shoe using cardboard and scrap materials. Use a variety of colors, shapes, and textures to create a highly decorative pattern. Your finished shoe will be a three-dimensional form. (See Figure 12–15.)

WHAT YOU WILL NEED

- Pencil and sheets of sketch paper
- Sheets of lightweight cardboard
- Scissors, heavy cardboard scraps, white glue, and stapler
- Pieces of brightly colored, richly patterned cloth
- Scrap materials, such as buckles, laces, bows, and sequins

▲ **Figure 12–14** This painting was created as a signboard for an art gallery in Paris. Notice the elegant patrons dressed in rich costumes of the times.

Jean-Antoine Watteau. *The Signboard of Gersaint.* c. 1721. Oil on canvas. 163 x 308 cm (64⅛ x 121¼"). Charlottenburg Palace, Berlin, Germany. Charlottenburg Castle. Staatliche Schoeloesser und Gaerten, Berlin, Germany.

188   Lesson 4   *Constructing a Rococo Shoe*

MEETING SPECIAL NEEDS

Assembling   The cardboard shoe assembly task may be difficult for students with some disabilities, such as neurological or orthopedic disabilities. You might pair these students with a non-disabled student. Together they will create two of the forms and then independently decorate and paint their own. Students who are shy might especially benefit from a class discussion of fashion, comparing contemporary sport shoe designs to examples of unique shoes and sandals, ties and belts, patterned shoelaces, and other trendy styles brought from a second-hand clothing store.

WHAT YOU WILL DO

1. Make several pencil sketches of a shoe as seen from the side. Make your design as elaborate and unusual as you can. Use exaggerated heels, soles, laces, and decorative features. Let your imagination guide you.
2. Choose your best sketch. Draw the outline of the shoe on a sheet of cardboard. Make the shoe lifesize. Carefully cut out the shoe.
3. Place your cutout on a second piece of cardboard. Holding it firmly in place, carefully cut around it, creating a second identical shoe.
4. Glue strips of heavy cardboard between the two shoe cutouts. These will be hidden inside, and will give you the basic form of a shoe.
5. Using pieces of cloth in different colors and patterns, cover the shoe form. Curve the cloth pieces around the heel of the shoe and across the top and the toe. Staple the cloth in place. (*Hint:* Cutting the cloth scraps small will help add to the decorative look of the shoe.) Glue buckles, bows, laces, and other scrap items in place as added decoration.
6. When the glue is dry, place your shoe on display. Compare your finished shoe with those of your classmates.

EXAMINING YOUR WORK

- **Describe**   Tell whether your finished object can be recognized as a shoe. State whether it has a heel, sole, and other shoe parts. Explain how your shoe is a three-dimensional form.
- **Analyze**   Point out the variety of colors, shapes, and textures in your work.
- **Interpret**   Identify the kind of person who would wear the shoe you designed. State whether you could imagine the shoe on the foot of a subject in Figure 12–14.
- **Judge**   Tell whether you feel you have succeeded in creating a Rococo shoe. State whether you feel it would win the shoe company contest. Explain why.

▲ Figure 12–15   Student work. Rococo shoe.

STUDIO OPTIONS

Try This!

- Create a shoe box with a design in the same Rococo style as your shoe. Follow the instructions given in Lesson 4 of Chapter 11.
- How would an ancient Egyptian, Greek, or Roman shoe differ from your Rococo shoe?

Select a period you have read about, and design a shoe that reflects that period in a humorous way. Create a painting of your own design using tempera colors. Display your work, and ask if anyone can identify the period you selected.

more about • • •

Rococo Style   In the eighteenth century, the French court at Versailles dictated the fashions of European footwear. Women were taught to lift their skirts to show off dainty shoes and ankles. Shoes had a curved heel and were frequently embellished with jewelry and embroidery. Buckles and ties over the instep were also typical. One of the most characteristic Rococo shoes was the backless silk and lace women's dress shoe. During the peak of the Rococo era, from 1740 to 1770, fashionable men wore heeled shoes with large silver or diamond buckles that complemented their colorful garments. By the 1780s footwear became more informal and facilitated a greater freedom of movement.

■ Cultural Diversity

Have students investigate and write a paragraph on a non-European style of clothing that possesses a highly decorative or ornate aesthetic. Some possibilities are the clothing of the Sioux, Latin American festival garments, Indian saris, and the imperial Chinese fashions.

• • • • • • • • • • • • •

ASSESS

■ Self-Assessment

Have students use Examining Your Work to evaluate their Rococo shoe created in this Studio Lesson. Responses may be written or oral.

■ Reteaching

Have students examine reproductions of Francois Boucher's paintings of Madame de Pompadour, a fashion trendsetter for European style. List on the board all of the elements of her dress and shoes and discuss how they are characteristic of the Rococo period.

■ Enrichment

Have students consider the question of whether people today are as concerned with fashion styles as they were in the 1700s. Students should consider factors such as the amount of money spent on clothing, how much people notice what others wear, how important it is to wear fashionable styles, and how often people discuss fashion. Have students write a page that states their conclusion and the reasons for them.

• • • • • • • • • • • • •

CLOSE

Have students compare the Rococo shoe style with shoe styles of today.

CONNECTIONS *Music*

☑ OBJECTIVES

After completing this feature, students will be able to:

- Understand the similarities between Baroque art and music.
- Name some of the composers of this period.

Teaching the Connection

- Have students read the feature on this page.
- Ask volunteers to share what they know about the art and music of the Baroque period. What kinds of music was written during this time? *(Composers wrote large-scale, expressive, elaborate pieces, rich in harmony and counterpoint. Cantatas, oratorios, and operas were popular forms, as was instrumental music.)* How was Baroque music similar to Baroque art? *(Both were more dramatic and more worldly than in earlier times. Both moved away from the restraint and order of the Renaissance.)* In this painting, how does the room itself have a Baroque feel? *(Its high ceiling and ornate furnishings share the same large-scale, expansiveness of the Baroque period.)*
- Tell students that Mozart went on tour as a child, performing for the rich and famous. He was still a child at the end of the Baroque period. His generation of artists and musicians built on the Baroque style to establish styles of their own.

Answers to Making the Connection

- They are rich aristocrats being entertained at tea.
- Responses will vary.
- Students' research will vary.

190

Oliver Michel Barthelemy. *Le Thé à l'Anglaise au Temple Chez le Prince de Conti.* 1766. Louvre, Paris, France. Lauros-Giraudon / Art Resource, New York.

How were Baroque Music and Art Similar?

From about 1600 to 1750, European music followed some of the same directions as art. It was vivid, expressive, and full of movement. The composers explored new avenues, using harmony and the major and minor scales more than before. For the first time, instrumental music was almost as popular as vocal music. As with art, much of the changes began in Italy with the introduction of the concerto and the opera.

Most composers of this time worked as organists and choirmasters in a church or were hired as musicians by aristocrats. Some of the most influential and successful composers of the time were Jean-Baptiste Lully of France, Henry Purcell of England, and Domenico Scarlatti and Antonio Vivaldi of Italy. Perhaps the most enduring musicians of the Baroque period, however, were Johann Sebastian Bach and Georg Friedrich Handel of Germany. In the late 1700s, the European middle class grew and public concerts became popular.

┌ MAKING THE CONNECTION

- ✔ How can you tell the social status of the audience pictured here in Barthelemy's painting? What are they doing?
- ✔ What music from this period have you listened to? How would you describe some of the works you have heard?
- ✔ Find out more about the life and work of one of the composers listed above. Listen to a few of that person's compositions.

INTERNET ACTIVITY

Visit Glencoe's Fine Arts Web Site for students at:

http://www.glencoe.com/sec/art/students

INTERNET ACTIVITY

Classrooms On-Line Share the experience of working together, exploring together, cooperating and learning with other teachers and classrooms who use the Glencoe Fine Arts programs. Make this connection work for you as you escape the walls of your classroom and join in the experience of many teachers who are doing the same projects and who want to share their thoughts.

Let us hear about your best ideas and share with others your successes. Promote the art and accomplishments of your own students. Find this connection within the *Teacher Resources* area of Glencoe's Fine Arts Site. Find links to kindred classrooms in this section of Glencoe's site to expand students' learning experiences. Find us at **http://www.glencoe.com/sec/art**

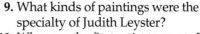
CHAPTER 12
REVIEW

BUILDING VOCABULARY

Number a sheet of paper from 1 to 5. After each number, write the term from the list that best matches each description below.

Baroque   portrait
etching   Rococo
facade

1. The outside front of a building.
2. An art style emphasizing movement, contrast, and variety.
3. A painting of a person.
4. An art style stressing free, graceful movement; a playful use of line; and bright colors.
5. An intaglio print made by scratching an image onto a specially treated copper plate.

 REVIEWING ART FACTS

Number a sheet of paper from 6 to 13. Answer each question in a complete sentence.

6. What architectural art style was practiced by Francesco Borromini?
7. What was a key contribution of Caravaggio to the art of the 1600s?
8. What kinds of paintings were in demand in Holland during the 1600s?

9. What kinds of paintings were the specialty of Judith Leyster?
10. Who was the first artist to create Rococo paintings?
11. To what post was Élisabeth Vigée-Lebrun named as a young woman?
12. What side of French life of the 1700s is revealed in the paintings of Jean-Baptiste Siméon Chardin?
13. What sorts of paintings did Francisco Goya create through his early forties?

 THINKING ABOUT ART

On a sheet of paper, answer each question in a sentence or two.

1. **Analyze.** Turn again to Caravaggio's painting of Christ's burial (Figure 12–2). Notice the artist's use of texture to add variety to the work. How many different textures can you find? On what objects in the work are these textures found?
2. **Compare and contrast.** Look once again at the portraits by Judith Leyster (Figure 12–5a) and Élisabeth Vigée-Lebrun (Figure 12–11). Tell in what ways the two works are alike. Explain how they are different. Which of these two artists' works do you find most successful? Explain.

MAKING ART CONNECTIONS

1. **Music.** The Baroque style was not limited to art. It is also found in music of the period. Working as part of a team of students, (1) find and tape-record a musical composition by the famous Baroque composer Johann Sebastian Bach (**yo**-hahn suh-**bast**-ee-uhn **bahk**), and (2) find and photocopy other works by several Baroque artists you learned about in this chapter. Stage a sound-and-sight presentation for your class.

2. **Social Studies.** Several of the painters you read about in this chapter created genre, rather than religious, works. Rembrandt, during the 1600s, was one. Chardin, during the 1700s, was another. Find a third genre artist from either of the two periods. Imagine that this person were living today. Based on what you know of the artist, describe what a twentieth-century work by him or her might look like. Give details about both the subject and style of the work.

Chapter 12 Review **191**

ANSWERS TO CHAPTER 12 REVIEW

■ **Building Vocabulary**

1. facade
2. Baroque
3. portrait
4. Rococo
5. etching

■ **Reviewing Art Facts**

6. The Baroque style of architectural art was practiced by Borromini.
7. Caravaggio's key contribution was the use of strong light and shadow.
8. Genre paintings were in demand in Holland during the 1600s
9. Judith Leyster specialized in portrait painting.
10. Antoine Watteau was the first artist to create Rococo paintings.
11. Élisabeth Vigée-Lebrun was named the queen's personal portrait painter.
12. Chardin painted scenes of the simple homes of everyday people.
13. Goya painted portraits of people from Spanish high society through his forties.

? THINKING ABOUT ART

1. Students should notice texture in the fabrics, flesh, hair, stone, plants.
2. Similarity exists in the artists' choice of women as portrait subjects, capturing the mood of the movement, showing detail. Differences lie in the area of how detail is shown, brush stroke technique, and how subject is presented. Answers will vary on which is preferred. Students should show they understand the aesthetic view they have chosen.

Native American Art

(pages 192–207)

Resources

- 13-10 Chapter Test, TRB page 277
- Transparency CC-13, *Onkto Mi Dreaming* by Oscar Howe
- Transparency 13, *Ceremonial House with Totem Decoration* (Inuit)
- Fine Art Print 14, *Kwakiutl Dance Mask*

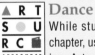

Dance
While studying this chapter, use Performing Arts Handbook page 329 to help students recognize the symbolism of a Native American legend represented in a performance by the American Indian Dance Theatre.

NATIONAL STANDARDS

This chapter addresses the following National Standards for the Visual Arts:

1. (a, b)	**4.** (a, b, c)
2. (a)	**5.** (a, b)
3. (a, b)	**6.** (a, b)

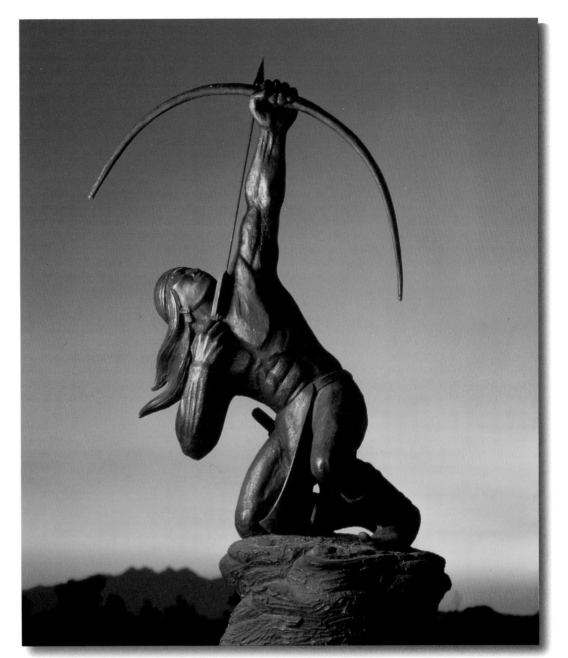

▲ This artist's father was the grandson of the Apache chief Mangus Colorado and a relative of Geronimo. Can you see any similarity when comparing this sculpture with the one by Byron in Figure 7–3?

Allan Houser. *Sacred Rain Arrow.* 1988. Bronze. 249 x 99 x 78.7 cm (98 x 39 x 31"). Glenn Green Galleries, Phoenix, Arizona.

192

FEATURED ARTISTS

T.C. Cannon	Lucy Lewis
Allan Houser	Dan Namingha
Oscar Howe	Margaret Tafoya
Kenojuak	Pablita Velarde

Native American Art

In history books the part of the globe we live in is called the New World. To the peoples who have dwelled in this region since earliest times, there is nothing new about it. Some of these groups—from Central and South America—you learned about in Chapter 6.

In this chapter you will read about the first people of North America. You will learn about their culture. You will learn, finally, about the proud traditions that have led to the making of art works like the one shown on the left.

PORTFOLIO IDEAS

Select one or more art works from the studio activities and lessons in this chapter that express something about your personality or a tradition that is meaningful to you. Describe how you created the art work to tell about you, in the way that Native American art represents the traditions and values of the artist who created it. Keep your chosen art work together with your notes in your portfolio.

OBJECTIVES

After completing this chapter, you will be able to:
- Name and describe five major groups of Native Americans.
- Identify the contributions to art the different Native American cultures have made.
- Identify Native American artists working today.
- Create art in the style developed by the Native Americans.

WORDS YOU WILL LEARN

coiled pot
cradle board
Kachina
loom
petroglyphs
polychrome
pueblos
sand painting
tepee
totem pole
warp
weft

■ Chapter Overview

Tell students that in this chapter they will learn about the different Native American cultures, their artists, and their contributions to art. They will also create their own art works in the Native American style.

■ Chapter Motivator

Ask students to look through the pages of this chapter and examine the art works illustrated. Ask them to count how many different forms of art works they see. Tell them that much of the traditional art of Native Americans has been handed down from ancient times and continues to flourish today.

■ Examining the Art Work

Direct students' attention to Allan Houser's *Sacred Rain Arrow*. Inform them that Allan Houser was a contemporary Apache Indian sculptor. Houser studied at the Indian School at Santa Fe, New Mexico, and then remained in Santa Fe and worked as a free-lance artist. His first job of notoriety was to paint a mural of the life of his people for the Department of the Interior in Washington, D.C. During World War II, Houser traveled to California, where he became interested in the media of sculpture. He worked successfully in a variety of styles and mastered the medium of bronze, metal, and stone in his sculptural designs. Houser's designs are modern yet firmly rooted in the special tradition of his Native American forefathers. Houser drew inspiration from both past and present, but like all successful artists, his sculpture transcends race and language.

DEVELOPING A PORTFOLIO

Organizing the Portfolio Providing students with an outline or checklist of the assignments that have been given over the grading period helps them keep track of what should be completed and can go into the portfolio. This outline may be posted in the room, but students should have their own copies. They can easily record assignments themselves and reflect on where they are with the assignments as they check the list. Throughout the grading period it is a good idea to set aside one or two times for students to update, reorganize or adjust their portfolio. Peer reviews and written reflection time work well at these times, too. These times for updates can be reinforced with a brief review of the established rubric for the portfolio.

• • • • • • • • • •

FOCUS

☑ OBJECTIVES

After completing this lesson, students will be able to:

• Name and describe four major groups of Native Americans.

• Identify the contributions to art made by the different Native American cultures.

• Draw narrative pictures in the style used by the Plains peoples.

☑ SUPPLIES

• Wall map of the world.

• Newspapers and news magazines, sheets of drawing paper, pencils, watercolor markers.

• Clay, sheets of newspaper, clay tools.

• Sheets of drawing paper or outline maps of the United States, pencils, fine-line markers.

Resources

■ 13-1 *History of the Mimbres Society*, TRB page 263 (art history)

■ 13-2 *Mimbres Designs*, TRB page 265 (reproducible master)

■ 13-3 *The Richness of Tribal Variety*, (cooperative learning) TRB page 267

194

Native American Art of the Past

When Christopher Columbus reached North America in 1492, he thought his ships had landed on the east coast of India. He referred to the natives he found living there as Indians. Today these first settlers are called Native Americans.

In this lesson you will study four of the major Native American groups: the Pueblo, Northwest Coast Indians, Plains Indians, and Woodlands Indians. You will look at the art they produced hundreds of years ago and see how their contributions influence Native American art today.

PUEBLO CULTURE

Pueblo tradition tells us that in ancient times the ancestors of this group settled in what is now known as the Four Corners region of the United States. Find this region on the map in Figure 13–1. Like other Native American groups, the Pueblo are believed to have come from Asia.

Scientific records show they probably came by way of the Bering Sea some 20,000 to 30,000 years ago.

"The People," as the early Pueblo called themselves, were farmers. They wore clothes woven from cotton, had a democratic form of government, and traded with other cultures.

Crafts

It was through trade with Mexico around A.D. 400 that the Pueblo learned to make pottery. The earliest kind of pot, called a **coiled pot**, was *a pot formed by coiling long ropes of clay in a spiral.* An example of such a pot is shown in Figure 13–2. The careful pinching together of the coils was meant to be both decorative and useful. In what ways is this type of pot similar to the ones made by the Chavín of South America? (See Figure 6–11 on page **88**). In what ways is it different?

▲ Figure 13–1   Native American Cultures.

▲ Figure 13–2   Pots like this had to be able to hold water, which was precious in the dry hot southwestern desert. The pots were also used to store food and were buried with the dead to help them in the afterlife.

Coil pot. Pueblo. A.D. 1050–1200. Exterior: coiled neck; pinched coil underbody and base; lug handles on each side of neck; smoothed interior. 27.9 x 26.7 cm (11 x 10½"). Courtesy of the School of American Research, Indian Arts Research Center, Santa Fe, New Mexico. Gift of Maria Chabot, Albuquerque, New Mexico.

CURRICULUM CONNECTIONS

Geography   The Four Corners region of the United States is located where the boundaries of Utah, Colorado, New Mexico, and Arizona come together. The Native Americans who settled in this region are thought to be Asians who traveled across the Asian continents to the Bering Sea. They crossed into what is now Alaska and made their way south along the West Coast and then inland. Have students look at the map of the world on pages 314 and 315 and estimate the number of miles these people traveled before settling in the Southwest United States. Let students reflect on the fortitude these early settlers must have had in order to travel thousands of miles on foot, carrying their belongings with them.

Petroglyphs

Although they were farmers, the early Pueblo also hunted for food. To ensure a good hunt, they made **petroglyphs** (peh-truh-glifs), or *rock carvings and paintings*, of their prey. This, they believed, would allow them to capture the animal's spirit. Can you think of another culture you learned about that shared this belief?

Examine the petroglyph of a bighorn sheep in Figure 13–3. Would you describe the work as realistic? Would you say it is stylized?

Architecture

The early inhabitants of the southwestern United States lived in round pit houses dug into the earth and covered with branches. Over the years the Indians learned to build with adobe, mud, and straw. When the Spanish arrived in the Southwest in 1540, they found *stacked, many-family dwellings made of adobe*. The Spaniards called these **pueblos**, after the Spanish word for "village." The same word was also used to refer to the Native American builders of these dwellings. Study the pueblo in Figure 13–4 on page **196**. Notice how the structure seems to grow out of the earth. What modern form of dwelling in our own culture has a purpose similar to the pueblo?

◄ **Figure 13–3   Petroglyphs like these have survived for many centuries. How are these rock paintings similar to the prehistoric cave paintings found in Lascaux (see Figure 4–1)?**

Petroglyph. Bighorn Sheep. A.D. 900–1100. Three Rivers Site, New Mexico.

NORTHWEST COAST INDIAN CULTURE

The coastal sections of British Columbia and the states of Washington, Oregon, and northern California are rich with plant and animal life. Rain is plentiful, and cooling sea breezes keep temperatures mild. It is understandable that these features appealed to several groups of people heading south before 7000 B.C.

Today the collected groups of the region are known by the name of Northwest Coast Indians. Find the area settled by these early cultures on the map in Figure 13–1.

Like the Pueblos, the Northwest Coast Indians made use of the resources around them. They used the tall trees of the area to make boats and logs for houses. They also used the trees to create art works.

Sculpture

No art form is more unmistakably Native American than the totem pole. A **totem pole** is *an upright log carving picturing stories of different families or clans*. The word totem means "spirit or guardian." Figure 13–5 on page **196** shows a totem pole carved by an artist of a Northwest Coast tribe. Typically, this pole is meant to be read from top to bottom. The top figure identifies the clan to which the pole belongs. Notice how the facial features have been stylized to fit the available space.

PLAINS INDIAN CULTURE

Not all peoples who arrived here in Pre-Columbian times set up permanent villages. Some were wanderers who moved from place to place, following the food supply. One such group was the people known as the Plains Indians.

Lesson 1   *Native American Art of the Past*   **195**

■ Aesthetics

Help students examine and discuss the totem pole shown in Figure 13-5. What do you see in this work? What visual elements can you identify? Which principles of art have been used to organize those elements? What message do you think the totem pole is intended to communicate? Are you able to fully understand that message? Why or why not?

■ Art Criticism

Have students discuss and compare two works by the Plains people: the cradle board shown in Figure 13-6 and the hide painting shown in Figure 13-7. What function was each work created to serve? How successfully does it serve that function? Is each a successful work of art? In terms of which aesthetic view do you consider the works successful? Why?

■ Cultural Diversity

Help students compare the cultures of the Pueblo people and the Plains people. What were the most important differences between the lives of people in these two groups? How was the architecture of the two groups different? What differences in their crafts can you identify? What do you think accounts for these differences? Encourage all students to participate in this discussion; ask interested students to do further research and to share their findings with the class.

▲ **Figure 13–4** Entrances to Pueblo dwellings were often holes in the roofs, with ladders leading down into the interiors.

Pueblo Dwellings. c. 1100. Taos, New Mexico.

The Plains Indians made their home in the large area bounded by the Mississippi River and the Rocky Mountains. Find these boundaries on the map in Figure 13–1. The Plains Indians hunted the bison. As the herds moved, so did the Plains people, dragging their possessions behind them on their custom-made sleds.

Architecture

Among the belongings the Plains people carried with them was the tepee. A **tepee** (**tee**-pee) was *a portable house.* As a rule, the tepee was cone-shaped and made of buffalo hide stretched over poles. The hides were covered with designs symbolizing the forces of nature.

At its base a tepee could range anywhere from 12 to 30 feet (4 to 9 m) in diameter. A large tepee contained about as much space as a standard living room of today. How many people do you think could live comfortably in such a space?

Crafts

Like the tepee, the crafts created by the Plains people were made to be easily carried. An example is the object pictured in Figure 13–6. This is a **cradle board,** a *harness worn on the shoulders and used to carry a small child.*

▶ **Figure 13–5** The figures on this totem pole represent a man, a bear, and a frog at the bottom. These figures show status and rights of the family for which it was carved.

Tlingit Totem Pole. Mid-19th Century. Wood and pigment. Museum of American History, Smithsonian Institution, Washington, D.C.

Notice the care that went into the woven design. What kinds of shapes—organic or geometric—has the artist used in this design? What natural materials are used to decorate it?

WOODLANDS CULTURE

The Woodlands made up the largest cultural group of Native Americans. They settled in North America east of the Mississippi River. The Woodlands people combined

196   Lesson 1   *Native American Art of the Past*

┌ *more about* ● ● ● ─

Totems   Tell students that the word *totem* was applied originally to an animal or other object held sacred by a tribe or individual. The animal or object was then adopted as their own symbol. This custom has its counterpart in the symbols of modern-day countries. The American eagle, the thistle of Scotland, and the lion of Great Britain are examples. Let each student choose a personal symbol or totem. The object or animal should be selected for its symbolic link to a personal skill or talent. Discuss what might have influenced the Native Americans to select the specific totems they chose. Have students draw their totem in the same stylized way the totem pole figures were designed. Let the class share their totems and what they symbolize.

hunting and gathering with simple farming. The Iroquois, made up of six different Woodlands groups, combined to form the highly organized Iroquois nation.

▲ **Figure 13–6   Even though their life was hard, the Plains Indians took great pride in their art. What features of this work reveal this pride?**

Ute Cradle Board. c. 1870. Buffalo hide, trade beads. Channing, Dale, Throckmorton Gallery, Santa Fe, New Mexico.

◀ **Figure 13–7   This hide tells stories from the artist's own life. Can you tell what is happening? A robe made from a decorated hide was highly prized. Often, the person wearing it thought it would protect him from harm.**

Exploits of a Sioux Leader. c. 1870–1875. Hide Painting. Philbrook Museum of Art, Tulsa, Oklahoma. Gift of Kills Eagle.

STUDIO ACTIVITY

Sketching an Event

Plains Indians painted tales of their battles on skins. Notice that the artist has used a birds-eye view in telling the tale shown in Figure 13–7.

Look through a newspaper or magazine for coverage of an important event in your city or in the world. On a sheet of paper, sketch the story behind this event. Carefully outline each object in your design. Color the work using watercolor markers.

P O R T F O L I O

Exchange finished art works with a classmate for peer evaluation. To evaluate a peer's work, use criteria preset by your teacher or class group, or evaluate the use of elements and principles of art, use of media, and how well the artist has followed the directions of the assignment. Keep the peer evaluation of your work and the art work together in your portfolio.

✔ CHECK YOUR UNDERSTANDING

1. In what region do the Pueblo people live? Where are they and other Native American groups believed to have come from?
2. What are coiled pots? What are petroglyphs?
3. What form of architecture gave one Native American group its name? Why was this word chosen?
4. For what unmistakably Native American form of art are the Northwest Coast Indians known?
5. What are tepees? Why did the Plains Indians have a need for tepees?

Answers to ✔ CHECK YOUR UNDERSTANDING

1. The Four Corners. They and other Native American groups are believed to have come from Asia.
2. Coiled pots were formed by coiling long ropes of clay in a spiral until a pot or vase had been made. *Petroglyphs* are rock carvings and paintings made by the Pueblo to ensure a good hunt.
3. Pueblo was the form of architecture that shared its name with one group of Native Americans. The stacked, many-family dwelling took its name from the Spanish word *pueblo,* which meant "village."
4. Totem poles.
5. A cone-shaped portable house. The Plains people were nomadic and needed to carry their shelters with them.

LESSON 2

Making a
Round
Weaving

(pages 198–199)

LESSON TIME: 120 minutes

. . . .
FOCUS

☑ OBJECTIVES

After completing this lesson, students will be able to:
- Plan and make round weavings on looms made from coat hangers.
- Describe, analyze, interpret, and judge their weavings.

☑ SUPPLIES

- Slides or large photographs of Native American blankets and rugs (including slides or photographs of looms).
- Small loom already warped or a simple loom made from cardboard.
- Wire coat hangers, masking tape, assorted fibers, blunt tapestry needles.
- Sheets of drawing paper, pencils, colored pencils or markers.

. . . .
TEACH

■ Motivator

Show slides or large photographs of several blankets and rugs woven by Native Americans; if possible, also show slides or photos of Native American weavers working at their looms. Let students describe and discuss what they see in each work. Then explain to students that they will be making their own weavings.

 LESSON 2

Making a Round Weaving

Some Native American craft styles and techniques are borrowed from other cultures. One you have learned about is Pueblo pottery, which came from artists in Mexico. Another craft, which also became an important art medium to many Native American cultures, is weaving. Woven materials were used for clothing and blankets. They were often highly decorated and expressed the artists' beliefs, customs, and traditions. Study the decorative weaving shown in Figure 13–8. It was created on a **loom**, or *frame holding a set of crisscrossing threads*. The loom holds two sets of threads. The **warp** threads are *threads running vertically and attached to the loom's frame*. The **weft** threads are those *threads passed horizontally over and under the warp*. The weaver of the object in Figure 13–8 was able to change colors and patterns by using different weaving techniques. This weaving was created on a circular loom.

▲ Figure 13–8　Student work. Round weaving.

WHAT YOU WILL LEARN

You will make a round weaving on a loom made from wire coat hangers. Plan a color scheme for your weaving, and use weaving techniques to change colors in your design. Use a complementary, monochromatic, or analogous color scheme.

WHAT YOU WILL NEED

- 2 wire coat hangers
- Masking tape
- Assorted fibers
- 2 or more blunt tapestry needles

WHAT YOU WILL DO

1. Make a frame for your loom by putting two wire coat hangers together and bending them to form a flat circle. Connect the hangers in two places around the circle with masking tape. Bend the hook on one of the hangers into a loop. This will be used to hang your completed work.
2. Pick the colors of fiber you will use in your weaving. Choose a complementary, monochromatic, or analogous color scheme. Set the fibers aside.
3. Tie a long strand of fiber to your frame using an overhand knot. Wrap the fiber strand completely around the frame using half-hitch knots. (See Figure 13–9.) Thread the end of your fiber strand through a needle. Pull it through several of the knot loops to keep the fiber from coming undone. Cut off any extra fiber.

TECHNIQUE TIP ▼

Warping　Before students string their warp threads, they must anchor the fiber to the frame. When they cross the circle to a point opposite the starting point, they will anchor the warp thread again. The fiber will then be wound around the frame until they reach the next "hour mark" on the frame. Then they will cross over to the opposite side, anchor, and wind around the frame again. They will use this method until they have finished, knotting the fiber at the center.

4. Create a warp by attaching a single long strand of fiber to the frame. Pass this across the circle at different points. Make sure each pass of the warp fiber crosses the center of the loom. (See Figure 13–10.) After six passes, begin a seventh. This time, take the warp strand only as far as the center. Tie all passes at this point.
5. Working from the center out, begin the weft using a tabby (over and under) weave. After several circuits, switch to one of the other techniques detailed in Figure 13–10. Experiment to create different color shapes or designs. You may leave some open spaces where the warp is not covered.
6. Display your weaving along with those done by classmates. See if you can identify the weaving techniques used in different works.

EXAMINING YOUR WORK

- **Describe**   Explain how you created a loom using two wire coat hangers. Identify the different color shapes you created by switching weaves.
- **Analyze**   Describe the shape of your loom. Tell what kind of color scheme you picked. Name the colors you used. Tell how you used weaving techniques to change the colors in your design.
- **Interpret**   Explain how the colors you chose help communicate a certain mood to viewers. Give your work a title.
- **Judge**   Tell whether your work succeeds. State what you might do differently in a second attempt at the assignment.

▲ Figure 13–9   Making the wire loom.

▲ Figure 13–10   Warping the loom. Examples of weaving techniques are detailed.

Try This! STUDIO OPTIONS

■ Make a second weaving, this time picking a different type of color scheme. Emphasize texture by using different fibers for your weaving.

■ Use a heavy-duty paper plate as a loom. Make an uneven number of notches around the edge. Warp it following the instructions in the lesson. Create another weaving.

Lesson 2   *Making a Round Weaving*   **199**

☑ OBJECTIVES

After completing this lesson, students will be able to:

• Identify Native American artists working today.

• Discuss works of both traditional and modern Native American art.

☑ SUPPLIES

• Photographs of pottery created by modern American artists, only some of whom are Native Americans; reproductions of paintings created by modern American artists, including some Native Americans.

• Sand, tempera paints, newspaper, cardboard, white glue, small brushes.

Resources

⬛ 13-4 *From Chief Seattle,* TRB page 268 (reproducible master)

⬛ 13-5 *Naming a Native American,* TRB page 269 (appreciating cultural diversity)

⬛ 13-7 *Coil Pot,* TRB page 271 (studio)

Native American Art Today

During the 1600s, 1700s, and 1800s, America was explored and settled by newcomers from Europe. Native Americans fought to keep the lands they had lived on for generations. Their efforts were unsuccessful. As the land was settled by Europeans, the Native American population dwindled. Those who remained were eventually forced to live in limited areas called reservations.

Although the original Native American way of life has changed through contact with European cultures, much of the artistic tradition remains. It can be seen in the work created by contemporary Native American artists.

TRADITIONAL NATIVE AMERICAN ART

Traditional art is based on past forms and ideas. Some designs and techniques used by traditional artists today date from over a thousand years ago.

Crafts

Pueblo legend tells of supernatural spirits called Kachina (kuh-**chee**-nuh) who once lived among the people. The Kachina taught the Pueblo how to live in harmony with nature. This legend gave rise long ago to the making of Kachina figures. A **Kachina** is *a hand-carved statuette that represents spirits in Pueblo rituals.* Figure 13–11 shows a Kachina created late in this century. Like the figures of old, this object uses formal balance. What idea or mood does the figure communicate to the viewer?

Another tradition carried forward by craftspeople today is pottery. The **polychrome,** or *many-colored,* pots in Figure 13–12 are by Lucy Lewis, a leading twentieth-century Native American potter. Lewis created these pots

using the same skills she learned as a child watching her elders. Each step was carefully done by hand, from digging the clay to grinding the minerals for the paints she used. She worked without the aid of a potter's wheel. Look closely at these works. The patterns on the surface are adaptations of prehistoric designs. What images do you see in these abstract decorations?

▲ Figure 13–11 **The Pueblo believe there are between 300 and 400 Kachinas. What other culture that you learned about believed in many spirits?**

Hopi Kachina. c. 1975. Mixed-media. San Diego Museum of Man, San Diego, California. John Oldenkamp.

TECHNOLOGY OPTIONS

National Gallery of Art Videodisc   Use the following images to discuss Native American portraits made by a nineteenth-century artist.

George Catlin
Catlin Painting the Portrait of Mah-to-toh-pa—Mandan

Search Frame 1902

George Catlin
See-non-ty-a, an Iowa Medicine Man

Search Frame 1906

▲ Figure 13–12   The artist learned to make pots from an aunt. What other skills besides art are learned through tradition?

Lucy Lewis. Polychrome Pots. Lewis Family. c. 1989/90. Acoma, New Mexico.

▲ Figure 13–13   In what ways is this water jar similar to the ones by Lucy Lewis? How are they different?

Margaret Tafoya. Jar, Santa Clara. Pueblo, N.M. c. 1965. Blackware. 43 x 33 cm (17 x 13"). National Museum of Women in the Arts. Gift of Wallace & Wilhelmina Holladay.

Margaret Tafoya is another Native American artist who has also preserved the traditional methods with modern experimental techniques. She has created the pottery water jar shown in Figure 13–13 using a method of intaglio molding and carving. Her jar is decorated with an ancient water-serpent design.

Painting

Some ancient art techniques still practiced today are associated with health and well-being. One of these, sand painting, is part of a healing ritual. **Sand painting** is *the pouring of different colors of powdered rock on a flat section of earth to create an image or design*. Examine the sand painting pictured in Figure 13–14. As with all creations of this type, this one is abstract in design.

▲ Figure 13–14   Works like this are temporary; a new one is made from scratch for each ritual.

Sand Painting. Medicine men placing feathers. American Museum of Natural History, New York, New York.

Lesson 3   *Native American Art Today*   **201**

Motivator

Show students photographs of pottery created by living American artists; some of the works should be by Native American artists, and others should be by Americans of other origins. Present each work, and let students describe and discuss it, but do not identify the artist. Ask: Were any of these pieces of pottery created by Native Americans? What makes you think so? Discuss various points of view; then identify the works by Native American artists. Follow the same procedure with modern paintings. Then explain that students will learn more about today's Native American artists and their works.

Sparking Creativity

For a fun hands-on, colorful activity, let students create their own sand paintings. They should begin by working together to color batches of sand; this can be done by kneading small amounts of tempera paint into the sand and then spreading the sand out on newspapers to dry. The sand should be mixed occasionally as it dries. Then have each student cover one side of a piece of cardboard with white glue, dip the glued side into plain sand, tap off any extra, and let their boards dry. Then have students apply white glue to areas on which they want to add color. Explain that they should sprinkle colored sand over the wet glue, tap off the extra sand, and allow the area to dry. This procedure should be repeated until students have completed their sand paintings.

■ **Art History**

Have students work in groups to research the history of specific Native American cultural groups. What art works were created in the past to record the stories of the people? Which modern artists from that culture are creating works today? Do those art works record the stories of the people— the way Allan Houser's works do, for example? If so, how? Do the art works reflect the stories and traditions of the people?

■ **Vocabulary**

Have students look up the combining forms of *poly-* and *chrome:* What does each word part mean? When the two word parts are put together to form the word *polychrome,* what does that word mean?

■ **Art Criticism**

Have students work in groups to compare and discuss the paintings by Oscar Howe, *Victory Dance,* Figure 13-16, and by Dan Naminga, *Hopi Dwelling,* Figure 13-17: How are the subjects of the two works different? What similarities can you identify? Compare their use of the elements and principles of art. What idea or feeling do you think each painting communicates? Are the message of the two works similar in some ways? If so, how? How would you judge the success of the three works in terms of the three aesthetic views?

MODERN NATIVE AMERICAN ART

Not all Native American artists of the twentieth century have been content to follow tradition. Many have studied at art schools and combined new media and techniques with their own cultural heritage.

Sculpture

One of the most influential Native American artists was Allan Houser (**ha**-oo-zohr). A Chiricahua Apache (chir-uh-**kah**-wuh uh-**pach**-ee), Houser was born in Oklahoma in 1914. As a child, he listened intently to stories about his people. After studying art, he went on to retell—usually in stone or bronze—the stories he had heard. Study the sculpture by Houser that opened this chapter, on page **192**. Can you imagine a story about this young warrior? How has Houser used line to move your eyes around the statue?

Painting

Portrait and landscape paintings are not parts of Native American art tradition. However, both played major roles in the brief life and career of twentieth-century painter T.C. Cannon. Cannon, a member of the Kiowa (**ky**-uh-waw) tribe, was born in 1946. A student of Allan Houser, he painted traditional subjects in brightly colored modern-day settings. Typical of his work is the portrait in Figure 13–15. Note the strong sense of design. What kind of detail has the artist shown in the man's clothing?

▶ **Figure 13–15** The artist skillfully incorporates traditional beliefs and symbols in his works. How has he done so in this painting?

T.C. Cannon. *Turn of the Century Dandy.* 1976. Acrylic on canvas. 152.4 x 132.1 cm (60 x 52″). Aberbach Fine Arts, New York, New York. Private Collection.

MEETING STUDENT DIVERSITY

Kinesthetic Learners Have students design a set of illustrated cards for each of the North American cultures described in this chapter. Have students begin by studying the map on page 194. Then have them gather information and create a card for each culture depicting geographical location, clothing, buildings and shelters, arts and crafts, and weapons.

Verbal/Linguistic Learners Have students research the life of a contemporary Native American artist. Have them prepare interview questions they would like to ask this artist about his or her art works, lifestyle, and cultural ties and traditions.

In the painting shown in Figure 13–16, another artist, Oscar Howe, breaks with painting traditions imposed upon Native Americans by European teachers. Traditionally, Indians did not use a realistic style. They often depicted the spirit of animals and plants in symbolic, stylized designs. Howe uses line, shape, and color to show excitement. He expresses the powerful energy of the spirit of victory.

The painting by Dan Naminga, Figure 13–17, is yet another example of the blending of contemporary subject and traditional styles. This time the artist paints Pueblo dwellings in a rich, colorful landscape.

▲ Figure 13–17　Does this dwelling remind you of one seen earlier? Can you see the tops of ladders extending upward? What were these used for?

Dan Naminga. *Hopi Dwelling*. Acrylic on canvas. 102 x 102 cm (40 x 40″).

▲ Figure 13–16　Compare this work with Figure 5–10. How are these two works similar? How do they differ?

Oscar Howe. *Victory Dance*. Philbrook Museum of Art, Tulsa, Oklahoma.

✔CHECK YOUR UNDERSTANDING

1. What is traditional art?
2. What is a Kachina?
3. What is sand painting? For what is sand painting used?
4. In what area of art did Allan Houser specialize?
5. What was the art specialty of T.C. Cannon?

Inuit-Style Print

(pages 204–205)

LESSON TIME: 90 minutes

• • • • • • • • • • • • • •

FOCUS

☑ OBJECTIVES

After completing this lesson, students will be able to:

• Design and make printing plates for Inuit-Style prints and make editions of three prints.

• Describe, analyze, interpret, and judge their own prints.

☑ SUPPLIES

• Photographs of several examples of Inuit art, including carved soapstone figures, carved ivory figures, masks, ivory record sticks, wood carvings, prints.

• Pencils; erasers; sheets of sketch paper; pieces of corrugated cardboard, 8 x 10 inches (20 x 25 cm); utility knives; white glue; water-based printing ink; shallow pans; soft brayers; sheets of paper for printing; tablespoons.

Resources

■ 13-8 *Kenojuak*, TRB page 273 (artist profile)

■ 13-9 *Inuit Sculpture*, TRB page 275 (art criticism)

LESSON 4

Inuit-Style Print

Another Native American group that has been around since earliest times is the Inuit (**in**-yuh-wuht). You probably know these people of Canada and Alaska better as Eskimos. The name "Eskimo" was used by explorers from other lands. The people from this group call themselves the Inuit. The Inuit have a tradition of carving bone, ivory, or stone to create abstract views of images from nature. This tradition is being upheld by artists working today. The print in Figure 13–18 is by a leading Inuit artist named Kenojuak (kuh-**noh**-joo-ak). Like all Native American artists, she combines nature, religion, and her own imagination.

WHAT YOU WILL LEARN

You will design a print based on your school mascot or some other school symbol. Your print will be abstract in design and should use line and shape to express your feelings about the animal. You will make an edition of three prints. (See Figure 13–19.)

WHAT YOU WILL NEED

• Pencil, eraser, and sheets of sketch paper
• 2 pieces of corrugated cardboard, 8 x 10 inches (20 x 25 cm)
• Paper-cutting knife and white glue
• Water-based printing ink
• Shallow pan and soft brayer
• Paper for printing
• Tablespoon

▶ Figure 13–18 What kind of balance has the artist used? Point to areas where different textures are shown.

Kenojuak. *Owls, Ravens and Dogs.* Courtesy of Dorset Fine Arts. Toronto, Ontario, Canada.

MEETING SPECIAL NEEDS

Using Examples   For self-expression, especially valuable for students with disabilities, the teacher and students could describe what characteristics in their own personalities are like those of animals and what qualities they would like to have even more of. For example, a lion's fierceness, a leopard's speed, the shyness of a deer, bird, or turtle, the sharp eyes of an owl, or the big ears of a rabbit could be shown in an imaginary animal design. If knives for cutting cardboard are considered too dangerous for some students with disabilities, substitute tagboard which is more easily cut and use blunt-ended scissors.

WHAT YOU WILL DO

1. On sketch paper, do a drawing of the animal you chose. On a second sheet of sketch paper, create an abstract design based on your first sketch. Leave out all unneeded details. Use line and shape to express feelings. Round shapes can express gentleness, diagonal lines can show danger or quick movement.

2. Transfer your design to a piece of corrugated cardboard. Using the paper-cutting knife, carefully cut out the design. Glue it to the second piece of cardboard to form a printing plate.

3. Squeeze out a small amount of ink into the pan. Roll the brayer back and forth in the ink to coat it evenly. Roll the brayer lightly over your printing plate. If you press down too hard, you might collapse the relief.

4. Place a clean sheet of paper on your plate. Gently rub the paper with the back of the spoon or your fingertips. Work quickly. Carefully remove the print. Set it aside to dry. Repeat the process twice more to make an edition of three prints. When all the prints are dry, sign and number them.

5. Display your finished prints alongside those of classmates. Decide which design you feel best captures the appearance and the spirit of your school mascot.

EXAMINING YOUR WORK

- **Describe** Identify the sources of your ideas for abstraction. Identify the unnecessary details you eliminated to create an abstract design.
- **Analyze** Tell which elements stand out most in your design.
- **Interpret** State what feelings toward your mascot your print expresses. Identify the features that help communicate those feelings.
- **Judge** Tell whether you feel your work succeeds. If you could redo your work, tell what changes, if any, you would make.

▲ **Figure 13–19   Student work. Inuit-style print.**

Try This! COMPUTER OPTION

■ Choose Mirror Symmetry tool or menu and small Brush size and shape. Draw an animal with simple, stylized lines and shapes to emphasize the mood of the animal. Continue adding other birds, animals, or fish to appear behind the first animal. Title and save work. Then use monochromatic colors, light and dark values of one color, to fill some spaces with solid color or color gradient. Add pattern and color to some areas. Leave some spaces white. Retitle, save, and print your work.

Lesson 4   *Inuit-Style Print*   **205**

TECHNOLOGY OPTIONS

Videocassettes   If you have access to a videocassette player in the classroom, you can take advantage of the many excellent videos available on Native American art and artists. Check with local natural history museums or museum catalogs to find out what they may have about tribal groups near your area. Contact the Native American museums of the southwestern states and ask if there are videos of Native American artists at work. Many subjects are available, including basket-weaving, pottery, and other traditional Native American crafts being created by authentic Native American artists and craftspeople.

TEACH

■ **Motivator**

Display photographs of Inuit art works of soapstone, ivory, wood, bone. Include carved figures, record rods, masks, and prints. Then ask: What group of people do you guess might have created these works? Guide students in identifying the Inuit people and in using the term *Inuit* rather than *Eskimo*.

■ **Vocabulary**

Review with students the definition of *print:* What steps are involved in making a print? What tools and equipment are needed? What is an edition? How are the prints in an edition numbered?

ASSESS

■ **Self-Assessment**

Have students use Examining Your Work to evaluate their Inuit-style prints created in this Studio Lesson. Responses may be written or oral.

■ **Reteaching**

Help groups of students discuss their own prints and compare them to Kenojuak's print, *Owl, Ravens and Dogs,* Figure 13-18. How does her print reflect the Inuit traditions? In what ways are your prints similar to hers?

■ **Enrichment**

Explain that Kenojuak, like many other Inuit artists, is a member of an artists' cooperative. Ask students to find out about Inuit artists' cooperatives. When, where, and why have they been formed? How do they function? What benefits do they offer to Inuit artists?

CLOSE

Have students tell what they learned about printmaking while working on this lesson.

☑ OBJECTIVES

After completing this feature, students will be able to:

- Explain the importance of storytelling to Native Americans.
- Understand the role of the Native American storyteller.

Teaching the Connection

- Have students read the feature on this page.
- Ask volunteers to share what they know about Native American storytelling. Why did Native Americans pass stories along orally? *(Most tribes did not have a written language; storytelling was a means of teaching values and history.)* Why is storytelling useful in any culture? *(It can preserve information and history that might otherwise be lost.)* In the painting, what is Old Father's relationship to the others? *(He is a respected elder.)*
- Tell students that like many Native Americans of her time, Pablita Velarde was educated at a boarding school where she was forbidden to speak her native Tewa language. She did study art at the U. S. Indian School in Sante Fe and went on to keep her heritage alive through her art.

Answers to Making the Connection

- Stars, sky, trees, mole, spider, eagle, bear, coyote, lion, turtle.
- She holds him in high regard; he is a large, strong, dominant figure. The upper arch of people and the horizontal section in the middle provide balance.
- Responses will vary. Students should give specific examples in their comparisons.

206

Pablita Velarde. *Old Father Story Teller.* 1960. Reprinted with permission from book titled *Old Father Story Teller* by Pablita Velarde, Clear Light Publishers.

Why Is Storytelling Important?

Storytelling has always been an important way for Native Americans to educate their people about their history and beliefs. For centuries, native peoples passed on stories orally from one generation to the next. The content of these oral narratives differed from tribe to tribe, but some of the themes were similar. One common theme was the creation of the world. Other stories dealt with heroes or tricksters. Many legends explained an aspect of nature or the universe. Many characters in the tales appeared as animals. In all stories, nature and the land were greatly cherished.

Pablita Velarde, the artist of this painting, grew up in a pueblo in New Mexico. She felt very fortunate to hear stories firsthand from her grandfather and great-grandfather. Today the Native American storytelling heritage continues, both orally and in writing. Entertaining and instructive, the stories help keep Native American cultures alive.

MAKING THE CONNECTION

- ✔ What elements of nature has the artist included in her work?
- ✔ What is the artist's opinion of the Old Father? How can you tell? How has the artist achieved balance in her painting?
- ✔ Find two books or stories that have been retold or illustrated by Native Americans. Compare the stories and illustrations.

INTERNET ACTIVITY

Visit Glencoe's Fine Arts Web Site for students at:

http://www.glencoe.com/sec/art/students

206   *Chapter 13 Connections*

INTERNET ACTIVITY

Student Museum Curators   Tell students they are about to become museum curators. They will work in virtual museums on the World Wide Web. Arrange students in small groups of 2 to 4 for each computer. Tell them to begin by choosing a theme for their exhibit. Give them time to browse some of the museum sites linked to the activity. As students tour each museum, have them determine which works of art they will include in the exhibit that will carry their chosen theme. Encourage students to take notes and prepare worksheets for pieces to be featured in their exhibits. If appropriate software capabilities are available, students can download images of the works and create their own virtual museum exhibit. Find us at **http://www.glencoe.com/sec/art**

REVIEW

BUILDING VOCABULARY

Number a sheet of paper from 1 to 12. After each number, write the term from the list that best matches each description below.

coiled pot   pueblos
cradle board   sand painting
Kachina   tepee
loom   totem pole
petroglyphs   warp
polychrome   weft

1. A pot formed by coiling long ropes of clay in a spiral.
2. Rock carvings and paintings.
3. Stacked, many-family dwellings made of adobe.
4. An upright log carving picturing stories of different families or clans.
5. A portable house.
6. A harness worn on the shoulders and used to carry a small child.
7. A hand-carved statuette that represents spirits in Pueblo rituals.
8. The pouring of different colors of powdered rock on a flat section of earth to create an image or design.
9. Having many colors.
10. A frame holding a set of crisscrossing threads.
11. Threads running vertically and attached to the loom's frame.
12. Threads passed horizontally over and under the warp.

REVIEWING ART FACTS

Number a sheet of paper from 13 to 19. Answer each question in a complete sentence.

13. In what areas did the early Pueblo people settle?
14. When did the Northwest Coast people reach the region they settled? What convinced them to remain in this region?
15. Which group of Woodlands people became organized as one large nation?
16. Which group of Native Americans is famous for its totem poles?
17. What are Kachina?
18. What Native American artist is famous for his portraits and landscapes?
19. Where do the Inuit live?

THINKING ABOUT ART

On a sheet of paper, answer each question in a sentence or two.

1. **Analyze.**   One of the three aesthetic views holds that the most important feature of a work is its composition. Tell how an art critic accepting this view would react to the sculpture that opened this chapter (page **192**). Explain why you believe the critic would have this reaction.
2. **Extend.**   Explain how the part of the world the Inuit live in is a factor in their artists' choice of media.

MAKING ART CONNECTIONS

1. **Science.**   Find all the works in this chapter that make use of geometric patterns. Identify the number and kind of motifs that appear in each one. Discuss the use of patterns from nature in Native American design.
2. **Language Arts.**   Enjoy the art of George Catlin as he captured the Native American culture in two books:

George Catlin: Painter of the Indian West by Mark Sufrin and *Buffalo Hunt* by Russell Freedman. You may also wish to read *When Clay Sings* by Byrd Baylor and Tom Bahti, or *Cities in the Sand: The Ancient Civilizations of the Southwest* by Scott S. Warren. How do these authors present the history of the Native American peoples?

Chapter 13 Review   **207**

ANSWERS TO CHAPTER 13 REVIEW

■ Building Vocabulary

1. coiled pot
2. petroglyphs
3. pueblos
4. totem pole
5. tepee
6. cradle board
7. Kachina
8. sand painting
9. polychrome
10. loom
11. warp
12. weft

■ Reviewing Art Facts

13. The Pueblo settled in what is known as the Four Corners section of the United States.
14. Northwest Coast people reached the area they settled around 7000 B.C. The good climate convinced them to stay.
15. Six groups of Woodlands groups combined to form the Iroquois Nation.
16. The Northwest Coast tribe carved totem poles.
17. The Kachina are supernatural spirits who taught the Pueblo how to live in harmony with nature. The spirits are represented by Kachinas.
18. T.C. Cannnon specialized in portrait and landscape painting.
19. The Inuit live in Canada and Alaska.

? THINKING ABOUT ART

1. A critic who bases his or her aesthetic view on composition would say this sculpture was beautifully balanced and well done. The viewer's eye travels diagonally from the feet up the body to the warrior's eye looking at the arrow and back down the curved bow to the body.

2. The Inuit artists are isolated in a cold climate and use bone, ivory, and stone because they are easy to obtain.

European Art of the Early 1800s

(pages 208–223)

Chapter Scan

Lessons

1 Neoclassic and Romantic Art

 2 Designing a Neoclassic Stage Set

3 European Art— Late 1800s

 4 Painting an Impressionist Landscape

Resources

- 14-8 Chapter Test, TRB page 295
- Transparency CC-14, *Nameless and Friendless* by Emily Mary Osborn
- Transparency 14, *Woman with a Parasol—Madame Monet and Her Son* by Claude Monet
- Fine Art Print 15, *Still Life with Bouquet* by Pierre Auguste Renoir

Dance

While studying this chapter, use Performing Arts Handbook page 330 to help students discover how the Joffrey Ballet's interpretation of *The Nutcracker* brings a classic musical composition of the 1800s into a performance universally loved to this day.

NATIONAL STANDARDS

This chapter addresses the following National Standards for the Visual Arts:

1. (a, b)   4. (c)
2. (a, b, c) 5. (b, c)
3. (a, b)   6. (a, b)

▲ The artist once stated that his desire was to paint pictures that were happy and pretty. Do you think this work demonstrates this mood? Explain your answer.

Pierre Auguste Renoir. *Dance at Bougival.* 1883. Oil on canvas. 181.8 x 98.1 cm (71⅝ x 38⅝"). Picture Fund. Courtesy Museum of Fine Arts, Boston, Massachusetts.

FEATURED ARTISTS

Jacques Louis David	Pierre Auguste Renoir
Eugène Delacroix	Auguste Rodin
Claude Monet	Joseph M.W. Turner
Berthe Morisot	Joseph Wright

CHAPTER 14

European Art of the Early 1800s

The 1600s, you have learned, was the age of Baroque art; the 1700s of Rococo art. The 1800s can be thought of as an age of change. No single art style dominated. One was hardly in place before it was first challenged and then replaced by another.

The century began with artists looking to the past for ideas. They modeled their own versions of grand heroes and noble deeds on the works of ancient Greek and Roman artists. By mid-century, however, artists were roaming city streets and the countryside, painting everyday scenes with dabs and dashes of paint. One work done in this manner is shown at the left.

PORTFOLIO IDEAS

Go through this chapter and select an art work that you like. Is it from the Neoclassic, Romantic, or Impressionist art period? Create an entry for your portfolio that demonstrates this style. Exchange finished works with a classmate for peer evaluation. Peers can tell you what they like about your art work and offer suggestions for revising the work. Based on the peer review, you may want to revise or change your art work. When your peer evaluation is returned, review the comments, and keep them in your portfolio with your sketch.

OBJECTIVES

After completing this chapter, you will be able to:
● Describe the Neoclassic, Romantic, and Impressionist styles of art.
● Discuss the importance of the Salon to artists of the day.
● Create art work in the Neoclassic and Impressionist style.

WORDS YOU WILL LEARN

art movement
Impressionism
landscape
Neoclassic
Romanticism
Salon

■ **Chapter Overview**

Tell students that in this chapter they will learn about Neoclassic, Romantic, and Impressionist styles of art, and create their own artworks in two of these styles.

■ **Chapter Motivator**

Instruct students to examine the painting of the dancing couple. Tell them that the artist, Pierre Auguste Renoir, was a French painter of the late nineteenth and early twentieth centuries. Write the word "Impressionism" on the board and tell them that artists who practiced this style were concerned with capturing the rapidly changing effects of light on their subjects.

■ **Examining the Artwork**

Tell students that Renoir's art is a joyous response to his love of life and the beauty he found in the world. This happiness illuminates each of his pictures—the sparkling landscapes, the radiant still lifes of flowers and fruit, the cheerful portraits of women and children, and the carefree scenes of holiday diversions. Explain that *The Dance at Bougival* shows a young couple moving with simple grace to the music of a band in a park setting. The blurring and lack of detail is exactly what we could expect to see in the background if we were seated at a table following with our eyes the movements of the two dancers as they swept by. Renoir does not show what he *knows to be there*; instead shows what *the eye actually sees in a given moment of time*.

National Museum of Women in the Arts

You may wish to use the National Museum of Women in the Arts videodisc and/or CD-ROM. The videodisc features a bar code guide, and the interactive CD-ROM provides stimulating activities.

DEVELOPING A PORTFOLIO

Whole Group Reviews When doing portfolio reviews in whole groups, you need to be sensitive to the risks the students have taken. Displaying work or allowing others to look closely can be very uncomfortable to students. Set guidelines for discussion and have some questions ready prior to the whole group portfolio review. The questions may ask students to assess in a positive manner the range or types of art work in the portfolio, the kinds of skills demonstrated in the art work, the feelings they get when they look at the art work or what they think the work symbolizes or means. Another suggestion for whole portfolio reviews is to have students each offer a compliment and a question about the portfolio in consideration. This works well for critiquing selected pieces of art work, too.

Neoclassic and Romantic Art

(pages 210–213)

• • • • • • • • • • • • • •
FOCUS

☑ OBJECTIVES

After completing this lesson, students will be able to:

• Describe the Neoclassic and Romantic styles of art.

• Explain what a landscape is.

• Create watercolor paintings evoked by specific sounds.

☑ SUPPLIES

• Slides or photographs of Baroque buildings and of ancient Greek temples.

• Sheets of drawing paper, pencils, watercolors, brushes, water.

• Recording of music by Richard Wagner, sheets of drawing paper, watercolors, brushes, water, black markers.

Neoclassic and Romantic Art

The late 1700s and early 1800s were stormy times in France. Outraged by the shameless greed of the wealthy ruling class, the poor people rose up in revolt. This uprising, known as the French Revolution, began with a bloody reign of terror. Thousands lost their heads on the guillotine. The following 20 years, marked by war and struggle, were no less bitter. Finally, the troubled French government was turned over to a popular young general. His name was Napoléon Bonaparte (nuh-**pol**-yuhn **boh**-nuh-part).

▲ **Figure 14–1** Notice how the artist arranged the three groups of figures. Do the arches and columns help unify the groups? Explain how dramatic contrasts of value help emphasize the most important parts of this work. In what way is this painting like a scene from a play?

Jacques Louis David. *The Oath of the Horatii*. 1786. Toledo Museum of Art, Toledo, Ohio.

TECHNOLOGY OPTIONS

National Gallery of Art Videodisc   Use the following images to more closely examine the art work presented on page 212.

Eugène Delacroix
Arabs Skirmishing in the Mountains

Search Frame 1130

Eugène Delacroix
Arabs Skirmishing in the Mountains

Search Frame 1132

Use Glencoe's *Correlation Bar Code Guide to the National Gallery of Art* to locate more art works.

NEOCLASSIC ART

Artists of the day believed these events were equal in importance to the rise and fall of ancient Greece and Rome. They even chose to show the events using an updated version of the styles of ancient Greece and Rome. As a result, their work became known as **Neoclassic** (nee-oh-**klas**-ik), meaning "new classic," *an art style that borrowed from the early classical period of ancient Greece and Rome.*

One of the most successful of the Neoclassic artists was Jacques Louis David (**zhahk** loo-**ee** dah-**veed**). Even though he later took part in the revolt against the French king, David was Louis XVI's painter. It was the king who asked David to paint what would become one of his most famous pictures. The painting, shown in Figure 14–1, shows two families living in neighboring ancient Roman cities. The families are related by marriage but divided by a war between their cities. A father and three sons of one family are shown pledging to fight to the death. All know their relatives will be among those they must battle. The women, helpless to prevent the tragedy, weep.

The picture is made up of three groups of figures. These are arranged across the canvas as though it were a stage. Notice David's skillful use of the background arches and columns to separate and frame these groups. The artist's careful painting of details—the swords, the helmets—adds to the picture's realism. His use of light adds drama to the picture.

ROMANTIC ART

As the 1800s wore on, people became weary of the political unrest and fighting. They looked for things that would take their minds off the upsetting events around them. Some artists shared this same desire. These artists were responsible for developing a new style of art called **Romanticism** (roh-**mant**-uh-siz-uhm). This is *a style of art that found its subjects in the world of the dramatic and exotic.*

France

To Romanticists, nothing stirred the imagination better than far-off places and colorful, action-filled adventures. The two are combined in the paintings of Eugène Delacroix (oo-**zhen** del-uh-**kwah**), a leader of the Romantic school. One of his paintings is pictured in Figure 14–2. In this work, Delacroix refused to allow his taste for action to interfere with his sense of design. He planned his painting so the viewer would miss none of its exciting details.

Study this work. Find the diagonal line beginning in the horse and rider at the lower left. This line leads your eye upward to the figures at the right. From there the gunsmoke pulls your gaze across the picture to the far-off figures and fortress.

England

Another artist who turned to his imagination for ideas was the English painter Joseph M. W. Turner. Unlike other Romanticists, however, Turner expected his viewers to use their imaginations as well. His glowing colors and blurred images free viewers to interpret his pictures in their own ways.

Turner spent his life painting landscapes. A **landscape** is *a drawing or painting focusing on mountains, trees, or other natural scenery*. He was fascinated in particular by sunlight and its shimmering reflection on water. This fascination can be seen in the painting in Figure 14–3. The work excites the viewer's curiosity with its dazzling sky and shimmering waters. There are ships in the center of the painting, and a church is visible on the right. With the use of light on the structures, the artist leads the viewer's eye down the canal and out to sea. As in all of Turner's best works, the real subjects are light and color.

---

more about • • •

New Styles   Explain that Neoclassicism was the official style of the French Academy throughout the century, particularly during the first half. This style made use of ancient Greek and Roman sculptures as models. It stressed the importance of balanced compositions, flowing contour lines, figures modeled in light and dark, subdued colors, and noble gestures and expressions. Romanticism was the style that developed and flourished during the first half of the century. It favored the use of rich, dramatic color and a sense of movement rather than balance. Paintings done in this style did not begin with contour lines, but with patterns of color which were used to create shapes and figures.

• • • • • • • • • • • • • •
TEACH

■ **Motivator**

Display slides or photographs of Baroque buildings that focus on Rococo details. Let students identify and describe what they see. Then ask: What style of art and architecture seems most different from the Baroque style? Let several students respond, and encourage them to give specific reasons to support their ideas. Then show slides or photographs of ancient Greek temples, and have students describe the differences. Artists reacted against the Baroque style and began working in a style intended to echo the works of ancient Greece and Rome, called Neoclassicism.

■ **Vocabulary**

Have students use dictionaries as they respond to these questions: To what culture does the word *classic* refer? What are some of the meanings of the adjective *romantic?* Which of those refer to art? Does romantic art relate more directly to facts or to imagination?

■ **Art Criticism**

Help students discuss and compare Jacques Louis David's *The Oath of the Horatii*, Figure 14-1, and Eugène Delacroix's *Arabs Skirmishing in the Mountains*, Figure 14-2: How do these two paintings differ in subject, in composition, and in content? How do these two works reflect the interests and concerns of the Neoclassic art movement and the Romantic art movement?

■ **Art History**

The works of artists in France reflected the impact of the French Revolution. Ask several volunteers to read about the life and works of Jacques Louis David. How did the French Revolution affect his life? How did it affect his works? Ask these volunteers to share these findings with the rest of the class.

211

TEACH
(continued)

Sparking Creativity

Remind students that music can influence or even inspire works of visual art. For example, the Romantic artist Gustave Dore reported that he painted one of his best known works, *Ship Trapped by an Iceberg,* in response to a musical composition by Richard Wagner. Play a recording of music by Wagner; let students listen for a while and then use watercolors to record their responses to the music. Remind them that they can use either the wet-on-wet technique employed in the Studio Activity or the wet-on-dry technique, in which they do not brush their papers with water. Once the watercolors have dried, let students use black markers to draw in lines separating the colors and defining the shapes and figures. How do these lines affect the impact of the paintings?

■ Cooperative Learning

Have students work in two groups. Ask one group to find reproductions of Romantic landscape paintings. Ask the other group to find reproductions of Japanese landscape prints and paintings. Then have the two groups share and discuss the art works they have chosen: How are they alike? What are the most important differences?

▲ **Figure 14–2** Delacroix often painted pictures that included action and adventure. Look at the figures in the foreground. Notice how they help to lead the viewer's eyes around the painting.

Eugène Delacroix. *Arabs Skirmishing in the Mountains.* 1863. Canvas. 92.5 x 74.6 cm (36⅜ x 29⅜"). National Gallery of Art, Washington, D.C. Chester Dale Fund.

212   Lesson 1   *Neoclassic and Romantic Art*

more about • • •

Delacroix Eugène Delacroix believed that art should electrify the viewer. He chose subjects filled with action, showing men and animals caught up in a conflict with nature or each other. The Romanticists were striving to show optical truth as well as things as they were in reality. Delacroix reflected the influence of David and Gericault. In addition, he chose to portray spectacular drama that would fire the imagination and appeal to a wide audience. He also realized that content was not the only concern. Of technique he said, "It is advisable not to fuse brush strokes, as they will [appear to] fuse naturally at [a]...distance." In this respect, he anticipated the Impressionists' experiments with light and color. His work might be said to be the precursor of the epic film.

212

1. Describe events in France in the late 1700s and early 1800s.
2. What is Neoclassic art? What led artists to begin creating art in this style?
3. What is Romantic art? What led artists to begin creating art in this style?

STUDIO ACTIVITY

Sketching a Sound

Using your imagination, sketch an image that goes with one of these sounds: a bird's song, the roar of the ocean, or breaking glass. Then brush water over your drawing and paint it with watercolors. Choose colors that best express the mood your work calls to mind.

P O R T F O L I O

Write a short paragraph explaining whether you communicated a mood with blurred images.

STUDIO ACTIVITY

Sketching a Sound
To prepare for this activity and set the mood, play a music box, wind chimes, or a similar recording as students come into the room.

• • • • • • • • • •
ASSESS

■ **Self-Assessment**
Have students complete the review questions on this page. Answers are provided below.

■ **Reteaching**
Work with small groups of students to review the differences between Neoclassicism and Romanticism: What political and social events helped shape Neoclassicism and Romanticism? How do the two art movements differ in subject and style? Then have group members browse through art books or collections of art reproductions. Ask each group member to find at least one Neoclassic art work and one Romantic art work.

■ **Enrichment**
Let students plan and create their own work in either the Neoclassic or Romantic style. Have them begin by selecting the style and then by deciding on a subject suitable to that style. Encourage students to present their work to the rest of the class.

▲ **Figure 14–3   Earlier in his career the artist painted pictures with more realistic subjects. What do you like about the way he painted this one?**

Joseph M. W. Turner. *The Grand Canal, Venice*. 1835. Canvas. 91.4 x 122.2 cm (36 x 48⅛"). The Metropolitan Museum of Art, New York, New York. Bequest of Cornelius Vanderbilt, 1899.

• • • • • • • • • •
CLOSE

Have students compare and contrast the paintings on these two pages by Delacroix and Turner.

Answers to ✔ CHECK YOUR UNDERSTANDING

1. Outraged by the shameless greed of the wealthy ruling class, the poor people rose up in a revolt called the French Revolution.
2. Neoclassic art is an art style borrowed from the early classical period of ancient Greece and Rome. Artists began using this style because they believed the events occurring during the French Revolution were equal in importance to the rise and fall of Greece and Rome.
3. Romanticism is a style of art that found its subjects in the world of the dramatic and exotic. People were weary of war and political unrest, and the artists began to develop works that would be uplifting.

LESSON 2

Designing a Neoclassic Stage Set

(pages 214–215)

LESSON TIME: 120 minutes

FOCUS

☑ OBJECTIVES

After completing this lesson, students will be able to:
- Design and build three-dimensional models for stage sets.
- Describe, analyze, interpret, and judge their own stage set models.

☑ SUPPLIES

- Pencils, sheets of sketch paper, mixing trays, tempera paint, wide-tipped brushes, Shoe boxes, sheets of mat board, scissors, white glue.
- Clay, wire, and/or other sculpting media.

Resource

14-5 *Step Back in Time,* TRB page 288 (art history)

TEACH

■ Motivator

Introduce this Studio Lesson by encouraging students to discuss their own experiences with theater productions—both in audiences and behind the scenes. Ask students to tell about plays or other live productions they have seen. If any students have participated in or helped with school or community productions, ask them to describe the stage setting.

214

LESSON 2

Designing a Neoclassic Stage Set

Look at the painting in Figure 14–4. It is by Jacques Louis David. As in the other work by this foremost Neoclassicist you studied (Figure 14–1), the figures appear almost as actors. The setting is like a stage.

Imagine for a moment that the stone dungeon in this work *is* part of a stage set. Imagine that just beyond the rightmost figure in the painting are wings — the area in a theater leading backstage. Imagine that to the left of the shadowed archway the set continues. What lies beyond the left edge of this painting? In this lesson you will invent a continuation of this scene.

WHAT YOU WILL LEARN

Design and build a three-dimensional model for a stage set. Your model will extend the stage in Figure 14–4. Match as closely as possible the colors, textures, and patterns of the walls and floor. Make two pieces of furniture to place in your model. These will emphasize the real space in the model. Your stage set will have the same feeling or mood suggested by David's painting.

▲ **Figure 14–4** Socrates, a great Greek philosopher, is shown in prison. He has been placed here after falsely being accused of denying the existence of Greek gods. His punishment is to drink poison.

Jacques Louis David. *The Death of Socrates.* 1787. Oil on canvas. 129.5 x 196.2 cm (51 x 77¼"). The Metropolitan Museum of Art, New York, New York. Catherine Lorillard Wolfe Collection.

RESOURCES BEYOND THE CLASSROOM

Exhibitions and Competitions   Community colleges, art schools, and universities sponsor exhibitions and competitions for their students. Younger students who view such exhibits and competitions will be exposed to a wide variety of skill levels, techniques, and media. On occasion, schools and colleges invite younger students to submit art works for exhibit; they may also invite students to participate in a competition, often in a special category. Though juried competitions are becoming more common, less formal methods of judging are still frequently used. Students who see and participate in such exhibits and competitions are more encouraged to continue to create art throughout their lives.

WHAT YOU WILL NEED

- Pencil and sheets of sketch paper
- Mixing tray, tempera paint, and 2 brushes—one wide, one fine-tipped
- Shoe box and 2 sheets of mat board
- Scissors and white glue

WHAT YOU WILL DO

1. Brainstorm with your classmates for possible answers to the question "What lies beyond the left border of this painting?" Then working by yourself, sketch several ideas for extending the stage. Create windows, doorways, stairs, arches, and other design features you like. Let your imagination and David's painting guide you. Choose your best sketch and set it aside.
2. Mix hues of tempera paint to match the lighted portions of the walls and the floor in David's painting. Create darker values of the same hue to match the shaded portions. Using the thick brush, paint the back, sides, and bottom of the shoe box. Using the fine-tipped brush, add the thin lines between stone blocks.
3. With scissors, cut from mat board doors, arches, and other design features appearing in your sketch. Make sure all added features match the colors, patterns, and textures found in the painting. Glue these features in place in your model.
4. Make furniture, such as a table, bench, or bed, to complete your design.

EXAMINING YOUR WORK

- **Describe** Tell whether the walls, floor, and other features of your model look real. Point out the features that help viewers identify your model as an extension of David's painting.
- **Analyze** State whether the colors and textures in your work match those in David's painting. Point out similarities between the patterns on the walls and floor in your model and those in the painting. Show ways in which you used real space in your model.
- **Interpret** Tell whether your stage set has the same mood or feeling as the one David's painting communicates. Decide what words you would use to describe that mood or feeling.
- **Judge** Decide in what way your model most succeeds. Tell whether it succeeds because of its realistic appearance, its composition, or its content.

5. When dry, display your model. Compare it with the stage set in the painting and with other student models. Decide which were most successful in matching the look of David's painting.

Lesson 2 *Designing a Neoclassic Stage Set* **215**

Try This!

STUDIO OPTIONS

- Look through a magazine to find figures to cut out and use as actors for your stage. Glue cardboard backings to your figures so they will stand. Pose them in your model so they appear to be relating to one another.

- Imagine the words each of your actors is speaking. Write these on pieces of white paper cut to look like the dialogue balloons in comic strips. Glue these to each actor so the words seem to be coming from his or her mouth.

MEETING SPECIAL NEEDS

Touching the Elements Provide photos or walk around the school with students to find architectural elements, such as arches or column capitals. Students with visual disabilities can feel the columns' roundness and, with their fingers, trace out the designs in reliefs or railings. Go to a stage in your school or community and view its lights and scenery. Students with vision or orthopedic disabilities especially can pull on the ropes to open and close the curtain and dim and brighten the lights. Students with speech disabilities or those otherwise embarrassed about speaking in public can portray on the stage what they think is happening in David's painting.

■ **Vocabulary**

Ask students to suggest several definitions of the noun *set*. Then ask: What is a stage set? How is the meaning of the noun *set* related to the noun *setting* (as in "the setting of the story")? Who works to create stage sets? How do you think you might create a model of a stage set?

■ **Art History**

Help students consider what makes David's *The Death of Socrates* a Neoclassic art work: What historical event does this work show? In what ways do the composition and the content reflect the interests of Neoclassic artists?

. . . .

ASSESS

■ **Self-Assessment**

Have students use Examining Your Work to evaluate their stage sets. Responses may be written or oral.

■ **Reteaching**

Present two or three paintings by artists of this period and have students evaluate them using the steps of art criticism.

■ **Enrichment**

Encourage groups of students to work together to create characters for one of the stage set models. What kinds of characters might appear on the stage set? What would those characters do? What would they say? Then have the group members model them in clay or form them from wire. Finally, have group members make the characters, place them in the stage set, and present their work to the rest of the class.

. . . .

CLOSE

Ask students to think of another scene from history that would be appropriate if placed in a stage set like the one they just created.

215

European Art—Late 1800s

Each age has its customs and fashions. One custom common in Paris and London during the 1800s was a yearly art show. The **Salon** (suh-**lahn**), *an annual exhibition of art*, was a major social event. An artist's reputation often depended upon whether or not his or her work was selected for showing at the Salon.

In this lesson you will read how the Salon led to the formation of an **art movement**, *a trend formed when a group of artists band together to create works of a single style.*

▲ **Figure 14–5** Cool colors — blues and greens — seem to move back in space. Warm colors — reds and yellows — seem to come forward. How has the artist used warm and cool colors in this work? Why do you think he made these choices?

Claude Monet. *Banks of the Seine, Vetheuil.* 1880. Canvas. 73.4 x 100.5 cm (28⅞ x 39⅝"). National Gallery of Art, Washington, D.C. Chester Dale Collection.

TECHNOLOGY OPTIONS

National Gallery of Art Videodisc   Use the following images to discuss additional paintings by artists covered in this lesson.

Claude Monet	Auguste Renoir	Berthe Morisot
The Artist's Garden at Vétheuil	*Oarsman at Chatou*	*In the Dining Room*

Search Frame 1388	Search Frame 1312	Search Frame 1268

Use Glencoe's *Correlation Bar Code Guide to the National Gallery of Art* to locate more art works.

IMPRESSIONIST PAINTING

In 1874 a group of discouraged artists decided to hold an exhibition of their own. They found an empty studio in Paris. There they hung pictures that had been rejected by the Salon. The people who came to view the exhibition reacted in different ways. Some were confused. Others laughed. Still others were angry. On one point most viewers were agreed: the paintings looked more like quick sketches than like finished art works. One angry critic, after viewing a painting titled *Impression: Sunrise*, referred to all the paintings as "impressionistic." The name stuck and continued to be used to identify paintings done in this new style.

This style, **Impressionism**, is *a style that attempted to capture the rapidly changing effects of light on objects.* Members of the Impressionist movement left their studios to paint outdoors. They looked at life around them and found subjects everywhere they looked. They painted landscapes and street scenes; they even set up their easels in cafes.

Claude Monet

The painting that gave Impressionism its name was the work of one of the movement's founders, Claude Monet (**klohd** moh-**nay**). Imagine Monet as he prepares to paint the landscape in Figure 14–5. He notes how the sunlight flickers on the gently swaying flowers. He notices how it reflects on rippling waters and glows through gray clouds. He observes, too, how the strongest sunlight blurs forms and blots out details. Now, taking brush in hand, he applies small dabs and dashes of paint to his canvas. He works quickly, trying to capture the effect of sunlight on every object. Each stroke of paint is a little different from the next in hue, value, and intensity. Monet knows the yellows and blues he is using will play against each other in the viewer's eye. They will give the painting a sparkle and brilliance to match that of the sun. Where does the artist use different values of yellow in the work? Where does he use different values of blue?

Pierre Auguste Renoir

One of the most productive of the Impressionists was a man named Pierre Auguste Renoir (pee-**ehr** oh-**goost** ren-**wahr**). Another of the movement's founders, Renoir painted right up to the day he died.

An area of painting Renoir explored using the Impressionist style was portraits. He was especially attracted to the eyes of his subject and often made these the focus of attention. Look at the portrait in Figure 14–6. The eyes, you will notice, are painted in sharp focus. The rest of the figure, meanwhile, is blurred. Renoir knew that when we look at a person or object, not all parts appear in focus at once. Only the part where our eyes rest at a given moment is seen sharply. Everything else appears fuzzy and slightly out of focus.

▲ Figure 14–6   The eyes in this work look right out at you. Even when you glance at other parts of the painting, your attention is always attracted back to the eyes.

Pierre Auguste Renoir. *Madame Henriot.* c. 1876. 65.9 x 49.8 cm (26 x 19⅝"). National Gallery of Art, Washington D.C. Gift of Adele R. Levy Fund, Inc.

Assign groups to work together to learn about the Salon and its impact on the art works of France. Have them find answers to these questions: Who sponsored the first Salon? When did juries begin to accept and reject art works submitted for exhibitions in the Salon? What was the Salon des Refuses? When was it started and what was its purpose? Where did Impressionist artists exhibit their works? Have groups prepare and present a discussion between Impressionist artists as they plan their own exhibit.

**Art in
Everyday Life**

Pose this question to students: Imagine that you have created some art works that you know are very good, but you are not allowed to participate in a major show. What would be your reaction, and what options would you have today to display your work?

■ **Cultural Diversity**

Impressionism was basically an art movement of France. Artists in other countries, however, were influenced by the ideas and works of the Impressionists. Ask students to work in groups to study the life and works of one of these artists: James A. M. Whistler, Mary Cassatt, John Singer Sargent, Childe Hassam, Philip Wilson Steer. To what extent could each artist be considered an Impressionist? How were the works of each influenced by the French Impressionists? After their research is complete, have the groups present examples of the artists' works and discuss what they have learned.

218

▶ **Figure 14–7** A writer once described this artist's painting technique as "Brushwork like fireworks." What do you think he meant by this? Do you agree? Why or why not?

Berthe Morisot. *Jeune Fille au Chien (Young Girl with a Dog).* c. 1887. Oil on canvas. 72.8 x 60.1 cm (28⅞ x 23⅝"). The Armand Hammer Collection, UCLA at the Armand Hammer Museum of Art and Cultural Center. Collection, Los Angeles, California.

Berthe Morisot

Another important member of the Impressionist movement, Berthe Morisot (**behrt** maw-ree-**zoh**), had strong family ties to art. Her great-grandfather, Jean Honoré Fragonard (**zhahnh** oh-nor-**ay** frah-goh-**nahrh**), was an important painter of the Rococo period. Her parents solidly supported her decision to follow a career as an artist. Like Renoir, Morisot chose portraits as a main avenue of expression for her work. One of these is pictured in Figure 14–7. Notice how the artist uses rapidly applied dabs of paint to capture her subject's expression. What mood does the artist communicate in this painting?

SCULPTURE

A sculptor working during the same time as the Impressionist movement was a man named Auguste Rodin (oh-**goost** roh-**dan**). Rodin used bits of wax or clay in his creations. Their rough, bumpy surfaces make his sculptures appear as though in a flickering light. Examine Rodin's work in Figure 14–8. Note how the sculpture looks as if it were created in an instant.

---

more about • • •

Rodin   Auguste Rodin was profoundly affected by the works of Michelangelo (Italy, 1475–1564). He created his first major work, *The Age of Bronze,* which depicts a naturalistic, lifelike figure. Viewers found the sculpture shockingly different from works to which they were accustomed, and some accused Rodin of taking a cast from a live model. Rodin was commissioned to create a huge bronze door for the Museum of Decorative Arts in Paris. The work was "The Gates of Hell," inspired by Dante's *Inferno.* Though he did not complete it, the complex work with nearly 200 separate figures is a masterpiece. Rodin deliberately left some of his sculptures incomplete, so that the figure merges into the stone from which it is cut. His *Balzac* is a moving example of this kind of sculpture.

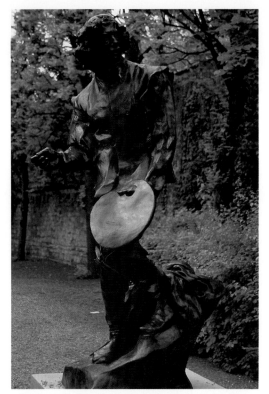

▲ **Figure 14–8** Does this figure look as though it is standing still or moving? Describe what it is doing at this moment.

Auguste Rodin. *Claude Lorrain*. Musee Rodin. Paris, France.

▲ **Figure 14–9** Student work. Center of interest.

STUDIO ACTIVITY

Emphasizing Center of Interest

Pick a familiar object. Working lightly in pencil, draw the object large enough to fill a sheet of paper 9 x 12 inches (23 x 30 cm). Decide what part of the drawing is to be the center of interest. Add more detail to this area. Use short strokes of crayon, chalk, or paint to add color to the drawing. Make the center of interest stand out by coloring it carefully using your brightest hues. Make the colors duller the farther you get from the center of interest. (See Figure 14–9.)

PORTFOLIO

Write an explanation of how you used the elements and principles of art to create a center of interest in your painting. Discuss the aspects of the art work you think are the most successful, and those you feel need improvement. Tell what you might do differently the next time. Keep your written explanation with your finished art work in your portfolio.

✔CHECK YOUR UNDERSTANDING

1. What was the Salon? How was the Salon tied to the beginning of the Impressionist movement?
2. What are some of the ways people reacted at the first showing of Impressionist works in 1874?
3. What did the Impressionists try to capture in their pictures? Where did they go to find subjects for their work?
4. What sorts of paintings did Renoir and Berthe Morisot specialize in?
5. In what area of art did August Rodin work? How did he give his works the look and feel of Impressionist paintings?

STUDIO ACTIVITY

Emphasizing Center of Interest

For an authentic Impressionist mood have students work outdoors for this activity. Let students try using oil pastels.

• • • • • • • • • • • • • •
A S S E S S

■ Self-Assessment

Have students complete the review questions on this page. Answers are provided below.

■ Reteaching

Work with groups of students to review and discuss the aims of Impressionism. After explaining that Camille Pissarro was a leading Impressionist, present this quote from a French critic: "Someone should tell M. Pissarro forcibly that trees are never violet, that the sky is never the color of fresh butter, and nowhere on earth are things to be seen as he paints them." Ask: What had this critic failed to understand about Impressionist paintings? What do you think Pissarro and other Impressionists might have said in reply to the critic?

■ Enrichment

Ask students to imagine themselves as French art critics during the 1870s; they are to review an exhibition of Impressionist paintings. Have each student write a newspaper article either supporting or against the Salon exhibitions.

• • • • • • • • • • • • • •
C L O S E

Go around the room and ask students to briefly describe the work of one of the Impressionist artists they have learned about in this lesson.

Answers to ✔CHECK YOUR UNDERSTANDING

1. A Salon was an annual exhibition of art. Artists whose work was rejected by the Salon decided to hold an exhibition of their own.
2. Some people were confused, some laughed, some were angry.
3. Impressionists tried to capture the rapidly changing effects of light on subjects. They looked at life around them and painted landscapes, street scenes, even cafe interiors.
4. Pierre Auguste Renoir specialized in portrait work as did Berthe Morisot.
5. Auguste Rodin was a sculptor. He used a rough, bumpy surface to make his works appear as if a flickering light were playing over the surface.

LESSON 4

Painting an Impressionist Landscape

Impressionist artists, you have learned, were interested in painting everyday scenes they saw around them. To Claude Monet, in particular, it made little difference whether he was painting a haystack, a few ordinary trees, or—as in Figure 14–10—a bridge. What mattered was how best to show the colors reflected from these subjects. Study the painting in Figure 14–10. Up close the picture appears to be little more than dabs of color.

Warm colors—yellows, reds, oranges—will be used to paint foreground objects. Cool colors—blues, purples, greens—will be used for background objects. Together these colors will be used to create an illusion of space. (See Figure 14–11.)

WHAT YOU WILL LEARN

Use tempera to paint a summer landscape. You will use a variety of colors, values, and intensities, applying these as dots of paint.

WHAT YOU WILL NEED

- Pencil and sheets of sketch paper
- Sheet of white paper, 9 x 12 inches (23 x 30 cm)
- Several brushes, tempera paint, and mixing tray

FOCUS

☑ OBJECTIVES

After completing this lesson, student will be able to:
- Use tempera to paint summer landscapes in the Impressionist style.
- Describe, analyze, interpret, and judge landscapes.

☑ SUPPLIES

- Slides or reproductions of paintings and drawings by Edgar Degas (if available).
- Pencils, sheets of sketch paper; sheets of white paper, 9 x 12 inches (23 x 30 cm); brushes; tempera paint; mixing trays.

Resource

■ 14-7 *Experiment in the Styles of the 1800s and 1900s*, TRB page 292 (studio)

▶ **Figure 14–10** Monet painted many views of rivers and bridges. The scenes show the bridges at all times of the day, in sunlight or sometimes in rain or heavy fog. What reason might the artist have had for making so many paintings of the same type of scene?

Claude Monet. *Bridge at Argenteuil*. 1874. Oil on canvas. 60 x 79.7 cm (23⅝ x 31⅜"). National Gallery of Art. Washington, D.C. Mr. and Mrs. Paul Mellon Collection.

TEACH

■ Motivator

Write the following quotation from Edgar Degas on the board: "One sees as one wishes to see, and it is that falsity that constitutes art." Let several volunteers restate the quotation in their own words. Then ask: What do these words tell you about the artist who said them? What do they tell you about Impressionism?

TECHNIQUE TIP ▼

Colors In this lesson students will be asked to match the colors, textures, and patterns of the walls and floor. See *Handbook* page 280 for tips on how to make lighter and darker values of the same color. Remind students to add small amounts of the basic color to white for a light value. If they want a darker value, a small amount of black should be added to the basic color. Stress small amounts. More can always be added, but too much means starting over.

WHAT YOU WILL DO

1. On a sheet of paper, list the different items that might be found in a landscape painting, such as a tree, stream, and valley. Pick three items from this list. Combine them in simple pencil sketches of warm, sunlit landscapes. Use the space technique of size to place some of the objects near to the viewer. Place others farther back. Draw only very light outlines or indications of your shapes.
2. Choose the best of your sketches. Draw it on the sheet of white paper. Fill the whole sheet with your drawing.
3. Without mixing colors, load a medium-pointed brush with a cool color of paint. Use dots and dabs of the brush to apply the paint to a background object. Pick a second cool hue that, when seen from a distance, will blend with the first to create a new hue. For example, dots of green placed next to dots of blue would create blue-green. Dots of complementary colors can be added to lessen or increase the intensity of the colors.
4. Use warm colors for foreground objects, applying paint in the same fashion. Stand back from your work from time to time. This will help you make sure the colors selected are blending as you expect them to.
5. When the paint is dry, display your work. View all the works, first from a distance, then close up.

COMPUTER OPTION

■ Choose the Airbrush tool and change the color settings to more transparent. Experiment with the Airbrush settings to produce a grainy effect for your landscape. Use Airbrush to build up layers of color to create a background that expresses the time of day, season, and place you have chosen. You will produce a very soft, hazy picture. Select finer and smaller Airbrush settings to draw simple objects on top of the background colors… buildings, plants, trees, or bridges. Redraw lines to darken edges or press heavily with drawing pen to emphasize the objects. Title, save, and print your work.

EXAMINING YOUR WORK

- **Describe** Identify the landscape objects you used.
- **Analyze** Point out the variety of hues you used in your work. Show the different values and intensities of paint. Tell whether you used warm colors for the foreground and cool ones for the background. State whether your use of warm and cool colors helps create a sense of space in your work.
- **Interpret** Point out the features that help viewers understand the scene is of a warm, sunny day.
- **Judge** Explain in what ways your painting shares the look and feel of the Impressionist work in Figure 14–11. Tell whether any part of your work is more successful than the rest. Explain.

▲ **Figure 14–11** Student work. Impressionist landscape.

■ Vocabulary

Review with students the meaning of the terms *warm colors* and *cool colors:* Why are some colors called warm and others called cool? Help students recall the definitions of *value* and *intensity:* What is the difference between the value of a hue and the intensity of that hue? What colors can you mix to change a hue's value? What colors can you mix to change a hue's intensity?

■ Aesthetics

Let students discuss their responses to Claude Monet's *Bridge at Argenteuil,* shown in Figure 14-11. Point out that this painting attempts to capture one moment in time. Does it succeed?

A S S E S S

■ Self-Assessment

Have students use Examining Your Work to evaluate their Impressionist landscapes. Responses may be written or oral.

■ Reteaching

Ask students to create second versions of their landscapes, this time using different media: colored markers, crayons, watercolors, or colored pencils. Let students compare and discuss their new works: How have the images and moods changed? Which of your two works most effectively suggests the style of Impressionist paintings?

■ Enrichment

Let small groups discuss which written works would best accompany Impressionist paintings: poems, stories, autobiographies, or essays. Then have each student write a short piece inspired by his or her own landscape painting.

C L O S E

Display the paintings. Have students analyze them following the instructions in Examining Your Work.

CONNECTIONS
Science

OBJECTIVES

After completing this feature, students will be able to:

*   Describe discoveries and inventions of the 1800s.
*   Understand the impact of the Industrial Revolution.

Teaching the Connection

*   Have students read the feature on this page.
*   Ask volunteers to share what they know about the Industrial Revolution. Why was the period of the late 1700s and early 1800s known as the Industrial Revolution? *(Many of the inventions of this time created a "revolution" in the ways goods were produced and transported.)* What inventions were particularly important? *(The steam engine and related machines had an impact on nearly every product, and new industries arose as a result.)* How is the ironworker portrayed here? *(He seems strong and confident.)*
*   Tell students that the Industrial Revolution affected the working classes immensely as machines replaced humans and animals as much more powerful sources of energy. Transportation and production systems changed completely.

Answers to Making the Connection

*   Iron could be forged more quickly and safely.
*   More (and better) goods and materials were more available, but many people experienced overcrowding in the cities and dismal working conditions.
*   Students' research will vary.

222

Joseph Wright of Derby. *The Iron Forge.* 1772. Broadlands Trust, Hants. Mountbatten Collection. Bridgeman Art Library, London, England. BAL 1561

What Discoveries Occurred During the 1800s?

Dramatic changes in science and industry occurred in the early 1800s, just as changes in the art world were also developing.

One of the most revolutionary inventions was James Watt's improved steam engine. It was the power source for ships, trains, and wondrous machines. Other key inventions were the spinning jenny, the power loom, and the cotton gin. Whole new industries sprang up because of such inventions. With the discovery of more metals, iron and steel production advanced. As the artist shows here, inventions like the mechanical

hammer made the ironworker's job easier.

In medicine, anesthetics like ether and chloroform were discovered. The beating of the human heart could now be heard with a stethoscope. Perhaps the most important medical discovery of the time was Edward Jenner's smallpox vaccine. Everyone was affected by the many inventions and discoveries of the time. All of these had a terrific impact on daily life. With the invention of the electric telegraph, the world was connected in a whole new way.

MAKING THE CONNECTION

*   In Wright's painting, notice how the white-hot iron is held as a mechanical hammer is about to strike and shape the iron. How do you suppose such a machine made work easier for the ironworker?
*   How did the increase in industry and mechanical inventions change people's lives?
*   Find out about some other advances in iron and steel production in England and America during the 1800s.

INTERNET ACTIVITY

Visit Glencoe's Fine Arts Web Site for students at:

http://www.glencoe.com/sec/art/students

222 *Chapter 14 Connections*

INTERNET ACTIVITY

Product Information Connect to the *Product Information* section to get a glimpse of the entire line of Glencoe's Secondary Fine Arts programs. Since you are using the *Understanding Art* textbook, you might want to investigate some of the excellent program components designed to accompany the Student Text and Teacher's Wraparound Edition. Check out the Teacher's Resource Binder, Fine Art Prints, and the Fine Art Transparency component, to which we have added cross-curriculum transparencies. You may also be interested in investigating Glencoe's entire line of art programs, which includes textbooks from middle school through high school—focusing on art media, art history, drawing, and painting. Find us at **http://www.glencoe.com/sec/art**

C H A P T E R 14
REVIEW

BUILDING VOCABULARY

Number a sheet of paper from 1 to 6. After each number, write the term from the list that best matches each description below.

art movement   Neoclassic
Impressionism   Romanticism
landscape   Salon

1. An art style that borrowed from the early classical period of ancient Greece and Rome.
2. A style of art that found its subjects in the world of the dramatic and exotic.
3. A drawing or painting focusing on mountains, trees, or other natural scenery.
4. An annual exhibition of art.
5. A trend formed when a group of artists band together to create works of a single style.
6. A style that attempted to capture the rapidly changing effects of light on objects.

REVIEWING ART FACTS

Number a sheet of paper from 7 to 14. Answer each question in a complete sentence.

7. How did the French Revolution help give rise to a new art style? What was the name of this style?
8. Name an important Neoclassic painter.
9. What events helped bring about the Romantic movement?
10. What sorts of themes are found in the paintings of Eugène Delacroix?

MAKING ART CONNECTIONS

1. **Social Studies.** You are looking at the painting by Eugène Delacroix (Figure 14–2) with two friends. One notes that some of the figures seem to be in awkward poses. The other remarks that the artist "probably had problems drawing these figures." How would you reply?

11. Why did Joseph M. W. Turner use glowing colors and blurred images in his works?
12. Name two artists whose works were turned down by the Salon. Tell what movement they went on to develop.
13. To what school of art did Berthe Morisot belong?
14. What is Auguste Rodin's special contribution to art?

THINKING ABOUT ART

On a sheet of paper, answer each question in a sentence or two.

1. **Analyze.** Imagine you lived in France during the 1800s. Which of the three art styles you learned about in this chapter would best fit your view of life? Explain your answer using information from the chapter.
2. **Compare and contrast.** Look at the landscape paintings by Joseph M. W. Turner (Figure 14–3) and Claude Monet (Figure 14–5). In what ways are the two works alike in subject matter, composition, and content? In what ways are they different in these three areas?
3. **Summarize.** What prompted the Impressionists to decide to hold their own art show in 1874?
4. **Extend.** Berthe Morisot's paintings were ignored by critics during her lifetime. Why do you think this was so?

2. **Language Arts.** Explore Monet's garden at Giverny in a book by Bjork Anderson, *Linnea in Monet's Garden*. As you enjoy photographs of Monet's paintings, you will follow Linnea's journey through the garden and her discovery of his paintings in a Paris gallery. Write an account of what she learned about being an Impressionist.

Chapter 14 Review **223**

 THINKING ABOUT ART

1. Answers will vary. Students should mention Impressionism, Neoclassicism, or Romanticism and demonstrate they know the characteristics of the style they name.
2. Answers will vary. Similarities include shimmering light and water with reflections. Differences include Turner's busy ship/dock scene vs. Monet's quiet nature setting.

3. Artists whose work had been rejected by the Salon decided to hold an exhibition of their own in 1874.
4. Perhaps she was rejected because the critics paid closer attention to the male artists. She was probably well regarded by her fellow Impressionists.

ANSWERS TO CHAPTER 14 REVIEW

■ **Building Vocabulary**

1. Neoclassic
2. Romanticism
3. landscape
4. Salon
5. art movement
6. Impressionism

■ **Reviewing Art Facts**

7. Artists began using a new style of art because they believed the events occurring during the French Revolution were equal in importance to the rise and fall of Greece and Rome. They called this the Neoclassic style.
8. Jacques-Louis David was an important painter of the Neoclassic school.
9. People were weary of war and political unrest, and the artists began to develop works that would be uplifting and portray life as it might be.
10. Two themes found in Delacroix's work are action-filled adventures and far-off places.
11. Turner felt that using blurred images and glowing colors would free viewers to interpret his pictures in their own ways.
12. Claude Monet and Pierre Auguste Renoir were turned down by the Salon. They developed Impressionism.
13. Berthe Morisot belonged to the Impressionist movement.
14. Auguste Rodin used a rough, bumpy surface to make his sculptures look as if a flickering light were playing over the surface.

Art of the Late Nineteenth Century

(pages 224–239)

Chapter Scan

Lessons

1 Art of the Post-Impressionists
2 Painting in the Style of Post-Impressionists
3 American Painting in the Late 1800s
4 Making an Expressive Watercolor Painting

Resources

- 15-9 Chapter Test, TRB page 317
- Transparency CC-15, *Interior with Portraits* by Thomas LeClear
- Transparency 15, *The Rocky Mountains, Lander's Peak* by Albert Bierstadt
- Fine Art Print 16, *Sloop, Nassau* by Winslow Homer

 Music/Dance
While studying this chapter, use Performing Arts Handbook page 331 to help students learn how the AMAN International Folk Ensemble preserves cultural dance and musical forms introduced to America during the late nineteenth century.

 NATIONAL STANDARDS

This chapter addresses the following National Standards for the Visual Arts:

1. (a, b)   5. (a, b, c)
2. (a, b, c)   6. (a, b)
3. (b)

224

▲ What type of balance is demonstrated in this painting? What is used to balance the dancers placed to the far right? Does this kind of balance make the picture look casual and unplanned?

Edgar Degas. *Ballet Dancers in the Wings.* 1900. Pastel on paper. 71.1 x 66 cm. (28 x 26″). Saint Louis Art Museum. St. Louis, Missouri. Quixis Collection.

FEATURED ARTISTS

Albert Bierstadt
Mary Cassatt
Paul Cézanne
Edgar Degas
Thomas Eakins
Paul Gauguin

Vincent van Gogh
Winslow Homer
Albert Pinkham Ryder
Georges Seurat
Henry O. Tanner

CHAPTER 15

Art of the Late Nineteenth Century

Toward the end of the 1800s, some artists felt that Impressionism was the perfect means of self-expression. To others, the new style raised as many questions as it answered. These artists, who had been working as Impressionists, felt that something was missing from their pictures. Their own works struck them, for one reason or another, as "unfinished."

In time, this dissatisfaction led to still newer forms of expression. One is showcased in the work at the left. In this chapter you will learn about such efforts and the pioneers behind them.

PORTFOLIO IDEAS

Select two art works from this chapter. Write the names of the two artists and two paintings. Evaluate one of the paintings. What is the subject? What mood does it create? How does it use the elements and principles of art? Then evaluate the other painting and compare the two. Place a star by those items that both paintings have in common. Keep your list in your portfolio and compare the characteristics to art works created during a different time period.

OBJECTIVES

After completing this chapter, you will be able to:
- Identify the artists who became known as the Post-Impressionists.
- Describe different ways the Post-Impressionists tried to solve the problems of Impressionism.
- Name artists who affected the development of American art of the 1800s.
- Create art works in the style of the Post-Impressionists.

WORDS YOU WILL LEARN

arbitrary colors
optical colors
Pointillism
Post-Impressionism
Realism

Art of the Post-Impressionists

Have you ever created something that pleased you at first but didn't seem right later? This was the case with several artists working toward the close of the 1800s. These artists worked as Impressionists but came to feel that there were problems with this style. The more they studied their art, the more dissatisfied they became. Art, they believed, should do more than just show the changing effects of light on objects. **Post-Impressionism** is *the name given to an art movement that appeared after the Impressionist movement.* The word *post* means "after."

▲ Figure 15–1   The artist repeated colors throughout this work to give it a sense of harmony. Can you find places where colors have been repeated?

Paul Cézanne. *Mont Sainte-Victoire.* 1902–04. Oil on canvas. 69.8 x 89.5 cm (27½ x 35¼"). Philadelphia Museum of Art, Philadelphia, Pennsylvania. George W. Elkins Collection.

FOCUS

☑ OBJECTIVES

After completing this lesson, students will be able to:
- Identify the artists who became known as the Post-Impressionists.
- Describe the different ways the artists tried to solve the problems of Impressionism.
- Distinguish between arbitrary colors and optical colors.
- Make paintings in the style of Paul Cézanne.

☑ SUPPLIES

- Sheets of sketch paper, colored pencils.
- One bottle (of dark glass, if possible), sheets of white paper, pencils, tempera paint, brushes.
- Art books that include reproductions of Impressionist and Post-Impressionist paintings.

Resources

TECHNOLOGY OPTIONS

National Gallery of Art Videodisc   Use the following images to demonstrate the style used by artists of the period.

Paul Gauguin	Paul Cézanne	Edgar Degas
Haystacks in Brittany	*Houses in Provence*	*Four Dancers*
Search Frame 1540	Search Frame 1436	Search Frame 1358

Use Glencoe's *Correlation Bar Code Guide to the National Gallery of Art* to locate more art works.

In this lesson you will learn about the key artists of the Post-Impressionist movement. You will also look at the important contributions they made to the history of art.

POST-IMPRESSIONIST ART

While the Post-Impressionists agreed that there were problems with Impressionism, their solutions to these problems differed. Some argued that art should be more carefully designed — that composition should not be forgotten. Others claimed feelings and emotions should be emphasized — that content deserved its rightful place. Still others championed design and mood — both composition *and* content — as important features.

Composition

One of the Post-Impressionists was also, interestingly, an original member of the Impressionist movement. This artist's name was Paul Cézanne (say-**zan**). Cézanne objected to the loss of composition arising from the Impressionist blurring of shapes. His solution was to use patches of color. These he joined together like pieces of a puzzle to create solid-looking forms.

The painting in Figure 15–1 illustrates Cézanne's technique. This mountain near the artist's home in southern France was one of his favorite subjects. He painted it more than 60 times and from nearly every angle.

◀ **Figure 15–2** Besides their bright colors, van Gogh's paintings are known for their rich textures. He often squeezed his colors from the tubes right onto the canvas. He would then use his brush, fingers, or anything else at hand to spread the paint with swirling strokes.

Vincent van Gogh. *Hospital at Saint-Remy.* 1889. The Armand Hammer Collection, Los Angeles, California.

■ **Motivator**

Introduce this lesson by having students review definitions of *composition* and *content*. Then have students experiment with drawings that emphasize either composition or content. Have students choose a particular section of the room or a specific object in the room, and ask all students to sketch that section or object. Let each student choose a primary objective either to show how he or she can use a principle of art (composition) or to show how he or she feels about the subject (content). Let students discuss their finished sketches: Which approach did each student use?

■ **Vocabulary**

Let students discuss the meanings of the words *arbitrary* and *optical,* using dictionaries if they like: What other words have about the same meaning as *arbitrary?* What sentence can you make up using the word *arbitrary?* What does the word *optical* mean? What part of the body is associated with the word *optical?* Then encourage students to speculate about the meanings of the terms *arbitrary colors* and *optical colors;* let a volunteer check the suggested definitions against the definitions given in the Glossary.

■ **Studio Skills**

Ask students to review the drawings they made for the Motivator activity, emphasizing either composition or content. Now have students draw the same object again, this time trying to give equal emphasis to composition and to content. How does the new drawing differ from the first?

more about • • •

Post-Impressionism   The term Post-Impressionism was first used in 1910, when Roger Fry arranged a London exhibit entitled "Manet and the Post-Impressionists." Some of the artists represented, such as Paul Cézanne, Paul Gauguin, and Vincent van Gogh, were dead and still unknown. The exhibition caused laughter among members of the public and anger among serious art critics. All the works in the exhibit seemed to attack traditional ideas of good art. The impact of Post-Impressionism influenced twentieth-century art movements such as Fauvism, Cubism, and the Nabis. Nonrepresentational artists, such as Wassily Kandinsky, and almost all modern graphic artists also developed largely from Post-Impressionism.

■ Aesthetics

Guide students in examining and discussing the three paintings reproduced in this lesson. Direct students' attention to Paul Cézanne's *Mont Sainte-Victoire,* Figure 15-1, and ask: What is the subject of this painting? What message or mood do you think it communicates? What indicates that Cézanne's main interest is the composition of this painting? Which elements and principles of art can you identify in this work?

Next, direct attention to Vincent van Gogh's *Hospital at Saint-Remy,* Figure 15-2, and ask: What is the subject of this work? How have the principles of art been used to organize the visual elements? What indicates that van Gogh's main interest is the content of his work? What idea or feeling does this work communicate to you?

Finally, have students examine Paul Gauguin's *Ancestors of Tehamana,* Figure 15-3, and ask: what is the subject of this painting? How has Gauguin used the principles of art to organize the elements in his work? What idea or feeling does this painting communicate to you? In this particular painting, do you think Gauguin was more interested in composition or content? Why?

■ Art Criticism

Ask students to compare the three paintings—Figure 15-1, Figure 15-2, and Figure 15-3. Have them consider the three aesthetic views: Does each painting depict its subject effectively? Does each painting succeed in terms of its composition? Does each painting succeed in communicating its message or mood? Then ask: Which painting do you consider the most successful work of art? Why is there no "correct" answer to this question?

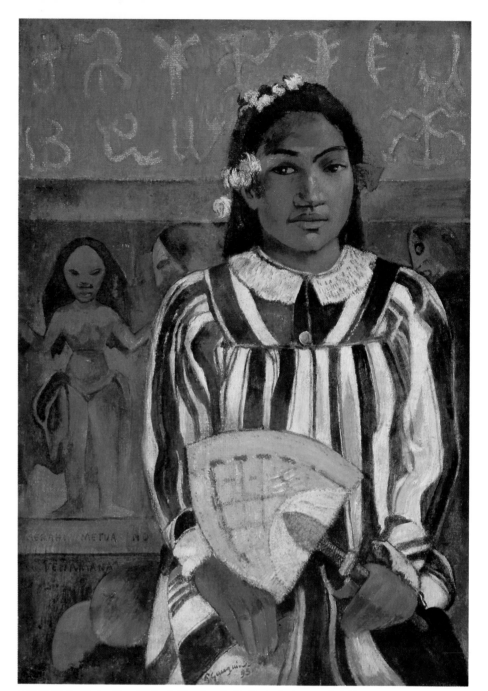

▲ **Figure 15–3   How has the artist directed the viewer's attention to the figure on the left? How does the use of color help show the difference between the figure in the foreground and the one in the background?**

Paul Gauguin. *Ancestors of Tehamana.* 1893. Oil on canvas. 76.3 x 54.3 cm (30 x 21"). Art Institute of Chicago, Chicago, Illinois. Gift of Mr. and Mrs. Charles Deering McCormick.

228   Lesson 1   *Art of the Post-Impressionists*

more about • • •

Gauguin   Paul Gauguin was a rebel. He took painting lessons and enjoyed painting as an amateur so much that he resigned from his successful brokerage business in 1883 to paint full time. His art never sold well enough in his lifetime to support his family. His attitude about color was as adventuresome as his willingness to change careers mid-life. He said. "A meter of green is greener than a centimeter if you wish to express greenness… And that shadow, a little bluish? Don't be afraid. Paint it as blue as you can." He chose to spend the later years of his life in the South Seas, where he painted primitive life and used his imaginative sense of color to convey his love of the simple life lived there.

Cézanne's main interest, however, was not showing the mountain as it really looked. It was to demonstrate how color patches could be turned in different directions to create a solid form. Notice how the artist uses the same color patches to form buildings, trees, and other objects. All are combined to create a richly colored pattern of geometric forms.

Content

The most famous of the Post-Impressionists was Vincent van Gogh (**goh**). Van Gogh's goal was not, like the Impressionists', to reproduce what the eye saw. It was to capture his own deepest feelings about a subject. He expresses these feelings with twisted lines and forms, intense colors, and rich textures.

Near the end of his short life, van Gogh suffered from mental illness. Hoping for a cure, he entered a private hospital. It was there that van Gogh painted the work in Figure 15–2 on page **227**. Take a moment to examine this picture. The artist treats the viewer to his private view of the world of the hospital. We see yellow walls and several small figures. But the twisting trees against a blue sky are the true focus of the painting. Through them, the artist communicates his mental agony and his sensitivity to the forces of nature. What principle of art is used to organize the curving lines of the trees?

Composition and Content

Paul Gauguin (goh-**ganh**) used color and shapes in new and exciting ways. He also created art works that could be enjoyed for their decorative appearance.

The painting in Figure 15–3 shows a scene in the South Seas, where Gauguin spent part of his life. The artist has portrayed his wife against a decorated background. The painting has two parts, a portrait and a scene from the past. The composition hints at the relationship between past and present. Notice how the fan points to the small figure painted on the wall. Like most of Gauguin's other works, this one is filled with meaningful colors. **Arbitrary (ahr**-buh-trehr-ee)

STUDIO ACTIVITY

Making a Simple Line Drawing

To Paul Cézanne, it didn't matter whether he was painting a mountain or a bottle. His goal each time was to use patches of color to create solid-looking forms.

Make a simple line drawing of a bottle. Draw the bottle big enough to fill a sheet of paper. Using a flat brush, apply patches of tempera paint to the bottle. Turn the patches in different directions—out, around, in—to show the solid, round form of the bottle.

P O R T F O L I O

Write a short paragraph to tell if this technique enabled you to create a solid, round form. If not, what would you do differently to improve its success? Keep your written paragraph with the painting in your portfolio.

colors are *colors chosen to communicate different feelings.* **Optical colors** on the other hand, are *colors viewers actually see.* What feelings do you associate with each of the different colors in Gauguin's painting?

✔ CHECK YOUR UNDERSTANDING

1. Define *Post-Impressionism.* Name two leading Post-Impressionists.
2. What were three different solutions Post-Impressionists found to the problems of Impressionism?
3. What was Cézanne's goal? What was van Gogh's goal?
4. What is arbitrary color? Which two Post-Impressionists used arbitrary color in their works?
5. What is optical color?

STUDIO ACTIVITY

Making a Simple Line Drawing

As an alternative, or extension to this activity, have students examine works by Vincent van Gogh. Then let them do a still-life drawing using oil pastels in the Post-Impressionist style.

ASSESS

■ Self-Assessment

Have students complete the review questions on this page. Answers are provided below.

■ Reteaching

Let each student show and discuss his or her Studio Activity painting: How is it similar to the paintings of Paul Cézanne? How is it different from Impressionist paintings? Then let group members browse through art books, identifying Impressionist works and Post-Impressionist works. What distinguishes the two styles?

■ Enrichment

Have students work in three groups; assign each group one of these artists: Paul Cézanne, Vincent van Gogh, Paul Gauguin. Ask group members to research the artist's life and to examine the reproductions of his work. Then have group members arrange a presentation, role playing each of these artists explaining how the artist's life affected his work as well as the effect his art had on his personal life.

CLOSE

Ask students to respond to this question: If you had been an artist in the period that spanned the change from Impressionism to Post-Impressionism, which style would you have chosen to paint? Explain why.

Answers to ✔ CHECK YOUR UNDERSTANDING

1. Post-Impressionism is an art movement that appeared after the Impressionist period. Two of its leading artists were Paul Cézanne and Vincent van Gogh.
2. Three solutions include making more clearly identifiable shapes, conveying more emotion, and creating art that could be enjoyed purely for its decorative appearance.
3. Cézanne: to use patches of color to create more solid forms. Van Gogh: to capture and convey his own deepest feelings about a subject.
4. Colors chosen to communicate different feelings. Cézanne and van Gogh.
5. Colors viewers actually see.

Painting in the Style of Post-Impressionists

(pages 230–231)

LESSON TIME: 45 minutes

• • • • • • • • • • • • •

FOCUS

☑ OBJECTIVES

After completing this lesson, students will be able to:

• Create paintings in the style of one of the Post-Impressionists.

• Describe, analyze, interpret, and judge their own paintings.

☑ SUPPLIES

• Sheets of white paper, tempera paints, brushes.

• Pencils; sheets of white paper, 9 x 12 inches (23 x 30 cm); tempera paint; brushes; mixing trays.

Resource

■ 15-5 *Post-Impressionist Self Portrait*, TRB page 308 (studio)

• • • • • • • • • • • • •

TEACH

■ Motivator

Allow students to try out the three painting techniques of this period. Ask each student to work with only two colors of paint and to work on a single piece of paper. On separate areas of the paper, have students try painting small dots, painting swirling and twisted lines, and painting flat, colorful shapes. Tell them to experiment with the feel and effect of each style of painting

230

Painting in the Style of Post-Impressionists

The painting in Figure 15–4 shows yet another Post-Impressionist solution to the problems posed by Impressionism. The work is by an artist named Georges Seurat (**zhorzh** suh-**rah**). Like Cézanne, Seurat felt the Impressionists' attempt to show the blurring effect of sunlight on forms was misguided. Seurat's solution was to use *a technique in which small, carefully placed dots of color are used to create forms*. This technique, called **Pointillism** (**poynt**-uh-liz-uhm), reached its height in Seurat's painting of a sunny summer day in a park. When seen from close up, the picture looks like a grouping of tiny dots. When the viewer stands back, however, the picture totally changes. The dots seem to blend together to create new colors and clear shapes.

WHAT YOU WILL LEARN

You will create a painting in the style of Seurat or one of the other Post-Impressionists. Use color, line, shape, or texture in the manner of the artist you choose. (See Figure 15–5).

WHAT YOU WILL NEED

• Pencil
• Sheet of white paper, 9 x 12 inches (23 x 30 cm)
• Tempera paint, several brushes, and mixing tray

═══════ **SAFETY TIP** ═══════

When an assignment calls for paints, use watercolors, liquid tempera, or school acrylics.

▶ **Figure 15–4** **This large painting is the artist's best known work. Thousands of colored dots are arranged with great precision to create the simple forms you see. Why do you suppose the artist made the work as large as he did? What kind of mood does it communicate to you?**

Georges Seurat. *Sunday Afternoon on the Island of La Grande Jatte.* 1884–86. Oil on canvas. 207.6 x 308 cm (81½ x 121¼"). Art Institute of Chicago, Chicago, Illinois. Helen Birch Bartlett Memorial Collection.

230 Lesson 2 *Painting in the Style of Post-Impressionists*

MEETING SPECIAL NEEDS

Holding a Brush Students with orthopedic disabilities who may have difficulty holding a brush can use pointers. Have them dip an object such as the eraser of a pencil or bit of foam on the end of a stick into paint and then print onto paper to achieve Post-Impressionistic effects. Also, students with difficulty holding small objects may be helped by wrapping the end of a paintbrush with masking tape or duct tape to increase its diameter, or a brush can be inserted into a short section of pipe insulation or a bicycle handle to make a comfortable grasping surface. Students with orthopedic disabilities will be interested in knowing about Toulouse-Lautrec's physical disability.

WHAT YOU WILL DO

1. Look once again at the paintings in Figures 15–2, 15–3, and 15–4. With classmates, discuss the main features of each artist's style.
2. Look through the pages of a magazine or newspaper. Look for a black-and-white illustration that has an interesting design or communicates a mood.
3. Using pencil, lightly redo the illustration on the sheet of white paper. Make your drawing large enough to fill the whole sheet. Keep the shapes in your drawing simple. Do not include details.
4. Finish and paint your work using one of the following styles: (a) With a fine-tipped brush, cover your drawing with closely spaced tiny dots of paint. Use colors opposite each other on the color wheel to create new hues and intensities. In this way, your work will resemble the Pointillist style of Seurat. (b) With a medium brush, apply paint in a swirling motion, creating twisted lines and shapes. Use bright, arbitrary colors to express a certain mood or feeling. In this way, your work will look like that of van Gogh. (c) Paint your drawing as a pattern of flat, colorful shapes. Paint dark outlines around these shapes. This will give your painting the same decorative look as Gauguin's.
5. When the paint is dry, display your work alongside those of classmates. See whether you can identify the Post-Impressionist style in the works of your fellow students.

 Try This! ## COMPUTER OPTION

■ Determine the mood you will create and what you will draw. Choose a color and medium Brush tool. Click but do not drag the Brush. Draw a simple object and background by making a series of dots with the Brush tool. Do not mix or blend colors, but place dots of colors next to each other so a new color is made when viewed from a distance. Create a small, miniature picture. Cover most of the white spaces. Title, save, and print your work.

EXAMINING YOUR WORK

- **Describe**   Hold your painting next to the illustration on which it is based. Tell whether you can identify the objects in the illustration.
- **Analyze**   Explain how you used color, line, shape, and texture. Tell which Post-Impressionist artist you used as a guide in using these elements. Point to places in your work where your use of elements was similar to that of your chosen artist.
- **Interpret**   State what mood or feeling, if any, you were attempting to express. Note whether others are able to pinpoint this mood or feeling.
- **Judge**   Compare your work with that of the artist who served as your guide. Tell whether your painting is similar in style to that work. Show in what ways, if any, your work is different.

▲ **Figure 15–5   Student work. Post-Impressionist painting.**

■ Aesthetics

Let students examine Georges Seurat's *Sunday Afternoon on the Island of La Grand Jatte*, shown in Figure 15-4, and discuss their responses: What do you notice first about this work? How do you feel when you look at it? How does the technique of Pointillism affect your responses to the painting?

■ Cultural Diversity

Japanese woodblock prints had an important influence on the works of certain Post-Impressionist artists, including works by Seurat. Ask volunteers to find reproductions of several Japanese prints and to share them with the rest of the class: How might these works have affected the paintings of the Post-Impressionists?

● ● ● ● ● ● ● ● ● ● ● ● ●

ASSESS

■ Self-Assessment

Have students use Examining Your Work to evaluate their paintings. Responses may be written or oral.

■ Reteaching

Have students work with partners to further explore the techniques of Post-Impressionist painting. Let each pair of students choose a subject and make three small paintings of it, each in a different Post-Impressionist technique.

■ Enrichment

Ask students: What was the primary intention of the painting you created in this lesson? Then have each student write a short story, poem, or essay that has the same intention.

● ● ● ● ● ● ● ● ● ● ● ● ●

CLOSE

Display works done by students in the Motivator activity and have them discuss which process they found most enjoyable to work with.

more about • • •

Seurat   The artistic career of Georges Seurat was brief but brilliant. He is regarded as having a pivotal role in the development of modern art. Seurat's first experiments were with light and color. He was interested in transferring the perfect combination of light and color, as seen in nature, to the canvas. To this end, Seurat studied not only the great art works of ancient and Renaissance times, but also the theory of color and the science of optics. He set himself the goal of developing what he called a "formula for optical painting." In 1884 Seurat met Paul Signac, who became his friend and his disciple. Together the two refined the techniques of Pointillism. Signac explained the theories of painting with scientific precision in his 1899 work, *From Delacroix to Neo-Impressionism.*

LESSON 3

American Painting in the Late 1800s

The 1800s was a period of great change and growth in the United States. The country grew in size as pioneers and the railroad pushed westward. It grew in wealth as trade and industry boomed. By the end of the century, America had taken its place as a world power. It had also emerged as a force to be reckoned with in the world of art.

In this lesson you will read about the artists who helped put America on the map.

AMERICAN REALIST ART

During the 1800s many American artists journeyed to the art centers of Europe to study. Some were greatly influenced by the art styles they encountered. Others were mainly unaffected by European art movements. They came home to develop styles that were unmistakably American. One of these was an artist named Thomas Eakins (**ay**-kuhnz).

▲ Figure 15–6   Everything in this picture is made to look real. The artist even included himself in the picture. He is the person in the center holding the oars.

Thomas Eakins. *Max Schmitt in a Single Scull (The Champion Single Sculls).* 1871. Oil on canvas. 81.9 x 117.5 cm (32¼ x 46¼"). The Metropolitan Museum of Art, New York, New York. Alfred N. Punnett Endowment Fund and George D. Pratt Gift.

▲ **Figure 15–7** Paintings like this capture the look and mood of the sea. With a little imagination, you can hear the roaring surf crashing against a rocky shore.

Winslow Homer. *Northeaster.* 1895. Oil on canvas. 87.4 x 127.6 cm (34⅜ x 50¼"). The Metropolitan Museum of Art, New York, New York. Gift of George A. Hearn.

Eakins, who painted only what he saw, is held to be one of America's first Realists. Realism was a movement that had its start in France in the mid-1800s. **Realism** is *a style of art in which everyday scenes and events are painted as they actually look.* Eakins, for example, stubbornly refused to show his subjects in a flattering light. As a result, he was scorned throughout his lifetime. His painting of a man in a racing boat in Figure 15–6 reveals Eakins's devotion to realism. The picture tells no story; it holds no suspense. What it does is offer a carefully studied and designed record of a simple scene that the artist witnessed. Note the care the artist took in painting even the reflections in the water.

Another artist who, like Eakins, painted exactly what he saw, was Winslow Homer.

Unlike Eakins, Homer painted pictures that often told stories, usually of people in the midst of some outdoor activity, such as hunting, fishing, or sailing.

Late in the 1880s Homer set up a studio on a rocky stretch of the Maine coast. There he painted scenes of the sea. At first his pictures were of action-filled struggles between nature and seafaring people. As time went on, the people in his works shrank in importance. His paintings began to focus instead on the power of the sea in its many moods. The work pictured in Figure 15–7 is from this later period. How would you describe the mood of the sea in this painting? What elements and principles of art help communicate this mood?

■ **Motivator**

Let students begin by observing small objects (either natural or manufactured) they have brought to class and then making drawings of those objects. Ask students to draw exactly what they see when they look at their objects—nothing more and nothing less.

■ **Vocabulary**

Let students discuss what kinds of works they would expect from an art style called Realism: What subjects would probably be depicted? How idealized would those subjects be? Then let students read the definition of Realism given on this page.

■ **Aesthetics**

Ask students about Thomas Eakins's approach to painting: Why do you imagine Eakins refused to paint his subjects in a flattering light? What response do you believe he expected from his subjects? What response did he usually get? Did Eakins believe that a work had to be beautiful in order to be an art work? Do you believe that all art should be beautiful? Why or why not? Encourage students to present and support varying points of view.

Lesson 3   *American Painting in the Late 1800s*   **233**

■ **Cooperative Learning**

Have students work in groups to investigate the social and political developments during the lifetimes of Eakins, Homer, Ryder, and Cassatt. Group members should begin by checking the dates of birth and death for the four artists; then they should decide how to divide the research among all group members. After students have completed their investigation, let group members share what they have learned and discuss the probable impact of American events on the works of the four artists.

Art in Everyday Life

Get students thinking about drawing everyday scenes. Suggest that they look closely to find the art in their lives. Have them notice lines, shapes, colors, textures. Tell them to listen to the sounds around them: voices, mechanical sounds, the shuffling of feet. Then have students draw a familiar scene, such as the school lunch room during lunchtime. Ask them to make their drawings as realistic as possible and, at the same time, to tell stories in their drawings. Let students compare and discuss their completed drawings: Why is it difficult to use the style of realism in creating narrative works? What styles work better for this type of drawing?

◀ **Figure 15–8   Light is important in the artist's paintings. He often showed the source of light in the form of the sun or, as here, the moon.**

Albert Pinkham Ryder. *Moonlight Marine (Toilers of the Sea)*. c. 1885. Oil on wood panel. 28.9 x 30.5 cm (11³⁄₈ x 12″). The Metropolitan Museum of Art, New York, New York.

▶ **Figure 15–9   Notice the looseness of the brush strokes. Does this take away from the impression of detail?**

Mary Cassatt. *Sewing Woman*. c. 1880–1882. Oil on canvas. 92 x 63 cm (36 x 25″). Musee d' Orsay, Paris.

234   Lesson 3   *American Painting in the Late 1800s*

RESOURCES BEYOND THE CLASSROOM

Television Programs   Although your students may already watch too much television, certain valuable programs found on public television or cable networks, such as A&E (Arts and Entertainment channel) and the Discovery Channel, can help students appreciate art and artists. These television channels often televise biographies of artists and documentaries describing movements in art. Sometimes programs will showcase a certain period of art. Historical documentaries produced by these networks often include social and artistic achievements of different societies. Often, videos of these programs can be obtained through the networks. Students can be encouraged to view these programs and write brief reviews of what they have seen to present to the class.

Portraying Realism

Two other artists who affected the development of American art in the 1800s were a colorful figure by the name of Albert Pinkham Ryder and Mary Cassatt.

A loner who paid little attention to the work of others, Ryder painted dreamlike images, often borrowed from literature. His style made use of large areas of color and thick layers of paint. The painting by him in Figure 15–8 shows the simple silhouette of a ship beneath a ghostly moon. The vessel seems to glide silently across the water, carrying its crew into a night filled with mystery and wonder.

Mary Cassatt, an American who studied at the Pennsylvania Academy of Fine Arts, went on to Paris for further training. There she met Degas and was influenced by his Impressionist paintings. She often chose women and children as her subjects, using the Impressionist play of light to enhance the gentle mood she created. Her work in Figure 15–9 shows why she is considered to be one of America's finest women painters.

✔CHECK YOUR UNDERSTANDING

1. What is Realism?
2. Why were the works of Thomas Eakins shunned during his lifetime?
3. What were favorite subjects of Winslow Homer?
4. Name four artists who affected the development of American art in the 1800s.
5. What kinds of works did Albert Pinkham Ryder create? Where did he get the ideas for his works?

STUDIO ACTIVITY

Creating Texture

One element that helps viewers sense the mood of the work in Figure 15–8 is texture. Look again at the painting. Notice how the sky and sea both appear alive, although in different ways.

Working lightly in pencil, sketch a nighttime landscape. Include trees, a lake, and the moon. Make your drawing large enough to fill a large sheet of paper. Switching to crayon, trace over all the pencil lines, pressing hard. Place a sheet of burlap beneath your paper. Using the side of an unwrapped crayon, rub over the sky in your drawing. Replace the burlap with bits of dried grass and leaves. Rub the crayon over the lake in your work. Examine the results. Use other materials with rough surfaces as a base for rubbing the remaining forms in your work. (For further information on rubbings, see Technique Tip **25**, *Handbook* page **286**.)

PORTFOLIO

Describe the results of each textural experiment. Write each technique and the words that describe its effects in chart form. Keep this chart and your sketch with texture samples in your portfolio for reference. Add new techniques and textures to your chart as you discover them.

STUDIO ACTIVITY

Creating Texture

Before beginning this activity, help students to think about textures in nature. Have them write a paragraph describing a landscape scene. Encourage them to use descriptive words to identify textures in the scene.

A S S E S S

■ **Self-Assessment**

Have students complete the review questions on this page. Answers are provided below.

■ **Reteaching**

Have students form four groups, and assign each group one of the artists presented in the lesson. Have group members work together to find reproductions of other works by their assigned artist. Then ask each group to share its reproductions with the rest of the class.

■ **Enrichment**

Let students work in groups to research and discuss the purposes of portrait painting: When did artists begin painting portraits? Why did those early artists paint portraits? Have the purposes of portrait painters changed since those earliest works? If so, how? Does an artist who paints a flattering portrait fulfill the purpose of portrait painting? Does an artist such as Eakins, who refused to flatter his subjects, fulfill the purpose of portrait painting? Let group members conclude their discussion by drawing and discussing portraits of one another: What is the purpose of each of these portraits?

C L O S E

Ask students to explain why American painters began painting in a realist style.

235

Answers to ✔CHECK YOUR UNDERSTANDING

1. A style of art in which everyday scenes and events are painted as they actually look.
2. Because he stubbornly refused to show his subjects in a flattering light.
3. Winslow Homer liked to paint pictures that told a story. At first he showed people engaged in outdoor activities; later he painted scenes showing the power of the sea in his works.
4. Thomas Eakins, Winslow Homer, Albert Pinkham Ryder, and Mary Cassatt.
5. He created dreamlike images using large areas of color and thick layers of paint. He often got his ideas from literature.

LESSON TIME: 90 minutes

· · · · · · · · · · · · · · ·
FOCUS

☑ **OBJECTIVES**

After completing this lesson, students will be able to:

• Use watercolor paints to create their own expressive scenes.

• Describe, analyze, interpret, and judge their own watercolor paintings.

☑ **SUPPLIES**

• Containers of water, sheets of white paper, 9 x 12 inches (23 x 30 cm); watercolor paints; brushes in several sizes; tempera paint in several hues; pen; India ink.

• Reproduction of one of Henry Tanner's paintings of a Bible scene (if available), sheets of drawing paper, pencils, wide-line and fine-tipped markers.

· · · · · · · · · · · · · · ·
TEACH

■ **Motivator**

Ask students to recall the work of Thomas Eakins: Why is Eakins called a Realist? What did Eakins paint? How important were story and mood in his paintings? Explain to students that they will study a work by a painter who became Eakin's student—and friend—at the Pennsylvania Academy of Fine Arts, Henry Tanner. Though Tanner worked in Realism, he usually created more expressive works, communicating a greater sense of mood and emotion.

236

Making an Expressive Watercolor Painting

Henry Tanner was a former student of Thomas Eakins and one of America's most talented black artists. Because his paintings did not sell in America, Tanner decided to move to Europe. Settling in Paris, he painted scenes from the Bible, which were well received. After one of his paintings was accepted in the Paris Salon, a highly respected French artist insisted that it be hung in a place of honor.

Although better known for his religious pictures, some of Tanner's best works were portraits and outdoor scenes. One of his scenes can be viewed in Figure 15–10. Notice the low-intensity hues, contrasting light and dark values, and fuzzy shapes in this painting. What kind of mood does Tanner create with these hues, values, and shapes?

WHAT YOU WILL LEARN

You will use watercolor paint to create your own expressive scene. Your scene will exhibit the same low-intensity hues, contrasting dark and light values, and fuzzy shapes found in Tanner's painting. Your painting will also express the same quiet stillness. (See Figure 15–11.)

▶ **Figure 15–10** The artist's interest in art was born when, as a child, he watched an artist at work in a park.

Henry O. Tanner. *The Seine*. 1902. Canvas. 23 x 32.9 cm (9 x 13"). National Gallery of Art, Washington, D.C. Gift of the Avalon Foundation.

more about • • •

Tanner   Henry Tanner was an American-born artist who studied briefly at the Pennsylvania Academy of Fine Arts, where Thomas Eakins became both his teacher and his friend. Tanner went to Paris in the 1890s, at least in part to escape racial prejudice, and he remained a resident of France until his death. In the early years of his career, Tanner used African-American life as his subject. Later, he turned to religious subjects, for which he is most famous. He traveled twice to Palestine, where he did research for his paintings of Bible scenes. Tanner chose the medium of watercolor over others because of its ability to capture light. He was especially concerned with the effects of light, particularly moonlight. Tanner used layers of glaze to capture the depth and intensity of light.

WHAT YOU WILL NEED

- Container of water
- Sheet of white paper, 9 x 12 inches (23 x 30 cm)
- Watercolor paint and several brushes
- Tempera paint in different hues
- Pen and India ink

WHAT YOU WILL DO

1. With water, completely wet the sheet of white paper.
2. Load a medium-pointed brush with a light color paint, and apply this carefully to the damp paper. The area painted might represent a lake or river. Add other areas of light colors to suggest sky and clouds.
3. Use the same technique to add dark shapes to your paper. These could suggest the shoreline, distant rooftops, boats, a bridge, or other objects. Do not worry about details. Concern yourself with creating areas of color with different dark values.
4. While your picture is drying, study it carefully. Use your imagination to identify the general outlines of the different objects.
5. When your painting is dry, use a pen and India ink to outline the objects. Add details.
6. Use white paint to create highlights and additional details.

EXAMINING YOUR WORK

- **Describe** Identify the different objects in your scene. Name the hues you used.
- **Analyze** Point out the low-intensity hues, contrasting light and dark values, and fuzzy shapes.
- **Interpret** Explain how your work expresses a quiet, still mood.
- **Judge** Compare your work with that of Tanner. Tell how your picture is similar in content and composition. Point out the differences.

▲ **Figure 15–11** Student work. Expressive watercolor painting.

Try This! COMPUTER OPTION

■ Choose light, transparent colors and a wide Brush tool to fill in areas representing sky and water. Select darker hues and roughly add shapes of objects such as buildings, bridges, shoreline, or trees. Use Water effect with mouse or drawing pen to smudge or soften the strokes and to create a watercolor effect. You may wish to use the Airbrush tool and transparent colors to build up layers of tints and shades. Use small Brush and a dark color to outline important objects in the picture. Title, print, and save your work.

TECHNIQUE TIP

Watercolors In this lesson, students are working with a piece of paper that has been dampened. Show how watercolors can be made to run. Apply a brushful of a light color to the sky area using enough paint and water to flood the area. Gently pick up the paper by the top edges and let the paint flow down, feathering as it goes. Explain that this can be used for foliage by picking the page up by its lower edge. Ask students for suggestions of other ways this technique could be applied.

■ **Vocabulary**

Review with students the definition of *intensity:* What are low-intensity hues? What are high-intensity hues? What effect do differences in intensity have?

■ **Aesthetics**

Let students share and discuss their responses to Tanner's painting shown in Figure 15-10: How does this work make you feel? What mood do you think the artist intended to communicate? How does his choice of medium contribute to that mood?

ASSESS

■ **Self-Assessment**

Have students use Examining Your Work to evaluate the paintings they created in this Studio Lesson. Responses may be written or oral.

■ **Reteaching**

Guide students in discussing Tanner's use of watercolor. Explain that some critics say "real artists" don't use watercolors, because watercolors are a medium for amateurs: Do you agree? Why or why not? How important is the choice of medium in creating a work of art? Then have students find and bring to class reproductions of other watercolor paintings. Help students compare and discuss the style of these works.

■ **Enrichment**

Ask students to identify important events in their own lives and to paint expressive scenes from these events. How can they depict their feelings and, in the same work, show what happened?

CLOSE

Have each student write a short interpretation of another group member's watercolor painting.

OBJECTIVES

After completing this feature, students will be able to:

- Describe life on the Western frontier.
- Understand the reasons why people went West.

Teaching the Connection

- Have students read the feature on this page.
- Ask volunteers to share what they know about the Westward movement. What other kinds of dangers did the adventurers experience? *(Encounters with Native Americans who resented this invasion of their lands; fire; broken wagons; dying livestock; typhoid, diphtheria, snake bite, infected cuts; freezing weather.)* Why did people leave their homes to go West? *(Overcrowding in cities, lack of jobs, failed farms in the East were some reasons.)* How does the painting compare with what you know about the true West? *(It is beautiful; the true image, though beautiful in many ways, was often marred by death and danger.)*
- Point out that Albert Bierstadt (1830–1902) was himself an immigrant, arriving in the U.S. as a baby. He first saw the West in 1859 as part of a surveying expedition and based his dramatic panoramic paintings on both sketches and photos.

Answers to Making the Connection

- Possible answers: color, line, emphasis, informal balance.
- Responses will vary. Most sought a more prosperous life with more opportunities.
- Answers will vary.

Albert Bierstadt. *Emigrants Crossing the Plains.* 1867. Oil. National Cowboy Hall of Fame and Western Heritage Center, Oklahoma City, Oklahoma.

What Adventures Awaited Frontier Settlers?

Life on the American frontier is portrayed in popular books and movies as an exciting, romantic adventure. Yet, the true picture was not very glamorous. If you could travel back in time, what would you discover?

During the 1800s, millions of emigrants ventured west. Some went in search of gold, others in search of cheap farm or ranch land. All dreamed of a better life, but the journey itself was treacherous. Accidents, disease, and exhaustion took their toll. Crossing wide, swollen rivers and steep mountains was life threatening. Along the trail, water was scarce. The sun and heat could be unbearable. There was no escaping the dust, wind, and rain. For many, this journey would be the last. Yet the brash hope and idealism of these individuals helped most survive.

The Homestead Act of 1862 granted free land to those who would farm it. Thousands more stampeded to the frontier. Many settlers were unprepared for the harsh life that awaited them. In Bierstadt's painting, we sense the rugged spirit of these emigrants paired with the awesome beauty of the landscape. How much of this image is real? How much is myth?

MAKING THE CONNECTION

- How has Albert Bierstadt used the elements and principles of art to direct the viewer's eye?
- The artist symbolized the hopes and dreams of the westward adventurers. What motivated these travelers to brave the hardships and continue onward?
- Locate examples of painting and photographs of the early West. Which ones are realistic, which ones seem idealistic? Why would an artist create a work with a certain point of view?

INTERNET ACTIVITY

Visit Glencoe's Fine Arts Web Site for students at:

http://www.glencoe.com/sec/art/students

INTERNET ACTIVITY

Artists Around the World Wide Web In Studio Cyberspace, Glencoe's Fine Arts Site will focus on art forms created in different countries in *Cultural Treasures.* Students view unique representative works from various cultures while learning about the cultural and social significance of the art form. Use this site with cultural or seasonal activities in your classroom.

Visiting an Artist Students can read about a contemporary artist and view featured work in *Visiting an Artist.* Images of the artist's work will be displayed, as well as the background and influences that inspired the artist. Use this site to discuss more career ideas for your students. Find us at **http://www.glencoe.com/sec/art**

REVIEW

 BUILDING VOCABULARY

Number a sheet of paper from 1 to 5. After each number, write the term from the list that best matches each description below.

arbitrary colors	Post Impressionism
optical colors	Realism
Pointillism	

1. An art movement that appeared after the Impressionists.
2. Colors viewers actually see.
3. Colors chosen to communicate different feelings.
4. A technique in which small, carefully placed dots of color are used to create forms.
5. A style of art in which everyday scenes and events are painted as they actually look.

 REVIEWING ART FACTS

Number a sheet of paper from 6 to 15. Answer each question in a complete sentence.

6. Name two problems and solutions some artists of the later 1800s found in the Impressionist style.
7. Which Post-Impressionist artist was a former Impressionist?
8. Which artist besides Cézanne was interested in making the forms in his paintings clearer and more solid-looking?
9. Which Post-Impressionist besides Gauguin used arbitrary colors in his works?
10. What painter filled his works with tiny dots of color? Why did he do this?
11. What was there about his works that made Eakins unpopular during his lifetime?
12. How did Homer's paintings change from his early to his later years in Maine?
13. Which two American artists of the late 1800s often painted pictures of the sea?
14. Name the artists who affected the development of American art in the 1800s.
15. Describe Ryder's painting techniques.

 THINKING ABOUT ART

On a sheet of paper, answer each question in a sentence or two.

1. **Analyze.** Paul Cézanne claimed that all forms in nature are based on three forms: the sphere, the cone, and the cylinder. Examine his painting in Figure 15–1. Tell how his work supports this idea.
2. **Compare and contrast.** Acting as a critic, interpret the works by Albert Pinkham Ryder (Figure 15–8) and Thomas Eakins (Figure 15–6). Tell how the two interpretations differ. Tell how they are alike.

MAKING ART CONNECTIONS

1. **Language Arts.** Read *Meet Edgar Degas* by Anne Newlands. In the book, Degas tells you about his paintings and what it was like to be an artist during the time he worked in Paris. Write a letter to Degas and tell him about being an artist in your town today. Compare what you read in Newlands' book with what you think he might experience if he lived in present-day United States.

2. **History.** Imagine that you lived in America during the 1800s. Using history and literature books for reference, write a short report on what life would have been like for a teen growing up in this time. Identify the area of the country where you might live, the lifestyle you would experience there, and the specific years you are writing about. List some events that would shape your life.

Chapter 15 Review **239**

1. Post-Impressionism
2. optical colors
3. arbitrary colors
4. Pointillism
5. Realism

6. Problems should include lack of composition and content. Solutions include making shapes more identifiable, conveying more emotion, and creating art that could be enjoyed purely for its decorative appearance.
7. Paul Cézanne was a former Impressionist.
8. Georges Seurat was also interested in making the forms in his painting clearer and more solid looking.
9. Van Gogh also used arbitrary colors.
10. Seurat used tiny dots of color. He used this technique to create new colors and clear shapes.
11. Eakins refused to show his subjects in a flattering light.
12. Homer's early paintings showed people engaged in outdoor activities. Later works focused on the power of the sea and its many moods.
13. Homer and Ryder both painted pictures of the sea.
14. Eakins, Homer, Ryder, and Mary Cassatt affected development of American art in the 1800s.
15. Ryder used large areas of color and thick layers of paint.

THINKING ABOUT ART

1. Students should mention that Cézanne has painted his mountain, trees, and buildings using patches of color to give his forms three dimensions, and that he has used the cone, sphere, and cylinder shapes in his paintings.

2. Students should discuss the content, describing Eakins's realism, lack of mystery, and photographic quality. They should see Ryder's heavy, mysterious mood, few details, simple composition. Similarities: boats, sky, water, and few people.

Art of the Early Twentieth Century

(pages 240–255)

Resources

- 16-9 Chapter Test, TRB page 337
- Transparency CC-16, *The Giant,* by N.C. Wyeth
- Transparency 16, *July Hay* by Thomas Hart Benton
- Fine Art Print 17, *Improvisation III* by Wassily Kandinsky

ART SOURCE **Dance**
While studying this chapter, use Performing Arts Handbook page 332 to help students see how a story from the American West is transformed for the first time into a classical dance form choreographed by Eugene Loring.

NATIONAL STANDARDS

This chapter addresses the following National Standards for the Visual Arts:

1. (a, b)   **4.** (c)
2. (a, b, c) **5.** (b, c)
3. (a, b)   **6.** (a, b)

▲ Notice that the wedding couple do not look at one another. How do you know that the groom in the work is a painter? How has the artist used color to draw attention to the bride?

Frida Kahlo. *Frida and Diego Rivera.* 1931. Oil on canvas. 100 x 78.7 cm (39⅜ x 31"). San Francisco Museum of Modern Art, San Francisco, California. Albert M. Bender Collection. Gift of Albert M. Bender.

240

FEATURED ARTISTS

George Bellows
Georges Braque
Allan Rohan Crite
John Steuart Curry
Frida Kahlo
Ernst Ludwig Kirchner

Käthe Kollwitz
Jacques Lipchitz
Henri Matisse
Diego Rivera
John Sloan
Alfred Stieglitz

Art of the Early Twentieth Century

Art has the power to delight. Art has the power to teach. Art also has the power, as history has shown time and again, to express emotion.

While some styles that developed early in the twentieth century shocked and surprised viewers, some styles were more easily recognized as expression of the artist's struggle. The painting at the left represents the life experience of the artist who created it. In the pages that follow you will learn about some of the many varied art styles of this period.

PORTFOLIO IDEAS

Select two examples from your portfolio that were done in the same media and that demonstrate your growth in the use of that media. Evaluate the works. Describe what you learned about using the media. What improvements did you make in using the media? What changes would you improve in using the media? Store your examples and evaluation in your portfolio.

OBJECTIVES

After completing this chapter, you will be able to:
● Identify the major art movements of the early twentieth century.
● Name the leaders of those movements.
● Describe art trends in the United States and Mexico in the early twentieth century.
● Use the elements and principles of art in the style of the Cubists.
● Create an art work showing rhythm and movement.

WORDS YOU WILL LEARN

Ashcan School
Cubism
The Eight
Expressionism
Fauvism
muralist
non-objective art
Regionalism

241

Art of the Early Twentieth Century in Europe

Every age, it has been said, learns from and builds on the one before it. The truth of these words is clear from developments in art in the early 1900s. Several new styles came along, each borrowing in a different way from Post-Impressionism. These styles, which stunned the art world, continue to affect art through the present day. In this lesson you will learn about the pioneers behind these innovative ways of making art.

FAUVISM

In 1905 a showing by a group of French artists started the art community buzzing. The most striking feature of the works in the show was their raw, sizzling colors. No effort had been made to paint realistic pictures. The artists' goal was to express their feelings through sharply contrasting colors and heavy outlines. One angry critic wrote that the paintings looked as though they had

▶ **Figure 16–1 This painting shows the artist's favorite model and her two brothers. Matisse's own presence is suggested by the empty armchair in the center where he would often sit, his violins hanging from the cabinet, and his art works tacked to the wall.**

Henri Matisse. *Pianist and Checker Players*. 1924. Oil on canvas. 73.7 x 92.4 cm (29 x 36⅜"). National Gallery of Art, Washington, D.C. Collection of Mr. and Mrs. Paul Mellon.

FOCUS

✓ OBJECTIVES

After completing this lesson, students will be able to:

- Identify the major European art movements of the early twentieth century.
- Name the leaders of those art movements.
- Create collages that capture the look and feel of twentieth-century American street scenes.

✓ SUPPLIES

- Sheets of drawing paper, colored markers.
- Old magazines with photographs and/or illustrations, scissors, white glue, sheets of white paper.
- Sheets of sketch paper; pencils; several objects with distinctive shapes, such as a basket, a vase, a small doll, a figurine.

Resource

■ 16-1 *Elements of Cubism*, TRB page 321 (reproducible master)

TECHNOLOGY OPTIONS

National Gallery of Art Videodisc   Use the following images to show examples of art of the early twentieth century.

Käthe Kollwitz *Self-Portrait*	Käthe Kollwitz *In God's Hands*	Wassily Kandinsky *Improvisation 31 (Sea Battle)*
Search Frame 2754	Search Frame 2567	Search Frame 2247

Use Glencoe's *Correlation Bar Code Guide to the National Gallery of Art* to locate more art works.

242

been done by *fauves* (**fohvs**). This term, which is French for "wild beasts," gave the movement its name: Fauvism (**fohv**-iz-uhm). **Fauvism** is *an art movement in which artists used wild, intense color combinations in their paintings*.

The leader of the Fauves was a law student who chose to become an artist. His name was Henri Matisse (ahnh-**ree** mah-**tees**). For his paintings, Matisse chose colors that communicated a joyous or happy mood. He then combined them, as in the picture in Figure 16–1, to create rich, decorative patterns. To understand the importance of color in Matisse's works, try to imagine Figure 16–1 in black and white. In what way would the painting be different? How would its mood change?

EXPRESSIONISM

Matisse and the Fauves wanted to show feelings in their art. In Germany the same goal was shared by another group of artists, who developed a movement known as Expressionism (ek-**spresh**-uh-niz-uhm). Artists using **Expressionism** worked in *a style that emphasized the expression of innermost feelings*. They ignored the contemporary rules of art. They had the strength to experiment with, to exaggerate, and in other ways to change, the proportions of figures and objects.

Painting

An early leader of the Expressionist movement was an artist named Ernst Ludwig Kirchner (**ehrnst lood**-vig **keerk**-nuhr). Figure 16–2 shows Kirchner's inner view of a street scene. Note his use of brilliant, clashing colors and sharp, twisted shapes. The people in Kirchner's world are crammed together in a small space. Yet they manage not to notice one another. How might you sum up the artist's feelings toward these people and their world?

Printmaking

The power of Expressionism can also be seen in the prints and drawings of Käthe

▲ **Figure 16–2** The artist has used twisted shapes to express his emotions. An earlier artist you read about did the same thing. Do you recall that artist's name?

Ernst Ludwig Kirchner. *Street, Berlin.* 1913. Oil on canvas. 120.6 x 91.1 cm (47½ x 35⅞"). Collection. The Museum of Modern Art, New York, New York. Purchase.

Kollwitz (**kay**-tuh **kohl**-vits). At a time when most artists were exploring color, Kollwitz created works mainly in black and white. Many, like the print in Figure 16–3, reveal her concern for the poor and her outrage at the horrors of war. In this moving work, she captures the sorrow and the despair of lower-class German mothers left alone to care for their children after World War I.

CUBISM

Paul Cézanne, you will remember, was interested in showing objects as solid-looking forms. A guiding idea behind one new style was Cézanne's notion that all forms in nature are made up of three shapes. Those three are the sphere, cone, and cylinder. This idea contributed to the development of **Cubism**, *an art style in which objects and the space around them are broken up into different shapes and then put back together in new relationships*.

■ Motivator

Explain to students that many works of modern art focus on expressing feelings. Ask students to try creating their own drawings that express feelings. Let students suggest several different feelings or emotions that might be depicted in art works—rage, joy, sorrow, disappointment, and so on. Then have each student choose one emotion and use colored markers to draw an expression of that emotion. Suggest that students may want to use colors, lines, and/or shapes to express the chosen emotion; remind them to depict the emotion itself, not a person causing or feeling that emotion. When students have finished their drawings, let them work in small groups to share their work. Can other group members identify the depicted emotion?

■ Vocabulary

Help students understand the meaning of the term *non-objective:* What is another word that has the same meaning as *object?* What does the prefix *non-* mean? What would you expect to see in a non-objective work of art?

■ Aesthetics

Explain that non-objective art has many detractors; some people feel that works without recognizable subjects are not art. Ask students for their opinions: Is non-objective art really art? Why or why not? Do you think that creating non-objective paintings or sculptures requires as much talent as creating representational art works? Why or why not?

CURRICULUM CONNECTIONS

Language Arts To help students have a better understanding of the naming of these art styles, discuss the origins of the names *Fauvism* and *Cubism.* Explain that *fauves* is a French word meaning "wild beast"; a critic used this word to describe the painters who created works with wild, intense color combinations. Ask students if they had been one of those painters, how would that critic's remark have made them feel? Would they have adopted the name *Fauvism* to identify their new art movement? Explain that another critic made this disparaging comment about a painting by Georges Braque: It "reduces everything to little cubes." Discuss how Braque would have felt about the critic's remark. Would they have adopted the name *Cubism* had they been in his shoes?

■ **Art Criticism**

Ask students to examine Figure 3-7, page 42, as they consider this quotation from Pablo Picasso: "When I paint, my object is to show what I have found and not what I am looking for." How does the quotation help make Picasso's intention in his painting clear? Encourage students to think about their own approach to creating art works. Ask them to think about whether they begin with an objective of what they will paint. Discuss how they might determine their own objectives.

Sparking Creativity

Challenge students to think about point of view. Remind students that Cubist works show objects from several different angles at once. Ask students to imagine how this might be accomplished.

Set out one or two objects with distinctive shapes—such as baskets, vases, figurines, and so on—at each of several work stations. Allow students to move about to the different work stations and sketch the object or objects from several different angles, making four or five different sketches of the same subject.

Then have students draw new pictures of their chosen subjects, combining the perspectives used in several of their sketches. How does making this new drawing help them understand the objects?

▲ Figure 16–3   Describe the expression on the faces of these people. What word would you use to describe the way these mothers act toward their children? How does this picture make you feel?

Käthe Kollwitz. *The Mothers.* 1919. Lithograph. 43.8 x 58.4 cm (17¾ x 23"). Philadelphia Museum of Art, Philadelphia, Pennsylvania. Anonymous donor.

Painting

The founder of Cubism was an artist you have met before in this book. Even if you had not met him here, his name is one you would instantly recognize. It is Pablo Picasso.

Picasso's early Cubist paintings were different arrangements of bits and pieces of his subject viewed from different angles. The subjects of these works are at times difficult to pick out. Later he began using brighter colors and larger shapes in his works. He also added texture and pattern, often by gluing found objects to his paintings. The picture in Figure 3–7 on page **42** is one of Picasso's later Cubist works. Are you able to identify the objects in this picture?

Sculpture

The Cubist style also found its way into sculpture of the early twentieth century. Jacques Lipchitz (**zhahk lip**-shuts), a Lithuanian-born sculptor who studied in Paris, used Cubism in his bronze castings. One of these works is pictured in Figure 16–4. Notice how the many fragments of a figure add up to a carefully designed three-dimensional whole. How has the artist used texture to give the work a sense of harmony?

Guest Speakers   Don't overlook the importance of guest speakers in the art classroom. Guest speakers can come from a variety of art-related areas and can speak on a wide range of topics. For example, a career counselor can discuss art careers and how to prepare for them. An artist can demonstrate certain techniques. An art historian can talk about a certain historical period, while an art critic can help students understand various aesthetic approaches to understanding art. A community college instructor can describe courses of study and can introduce students to non-credit courses designed for their age group. Speakers can be found at nearby community colleges, area art councils, and in community organizations.

▲ **Figure 16–4** What has the artist done to create value?

Jacques Lipchitz. *Bather*. 1923–25. Bronze. 198.5 x 79.1 x 70.5 cm (78⅛ x 31⅛ x 27¾"). Dallas Museum of Art, Dallas, Texas. Gift of Mr. & Mrs. Algur H. Meadows and the Meadows Foundation, Inc. © 1998 Estate of Jacques Lipchitz/Licensed by VAGA, New York, NY/Courtesy Marlborough Gallery, New York.

NON-OBJECTIVE ART

One evening in 1910 after painting outdoors all day, a weary artist returned to his studio. There he was greeted by a surprise that changed the course of art history. Perched on his easel was a painting unlike anything he had ever seen. Its brightly colored shapes and lines seemed to glow and shimmer in the dim light. Rushing to the canvas, the artist had his second surprise of the night. The work was his own; he had carelessly placed it upside down on the easel! The artist's name was Wassily Kandinsky (**vahs**-uh-lee kuhn-**din**-skee). His discovery led to the birth of a new style called **non-objective art**. These are *works in which no objects or subjects can be readily identified*.

STUDIO ACTIVITY

Making a Collage

Look through the pages of a magazine for street scenes. Cut any pictures you find into angled shapes of different sizes. Arrange these shapes into a collage. Your work should capture the look and feel of a twentieth-century American street scene. Glue the shapes to a sheet of white paper. Compare your street scene with the one in Figure 16–2. Is your collage as successful in expressing a mood or feeling? Why or why not?

PORTFOLIO

For your portfolio, you may wish to mount or mat your collage. Include your written comparison telling whether your collage expresses the mood or feeling you were trying to capture.

In the experiments that followed, Kandinsky found he could express feelings using only colors, shapes, and lines. These elements could be arranged, just as the notes of a song are, to create a mood.

✔ CHECK YOUR UNDERSTANDING

1. What is Fauvism? Who was the leader of the Fauves?
2. What is Expressionism? In what way did the Expressionists ignore the rules of art?
3. To what movement did the artist Käthe Kollwitz belong? What media did she favor?
4. Define *Cubism.* Name the Post-Impressionist artist whose ideas influenced the Cubist movement.
5. Tell in what area of art Jacques Lipchitz worked. By what art movement was he influenced?
6. Tell how non-objective art got its start. Name the originator of the movement.

Lesson 1   *Art of the Early Twentieth Century in Europe*   **245**

Answers to ✔ CHECK YOUR UNDERSTANDING

1. An art movement in which artists use wild, intense color combinations in their paintings. Henri Matisse.
2. The style that emphasizes the expression of innermost feelings. They ignored the rules of art by changing the proportions of figures and objects.
3. Käthe Kollwitz was an Expressionist. She worked mainly in black and white.
4. A style in which objects and the space around them are broken up into different shapes and put together in new relationships. Paul Cézanne.
5. A sculptor; influenced by the Cubist movement.
6. Non-objective art is work where no objects or subjects can be readily identified. Kandinsky.

STUDIO ACTIVITY

Making a Collage

Have students bring magazines from home that they can share with classmates to create this collage.

■ Cultural Diversity

Several influences on the development of Cubism have been acknowledged; these include African tribal sculptures and the low-relief sculptures of the ancient Egyptians. Ask two groups of volunteers to find examples of these works and demonstrate how the works might have influenced Cubism.

• • • • • • • • • • • • • • • •

ASSESS

■ Self-Assessment

Have students complete the review questions on this page. Answers are provided below.

■ Reteaching

Have students find examples of Expressionist and/or non-objective art in magazines and newspapers. Give students an opportunity to share what they have found with the rest of the class. Ask: How easy—or difficult—was it to find examples of Expressionist and non-objective art?

■ Enrichment

Have students form seven groups, and assign each group one of these artists: Henri Matisse, Ernst Ludwig Kirchner, Käthe Kollwitz, Paul Cézanne, Pablo Picasso, Jacques Lipchitz, Wassily Kandinsky. Have the members of each group learn about the life and works of their assigned artist and plan a presentation of their findings.

• • • • • • • • • • • • • • • •

CLOSE

Ask students to describe Fauvism, Expressionism, and Cubism, and name one artist who created works in each.

245

Making a Cubist Chalk Drawing

A co-founder of the Cubist movement was an artist named Georges Braque (**zhorzh brahk**). A favorite form of expression for Braque was the still life. Instead of fruits or flowers, he usually chose household objects as subjects. Figure 16–5 shows one of his still lifes. Notice how the table, other objects, and background are combined to make a flat, decorative design. All parts of the work are equally interesting to look at. The different colors, shapes, lines, and textures are organized into an interesting whole.

In this lesson you will use the elements and principles of art in the same way.

WHAT YOU WILL LEARN

You will create a still life with chalk in the later style of the Cubists. You will repeat colors, shapes, lines, and textures to make a flat, decorative pattern. Your pattern will fill the paper. A warm or cool color scheme will be used to add harmony and express a mood. (See Figure 16–6.)

WHAT YOU WILL NEED

- Pencil and sheets of sketch paper
- Sheet of white paper, 18 x 24 inches (46 x 61 cm)
- Colored chalk and spray fixative
- Sheets of facial tissue

▶ **Figure 16–5** How many different objects can you identify? What other objects could be used to make an interesting still life? Describe the different textures. How has the artist added unity to this design?

Georges Braque. *Still Life:Le Jour.* 1929. Canvas. 115 x 146.7 cm (45¼ x 57¾"). National Gallery of Art, Washington, D.C. Chester Dale Collection.

FOCUS

☑ OBJECTIVES

After completing this lesson, students will be able to:
- Create still-life drawings in the later style of the Cubists.
- Describe, analyze, interpret, and judge their own drawings.

☑ SUPPLIES

- Potted plant, cut flowers in a vase, or another object; pencils; sheets of sketch paper.
- Pencils; sheets of sketch paper; sheets of white paper, 18 x 24 inches (46 x 61 cm); colored chalk; spray fixative; sheets of facial tissue.
- Several art books that include reproductions of Cubist works.

Resource

◼ 16-2 *American Realism in Art*, TRB page 324 (aesthetics/art criticism)

TEACH

◼ Motivator

Place a potted plant, a small bouquet, or some other object in a central location. Ask students to stay in their seats, look closely at the object, and then draw a quick sketch of it, concentrating on an interesting shape or detail. Then let students compare and discuss their sketches: How is each drawing different from the others?

246

more about • • •

Cubism   The Cubist art movement is generally considered to have been founded by two artists: Pablo Picasso and Georges Braque. Picasso created the first Cubist work, *Les Demoiselles d'Avignon,* in 1907. Braque was one of the few artists who apparently understood and appreciated the work; he stopped working in the Fauvist style and became a Cubist. The two worked together closely during the early years of the movement. After several years Picasso and Braque developed a style called Analytic Cubism. Each work consisted of many carefully analyzed facets of the same subject, superimposed over one another. The colors used were generally muted. The next Cubist style, Synthetic Cubism, emerged around 1912 and used brighter colors and more decorative devices.

WHAT YOU WILL DO

1. Bring to class an object with an interesting shape. Some possibilities are an old violin or guitar, an oddly shaped bottle, or a house plant. Working with three other students, arrange the objects on a tabletop. Each student should have a clear view of the objects.

2. Make several rough pencil sketches for a still life. You may exaggerate or in other ways change shapes and lines for added interest. Shapes should be shown as simple, flat planes. Repeat the lines of the objects in the background areas.

3. Working lightly in chalk, transfer your best sketch to the sheet of white paper. Fill the whole sheet with your design.

4. Choose four or five sticks of chalk to create either a warm or cool color scheme. As you choose, keep in mind the mood you want your work to communicate.

5. Color your still life. Color some shapes by blending two or more hues with facial tissue. Repeat colors throughout the picture to add harmony. Make some shapes stand out clearly by adding heavy contour lines. Use the chalk to create different textures in some shapes.

6. Spray your still life with fixative. Compare it with the one in Figure 16–5 and those by other students.

SAFETY TIP

Remember to use chalk in a place with plenty of ventilation. If you begin to have breathing problems, finish the lesson using crayon. Use spray fixative outdoors or in a space with plenty of ventilation.

Try This! COMPUTER OPTION

■ Use the Pencil tool to sketch a still life with varied, simple lines and shapes to make the objects appear flat. Use the Straight Line tool to draw horizontal and vertical lines across the still life. Fill in each space with a solid or patterned color. Repeat colors to create harmony. Emphasize some shapes by using a thick Brush to outline. Title, save, and print your work.

EXAMINING YOUR WORK

- **Describe** Point to and name the different objects in your picture. Explain how and why you changed the shapes and lines of those objects.
- **Analyze** Point out places where you have repeated colors, shapes, and lines. Explain how these elements have been used to create a flat, decorative pattern. Tell whether your design fills the whole sheet of paper.
- **Interpret** Tell how the warm or cool color scheme adds a mood to your work. Identify this mood.
- **Judge** Tell whether you feel your work succeeds. Explain your answer.

▲ **Figure 16–6   Student work. Cubist chalk drawing.**

■ Vocabulary

Help students review the definition of *Cubism*. Ask students how their sketches from the Motivator activity relate to Cubism.

■ Art Criticism

Present the following quote from Guillaume Apollinaire, a poet and critic during the early modern art era: "Cubism differs from the old school of painting in that it aims not at an art of imitation but at an art of conception." Ask: What do you think Apollinaire meant? Have students support their responses by pointing out specific examples in modern works reproduced in this chapter.

ASSESS

■ Self-Assessment

Have students use Examining Your Work to evaluate their Cubist chalk drawings. Responses may be written or oral.

■ Reteaching

Have small groups of students browse through art books. Let each student select and share reproductions of two Cubist paintings or sculptures. Ask: Why did you choose this work of art? What made you identify it as an example of Cubism? Which art elements did you find most interesting in this work?

■ Enrichment

Ask each student to choose a favorite object and create two drawings or paintings of it: one as realistic as possible and the other in the style of later Cubism. Display the pairs of paintings or drawings, and encourage students to discuss and compare the two works in each pair.

CLOSE

Let students work with partners to compare and discuss their Cubist chalk drawings. Then have students write short descriptions of their partners' drawings.

LESSON 3

Art of the
Early
Twentieth
Century in
America

(pages 248–251)

Art of the Early Twentieth Century in America

• • • • • • • • • • • • • • •
FOCUS

☑ OBJECTIVES

After completing this lesson, students will be able to:

• Describe art trends in the United States and Mexico in the early twentieth century.

• Name leading artists in those trends.

• Create abstract drawings with images that capture specific concepts.

☑ SUPPLIES

• Wall map of the United States.

• Current and old magazines, pencils, tracing paper, pens, India ink.

• Sheets of drawing paper, colored pencils.

• Sheets of butcher paper, pencils, tempera paints, brushes.

Resources

248

In the early twentieth century the pace of life quickened in the United States. The airplane, assembly line, and telephone were all part of a new fascination with speed. A search for new formulas in American art mirrored the restlessness of the age. In this lesson you will learn about the most important of the new art movements. You will also learn about developments in the art of Mexico.

THE ASHCAN SCHOOL

As the 1800s gave way to the 1900s, the important names in American art remained unchanged. Homer, Eakins, and Ryder continued on as the unchallenged leaders. In New York a group of lesser-known painters felt a change was overdue. Since there were eight members in all, they called themselves, simply, **The Eight**. This was a *group of artists who created art work that reflected the spirit of the times in which they lived, the early 1900s.*

The members of The Eight were all one-time newspaper cartoonists or magazine illustrators. These experiences influenced their choice of subjects for their paintings. Their works drew on images from everyday life in the big city. These pictures of crowded city streets, dark alleys, and gray slums were recorded in a no-nonsense, realistic style. When The Eight held their first public showing in 1908, viewers politely examined their works. Then they laughed. A more fitting name for these chroniclers of working-class American life, some decided, was the **Ashcan School**. This became *the popular name given to the group of artists who made realistic paintings of working-class America.*

Painting

One of the most talented members of the Ashcan School was John Sloan. His pictures capture the color, movement, and humor of big-city life. Look at the painting by Sloan in Figure 16–7. The hairdresser in the picture goes about her business with hardly a care. Below, meanwhile, passersby stop and stare as if witnessing an important event. Locate the girls at the bottom of the picture. One, you will notice, seems to be talking excitedly. What do you suppose she is saying?

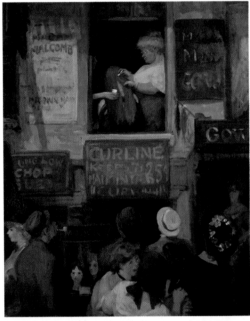

▲ Figure 16–7   **What has the artist done to emphasize the figures in the second-story window? How has movement been introduced?**

John Sloan. *Hairdresser's Window.* 1907. Oil on canvas. 81 x 66 cm (31⅞ x 26"). Wadsworth Atheneum, Hartford, Connecticut. Ella Gallup Sumner and Mary Catlin Sumner Collection.

TECHNOLOGY OPTIONS

National Gallery of Art Videodisc   Use the following images to examine works by artists discussed in this lesson.

John Sloan
The City from Greenwich Village

Search Frame 2090

George Bellows
My Family

Search Frame 2074

Alfred Stieglitz
Georgia O'Keeffe

Search Frame 3302

Use Glencoe's *Correlation Bar Code Guide to the National Gallery of Art* to locate more art works.

248

◄ **Figure 16–8** What do you think the artist wanted to show in this painting: the poverty and hopelessness of city dwellers, or the vitality and pleasures of life in the inner-city? What sounds do you associate with this scene? What aesthetic views would you use when judging this work?

George Bellows. *Cliff Dwellers.* 1913. Oil on canvas. 102.0 x 106.8 cm (40³⁄₁₆ x 42¹⁄₁₆″). Los Angeles County Museum of Art, Los Angeles, California. Los Angeles County Fund.

An artist who was closely tied to the Ashcan School, though not one of The Eight, was George Bellows. His painting in Figure 16–8 makes use of the same urban subject matter. Groups of young men, women, and frolicking children hold center stage in the sunlit foreground. In the background are shadowed tenements with balconies crowded with figures peering down at the constant bustle that is a part of life in the heart of a great city.

Photography

The Ashcan painters were not alone in using city scenes as subjects for art. The same look and feel was achieved in the works of artist Alfred Stieglitz (**steeg**-luhts). Stieglitz played an important part in the early development of photography as a new art form. Examine his photograph in Figure 16–9. What details in the work reveal it to be of a bitterly cold winter day? What mood does the picture communicate?

◄ **Figure 16–9** Find the curving and diagonal lines that help pull the viewer in. How does the variety of light and dark values add interest to the work?

Alfred Stieglitz. *The Terminal.* c. 1892. Photogravure. 25.4 x 33.7 cm (10 x 13¼″). The Art Institute of Chicago, Chicago, Illinois. The Alfred Stieglitz Collection.

Lesson 3   *Art of the Early Twentieth Century in America*   **249**

--- *more about* ● ● ● ----

The Eight   This group of eight artists who joined together and painted in the early 1900s chose subjects from everyday life in the big city. The criticism of their choice of style and subject matter was obvious from the word chosen to characterize it, "Ashcan School." However, these artists, who had all come from the same newspaper or magazine background, were accustomed to extracting the essence of a scene and communicating it in an easily understandable form. A cartoon must capture an amusing contradiction; a magazine illustration must contain an essential moment of truth. These artists were trained to take a basic approach to art. Let students ask themselves to consider the most important thing they wish to communicate in their art, and how they can accomplish this task.

■ **Studio Skills**

Most American art of the early twentieth century suggested speed and restlessness. Let students experiment with capturing the feelings of speed and movement in line drawings. Ask each student to choose a familiar action or sport and make a colored-pencil drawing in which line conveys that sense of movement. When students are satisfied with their drawings, let them share their work with the class, and have them discuss their experiments: What different techniques have you used to convey movement and speed? Which techniques seem most successful? What approaches would you try if you wanted to use shape or color to convey movement?

■ **Cultural Diversity**

Let students work in groups to explore the art works created in other parts of the world during the first part of the twentieth century. Have groups select one of these areas: Africa, India, South America, Japan, China, or the Middle East. Encourage them to use online computer resources as part of their research. Then have them plan an interesting presentation of their findings, perhaps using computer or video technology.

▶ **Figure 16–10** Point to the lines that lead to the figures of the preacher and the girl. Where is the circle shape formed by the windmill blades repeated? How is deep space suggested?

John Steuart Curry. *Baptism in Kansas.* 1928. Oil on canvas. 101.6 x 127 cm (40 x 50"). Whitney Museum of American Art, New York, New York. Gift of Gertrude Vanderbilt Whitney.

REGIONALISM

After World War I a different brand of realistic art enjoyed brief popularity in the United States. Several artists used a style that became known as **Regionalism** (**ree**-juh-nuh-**liz**-uhm) to record *local scenes and events from the artist's own region, or area, of the country.*

An example of the Regionalist style may be found in Figure 16–10. The artist of the work, John Steuart Curry (**stoo**-urt **ker**-ee), was a native of Kansas. In this painting he shows a preacher about to baptize, or spiritually cleanse, a young girl. The setting is a Kansas farm. Relatives and friends have gathered to witness this ritual of passage. They all look at the preacher and the girl, automatically directing the viewer's eyes there. The legs of a windmill point to the scene as well as to the glowing clouds in the sky.

ART IN MEXICO

The early twentieth century was a time of unrest and revolution in Mexico. Hard-working peasants, treated like slaves by rich landlords, struggled to free themselves. Several artists witnessed the struggle. They used their art to lend their support to the people.

One who did so was Mexico's foremost muralist (**myoor**-uh-list) Diego Rivera. A **muralist** is *an artist who paints large art works directly onto walls or ceilings.* In the mural in Figure 16–11, the artist tells of the only true escape for the poor: death. Several soldiers of the common people kneel around one of their own who has fallen in battle. In the distance flames rise from the landlord's house; the peasant's death has already been avenged.

Two years before he painted *Liberation of the Peon,* Rivera married the painter Frida Kahlo, judged by many to be Mexico's most famous woman artist. Seriously injured in a bus accident when she was a teenager, Kahlo never fully recovered, and lived in almost constant pain until her death some 30 years later. She took up painting while recovering from her accident even though her injuries were so severe she had to learn to paint lying down. The Chapter Opener on page **240** shows the wedding portrait Kahlo painted shortly after her marriage. Neither seems happy, although this should be a joyous moment in both their lives. Perhaps Kahlo realized that her marriage would be a stormy one, marred by many disputes.

─ *more about* • • • ─

Diego Rivera   The work of Diego Rivera was influenced by native Mexican sculpture and Pre-Columbian art of Central America. From these influences he took the large, simplified forms and massive shapes. Another major influence on his work came when he went to Europe to study, work, and travel. There, he was strongly influenced by Expressionism. When he returned to Mexico, he and his friends and fellow artists, José Orozco and David Siqueiros, tried to use art to instruct and educate the poor and illiterate. The artists tried to give these people incentives to bring about revolutionary changes. At this time Rivera worked on murals that depicted the history of Mexico and the life and problems of the people.

1. Who were The Eight? What were their backgrounds as artists? What kinds of paintings did they create?
2. When did The Eight stage their first showing? How did the public react? What nickname were The Eight given?
3. What art form was the specialty of Alfred Stieglitz?
4. What style of art became popular after World War I? Name an artist who created works in this style.
5. What is a muralist? Who was Mexico's foremost muralist?
6. What theme appears in the work of Diego Rivera?

STUDIO ACTIVITY

Creating Abstract Effects

Look again at Figure 16–11. The work, you will notice, is both abstract and expressive. Choose one of the following words: *war, hunger, anger.* Look through magazines, tearing out pages showing objects that capture the idea of this word. Using pencil and tracing paper, carefully transfer the images you have found to a sheet of paper. Overlap the drawings to create an abstract effect. Use India ink to create contrasts of light and dark shapes.

PORTFOLIO

You might want to practice for portfolio presentation by presenting this art work to classmates. Display the work, and describe how you used the elements and principles of art to create a theme. Evaluate your success by asking classmates to tell the theme suggested by your work.

◀ Figure 16–11 Describe the way in which these soldiers care for the dead. What feelings do you think this painting stirred up in Mexican viewers of the artist's day?

Diego Rivera. *Liberation of the Peon.* 1931. Fresco on plaster. 187.9 x 241.3 cm (74 x 95"). Philadelphia Museum of Art, Philadelphia, Pennsylvania. Gift of Mr. & Mrs. Herbert Cameron Morris.

Lesson 3   *Art of the Early Twentieth Century in America*   **251**

STUDIO ACTIVITY

Creating Abstract Effects

Remind students to consider the elements of line, color, and shape as they work on this Studio Activity. Have them turn back to pages 2–5, if necessary, to review these elements of art. Then as they make their abstract compositions, tell them to use these elements to emphasize the expressive quality of their work.

ASSESS

■ Self-Assessment

Have students answer the review questions on this page. Answers are provided below.

■ Reteaching

Work with small groups to review the art trends of the early twentieth century in the United States and Mexico. Then let group members select one of the paintings reproduced in this lesson and compare it to the work of Eakins, Homer, or Ryder shown on pages 232–234.

■ Enrichment

Have students work in groups to plan and paint murals that suggest the work of Diego Rivera. This may develop into an extended school project. Group members should begin by selecting a story and a message that they want to depict in their mural. Then have them work together to plan, sketch in, and paint all the parts of the mural. Let group members display their completed murals, answering any questions other students may have about the story or the message.

CLOSE

Display and discuss the line drawings students created to express speed and movement.

251

Answers to ✔ CHECK YOUR UNDERSTANDING

1. A group of lesser-known painters who were all newspaper cartoonists or magazine illustrators who created art works that reflected the spirit of the times in which they lived, the early 1900s.
2. The Eight staged their first showing in 1908. The public reacted politely, then they laughed. The Eight were given the nickname, "The Ashcan School."
3. Photography.
4. A style of art called "Regionalism" became popular after World War I. John Steuart Curry.
5. An artist who paints large art works directly onto a wall or ceiling. Diego Rivera.
6. The struggle for liberty.

LESSON 4

Making a
Print of a
Figure in
Action

(pages 252–253)

LESSON TIME: 90 minutes

Making a Print of a Figure in Action

Figure 16–12 shows another action scene by George Bellows. This is one of six paintings the artist made on the subject of prizefights. He also made many prints and countless drawings. Here, as elsewhere, he uses slashing diagonal lines to show movement. In this lesson you will do the same.

WHAT YOU WILL LEARN

You will overlap a series of prints showing a figure in action. You will use diagonal lines to complete the figure. These lines will add to a feeling of rhythm or movement. (See Figure 16–13.)

WHAT YOU WILL NEED

- Pencil and sheets of sketch paper
- Ballpoint pen and paper towels
- Styrofoam meat tray
- Brayer
- Water-based printing ink and shallow tray
- Scissors
- Sheet of drawing paper, 10 x 12 inches (25 x 30 cm)

▶ Figure 16–12 What has been done to emphasize the two figures? What kinds of lines have been used?

George Wesley Bellows. *Stag at Sharkey's.* 1909. Oil on canvas. 93 x 122.5 cm (36¼ x 48¼"). The Cleveland Museum of Art, Cleveland, Ohio. Hinman B. Hurlbut Collection.

FOCUS

☑ OBJECTIVES

After completing this lesson, students will be able to:
- Make prints showing figures in action.
- Describe, analyze, interpret, and judge their own prints.

☑ SUPPLIES

- Pencils, sheets of sketch paper.
- Ballpoint pens and paper towels; Styrofoam meat trays; brayers and water-based printing ink; shallow trays; scrap paper; sheets of drawing paper, 10 x 12 inches (25 x 30 cm).

TEACH

■ Motivator

Let students work together to draw and discuss lines that convey movement. Have members of each group experiment with different kinds of lines. Demonstrate for them how to use both the tips and the sides of their pencils, and show them how to experiment with thick lines and thin lines, straight lines and diagonal lines, curved lines, and jagged lines. Point out the kinds of movement the different lines convey.

252   Lesson 4   *Making a Print of a Figure in Action*

MEETING STUDENT DIVERSITY

Kinesthetic Learners   Display for the class examples of more murals by Diego Rivera and José Orozco. Have students identify aspects of life in Latin America and illustrate them by creating their own paintings. Display the works in a colorful classroom mural using all of the illustrations and paintings.

Visual/Spacial Learners   To help students remember the many art styles introduced in this chapter, chart the styles and periods with color cues or graphic symbols. Provide students with colored pencils, markers, or colored paper. Have them list and then code each of the various art styles with a color or symbol. Reinforce the use of these color codes in overhead transparencies or as study aids.

WHAT YOU WILL DO

1. Take turns with your classmates in acting as models. Each model will strike an action pose, such as running, reaching, or pushing.
2. Make a series of gesture drawings of students in different poses. Quickly drawn diagonal lines will help you catch a sense of action. Avoid details. Focus on showing movement. (For more on gesture drawing, see Technique Tip 1, *Handbook* page 277.)
3. Select your best drawing. Place it on top of the styrofoam meat tray and transfer the figure to the tray by tracing over it firmly with a ballpoint pen. Cut your figure out of the tray with scissors. This is to be your printing plate.
4. Squeeze a small amount of water-based printing ink into the tray. Roll the brayer back and forth through the ink until the whole brayer is covered with ink.
5. Put the figure on a paper towel. Roll the brayer over the figure. Pick up the figure by the edges and place it ink-side down on your sheet of drawing paper. Press the back of the figure firmly all over to transfer ink.
6. Ink the plate again and make another print. This time overlap images on your paper until you are satisfied with your design. Arrange your images in a horizontal or vertical line to add a feeling of rhythm.
7. Title your work, sign it, and place it on display.

EXAMINING YOUR WORK

- **Describe** Identify the figure in your print. Point out different features of the figure.
- **Analyze** Explain how the diagonal lines in your print carry a sense of rhythm.
- **Interpret** Find out whether viewers can identify the action in your print. Reveal the action you were trying to show.
- **Judge** Tell whether you feel your work succeeds. Tell what you would do to improve your work on a second effort.

▲ Figure 16–13   Student work. Figure in action.

Try This! COMPUTER OPTION 🖳

■ Using Pencil or Brush tool, create a gesture drawing of a figure in action. Use the Lasso Selection tool to Copy and Paste multiple copies on the page, arranging and overlapping the figures to show action and rhythm. Title and save. Then choose colors that go from light to dark and Flood-fill each shape to create the illusion of depth and movement. Try several color schemes. Choose the best, then retitle, save and print one drawing.

Lesson 4   *Making a Print of a Figure in Action*   **253**

more about ...

Realism   In the United States, especially during the early modern period, Realism was the style most often taught and practiced in schools of art. Yet the ideas of speed and movement were so strong that they eventually led to an American form of Abstract Expressionism, which has become known as Action Painting. In this style of art, the process of painting is as important as the product of painting. The artist becomes part of the art work. Action Painting retains the dynamism found in art styles such as Futurism, but its works are non-objective. Jackson Pollock is the artist most often associated with Action Painting.

■ Vocabulary
Review with students the definition of the term *print*; How is a print created? How is a print different from a reproduction of an original painting?

■ Studio Skills
Let each student carve several linoleum blocks into printing plates that show basic shapes, either geometric or organic. Then have students create several printed designs, each demonstrating a different principle of organizing the shapes and colors.

Art on a Shoestring
Don't forget you can use foam food trays instead of linoleum blocks to carve shapes for this activity.

ASSESS

■ Self-Assessment
Have students use Examining Your Work to evaluate their prints created in this Studio Lesson. Responses may be written or oral.

■ Reteaching
Review with students the principle of movement (see page 11). Then have them select from the text at least two works that convey a sense of movement.

■ Enrichment
Let individual students carve shapes of different styles of houses and make separate prints of each house. When completed, they can then be mounted together to create a neighborhood.

CLOSE
Display all the prints. Ask: What do some of the prints suggest? Discuss how some of the prints seem to work together to suggest a narrative.

CONNECTIONS *Social Studies*

Allan Rohan Crite. *School's Out*. 1936. Oil on canvas. 76.8 x 91.8 cm (30¼ x 36⅛"). National Museum of American Art, Smithsonian Institution, Washington, D.C.

How Did the WPA Help Artists?

The stock market crash of 1929 created an economic disaster called the Great Depression. Panic and despair gripped the nation as thousands of businesses failed and workers were laid off. Banks had invested their depositors' money in the stock market. When the market crashed, there was no money to return to depositors. Millions of people lost their jobs and their life savings. By 1932, twenty-five percent of the work force was unemployed. Among the unemployed were many, many artists.

The government set up relief programs to provide jobs for the unemployed. As part of his "New Deal" for worker relief, President Franklin D. Roosevelt created a national program called the Works Progress Administration (WPA).

Artists urged the president to set up a job program for artists, so Roosevelt authorized the federal Public Works of Art Project and the Federal Art Project. These programs employed artists to paint murals on public buildings, to create public sculptures and pottery, and to teach arts and crafts. Among the artists who participated was Alan Rohan Crite, who painted neighborhood scenes like the one pictured here.

MAKING THE CONNECTION

- How would you describe the artist's style in this painting, *School's Out*?
- Crite painted this work in the midst of the Depression. He wanted to show people "enjoying the usual pleasures of life with its mixture of both sorrow and joys." Do you think he was successful? Explain.
- Find out more about artists who worked during the Depression. Identify two artists and compare their art works and their lives.

INTERNET ACTIVITY

Visit Glencoe's Fine Arts Web Site for students at:

http://www.glencoe.com/sec/art/students

INTERNET ACTIVITY

Additional Studios   You can access additional studio lessons in Glencoe's Fine Arts Site on the World Wide Web. Use these studios to supplement the lessons found in the textbook or to challenge students further in specific art techniques. An overview stating the learning objectives, lists of materials, and step-by-step instructions are provided, as well as occasional examples of student art that demonstrates the completed project. You can print out the studio lesson instructions and duplicate them for student use. Once your students have completed the lesson, consider contacting us to submit their works for possible inclusion in future versions of lessons on the World Wide Web. Find us at **http://www.glencoe.com/sec/art**

After completing this feature, students will be able to:
- Understand the effects of the Great Depression.
- Explain how the government helped artists.

Teaching the Connection

- Have students read the feature on this page.
- Ask volunteers to share what they know about the Great Depression. What was life like for most people during the Great Depression? *(Nearly everyone was affected. For the first time, the government had to provide financial relief to people for basic necessities. People learned to "make do" with what they had or go without. Some families were separated.)* How did the government help? *(Programs like the Federal Art Project enabled artists to make a living doing what they did best.)* What did the artists do? *(Needy artists were asked to paint murals or paintings of American scenes, like Crite's painting.)*
- Explain that Alan Rohan Crite was one of only a handful of African-American artists (out of 3,500 total) who participated in the short-lived Public Works of Art Project. The artists were able to continue their art, and the public benefitted as well.

Answers to Making the Connection

- Answers may vary. Realistic.
- Possible response: Yes, because the people here look natural; their expressions reflect what you would expect.
- Responses will vary.

BUILDING VOCABULARY

Number a sheet of paper from 1 to 8. After each number, write the term from the list that best matches each description below.

Ashcan School   Fauvism
Cubism   muralist
The Eight   non-objective art
Expressionism   Regionalism

1. An art movement in which artists used wild, intense color combinations in their paintings.
2. A style that emphasized the expression of innermost feelings.
3. A style in which objects and the space around them are broken up into different shapes and then put back together in new relationships.
4. A style in which no objects or subjects can be readily identified.
5. A group of New York artists who created art work that reflected the spirit of the times in the early 1900s.
6. The popular name given to the group of artists who made realistic paintings of working-class America.
7. A style that records local scenes and events from an artist's own region, or area, of the country.
8. An artist who paints large art works directly onto walls or ceilings.

 REVIEWING ART FACTS

Number a sheet of paper from 9 to 14. Answer each question in a complete sentence.

9. What feature did Expressionism and Fauvism have in common?
10. Identify the artist whose idea led to the forming of the Cubist movement.
11. What artist is credited with developing the non-objective style?
12. In what way were the photographs of Alfred Stieglitz linked to the work of the Ashcan painters?
13. When did the Regionalist movement begin? Name a member of the movement.
14. Which artist that you read about in this chapter was a muralist?

 THINKING ABOUT ART

On a sheet of paper, answer each question in a sentence or two.

1. **Extend.** Imagine that Käthe Kollwitz had chosen to do her print *The Mothers* (Figure 16–3) in color. Do you think such a decision would have added to the power of the work? Explain your answer.
2. **Analyze.** The work by John Steuart Curry (Figure 16–10) shows the use of emphasis. Find another work in this chapter that uses emphasis. Explain how the artist leads the viewer's eye to the most important feature.

— MAKING ART CONNECTIONS —

1. **Language Arts.** Divide a sheet of paper into three columns. Label one column *Subject*, one *Composition*, and one *Content*. Then, going through the art works in this chapter one by one, decide in which column or columns each artist's name belongs. Compare your completed list with those of other students in your class.

2. **Language Arts.** Examine the historical and artistic influences that shaped the art of Pablo Picasso in a book by Juliet Heslewood, *Introducing Picasso: Painter, Sculptor.* What do you think most influenced his particular style?

Chapter 16 Review   **255**

Art of Today

(pages 256–273)

Resources

- 17-8 Chapter Test, TRB page 351
- Transparency CC-17, *Granite Weaving* by Jesus Morales
- Transparency 17, *Peaceable Kingdom* by John August Swanson
- Fine Art Print 18, *Diner* by Richard Estes
- Fine Art Print 19, *Actor in a Ruff* by Jean Dubuffet
- Fine Art Print 20, *I'll Fly Away* by Michael Cummings

A R T
S O U
R C E **Theatre**
ARTSOURCE While studying this chapter, use Performing Arts Handbook page 333 to help students recognize the struggle of a young girl's life as expressed by the performance of Josefina López in the play *Simply Maria, or The American Dream.*

NATIONAL STANDARDS

This chapter addresses the following National Standards for the Visual Arts:

1. (a, b)   **4.** (c)
2. (a, b, c) **5.** (b, c)
3. (a, b)   **6.** (a, b)

▲ Can you find any signs of life in this painting? What do you think these structures represent? What purpose do they serve? How does this painting make you feel?

Kay Sage. *I Saw Three Cities.* 1944. Oil on canvas. 91.5 x 71.0 cm (36 x 27⅞"). The Art Museum, Princeton University, Princeton, New Jersey. Gift of the Estate of Kay Sage Tanguy.

FEATURED ARTISTS

Patrick Boyd	Barbara Hepworth	Joan Miró	Sandy Skoglund
Alexander Calder	Ellsworth Kelly	Henry Moore	Andrew Wyeth
Giorgio de Chirico	Paul Klee	Louise Nevelson	
Gene Davis	Jacob Lawrence	Nam June Paik	
Arshile Gorky	René Magritte	Judy Pfaff	
Duane Hanson	Marino Marini	Kay Sage	

Art of Today

The long story of art is a story marked by change. With each passing age, the search for original forms of expression is renewed. A style that startled viewers of one generation becomes a part of the mainstream as another shocking style makes its appearance.

At no time in history has the search for new directions been more visible than now. The last 100 years have seen more changes in art styles, media, and techniques than all the thousand years before. One style appears in the work at the left. Can you see any similarities with art works created earlier? In this chapter you will learn how this and other recent art styles originated.

PORTFOLIO IDEAS

Select five examples of art work that demonstrate how you have grown as an artist in your ability to communicate feelings, moods, or thoughts in your art work. For each piece, state what you have learned and explain why this piece is a good example of your skills. Include your personal reflection for each piece in your portfolio.

OBJECTIVES

After completing this chapter, you will be able to:
● Identify major art movements of the last 100 years.
● Identify the characteristics and leaders of those art movements.
● Create a painting in the Surrealist style.
● Create a work using contemporary styles and techniques.

WORDS YOU WILL LEARN

Abstract
   Expressionism
Dada
Hard-Edge painting
kinetic art
mobile
multi-media art
New Realism
Op-Art
social protest painting
Surrealism

257

■ **Chapter Overview**
Tell students that in this chapter they will learn about the major artists and art movements of the last 100 years. They will also create art works based on two of these contemporary art movements.

■ **Chapter Motivator**
Tell students that Kay Sage and her husband Yves Tanguy were Surrealist artists. Ask them what they know about this art style. Explain that Surrealist artists tried to express the subconscious, the irrational, the world of dreams, and the inner workings of the mind. These artists sought inspiration for their art *not* from the outside world, but from within their own minds.

■ **Introducing the Art Work**
Sage's painting *I Saw Three Cities* both resembles and differs from the works of other Surrealists. It does not include living creatures nor does it suggest complicated and confusing ideas. She creates a totally believable, but mysterious world in which every geometric shape, every cast shadow, every fold of fabric is carefully created with a few cool colors. Point out how the forms in her painting seem insecure, as if they could easily be pushed over. Ask students what they think these forms represent. If they have difficulty, tell them that this is not surprising, *everyone* has difficulties trying to describe them or identify their purpose. Sage explains: "Why should anything mean more than its own statement?" Do students agree or disagree?

National Museum of Women in the Arts
You may wish to use the National Museum of Women in the Arts videodisc and/or CD-ROM. The videodisc features a bar code guide, and the interactive CD-ROM provides stimulating activities.

DEVELOPING A PORTFOLIO

Teacher Feedback As much as the students enjoy and appreciate hearing good comments from their friends and peers, positive teacher feedback can be more powerful. Keeping a portfolio of one's work over a period of time and then going back seeing for oneself the actual growth is enlightening for the students. Written comments by the teacher can inspire students to do so much more or give up completely. Your challenge in the portfolio review process is to motivate students to pursue standards of good, thoughtful art work. The established rubrics offer a framework for this and the written reflections play a supporting role. Feedback could include recognition of demonstrated strengths in the portfolio, areas for future focus, and recognition of specific examples that stood out.

LESSON 1

European Art Today

• • • • • • • • • • • • • • • •
FOCUS

☑ OBJECTIVES

After completing this lesson, students will be able to:

• Describe the Dada and Surrealist art movements.

• Name three twentieth-century European artists whose art was based on the inner workings of the human mind.

• Describe some of the new explorations undertaken by twentieth-century sculptors.

• Name three twentieth-century sculptors.

☑ SUPPLIES

• Sheets of paper.

• Pencils.

• Crayons, colored pencils, or felt tip markers.

• Reproductions of Marino Marini's prints and paintings.

• Modeling clay.

• Clay modeling tools.

Resource

☐ 17-1 *A Personal Aesthetic*, TRB page 341 (aesthetics)

The Impressionists went outdoors to find ideas. The Expressionists looked to their own hearts. The second decade of the twentieth century found artists exploring still another source for art ideas. That was the inner workings of the mind.

FANTASY ART

Imagine yourself a visitor at a showing of new art. Suddenly your eye falls upon a work that is at once familiar and shocking. It is familiar because it is a photograph of the *Mona Lisa*. It is shocking because someone has drawn a mustache on Leonardo da Vinci's world-famous portrait.

It was this very experience that outraged members of Europe's art community in 1916. The artist behind the work was a one-time Cubist named Marcel Duchamp (mar-**sel** doo-**shahnh**). The movement he belonged to, **Dada** (**dahd**-ah) was *founded on the belief that Western culture had lost its meaning*. For Dadaists (**dahd**-uah-ists), the beauty of art was in the *mind*, not the eye, of the beholder. Art, in other words, did not have to be beautiful or express important ideas. Usually the point was driven home, as in Duchamp's photograph, by poking fun at art of the past.

SURREALISM

Although Dada lasted only six years, it paved the way for other art explorations of the mind. The most important of these was **Surrealism** (suh-**ree**-uh-liz-uhm). This movement *probed the subconscious world of dreams* for ideas, and was touched off by the works of a Greek-born Italian artist named Giorgio de Chirico (**jor**-joh duh **kir**-ih-koh). Like the artists who followed him, de Chirico created mysterious, nightmarish landscapes

▲ Figure 17–1 **What gives this picture its dreamlike appearance? What kinds of feelings does it arouse in you?**

Giorgio de Chirico. *The Nostalgia of the Infinite.* (1913–14; dated on painting 1911). Oil on canvas. 135.2 x 64.8 cm (53¾ x 25½"). Collection, The Museum of Modern Art, New York. Purchase.

TECHNOLOGY OPTIONS

National Gallery of Art Videodisc   Use the following images to demonstrate different works by artists of this period.

Paul Klee	Marino Marini	Frank Stella
The White House	*Horseman*	*Chyrow II*
‖‖‖‖‖‖‖‖‖	‖‖‖‖‖‖‖‖‖	‖‖‖‖‖‖‖‖‖
Search Frame 2165	Search Frame 2569	Search Frame 2331

Use Glencoe's *Correlation Bar Code Guide to the National Gallery of Art* to locate more art works.

where time had no meaning. One of these is shown in Figure 17–1. Notice the two small figures seen as silhouettes at the center of the work. Their importance seems to shrink before the huge tower looming behind them. What is the meaning of the tower and the flags? Like a dream, the painting raises many unanswerable questions. Attempts to answer these questions only adds to the feeling that viewers are experiencing a nightmare from which they cannot awaken.

By the end of the 1920s the Surrealist movement had spread to many countries. One artist who seemed comfortable with the movement was the Spanish painter Joan Miró (**zhoo**-ahn mee-**roh**). Miró created fantasy worlds that were free not only of rhyme and reason but also of realism. In the work in Figure 17–2 he brings the viewer face-to-face with a scene depicting strange, imaginary creatures.

Several women artists were also active in the Surrealist movement. One American painter, Kay Sage, created pictures like the one in the Chapter Opener, showing a silent deserted world bathed in a cool, mysterious light. Strange architectural forms are scattered about, but there are no clues to tell us how large these forms are, what purpose they serve, or who built them. One wonders how long they have been here—and then comes the question that arouses anxiety, even fear: Where is *here?*

◀ **Figure 17–2   How do the foreground shapes differ from the background? Can you find any shapes that look like people, animals, or musical instruments? What aesthetic views would you use when judging this painting?**

Joan Miró. *Dutch Interior II.* 1928. Oil on canvas. 92 x 73 cm (36¼ x 28¾"). Solomon R. Guggenheim Museum, New York. Photograph by David Heald, © The Solomon R. Guggenheim Foundation.

Lesson 1   *European Art Today*   **259**

■ Motivator

Have students play the Surrealist game known as "Exquisite Corpse." Give each student a sheet of paper to fold into three equal sections. On the top third, students should draw a head and neck of any animal, person, or creature, making sure that the necklines extend slightly into the middle section. Students should fold the paper so only the middle section shows and pass it to someone else. Students should then draw a body down to the waist, once again leaving starting lines. Pass the papers again and fill in the rest of the body. At each stage the papers should be folded under so that students cannot see other parts of the drawing. Then students should open the drawings and view them. According to the Surrealists, games like this reveal subconscious truths that people generally ignore.

■ Vocabulary

Tell students that Surrealist Andre Breton once defined Surrealism as "Thought's dictation, free from any control by the reason, independent of any aesthetic or moral preoccupation." Discuss this definition and have students try a Surrealist writing exercise. Instruct them to write down the flow of whatever comes into their minds. Encourage them to write everything, no matter how bizarre or ungrammatical and assure them that you will not collect the results. Discuss students' experience of writing in a Surrealist manner.

---

more about • • •

Miró   Joan Miró was a forgetful, modest man who lived on the island of Majorca off the coast of Spain. Because he never lost his childhood curiosity, his house was filled with toys that he collected and studied with enthusiasm and amusement. He owned hundreds of jack-in-the-boxes. While he was still a student, a teacher made him draw objects by feeling them and thinking about them rather than by looking at the objects. This technique suited him superbly, and Miró went on to become a leading Surrealist painter. His works carry the viewer into a world of dreams and half-forgotten memories where time is meaningless, space is ignored, and imaginary creatures frolic. They are fantasy ballets in which familiar figures and objects have been transformed into new, extraordinary shapes.

■ Art Criticism

Have students imagine that they are art critics assigned to write a review of Figure 17-3. Their reviews should incorporate information from carrying out the four steps of art criticism.

■ Cooperative Learning

Show students reproductions of Marino Marini's many prints and paintings of peasants and horses. Have groups hold a discussion of the similarities and differences of a subject that had been rendered in two and three dimensions. Have them consider events or images that are so powerful that it would be worthwhile to explore them in several media, as Marino Marini did.

■ Cultural Diversity

Ask students to explore the founding of the National Museum for Women in the Arts. Then have them find out how many works by men and by women are in the collection of a local art museum in their community. Discuss why a museum just for art works by women artists was created.

■ Studio Skills

Have students examine Figure 17-5 and discuss Barbara Hepworth's use of art elements and principles. Students can explore her style further by using clay to model a non-objective work that has rounded forms and small, curved openings.

Fantasy and humor are key ingredients also in the art of Swiss-born Paul Klee (**klay**). Though not a Surrealist, Klee based his work on images glimpsed through his mind's eye. Most, like his picture of a tightrope walker (Figure 17–3), are like simple, childlike creations. Notice how the walker makes his way boldly across a wire supported by a flimsy network of thin lines. These lines look as though they will collapse at any second. What statement might the artist be making about people who foolishly enter situations without weighing the consequences?

▲ **Figure 17–3** What has the artist done to add a sense of harmony? Can you point to places where variety is used? What property of this work is most important—its realism, its design, or its meaning?

Paul Klee. *Tightrope Walker.* 1923. Color lithograph. 43.1 x 26.7 cm (17 x 10½"). McNay Art Museum, San Antonio, Texas.

SCULPTURE

Over the last 40 years sculptors have also explored new areas of self-expression. Some have continued to create recognizable images. Others have taken the path toward non-objective art.

The works of Marino Marini (muh-**reen**-oh muh-**reen**-ee), an Italian sculptor, draw on a single haunting image. That image—peasants fleeing their villages on horseback during bombing raids—was one the artist witnessed during World War II. Sculptures like the one in Figure 17–4 are attempts to capture the suffering of civilians during wartime.

▲ **Figure 17–4** What kinds of real and imaginary lines help add a feeling of tension? Is this a successful work of art?

Marino Marini. *Horse and Rider.* 1951. Bronze. 55.7 x 31.1 x 43.5 cm (21⅞ x 12¼ x 17⅛"). Hirshhorn Museum and Sculpture Garden, Smithsonian Institution, Washington, D.C. Gift of the Lily Harmon Foundation. © 1998 Estate of Marino Marini/Licensed by VAGA, New York, NY

An artist best known for her non-objective creations was English sculptor Barbara Hepworth. A trademark of her work is the use of holes. As in the work in Figure 17–5, these create centers of interest within gently curving forms.

RESOURCES BEYOND THE CLASSROOM

Public Spaces   Public spaces provide ample opportunity to see showcased art in the community. Many buildings have displays of art that students can be encouraged to view individually, or a group tour could be arranged if several buildings house works of art. Cities often purchase works of art from their local artists; these can be seen on display at city halls and in courthouses. Outdoor sculpture can be seen in downtown areas and along main streets. Malls and other large commercial buildings often have sculptures housed inside, especially near resting areas. They also boast wall hangings of infinite variety, often suspended from the ceiling.

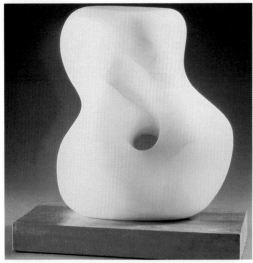

▲ **Figure 17–5** Notice the smooth texture of the alabaster. Would you be tempted to run your hands over the surface of the work?

Barbara Hepworth. *Merryn*. 1962. Alabaster. 33 x 29 x 20 cm (13 x 11½ x 8¼"). National Museum of Women in the Arts. Washington, D.C. Gift of Wallace and Wilhelmina Holladay.

▲ **Figure 17–6** Notice how the sculptor gave the family members a feeling of unity. How did he provide variety?

Henry Moore. *Family Group*. 1948–49. Cast 1950. Bronze. 150.5 x 118.1, base 114.3 x 75.9 cm (59¼ x 46½, base 45 x 29⅞"). Museum of Modern Art, New York, New York. A Conger Goodyear Fund.

STUDIO ACTIVITY

Capturing a Surrealist Scene

Using your imagination, picture a scene you might expect to find in a dream or nightmare. In your sketchbook, list objects you imagine. Do not include people. Using pencil, draw the scene as a Surrealist might. Try to capture the feeling of confusion the image stirs up in you. Reproduce your sketch onto another sheet of paper and use crayon or chalk to color your picture. Make sure you choose hues that help emphasize the fear or other emotion you are trying to express.

P O R T F O L I O

Exchange paintings with a classmate for peer evaluation. Use the steps of art criticism for peer assessment. Include the peer evaluation, any responses you have for your self-reflection, and your art work in your portfolio.

Another sculptor, Henry Moore, created both non-objective works and works that were sometimes nearer to realism. The close relationship of family members is expressed in Figure 17–6. Moore stylized the figures and yet clearly defined them as mother, father, and child. The figures of the parents are linked by the child, the touching knees, and the husband's hand on his wife's shoulder, providing a unified whole.

✔CHECK YOUR UNDERSTANDING

1. What did the Dadaists believe? How did they usually give expression to this belief?
2. What is Surrealism? What artist's works initiated the movement? Name another Surrealist.
3. For what kinds of works is Paul Klee best known?
4. What image turns up again and again in the works of Marino Marini?
5. What is the trademark of sculptor Barbara Hepworth?

STUDIO ACTIVITY

Capturing a Surrealist Scene

If students are interested, have them keep a "dream journal" for a few nights. Then they may refer to these notes about their own dreams to make their sketches and drawings for this activity.

• • • • • • • • • •

ASSESS

■ **Self-Assessment**

Have students complete the review questions on this page. Answers are provided below.

■ **Reteaching**

Point out to students that many of the artists whose works are illustrated in this lesson have been described as working in a "childlike" or "primitive" style. Discuss the meaning of these terms. Ask why they have been applied to the works of Miró, Klee, Marini, and Moore.

■ **Enrichment**

Tell students that Henry Moore, whose work is pictured in Figure 17-6, had a serious, long-standing interest in Egyptian, Sumerian, African, and Mexican Pre-Columbian sculpture. Have groups of students research one of these sculptural traditions and discover how the various styles are reflected in Henry Moore's art. Students should summarize their findings in a brief written report.

• • • • • • • • • •

CLOSE

Have students briefly state which art work reproduced in this lesson is their favorite and which one they like the least. Have students explain their responses.

Answers to ✔CHECK YOUR UNDERSTANDING

1. The Dadaists believed that Western culture had lost its meaning. They gave expression to this belief by poking fun at the art of the past.
2. Surrealism probed the subconscious world of dreams. Giorgio de Chirico's work launched the movement. Joan Miró was another Surrealist.
3. Paul Klee is best known for works of a simple, childlike nature filled with fantasy and humor.
4. The image of peasants fleeing their villages on horseback during raids is a recurring theme in art of Marino Marini.
5. Sculptor Barbara Hepworth's trademark is the use of holes.

● ● ● ● ● ● ● ● ● ● ● ● ● ●
FOCUS

☑ **OBJECTIVES**

After completing this lesson, students will be able to:

- Describe the characteristics of René Magritte's art.
- Create a painting in the Surrealist style.

☑ **SUPPLIES**

- Pencils.
- Sketch paper.
- Sheets of white drawing paper, 10 x 12 inches (25 x 30 cm).
- Tempera paints.
- Assorted brushes.
- Mixing trays.

Resource

○ ◼ 17-2 *Art—The Heartbeat of*
○   *the World*, TRB page 342
○   (art history)

● ● ● ● ● ● ● ● ● ● ● ● ● ●
TEACH

◼ **Motivator**

Invite students to share accounts of dreams they have had. Ask: Did you dream last night? Have students do quick sketches of a recent dream. Then ask them if their sketches make sense in the "real" world.

262

Painting in the Surrealist Style

Another artist who painted in the Surrealist style was Belgian painter René Magritte (ren-**ay** muh-**greet**). Magritte was a painter of riddles. In his pictures, familiar objects turn up together in unusual relationships or strange settings. Look at the work in Figure 17–7. At first glance this appears to be little more than a realistic painting of an ordinary looking room with a fireplace suggesting stillness and peace. The clock on the mantle notes the slow, regular passing of time. But bursting out of the wall is a steaming locomotive! This is an image of speed, energy and noise that disturbs the peacefulness of the room. What does it mean? Perhaps the only purpose here is to create surprise. We are shocked to see ordinary objects put together in ways that make no sense at all.

WHAT YOU WILL LEARN

You will draw and paint a work in the Surrealist style. You will combine familiar objects in strange, surprising ways. Objects will be painted realistically with a variety of hues, values, and intensities. (See Figure 17–8.)

WHAT YOU WILL NEED

- Pencil and sheets of sketch paper
- Sheet of white drawing paper, 10 x 12 inches (25 x 30 cm)
- Tempera paint
- Assorted brushes
- Mixing tray

▲ **Figure 17–7** How does Magritte's dream world differ from de Chirico's (see Figure 17–1)? Does the realistic painting style add to or take away from the idea the work communicates?

René Magritte. *Time Transfixed*. 1938. Oil on canvas. 147 x 98.7 cm (58 x 39"). The Art Institute of Chicago, Chicago, Illinois. Joseph Winterbotham Collection.

262   Lesson 2   *Painting in the Surrealist Style*

MEETING SPECIAL NEEDS

Small Group Discussion   Divide the class into small groups to facilitate each student telling the others in the group a story about his picture. For students who are reluctant to speak in front of the class, working in small groups of three or four will help these students feel more comfortable talking with their peers. Students with moderate or severe retardation or visual perception difficulties may wish to use pre-selected magazine pictures to paste together in unusual combinations. They may then decorate the picture with markers.

WHAT YOU WILL DO

1. Pick a common object to be featured in your picture. Using your imagination, sketch this object in a setting that makes little or no sense. You might, for instance, feature a thumbtack as tall as a house. You might choose to draw a bed on which eggs are frying. Make your image as offbeat and surprising as you can.

2. Carefully transfer your best sketch to the sheet of drawing paper. Make your finished drawing as realistic as possible. Using tempera, paint your work. Add details. Mix and blend hues, values, and intensities of color to make your objects lifelike.

4. Give your work a title unrelated to the objects in it. Write this title on the back of the picture.

5. Exchange paintings with a classmate. Write a brief explanation of the painting you receive. Your explanation, like the painting itself, can be offbeat.

6. Display your work along with its explanation. Compare it with those done by other students. Which were most surprising? What qualities in them caused you to react this way?

EXAMINING YOUR WORK

- **Describe** Identify the objects in your picture. Explain what steps you took to make these objects appear lifelike.
- **Analyze** Point to the variety of hues, values, and intensities in your work. Identify any other elements and principles you used to make objects more real-looking.
- **Interpret** Explain what steps you took to surprise and shock viewers.
- **Judge** Tell whether you feel your work succeeds. State what aesthetic view you feel would be best for judging your work.

▲ Figure 17–8 Student work. Surrealist painting.

Try This! COMPUTER OPTION

■ Scan into your computer program pictures of two dissimilar objects. Use the Resizing tool or menu to change the objects to create an unexpected size relationship. Use other tools available to add shadows, background, and details to make the images look real. Title, save, and print your work. Images can be scanned into the computer using a digital, analog, or *Quick-cam* camera, or a handheld or flatbed scanner.

---

more about . . .

Magritte The Belgian artist René Magritte began his association with the Surrealist group in 1930. His images are mysterious and derived from fantasy, but they are executed in a highly naturalistic style that is entirely opposed in spirit to the spontaneous, automatic handwriting art style that was cultivated by more central members of the Surrealist movement. Besides painting, Magritte also experimented with photography. Although he did not pursue this medium for very long, his influence on Surrealist photography was considerable. Photographers such as Herbert Bayer have translated Magritte's paradoxical pictures into photomontaged visual riddles that question everyday conceptions of reality.

■ Art Criticism

Have each student show Figure 17-7 to at least three people who are unfamiliar with Surrealist art and ask their interpretation. Students should write this information down. Discuss the various responses and categorize them by the three aesthetic theories. Then discuss whether people's opinions varied according to their age, gender, or personality.

• • • • • • • • • • • • • • •
ASSESS

■ Self-Assessment

Have students use Examining Your Work to evaluate their art works. Responses may be written or oral.

■ Reteaching

Give each student three slips of paper on which they are to write a brief description of a person, a goal, and an obstacle. Put the slips into three paper bags and have students draw out one in each category. Then students should write a Surrealist short story based on the character, goal, and problem on their slips. Discuss the similarities between their stories and the style of Figure 17-7.

■ Enrichment

Have groups of students investigate a woman Surrealist artist such as Frida Kahlo, Kay Sage, Dorothea Tanning, Leonor Fini, Remedios Varo, Leonora Carrington, and Lee Miller. The groups should prepare a brief oral presentation on their artist and the themes of her art.

• • • • • • • • • • • • • • •
CLOSE

Have students write a paragraph that states whether the strange juxtapositions in art by Magritte and other Surrealists are appealing. Do they find Surrealist art meaningless and confusing, or does it strike a chord in their own experience?

American Art Today

• • • • • • • • • • • • •
FOCUS

☑ OBJECTIVES

After completing this lesson, students will be able to:

• Describe the style of Abstract Expressionism.
• Explain why some artists were dissatisfied with Abstract Expressionism.
• Name three styles of painting that emerged soon after Abstract Expressionism.
• Name two artists who created new forms of non-objective sculpture.

☑ SUPPLIES

• Sheets of dark-colored construction paper.
• Reproductions of works by Duane Hanson.
• Scissors.
• Colored paper, sheets of plain paper.
• Medium-weight wire, aluminum cans.
• Cutting pliers, tin snips, or heavy duty scissors.
• Hammer, nails, spray enamel paint.

Resources

⊓ ▪ 17-3 *Jacob Lawrence*, TRB
⊓ page 343 (artist profile)
⊓ ▪ 17-4 *The American Art*
⊓ *Image*, TRB page 344
⊓ (reproducible master)
⊓

In the late 1800s the United States was recognized as a global power. It began slowly but surely to emerge as a world leader in art. By 1950 the change was complete. New York replaced Paris as the center of painting and sculpture.

Art since that time has been rocked by one new style after another. Countless new materials and techniques have been tried as artists attempt to solve an age-old problem. That problem is how best to speak to viewers through the language of art. In this lesson you will look at some solutions.

ABSTRACT EXPRESSIONISM

The first new form of expression was a bold style that was influenced by several past styles. Its name is **Abstract Expressionism**. In this art style, *paint was dribbled, spilled, or splashed onto huge canvases to express painting as an action.* Abstract Expressionist artists rejected the use of subject matter in their work. They dripped, spilled, and splashed rich colors on canvas to create their paintings. The *act* of painting was so tied to their work that the Abstract Expressionists became labeled "action painters."

One of the first members of the Abstract Expressionist movement was an Armenian-born artist named Arshile Gorky (**ar**-shuhl **gor**-kee). Gorky's early works show strong traces of Surrealism. By the mid-1940s, however, he was showing real objects as doodle-like lines and shapes in his paintings. Figure 17–9 shows a painting completed a year before his death. To appreciate such works demands that viewers open themselves to the artist's one-of-a-kind blending of colors, shapes, and lines.

▲ **Figure 17–9 Does a viewer need to see things in a painting to enjoy it? Can a painting be enjoyed for the beauty of the visual elements?**

Arshile Gorky. *Golden Brown.* c. 1943–44. Oil on canvas. 110.8 x 141.3 cm (43⅝ x 55⅝"). Washington University Gallery of Art, St. Louis, Missouri. University Purchase, Bixby Fund, 1953.

▲ **Figure 17–10   What is the positive shape in this work? What is the negative shape?**

Ellsworth Kelly. *Red/White.* 1964. Oil on canvas. 95.3 x 91.4 cm (37½ x 36"). Courtesy Blum Helman Gallery, New York, New York.

TECHNOLOGY OPTIONS

National Gallery of Art Videodisc   Use the following images to discuss the varied art and styles of this century.

Arshile Gorky	Andrew Wyeth	Alexander Calder
The Artist and His Mother	*Hawk Mountain*	*Untitled*

Search Frame 2303   Search Frame 3011   Search Frame 2607

Use Glencoe's *Correlation Bar Code Guide to the National Gallery of Art* to locate more art works.

Equally dazzling in their use of color are the paintings of Helen Frankenthaler (**frank-uhn-tahl-uhr**), another Abstract Expressionist. Frankenthaler's action paintings often begin on the floor of her studio. Standing above a blank canvas, the artist pours on layer after layer of thinned color. With each new addition, the work grows. Study the painting by Frankenthaler in Figure 2–5 on page **20**. Like most works by the artist, edges of shapes are sometimes sharp, sometimes blurred. Find the flamelike shape at the center. Notice how it appears to be spreading outward to other parts of the canvas.

OTHER DIRECTIONS IN PAINTING

It was not long after Abstract Expressionism appeared on the scene that other artists began challenging it. The style, they argued, was too personal—too much in the mind of the artist. Among the solutions that arose were:

- **Hard-Edge painting**. This was *a style that emphasized clear, crisp-edged shapes*. The work shown in Figure 17–10 is by Hard-Edge painter Ellsworth Kelly. Notice how the square shape of the canvas shows off the simple positive and negative shapes. What would you see first if the colors were reversed?
- **Social protest painting**. Emerging in the 1930s, this was *an art style that attacked the ills of big-city life*. It remained alive through the 1960s in the works of Jacob Lawrence, a black artist. Study the painting by Lawrence in Figure 17–11. Like the artist's other works, this one tells a story. What words would you use to describe the story?
- **New Realism**. Not all artists of the past few decades have been content to use non-objective styles. Some formed a movement called **New Realism**, *an art movement that rediscovered the importance of realistic detail*. Figure 17–12 shows a work by Andrew Wyeth, who has been a realist throughout his long career. The painting, you will notice, offers more than just a photographic record of its subject. It gives a glimpse of the kind of person the man is. Notice that he is turned away from the viewer. In this way he cannot see the pity in our eyes. Alone in his empty room he stubbornly guards the possessions left to him — his pride and dignity.

◀ **Figure 17–11 This is an example of social protest painting. What symbols did the artist use to convey his ideas?**

Jacob Lawrence. *Toussaint L'Overture Series*. 1938. Tempera on paper. 46.4 x 61.6 cm (18¼ x 24¼"). Fisk University.

Lesson 3 *American Art Today* **265**

••••••••••••••••
TEACH

■ **Motivator**

Point out to students that each of the artists in this lesson was working at a time when artists developed very unique and individual styles. Have students compare the experiences of these artists with that of Italian Renaissance artists, whose artistic styles were much more consistent. Is it harder for artists to develop a style of their own than to work in the same style as others?

■ **Art Criticism**

Have students select the art work that they like the least in this lesson and write a four-part art critical discussion about it. Challenge students to arrive at a positive judgment of the work. Invite students to read aloud their evaluations. Discuss the reasons why certain works are less appealing and whether it was difficult to see their positive elements.

■ **Studio Skills**

Tell students that art historians believe that Ellsworth Kelly developed his sensitivity to shape and color from his childhood experience of bird watching with his grandmother. Have students experiment with reducing the formal qualities of an object in their own environment to a non-objective, two-dimensional design. They should select an item and play with various ways to incorporate two or three of its colors into a simple two-dimensional work. When students have arrived at a final version, they should cut the shapes out of colored paper and glue them onto a plain backing sheet.

CURRICULUM *CONNECTIONS*

Social Studies Jacob Lawrence's paintings communicate his feelings about black culture and consciousness, often in the form of visual stories. Born in New Jersey in 1917, Lawrence moved to Harlem in the 1920s during the tremendous upswing in black culture that has come to be known as the Harlem Renaissance. Although the Harlem Renaissance was beginning to fade by the time Lawrence arrived, the seeds of his artistic career were sown there. In the Harlem Community Art Center and Harlem Art Workshop, Lawrence gained valuable experience and encouragement. In 1939 he had his first one-man show. He found that he often needed more than one frame of a painting to tell a story. Many of his works, including Figure 17-11, speak of the experience of African-Americans.

Have students create Calder-style mobiles out of wire and aluminum cans. Students should use tin snips or heavy duty scissors to cut abstract shapes out of the cans. They can make holes in them by hammering the point of a nail through the aluminum and then banging the reverse side to smooth it. Then the shapes may be sprayed with enamel paint. After the shapes dry, students can use small pieces of wire to suspend them from the main wire arc at the top.

■ **Cultural Diversity**

After examining Figure 17-10, students may wish to write a short report on the use of boldly colored, two-dimensional design outside of the United States. Some possibilities are the beadwork of the Pacific Northwest Coast Athapaskan Indians, patchwork textiles by the Maroons in the Suriname rain forest of South America, and the traditional mud wall paintings that are repainted every year in Ghana after the rainy season.

■ **Art History**

Show students pictures of other sculptures by Duane Hanson to familiarize them with their range of his subjects. Ask students who think they would make a good Duane Hanson sculpture to assume the pose and expression they would strike for Hanson. Discuss how the student sculptures would fit into Duane Hanson's profile of American culture.

▲ **Figure 17–12**   Notice how the man in the picture is turned away from the viewer. What reason might the artist have had for positioning him this way?

Andrew Wyeth. *That Gentleman*. 1960. Tempera on panel. 59.7 x 45.1 cm (23½ x 17¾"). Dallas Museum of Art, Dallas, Texas.

SCULPTURE

Painters have not been alone in the search for new methods of self-expression. Sculptors, too, have experimented with new styles. One of them, Alexander Calder, was able to number among his contributions the invention of a new term. That term, **mobile** (**moh**-beel), was used to describe a *sculpture made of carefully balanced shapes hung on wires*. Most of Calder's mobiles, like the one in Figure 17–13, are non-objective. Imagine this moving sculpture as it might appear as you stand near it. Try to picture the ever-changing patterns created by the bobbing and twisting of the shapes. What images do you think might come to mind?

A different approach to non-objective sculpture is found in the three-dimensional collages of Louise Nevelson (**nev**-uhl-suhn). Her works, one of which appears in Figure 17–14, were assembled from found objects and wood scraps. Viewers often experience these sculptures as at once familiar and foreign. The wood scraps in Figure 17–14 are easily identified. They are combined in such a way, however, that they create something entirely new and different. Are they gates or doors? If so, what kind of fascinating world lies beyond?

Just as some painters of recent times have made realism their goal, so have some sculptors. One is artist Duane Hanson. Hanson's sculptures are so lifelike they are often mistaken for real people. Imagine yourself

▲ **Figure 17–13**   What shape is emphasized in this mobile? How is this emphasis achieved? Is pattern an important principle? How is pattern shown?

Alexander Calder. *Zarabanda* (Un Disco Blanco). 1955. Painted sheet metal, metal rods and wire. 106.6 x 166.1 cm (42 x 65⅜"). Hirshhorn Museum and Sculpture Garden, Smithsonian Institution, Washington, D.C. Gift of Joseph H. Hirshhorn.

TECHNIQUE TIP ▼

Materials for Mobile   Many of the materials used in the Calder mobile activity in the Studio Skills activity can be obtained at a hardware store, including the wire, tin snips, paint, and sturdy pliers that have a cutting edge, such as electrician's pliers. If you wish to increase the longevity of the finished mobiles, consider also purchasing metal primer. First rinse the aluminum cans and cut out the desired shapes. Then roughen the surface slightly with cleansing powder or fine-grade sandpaper so that the paint will adhere better. Paint or spray the primer and allow it to dry before applying the color coat. Be certain to allow proper ventilation while priming and painting.

▲ **Figure 17–14** What would happen if this sculpture were painted in several different colors? Would it be as successful? Why or why not?

Louise Nevelson. *Mrs. N's Palace*. 1971. Painted wood, mirror. 355.6 x 607 x 457.2 cm (140 x 239 x 180″). The Metropolitan Museum of Art, New York, New York. Gift of the artist.

▲ **Figure 17–15** The people in this work are types you might pass on the street or at a shopping mall. Why do you think the artist has chosen to freeze these types in time? What are we able to learn about them? What can we learn about ourselves?

Duane Hanson. *Tourists*. 1970. Polyester and fiberglass. Lifesize. OK Harris Works of Art, New York, New York.

![pencil icon] **STUDIO ACTIVITY**

Creating an Action Painting

Experiment with your own action painting using watercolor paints and cotton swabs. Moisten a cotton swab with water and a single hue of color. Rub the swab across a large sheet of paper to make varied paint strokes. Use a fresh cotton swab and choose another hue. Put feeling and expression into your work by including drips and dabs of color.

Use this technique to complete several works, each expressing a different feeling. Display your finished works along with those of classmates.

PORTFOLIO

For your portfolio, write a detailed description of the techniques you used in your experiments. Tell which results you thought were most successful and why. Include your written summary with your finished works in your portfolio.

standing before Hanson's sculpture of tourists in Figure 17–15. Typical of his work, these people are average-looking and wear everyday clothing. What reaction do you suppose the artist wants viewers to have? What message about life in present-day America might he be sending?

✔ CHECK YOUR UNDERSTANDING

1. What is Abstract Expressionism? Name two members of the movement.
2. Besides Abstract Expressionism, name three directions painting has taken in the last 40 years. Define each school.
3. What term did Alexander Calder invent? Describe the kinds of sculptures he created.
4. Which of the artists you learned about in this lesson created three-dimensional collages?

Lesson 3   *American Art Today*   **267**

LESSON TIME: 90 minutes

• • • • • • • • • • • • • • •
FOCUS

☑ OBJECTIVES

After completing this lesson, students will be able to:

• Explain how Op artists create optical illusions.

• Create an art work that combines elements of Op Art and Hard Edge painting.

☑ SUPPLIES

• Pencils.
• Sketch paper, rulers.
• Pieces of illustration board, 12 x 12 inches (30 x 30 cm).
• India ink.
• Assorted pen points or nibs.
• Copies of works by Victor Vasarely and other Op artists.

• • • • • • • • • • • • • • •
TEACH

■ Motivator

Have students discuss the following quote by Gene Davis: "Far from being narrow and confining, the stripe has an astonishing potential for breadth and complexity...If I worked for fifty more years, I wouldn't exhaust the possibilities." Ask students whether they agree with Davis's attitude toward stripes.

■ Vocabulary

Explain to students that Op Art sought to create a sense of movement on the picture surface by means of optical illusion. Have students examine Figure 17-16 and show other examples of Op Art. Ask them how Op Art's optical illusionism differs from that of other art works in this text.

268

LESSON 4

Making a Hard-Edge Op Art Work

The painting in Figure 17–16, by artist Gene Davis, is typical of another movement of the second half of the twentieth century. The movement's name is **Op Art**. Artists working in this style *made use of precise lines and shapes to create optical illusion.* Stare at Davis' painting for a moment. Notice how the vertical lines in the picture appear to vibrate with color.

Compare this work with the Hard-Edge painting on page **264**. Imagine the artists of the two had decided to combine their styles in a single painting. What would it look like?

WHAT YOU WILL LEARN

Using India ink, you will create a pattern of black and white values. You will create this design over another made up of simple positive and negative shapes. The finished work—a blend of Op Art and Hard-Edge styles—will give a feeling of dizzying movement. (See Figure 17–17.)

WHAT YOU WILL NEED

• Pencil, sheets of sketch paper, and ruler
• Piece of illustration board, 12 x 12 inches (30 x 30 cm)
• India ink
• Pen holder and assorted points, or nibs

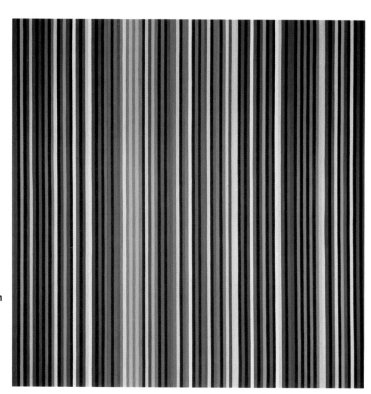

▶ **Figure 17–16 How does the artist add variety to this composition? Where are the most intense colors found? When you stare at it, does this picture seem to vibrate?**

Gene Davis. *Cool Buzz Saw.* 1964. Acrylic on canvas. 189.9 x 291.1 cm (113¾ x 115″). San Francisco Museum of Modern Art, San Francisco, California. Gift of the Women's Board.

268   Lesson 4   *Making a Hard-Edge Op Art Work*

— more about • • • —

Ellsworth Kelly Ellsworth Kelly's paintings are perfect examples of the Hard Edge movement's love of smooth surfaces, hard edges, pure colors, and simple geometric shapes rendered with great precision. Kelly does not base his paintings on any mathematical formula. He simply arranges the forms according to his eye, although the design is often abstracted from his nature photographs. Best known for his bold canvases, Kelly also intermittently has made sculptures, some of which are composed of his familiar geometric forms painted with primary colors. He later forsook almost all color and created works that had polished metal surfaces. In both his paintings and his sculpture, Kelly betrays a fascination with edges and how they slice through space.

WHAT YOU WILL DO

1. Look once again at the Hard-Edge painting by Kelly on page **264**. Draw several pencil sketches of a single Hard-Edge shape. The negative and positive shapes on your paper should be equally interesting.
2. Pick your best sketch. Using pencil and ruler, draw it on the piece of illustration board.
3. Study the Op Art painting by Gene Davis in Figure 17–16. Again working with ruler and pencil, cover the illustration board with closely spaced vertical lines. The spaces between the lines need not be exact. No two lines, however, should be more than a half inch apart.
4. With a pen and India ink, fill in the shape at the top left corner of your design. Be careful to stay within the lines. Working downward, leave the next shape white. Ink in every other shape until you reach the bottom of the illustration board. Repeat the process for the next vertical strip, this time leaving the topmost shape white. Continue in this fashion until all the strips have been completed.
5. Display your work alongside those of classmates. Which have the most interesting Hard-Edge designs? Which give the same kind of vibrating effect found in Figure 17–16?

▲ Figure 17–17   Student work. Hard-Edge Op Art.

Try This! ## COMPUTER OPTION

■ Flood-fill page with a light color. Choose a darker, complementary color and a wide Brush or Straight Line tool. Draw parallel horizontal, diagonal, or vertical lines to create stripes from side to side on the page. Use a variety of Selection tool shapes to select round or rectangular areas. Flip, Turn, or Rotate selections so lines within the shape move in a different direction from the background stripes. Title, save, and print your work. Try another option: Begin with a variety of parallel line colors and follow the steps. Compare. Is the effect as dramatic as using two contrasting colors?

Lesson 4   *Making a Hard-Edge Op Art Work*   **269**

more about • • •

Op Art   Developed in the United States after 1960, this non-objective art movement had parallels in several European countries including Germany and Italy. Op artists sought to create an impression of movement on the picture surface by means of optical illusion. In traditional paintings, the aim was to draw the viewer into the work. In contrast, Op pictures seem to vibrate and reach out to the spectator. Victor Vasarely is generally regarded as the founder of this movement. He used dazzling colors and precise geometric shapes to create surfaces that appear to move. They seem to project forward in some places and to recede in others. Op Art extended illusionism into the realm of non-representational art.

Art of the Next Frontier

(pages 270–271)

• • • • • • • • • • • • • • •

FOCUS

✔ OBJECTIVES

After completing this lesson, students will be able to:

• Describe some recent development in American art.

• Explain how contemporary artists are using new technologies.

✔ SUPPLIES

• Sheets of paper.

• Pencils.

• Materials for a class-designed and staged photograph.

• Good quality camera and color film.

Resources

■ 17-5 *Look to the Future,* TRB page 345 (cooperative learning)

■ 17-6 *Will Art Become Universal?,* TRB page 347 (appreciating cultural diversity)

■ 17-7 *Your Shared Culture,* TRB page 349 (studio)

• • • • • • • • • • • • • • •

TEACH

■ Motivator

Have students brainstorm ideas for creating a staged photograph. If they wish, the photo can mimic the Surrealist overtones of Figure 17-18. Help students set up the scene in a corner of the classroom or outdoors. Photograph a final version, have the picture enlarged, and display it in the classroom. Discuss the difficulties and potential of creating staged photographs.

270

Art of the Next Frontier

Artists have never been content to stay in one place for long. They are a restless breed, forever moving on, thirsting after new challenges. As we enter the twenty-first century, questions arise: What challenges will open themselves to the artists of tomorrow? What will art be like in the new century?

Answering these questions would take a crystal ball. Still, possible glimpses of the art of tomorrow are afforded by innovative developments in the art of today. In this lesson you will look at some of these developments.

ART AND TECHNOLOGY

If there is one word most closely identified with art of today, it is *technology*. Technology is the use of science to make life better. Art of the past few years has drawn on such technological advances as the computer and laser. It has also redefined the boundaries between one branch of art and the next.

Staged Photography

In the late 1800s the new art of photography changed the way painters looked at their subjects. In more recent times another new art—filmmaking—has had the same effect on photographers. Some have begun staging pictures in much the way movie directors set up a scene.

Figure 17–18 shows a staged photograph by artist Sandy Skoglund (**skoh**-gluhnd). For this work the artist sculpted each of the goldfish individually from clay. She also painted the room and directed the location of the two people. What twentieth-century style of painting does this work call to mind? What message might the photographer be sending to viewers?

▲ Figure 17–18   How would you describe the artist's use of color? Would this work have a different appearance if it had been shot in black and white?

Sandy Skoglund. *Revenge of the Goldfish.* 1981. Staged Photograph. Lorence Monk Gallery. New York, New York.

Multi-Media Art

The ancient Hindus, you may recall, believed temples to be as much sculpture as architecture. This idea has been carried forward in recent years by artists of multi-media works. **Multi-media art** is *a work that makes use of tools and techniques from two or more areas of art.*

A careful merging of architecture and sculpture is found in the expressions of sculptor Judy Pfaff (**faf**). Study the multi-media work by her in Figure 17–19. Parts of the work are the floor of the room, walls, and ceiling themselves. The viewer is able to move not only around this sculpture but also *within* it.

Kinetic Art

Examine the "sculpture" in Figure 17–20 by Nam June Paik. This work loosely belongs to a movement begun in the 1960s called **kinetic** (kuh-**net**-ik) **art.** This is *a style in which parts of works are set into motion.* The motion can be triggered by a form of energy or by

270   Lesson 5   *Art of the Next Frontier*

MEETING STUDENT DIVERSITY

Verbal/Linguistic Learners   Have students with strong linguistic abilities create crossword puzzles using the art terms, art movements, and names of artists who are covered in this chapter. Have them work with large squared graph paper and arrange the words vertically or horizontally in the squares. Then have students number each name or term and write clues for classmates so that classmates can successfully complete the crossword puzzle. Provide copies of the puzzles for each member of the class.

▲ **Figure 17–19** In what ways has the artist created a "real" landscape? What other branches of art besides sculpture and architecture are brought into play in this multi-media work?

Judy Pfaff. *Kabuki (Formula Atlantic)*. 1981. Mixed media. Hirshhorn Museum and Sculpture Garden, Smithsonian Institution, Washington, D.C.

the viewer moving past the work. Some art gives the impression of movement without actually moving. The work in Figure 17–20 is made up in part of 300 television screens. The viewer experiences a number of different images and sounds all at the same time. What do you imagine this experience would be like? What statement might the artist be making about the age of television?

A Futuristic Dwelling

Art, it has been said, mirrors the time in which it is created. This holds especially true for the branch of art called architecture.

On a sheet of paper, make a pencil drawing of a dream dwelling of the future. Provide solutions to such growing problems as pollution and thinning of the ozone layer. Share your finished work with classmates. Which design is the most interesting? Why?

P O R T F O L I O

Provide information for art historians of the future. Include this information with your drawing in your portfolio.

✔CHECK YOUR UNDERSTANDING

1. What is technology? What part has technology played in art of the present?
2. What is a staged photograph?
3. Define *multi-media art*.
4. To what two art movements does the painting in 17–16 belong?

▲ **Figure 17–20** A computer is used to "flip" and enlarge images on the different screens in this work. How many different images can you count? In what way is being bombarded by all these images at once similar to a typical day in our lives?

Nam June Paik. *Fin de Siècle II*. 1989. Video installation: Approximately 300 television sets. Originally shown at the Whitney Museum of American Art, New York, New York.

Lesson 5   *Art of the Next Frontier*   **271**

Answers to ✔CHECK YOUR UNDERSTANDING

1. Technology is the use of science to make life better. Art of the present has drawn on the use of the computer and the laser.
2. Some photographers have staged their pictures in the same way a movie director sets up a scene.
3. A multi-media piece is a work that makes use of tools and techniques from two or more branches of art.
4. The figure in 17-16 belongs in Op Art and Hard Edge art movements.

A Futuristic Dwelling

To extend this activity, you may assign students to develop their plans into a three-dimensional model. Suggest using cardboard, shoeboxes, or plastic foam as modeling media.

• • • • • • • • • •

ASSESS

■ **Self-Assessment**

Have students complete the review questions on this page. Answers are provided below.

■ **Reteaching**

Have groups of students research how various new technologies are used by artists. Students may explore the relationship between art and computers, lasers, video, copy machines, and fax machines. Each group should make a brief oral presentation that describes examples of the kinds of art that are possible by using a particular technology.

■ **Enrichment**

Have students select an artist from this chapter and one from either Chapter 11 or 12 and write a dialogue between the two artists that reveals what is different about life as an artist in the twentieth century and life as an artist in past times. The dialogues can touch on issues such as patronage, lifestyle, society's attitude toward artists, materials and techniques, and whether beauty and religious truth are among the artists' goals.

• • • • • • • • • •

CLOSE

Briefly review all of the movements discussed in this chapter. Have students identify the time and place in which a given style was popular. Then have students create a word web to characterize each movement in terms of its style and goal.

CONNECTIONS *Technology*

- Define a hologram.
- Understand how holograms are used.

Teaching the Connection

- Have students read the feature on this page.
- Ask volunteers to share what they know about holograms and holographic technology. How are holograms made? *(With laser light.)* What everyday uses of holograms have you observed? *(Holograms on book covers, cards, pencils, and so on.)* How are holograms useful to the artist? *(Holograms create the sensation that you could reach out and touch something within the image.)*
- Tell students that some art critics had a hard time accepting holographic art as genuine art when it first began to appear. Today, however, such art forms are viewed as authentic. It is still the artist who decides what the idea of the art will be and how to execute that idea.

Answers to Making the Connection

- The light hits them as though they were suspended. They seem to have form, as though you could hold the sculpted pieces.
- Responses will vary: medical technology, architectural design, and to detect flaws in manufactured goods. Computer and video games, pictures, and cards.
- Student research will vary.

Patrick Boyd. *Hato no Naka no Neko (Cat Among the Pigeons)*. 20.3 x 25.4 cm (8 x 10"). Photomontage stereogram on glass, with life-size display stand. Holos Gallery, San Francisco, California.

What Do You See in a Hologram?

A hologram is a three-dimensional record of an image made with laser light. Holograms look so real that the viewer has the sensation of being able to reach out and touch the image.

Holography is similar to photography. Precision optical instruments are used to expose special photo-sensitive materials to laser light. Although a hologram is a "flat" picture, when a beam of light strikes it at the proper angle, a three-dimensional image will appear. The hologram displays an image that can be viewed from many different angles and depths, just like solid objects in the real world.

Holograms have many uses in science and engineering, especially when combined with computer graphics. Medical scientists can record three-dimensional views of living cells. Pilots can use holographic instruments to land planes in bad weather. Holograms even appear on credit cards to prevent forgery.

Artists can create new art forms using holographic imaging. In *Cat Among the Pigeons*, Patrick Boyd has produced a kind of hologram, called a stereogram, on a glass plate. The technique makes you feel as though you could reach right into the picture.

MAKING THE CONNECTION

- In the hologram shown here, what makes the images appear to be floating in mid-air? What makes them look like sculptures?
- How are holograms used in science and in everyday life? Where have you seen holograms used?
- Laser light is different from ordinary light. Find out more about laser technology and its benefits.

INTERNET ACTIVITY

Visit Glencoe's Fine Arts Web Site for students at:

http://www.glencoe.com/sec/art/students

INTERNET ACTIVITY

Getting Your School Connected   The technology that opened the Internet to businesses and private individuals has also increased its potential for educational use. This great potential was recognized by the president, who challenged the nation to connect every classroom in America to the Internet by the year 2000. Problems such as cost, installation of telephone lines, availability of local service providers, and acceptable use by students are all challenges that educators face, but these challenges are being overcome. Work with your school district and your administrators. Show them examples from this program that guarantee the learning experience and benefits available to your students once your classroom is on-line. Find us at **http://www.glencoe.com/sec/art**

REVIEW

BUILDING VOCABULARY

Number a sheet of paper from 1 to 10. After each number, write the term from the list that best matches each description below.

Abstract Expressionism
Dada
Hard-Edge painting
kinetic art
mobile
multi-media art
New Realism
Op Art
social protest painting
Surrealism

1. An art movement founded on the belief that Western culture had lost its meaning.
2. An art movement that probed the subconscious world of dreams.
3. An art style in which paint was dribbled, spilled, or splashed onto huge canvases to express painting as an action.
4. An art style that emphasized clear, crisp-edged shapes.
5. An art style that attacked the ills of big-city life.
6. An art movement that rediscovered the importance of realistic detail.
7. A style made of carefully balanced shapes hung on wires.
8. An art style that made use of precise lines and shapes to create optical illusion.
9. A work that makes use of tools and techniques from two or more areas of art.
10. An art style in which parts of works are set into motion by a form of energy.

REVIEWING ART FACTS

Number a sheet of paper from 11 to 18. Answer each question in a complete sentence.

11. Name an artist of the Dada movement.
12. Describe the works of Paul Klee.
13. What sculptor did works of Italian peasants fleeing a bombing raid?
14. For which type of sculpture was Barbara Hepworth best known?
15. In what art movement was Arshile Gorky a pioneer?
16. What sculptor you learned about created three-dimensional collages?
17. Name an artist who works in the area of staged photography.
18. For what kinds of works is Judy Pfaff known?

❔ THINKING ABOUT ART

On a sheet of paper, answer each question in a sentence or two.

1. **Analyze.**   React to the opinion that art must be serious to be good. Find works from the chapter that support your position.
2. **Compare and contrast.**   Compare the works in Figure 17–2 and Figure 17–13. Aside from the fact that one is a painting and the other a sculpture, how do they differ? What do they have in common? Would you use the same aesthetic view in judging the two? Explain.

MAKING ART CONNECTIONS

1. **Language Arts.**   Choose one of the non-objective works you learned about in this chapter. Make a list of points about this work you would bring up in a debate with someone who claimed a two-year-old could create the same "art."
2. **History.**   In this chapter you learned of some art movements that appeared in the late twentieth century. The following are several others: Pop Art, Earth Art, and Conceptual Art. Using an encyclopedia or other library resource, find out the names of artists who worked in the movement, and identify their goals. Report your findings to the class.

■ Building
Vocabulary

1. Dada
2. Surrealism
3. Abstract Expressionism
4. Hard-Edge painting
5. social protest painting
6. New Realism
7. mobile
8. Op Art
9. multi-media art
10. kinetic art

■ Reviewing
Art Facts

11. Marcel Duchamp was a member of the Dada movement.
12. Paul Klee's works were simple and childlike, filled with fantasy and humor.
13. Marino Marini sculpted peasants fleeing a bombing raid.
14. Barbara Hepworth is known for non-objective sculpture.
15. Arshile Gorky was one of the first Abstract Expressionists.
16. Louise Nevelson created three-dimensional collages.
17. Sandy Skoglund uses staged photography.
18. Judy Pfaff is known for multi-media architecture/sculpture.

❔ THINKING ABOUT ART

1. Answers may vary. Students should show they understand playful and experimental art can be well done. Students' choices of art works should support their stated opinion.

2. Students should show they know the mobile is a free-floating, moving piece and the Miró is a painting. The common characteristics are the use of non-objective shapes. Answers will vary on the use of an aesthetic view.

Using the Handbook

The Handbook is a convenient reference section which offers students step-by-step procedures, additional career and artist profile information, and optional studio lessons. This material is designed to complement and enrich the narrative and studio lessons that appear earlier in the book.

The Handbook is divided into the following sections:

PART 1: Technique Tips
PART 2: Artist Profiles
PART 3: Career Spotlights
PART 4: Additional Studios

The Handbook can be used in conjunction with specific chapters and lessons, or you may wish to use each section of the Handbook for independent study. For example, if you want to cover careers or art history in two separate weeks, you can use the Artist Profiles for one week and Career Spotlights for the next week. Regardless of the way you integrate the material, the *Teacher's Wraparound Edition* offers additional information in the outside column to help you teach, apply, and reinforce these materials.

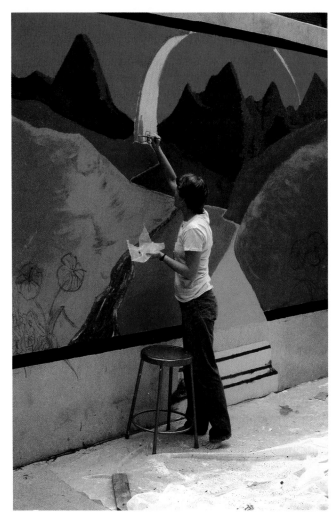

▲ Working on group murals is an excellent way to practice artistic skills, gain recognition, and at the same time, have fun.

HANDBOOK CONTENTS

■ PART 1:
Technique Tips

This section offers students step-by-step procedures of how to do specific skills related to the areas of drawing, printmaking, painting, and sculpting. General techniques in these areas are described and, when appropriate, illustrated with line drawings. Other general skills, such as making a mat or using glue, are included in this reference section.

■ PART 2:
Artist Profiles

The Artist Profiles provide students with background information of fourteen artists whose works appear in the text. The information gives a short biographical sketch about the artist and gives the reader an account of world events which occurred during the artist's life. The material is written in a warm, personal tone and will motivate students to seek more in-depth outside information about the artist.

■ PART 3:
Career Spotlights

This section introduces students to fourteen careers within the art-related fields. Students are presented with an overview of the type of work and personal qualifications required of a person working in the featured occupation. In the *Teacher's Wraparound Edition*, addresses are provided so that students can research and obtain further information about the careers that interest them.

■ PART 4:
Additional Studios

Five additional studio lessons are provided as extensions to chapter content. These lessons can be used as independent practice for gifted and talented students, as cooperative learning projects, or to practice and enhance computer art skills. In contrast to the lessons which appear within the text, these lessons generally take an extended period of time to complete. Each studio lesson has been reviewed and given an approximate time allotment that should be allowed.

TECHNIQUE TIP

Stretch Your School Budget Check with the local art club to see if it has a benevolence fund for aid to education. Check with the local art directors' club, designers' association, or society of illustrators (in cities larger than 300,000).

Tracing vellum and some watercolor rendering papers can be bought less expensively in rolls or by the foot than by the sheet or pads. A 100% rag, twenty-pound vellum is pretty tough—and you can iron the back of it to smooth it after using liquid media.

1. Making Gesture Drawings

Gesture drawing is a way of showing movement in a sketch. Gesture drawings have no outlines or details. You are not expected to draw the figure. Instead, you are expected to draw the movement, or what the figure is doing. Follow these guidelines:

- Use the side of the drawing tool. Do not hold the medium as you would if you were writing.
- Find the lines of movement that show the direction in which the figure is bending. Draw the main line showing this movement.
- Use quickly drawn lines to build up the shape of the person.

2. Making Contour Drawings

Contour drawing is a way of capturing the feel of a subject. When doing a contour drawing, remember the following pointers:

- If you accidentally pick up your pen or pencil, don't stop working. Place your pen or pencil back where you stopped. Begin again from that point.
- If you have trouble keeping your eyes off the paper, ask a friend to hold a piece of paper between your eyes and your drawing paper. Another trick is to place your drawing paper inside a large paper bag as you work.
- Tape your paper to the table so it will not slide around. With a finger of your free hand, trace the outline of the object. Record the movement with your drawing hand.

- Contour lines show ridges and wrinkles in addition to outlines. Adding these lines gives roundness to the object.

3. Drawing with Oil Pastels

Oil pastels are sticks of pigment held together with an oily binder. The colors are brighter than wax crayon colors. If you press heavily you will make a brilliant-colored line. If you press lightly you will create a fuzzy line. You can fill in shapes with the brilliant colors. You can blend a variety of color combinations. For example, you can fill a shape with a soft layer of a hue and then color over the hue with a heavy layer of white to create a unique tint of that hue.

If you use oil pastels on colored paper, you can put a layer of white under the layer of hue to block the color of the paper.

4. Drawing Thin Lines with a Brush

Drawing thin lines with a brush can be learned with a little practice. Just follow these steps:

1. Dip your brush in the ink or paint. Wipe the brush slowly against the side, twirling it between your fingers until the bristles form a point.
2. Hold the brush at the beginning of the metal band near the tip. Hold the brush straight up and down.
3. Imagine that the brush is a pencil with a very sharp point. Pretend that pressing too hard will break the point. Now touch the paper lightly with the tip of the brush and draw a line. The line should be quite thin.

   To make a thinner line still, lift up on the brush as you draw. After a while, you will be able to make lines in a variety of thicknesses.

5. Making a Grid for Enlarging

Sometimes the need arises to make a bigger version of a small drawing. An example is when you create a mural based on a small sketch. Follow these steps:

1. Using a ruler, draw evenly spaced lines across and up and down your original drawing (Figure T–1). Count

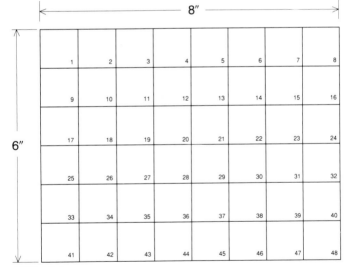

▲ **Figure T–1**

Drawing Some drawings look better without a mat. A backing board with a lightweight acetate covering will do the trick. If the drawing is on tracing paper or vellum, however, there needs to be a piece of inexpensive white poster or tagboard between the corrugated board and the drawing. The corrugated board will discolor any drawing in a few years. Thin paper will show the corrugation ridges from the backing.

Using the Technique Tips

The technique tips listed on these pages give students helpful hints for handling different media and tools. The technique tips offer students step-by-step procedures to assist them with their art production skills. Each technique tip contains procedures that should be followed in sequential order for maximum success.

USING THE DRAWING TIPS

1. Making Gesture Drawings
   Use with:
   - Drawing Your Personality, Studio Activity, page 133
   - Creating Abstract Expressionism, Studio Activity, page 251
   - Making a Print of a Figure in Action, page 253
2. Making Contour Drawings
   Use with:
   - Drawing a Still Life, page 167
   - Designing a Visual Symbol, page 172
   - Drawing Expressive Hands, page 182
3. Drawing with Oil Pastels
   Use with:
   - Illustrating a Story, Studio Activity, page 149
   - Still Life, page 167
   - Cubist Chalk Drawing, page 247
4. Drawing Thin Lines with a Brush
   Use with:
   - Perceiving an Object, Studio Activity, page 69
   - Making a Painting for a Greek Vase, page 102
   - Designing a Neoclassic Stage Set, page 214
5. Making a Grid for Enlarging
   Use with:
   - Making a Stylized Motif, page 93

the number of squares you made from side to side. Count the number of squares running up and down.

2. Measure the width of the surface to which the drawing is to be transferred. Divide that figure by the number of side-to-side squares. The resulting number will be the horizontal measure of each square. You may work in inches or centimeters. Using a ruler or yardstick, mark off the squares. Draw in light rules.

3. Measure the height of the surface to which the drawing is to be transferred. Divide that figure by the number of up-and-down squares. The resulting number will be the vertical measure of each square. Mark off the squares. Draw in pencil lines.

4. Starting at the upper left, number each square on the original drawing. Give the

same number to each square on the large grid. Working a square at a time, transfer your image. (See Figure T–2.)

6. Using Shading Techniques

When using shading techniques, keep in mind the following:

- Lines or dots placed close together create dark values.
- Lines or dots placed far apart, on the other hand, create light values. To show a change from light to dark, start with lines or dots far apart and little by little bring them close together.
- Use care also to follow the shape of the object when adding lines. Straight lines are used to shade an object with a flat surface. Rounded lines are used to shade an object with a curved surface.

7. Using Sighting Techniques

Sighting is a technique that will help you draw objects in proportion.

1. Face the object you plan to draw. Hold a pencil straight up and down at arm's length. Your thumb should rest against the side of the pencil and be even with the tip.
2. Close one eye. With your other eye, focus on the object.
3. Slide your thumb down the pencil until the exposed part of the pencil matches the object's height. (See Figure T–3.)

▲ Figure T–3

4. Now, without moving your thumb or bending your arm, turn the pencil sideways.
5. Focus on the width of the object. If the height is greater, figure out how many "widths" will fit in one "height." If the width is greater, figure out how many "heights" will fit in one "width."

▲ Figure T–2

TECHNIQUE TIP

Thumbnail Sketches Thumbnail sketches are small sketches drawn quickly to record ideas and information for a finished drawing. They are called thumbnail because they are almost small enough to have been drawn on a thumbnail. They are usually done with pen and ink. Graphic artists and illustrators use them to record ideas and also to show ideas to other artists, art directors, and executives. Have students work in small groups and develop a series of thumbnail sketches that could be used to plan a series of paintings of animal totems or symbols of ancestry. When students have completed their sketches, have them display their work.

8. Using a Viewing Frame

Much in the way a camera is used to focus on one area of a scene, you can better zero in on an object you plan to draw by using a viewing frame (Figure T–4). To make a viewing frame do the following:

1. Cut a rectangular hole in a piece of paper about 2 inches (3 to 5 cm) in from the paper's edges.
2. Hold the paper at arm's length and look through the hole at your subject. Imagine that the hole represents your drawing paper.
3. Decide how much of the subject you want to have in your drawing.
4. By moving the frame up, down, sideways, nearer, or farther, you can change the focus of your drawing.

9. Using a Ruler

There are times when you need to draw a crisp, straight line. By using the following techniques, you will be able to do so.

1. Hold the ruler with one hand and the pencil with the other.
2. Place the ruler where you wish to draw a straight line.
3. Hold the ruler with your thumb and first two fingers. Be careful that your fingers do not stick out beyond the edge of the ruler.
4. Press heavily on the ruler so it will not slide while you're drawing.
5. Hold the pencil lightly against the ruler.
6. Pull the pencil quickly and lightly along the edge of the ruler. The object is to keep the ruler from moving while the pencil moves along its edge.

▲ Figure T–4

PAINTING TIPS

10. Cleaning a Paint Brush

Cleaning a paint brush properly helps it last a long time. *Always*:

1. Rinse the thick paint out of the brush under running water. Do not use hot water.
2. Gently paint the brush over a cake of mild soap, or dip it in a mild liquid detergent (Figure T–5).

▲ Figure T–5

Technique Tips **279**

more about • • •

Perceptual Skills Tell students that seeing the item they are drawing as a whole rather than just a collection of parts results in more successful drawings. Explain that the fact that we naturally see things as a whole was discovered in Germany in 1912 by a psychologist named Max Wertheimer. He founded a branch of psychology called Gestaltism. The German word *gestalt* means pattern or form. According to Gestalt psychology, we only recognize objects by seeing total patterns or forms, not by adding up the individual parts we see. Tell students that in making most drawings, they should do the large shapes first and add the details later. Encourage them to think in terms of the Gestalt view of life.

3. Gently scrub the brush against the palm of your hand to work the soap into the brush. This removes paint you may not have realized was still in the brush.

4. Rinse the brush under running water while you continue to scrub your palm against it (Figure T–6).

▲ **Figure T–6**

5. Repeat steps 2, 3, and 4 as needed.

When it is thoroughly rinsed and excess water has been squeezed from the brush, shape your brush into a point with your fingers (Figure T–7). Place the brush in a container with the bristles up so that it will keep its shape as it dries.

▲ **Figure T–7**

11. Making Natural Earth Pigments

Anywhere there is dirt, clay, or sand, there is natural pigment. To create your own pigments, gather as many different kinds of earth colors as you can. Grind these as finely as possible. (If you can, borrow a mortar and pestle.) (See Figure T–8.) Do not worry if the pigment is slightly gritty.

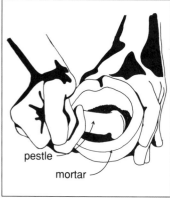

pestle

mortar

▲ **Figure T–8**

To make the binder, mix equal parts of white glue and water. Place a few spoonfuls of your powdered pigment into a small jar. Add a little of the binder. Experiment with different amounts of each.

When you work with natural pigments, remember always to wash the brushes before the paint in them has a chance to dry. The glue from the binder can ruin a brush. As you work, stir the paint every now and then. This will keep the grains of pigment from settling to the bottom of the jar.

Make a fresh batch each time you paint.

12. Mixing Paint to Change the Value of Color

You can better control the colors in your work when you mix your own paint. In mixing paints, treat opaque paints (for example, tempera) differently from transparent paints (for example, watercolors).

- *For light values of opaque paints.* Mix only a small amount of the hue to white. The color can always be made stronger by adding more of the hue.
- *For dark values of opaque paints.* Add a small amount of black to the hue. Never add the hue to black.
- *For light values of transparent paints.* Thin a shaded area with water (Figure T–9). This allows more of the white of the paper to show through.
- *For dark values of transparent paints.* Carefully add a small amount of black to the hue.

▲ **Figure T–9**

13. Working with Poster Paints (School Tempera)

When using poster paints (school tempera) remember the following:

- Poster paints run when wet. To keep this from happening, make sure one shape is dry before painting a wet color next to it.

14. Working with Watercolors

- If you apply wet paint to damp paper, you create lines and shapes with soft edges.
- If you apply wet paint to dry paper, you create lines and shapes with sharp, clear edges.
- If you dip a dry brush into damp paint and then brush across dry paper, you achieve a fuzzy effect.
- School watercolors come in semi-moist cakes. Before you use them, place a drop of water on each cake to let the paint soften. Watercolor paints are transparent. You can see the white paper through the paint. If you want a light value of a hue, dilute the paint with a large amount of water. If you want a bright hue, you must dissolve more pigment by swirling your brush around in the cake of paint until you have dissolved a great deal of paint. The paint you apply to the paper can be as bright as the paint in the cake.

PRINTMAKING TIP

15. Making a Stamp Printing

A stamp print is an easy way to make repetitive designs. The following are a few suggestions for making a stamp and printing with it. You may develop some other ideas after reading these hints. Remember, printing reverses your design, so if you use letters, be certain to cut or carve them backwards.

- Cut a simple design into the flat surface of an eraser with a knife that has a fine, precision blade.
- Cut a potato, carrot, or turnip in half. Use a paring knife to carve a design into the flat surface of the vegetable.
- Glue yarn to a bottle cap or a jar lid.
- Glue found objects to a piece of corrugated cardboard. Make a design with paper-clips, washers, nuts, leaves, feathers, or anything else you can find. Whatever object you use should have a fairly flat surface. Make a handle for the block with masking tape.
- Cut shapes out of a piece of inner tube material. Glue the shapes to a piece of heavy cardboard.

There are several ways to apply ink or paint to a stamp:

- Roll water-based printing ink on the stamp with a soft brayer.
- Roll water-based printing ink on a plate and press the stamp into the ink.
- Apply tempera paint or school acrylic to the stamp with a bristle brush.

SCULPTING TIPS

16. Working with Clay

To make your work with clay go smoothly, always do the following:

1. Dip one or two fingers in water.
2. Spread the moisture from your fingers over your palms.

Never dip your hands in water. Too much moisture turns clay into mud.

17. Joining Clay

If you are creating a piece of sculpture that requires joining pieces, do the following:

1. Gather the materials you will need. These include clay, slip, (a creamy mixture of clay and water), a paint brush, a scoring tool, (perhaps a kitchen fork) and clay tools.
2. Rough up or scratch the two surfaces to be joined (Figure T–10).

▲ Figure T–10

Technique Tips **281**

SAFETY TIPS

Printing Remind students to always wipe any remaining ink from a block and brayer after they have finished printing. If they have used a water-based printing ink, they can use water for cleaning. If they have used oil-based ink, however, they should use a solvent such as turpentine. Remember that if they use a solvent, they should be careful not to get the solvent on their skin, or in their eyes.

Using Kilns Place kilns in a separate room. If that is not possible, locate the kiln in an out-of-the-way part of the room where students are not likely to come into contact with it when it is in operation. In addition, all kilns should have local exhaust ventilation.

3. Apply slip to one of the two surfaces using a paint brush or your fingers (Figure T–11).

▲ **Figure T–11**

4. Gently press the two surfaces together so the slip oozes out of the joining seam (Figure T–12).

▲ **Figure T–12**

5. Using clay tools and/or your fingers, smooth away the slip that has oozed out of the seam (Figure T–13). You may wish to smooth out the seam as well, or you may wish to leave it for decorative purposes.

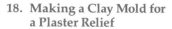

▲ **Figure T–13**

18. Making a Clay Mold for a Plaster Relief

One of the easiest ways to make a plaster relief is with a clay mold. When making a clay mold, remember the following:

- Plaster poured into the mold will come out with the opposite image. Design details cut into the mold will appear raised on the relief. Details built up within the mold will appear indented in the relief.
- Do not make impressions in your mold that have *undercuts* (Figure T–14). Undercuts trap plaster, which will break off when the relief is removed. When cutting impressions, keep the deepest parts the narrowest.
- In carving a raised area in the mold, take care not to create a reverse undercut (Figure T–15).

If you want to change the mold simply smooth the area with your fingers.

19. Mixing Plaster

Mixing plaster requires some technique and a certain amount of caution. It can also be a very simple matter when you are prepared. Always do the following:

- Use caution when working with dry plaster. Wear a dust mask or work in a well-ventilated room.
- Cover your work space to keep the dust from spreading.
- Always use a plastic bowl and a stick for mixing. Never use silverware you will later eat from.
- Always use plaster that is fine, like sifted flour. Plaster should never be grainy when dry.
- Always add the water to the bowl first. Sift in the plaster. Stir slowly.
- Never pour unused plaster down a drain. Allow it to dry in the bowl. To remove the dried plaster, twist the bowl. Crack the loose plaster into a lined trash can.

▲ **Figure T–14**

▲ **Figure T–15**

more about • • •

Pottery   Before becoming pottery, clay takes six forms:
- *Plastic Clay*—clay wet enough to be worked but dry enough to hold its shape.
- *Slip*—clay with enough water added to make it runny. Slip is used to glue together shaped pieces of damp clay.
- *Leather hard clay*—clay which is still damp but too hard to model.

- *Greenware*—very dry clay that will break easily. An object at the greenware stage is ready to be fired.
- *Bisqueware*—fired pottery that is hard but not ready to use.
- *Glazeware*—pottery coated with powdered chemicals that melt during firing into a hard, glass-like finish.

20. Working with Papier-Mâché

Papier-mâché (**pay**-puhr muh-**shay**) is a French term meaning "chewed paper." It is also the name of several sculpting methods using newspaper and liquid paste. These methods can be used to model tiny pieces of jewelry. They can also be used to create life-size creatures.

In creating papier-mâché sculptures, the paper-and-paste mixture is molded over a support. You will learn more about supports shortly. The molded newspaper dries to a hard finish. The following are three methods for working with papier-mâché:

- **Pulp Method.** Shred newspaper, paper towels, or tissue paper into tiny pieces. (Do not use glossy magazine paper; it will not soften.) Soak your paper in water overnight. Press the paper in a kitchen strainer to remove as much moisture as possible. Mix the mashed paper with commercially prepared papier-mâché paste or white glue. The mixture should have the consistency of soft clay. Add a few drops of oil of cloves to keep the mixture from spoiling. A spoonful of linseed oil makes the mixture smoother. (If needed, the mixture can be stored at this point in a plastic bag in the refrigerator.) Use the mixture to model small shapes. When your creations dry, they can be sanded. You will also be able to drill holes in them.
- **Strip Method.** Tear newspaper into strips. Either dip the strips in papier-mâché paste or rub paste on them. Apply the strips to your support (Figure T–16). If you do not want the strips to stick to your

▲ **Figure T–16**

support, first cover it with plastic wrap. Use wide strips for large shapes. Use thin strips for smaller shapes. If you plan to remove your finished creation from the support, apply five or six layers. (Change directions with each layer so you can keep track of the number.) Otherwise, two or three layers should be enough. After applying the strips to your support, rub your fingers over the surface.

As a last layer, use torn paper towels. The brown paper towels that are found in schools produce an uncomplicated surface on which to paint. Make sure no rough edges are sticking up. Store any unused paste mixture in the refrigerator to keep it from spoiling.

- **Draping Method.** Spread papier-mâché paste on newspaper. Lay a second sheet on top of the first. Smooth the layers. Add another layer of paste and another sheet of paper. Repeat until you have four or five layers of paper. Use this method for making drapery on a figure. (See Figure T–17.) If you allow the lay-

▲ **Figure T–17**

ers to dry for a day or two, they will become leathery. They can then be cut and molded as you like. Newspaper strips dipped in paste can be used to seal cracks.

Like papier-mâché, supports for papier-mâché creations can be made in several different ways. Dry newspaper may be wadded up and wrapped with string or tape (Figure T–18). Wire coat hangers may be padded with rags. For large figures, a wooden frame covered with chicken wire makes a good support.

▲ **Figure T–18**

20. Papier-Mâché
Use with:
- Making a Mood Mask Relief, page 140
- Material in the Teacher's Resource Binder

Technique Tips **283**

MEETING SPECIAL NEEDS

Physical Disabilities and Safety   At the beginning of each school year or new term, determine if any of your students are asthmatic, visually or hearing impaired, or on prescribed medication. Asthmatic students should not be exposed to dusts, fumes, or vapors because of breathing difficulties. Visually impaired students understandably operate very close to their art work, and as a consequence, are more likely to inhale dusts, vapors, and fumes. Students with hearing impairments should not be exposed to activities requiring loud hammering or noisy machinery. If students are found to be on medication, seek a physician's advice regarding the potential harmful interaction between the prescribed medicine and art materials used in the class.

TECHNIQUE TIPS

21. Making a Paper Sculpture
Use with:
- Making a Clay Urn, Studio Options, page 87
- Constructing a Mask, Studio Activity, page 139
- Making a Rococo Shoe, page 189

OTHER TIPS

22. Measuring Rectangles
Use with:
- Designing a Visual Symbol, page 172
- Making a Stylized Motif, page 93

23. Making a Mat
Use with:
- Painting an Expressive Scene, page 38
- Painting Using Earth Pigments, page 53
- Creating a Picture Story, page 63
- Making a Scroll, page 70
- Making a Stylized Motif, page 93
- Making a Painting for a Greek Vase, page 103
- Illustrating Your Tree of Life, Studio Activity, page 117
- Drawing a Still Life, page 167

▲ Figure T–19

To create a base for your papier-mâché creations, tape together arrangements of found materials. Some materials you might combine are boxes, tubes, and bowls. (See Figure T–19.) Clay can also be modeled as a base. If clay is used, be sure there are no undercuts that would keep the papier-mâché from lifting off easily when dry. (For an explanation of undercuts, see Technique Tip **18,** *Handbook* page **276.**)

Always allow time for your papier-mâché creations to dry. The material needs extra drying time when thick layers are used or when the weather is damp. An electric fan blowing air on the material can shorten the drying time.

21. Making a Paper Sculpture

Another name for paper sculpture is origami. The process originated in Japan and means "folding paper." Paper sculpture begins with a flat piece of paper. The paper is then curved or bent to produce more than a flat

surface. Here are some ways to experiment with paper.
- **Scoring.** Place a square sheet of heavy construction paper, 12 x 12 inch (30 x 30 cm), on a flat surface. Position the ruler on the paper so that it is close to the center and parallel to the sides. Holding the ruler in place, run the point of a knife or a pair of scissors along one of the ruler's edges. Press down firmly but take care not to cut through the paper. Gently crease the paper along the line you made. Hold your paper with the crease facing upward.
- **Pleating.** Take a piece of paper and fold it one inch from the edge. Then fold the paper in the other direction. Continue folding back and forth.
- **Curling.** Hold one end of a long strip of paper with the thumb and forefinger of one hand. At a point right below where you are holding the strip, grip it lightly between the side of a pencil and the thumb of your other hand. In a quick motion, run the pencil along the strip. This will cause the strip to curl back on itself. Don't apply too much pressure, or the strip will tear. (See Figure T–20.)

▲ Figure T–20

OTHER TIPS

22. Measuring Rectangles

Do you find it hard to create perfectly formed rectangles? Here is a way of getting the job done:

1. Make a light pencil dot near the long edge of a sheet of paper. With a ruler, measure the exact distance between the dot and the edge. Make three more dots the same distance in from the edge. (See Figure T–21.)

▲ Figure T–21

2. Line a ruler up along the dots. Make a light pencil line running the length of the paper.
3. Turn the paper so that a short side is facing you. Make four pencil dots equally distant from the short edge. Connect these with a light pencil rule. Stop when you reach the first line you drew. (See Figure T–22.)
4. Do the same for the remaining two sides. Erase any lines that may extend beyond the box you have made.
5. Trace over the lines with your ruler and pencil.

The box you have created will be a perfectly formed rectangle.

TECHNIQUE TIP

Classroom Demonstrations The instructional strategy that is probably most familiar to art teachers is demonstration. This is an especially effective method of instruction when applied to studio activities. When preparing for a demonstration, always practice beforehand using the same materials students will be expected to use.

Include continuous commentary with the demonstration explaining in detail what you are doing and why you are doing it this way. Detailed explanation increases the likelihood that the information will be better understood and assimilated by students.

▲ Figure T–22

▲ Figure T–23

23. Making a Mat

You can add appeal to an art work by making a mat, using the following steps.

1. Gather the materials you will need. These include a metal rule, a pencil, mat board, cardboard backing, a sheet of heavy cardboard to protect your work surface, a mat knife with a sharp blade, and wide masking tape.
2. Wash your hands. Mat board should be kept very clean.
3. Measure the height and width of the work to be matted. Decide how large a border you want for your work. (A border of approximately 2½ inches on three sides with 3 inches on the bottom is aesthetically pleasing.) Your work will be behind the window you will cut.
4. Plan for the opening, or window, to be ¼ inch smaller on all sides than the size of your work. For example, if your work measures 9 by 12 inches, the mat window should measure 8½ inches (9 inches minus ¼ inch times two) by 11½ inches (12 inches minus ¼ inch times two). Using your metal rule and pencil, lightly draw your window rectangle on the back of the board 2½ inches from the top and left edge of the mat. (See Figure T–23.) Add a 2½ inch border to the right of the window and a 3 inch border to the bottom, lightly drawing cutting guidelines.

   Note: If you are working with metric measurements, the window should overlap your work by 0.5 cm (centimeters) on all sides. Therefore, if your work measures 24 by 30 cm, the mat window measures 23 cm (24 − [2 x 0.5]) by 29 cm (30 − [2 x 0.5]).

▲ Figure T–24

5. Place the sheet of heavy, protective cardboard on your work surface. Place the mat board, pencil marks up, over the cardboard. Holding the metal rule firmly in place, score the first line with your knife. Always place the metal rule so that your blade is away from the frame. (See Figure T–24.) In case you make an error you will cut into the window hole or the extra mat that is not used for the frame. Do not try to cut through the board with one stroke. By the third or fourth stroke, you should be able to cut through the board easily.
6. Working in the same fashion, score and cut through the board along all the window lines. Be careful not to go beyond the lines. Remove the window.
7. Cut a cardboard backing for your art work that is slightly smaller than the overall size of your mat. Using a piece of broad masking tape, hinge the back of the mat to the backing. (See Figure T–25.)

▲ Figure T–25

SAFETY TIP

Art Safety Precautions   The need to direct time and effort to safeguarding the health of students in the art studio cannot be ignored. Art teachers, aware of this responsibility, may feel that assistance is needed. Many instructors have turned to the Arts, Crafts, and Theater Safety (ACTS) group for this assistance. ACTS is an international clearinghouse for research and information on health hazards in the arts. It publishes a newsletter which covers a range of topics including new hazards, precautions, government regulations, lawsuits, and a calendar of events. Interested teachers can write to the following address: Arts, Crafts, and Theater Safety (ACTS)
181 Thompson St., #23
New York, New York 10012-2586

Position your art work between the backing and the mat and attach it with tape. Anchor the frame to the cardboard with a few pieces of rolled tape.

24. Mounting a Two-Dimensional Work

Mounting pictures that you make gives them a professional look. To mount a work, do the following:

1. Gather the materials you will need. These include a yardstick, a pencil, poster board, a sheet of heavy cardboard, a knife with a very sharp blade, a sheet of newspaper, and rubber cement.
2. Measure the height and width of the work to be mounted. Decide how large a border you want around the work. Plan your mount size using the work's measurements. To end up with a 3-inch (8 cm) border, for example, make your mount 6 inches (15 cm) wider and higher than your work. Record the measurements for your mount.
3. Using your yardstick and pencil, lightly draw your mount rectangle on the back of the poster board. Measure from the edges of the poster board. If you have a large paper cutter available, you may use it to cut your mount.
4. Place the sheet of heavy cardboard on your work surface. Place the poster board, pencil marks up, over the cardboard. Holding the yardstick firmly in place along one line, score the line with your knife. Do not try to cut through the board with one stroke. By the third try, you should be able to cut through the board.

▲ Figure T–26

▲ Figure T–27

5. Place the art work on the mount. Using the yardstick, center the work. Mark each corner with a dot. (See Figure T–26.)
6. Place the art work, face down, on a sheet of newspaper. Coat the back of the work with rubber cement. (*Safety Note:* Always use rubber cement in a room with plenty of ventilation.) *If your mount is to be permanent, skip to Step 8.*
7. Line up the corners of your work with the dots on the mounting board. Smooth the work into place. *Skip to Step 9.*
8. After coating the back of your art work, coat the poster board with rubber cement. Be careful not to add cement to the border area. Have a partner hold your art work in the air by the two top corners. Once the two glued surfaces meet, you will not be able to change the position of the work. Grasp the lower two corners. Carefully lower the work to the mounting board. Line up the two corners with the bottom dots. Little by little, lower the work into place (Figure T–27). Press it smooth.

9. To remove any excess cement, create a small ball of nearly dry rubber cement. Use the ball of rubber cement to pick up excess cement.

25. Making Rubbings

Rubbings make interesting textures and designs. They may also be used with other media to create mixed-media art. To make a rubbing, place a sheet of thin paper on top of the surface to be rubbed. Hold the paper in place with one hand. With the other hand, rub the paper with the flat side of an unwrapped crayon. Always rub away from the hand holding the paper. Never rub back and forth, since this may cause the paper to slip.

26. Scoring Paper

The secret to creating neat, sharp folds in cardboard or paper is a technique called scoring. Here is how it is done:

1. Line up a ruler along the line you want to fold.
2. Lightly run a sharp knife or scissors along the fold line. Press down firmly enough to leave a light crease. Take care not to cut all the way through the paper (Figure T–28).

SAFETY TIP

Cleanup Routines   Remind students to clean up thoroughly and often. They should make certain to clean up spills immediately to prevent accidents. If dust results, have them use a wet mop or vacuum rather than a broom. Sweeping stirs up dust that could prove harmful to some students, particularly those who are asthmatic.

▲ **Figure T–28**

3. Gently crease the paper along the line you made. To score curved lines, use the same technique. Make sure your curves are wide enough to ensure a clean fold. Too tight a curve will cause the paper to wrinkle (Figure T–29).

▲ **Figure T–29**

27. Making a Tissue Paper Collage

For your first experience with tissue, make a free design with the tissue colors. Start with the lightest colors of tissue first and save the darkest for last. It is difficult to change the color of dark tissue by overlapping it with other colors. If one area becomes too dark, you might cut out a piece of white paper, glue it over the dark area carefully, and apply new colors over the white area.

1. Apply a coat of adhesive to the area where you wish to place the tissue.
2. Place the tissue down carefully over the wet area (Figure T–30). Don't let your fingers get wet.
3. Then add another coat of adhesive over the tissue. If your brush picks up any color from the wet tissue, rinse your brush in water and let it dry before using it again.
4. Experiment by overlapping colors. Allow the tissue to wrinkle to create textures as you apply it. Be sure that all the loose edges of tissue are glued down.

▲ **Figure T–30**

28. Working with Glue

When applying glue, always start at the center of the surface you are coating and work outward.

• When gluing papers together don't use a lot of glue, just a dot will do. Use dots in the corners and along the edges. Press the two surfaces together. Keep dots at least ½ inch (1.3 cm) in from the edge of your paper.
• Handle a glued surface carefully with only your fingertips. Make sure your hands are clean before pressing the glued surface into place.
• *Note:* The glue should be as thin as possible. Thick or beaded glue will create ridges on your work.

Using Spray Fixatives To protect drawings you can spray them with fixative to keep them from smearing. Spray fixative is sold both in aerosol cans and in small bottles with atomizers. Test the spray first on a piece of scrap paper marked with the same drawing medium used in the drawing. Avoid getting the spray device too close to the drawing. Hold the spray device 12 to 18 inches (30 to 46 cm) from it. Keep the sprayer moving. Several light coats are better than one heavy one. Fixative dries rapidly. Spray fixative labeled *workable* is best. This term means that after you spray an area of a drawing lightly, you can still draw on it. Always use spray fixatives outside the studio in a well-ventilated area—outdoors, if possible. Breathing the fixative over a long period of time can be lethal.

Using the Artist Profiles

Role playing, games, and bulletin boards can be effective ways to involve students and to help them grasp information about the various artists, the time in which the artists lived, their particular art style and techniques, and their contributions to the world of art. On the following pages are teaching strategies designed to help you introduce, reinforce, and teach students about artists and their works.

▲ Artists, down through the ages, have helped us visualize what we learn about history. Art historians are responsible for much of what we know about the artists who have lived in the past.

Paul Cézanne

1839–1906
French Painter

The Card Player
page **19**

Mont Sainte-Victoire
page **226**

In 1839 the art of photography was born in France. Another French birth the same year — that of Paul Cézanne — would lead to equally important developments in the future of pictures.

Cézanne was born in the town of Aix (**ex**) in southern France. At the age of 22 he journeyed to Paris to study with the Romantics. He soon learned of other styles of painting that held even greater appeal for him.

By the end of the 1870s Cézanne began experimenting with an art style all his own. He returned to the south of France to perfect it. His goal, as he described it, was "to make of Impressionism something solid and permanent, like the art of the museums."

A loner, Cézanne struck the people of his little town as a strange figure. Who, they wondered, was this man who spent his days alone in the fields, making paintings no one bought? It was while out in the fields one rainy day during his sixty-seventh year that Cézanne developed a bad cough. A few days later he died of pneumonia.

Cézanne's one-of-a-kind use of color patches to create solid forms is showcased in *Mont Sainte-Victoire* (page **226**). This is one of over 60 views of a favorite subject the artist painted.

The widespread availability in the early 1300s of a product called paper ushered in a new era in writing. A new era in painting came about during this same period. The person responsible for this second development was a gifted Italian artist named Giotto di Bondone (**jah**-toh dee-bahn-**dohn**-ee).

Giotto's lifelong calling as an artist was clear from the time he was 10. The son of a shepherd, he liked to pass the time drawing on flat stones in the fields. According to a popular story, one day a famous artist named Cimabue (chee-muh-**boo**-ay) came across young Giotto at work. Amazed at the boy's skill, Cimabue took him into his studio. Soon Giotto's skill as a painter was recognized throughout Italy.

In the early 1300s Giotto was asked to paint a series of frescoes on the walls of a church in Padua, Italy. One of these, *The Flight into Egypt*, is shown on page **154**. Like other religious paintings of the day, Giotto's works focused on familiar stories from the Bible. Unlike anything ever done before, however, Giotto's paintings were peopled with flesh-and-blood figures. These figures moved about in what appeared to be real space. They also exhibited feelings and emotions with their facial expressions and gestures. Painting had taken a giant step forward.

So great was Giotto's contribution that when he died, a statue was created in his honor. On its base were the words "I am Giotto, that is all. The name alone is a victory poem."

Giotto (di Bondone)

1266–1337
Italian Painter

The Flight into Egypt
page **154**

■ Visual Presentation

Divide the class into groups of two or three and assign different time periods to each group. Have each group research that period and report on it to the class. Encourage students to use as many visual aids as they can, and to use the school media center and local library. Suggest that they use large prints of art works if they are available; the library is a good source of either prints or oversize art books. The media center might have equipment with which the students can make slides from books to use in the report. Slides ensure that everyone in the class can see the works being discussed. Dressing up in costumes, role playing, or presenting a dramatization can also make a report more enjoyable and meaningful for everyone.

■ Dramatization

A good choice for a dramatization is one event from the artist's life. Dramatizations make stronger impressions than straight reports. For example, a debate on style between the Impressionists and Post-Impressionists would be interesting, especially if students took on the roles of real characters, such as Monet, Renoir, Cézanne, or van Gogh.

Artist Profiles **289**

┌ *more about* • • • ┐

Paul Cézanne By creating multiple variations of a landscape instead of rendering a single perspective, Paul Cézanne asserts that nature—and all objects—may be seen from a number of views. Even within each individual image, such as his *Mont Sainte-Victoire*, Cézanne provokes his viewers into creating their own perspectives by providing details that suggest qualities rather than illustrate them. The rolling quality of the mountain is instilled by the same brush strokes that delineate houses and yield bushes. Depth and texture are implied rather than depicted. For example, when Cézanne uses bright and unshaded colors to paint an apple, the viewer singles out the distant fruit regardless of its relative placement in the work's composition.

■ Puzzles

Turn some extra prints found in magazines into puzzles. Dry mount the print on a strong backing, such as poster board or mat board. If you are going to make more than one puzzle, put each on a different color backing so that if the pieces get mixed up, they can be separated by color. Laminate the work, if possible, to protect the surface. Then, using a sharp cutting blade, cut the print into puzzle pieces. Try to keep the puzzle pieces large to help students become familiar with the art work. Use a separate storage container for each puzzle.

Puzzles can help slower learners, or you can use them to hold a puzzle speed competition. Teams of students can compete to see which team can assemble a puzzle the fastest.

Francisco Goya

1746–1828
Spanish Painter

Cornered (From the Disasters of War)
page 187

The early 1800s found the world on the move. The invention of the steamboat was followed quickly by the building of the first railroad. The art world, too, was on the move — into a realm of self-expression where it has stayed to this day. The artist most identified with this move is a free spirit named Francisco Goya (fran-**sis**-koh **goy**-uh).

Goya was born in Saragossa (sar-uh-**goh**-suh), Spain. As a young man he traveled to Italy. He was not impressed by the Renaissance masterpieces and returned home. There he went to work as a portrait painter. His works flattered the members of the Spanish ruling class, who were his subjects. In 1786 he was named personal painter to King Charles IV.

An illness four years later left the artist deaf. Far from plunging him into despair, his handicap seemed to fuel his imagination. When war broke out in 1808, the artist created a series of prints unlike anything done before. Goya's view of war has no heroes or acts of glory. Like *Cornered* (page **187**), the prints in this series speak, rather, of senseless waste and brutality.

As Goya grew older, his view of the world grew grimmer still. His later works drew more and more on his own inner dreams and visions.

By the mid-1890s the United States had entered the age of communication. The newly invented telephone and wireless telegraph made it possible for people to communicate with one another over great distances. Not all people benefited from these inventions, however. To Native Americans tucked away in the New Mexico wilderness, time had stood still. It was in that quiet place at this not-so-quiet time that an artist named Lucy Lewis was born.

Lucy Lewis was raised in a pueblo in the town of Acoma (uh-**coh**-muh). She learned early of the importance of pottery to her people. As a child, Lewis watched her aunt make wide-mouthed pots called *ollas* (**oy**-uhs). She was taught where to dig for the best clay and how to mix the clay with water. As she grew, she began to experiment with different natural pigments. The pots she designed and crafted were unusually lightweight and handsome.

In time, people in the pueblo became aware that Lucy Lewis had a special gift. They encouraged her to enter craft fairs and shows. She followed their advice — and came away with many awards.

Today Lewis still lives in the Acoma area with her family. There she and her daughters teach others the fine craft of pottery.

Lucy Lewis

1897–
Native American Craftsperson

Polychrome Pots
page 201

more about • • •

Francisco Goya   While Francisco Goya demonstrates his insightful mind and deft talent in paintings such as the compassionate *Third of May, 1808* and the sarcastic *The Family of Charles IV*, he created what might be his most unique works in etching. In his *Caprices*, finished in 1799, Goya made succinct points about the foolishness of humankind. Inspired by experiences with corrupt politicians and war, the mature Goya later returned to the black and white medium to further criticize the stupidity of humankind in *The Disasters of War* and *The Proverbs*. Focusing on the vileness of warfare, Goya spares no one. He castigates soldiers in "Why?" and "That Is Wrong" but reveals the peasants—whom he celebrates in *Third of May, 1808*—to be as barbaric as warriors.

Judith Leyster

1609–1660
Dutch Painter

Self-Portrait
page 181

The late 1800s were a time of great discovery. In Germany a scientist named Roentgen (**rent**-guhn) discovered X-rays. In France a husband and wife named Curie (**kyu**-ree) discovered the element radium. Another discovery in France at the time had important consequences for the art world. It was the discovery of a signature on a painting long thought to be by the great Dutch artist Franz Hals. The surprising signature read "Judith Leyster" (**ly**-stuhr), not Franz Hals.

This "mystery" artist had been born some 250 years earlier in the Dutch city of Haarlem (**har**-luhm). At a time when women seeking art careers were often helped by artist fathers, Leyster—a brewer's daughter—had to rely on talent alone. Another difference between her and other female painters was her choice of subject matter. Instead of delicate still lifes, Leyster did robust genre paintings and portraits. One of these, her now-famous *Self-Portrait*, appears on page **181**. By 17 she had gained a reputation as an artist of great promise.

Leyster learned—and learned well—from other major painters of her day. Most notable among these are Hals, for his brush technique, and Caravaggio (see page **179**), for his use of light. Still, her works have a look that on careful inspection is unmistakably hers. Her portraits, especially, seem to invite the viewer in as if subject and viewer were close friends.

The voyages in the late 1400s of Christopher Columbus and Vasco da Gama broadened the world's horizons. So did the birth during that period of possibly the greatest artist the world has ever known. His name was Michelangelo Buonarroti (my-kuh-**lan**-juh-loh bwohn-uh-**rah**-tee).

Michelangelo was born in Florence to a poor family. At the age of six he was sent to live with the family of a stonecutter. There he came to love the feel of a sculptor's chisel and hammer in his hands. Art had found its way into his life.

Over the next 10 years Michelangelo's genius was given shape and direction through study with Florence's foremost artists. By the time he was 24, he had completed his first masterpiece, the *Pietà* (page **165**).

Despite his great talents, Michelangelo was hampered by some very human shortcomings. One was a hot temper, which made him hard to work with. Another was a need to see every project he took on in larger-than-life terms. Because of this second weakness, many of his works were never finished. One that was completed—and one of his most famous achievements—was his magnificent painting of the ceiling of the Sistine Chapel in Rome. The heroic job took four years to complete. During that time Michelangelo worked flat on his back on a platform he had built 68 feet (20 m) above the chapel floor!

Michelangelo (Buonarroti)

1475–1564
Italian Sculptor, Painter

Pietà
page 165

■ Card Games

Use prints in card games to help students become familiar with the names of artists and the titles of the works. To make a card game, mount medium-size prints on poster board, leaving a small margin around the print. Cut the print in fourths. Print the name of the artist and the title in the margin of each section of the print. Laminate the sections to make them last longer.

Using about 10 prints (40 sections), create a deck of cards with which the students can play a variation of the card game, "Go Fish." The students must ask for the cards by artist and/or title. If you have many works by one artist, they must always use titles, but if you only have one print from each artist, they may use just artist. The students should request the work by saying, "Do you have any Picasso?" After a player has collected all four sections of a print, that print must be placed on the table for all to see. This exposes all players and observers to the print. The more times the students hear the names repeated, the more they learn. Use artists and works that you think are worth learning about.

✦ more about • • •

Michelangelo Although Plato himself distrusted artists (and poets) discrediting them as irrational and subversive to reason, the works of Michelangelo have been rightfully described as Platonic. Always concerning himself with "formal" and "ideal" notions, Michelangelo shared unlikely perspectives with the art-loathing philosopher. As Plato attempted to associate language, ideas, and forms, Michelangelo attempted to capture the ideal form of his subjects with sculpture. He viewed sculpting as a discovery process. Instead of trying to create a form by shaping stone, Michelangelo removed excess stone to reveal an existing essence that represented both truth and beauty.

Time-Period Recognition Game

If you can find individual prints that are small enough, you might organize them into a time-period recognition game. For example, you might set up one deck with four Ancient Egyptian works, four Gothic, four Renaissance, four African-American, four Near East, and so forth. At the beginning of the year you can use stick-on labels that identify the periods. Later you can remove the labels. Be careful that each set of four in a deck is distinctly different from every other set in that deck.

Time-Style Recognition Game

For a more advanced game than the one above, organize the cards by style. In this deck you might include four Impressionist works, four Cubist works, four Surrealist works, and so forth. Again, be careful not to use two styles that might be confused, such as American Regionalist and English Landscape.

Joan Miró
1893–1983
Spanish Painter

Femme (Woman)
page 27

Dutch Interior
page 259

The year was 1925. The world had scarcely recovered from "the war to end all wars" when it was shaken again. This time the explosion took place within the art world of Paris. It was caused by paintings like *Dutch Interior* (page **259**), created by a shy little Spanish artist named Joan Miró (zhoo-**ahn** meer-**roh**).

Miró was born in a town outside of Barcelona (bahr-suh-**loh**-nuh), Spain. As an art student, he was made to draw objects by "feeling" them rather than looking at them. For someone more fascinated by the world within than the one outside, the exercise was perfect training.

In 1919 Miró traveled to Paris, the capital of the art world. There he fell upon hard times. He was forced to get by on one meal a week. In between he ate dried figs to keep up his strength. It may have been the visions brought about by hunger that led to his first important Surrealist pictures.

After his first showing, Miró was hailed as a major new talent. He went to live on the island of Majorca (muh-**yor**-kuh), off the coast of Spain. There he painted in a room so small he had trouble moving around in it.

Later in his long career Miró broadened his interests to include sculpture. He also created huge weavings that, like *Femme* (page **27**), mirror the colorful designs of his paintings.

After the Brooklyn Bridge opened in the late 1800s, bridge building would never be the same. After a showing of paintings in Paris during this same period, art would never be the same. The showing was by a group of artists who had been turned down by the Salon. Their style, which became known as Impressionism, took its name from a work by one of the group's founders. The artist's name was Claude Monet (**klohd** moh-**nay**).

Monet was born in Paris in 1840. His father, a grocer, moved the family to the port city of Le Havre (luh **hahv**-ruh) soon after his son's birth. Even as a child, Monet saw something magical in sunlight's effects on water. He studied with a noted landscape artist, who taught him the basics of Realist painting.

It was while a student that Monet met two other young artists, Pierre Auguste Renoir (oh-**guste** ren-**wahr**) and Alfred Sisley. The three soon became friends. They also began experimenting together, making paintings outdoors in natural sunlight. At first their works were laughed at by critics. Today the works of these three artists are among the most admired in the history of art.

During a stay along the river front Monet painted *Bridge at Argenteuil* (page **220**). Like his other mature works, this work contains no solid lines or forms. Rather, these elements are hinted at through dabs and dots of color.

Claude Monet
1840–1926
French Painter

Banks of the Seine, Vetheuil
page 216

Bridge at Argenteuil
page 220

— *more about* • • • —

Joan Miró As one of the first successful Surrealist painters, Miró has had a profound impact on the art community, lending his talents to painting, sculpting, and mural making. Miró transformed his subjects into organic shapes to create symbolic images. The meaning of Miró's *The Harlequin's Carnival* is complex. While the actual objects in the composition are mostly unrecognizable, the mood is undeniably buoyant. The painting is divided into symbolic black and white halves. Still, the viewer's eye is lifted upward by unrestrained vertical movement. An open window and floating objects reinforce the sense of freedom, while various eyes, ears, and mouths add a sensuous element.

Berthe Morisot
1841–1895
French Painter

*Jeune Fille au Chien
(Young Girl with her Dog)*
page 218

The last decade of the 1800s was a time of change. In 1896 Thomas Edison burst on the scene with the invention of the motion picture. A year earlier the art world mourned the passing of a maker of pictures of a different sort. The artist's name was Berthe Morisot (**behrt maw-re-zoh**).

Berthe Morisot was born into an art family. Her parents were art lovers and Jean-Honoré Fragonard (**zhahnh** oh-nor-**ay** frah-goh-**nahrh**), an important painter of the 1700s, may have been her great-grandfather. From the time she was a young girl, she knew she would become a painter. At 15 she met and became good friends with Edouard Manet (ay-doo-**ahrh** mah-**nay**), a leading artist of the day. Several years later she married Manet's brother.

Like Manet, Morisot focused on indoor scenes and portraits. Her portrait titled *Jeune Fille au Chien* (page **218**) is one of her best-known art works.

Although other artists praised her work, during her lifetime Morisot was ignored by critics. Many did so merely because she was a woman. It was not until her death that her work began receiving the respect it had always deserved.

In 1905 Albert Einstein published his theory of relativity. In so doing, he challenged age-old beliefs about the meaning of time and space. In that same year a young girl moved with her family from Russia to America. She would grow up to create art that would challenge age-old beliefs about the meaning of sculpture. Her name was Louise Nevelson (**nev**-uhl-suhn).

As a child in Maine, Nevelson spent long hours playing in her father's lumberyard. She loved to carve and build using the scraps of wood she found.

At the age of 20 Louise married and two years later gave birth to a child. In time, she came to resent the responsibilities of marriage and motherhood that took time away from her art. In 1931 she left her son with her parents and headed to Europe to study art.

Nevelson's first showing came in 1941. The reviews, which were favorable, spurred her on. In the decades that followed, she began more and more to experiment with "found" media. It was not uncommon to find her studio littered with wood scraps very much like the ones she had played with in her father's lumberyard. Most of Nevelson's works from the 1960s on are, like *Mrs. N's Palace* (page **267**), three-dimensional collages. Most invite viewers to use their imaginations as well as their eyes.

Louise Nevelson
1900–1988
American Sculptor

Mrs. N's Palace
page 267

■ Bulletin Boards

Divide the class into groups and have each group choose one of the artists from the Artist Profiles, Handbook pages 289–295. Set aside one small bulletin board as an "Artist of the Week" board and assign each group the responsibility of featuring their artist for one week. Set up some guidelines for the student displays and share these with the class. Some criteria for the display could be:

- catchy title and neat lettering
- quantity and accuracy of information
- creativity and aesthetic quality.

The minimum information would include artist's name, country, dates of birth and death, style, and titles of works displayed, example of artist's works, information about the artist, and portrayal of the artist's style or of the time and place in which the artist lived. Grade the display according to the guidelines established.

Artist Profiles **293**

more about • • •

Louise Nevelson While it may at first seem nonsensical, assemblage sculpture is a natural medium for affecting an audience. Using common objects that have not been designed for artistic purposes, the artist effectively bridges the gap between the viewer's world and the artistic world. When the viewer sees an everyday object in the context of art, he or she is forced to consider its place in the work and in society.

Louise Nevelson is known for her use of household items and pieces of old Victorian houses. Painting them and arranging them in boxes or other frames, Nevelson questions notions about homes, tradition, and antiquity. She has complemented her works with the experimental use of such visual components as aluminum and clear plastic.

Maps

Have world maps and globes available to help students locate cities and countries where the artists lived and worked. This helps students visualize the geographical features that influenced the artists' work.

Time Line

Display a time line in the class. Have students attach sketches of the masterpieces shown in the text in the proper spot on the time line. They might even add small prints of works that are not in the text or photocopy works from books, color the photocopies, and add the name of the artist and the title of the work. If there is not enough room for all the pieces at one place in time, strings of yarn can be attached to the photocopy and pictures arranged above or below the proper place with yarn leading to the proper place on the time line.

Albert Pinkham Ryder

1847–1917
American Painter

Moonlight Marine (Toilers of the Sea)
page **234**

The first two decades of the twentieth century were a politically stormy time. The winds of revolution swept through Russia and China. In 1914 the world went to war. To take their minds off gloomy events of the day, some people turned inward. One who did—and came back to the world with a rare gift of art—was Albert Pinkham Ryder.

Ryder was born in New Bedford, Massachusetts. When he was a young man, his family moved to New York City. There an older brother helped pay his way through art school. Showing little interest in the works of other artists, Ryder forged his own one-of-a-kind style. Among the features of his style were paint layers so thick that his pictures sometimes looked three-dimensional.

Always given to strange personal habits, Ryder developed still odder ways during his middle years. He gave up his Greenwich Village apartment and moved into a run-down rooming house. Burdened by poor eyesight, he spent his days indoors, his nights roaming the streets alone. After 1900 he became a hermit altogether.

It may have been during his silent night walks that Ryder dreamed up ideas for his pictures. Most, like *Moonlight Marine* (page **234**), are glimpses of a dream world, which capture the viewer's imagination.

In 1921 a bitterly fought revolution in Mexico ended. Honest, hard-working people, long treated as slaves by rich landlords, were free at last. In that same year a talented Mexican artist returned from abroad. He began the first of many larger-than-life chronicles of the struggle for freedom. His name was Diego Rivera (dee-**ay**-goh rih-**vehr**-uh).

Rivera was born in the city of Guanajuato (gwahn-uh-**waht**-oh). As a young man, he journeyed to Paris, where he met Picasso and Matisse. While in Europe he also studied the art of the great Italian fresco painters. The size of the frescoes—some covered entire walls—appealed to him. Such an art form, he felt, would be a fitting tribute to those who had fought so bravely in the Mexican Revolution. It would also be a reminder to Mexico's rich of the power of the people.

Murals like *The Liberation of the Peon* (page **251**) reveal Rivera's skill as a storyteller. They also reveal the influences of both Giotto and Rivera's pre-Columbian ancestors.

After making a name for himself, Rivera was asked to paint murals in the United States. He created works that, like those in Mexico, were filled with people and action. These illustrated the American fascination with speed and the machine. Unfortunately, many of these magnificant murals were destroyed.

Diego Rivera

1886–1957
Mexican Painter

The Liberation of the Peon
page **251**

294 *Artist Profiles*

more about • • •

Diego Rivera Although Diego Rivera had dabbled in the early Cubist movement, today he is best known for his accomplishments in mural making. Commissioned by the government of Mexico shortly after a revolution in the 1920s, Rivera began a series of national murals. In an effort to stir national pride, he borrowed from the style indigenous to Mexico before its colonization and conveyed the spirit of the new revolution. Combining his aesthetic ideals with social goals, Rivera's art is aimed not only at the art community, but at Mexico as a whole. When Rivera's socially-inspired art earned him wide recognition, he refused to compromise his beliefs.

Alfred Stieglitz
1864–1946
American Photographer

The Terminal
page 249

Around 1900 the United States opened its doors to Americans-to-be from all nations. To young Abstract painters hoping to enter the art world of the day, the door was firmly shut. Abstract painting was misunderstood and unappreciated by the public and most art critics. One free thinker who provided an outlet for these brave new talents was himself an artist. He was photographer Alfred Stieglitz (**steeg-luhts**).

Stieglitz was born in Hoboken, New Jersey. His interest in photography began when he was young. Early in his career he began seeing photography's potential as an art medium. He spent long hours—sometimes in swirling snow—waiting for just the right shot.

In 1902 he formed Photo-Secession, an organization devoted to the art of photography. Three years later he opened a gallery at 291 Fifth Avenue in New York City. Known as 291, the gallery became a haven for struggling young artists from all areas of art. One artist whose work was displayed at 291 was a native of Wisconsin named Georgia O'Keeffe. Stieglitz and O'Keeffe developed a friendship that grew over time. Despite an age difference of 23 years, the two were married in 1924.

Stieglitz spent his life championing the world of other photographers. Still, his own photographs are among the most sensitive ever taken. Through instant human studies, like *The Terminal* (page **249**), he carried photography to new heights.

Name That Artist
Place in a brown paper bag the names of each of the artists who appear in the Artist Profiles. Pass the bag around the room and have each student blindly select one of the cards within. Have the student list one characteristic that is associated with the artist. For example, if the artist Picasso is picked, the student may say Cubism or Spanish-born. The name is put back into the bag and shaken for the next student to select an artist name. If the student is able to successfully identify a characteristic that has not already been mentioned about the artist, he or she stays in the game. If not, the player sits on the sidelines until a new game begins.

In 1875 Congress passed an act giving African Americans the right to serve on juries. Eight years later the Supreme Court declared the act unconstitutional. It was not long after that decision that artist Henry Tanner made a decision of his own. Tanner, an African American artist having little success selling paintings in America, decided to set sail for Europe.

Tanner had been born 32 years earlier in Philadelphia, Pennsylvania. His father was a minister, who later became a bishop. Tanner's interest in art began when he was only 12. Walking through a park with his father, he saw a landscape painter at work. Tanner watched in fascination. As his fascination grew, so did his desire to become a painter.

Tanner entered the Pennsylvania Academy of Fine Arts, where his teacher was Thomas Eakins. Eakins advised his student to turn from landscapes to genre scenes—which Tanner did. But Tanner found there was little market for paintings of any kind by an African American. Wanting, in any case, to focus on Biblical subjects, he headed for Paris. Within five years one of his Biblical pictures was hanging in a place of honor at the Paris Salon.

While Tanner painted mostly religious works, he still found time now and then to exhibit his skills at painting landscapes. *The Seine* (page **236**) is one of these works.

Henry O. Tanner
1859–1937
American Painter

The Seine
page 236

Artist Profiles **295**

more about • • •

Alfred Stieglitz Alfred Stieglitz was a leader in establishing photography as a fine art. He was trained in photographic technology in Berlin, where he first established himself as a photographer of technical excellence and penetrating insight. Stieglitz returned to the United States and continued his work as a photographer and as a promoter of other visual artists, both photographers and painters. He published a magazine, *Camera Work*, largely as a vehicle for promoting photography as art. He also helped other American photographers by exhibiting their work in his galleries. Among Stieglitz's most famous works are his series of portraits of painter Georgia O'Keeffe, to whom he was married, and his cloud studies, which he titled *Equiivalents*.

Try the following teaching strategies to introduce students to the many art-related job opportunities and careers. At the bottom of the pages are addresses of organizations that students can write to for additional career information.

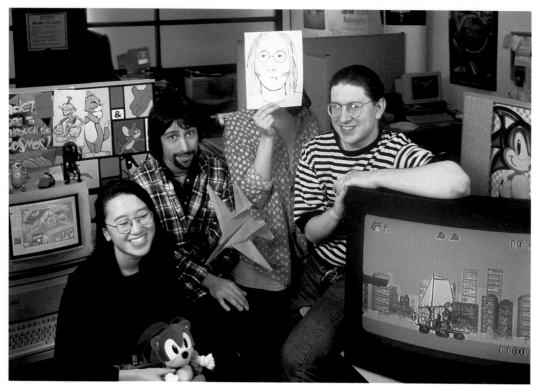

▲ There are many career opportunities in art and art-related fields.

296

RESOURCES BEYOND THE CLASSROOM

Guest Speakers Bring in resource people during the time that you are presenting careers to make the material more meaningful to students. Students will be interested in learning from people who work directly in the art-related field. You may also invite the guidance counselor to discuss art-related careers and to talk about the various schools and colleges that specialize in art-related careers. If you live in an urban area, it will not be difficult to find people who work at some of these careers. Even the smallest newspaper in a rural area needs a layout person. The local television station will also employ someone who fits one of the career categories mentioned in this section. Consider florists or window display people who can demonstrate how the elements and principles of art are used in their jobs.

Art Director

You may know that movies are the work of hundreds of people. You may also know there is one person in charge of all others, called the director. But did you know that advertisements, books, and magazines also have directors?

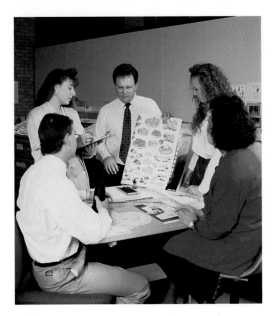

Art directors are experienced artists whose job is to lead or supervise other artists. Like film directors, art directors are responsible for seeing that all other jobs in a project are done.

Art directors are hired by advertising agencies, book publishers, and television or radio stations. The specific tasks of the job may differ slightly from place to place. In general, the art director hires and oversees the work of illustrators, photographers, and graphic designers. Together, the art director and the people who report to him or her are called a team. The art director has the responsibility for signing off, or approving, all work done by team members.

Art Teacher

Many people with an interest in art and a desire to share their knowledge become art teachers.

A career in art teaching requires a college education. Part of that education is devoted to methods of teaching. Part is devoted to developing a broad background in the history of art and the use of art materials and techniques.

Good art teachers open their students to a wide variety of art experiences. They give students the chance to create their own art and to react to the art of others. They also make sure their students learn about such important areas as aesthetics, art criticism, and art history.

While most art teachers work in schools, some find employment opportunities in other areas. Some art teachers work in museums or hospitals. Some teachers work in retirement centers. Still others work in nursery schools and day-care centers.

■ Analyzing Advertisements

Divide students into small groups and explain that art directors supervise advertising campaigns used to market and promote products. Have students select a variety of magazines from different interest areas, such as fashion, mechanics, photography, architecture, teen life, current events, health, sports, science, science fiction, television, and so forth. Have each group compare such things as the types of advertisements and the types of advertising techniques used to capture the attention of the specific audience. Have them present their findings to the class.

■ Art Teacher

Invite a school counselor to speak to the class and explain the requirements (grade point averages and portfolio requirements) for attending art and design schools. Have the counselor explain the additional requirements for becoming an art teacher in your state.

more about • • •

Advertising Careers You may wish to have students write to the following for information about careers in advertising management.

American Advertising Federation
1101 Vermont Ave NW
Washington, D.C. 20005-3521

Teachers' Associations Have students contact the following organizations to learn more about teachers' unions and education-related issues:

American Federation of Teachers
555 New Jersey Avenue, NW
Washington, D.C. 20001

■ Editorial Cartoonist

Distribute magazines which have a variety of editorial cartoons. Have students select their favorite cartoon and pair up with another student who selected the same cartoon. Direct students to analyze the style, content, and technique that the artist uses in order to get the message across. Have students present their findings to the class and, if possible, provide background information about the artist who produces the editorial cartoon.

■ Animation Research

If a group cannot decide on a "favorite" cartoon, you may want them to research the field of animation at the library, or have them find out how to make a flip book, make one, and show it to the class.

Computer Graphics Specialist

What do computers have to do with art? To the person known as a computer graphics specialist, the answer is "everything!"

Computer graphics specialists are skilled professionals who use state-of-the-art electronic equipment to create designs. The work they do has brought the world of commercial art into the space age. A career in this field combines a strong background in design with a knowledge of computers.

The computer graphics specialist works with tools such as electric light pens on electronic tablets. With these tools, any image may be drawn and colored in. Such computer drawings may be stored permanently in the computer's memory. They can then be called up and reworked by the designer as needed.

Some computer graphics specialists work with systems that allow them to see their finished work in different sizes and colors. Computer-made designs can also be sent along telephone lines around the world.

Editorial Cartoonist

Newspaper editorials are written accounts that invite readers to form an opinion about important news topics. Editorial cartoons do the same work in pictures.

Editorial cartoonists, the people who create such pictures, work for newspapers and magazines. Their creations usually appear as single drawings without titles or captions. Sometimes editorial cartoons go hand-in-hand with the main editorial, which is printed nearby. At other times they comment on other issues figuring in current events.

Many editorial cartoonists use a style of art called *caricature* (**kar**-ih-kuh-chur). This is the exaggerating of facial features or expressions to poke fun at well-known figures. Some editorial cartoonists use symbols to communicate their meanings. What familiar figures are used to symbolize the two political parties in the United States?

298   *Career Spotlights*

― *more about* • • •

Computer Graphics Careers Students may wish to write for more information on education and career resources in the field of computer graphics, art, and design. Have them contact the Special Interest Group on Computer Graphics (SIGGRAPH) at:

ACM SIGGRAPH
1515 Broadway, 17th floor
New York, New York 10012

Exhibit and Display Designer

The next time you pass a display of clothing or other goods in a department store, look carefully. Somewhere within that display will be a hidden message: artist at work.

Exhibit and display designers work in a number of retail and non-profit settings. Some of these settings are trade shows, department stores, showrooms, art galleries, and museums. Such designers plan presentations of collections, exhibits, and traveling shows of all kinds. They are responsible for such matters as deciding what items should be grouped together. They also take into account how displays should be arranged and lighted.

The display designer is an important part of the sales team. Displays attract customers. They can affect a customer's decision to buy. The way the display designer does his or her job can make all the difference between whether or not a sale is made.

Graphic Designer

There are artists all around us. They are there behind every billboard, street sign, and soup can label. These artists are called graphic designers. They use pictures and words to inform or decorate.

Graphic designers work in a great many areas. Each area has its own special tasks and title. Technical illustrator is one of these titles. Sign maker is another.

The field of graphic design has its roots in the 1500s. It was in that century that the printing press was invented. People were needed to arrange words and pictures on the printed page. To this day that task, known as layout, is a job of graphic designers. Graphic designers also pick type faces, or styles of lettering, for printed material. They must also decide how drawings or photographs will be used as illustrations.

■ Display Designer

Divide students into small groups and assign them to create either a window display, point-of-purchase display, or exhibit display. Have them select a product of their choice and create a three-dimensional display. Set up criteria for evaluating the display such as: neatness, product identity, eye-catching, informative, and so forth. Set up a panel of students to judge the displays.

■ Graphic Designer

Invite a graphic designer to visit and speak to your students. If you cannot find a commercial artist, a local art hobbyist or craftsperson may substitute, as well as a college art student who may be home on vacation. If there is a local artist in your area, a field trip to this person's studio can be exciting.

Career Spotlights **299**

⌐ *more about* • • • ┐

Art and Design For a list of accredited schools of art and design, contact:

National Association of Schools of Art and Design
11250 Roger Bacon Drive, Suite 21
Reston, Virginia 22090

Industrial Designer

What do toys, vacuum cleaners, and cars have in common? All are designed to work easily and have a pleasing look. These and countless other items you see and use each day are the work of industrial designers.

Industrial designers work for makers of products. These artists work closely with engineers who develop the products. Sometimes industrial designers are asked to work on things as simple as tamper-proof caps for medicines. At other times they are asked to work on projects as complicated as space vehicles. Before they begin work, industrial designers need to know how the product is to be used.

Because different brands of the same product are sold, industrial design sometimes crosses over into advertising. The appearance of a design becomes especially important in the case of very competitive products such as cars and entertainment systems, for example.

Interior Designer

Architects give us attractive, functional spaces in which to live, work, and play. Interior designers fill those spaces with attractive and useful furnishings and accessories.

The job of the interior designer is to plan the interior space. This includes choosing furniture, fabrics, floor coverings, lighting fixtures, and decorations. To do this job well, the designer must take into account the wants and needs of the users of the space. In planning a home, for example, the interior designer will learn as much as possible about the lifestyle of the family that lives there.

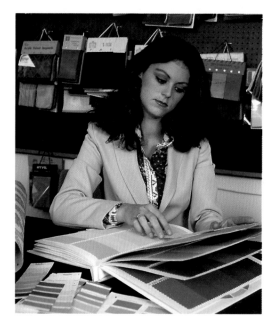

Interior designers help their clients envision their ideas through the use of floor plans, elevations, and sketches—sometimes using special computer software programs. Once a client has agreed to a plan, the designer makes arrangements for buying materials. He or she also oversees the work for builders, carpenters, painters, and other craftspeople.

■ Interior Designer

Divide students into small groups and have each group imagine that they are interior designers who have been asked to plan a student lounge for the school. Before they make their design, they should survey their friends to see what they would like in a lounge. Have them try to think of the lounge as a multipurpose area that could serve as space for a party, a meeting, art exhibits, and so on. What areas will they need to include? Have them make sketches for their lounge and include paint chips, wallpaper and floor covering samples to show the color scheme for the room.

— *more about* • • • —

Designers   For information about careers in interior design, contact:

American Society of Interior Designers
200 Lexington Ave.
New York, New York 10016

A brochure that describes careers in industrial design and lists academic programs in the field is available from the Industrial Designers Society of America. For price and ordering information write:

Industrial Designers Society of America
1142 Walker Road
Great Falls, Virginia 22066-1836

Magazine Designer

Magazine designers are graphic designers who work for publications called *periodicals*. These are booklets or pamphlets that come out on a regular basis in issues.

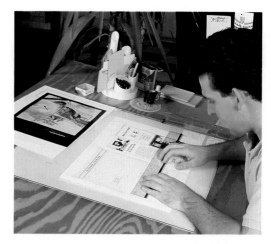

There are two parts to a magazine design — the fixed design and the variable design. The fixed design includes the features of the magazine that seldom change. These include the different type faces and decorative elements such as page borders. The magazine designer works mostly on the variable design. This includes making sure all the pages in an issue are a standard length. Another part of variable design is figuring out where illustrations should go and how large they should be.

At times a magazine designer is called upon to create special features for a periodical. These are used to highlight a theme running throughout the issue.

Medical Illustrator

Among Leonardo da Vinci's many achievements were his drawings of *anatomy* or human body parts. Ever since his time there has been a call for medical illustrators.

Medical illustrators work for medical schools, teaching hospitals, and publishers of medical journals and textbooks. All have a basic knowledge of medicine and an ability to work with many different art media. Among these are transparencies (trans-**pare**-uhn-sees), or illustrations that are placed on overhead projectors.

The work of medical illustrators falls into two main areas. One is the drawing of diagrams showing various details, such as the heart and limbs. The second is doing step-by-step illustrations of surgical and other medical procedures.

At times medical illustrators are called upon to work with such medical equipment as X-ray machines, microscopes, and scanners.

Career Spotlights **301**

■ Field Trips

Field trips contribute greatly to a course. If class field trips are not possible, individual trips which one or more students may take after school or on weekends might be arranged.

All trips will be more successful if guidelines are set up to help students understand the objectives. Research done prior to the trip and a follow-up evaluation will add to the value of the experience. Students should know what to look for and what to expect to gain from the experience. It might be pointed out that the business people they visit may be possible employers and that appropriate conduct and dress on a trip may make a future interview more likely. Students should know what kind of follow-up will be expected. For example, a written evaluation, quiz, or participation in a class discussion might be required.

The instructor should make the necessary arrangements well in advance to ensure the students' welcome. A time schedule should be established and carefully followed. While museums, organizations, and industries are happy to conduct tours of their facilities, the staff members usually have other responsibilities, and group tours must be prearranged.

Field trip possibilities vary in each community. Suggestions for possible field trips: display rooms in furniture stores; model apartments in new apartment buildings; rug and carpet salesrooms; wallpaper stores; interior design studios; decorator showrooms; historic houses and museums; advertising agencies.

more about • • •

Illustrators For information on careers in illustration have students contact:

The Society of Illustrators
128 East 63rd Street
New York, New York 10021-7303

■ Photojournalist

Have students look through local newspapers and notice the credit lines under the photographs. They should note that some have come in over the wires, and they carry labels such as "UPI." Others have been taken locally. Have students note the name of the photographer. Ask: Is there just one photographer working for the paper or can you find many different names on the credit lines? Does one person seem to specialize in one type of photography, such as sports or entertainment?

Museum Curator

Like universities and libraries, museums have the job of preserving and passing on culture. The person in charge of seeing that the museum does its job is called the museum curator (**kyoor**-ayt-uhr).

Curators are part custodian, part scholar, and part historian. The tasks of the curator are many. They include securing, caring for, displaying, and studying works of art. The curator makes sure works are arranged so they teach, inform, and delight.

As holders of advanced college degrees, curators carry on research in their own areas of interest. They report their findings in books, lectures, and journals.

Photojournalist

Photography, as you have learned, was unheard of until the mid-1800s. No sooner had photography emerged on the scene, however, than the field of photojournalism was born. Photojournalism is the taking of pictures for newspapers and magazines.

One of the earliest photojournalists was a photographer named Mathew Brady. Brady lived in America during the Civil War. His early black-and-white snapshots offer dramatic glimpses of life on and off the battlefield.

Since Brady's time the field of photojournalism has grown and with it, the responsibilities of the photographer. Photojournalists are expected to seek out and record newsworthy scenes. They must also be able to take action pictures quickly and process them with equal speed.

Some photojournalists in recent decades have chosen specialties for themselves. Two of these areas are politics and sports.

more about • • •

Museum Curators   For general information about careers as a curator and schools offering courses in curatorial science, contact:

American Association of Museums
1225 I Street NW, Suite 200
Washington, D.C. 20005-3914

Special Effects Designer

Are you the sort of person whose imagination works overtime? Then maybe the field of special effects design is for you.

Unlike people in other art careers, special effects designers may not attend special schools. The field is very new. The people who have created film and television magic to date have come up through the ranks. They may have started by building sets for plays or designing film backgrounds.

Special effects artists are one part painter, one part sculptor, and one part engineer. They have the ability to imagine, and then create, fantasy scenes or creatures. They are masters of make-believe.

There is no limit to the tools used by special effects designers. Depending on the needs of a project, they might use papier-mâché, plaster, plastic molds, or paint. Makeup, trick photography, and computers are just a few of the other media they use.

Urban Planner

Have you ever wondered how big cities come to look the way they do? The two-word answer to this question is urban (or city) planners.

City planners are people whose job is to supervise the care and improvement of a city. Every large American city has a planner.

A main task of city planners is to enforce zoning laws. These are laws controlling what part of a city may be used for what purposes. Thanks to city planners, garbage dumps are not located in residential communities.

A second task of the city planner is to look after the growth and development of the urban areas. The planner works with the mayor and other city officials to create parks, harbors, and shopping malls.

City planners are trained as architects. Their knowledge of design helps them to plan a pleasing cityscape.

■ Urban Planner

Have students work in small groups and imagine that they have been hired as a city planning team to improve their town. If they live in a big city, have them limit the area to their own neighborhood. Ask them to prepare a survey to ask people what they like most and what they like least about the town or neighborhood. They should find out which building is considered the most important and which is considered the most attractive. Ask about traffic flow, stores, recreation, entertainment, health services, police protection, and water and sewerage. They can add other questions to the survey. Then they should carry out the survey. Have them talk to students at their school and adults who live in the area. Have them put all of their findings in graph or chart form. Compare adult and teen replies. Do the two groups agree or disagree on each item?

more about • • •

Urban Planning For additional information on careers in urban and regional planning, have students contact:
American Planning Association
1776 Massachusetts Avenue, NW
Washington, D.C. 20036-1904

LESSON 1

Creating a Computer Quilt Design

Creating a Computer Quilt Design

(pages 304–305)

LESSON TIME: 60 minutes

☑ OBJECTIVES

After completing this lesson, students will be able to use the computer to:

- Combine lines and shapes to make a geometric motif.
- Use repeated motifs to make a quilt design.
- Flip or rotate the motif to vary the designs.

☑ SUPPLIES

- Computer with an art application.
- Mouse or graphics tablet with a stylus or drawing pen.
- Floppy disk to save work.
- Color printer (for black-and-white printer, add color with pen, pencils, or markers).

■ Lesson Review

Suggest that students review the following lesson before beginning the Studio Lesson:

- Chapter 6, Lesson 4, Making a Stylized Motif, pages 92–93, to discover how artists use color, lines, and shapes to make stylized motifs for textile or wallpaper design.

■ Motivator

Show students examples of *geometric* quilt designs. Explain that quilts were first made for warmth by combining layers of fabric. Quilts became more decorative and some patterns were so popular they became standard designs. Today, artists use the computer to create fabric designs.

304

Artists use the computer as a design tool to make patterns for application to other media such as silk screen or tapestry. Christopher Pallotta created these two quilt patterns on the computer. The designs can be displayed and enjoyed as art works or they can be used to make quilts from fabric.

You can create quilt patterns by designing a motif for a quilt square and adding solid colors, patterns, and textures. To make the quilt pattern, repeat the motif, using the same combination of colors or include contrasting colors. You can then emphasize the design with the addition of intricate details.

WHAT YOU WILL LEARN

You will use the principle of rhythm by repeating a geometric motif to make a decorative quilt pattern. First you will explore the Shape and Line tools to design a geometric motif. Next, you will use the Bucket tool to add color. Then you will learn how to Copy, Paste, and arrange copies of the square motifs to create a quilt design. Discover how rotating or inverting copies of the motif creates varying quilt designs. Make several examples showing different arrangements of the original motif.

WHAT YOU WILL NEED

- Computer with an art application
- Mouse or graphics tablet with a stylus or drawing pen

- Floppy disk to save work
- Color printer (for black-and-white printer, add color with pen, pencils, or markers)

WHAT YOU WILL DO

1. Look at Pallotta's quilt designs or recall other quilts you have seen. On the computer, make two or three geometric motifs. Hold down the Shift or Option key and draw an open square with the Rectangular Shape tool. (Choose the No Fill setting for an open square.) Choose from the Shape tools to add more open shapes. Use a variety of shapes and sizes, including circles, triangles, or hexagons.

▶ **Figure S–1**

Christopher Pallotta. *Collideoscope Quilt, Kaleidoscope Quilt*

---

more about • • •

Computer Technology Many fabric artists use computer art applications because they can make variations of a design faster than using other art techniques. Some art applications provide tools or menus to add textures that change the surface quality of the image to imitate fabric and other surfaces. Quilt designs made on the computer can be printed in large sizes and displayed without using fabric. In factories where cloth is produced, machines are controlled by programmed computers that choose the colors of thread and yarn, determine the patterns, and run the giant looms that make the fabric.

2. Select the Straight Line tool to divide the area into smaller spaces or shapes. Add smaller lines and shapes to create details. Title and Save this geometric motif.

3. Create a different motif, beginning again with an open square. Title and Save.

4. Choose the motif you like the best. Select several hues—solid, gradients, or mixed with a pattern. Fill in spaces of the motif with color using the Bucket Flood-fill tool. (You may begin with the original line motif and fill with another color choice.) Title and Save your work.

5. Use the Lasso or Rectangular Selection tool to Select the geometric motif. From the Edit menu, click, drag, and choose Copy to copy the motif in the Clipboard.

6. From the Edit menu, click, drag, and choose Paste to place a copy on the screen. Note the keyboard shortcut key in the menu command box. You may wish to use this key later.

7. Notice the moving dotted lines around the selection. These indicate the motif is Selected and now can be moved or changed. Put the cursor on top of the motif and drag it into position. While the motif is still Selected, choose Flip, Rotate, or another command from the menu that allows you to transform selected graphics. To Paste selection into position, click the cursor on another area of the screen outside the selection.

8. Continue to Paste additional copies and arrange them to complete a repeating rhythm. Decorate with a frame or border, if needed. Retitle, save, and print.

EXAMINING YOUR WORK

- **Describe**   Name the colors in your motif. Identify the geometric shapes used.
- **Analyze**   Explain how you arranged the individual motif to make the quilt; identify the tools and menus. Tell why you chose the color scheme. Identify any combinations of color and patterns you used.
- **Interpret**   Compare and explain the varying appearance of the quilt designs caused by flipping, rotating, and arranging the original motif differently. What is the mood or feeling created by the shapes, colors, and textures? Title your work.
- **Judge**   Tell if you have used the principle of rhythm by repeating a geometric motif to make a decorative quilt. What part do you like best? Would you make any changes? How?

▲ Figure S–2   Student work. Computer quilt.

Try This! STUDIO OPTION

■ Make a storytelling quilt. Choose a theme for your quilt to record an event, a celebration, or a favorite folk tale. Begin by using the Pencil or Brush tools to draw a picture. Choose hues and patterns to emphasize the mood of the quilt. Apply color directly using Brush tools or fill in line drawings with the Bucket tool. Title and Save. Follow Studio Lesson directions to create a repeating geometric border design. Retitle, save, and print the storytelling quilt pattern.

Lesson 1   *Creating a Computer Quilt Design*   **305**

■ Studio Skills

Following are suggestions for expanding studio skills.

- Have students use the Shape tools to make a motif. Remind them to hold down the Shift key to restrict a shape, making a perfect square or circle.
- To align shapes, have students practice placing the cross hair at the origin of the previously drawn shapes. Explore various line thicknesses.
- Suggest that students explore both informally and formally balanced geometric motifs. Consider using a corner as the center of interest.
- Have them use the Lasso selection tool when copying specific shapes because it only captures the object and does not include any background space.
- Encourage students to save as they work so earlier ideas can be retrieved or different color schemes can be explored.
- Some art applications provide tools or menus to add textures such as changing the surface quality of the image or changing the paper when drawing to simulate rough or smooth papers. Try these options if available.

■ Self-Assessment

- Did you use straight lines and geometric shapes to create a motif?
- Does your quilt design have repeated geometric motifs that create a rhythm?
- Have you made more than one quilt design with the same motif by flipping or rotating the motif or changing hues?
- Identify the tools or menus on the computer that you found most useful.

CURRICULUM CONNECTIONS

Social Studies   Artists from many cultures create storytelling quilts to communicate traditional tales and stories or to express ideas about events. The Kinglist cloth from Benin, a small African country, features plant, animal, and people cloth shapes which are appliqued onto fabric. Before this century, only kings could own the cloth and these earlier designs were made to show events in the life of the king. Symbols were used to represent the many names of the king. The king's importance was shown by making him much larger than other people shapes on the cloth. In America, the German people, especially the Amish, are known for their beautiful geometric quilt designs. Many designs are based on the square and smaller fractions of the square.

LESSON 2

Coil Pot

(pages 306–307)

LESSON TIME: 90 minutes

☑ OBJECTIVES

After completing this lesson, students will be able to:

- Identify principles of art in Native American pottery.
- Use clay to form coils into a coil pot.

☑ SUPPLIES

- Clay and slip.
- Canvas-covered clay board.
- Plastic bags, bowl of water.
- Scraps of heavy cardboard.

■ Lesson Review

Suggest that students review the following lessons before beginning the Studio Lesson:

- Chapter 1, Lesson 3, The Principles of Art, page 8, to describe the purpose of rhythm and be able to explain how rhythm can be created in pottery.
- Chapter 13, Lesson 3, Native American Art Today, page 200, to look at pottery created by Native American artists.

■ Motivator

Supply a variety of clay pots, or have students bring in samples. Compare the differences between the clay pieces. Do they have a sense of rhythm or texture? Is color used? Bring in pictures of various clay artifacts and discuss the principles of art and how they are used.

 LESSON 2

Coil Pot

Look at the object in Figure S–3. This is an example of an early Native American coil clay pot. Scientific dating of artifacts like this helps experts estimate the earliest time ancient people may have arrived on this continent. Works like this also provide a window on the way of life of those people.

WHAT YOU WILL LEARN

You will create a clay pot in the style of prehistoric Native Americans. You will give the work a sense of rhythm by increasing and then decreasing the size of coils. Your finished pot should be both useful and decorative.

WHAT YOU WILL NEED

- 2 pounds of clay, and slip
- Canvas-covered clay board
- Large plastic bag and bowl of water
- Scrap piece of heavy cardboard

WHAT YOU WILL DO

1. Review Technique Tip **16**, *Handbook* page **281**. It will give you some general background information on working with clay.
2. Gently throw your clay against the clay board. Doing this will remove any air pockets that might cause your work to explode when fired.

▶ **Figure S–3** **What do you suppose were some of the functional uses of a pot like this in the Pueblo culture?**

Pueblo. Ceramic Jar. Prehistoric. White slip with black painted decoration. 10.8 x 15.8 cm (4¼ x 6¼"). Indian Arts Research Center, Santa Fe, New Mexico.

more about • • •

Coil Pots Native American pottery was not produced in any quantity in America until about A.D. 500. The first pottery was molded from slabs and set in the sun to dry. Most later pottery was made using the coil technique and variations on this technique were used throughout the centuries. Native Americans did not develop a wheel and most did not develop a high-firing clay. After the coil technique was invented, the Native Americans experimented with different kinds of surface treatment. Sometimes the coils were smoothed over, and the piece was shaped and polished with a smooth stone. Sometimes the coils were left partially or completely unsmoothed. Early decorations were simply black shapes over a white surface.

3. Pinch off a lump of clay about the size of a lemon. With the heel of your hand, flatten the lump into a circle about ½ inch (13 mm) thick. Set it aside. (See Figure S–4.)

4. Pinch off a second smaller lump, and roll it into a rope. The rope should be about ½ inch (13 mm) thick and 12 inches (30 cm) long. Form the rope into a ring, joining the two ends with slip. Seal the ring to the circle you made. This is to be the base of your pot.

5. Create four more ropes. All should be the same thickness as the first rope. Each, however, should be slightly longer than the one before it. Form the shortest rope into a ring, as you did earlier. Using slip, attach it to your base. Form the next longest rope into a ring. Attach it to the outer edges of the last coil. Continue to work in this fashion until your work is five coils high.

6. Roll out five more ropes, this time making each slightly shorter than the one before it. Form the longest into a ring. Attach it to the inner edges of the last coil on your pot. Continue working in this manner until you have used all your ropes. (*Hint:* If it takes longer than one class period to finish your pot, store it in the plastic bag. This will keep it moist until you are ready to work with it again.)

7. Allow your pot to dry to the greenware stage. Use the scrap of cardboard as a scraper to smooth out any bumps. Fire the pot in a kiln. Display your finished pot alongside those of classmates. Which pots succeed in showing a sense of rhythm?

EXAMINING YOUR WORK

- **Describe** Tell whether all the coils in your pot have the same thickness. Describe the form of your pot. Explain what you did to obtain this form.
- **Analyze** Tell which principles were used to organize the elements in your work. State whether your pot has a sense of rhythm. Explain how this sense of rhythm is realized.
- **Interpret** Point out in what ways your pot is similar to a prehistoric Native American coil pot.
- **Judge** Tell whether you have succeeded in creating a work that is both useful and decorative. Tell what changes you would make if you were going to redo your pot.

▲ Figure S–4   Student work. Coil pot.

Try This! STUDIO OPTIONS

■ Make a second pot similar to the first one. This time, use your fingernails or a pencil point to dent each coil every inch (2.5 cm) or so. This will add an interesting texture. Compare your pot with the coiled pot in Figure 13–2 on page **194.**

■ Make a second pot similar to the first one. This time, use your cardboard scraper to smooth out the coils. Using a sharp clay tool, carve a geometric design in the surface of your pot. This design should be made so that it fits comfortably within the shape of your pot.

■ Studio Skills

- Many artists prefer to work clay by hand instead of using a wheel. Discuss with students the reasons why an artist might use a wheel, and also why an artist might prefer to use his or her hands to create a piece of pottery.
- Have students keep their clay in the plastic bag, and take out only as much as they need to shape one coil at a time. This way, the clay will not dry out while they are in the middle of a project.
- Emphasize to students the importance of eliminating air bubbles from the clay. Be sure they are using the proper technique for doing this thoroughly, and assist them as necessary.

■ Self-Assessment

- Have students use Examining Your Work to evaluate their pottery creations.
- Ask students to describe how they used the principle of rhythm in their coil pots.
- Have students prepare a display of the coil pots created in this lesson in an area where others may view their works.

Lesson 2   *Coil Pot*   **307**

TECHNIQUE TIP

Polishing Clay To polish the clay pots created in this Studio Lesson, students should wait for the clay to become leather hard. Remind students that leather-hard clay is clay that is still damp to the touch but too hard to model. When clay has reached this stage, have them rub the surface of the pot with the back of a metal spoon or a polished stone. As they rub, students will notice a shiny appearance on the surface of the clay. This smooth, shiny surface will remain through all firings.

LESSON 3

Making Silk Screen Prints

LESSON TIME: 180 minutes

☑ OBJECTIVES

After completing this lesson, students will be able to:
- Make a screen plate, block out a design on the plate, and print an edition.
- Describe, analyze, interpret, and judge their own work.

☑ SUPPLIES

- Photograph of Andy Warhol.
- Pencils, rulers, shoe box lids, utility knives or scissors, masking tape, nylon net fabric, wax crayons, colored water-based printing inks or school acrylic paints, squeegees or pieces of heavy-duty cardboard.

■ Lesson Review

Suggest that students review the following lessons before beginning this Studio Lesson:
- Chapter 1, Lesson 1, The Elements of Art, pages 2-5.
- Chapter 2, Lesson 1, Drawing, Painting, Printmaking, and Computer Art, pages 18-21.

■ Motivator

Display a photograph of Andy Warhol. Then have students look at his self-portrait screen print. Ask: How are the photograph and the print different? How do you think this art work was created? What mood does the repetition of the double print create? How do you think the technique used to create the print contributes to the mood or idea?

Screen printing is the easiest technique to use when making a print using many colors. Study the screen print in Figure S–5. This was done by American artist Andy Warhol. How many different colors of ink do you think the artist used? How do the colors affect the mood of the work?

WHAT YOU WILL LEARN

You will make a screen plate out of cardboard, masking tape, and net fabric. You will block out a design with a wax crayon. The design will use the principle of rhythm to organize the element of shape. Give your print a title that describes the mood or feeling you want to capture. You will print an edition of three prints.

WHAT YOU WILL NEED

- Pencil and ruler
- Shoe box lid
- Utility knife and scissors
- Sheets of sketch paper
- Masking tape and nylon net fabric
- Wax crayon
- Colored water-based printing ink or school acrylic paint
- Squeegee or a piece of heavy-duty cardboard the size of the screen opening
- Sheets of white paper

▲ **Figure S–5**

Andy Warhol. *Double Self Portrait.* Screen print in paint on canvas. 1.8 x 1.8 m (6 x 6'). The Detroit Institute of Arts, Detroit, Michigan. Founders Society Purchase, Friends of Modern Art.

more about • • •

Screen Printing   Point out to students that some of the techniques used for printing on paper are similar to those used to print on fabric. Silk screen and block printing are most widely used. For this process, designs for fabric must be planned as a continuous repeat pattern. Often the designs interlock so that a break is not apparent. Have students look at examples of printed fabric to notice the design units. Tie-dye and batik are other versatile techniques for fabric design. A rich heritage of design in batik and tie-dye comes from cultures of the Far East as well as Africa. For example, a kind of wood block, called adinkra, comes from the Ashanti tribe of Ghana.

WHAT YOU WILL DO

1. With pencil and ruler, measure a 3 x 5 inch (8 x 13 cm) square on the shoe box lid. Using the utility knife, carefully cut out the rectangle. Protect the table with a thick piece of cardboard.

2. Trace the size of the opening in the shoe box lid on sheets of sketch paper. Experiment drawing rhythmic designs that lead the eye around the space. One way to do this is by repeating shapes. Change the size, however, to add interest to these shapes. Choose the best of your designs. Shade the space between the shapes with a pencil. Set your sketch aside.

3. Cut a rectangle of net fabric slightly larger than the opening. With masking tape, fasten the fabric securely to the inside of the lid. Cut a piece of cardboard that will fit inside the lid but cover the opening. The cardboard will act as a squeegee later.

4. Place the screen over your design. Hold it firmly in place. Pressing heavily with the crayon, plug the holes in the net over the shaded areas.

5. Place the screen over a sheet of white paper. Choose a color of ink. Squeeze a small amount of ink at the top of the screen. With your cardboard squeegee, pull ink from the top of the screen to the bottom. As you do, press down heavily.

EXAMINING YOUR WORK

- **Describe** Tell how this print technique is different from the other types of printmaking. Tell how the finished work is different. Show how you repeated the same shape in different sizes to add interest.
- **Analyze** Explain how you used the principle of rhythm to organize the shapes. Tell whether the element of texture plays an unplanned role in the finished work. Discuss what this reveals about printmaking.
- **Interpret** Tell how the title describes the mood you wanted to express in your art work.
- **Judge** Tell whether you feel your work succeeds. Explain your answer.

---

6. Lift the screen carefully off the paper so as not to smear the ink. Make a second and third print.

7. Display one of your finished prints. Discuss any interesting textures you created.

Try This! STUDIO OPTION

- Make a screen print using crayon to draw a line design on the screen.
- Borrow a classmate's printing plate. Using a second color of ink, add a second color to one of your dried prints. Line up the outlines of your print and the plate opening. Describe the results.

■ **Studio Skills**

- Let students experiment with gluing paper shapes onto the bottom side of their screens. The paper blocks the screen completely and produces sharp images.
- Help students identify some commercial products—such as their own T-shirts—that are decorated with silk screening. Then display reproductions of several art works created by silk screening.
- Have students explore other materials that can be used to block the screen and create stenciled images. Ask: How might school acrylics be used? What effects can be created with white glue? How might liquid wax resist be used? How long must each material dry before you try to print from the screen? Let students experiment with their ideas.

■ **Self-Assessment**

- Ask students to review the prints they made for this Studio Lesson and discuss the use of the elements and principles of art.
- Let them discuss their responses to these questions: Which of the prints is most successful? Why? What do you like most about each of the other prints?
- Review students' silk screen prints, and consider their evaluations of their own work as printmakers.

Lesson 3 *Making Silk Screen Prints* **309**

more about • • •

Andy Warhol Andy Warhol was probably the best-known American Pop artist. He illustrated popular culture by mass-producing art. Warhol was trained at the Carnegie Institute of Technology, and during the 1950s he worked as an advertising illustrator. During the next decade he used innovative silk screening techniques to create images of such subjects as Campbell's soup cans, Coca-Cola bottles, and the faces of Hollywood celebrities. Warhol mass-produced representations of mass-produced consumer goods, and called his work art. He defended his creations by pointing out that mechanical reproduction was an important part of American society and a legitimate means of creating art. His use of the idea of duplication conveys the message of coolness and detachment that is a distinct feature of modern life.

Computer Cartooning

LESSON 4

Computer Cartooning

(pages 310–311)

LESSON TIME: 90 minutes

☑ OBJECTIVES

After completing this lesson, students will be able to:
- Use simple lines, shapes, and exaggeration to create an original cartoon character.
- Communicate an idea or message through a cartoon.

☑ SUPPLIES

- Pencil and sketchbook.
- Computer with art application.
- Mouse or graphics tablet with a stylus or drawing pen.
- Scanning device such as a hand-held or flatbed scanner.
- Floppy disk to save work.
- Color printer (or add color with pen, pencils, or markers).

■ Lesson Review

Suggest that students review the following lessons before beginning the Studio Lesson:
- Chapter 4, Lesson 5, Creating a Picture Story, pages 62–63, to explore how early artists used pictures to tell a story.
- Chapter 16, Lesson 1, pages 243–244, to review how artists use color, lines, and shapes to express mood.

■ Motivator

Have students name a favorite cartoon character from newspapers, magazines, or film, including computerized characters. Have students identify the shapes, sizes, colors, and details artists use to create the mood of the character. Then brainstorm descriptive words associated with different moods.

310

Cartoons represent objects with simple lines, shapes, and colors. Cartoon characters can be human, animal, or objects. They often appear as exaggerated caricatures portrayed with human characteristics: shy, bold, clumsy, athletic, villainous, or heroic. Cartoonists usually combine characters, action, setting, and message in one pictorial frame or a series of frames, called a comic strip, to tell a story. Newspapers have popularized cartoon characters since the early twentieth century. The computer saves artists many hours of hand labor by quickly replicating cartoon characters and settings. Artists like Mike Pantuso create cartoons for young children. His pictures are cartoons created by using simple shapes and primary and secondary colors.

WHAT YOU WILL LEARN

You will create an original cartoon character on the computer, using simple lines and shapes. You will either scan a sketch of your character into the computer or use the mouse or drawing pen to draw the character directly into an art application. Once the image is on the screen, you will manipulate it, change the size, or make variations to improve your character. Your final cartoon may be one picture or several frames put together to create a strip.

WHAT YOU WILL NEED

- Pencil and sketchbook
- Computer with art application
- Mouse or graphics tablet with a stylus or drawing pen
- Scanning device, hand-held or flatbed scanner (optional)
- Floppy disk to save work
- Color printer (for black-and-white printer, add color with pen, pencils, or markers) *Optional:* If scanning devices are not available, draw image directly into computer application. If a computer is not available, use pencil, pens, and paints.

WHAT YOU WILL DO

1. Choose a favorite animal or figure for your sketch. Think of the characteristics you want to express: bold, cunning, shy, or heroic, for instance. Make several sketches on paper. Use simple lines and shapes to draw the figure. Emphasize each characteristic by exaggerating proportion, shape, and size.

▶ **Figure S–6**

Mike Pantuso. *Banana Man.* Computer art, appears in the following publication: *Adobe Photoshop, Creative Techniques.* Salles, Denise, Gary Poyssick, and Ellenn Behoriam. 1995. Macmillan Computer Publishing and Shepard Poorman Communications Corporation, Indianapolis, Indiana.

310   Lesson 4   *Computer Cartooning*

---

more about • • •

Technology   Many artists and illustrators use computer art applications to quickly combine images and make multiple copies in varying sizes faster than with other art techniques. The computer offers filmmakers advantages over conventional techniques because it can control lighting effects and make two-dimensional objects look three-dimensional. Have students explore simple animation techniques. Staple about 12 small empty sheets of paper together at one end to make a flip book. Draw a dot, circle, or simple shape on the first page. Redraw the shape on the next page moving the dot or shape to a slightly different position. Continue repeating the shape but move it slightly each time. Also consider adding details or slightly changing the shape each time. Flip the pages. Watch the action.

2. Draw your cartoon character directly into the computer using a mouse or stylus pen and the Pencil or a small Brush tool. Scan your original sketch into the computer as Line Art with a hand-held or flatbed scanner, if available. You may also lay your sketch on a graphics tablet and trace around lines of the cartoon character with the stylus or drawing pen. When the image is in the computer, Title and Save your work to a file or disk.

3. Explore variations of the character by manipulating and altering the position and size. Choose a Selection tool such as the Lasso to select the image and pick options from the Transformation or Special Effects menu to change size, flip, rotate, or distort the image. Retitle and save variations you like.

4. Think of a message you want to express or a problem that needs to be solved. Include humor if possible. Decide whether you can accomplish your idea in one frame or if you need several frames to convey the action and the message. Add objects, figures, and details to help convey the message. Retitle and save your work.

5. Select three or four primary and secondary colors and use the Bucket tool to flood-fill shapes and spaces with hues. If the color leaks into other spaces, use the Undo command from the Edit menu, or the keyboard shortcut. Then choose the Fatbits or Zoom-in tool or command to find the missing pixels in the outline. Fill these in with Pencil or small Brush tool to close the outline. Imitate the comic strip look by clicking the Brush tool to add dots of color.

6. Retitle, save, print, and display your cartoon.

EXAMINING YOUR WORK

- **Describe**   Identify your cartoon character. Name the colors you used. Describe the setting.
- **Analyze**   Tell what elements you used to emphasize the character's personality. Show how you exaggerated the character's features.
- **Interpret**   What is the mood? How do the colors and composition help to convey this mood? What title did you choose to name your work?
- **Judge**   Did you create an expressive cartoon using exaggeration and simple lines, shapes, and colors? How did you make use of computer tools in your work? What would you change to improve it?

▲ **Figure S–7   Student art. Computer cartoon character.**

Try This!

STUDIO OPTION

■ If you have a slide show option you can animate your cartoon by creating a strip and displaying it frame by frame. Select one frame of a cartoon you like. Redraw the frame making it larger using the Pencil or small Brush tool. Use simple lines and shapes.

Redraw several times, making changes in each successive frame. Add details but do not include any words. Title and save. Add color using the Bucket or Brush tools. Try using dots of color to imitate the dot patterns used in comic strips. Retitle, save, and print your strip.

Lesson 4   *Computer Cartooning*   **311**

■ Studio Skills

- Have students list the words that describe the qualities they would like to use to create a cartoon character.
- Then have students make several sketches on paper or directly on the computer that explore combinations of simple shapes and exaggerated features to express these qualities.
- Most computer art programs offer commands to flip, rotate, and distort selected objects. Some art applications provide tools and menus for resizing or changing the scale of the object. These menus and tools give students additional opportunities to develop their cartoon idea.

■ Self-Assessment

- Can other students immediately identify the mood of your cartoon character?
- Did you use shape, size, color, detail, and exaggerated features to create this mood?
- Have you included a setting which provides more information for the viewer about the idea you want to communicate?
- Does the cartoon convey a message in one or more frames with very few, if any, words?
- Identify the computer tools or menus you found were most useful.

CURRICULUM CONNECTIONS

Language Arts   Write a story about the character you have created. If you have included dialog in the cartoon, redo the cartoon so that "the picture tells the story" without any dialog.

Math   Determine how proportion and scale have been altered in your character's features. Identify the changes by making a ratio between the normal size of the feature and the exaggerated one.

Social Studies   Discuss how early primitive artists used a cartoon style to tell a story about people, animals, and events on the walls of caves, rocks, and hides of animals.

LESSON 5

Computer-Designed Advertisement

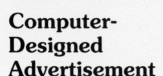

LESSON 5

Computer-Designed Advertisement

(pages 312–313)

LESSON TIME: 90 minutes

☑ OBJECTIVES

After completing this lesson, students will be able to:

- Explain how graphic artists combine images and text to create advertising designs.
- Use the principles of harmony, variety, and unity in a commercial design.

☑ SUPPLIES

- Pencil and sketchbook.
- Computer with art application.
- Mouse or graphics tablet with a stylus or drawing pen.
- Scanning device such as a hand-held or flatbed scanner (optional).
- Floppy disk to save work.
- Printer.

■ Lesson Review

Suggest that students review the following lessons before beginning this Studio Lesson:

- Chapter 1, Lesson 1, The Elements of Art, pages 2-5.
- Chapter 1, Lesson 3, The Principles of Art, pages 8-11.
- Chapter 2, Lesson 1, Drawing, Painting, Printmaking, and Computer Art, pages 18-21.

■ Motivator

Have students select their favorite advertisement from a newspaper, magazine, or brochure and bring it to class. Analyze the product or service to discover which elements of art are used.

312

Graphic artists use the computer to create product package designs, brochures, advertisements, and company logos. Look at the work shown in Figure S–8 by Philip Nicholson. The entire piece was created using a computer.

Today, art applications are easier to use. Artists may work directly on the computer or begin with pencil and paper sketches. The computer makes some tasks easier because it can retrieve, reproduce, recombine, and alter images with ease. Some software programs simulate textures and appearance of traditional art media, such as watercolors and oil paints. Artists combine photographs and scanned images with textures and collage effects. Commercial illustrators use a combination of media including computer graphics applications, clip art, and traditional art materials to create exciting images for product marketing.

WHAT YOU WILL LEARN

You will design a product package or advertisement on the computer using a variety of fonts, styles, and sizes. Choose a theme and select hues to emphasize the mood. Decide whether you will draw objects or import and combine clip art images. You will then create harmony by using repeating colors, textures, shapes, and letters. Add variety by changing the size or rotating the shapes. After you design your package, you may wish to include a frame or border to create unity.

▲ **Figure S–8**

Philip Nicholson. *Poster Series*

RESOURCES BEYOND THE CLASSROOM

Computer Artists Locate a graphic artist in your community who uses the computer as part of his or her design process. Invite the artist to class to demonstrate and explain the processes, techniques, and products he or she uses. Have students prepare questions ahead of time so that they can make the most of the artist's visit. You might wish to have students complete some computer lessons ahead of time and have them on display for the visitor to review.

WHAT YOU WILL NEED
- Pencil and sketchbook
- Computer with art application
- Mouse or graphics tablet with a stylus or drawing pen
- Floppy disk to save work
- Color printer (for black-and-white printer, add color with pen, pencils, or markers)

WHAT YOU WILL DO
1. Choose the kind of product or promotion you wish to represent. Design a package cover or an advertisement representing a product or products, such as the one shown in Figure S–8.
2. Make pencil sketches of the layout. Include fictitious product names, images, or symbols that represent your product and illustrate the message of the advertisement. Choose simple shapes and colors.
3. On the computer, begin with the letters of the product name. Select the Text tool and choose a Font, Style, and Size. Use a Selection tool to manipulate the letters by stretching, rotating, or distorting them. Add shadows to give perspective or emphasis to the letters. Title and save your work at intervals, so you can return to different points of the design process. Try other tools, menus, and designs.
4. Draw symbols or objects with the Pencil or Brush tools. Combine with Clip Art, if available. Add color directly with the Pencil or Brush tool or use the Bucket tool to Flood-fill spaces with color and texture. Title and save your work again.
5. Examine the words and images you have created. Select, Copy, and Paste words, letters, shapes, or objects to repeat

EXAMINING YOUR WORK
- **Describe** Identify the products in the package or advertisement. Point to your color choices and the use of images in your design.
- **Analyze** Discuss the layout. Explain how the advertisement is organized and the sequence you followed. Tell what you drew first, what you added next, and how you organized the design.
- **Interpret** Describe how the choice of font, style, size, and color help to emphasize the message in your design. Explain which elements and principles you used to organize the layout.
- **Judge** Did you use the principles of unity, harmony, and variety in your design? Did you manipulate fonts, shapes, and colors to make a successful product design?

images and create harmony through repetition. While objects are selected, add variety with changes in color, size, or position. Try overlapping images. Fill the page.
6. You may wish to make a frame or border around the design to create unity. Make a frame using lines, shapes, letters, or objects. Draw an object with a Pencil and then Select, Copy, and Paste image at regular intervals around the perimeter.
7. Retitle, save, and print your work. Try printing on different types of paper for different effects.

How does the artist communicate the message or emphasize the product? Have students make a chart and compare the colors to discover which hues are more frequently used. Ask: What kinds of advertisements use informal or formal balance? How is emphasis achieved?

■ Studio Skills
- First, have students list the kinds of products or services they would like to advertise.
- Next, have students make several sketches, on paper or directly on the computer. Explore fonts, sizes, and styles, combined with drawn images, clip art, photographs, or scanned images.
- If available, use a scanner to digitize photographs. Consider using a digital or analog camera to capture objects around you that can be included in your design.
- Explore several layouts that use formal or informal balance.
- Repeat colors, images, or letters to create harmony. Add a frame to unify the design.

■ Self-Assessment
- Can you explain to other students how graphic artists use the art elements and principles to combine images and text when making a design?
- Did you effectively combine letters or words with images to communicate the mood and message?
- Have you repeated shapes, colors, textures, and letters to create harmony?
- Does your design balance harmony and variety to create unity?
- Identify the computer's tools or menus you found were the most useful.

Try This! STUDIO OPTION

■ Design a travel brochure to promote a city or a vacation or recreation spot. Decide what popular and attractive points would promote the location, such as climate or activities. Include information in your brochure that would attract potential customers. Create a name or logo. Draw objects or include clip art. Choose colors to augment the mood of the resort. Title, save, and print your brochure.

CURRICULUM CONNECTIONS

Language Arts Have students use the computer to design their own alphabet or code. Combine lines and shapes to make different symbols or create a system that uses pictures.

Math Symbols are used to identify mathematical language and functions. Have students list common math symbols. Students may wish to investigate the binary code which translates all text, sound, and graphics into two digits—1 and 0.

Social Studies Have students research the first advertisement. Discover the culture, date, product, and purpose. (Hint: Students may begin by looking up the Medieval street signs used in England c. 10–12th century to identify their shops. How did the Romans advertise?)

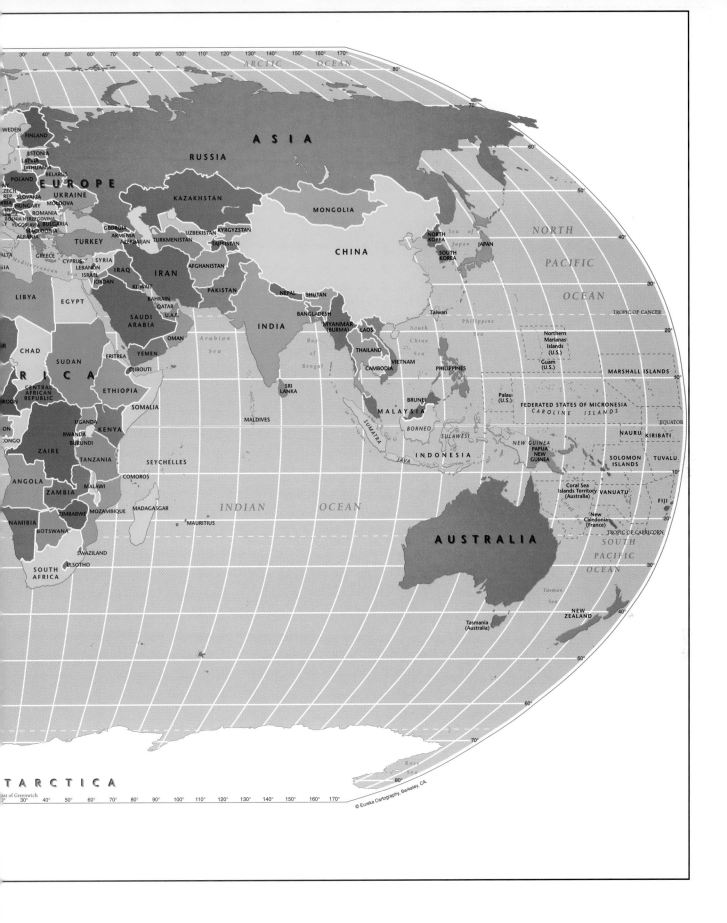

ARCTIC   OCEAN

SWEDEN
FINLAND
ESTONIA
LATVIA
LITHUANIA
BELARUS
POLAND EUROPE
CZECH
REP. SLOVAKIA UKRAINE
ARIA HUNGARY MOLDOVA
BOSNIA HERZEGOVINA ROMANIA
Y YUGOSLAVIA BULGARIA
ALBANIA MACEDONIA
GREECE
ALTA CYPRUS
Mediterranean LEBANON SYRIA
Sea ISRAEL
JORDAN
TURKEY
GEORGIA
ARMENIA
AZERBAIJAN TURKMENISTAN
IRAQ
IRAN
KUWAIT
BAHRAIN
QATAR
U.A.E.
OMAN
SAUDI
ARABIA
YEMEN
ERITREA
DJIBOUTI

ASIA

RUSSIA

KAZAKHSTAN

UZBEKISTAN KYRGYZSTAN
TAJIKISTAN

MONGOLIA

AFGHANISTAN

PAKISTAN

CHINA

NORTH
KOREA
SOUTH
KOREA

Sea of
Japan

JAPAN

NORTH

PACIFIC

OCEAN

TROPIC OF CANCER

LIBYA
EGYPT

CHAD
SUDAN

RICA

CENTRAL
AFRICAN
REPUBLIC

Arabian
Sea

NEPAL BHUTAN
BANGLADESH
INDIA
MYANMAR
(BURMA) LAOS
THAILAND
CAMBODIA VIETNAM
SRI
LANKA
MALDIVES

Bay
of
Bengal

Taiwan

PHILIPPINES

South
China
Sea

Philippine
Sea

Northern
Marianas
Islands
(U.S.)
Guam
(U.S.)

MARSHALL ISLANDS

ETHIOPIA
SOMALIA

Palau
(U.S.)

FEDERATED STATES OF MICRONESIA
CAROLINE   ISLANDS

EQUATOR

ON
CONGO
UGANDA
RWANDA
BURUNDI
ZAIRE
KENYA
TANZANIA

SEYCHELLES

MALAYSIA
BRUNEI
SUMATRA
BORNEO
SULAWESI
JAVA
INDONESIA

NEW GUINEA
PAPUA
NEW
GUINEA

NAURU KIRIBATI

SOLOMON
ISLANDS

TUVALU

ANGOLA
ZAMBIA
MALAWI
COMOROS
NAMIBIA
ZIMBABWE MOZAMBIQUE
BOTSWANA
MADAGASCAR
MAURITIUS

INDIAN   OCEAN

Coral Sea
Islands Territory
(Australia)

VANUATU

New
Caledonia
(France)

FIJI

TROPIC OF CAPRICORN

SWAZILAND
LESOTHO
SOUTH
AFRICA

AUSTRALIA

SOUTH

PACIFIC

OCEAN

Tasman
Sea

NEW
ZEALAND

Tasmania
(Australia)

TARCTICA
st of Greenwich

Ross
Sea

© Eureka Cartography, Berkeley, CA.

Artsource®: Performing Arts Handbook

(pages 316–333)

■ Purpose

The 17 features in the Performing Arts Handbook are designed to enrich students' learning by correlating what they learn about the visual arts to the performing arts—dance, music, and theatre. The featured performers and groups in this handbook were specifically chosen to supplement the chapters in the student text.

■ Using the Handbook

The following categories suggest ways to use the Performing Arts Handbook.

- **Mini-lessons** Use the features as stand-alone lessons about dance, music, and theatre.
- **Motivator** Use the features to introduce related chapters. Listed on each chapter opening page of your Teacher's Wraparound Edition is a segment that correlates each chapter to this section. As you plan lessons, consider how you might use the Performing Arts Handbook as a way of introducing the chapter's contents.
- **Extension** Refer to the recommended Artsource® feature found on the chapter opening page of the Teacher's Wraparound Edition, and use the appropriate feature to expand the study of that chapter. Students may volunteer for this Extension activity, or you might assign groups of students to read the feature then complete the questions and activities on their own.

316

Performing Arts Handbook

The following pages of content were excerpted from *Artsource®: The Music Center Study Guide to the Performing Arts,* developed by the Music Center Education Division, an award-winning arts education program of the Music Center of Los Angeles County.

The following artists and groups are featured in the Performing Arts Handbook.

more about • • •

Artsource®   The materials provided in this Performing Arts Handbook are excerpted from *Artsource®: The Music Center Study Guide to the Performing Arts,* a project of the Music Center Education Division. The Music Center of Los Angeles County, the largest performing arts center in the western United States, established the Music Center Education Division in 1979 to provide opportunities for life-long learning in the arts, and especially to bring the performing and visual arts into the classroom. The Education Division believes the arts enhance the quality of life for all people, but are crucial to the development of every child.

The Alvin Ailey American Dance Theater

The Alvin Ailey American Dance Theater. Alvin Ailey, founder and choreographer. "Revelations." Photo: Bill Hilton.

The Alvin Ailey Company performs classical ballet and modern works by well-known choreographers, but the group is best known for dances drawn from Alvin Ailey's African-American background. These masterpieces capture the essence of his black experience in America and feature musical themes based on African-American cultural heritage such as blues, spirituals, and jazz. "Revelations," the dance shown on this page, has become the signature piece for the company because it clearly captures the spirit and aesthetics of the company and its creator. The choreography includes different dances, all of which celebrate the human spirit and its ability to overcome adversity.

■ **DISCUSSION QUESTIONS**

1. The word *revelation* means something that was unknown and is now revealed. Discuss a revelation a person might have while struggling through a difficult situation.

2. Look at the photo on this page. What images come to mind as you study the positions of the dancers? Discuss how unity and variety are demonstrated.

3. Imagine you are going to create a signature piece to represent yourself. Identify three to five traits that describe different parts of yourself. Demonstrate these traits with a gesture or expressive movement. Which ones seem appropriate for your signature piece? Why?

■ **CREATIVE EXPRESSION ACTIVITIES**

Language Arts   Think about Discussion Question 1. Write about a time when you or someone you know had a revelation.

Dance/Theatre   After discussing Question 3, find gestural movement that can express each of the personal traits you listed. Choose one you like and abstract it in several different ways by exaggerating the size, doing it in slow motion, giving it a rhythmic pattern, adding a turn or change of level, or performing it as you walk. Share ideas with a partner and discuss what worked best.

Setting the Stage

Direct students to read the paragraph about The Alvin Ailey American Dance Theater and view the *Artsource®* selection if available.

O P T I O N A L

Artsource®: **Performing Arts Package 3**

- VHS tape segment 3-1 (Playing time 4:26)

■ **Connecting the Arts**

Using the Discussion Questions on this page, help students recognize that many artists have used difficult experiences to express a "revelation" in their work. Possible responses:

1. Circumstances may cause the difficulty; after struggle, life can often seem more precious.

2. Flock of birds—position of arms and their grouping; different level of dancers; people working together show a sense of unity and repetition.

3. Sense of humor, always late, caring, a good friend, likes basketball.

■ **Extensions**

- After students have examined the photograph and, if possible, viewed the video, have them complete the Creative Expression Activities.

- Encourage students to share experiences with dance. These might include taking lessons, seeing a live concert, social dancing or seeing dance on TV or in the movies.

- Use *Artsource®* package 3, Unit 1, for more information about The Alvin Ailey American Dance Theater and for additional related activities.

Appreciating the Performing Arts

Dance   As a child, Alvin Ailey attended Sunday school and The Baptist Young People's Union. It was these experiences that inspired "Revelations," choreographed in 1960. In it there are several sections that evoke strong emotions by expressing through movement the joy and strength of the music and capturing a sense of personal freedom, wit, and humanity. The beginning formation of the dance (shown on student page) is particularly memorable. A tight grouping of men and women reach out in unison, conveying powerful feelings of support, dignity, and hope. Alvin Ailey allowed the music he selected to influence his ideas and his choreography. Since his death in 1989, Judith Jamison, one of his most well-known dancers, has taken over as artistic director.

317

In the Heart
of the Beast
Puppet and
Mask Theatre

PERFORMING
ARTS

Theatre

In the Heart of the Beast Puppet and Mask Theatre

Direct students to read the paragraph about Sandy Spieler and Debra Frasier and view the *Artsource®* selection, if available.

OPTIONAL

Artsource®:
**Performing Arts
Package 3**

- VHS tape segment 3-2
  (Playing time 8:30)

■ Connecting the Arts

Using the Discussion Questions on this page, help students recognize that artists can work in one medium or combine media in a variety of ways to express ideas. Possible responses:

1. Childhood to adolescence; graduating from school into work force; moving out of the family home; weddings; birthdays.
2. Painting; decorated fabric; cut-out art; 3-D construction
3. Celebrate the arrival with music and feeling of joy; the sun rose in happiness on the day you were born; the wind sang a song to welcome you.

■ Extensions

- After students have examined the photograph and, if possible, viewed the selection, have them complete the Creative Expression Activities.
- Encourage students to find out about and share events, experiences connected with the day of their birth.
- Use *Artsource®* package 3, Unit 2, for more information about In the Heart of the Beast Puppet and Mask Theatre and its production of *On the Day You Were Born* and for additional related activities.

318

In the Heart of the Beast Puppet and Mask Theatre. Sandy Spieler, artistic director. *On the Day You Were Born,* by Debra Frasier.

The idea for the production of *On the Day You Were Born* began when author/illustrator Debra Frasier approached Sandy Spieler and In the Heart of the Beast Puppet and Mask Theatre to make a mask or puppet to celebrate the publication of her book. The theatre wanted to do a play about the natural wonders of the world and Frasier's book was perfect in both theme and visual style. The story is based on the natural events that unfold on the day a child enters the world. The play combines puppetry, painting, poetry, dance, and music. It celebrates the natural miracles of the earth and extends an enthusiastic welcome to each member of our human family.

■ DISCUSSION QUESTIONS

1. What other rites of passage, in addition to birth, are causes for celebration in our lives?
2. Look at the photo on this page. Identify and describe as many different forms of media as you can.
3. What ideas would you include in a song, book, or poem that welcomes a new child into the world? Think of ways to include some natural forces such as wind or sun in your welcome.

■ CREATIVE EXPRESSION ACTIVITIES

History Research how different cultures celebrate birth. Make a list of the various rituals or customs.

Language Arts Visit the library to locate and read a newspaper published on the day you were born. Select ten items from that issue to describe in a journal or story.

Art Topics in the glossary of Frasier's book include: migration, rotation, gravity, the moon's phases, rising and falling tides, sunlight, and photosynthesis. Using mixed media, design a collage that captures one of these themes from nature.

Appreciating the Performing Arts

Theatre Ms. Spieler worked in close collaboration with Ms. Frasier, becoming midwife to the creative process in bringing the book off the page and onto the stage. She began by storyboarding the book into sections: a prologue, an invocation, the revelation of wonders, and finally the birth and welcome song.

They then constructed tag board models of the show's three large boxes that open to reveal the text and action of the story. The boxes incorporate mural techniques, banners, animated tableaux, and whimsical fabrics in harmony with Frasier's colorful illustrations.

Duke Ellington is an American Jazz legend who composed his first piece, "Soda Fountain Rag," while still a teenager. Born in 1899, he showed promise in art as well as music. He decided to pursue a career in music, eventually organizing his own band that he led for 50 years. He and his band revolutionized the concept of jazz, elevating it to a new level. One of his compositions, "The Prowling Cat," is a short, playful, swinging tune for solo trumpet. The piece begins with trumpet sounds like a cat howling in the night. At the end, the trumpet plays its highest notes and then the full band joins in for the finale.

Duke Ellington with singer Vikki Carr. Photo: Courtesy of The Music Center Operating Company Archives. Otto Rothchild Collection.

■ DISCUSSION QUESTIONS

1. What qualities of the trumpet could be used to capture the sounds of a prowling cat? What other instruments could also be used?

2. Think of the characteristics of a cat. What words or phrases describe the quality, actions, and tempo of a prowling cat?

3. The basic elements of jazz include: *syncopation, improvisation, blue notes, break,* and *riff.* Find a definition and give an example of each. Listen to jazz music and see if you can identify any of these elements.

■ CREATIVE EXPRESSION ACTIVITIES

Music   Listen to some examples of Duke Ellington's work. Identify the basic elements of syncopation, improvisation, blue notes, break, and riff. Explain how they impact the music.

Music   Listen to music about cats written by other composers, such as: "The Waltzing Cat" by Leroy Anderson; "Gellico Cats" from the musical *Cats* by Andrew Lloyd Webber; "Royal March of the Lions" from *Carnival of the Animals* by Saint-Saens. Notice how each composer used voices and/or instruments to suggest the sounds and movements of cats. Select two, then compare and contrast your findings.

Performing Arts Handbook **319**

■ Setting the Stage

Direct students to read the paragraph about Duke Ellington and listen to the *Artsource*® selection, if available.

O P T I O N A L

Artsource®:
Performing Arts Package 3

• Audio tape segment 3-1 (Playing time 2:44)

■ Connecting the Arts

Using the Discussion Questions on this page, help students recognize that in order to appreciate a work of art, it is important to learn about it and know what to look for or to listen to. Possible responses:

1. High, harsh, blaring tones; violin, cello; clarinet.

2. All senses are on alert, tension, taut; sneaking, cautious, crouching.

3. *Syncopation:* a shifting of accent; *improvisation:* performing spontaneously off a stated melody; *blue note:* slightly out of tune note; *break:* a virtuoso passage for a solo; *riff:* a short rhythmic ostinato pattern played on percussion.

■ Extensions

• After students have examined the photograph and, if possible, listened to the audiocassette, have them complete the Creative Expression Activities.

• Have students bring in a variety of musical styles and provide historical and cultural background.

• Use *Artsource*® package 3, Unit 3, for more information about Duke Ellington and for additional related activities.

Appreciating the Performing Arts

Music   As the twentieth century dawned, a new style of music was taking form—jazz. As the century progressed, jazz inspired big band swing, cool jazz, rhythm and blues, bebop, rock 'n' roll, and soul. Each of these styles produced musicians who reached musical stardom because of their immense talent and creative musicianship. Duke Ellington is one who achieved this status and maintained it throughout his lifetime. Today, even after his death, his name commands respect in the music world. He was one who managed to elevate a popular form of music into the respected sphere of serious art.

■ Setting the Stage

Direct students to read the paragraph about Bali and Beyond and listen to the *Artsource®* audiocassette if available.

> **OPTIONAL**
>
> *Artsource®:*
> **Performing Arts Package 3**
> • Audio tape segment 3-2 (Playing time 6:25)

■ Connecting the Arts

Using the Discussion Questions on this page, help students recognize that music has been a form of expression from ancient times, but is constantly changing as people discover new ways to make and combine sounds and rhythm. Possible responses:

1. Glockenspiel, vibraphone, marimba, song bells.
2. Jazz groups often have marimbas, reed horns, non-reed horns, flutes, drums, cymbals, and stringed instruments such as an electric guitar or bass. An orchestra also has violins, cymbals, cellos, or harps.
3. Drums with two heads (membranophones); bass (chordophones); Gamelan (idiophones); horn (aerophones).

■ Extensions

• After students have examined the photograph and, if possible, listened to the selection, have them complete the Creative Expression Activities.
• Challenge students to recognize cultural influences in modern music. For example, Salsa (Latin and African). Use *Artsource®* package 3, Unit 4, for more information about Bali and Beyond.

320

Bali and Beyond, Creative World Cultures. Cliff DeArment and Maria Bodmann. "Sumer Time." Photo: Cliff DeArment.

The musical group called Bali and Beyond embraces music from the East Indies and combines it with American music. This unique style creates extraordinary sounds that go beyond the familiar aspects of Western music. Fusing the ancient tradition of Hindu-Buddhist Asia with a contemporary spirit, Bali and Beyond creates new and exciting pieces from early cultural sources. One of their pieces, "Sumer Time," is a version of George Gershwin's classic "Summertime" from the musical *Porgy and Bess.* The group incorporates many different combinations of ancient instruments. For example, the sound of the Gamelan Gender Kantilan (a metal bar instrument like the xylophone) is combined with the modern sound of the saxophone.

■ DISCUSSION QUESTIONS

1. Name and describe some familiar bar instruments such as the xylophone, similar to the Indonesian ones described.
2. The traditional Gamelan Indonesian ensemble is made up of bar instruments, bamboo flutes, gongs, zithers, Indonesian violins, cymbals, balls, reed horns, log drums and a variety of other percussion instruments. What instruments might an American jazz ensemble use?
3. Study the photo on this page. Describe the instruments pictured. Put each instrument into one of the following four categories: metal and wood; drums; flutes, saxophone, and bassoon; violin and cello.

■ CREATIVE EXPRESSION ACTIVITIES

Language Arts   Shadow puppetry has been a part of the Balinese culture for over one thousand years. Read about this ancient art form and learn about the significance of the Gamelan in relationship to this art form.

Art   Just as visual artists work with a palette of colors in creating their works of art, musicians also have a variety of sounds with which to work. Find sound sources in your environment by experimenting with ordinary objects and hitting, blowing, plucking, or shaking them to hear their tone color. Try using wooden pencils tapped on tables or running fingers up and down venetian blinds.

Appreciating the Performing Arts

Music   The fusion of ancient cultural musical styles with contemporary styles is popular with a number of ethnic jazz ensembles. In addition to blending styles, these modern groups create new and different musical sounds by combining ancient instruments with contemporary acoustic and electronic instruments. For example, when "Sumer Time" is played by Bali and Beyond, the melody begins in an ancient Indonesian style, then the mood changes as the group shifts into a modern jazz style. Like Cliff DeArment, composers have employed an assortment of musical ideas to vary a basic theme, a musical form known as "theme and variations."

Japanese Festival Sounds. John Y. Mori, artistic director.
Photo: Craig Schwartz © 1989.

John Y. Mori was fascinated by the Taiko drummer who accompanied the folk dancers at the annual Obon Buddhist Festival in Los Angeles. This inspired him to learn to play the drums. Today he blends traditional Taiko drumming with a modern Japanese-American style. Taiko drumming originated in ancient India as part of religious ceremonies and celebrations. This form eventually found its way to Korea, China, and Japan. Traditionally, Taiko drums were included in ensembles with other instruments. In some cultures the drums were also used to perform functional roles, such as announcing the time of day or calling people to special gatherings. Today, Taiko is featured in performances with some ensembles composed solely of various sized drums.

■ Setting the Stage

Direct students to read the paragraph about John Y. Mori and Japanese Festival Sounds and view the *Artsource®* selection, if available.

OPTIONAL

Artsource®:
Performing Arts Package 3
• VHS tape segment 3-3 (Playing time 8:55)

■ Connecting the Arts

Using the Discussion Questions on this page, help students recognize that while artistic forms and styles may begin in one culture, they are carried to other places in the world as people migrate. Possible responses:
1. India to Korea, China, Japan, and United States.
2. Athletes and dancers must show great discipline over mind, body, and spirit.
3. Many traditional cultures of Africa and Native Americans. Drumming is used for ritual, dance, ceremonies, battle, healing, and recreation.

■ Extensions
• After students have considered the discussion questions and, if possible, viewed the video, have them complete the Creative Expression Activities. Guide them with information about the five basic drum strokes provided below.
• Encourage students to understand how traditions change and evolve the further they are from their source.
• Use *Artsource®* package 3, Unit 5, for more information about John Y. Mori and his musical group.

■ DISCUSSION QUESTIONS

1. Where did Taiko drumming originate? To what other countries did it spread?
2. Taiko performers demonstrate great skill and control in movement and drum technique. Their performance skills are a result of many hours of concentrated, vigorous work involving the mind, body, and spirit. Discuss how Taiko drummers are like athletes and dancers.
3. What other cultures place an emphasis on drumming? For what purposes are the drums used?

■ CREATIVE EXPRESSION ACTIVITIES

Language Arts The technique of learning drum patterns by vocalizing the sounds began in India and was transferred to many Asian cultures. Five basic syllables used in Taiko are: KA; KARA; DON; DOGO; and SU (which means *rest*). Combine the syllables in different patterns, saying them as you clap or beat out the rhythms. Repeat each pattern several times.
Geography Using a map or globe, trace the geographical and historical route of the Taiko drums from India through Asia to the United States.
Music Learn about and try the three basic techniques for playing percussion instruments: striking, shaking, or scraping.

Appreciating the Performing Arts

Music Humans have created musical instruments from a variety of materials found in their environment to produce many different sounds. Taiko drums are part of the percussion family of instruments that produce sounds when they are either hit, shaken, or scraped. Like other musical instruments, drums are designed in many sizes and shapes. The five basic drum strokes are: KA (a quarter note struck on the drum rim); KARA (two eighth notes struck on the rim); DON (a quarter note struck on the drum head); DOGO (two eighth notes on the head); SU (a rest). By learning these five sounds, students can be taught a few very simple drumming patterns using two pencils, erasers downward.

Ballet Folklorico de Mexico

Setting the Stage

Direct students to read the paragraph about the Ballet Folklorico de Mexico and examine the photograph of the dancers. View the *Artsource®* video if available.

OPTIONAL

Artsource®:
Performing Arts Package 3

• VHS tape segment 3-4 (Playing time 8:45)

Connecting the Arts

Using the Discussion Questions on this page, help students recognize the connections between visual and performing arts and that they are both expressions of a culture. Possible responses:

1. Elaborate decorations, patterns, design.
2. The sphere, or sun.
3. Circle, rectangles, intersecting lines.

Extensions

• After students have examined the photograph and, if possible, viewed the video, have them complete the Creative Expression Activities.

• Have students work in groups to create three sun motifs. Then choose one and make a design that shows movement using eight repetitions of the motif.

• Use *Artsource®* package 3, Unit 6, for more information about the Ballet Folklorico de Mexico and for additional related activities.

For over 25 years, the Ballet Folklorico de Mexico has presented authentic folk dances from different ethnic groups within Mexico. Amalia Hernández, the featured director of the dance group shown on this page, creates exciting dances based on ancient traditions. From the time of the Olmec Indians to the birth of modern Mexico, more than thirty distinct cultures have influenced Mexican culture. The dance shown in this photo is called "Los Mitos" and features the pageantry and ritual of these cultures before the arrival of the Spaniards.

Ballet Folklorico de Mexico. "Los Mitos." Amalia Hernández, artistic director.

■ DISCUSSION QUESTIONS

1. Compare the headdress of the dancers to the headdress of the Zapotecan goddess on page 80 in your book. What similarities do you see in the patterns and symbols?
2. What symbolism do you see in the photo on this page that inspired ancient cultures of Mexico? What characteristics of the symbol can you name?
3. After viewing the video, describe how the dancers used geometric spatial designs.

■ CREATIVE EXPRESSION ACTIVITIES

Dance   Stand in an open area with 6–8 students and organize yourselves into three different geometric shapes, selecting from a circle, square, triangle, or the letter X. After your designs are organized, choose two that you like and walk or skip from one figure into another using 8 counts to travel.

Language Arts   Write a personal reflection of your impressions and feelings about either the images you see in the illustration on this page or of the dance in the video.

Appreciating the Performing Arts

Dance   "Los Mitos" (the myths) is part of a suite of dances called *Los Concheros*. The suite is based on the ancient rituals of some of the indigenous cultures, such as the Toltecs and the Aztecs. These rituals connect each dancer to life and the universe. The title of the suite, *Los Concheros*, refers to the people who blow large conch shell trumpets during the ceremonial rites. Although the Concheros still enact their rituals today, the ceremonies now reflect the Spanish influence and have become a fusion of Christian and pre-Hispanic traditions.

Faustwork Mask Theater was founded in 1983 by Robert Faust, artistic director, actor, athlete, dancer, choreographer, and mask-maker. *The Mask Man* is a solo performance about masks that simultaneously entertains and educates. The set is a wall of masks, all original creations by Robert Faust. First comes a brief introduction about the many uses of masks throughout the world. Then the performer demonstrates their power by removing the masks from the wall one by one, and assuming the character expressed in each face. A variety of characters spring to life. Through the parade of almost twenty characters, the audience glimpses human nature at its silliest and most touching.

Faustwork Mask Theater. *The Mask Man.*
Robert Faust, artistic director.
Photo: Craig Schwartz, © 1993.

■ DISCUSSION QUESTIONS

1. The photo on this page shows Robert Faust with masks from *The Mask Man.* Study the expression of the masks. What kinds of personalities are being shown? What can you tell about the character's age, culture, and personality traits from the mask alone?
2. How might a mask be used in the theatre?
3. The first Greek masks were used in plays to impersonate gods. What Greek gods and goddesses can you name? What were their attributes or symbols?
4. Masks are often part of festivals, celebrations, and rituals. Describe activities you have participated in that used masks.

■ CREATIVE EXPRESSION ACTIVITIES

Language Arts   Read Greek myths or Greek stories such as "Theseus and the Minotaur" or "The Golden Fleece." How might masks be used in these works?

Physical Education   The ancient Greeks invented the first Olympic Games over 2,500 years ago. Plan a classroom Olympics with events from the original Greek games such as running, long-jump, and javelin.

Art   Create a two-sided mask showing contrasting feelings on each side. You might choose happy and sad, or good and evil. Think of movements to go with your mask to express each emotion.

Appreciating the Performing Arts

Theatre   As a device for theatre, masks evolved from religious practices of ancient Greece. The traditional masks depicting Tragedy and Comedy are derived from Greek theatrical traditions. One advantage of using masks in a performance is that they can be seen from a distance because they are often larger than the human head. The mask holds enchantment and fascination, and still retains a deep and complex meaning in tribal cultures. Faustwork Mask Theater celebrates the ancient art of the mask and its roots in theatre by taking it to an entirely different, almost startling dimension.

■ Setting the Stage

Direct students to read the paragraph about Faustwork Mask Theater and examine the photograph. If you have the *Artsource®* selection, have students view it.

> **O P T I O N A L**
> *Artsource®:*
> **Performing Arts Package 3**
> • VHS tape segment 3-5 (Playing time 5:13)

■ Connecting the Arts

Discuss the use and history of masks in theatre, and celebrations. Concentrate on the mask's power of transformation and the performer's ability to convey a variety of characters using masks. Possible responses:

1. The man is powerful; he poses in a strong, confident stance.
2. A mask might be used to create a visual effect; to allow one actor to play many roles. Children's plays, ghost stories, or mysteries.
3. Athena, warrior goddess, carries a spear and shield; Zeus, father of the gods, carries a thunderbolt and scepter; Hermes, wears winged sandals.
4. Halloween, Mardi Gras, Chinese New Year, Day of the Dead.

■ Extensions

• After students have examined the photograph and, if possible, viewed the selection, assign the Creative Expression Activities.
• Encourage students to share their personal experiences making and wearing masks.
• Use *Artsource®* package 3, Unit 7, for more information about Faustwork Mask Theater and for additional related activities.

Setting the Stage

Direct students to read the paragraph about Ranganeketan and view the *Artsource®* selection, if available.

O P T I O N A L

Artsource®:
Performing Arts Package 3

• VHS tape segment 3-6 (Playing time 9:09)

Connecting the Arts

Using the Discussion Questions on this page, help students recognize many cultures that have existed for thousands of years and have preserved their culture and arts through music and dance. Possible responses:

1. The bottom of skirt is round and looks like a lampshade; middle part is shaped in permanent ruffles; colors are bright.
2. Spiritual forces or gods create everything and place these ideas into the minds of people.
3. Ideas may include: truth, discipline, hard work, importance of study, respect for self and others.

Extensions

• After students have thought about the Discussion Questions and, if possible, viewed the video, have them complete the Creative Expression Activities.
• Encourage students to learn about and respect the beliefs of people from cultures different from their own.
• Use *Artsource®* package 3, Unit 8, for more information about Ranganeketan and the arts of Manipur, India.

324

The tiny community of Manipur, called the "Jewel of India," is a secluded state. It is tucked into an oval-shaped valley in the Himalayan mountains of India. The ancient culture here has been preserved intact for thousands of years. Traditions are carefully passed on from one generation to the next by master artists and teachers. "Rasa Lila" is a classical dance believed to have been created by the Hindu god Krishna. The specific form of the dance was communicated to King Jai Singh through a dream with specific descriptions of movements, style, and costumes. Performed in the spring at the Festival of Colors, the dance begins in the early evening and continues for eighteen hours.

Ranganiketan Manipuri Cultural Arts Troupe. Dr. T.D. Singh, founder and director. "Vansanta Rasa Lila." Photo: Craig Schwartz, © 1992.

DISCUSSION QUESTIONS

1. Study the photo of the costumed dancer performing "Vansanta Rasa Lila." Describe the details of her dress.
2. The people of Manipur believe that everything is divinely inspired, including all of their artistic expressions. What do you think this means?
3. From an early age, young children commit to an honored and respected relationship with a specific master teacher. If you were a master teacher to a young child, what important ideas would you want to teach him or her?

CREATIVE EXPRESSION ACTIVITIES

Dance The dances of India incorporate gestures that symbolize an idea or image. Create gestures to show the concept of the following words: tree, mountain, stream, rain, boat, friend, fish. Make up three more words and gestures. Share and combine them with gestures from classmates.

Language Arts Select a simple story or poem about something in nature. Make up gestures and movement that are performed as the story is told. Add music if you wish.

Appreciating the Performing Arts

Dance/Music Visitors are forbidden to travel freely within Manipur, so it is especially significant that Ranganiketan shares their culture with outsiders, building friendship and understanding. Legend tells how the dance, "Rasa Lila," was given in a dream to Jai Singh, a popular king in Manipur around 1750. He was forced to meet an impossible task—to subdue and ride upon the back of a wild elephant to prove he was the rightful king. He was aided by Krishna, who asked in return that the king build the Govinda Temple. When the king accomplished this task, Krishna is said to have given him the "Rasa Lila" dance, through a dream, that communicates pure love and unselfishness. Already performed in the world of the gods, the dance could now be recreated on earth.

324

During the infamous Middle Passage of the 1700s, black people from Africa were transported to many different lands. They carried the traditions and customs of several different racial and ethnic groups with them. All of the dance styles from countries such as Brazil, the Caribbean, and black Africa, as well as those from black America, were impacted by this movement of peoples. Every year Chuck Davis journeys to Africa and "sits at the feet of the elders." He researches the history of specific ethnic groups and their dances, music, and songs. His work is an African-American interpretation of authentic material from Africa. The result is a blending of styles and movement in the dances he creates.

The African American Dance Ensemble. Chuck Davis, artistic director and choreographer. "African Diaspora." Photo: Lee Hanson.

■ DISCUSSION QUESTIONS

1. The dance called "African Diaspora," which means "scatter widely," expresses a connection to Africa wherever black people traveled. Name the countries where you think African culture has had a major impact.
2. Study the photo of Mr. Davis. Describe what he is wearing and discuss how it is similar to or different from American outfits. What ideas or words would you use to describe his facial expressions and arm gestures?
3. What dance styles do you think have their roots in traditional African cultures?

■ CREATIVE EXPRESSION ACTIVITIES

Language Arts   In many African ethnic groups, it is believed that wise people speak in proverbs and that everything has a place in life and a reason for being. Read the following proverbs, and then think of English equivalents: "Rain beats a leopard's skin, but it does not wash out the spots."(Ashanti); "When spider webs unite, they can tie up a lion." (Ethiopia); "Cross the river in a crowd and the crocodile won't eat you." (Kenya).

Social Studies   Most African groups have ceremonies that celebrate life passages. Create a Naming Ceremony for you and your classmates. Select a name for yourself that tells something of your character, appearance, accomplishments, or history. Include a special song and movements.

Appreciating the Performing Arts

Dance   Chuck Davis researches the history of specific ethnic groups and strives to learn how each dance is connected to the society and performed for specific occasions. Only when he knows this information can he incorporate the authentic movements into original African-American work. Although he recognizes that movement takes on other meanings when it is removed from its roots, he is conscientious about paying homage to its origin. He sees himself as a "griot," or teacher and historian. He states, "I have gone to Africa and I have sat at the feet of elders and I have listened as their words poured like raindrops onto and into my being."

■ Setting the Stage

Direct students to read the paragraph about Chuck Davis and view the *Artsource* selection if available.

OPTIONAL

Artsource®:
Performing Arts Package 3

- VHS tape segment 3-7 (Playing time 12:30)
- Audio tape segment 3-4 (Playing time 14:47)

■ Connecting the Arts

Help students recognize that people from different African cultural groups have influenced new cultures in places to which they traveled. Possible responses:
1. Brazil, Cuba, Haiti, North America.
2. A long tunic top that comes past his hips; pants that are wide at the top and narrow at the ankles; close fitting hat. Ideas are happy, open, welcoming, greeting.
3. Students may mention any of the dance styles from Brazil, Cuba, Haiti, black Africa, black American popular dances.

■ Extensions

- After students have completed the Discussion Questions and, if possible, viewed the video, have them complete the Creative Expression Activities.
- Encourage students to recognize that even though most immigrants come with their own language and culture, the slave trade separated black Africans from their language, songs and dances.
- Use *Artsource®* package 3, Unit 9, for more information about Chuck Davis and his work.

■ Setting the Stage

Direct students to read the paragraph about Paul Salamunovich and his experiences with Gregorian Chant and listen to the *Artsource®* audiocassette, if available.

OPTIONAL

Artsource®:
Performing Arts Package 3

• Audio tape segment 3-5 (Playing time 1:15)

■ Connecting the Arts

Using the Discussion Questions on this page, help students recognize that Gregorian Chant, an ancient music style, has connections with modern music and musicians. Possible answers:

1. The simplicity, smooth melodic lines and purity of tone often serve to soothe the listener.
2. Game songs and chants, sports chants, cheers.
3. Pop, rock, jazz, blues, Gospel, Spirituals, ballads.

■ Extensions

• After students have examined the photograph and, if possible, listened to the audiocassette, have them complete the Creative Expression Activities.
• Ask students to discuss their experiences with vocal music, either as performers or listeners.
• Use *Artsource®* package 3, Unit 10, for more information about Paul Salamunovich and vocal music.

326

When Paul Salamunovich joined the Boys Choir of St. James Catholic Church he was first exposed to Gregorian Chant. His early experience with music of the Middle Ages became a lifelong devotion. Salamunovich met famed choral director Roger Wagner when he served at St. James Church as guest conductor. Thus began a close lifetime association. Salamunovich joined Wagner's Los Angeles Youth Choir, a choral group that formed the nucleus for the Roger Wagner Chorale. The Chorale eventually became the Los Angeles Master Chorale with Salamunovich as its director. With mutual respect for Gregorian Chant, both Wagner and Salamunovich have infused the sounds of the Chorale with the beauty and basic traditions of Gregorian Chant.

The Los Angeles Master Chorale. Paul Salamunovich, director. Gregorian Chant. Photo: Robert Millard, Courtesy of the Los Angeles Master Chorale.

■ DISCUSSION QUESTIONS

1. Gregorian Chant is known for its pure, unaccompanied, non-rhythmic melodic lines. This is in direct contrast to most contemporary music. Why do you suppose Gregorian Chant has recently become popular again?
2. Early Gregorian Chants were performed solo or by groups of voices singing in unison. Name some chants, usually performed in unison, that you might hear today.
3. One style of Gregorian Chant—called Melismatic—is when the singer(s) sing several notes on one syllable of a word. Identify some modern music styles that also use this style.

■ CREATIVE EXPRESSION ACTIVITIES

History   It is believed that Gregorian Chant was named for Pope Gregory I, who organized existing chant into a unified body. Identify another historical figure who has influenced an event that was then named for that person.

Music   Trained singers are able to ornament, or add extra notes, to a simple Gregorian Chant, adding interest to the performance. Compare this practice with performances by contemporary popular singers.

Art   Discuss the contributions of music and art to the Church during the Middle Ages.

Appreciating the Performing Arts

Music   Gregorian Chant evolved during the early Middle Ages. With the growth of the Catholic Church during that period the chant or plainsong was elevated to prominence by Pope Gregory. The foundation of Gregorian Chant, however, developed from a beautiful cultural mix. Middle Eastern and early Jewish music influenced its development. In addition, from Greece came the Byzantine chant and from Italy the Ambrosian chant. The Gallican chant had been in use in France and Spain, influenced by the Moors, developed the Mozarabic chant. The Los Angeles Master Chorale is known worldwide today for its purity of tone, treatment of high notes, and flawless shape of phrase—all greatly influenced by the basic sounds of Gregorian Chant.

The Guthrie Theatre Ensemble and Cityscape. Jennifer Tipton, director. *The Tempest*, by William Shakespeare, 1991 Production. Photo: Michal Daniel

The story in *The Tempest,* a play by William Shakespeare, unfolds on an enchanted island where Prospero, the rightful Duke of Milan, has found refuge with his daughter Miranda. With his art and magic, and the help of the spirit Ariel, Prospero brings his enemies to the isle. There he brings them to justice and spiritual redemption. In this world of fantasy, Shakespeare brings to life a story of love, revenge, despair, hope, and wisdom. These elements are combined in a delicate web of poetry, imagination, and charms. Director Jennifer Tipton assembled a team of internationally acclaimed artists for this production. She created an island world reflecting the elements of nature and art, inspired by their interpretation of Shakespeare's play.

■ DISCUSSION QUESTIONS

1. The photo on this page depicts a scene from *The Tempest.* Study the characters and their postures and relationships to each other. Discuss what you think might be happening between them.
2. At the end of *The Tempest* Prospero gives up his magical powers and returns to the world of men. Discuss reasons why someone would want to give up magic and return to the real world.
3. Themes highlighted by the director of the play includes mirrors, shadows, and dreaming. The island in *The Tempest*, like a stage, is a place for dreams. Think about this statement and discuss whether or not you agree.

■ CREATIVE EXPRESSION ACTIVITIES

Language Arts Work with a group to select a Shakespearean sonnet and perform it as choral reading. Highlight the poetry and rhythm of the verse. You may have all voices reading in unison, solos, or combinations.

Dance The Guthrie Theatre production of *The Tempest* incorporates the movement technique of mirroring in the staging of the play. With a partner, practice creating mirror images and movements.

Language Arts Explore some of Shakespeare's most well-known quotations and discuss their meanings. For example, consider Jaques' statement in a scene from *As You Like It,* "All the world's a stage, and all the men and women merely players." (Act 2, Scene 7)

Appreciating the Performing Arts

Theatre "As a designer, the directors I have come to admire always allow me to bring some part of myself—as an artist—to the creation of the work," states Jennifer Tipton. She used the technique of mirroring in her staging of *The Tempest* to reveal Shakespeare's characters and provide insights into their relationships. She said, "This play is about mirrors and shadows—about itself reflected brightly and darkly. Each person represented is found within another or has characteristics deeply buried in the dark side of the other. It is only when we face the mirror and are able to see our own shadow within and without that we can become all of ourselves."

■ Setting the Stage

Direct students to read the paragraph about *The Tempest* and the version directed by Jennifer Tipton for the Guthrie Theatre and listen to the *Artsource®* selection, if available.

OPTIONAL

Artsource®: **Performing Arts Package 3**

• Audio tape segment 3-6 (Playing time 10:00)

■ Connecting the Arts

Help students recognize the role of a director and the teamwork involved in interpreting plays and presenting them as theatre. Possible responses:

1. The woman and the man look like they're in love; the man in the background looks like the father and he isn't certain whether or not he approves.
2. Magic can be overpowering; it gives the person an unfair advantage over others; a person might want to test their powers without magic; afraid of what might happen.
3. Students may agree because distortions can take place; you can be any character you wish.

■ Extensions

• After students have examined the photograph and, if possible, listened to the audiocassette, have them complete the Creative Expression Activities.
• Encourage students to share knowledge about the works of Shakespeare.
• Use *Artsource®* package 3, Unit 11, for more information about *The Tempest,* directed by Jennifer Tipton.

Diana Zaslove

■ Setting the Stage

Direct students to read the paragraph about Diana Zaslove and music of the 16th and 17th centuries, and listen to the *Artsource®* selection if available.

O P T I O N A L

Artsource®:
Performing Arts Package 3

- Audio tape segment 3-7 (Playing time 4:27)

■ Connecting the Arts

Using the Discussion Questions on this page, help students recognize how music was an expression of the times. Possible responses:

1. Expression is peaceful and relaxed.
2. People felt that established rules could be bent or broken and new ways were not seen as being wrong, but rather as interesting and inventive.

■ Extensions

- After students have completed the Discussion Questions and, if possible, listened to the *Artsource®* selection, have them complete the Creative Expression Activities.
- Encourage students to recognize the impact of the Renaissance. Have them identify where they feel freedom of expression is encouraged and where it is most challenged in today's world.
- Use *Artsource®* package 3, Unit 12, for more information about the music and dance of the period.

328

Music

Diana Zaslove

Singer Diana Zaslove performs popular songs of the sixteenth and seventeenth centuries. The mood of this dynamic time following the Renaissance was one of optimism and discovery. During this period composers began to emphasize the expressiveness of the human voice as a solo instrument. Poetry and music were combined to express a variety of emotions, especially aspects of love. Before the Renaissance, most music was written for the church to express religious, or sacred, themes. Now, for the first time, music was written to express the human spirit and worldly, or secular, themes. The lute, similar to the guitar, was the most popular instrument of this period and was often used to accompany singers.

Diana Zaslove, Lyric Soprano. 16th- and 17th-Century Music. Photo: Courtesy of Diana Zaslove.

■ DISCUSSION QUESTIONS

1. Notice the relaxed quality of the singer's dress. Discuss how the type of music she sings is reflected in her dress and manner.
2. Composers of this period wrote music for more than one solo voice, sometimes for up to four or five voices in harmony. Before this time, the instruments usually played the same part that was being sung. Now the vocalist would sing the melody while the lute player carried the parts of all the other voices. This allowed the beauty of *all* the harmony parts to be heard. Discuss how Renaissance ideas allowed for the development of harmony.

■ CREATIVE EXPRESSION ACTIVITIES

Language Arts Write a rhythmical poem that expresses an aspect of love, such as friendship, loss, devotion, or romance. If you wish, set it to music.

Music/Dance Instrumental music and dance of this period were intimately connected. Many of the patrons who supported musicians were people of wealth and power. They commissioned works for special occasions that often included dancing. Research some dance forms such as the galliard, pavane, ronde, or bergerette. Make a comparison between these and other popular folk dance forms such as the jig and reels that use partners, lines, and circles.

328   *Performing Arts Handbook*

Appreciating the Performing Arts

Music One of the most interesting aspects of this period of music was the collaboration between exceptional lyric poets and composers. During this time words took on new importance and were carefully selected to express different emotions, especially love. Much of the music was written for the theatre to be performed in plays. This musical Renaissance started in the Netherlands, but the composers and poets were so popular that they were enticed to perform their music in Spain, Bohemia, Austria, Germany and the cities of northern Italy. Each country had a specific Renaissance style; however, as composers moved fluidly between these countries, the character of each style was influenced by the others.

PERFORMING ARTS

Hanay Geiogamah was born in Anadarko, Oklahoma. He was raised with the traditions of the Kiowa Tribe. As he grew up, his interest in his traditional culture increased. At first he sought ways to express himself and communicate about his culture through drama. In 1987, Geiogamah and Barbara Schwei formed the American Indian Dance Theatre. The dance shown in the photo on this page is the "Hoop Dance." It is based on a legend of a dying man who wished to leave something on earth. The Creator gave him a hoop of wood and told him that for each natural form he could recreate, one more hoop would be added. As he danced, he grew stronger, for each additional hoop allowed him to create other designs.

American Indian Dance Theatre, Hanay Geiogamah, artistic director. Eddie Swimmer performing "Hoop Dance." Photo: Don Perdue.

■ DISCUSSION QUESTIONS

1. Study the photo of the hoop dancer. Describe what natural form he appears to be showing. What other natural forms might be included in the hoop dancer's repertoire?
2. The "Hoop Dance" was originally designed to teach stories of creation. As many as 40 reed hoops are manipulated to show how all natural things are connected, yet everything grows and changes. Discuss how a dancer might move with the hoops to create different ideas without ever losing the beat of the music.
3. Mr. Geiogamah has developed a system for categorizing American Indian dance. These categories are: *seasonal/functional; spiritual/ceremonial;* and *celebrational/ bravura.* Discuss what you think each of these categories means and the type of dance that would be included.

■ CREATIVE EXPRESSION ACTIVITIES

Art   Make a drawing of a hoop dance. Start with the pose of the hoop dancer shown in the photo. Then draw a series of ten or more drawings showing the dancer in slightly different positions. Combine the drawings to create an animated progression of positions.

Language Arts   Read this statement by the hoop dancer and expand on it, "When I started dancing, I discovered that my hoops had stories in them and the shapes I made could…"

Performing Arts Handbook   **329**

■ **Setting the Stage**

Direct students to read the paragraph about the American Indian Dance Theatre and view the *Artsource®* selection, if available.

OPTIONAL

Artsource®:
Performing Arts Package 3
• VHS tape segment 3-8 (Playing time 3:37)

■ **Connecting the Arts**

Help students recognize that there are 430 Native American cultural groups in the United States. Each has its own language, customs, and traditions. Possible responses:
1. Large bird, possibly an eagle or hawk; turtle, flowers, squirrels, snake, or butterfly.
2. Step in and out of the hoops; slide them up and down his body; circle them to add or subtract them; switch them from arm to arm or legs to arms.
3. *Seasonal/functional:* connect to seasons or preparation for hunt, or burial; *spiritual/ceremonial:* have a ceremonial function; *celebrational/bravura:* challenge and competition.

■ **Extensions**
• After students have completed the Discussion Questions and, if possible, viewed the selection, have them complete the Creative Expression Activities.
• Encourage students to recognize the benefit of understanding and respecting the cultural heritage of others.
• Use *Artsource®* package 3, Unit 13, for more information about the American Indian Dance Theatre.

Appreciating the Performing Arts

Dance   Another dance performed by the American Indian Dance Theatre is the "Eagle Dance." The eagle is sacred to all tribes and is a symbol of wisdom, strength and vision. The "Eagle Dance" varies from region to region, but this interpretation is a blending of two styles: one from the Northern Plains and the other from the Zuni Pueblo. The dances reflect the life cycle of the eagle from its first steps and attempts to fly, through maturity and into the spirit world. It is believed that eagles are messengers between man and the Creator. The dancers mime the movements of this creature in order to take the thoughts and messages of humans to the 'higher above.'

■ Setting the Stage

Direct students to read the paragraph about The Joffrey Ballet. If you have a recording of "The Nutcracker Suite," play the selection for students.

OPTIONAL

Artsource®:
Performing Arts Package 3

• Audio tape segment 3-8 (Playing time 6:30)

■ Connecting the Arts

Help students recognize that good stories are universal and can be changed and adapted to fit different historical and cultural settings. Possible responses:

1. Answers should include details from the Christmas story about Clara and the Nutcracker that comes to life.
2. Dresses are full of ruffles and lace to resemble flowers. All decoration should be firmly attached and able to move easily so that dancers can concentrate on their positions without being hindered by the costume.

■ Extensions

• After students have examined the photograph, assign the Creative Expression Activities.
• Encourage students to share experiences connected with *The Nutcracker,* discussing the different versions of the story, time period, and the dance movements.
• Use *Artsource®* package 3, Unit 14, for more information about The Joffrey Ballet and their interpretation of *The Nutcracker.*

330

The Joffrey Ballet. Gerald Arpino, artistic director. *The Nutcracker,* "Waltz of the Flowers." Photo: Herbert Migdoll.

The Nutcracker is a traditional holiday ballet, treasured all over the world. The dance was inspired by the musical score of Tchaikovsky and based on a delightful story by E.T.A. Hoffman, *The Nutcracker* and *The King of the Mice.* Hoffman's story was written in 1851 and then rewritten and simplified in 1890 by the Russian choreographer Marius Petipa. Petipa then presented the script to Tchaikovsky for the score. This production of the ballet was conceived and directed by Robert Joffrey with special choreography by Gerald Arpino. The Joffrey Ballet gives an American interpretation of the story. Their special production emphasizes its international cultural heritage by combining the classic tale with modern dance concepts.

■ DISCUSSION QUESTIONS

1. Have you seen a version of *The Nutcracker*? If so, describe what you remember of the story and the dance interpretation.
2. Study the photo of the dancers performing "The Waltz of the Flowers." Describe the costumes and discuss how a costume designer might create outfits so that performers can move and dance easily.

■ CREATIVE EXPRESSION ACTIVITIES

Art In a small group, listen to a specific section of the music or take a specific section of the story. Brainstorm ideas on how to create the sets, props, costumes and lighting. Each person should take one of the roles and all group members then work in collaboration to draw sketches and discuss their vision of the scene.

Mime Create a mime or movement study based on toys and how they might move if animated. These might include: yo-yos, kites, balls, plastic clay, different types of dolls, jack-in-the-box; or action figures.

330   *Performing Arts Handbook*

Appreciating the Performing Arts

Dance One of the most highly acclaimed companies in the world, Joffrey conveys a specifically American energy and style. Its purpose is twofold: to revive major historical ballets and to present new choreography that draws from American life. The company today is the outgrowth of a vision begun in 1956, when six dancers joined together to perform. They took turns driving, setting the stage, ironing the costumes and playing musical instruments. Today, as many as 75 people travel with the company including 40 dancers and nine semi-trailers containing crates of costumes, props, scenery, and 4,000 pairs of ballet shoes.

Music/Dance   *AMAN International Folk Ensemble*

ART
S★U
RC■
ARTSOURCE

PERFORMING ARTS

AMAN International Folk Ensemble. Jerry Duke, choreographer. "Suite of Appalachian Music and Dance." Photo: Craig Schwartz.

AMAN International Folk Ensemble was founded in 1964. Its purpose is to research, preserve, and present traditional dance, music, and folklore of the many diverse ethnic groups in America. The "Suite of Appalachian Music and Dance" shown in the photo gives a perspective on different dance forms found in the Appalachians, a far-reaching geographical area east of the Mississippi. The style and costuming is set around the turn of the nineteenth century. Dance styles range from stiff and formal postures of the north to stronger upper body movements of southern dances. The later dances have a West African influence.

■ DISCUSSION QUESTIONS

1. Study the photo of dancers on this page. What do the costumes tell you about the historical time period of the dance?
2. Find a book of Appalachian folksongs and study the lyrics. Discuss the lyrics and how they often tell a story.
3. Discuss how dance and music help a community establish common traditions that form a culture.

■ CREATIVE EXPRESSION ACTIVITIES

Dance   Circle dances were often used in Appalachian dances. Create a circle dance that uses some of the following ideas: around, moving in and out, bridges, spirals, circles inside of circles. Choose 8 counts or 16 counts for each movement.

Art   A wooden, jointed dancing puppet is used as the rhythmic accompaniment to the dance. Use wood and paint to create your own simple dancing puppet. Loosely attach arms and legs to the body with nails or screws. Use a dowel to wedge through a hole in the center of the puppet and a flexible piece of wood or plastic to place under it. Use a rhythmic flicking motion to animate the puppet as you move it up and down.

Appreciating the Performing Arts

Music/Dance   When the AMAN Folk Ensemble commissions work, the process begins with the Artistic Director. He decides upon a specific cultural group within a geographic region, researches the material, and then contacts the folklorists and choreographers who exemplify the best work in each area. The "Suite of Appalachian Music and Dance" needs to be viewed in a broad historical and geographical perspective. A costumer, lighting designer, and a music director worked collaboratively to complete the work under the leadership of the artistic director. There is also a clogging doll used in this dance which is not only a toy, but also serves as a rhythmical musical instrument.

Direct students to read the paragraph about AMAN and Appalachian dance, as represented in the suite. Present the *Artsource*® selection, if available.

O P T I O N A L

Artsource®:
Performing Arts Package 3

- VHS tape segment 3-9 (Playing time 8:10)
- Audio tape segment 3-9 (Playing time 4:17)

■ Connecting the Arts

Help students recognize that as people migrated, they brought their music and dance with them and it gradually changed as other cultures impacted it. Possible responses:

1. Answers will vary, but should indicate early American or turn-of-the century.
2. People wrote simple songs about the events of ordinary life, exceptional characters, events, feelings, and humor.
3. When people know and love the same songs and dances it gives them something in common and they feel a cultural connection.

■ Extensions

- After students have completed the Discussion Questions and, if possible, viewed the selection, have them complete the Creative Expression Activities.
- Encourage students to recognize that cultural traditions have a source, but are constantly changing as they travel with the people.
- Use *Artsource*® package 3, Unit 15, for more information about AMAN and "Suite of Appalachian Music and Dance."

■ Setting the Stage

Direct students to read the paragraph about Eugene Loring, Aaron Copland and *Billy the Kid*, and view the *Artsource®* selection, if available.

O P T I O N A L

Artsource®:
Performing Arts Package 3

• VHS tape segment 3-10 (Playing time 9:25)

■ Connecting the Arts

Help students recognize that some works of art are associated with historical times or events and represent a change in thinking that takes place in a specific culture. Possible responses:

1. Driving covered wagons, hauling wood or water, spinning, cooking, chopping and sawing wood.
2. Change the instruments from guitar to orchestral instruments; eliminate the lyrics.
3. Boots with flowers, striped pants with a belt, gloves with the fingers cut out, shirt with flowers and lines.

■ Extensions

• After students have thought about the Discussion Questions and, if possible, viewed the video, have them complete the Creative Expression Activities.

• Encourage students to recognize that preserving classical dance is a big job. It takes an expert 100 hours to reconstruct (stage, teach and rehearse) *Billy The Kid.*

• Use *Artsource®* package 3, Unit 16, for more information about Eugene Loring and his ballet, *Billy The Kid.*

This ballet is based on the notorious outlaw Billy the Kid. It is the first time that American themes, music, and movements were used in a classical ballet. Choreographer Eugene Loring began the process of choreographing by organizing the events of Billy's life. He placed events sequentially into scenes and then determined their dramatic impact and length. He then sent these plans to Aaron Copland in Paris. Copland used them to create his musical score which is based on themes from cowboy songs. The work was premiered by a small group who danced all the parts, changing both their costumes and the lighting each time the scene changed. The score was played on two pianos. The ballet was so successful that Mr. Loring was featured on the cover of *Life Magazine* in 1938.

The Joffrey Ballet. Eugene Loring, choreographer. Tom Mossbrucker dancing *Billy the Kid,* composed by Aaron Copland. Photo: Herbert Migdoll.

■ DISCUSSION QUESTIONS

1. The ballet begins with the "Opening March" showing pioneers traveling westward, and is composed of various actions, or motifs, inspired by the activities in their daily life. Discuss what activities would be shown. Describe some of the basic movements involved with each activity.

2. Discuss how a composer might translate a cowboy song into the classical music style for an orchestra. What changes would need to be made to the song?

3. Study the photograph on this page and describe the costume. Discuss how it has been stylized to represent a cowboy of the old West. What ideas does it capture?

■ CREATIVE EXPRESSION ACTIVITIES

Theatre   Choose characters from the Old West and show three different poses for each. Move from one position to the next, making four-count transitions. Combine characters to form group portraits.

Mime   List activities of pioneer life, such as chopping, sawing, baking, sewing, and pulling a cart. Mime each of these ideas separately. Then develop a sequence of movements that includes four or five of these activities.

History   Sometimes dances have to be reconstructed. *Billy the Kid* is a ballet that has been preserved as a historical piece. Each time a company wants to perform it, they must get permission and then have a reconstructionist come. Research how dances are reconstructed and find out how technology helps this process.

Appreciating the Performing Arts

Dance   Eugene Loring felt there was no true movement unless there was an emotional impetus behind it. His dancers were directed to feel the emotion before doing the movement. At rehearsals he asked them to get inside themselves and analyze their own likes and dislikes. When dancing any role, they explored all aspects of the characters in order to fully understand their motivations. Patrice Whiteside, a student of Loring and formerly a principal dancer with the Oakland Ballet Company, safeguards the integrity of his life's work and reconstructs and teaches the ballets.

Simply Maria, or The American Dream. Josefina López, playwright. Actors left to right: Margarita Cota, Daniel Mora, Claire Engel, Andres Monren, Albert Loredo, Leila Knox, Connie Collier, Don Loper. Photo: Courtesy of the Playwrights Project.

Simply Maria, or The American Dream is a one-act play about a young Hispanic girl's struggle to find her own sense of self. She finds freedom by challenging the traditional part of her heritage. The main character, Maria, finds herself living in dual cultures—the Mexican traditions of her former homeland and the newfound liberty of the United States. Ms. López weaves her tale between dream sequences and realistic experiences. The play includes a range of characters from the familiar to the symbolic. *Simply Maria* gives a unique perspective on the universal journey of adolescence with a powerful and inspirational message.

■ DISCUSSION QUESTIONS

1. Have you ever felt that you needed to free yourself from a gender or cultural stereotype? Describe the situation and discuss the limitations involved.
2. Do you feel women are expected to fulfill traditional or cultural roles? Has this changed throughout history or in different cultures?
3. Study the photograph and create a simple scenario of what you think is happening. Keep your idea connected to the basic premise of the play, as described above.

■ CREATIVE EXPRESSION ACTIVITIES

Language Arts   Make a list of all the roles a person plays in life. Choose one role and write a brief paragraph describing a problem you might face in that role.

History   Select a social studies unit to dramatize. Choose characters of historical interest to portray. For example, if the American Revolution were selected, historical characters could be John and Abigail Adams, Ben Franklin, or Thomas Jefferson. Scenes might include the Boston Tea Party or signing of the Declaration of Independence.

Art   Use illustrations or paintings of different settings to make up stories that could only happen in those settings.

Performing Arts Handbook   **333**

■ Setting the Stage

Direct students to read the paragraph about Josefina López and her play and view the *Artsource* video if it is available.

OPTIONAL

Artsource®:
Performing Arts Package 3

- VHS tape segment 3-11 (Playing time 10:21)

■ Connecting the Arts

Using the Discussion Questions on this page, help students recognize that people who share an ethnic and American culture are often challenged to find an acceptable balance between them or to choose one over the other. Possible responses:

1. Answers will vary, encourage students to discuss cultural experiences but be certain to respect personal privacy.
2. Even though there have been many more options possible, many cultures still think in traditional terms.
3. Ideas and plans will vary.

■ Extensions

- After students have completed the Discussion Questions and, if possible, viewed the video, have them complete the Creative Expression Activities.
- Encourage students to recognize that we all have many choices to make about our lives. There are no right answers, but most choices are based on basic beliefs, cultural values, talents and desires.
- Use *Artsource®* package 3, Unit 17, for more information about Josefina López and her play, *Simply Maria, or The American Dream.*

Appreciating the Performing Arts

Theatre   Josefina López moved to Los Angeles from Cerritos, in the state of San Luis Potosi, Mexico when she was five years old. One of eight children, her parents hoped that she might someday earn a good living as a secretary, marry a nice man, and have children. At seventeen, however, Josefina aspired to go to college and be a writer or an actress. She was moved by seeing Luis Valdez's play, *I Don't Have to Show You No Stinking Badges*, which portrays a Mexican-American who wants to be an actor but can't get cast. This inspired her to write the play, *Simply Maria, or The American Dream*, from an Hispanic woman's point of view.

Artists and Their Works

Glossary

A

Abstract Expressionism   An art style in which paint was dribbled, spilled, or splashed onto huge canvases to express a feeling. (Ch. 17–3)

Abstract work   A work in which the artist uses a recognizable subject but portrays it in an unrealistic manner. (Ch. 9–1)

Adobe (uh-**doh**-bee)   Sun-dried clay. (Ch. 6–3)

Aesthetic view (ess-**thet**-ik)   An idea, or school of thought, on what is important in a work of art. (Ch. 3–1)

Amphora (**am**-fuh-ruh)   A twin-handled vase. (Ch. 7–1)

Aqueduct (**ak**-wuh-duhkt)   A network of channels meant to carry water to a town or city. (Ch. 7–3)

Arabesques (ar-uh-**besks**)   Swirling geometric patterns of plant life used as decoration. (Ch. 8–3)

Arbitrary colors (**Ahr**-buh-trehr-ee)   Colors chosen to communicate different feelings. (Ch. 15–1)

Architecture   The planning and creating of buildings. (Ch. 2–3)

Art criticism   Studying, understanding, and judging works of art. (Ch. 3–1)

Art history   The study of art from past to present. (Ch. 3–3)

Artifacts   Simple handmade tools or objects. (Ch. 6–1)

Art movement   A trend formed when a group of artists band together to create works of a single style. (Ch. 14–3)

Ashcan School   The popular name given to the group of artists who made realistic paintings of working-class America. (Ch. 16–3)

B

Balance   A principle of art concerned with arranging the elements so that no one part of a work overpowers, or seems heavier than, any other part. (Ch. 1–3)

Baroque (buh-**rohk**)   An art style emphasizing movement, contrast, and variety. (Ch. 12–1)

Binder   A liquid that holds together the grains of pigment in paint. (Ch. 2–1)

Buttress   A brace or support placed on the outside of a building. (Ch. 10–3)

C

Calligraphy (kuh-**ligg**-ruh-fee)   A method of beautiful handwriting sometimes using a brush. (Ch. 8–3)

Castles   Fortlike dwellings with high walls and towers. (Ch. 10–1)

Cathedral   A large, complex church created as a seat of office for a bishop. (Ch. 10–3)

Coiled pot   A pot formed by coiling long ropes of clay in a spiral. (Ch. 13–1)

Collage (kuh-**lahzh**)   An art work made up of bits and pieces of two-dimensional materials pasted to a surface. (Ch. 8–4)

Color   An element of art that refers to what the eyes see when light is reflected off an object. (Ch. 1–1)

Composition   The way the art principles are used to organize the art elements of color, line, shape, form, space, and texture. (Ch. 3–1)

Concrete   A finely ground mixture of small stones and powdered minerals used in building. (Ch. 7–3)

Content   The idea, feeling, mood, or message expressed by an art work. (Ch. 3–1)

Contour drawing (**kahn**-toor)   Drawing an object as though your drawing tool is touching the edges of the form. (Ch. 11–2)

Cradle board   A harness worn on the shoulders and used to carry a small child. (Ch. 13–1)

Crafts   The different areas of applied art in which craftspeople work. (Ch. 2–3)

Cubism   An art style in which objects and the space around them are broken up into different shapes and then put back together in new relationships. (Ch. 10–1)

Culture   The ideas, beliefs, and living customs of a people. (Ch. 4–1)

D

Dada (**dahd**-ah)   An art movement founded on the belief that Western culture had lost its meaning. (Ch. 17–1)

E

Edition   A series of identical prints made from a single plate. (Ch. 2–1)

Effigy (**eff**-uh-jee)   An image that stands for ideas or beliefs. (Ch. 6–1)

The Eight   A group of New York artists who created art work that reflected the spirit of the times in which they lived, the early 1900s. (Ch. 16–3)

Emphasis   A principle of art concerned with making an element or object in a work stand out. (Ch. 1–3)

Etching   An intaglio print made by scratching an image onto a specially treated copper plate. (Ch. 12–3)

Expressionism   (ek-**spresh**-uh-niz-uhm) A style that emphasized the expression of innermost feelings. (Ch. 16–1)

F

Facade (fuh-**sahd**)   The outside front of a building. (Ch. 12–1)

Face mask   A mask worn to hide the identity of the wearer. (Ch. 9–3)

Fauvism (**fohv**-iz-uhm)   An art movement in which artists use wild, intense color combinations in their paintings. (Ch. 16–1)

Form   An element of art that refers to an object with three dimensions. (Ch. 1–1)

Freestanding sculpture   Sculpture surrounded on all sides by space. (Ch. 2–3)

Fresco (**fres**-koh)   A painting created when pigment is applied to a section of wall spread with fresh plaster. (Ch. 10–3)

Frieze (**freez**)   A decorative band running across the upper part of a wall. (Ch. 7–1)

Funerary urns (**fyoo**-nuh-rehr-ee)   Decorative vases or vessels found at burial sites. (Ch. 6–2)

G

Gargoyle   A projecting ornament on a building carved in the shape of a fantastic animal or grotesque creature. (Ch 10–4)

Genre pieces (**Zhahn**-ruh)   Art works that focus on a subject or scene from everyday life. (Ch. 6–1)

Glaze   Glass-like finish on pottery. (Ch. 5–1)

H

Hard-Edge painting   An art style that emphasized clear, crisp-edged shapes. (Ch. 17–3)

Harmony   A principle of art concerned with blending elements to create a more calm, restful appearance. (Ch. 1–3)

Headpieces   Masks carved of wood and worn on the head like a cap. (Ch. 9–3)

Hieroglyphic (**hy-ruh**-glif-**ik**)   An early form of picture writing. (Ch. 4–3)

I

Illuminations   Hand-painted book illustrations. (Ch. 10–1)

Impressionism   An art style that attempted to capture the rapidly changing effects of light on objects. (Ch. 9–2)

K

Kachina   A hand-carved statuette that represents spirits in Pueblo rituals. (Ch 13–1)

Kinetic art (kuh-**net**-ik)   An art style in which parts of works are set into motion by a form of energy. (Ch. 17–5)

L

Landscape   A drawing or painting focusing on mountains, trees, or other natural scenery. (Ch. 14–1)

Line   An element of art that refers to the path of a moving point through space. (Ch 1–1)

Linear perspective (puhr-**spek**-tiv)   The use of slanted lines to make objects appear to extend back into space. (Ch. 11–1)

Loom   A frame holding a set of crisscrossing threads. (Ch. 13–2)

M

Madonna   A work showing the Virgin Mary with the Christ Child. (Ch 11–1)

Media   The plural of *medium*. (Ch 2–1)

Medium of art   A material used to create a work of art. (Ch. 2–1)

Megaliths   Large stone monuments, such as Stonehenge in England. (Ch. 4–1)

Menus   Drop-down boxes on the computer screen that list selections available in software programs. (Ch. 2–4)

Mihrab (**meer**-ahb)   A highly decorated nook found in a mosque. (Ch. 8–3)

Minaret (min-uh-**ret**)   A slender tower from which Muslims are called to prayer. (Ch. 8–3)

Mixed media   The use of more than one medium in a work of art. (Ch. 3–1)

Mobile (**moh**-beel)   A sculpture made of carefully balanced shapes hung on wires. (Ch. 17–3)

Monolith (**mahn**-uh-lith) A structure created from a single stone slab. (Ch. 6–3)

Mosque   A Muslim house of worship. (Ch. 8–3)

Motif (moh-**teef**)   Part of a design that is repeated over and over in a pattern or visual rhythm. (Ch. 6–2)

Movement   A principle of art used to create the look and feeling of action and to guide a viewer's eye throughout the work. (Ch. 1–3)

Multi-media art   A work that makes use of tools and techniques from two or more areas of art. (Ch. 17–5)

Muralist   An artist who paints large art works directly onto walls or ceilings. (Ch. 16–3)

N

Neoclassic (nee-oh-**klas**-ik)   An art style that borrowed from the early classical period of ancient Greece and Rome. (Ch. 14–1)

New Realism   An art movement that rediscovered the importance of realistic detail. (Ch. 17–3)

Non-objective   Having no recognizable subject matter. (Ch. 2–1)

Non-objective art (nahn-uhb-**jek**-tiv)   Art works in which no objects or subjects can be readily identified. (Ch. 1–2), (Ch. 16–1)

O

Oil paint   A mixture of pigment, linseed oil, and turpentine. (Ch. 11–3)

Op art   An art style that made use of precise lines and shapes to create optical illusion. (Ch. 17–4)

Optical colors   Colors viewers actually see. (Ch. 15–1)

P

Pagoda (puh-**gohd**-uh)   A tower several stories high with roof curving slightly upward at the edges. (Ch. 5–3)

Papier-mâché (pap-yah-muh-**shay**)   A sculpting technique using newspaper and liquid paste. (Ch. 9–4)

Perceive   To become aware of through the senses of the special nature of objects. (Ch 5–1)

Perceiving   To become aware of through the senses.

Petroglyphs (**peh**-truh-glifs)   Rock carvings and paintings. (Ch. 13–1)

Pietà (pee-ay-**tah**)   A work showing Mary mourning over the body of Christ. (Ch. 11–1)

Pigment   A finely ground powder that gives every paint its colors. (Ch. 2–1)

Pixels   Individual squares on the computer screen. (Ch. 2–1)

Pointed arch   A curved arrangement of stones reaching up to a central point. (Ch. 10–3)

Pointillism (**poynt**-uh-liz-uhm)   A technique in which small, carefully placed dots of color are used to create forms. (Ch. 15–2)

Polychrome (**pahl**-ee-krohm)   Having many colors. (Ch. 13–3)

Porcelain (**pore**-suh-luhn)   A fine-grained, high-quality form of pottery. (Ch. 5–1)

Portfolio   A pad of drawing paper on which artists sketch, write notes, and refine ideas for their work. (Ch 1–1)

Portrait   A painting of a person. (Ch. 12–1)

Post and lintel system (**lint**-uhl)   An approach to building in which a crossbeam is placed above two uprights. (Ch. 4–3)

Post-Impressionism   An art movement that appeared after the Impressionists. (Ch. 15–1)

Printing plate   A surface onto or into which the image is placed. (Ch. 2–1)

Printmaking   A technique in which an inked image from a prepared surface is transferred onto another surface. (Ch. 2–1)

Proportion   A principle of art concerned with the relationship of one part to another and to the whole. (Ch. 1–3)

Pueblos   Stacked, many-family dwellings made of adobe. (Ch. 13–1)

R

Realism A style of art in which everyday scenes and events are painted as they actually look. (Ch. 15–3)

Regionalism (**reej**-uhn-uhl-iz-uhm) An art style that records local scenes and events from an artist's own region, or area, of the country. (Ch. 16–3)

Relief sculpture Sculpture partly enclosed by space. (Ch. 2–3)

Renaissance (ren-uh-**sahns**) A period of great awakening. (Ch. 11–1)

Rhythm A principle of art concerned with repeating an element to make a work seem active or to suggest vibration. (Ch. 1–3)

Rococo (ruh-**koh**-koh) An art style stressing free, graceful movement; a playful use of line; and bright colors. (Ch. 12–3)

Romanticism (roh-**mant**-uh-siz-uhm) A style of art that found its subjects in the world of the dramatic and exotic. (Ch. 14–1)

Round arch A curved arrangement of stones over an open space. (Ch. 7–3)

S

Salon (suh-**lahn**) An annual exhibition of art. (Ch. 14–3)

Sand painting The pouring of different colors of powdered rock on a flat section of earth to create an image or design. (Ch 13–3)

Screen A partition used as a wall to divide a room. (Ch. 5–3)

Scroll A long roll of illustrated parchment or silk. (Ch. 5–1)

Shape An element of art that refers to an area clearly set off by one or more of the other elements of art. (Ch. 1–1)

Shoulder masks Large, carved masks made to rest on the shoulders of the wearer. (Ch. 9–3)

Sketchbook A carefully selected collection of art work kept by students and professional artists. (Ch. 2–1)

Social protest painting An art style that attacked the ills of big-city life. (Ch. 17–3)

Solvent A material used to thin a paint's binder. (Ch. 2–1)

Space An element of art that refers to the distance between, around, above, below, and within things. (Ch. 1–1)

Stained glass Colored glass pieces held in place with lead strips. (Ch. 10–3)

Stele (**stee**-lee) A carved upright stone slab used as a monument. (Ch. 4–3)

Stupas (**stoop**-uhs) Beehive-shaped domed places of worship. (Ch. 8–1)

Style An artist's personal way of using the elements and principles of art and expressing feelings and ideas in art. (Ch. 3–3)

Stylized Simplified or exaggerated to fit the rules of a specific type of design. (Ch. 6–3)

Subject The image viewers can easily identify in an art work. (Ch. 3–1)

Surrealism (suh-**ree**-uh-liz-uhm) An art movement that probed the subconscious world of dreams. (Ch. 17–1)

Symbolism The use of an image to stand for a quality or an idea. (Ch. 11–3)

T

Tempera (**tem**-puh-ruh) A painting medium in which pigment mixed with egg yolk and water is applied with tiny brush strokes. (Ch. 10–1)

Tepee (**tee**-pee) A portable house. (Ch. 13–1)

Texture An element of art that refers to the way a thing feels, or looks as though it might feel, if touched. (Ch. 1–1)

Totem pole An upright log carving picturing stories of different families or clans. (Ch. 13–1)

Triumphal arch (try-**uhm**-fuhl) A monument built to celebrate great army victories.

U

Ukiyo-e (oo-**kee**-yoh-ay) An art style meaning "pictures of the floating world." (Ch. 5–3)

Unity The arrangement of elements and principles with media to create a feeling of completeness or wholeness. (Ch. 1–3)

Urban planning Arranging the construction and services of a city to best meet its people's needs. (Ch. 4–4)

Glossary

Variety A principle of art concerned with combining one or more elements to create interest by adding slight changes. (Ch. 1–3)

Warp Threads running vertically and attached to the loom's frame (Ch. 13–2)

Weaving A craft in which fiber strands are inter-locked to make cloth or objects. (Ch. 13–1)

Weft Threads passed horizontally over and under the warp. (Ch. 13–2)

Woodblock printing Making prints by carving images in blocks of wood. (Ch. 5–3)

Yamato-e (yah-**mah**-toh-ay) An art style meaning "pictures in the Japanese manner." (Ch. 5–3)

Ziggurat (**zig**-uh-raht) A stepped mountain made of brick-covered earth. (Ch. 4–4)

Glossary/Glosario

A

Abstract Expressionism/Expresionismo abstracto
Un estilo artístico en el que se salpicaba, derramaba y chorreaba pintura sobre lienzos inmensos para expresar una emoción. (Capítulo 17–3)

Abstract work/Obra abstracta Una obra en la cual el artista presenta un sujeto fácil de identificar de una manera que no es realista. (Capítulo 9–1)

Adobe/Adobe Arcilla que se ha secado al sol. (Capítulo 6–3)

Aesthetic view/Opinión estética Lo que una persona o escuela considera importante en una obra de arte. (Capítulo 3–1)

Amphora/Ánfora Jarra de dos asas. (Capítulo 7–1)

Aqueduct/Acueducto Un sistema de canales por donde se transporta el agua hasta una ciudad o pueblo. (Capítulo 7–3)

Arabesques/Arabescos Adornos geométricos de plantas que se repiten en espirales o remolinos. (Capítulo 8–3)

Arbitrary colors/Colores arbitrarios Colores que han sido seleccionados para comunicar distintas emociones. (Capítulo 15–1)

Architecture/Arquitectura El planear y crear edificios. (Capítulo 2–3)

Art criticism/Crítica del arte Estudiar, comprender y evaluar obras de arte. (Capítulo 3–1)

Art history/Historia del arte El estudio del arte desde el pasado al presente. (Capítulo 3–3)

Artifacts/Artefactos Objetos o instrumentos sencillos, hechos a mano. (Capítulo 6–1)

Art movement/Movimiento artístico Una tendencia que se produce cuando un grupo de artistas se reúne para crear obras en un estilo en particular. (Capítulo 14–3)

Ashcan School/Escuela del basurero El nombre popular que se le dio a un grupo de artistas que pintaron cuadros realistas de gente de clase obrera. (Capítulo 16–3)

B

Balance/Equilibrio El principio artístico que trata de la disposición de los elementos artísticos de tal manera que ninguna parte de una obra domine a otra. (Capítulo 1–3)

Baroque/Barroco Un estilo artístico que enfatiza el movimiento, el contraste y la variedad. (Capítulo 12–1)

Binder/Aglutinante El líquido en que se disuelven los granos de pigmento. (Capítulo 2–1)

Buttress/Contrafuerte Un pilar que se pone en la parte de afuera de un edificio para apuntalaro o reforzarlo. (Capítulo 10–3)

C

Calligraphy/Caligrafía Un método de escribir con letra bella, a veces con pincel. (Capítulo 8–3)

Castles/Castillos Fortalezas que servían de viviendas, con murallas altas y torres. (Capítulo 10–1)

Cathedral/Catedral Una iglesia grande y complicada que es la sede de un obispo. (Capítulo 10–3)

Coiled pot/Vasija enrollada Una vasija que se forma colocando rollos de arcilla en forma de espiral. (Capítulo 13–1)

Collage/Collage Una obra de arte hecha de pedazos de materiales de dos dimensiones pegados a una superficie. (Capítulo 8–4)

Color/Color Uno de los elementos del arte que se refiere a lo que ven los ojos cuando un objeto refleja la luz. (Capítulo 1–1)

Composition/Composición La manera en que se usan los principios del arte para organizar los elementos de color, línea, contorno, forma, espacio y textura. (Capítulo 3–1)

Concrete/Concreto Una mezcla de piedras pequeñas y minerales en polvo que se muele finamente y se utiliza en la construcción de edificios. (Capítulo 7–3)

Content/Contenido La idea, sentimiento, atmósfera o mensaje que expresa una obra de arte. (Capítulo 3–1)

Contour drawing/Dibujo de contorno Dibujar un objeto como si el instrumento de dibujar estuviera tocando los bordes de la figura. (Capítulo 11–2)

Cradle board/Tabla de acunar Un armazón de cuero que se lleva en las espaldas para cargar a un niño chiquito. (Capítulo 13–1)

Crafts/Artesanía Las artes aplicadas en que trabajan los artesanos. (Capítulo 2–3)

Cubism/Cubismo Un estilo artístico en el que se quiebra la forma de los objetos y del espacio que los rodea, y se vuelven a reunir los pedazos de manera que formen un conjunto nuevo. (Capítulo 16–1)

Culture/Cultura   Las ideas, creencias y costumbres vivas de un pueblo. (Capítulo 4–1)

D

Dada/Dadaísmo   Un movimiento artístico que se basó en la creencia de que la cultura Occidental ya no tenía sentido. (Capítulo 17–1)

E

Edition/Edición   Una serie de grabados idénticos que están hechos de una misma placa. (Capítulo 2–1)

Effigy/Efigie   Una imagen que representa ciertas ideas o creencias. (Capítulo 6–1)

The Eight/Los Ocho   Un grupo de artistas neoyorquinos que creaban obras que reflejaban el espíritu de la época en que vivían, el comienzo de los años 1900. (Capítulo 16–3)

Emphasis/Énfasis   El principio artístico que trata de la manera en que se puede hacer resaltar un elemento u objeto en una obra. (Capítulo 1–3)

Etching/Aguafuerte   Un tipo de grabado entallado en el que se hacen cortes en una placa de cobre que ha sido tratada con substancias químicas para producir la imagen. (Capítulo 12–3)

Expressionism/Expresionismo   Un estilo que enfatiza la expresión de los sentimientos más profundos. (Capítulo 16–1)

F

Facade/Fachada   El frente de un edificio. (Capítulo 12–1)

Face mask/Máscara facial   Una careta que usa una persona para esconder su identidad. (Capítulo 9–3)

Fauvism/Fauvismo   Un movimiento artístico en el cual los artistas usan combinaciones extrañas de colores intensos en sus pinturas. (Capítulo 16–1)

Form/Forma   El elemento del arte que se refiere a un objeto de tres dimensiones. (Capítulo 1–1)

Freestanding sculpture/Escultura de pie   Escultura que está completamente rodeada por espacio vacío. (Capítulo 2–3)

Fresco/Fresco   Una pintura en la que el pigmento se aplica a una sección de pared que está recién cubierta de yeso. (Capítulo 10–3)

Frieze/Friso   Una franja decorativa a lo largo de la parte superior de una pared. (Capítulo 7–1)

Funerary urns/Urnas fúnebres   Vasijas decoradas que se encuentran en lugares de sepultura. (Capítulo 6–2)

G

Gargoyle/Gárgola   Un ornamento que sobresale de un edificio en la forma de un animal fantástico o criatura grotesca. (Capítulo 10–4)

Genre pieces/Obras de género   Obras que enfocan en un sujeto o escena de la vida diaria. (Capítulo 6–1)

Glaze/Vidriado   Un barniz que parece cristal que se le pone a los objetos de cerámica. (Capítulo 5–1)

H

Hard-Edge painting/Pintura con bordes definidos   Un estilo artístico en el que los contornos están muy nítidos. (Capítulo 17–3)

Harmony/Armonía   El principio artístico que trata de la combinación de elementos para crear una apariencia más tranquila y relajante. (Capítulo 1–3)

Headpieces/Cascos con máscaras   Caretas talladas en madera que se llevaban en la cabeza como una gorra. (Capítulo 9–3)

Hieroglyphic/Jeroglíficos   Un tipo de escritura antigua que usaba dibujos para expresar ideas. (Capítulo 4–3)

I

Illuminations/Iluminaciones   Ilustraciones pintadas a mano que se usaban en los libros. (Capítulo 10–1)

Impressionism/Impresionismo   Un estilo artístico en el que se trataba de capturar los efectos de la luz sobre los objetos, efectos que cambian rápidamente. (Capítulo 14–2)

Intaglio/Entallar   Un método de imprimir en el cual la imagen que se va a grabar se corta en una superficie.

K

Kachina doll/Muñeca Kachina   Una pequeña estatua tallada a mano que se usa para enseñarle a los niños acerca de las ceremonias de los indios pueblo. (Capítulo 13–1)

Kinetic art/Arte cinético Un estilo artístico en el que partes de las obras se mueven por medio de algún tipo de energía. (Capítulo 17–5)

Landscape/Paisaje Un dibujo o pintura principalmente de montañas, árboles u otras escenas de la naturaleza. (Capítulo 14–1)

Line/Línea El elemento del arte que se refiere a la trayectoria de un punto que se mueve a través de un espacio. (Capítulo 1–1)

Linear perspective/Perspectiva lineal El uso de líneas inclinadas para hacer parecer que los objetos están más atrás en el espacio. (Capítulo 11–1)

Loom/Telar Un bastidor que sujeta una serie de hilos entrecruzados. (Capítulo 13–2)

M

Madonna/Madona Una obra que representa a la Virgen María y al Niño Jesús. (Capítulo 11–1)

Media/Medios En inglés, el plural de "medium" que significa medio o recurso. (Capítulo 2–1)

Medium of art/Medio de expresión El material usado para crear una obra de arte. (Capítulo 2–1)

Megalith/Megalito Monumento inmenso de piedra, como Stonehenge en Inglaterra. (Capítulo 4–1)

Menus/Menús Casillas que enumeran las selecciones que ofrece un programa de software. (Capítulo 2–4)

Mihrab/Mihrab Un nicho muy decorado en una mezquita. (Capítulo 8–3)

Minaret/Minarete Una torre delgada desde donde los musulmanes son llamados a rezar. (Capítulo 8–3)

Mixed media/Técnica mixta El uso de más de un medio de expresión en una obra de arte. (Capítulo 3–1)

Mobile/Móvil Una escultura hecha de piezas bidimensionales colgadas de alambres y equilibradas con mucho cuidado. (Capítulo 17–3)

Monolith/Monolito Una estructura hecha de un solo pedazo de piedra. (Capítulo 6–3)

Mosque/Mezquita Un edificio religioso islámico. (Capítulo 8–3)

Motif/Motivo Parte de un diseño que se repite de acuerdo a un patrón o ritmo visual. (Capítulo 6–2)

Movement/Movimiento El principio artístico que trata de cómo crear una sensación de acción y que guía la mirada del observador a través de la obra. (Capítulo 1–3)

Multi-media art/Arte multimedia Una obra que utiliza los instrumentos y las técnicas de dos o más tipos de arte. (Capítulo 17–5)

Muralist/Muralista Un artista que pinta obras grandes directamente en paredes o techos. (Capítulo 16–3)

Neoclassic/Neoclásico Un estilo artístico basado en las artes clásicas de Grecia y Roma antiguas. (Capítulo 14–1)

New Realism/Nuevo realismo Un movimiento artístico que volvió a descubrir la importancia de los detalles realistas. (Capítulo 17–3)

Non-objective/Sin objeto Que no tiene ningún sujeto que se pueda reconocer. (Capítulo 2–1)

Non-objective art/Arte sin objeto Obras que no tienen objetos o sujetos que se puedan identificar con facilidad. (Capítulo 1–2), (Capítulo 16–1)

O

Oil paint/Pintura al óleo Una mezcla de pigmento, aceite de linaza y trementina. (Capítulo 11–3)

Op art/Op-art Un estilo artístico que utiliza líneas y contornos muy precisos para crear ilusiones ópticas. (Capítulo 17–4)

Optical colors/Colores ópticos Los colores que los observadores ven en realidad. (Capítulo 15–1)

Pagoda/Pagoda Una torre que tiene varios pisos de altura y techos cuyos bordes hacen una pequeña curva hacia arriba. (Capítulo 5–3)

Papier-mâché/Papel maché Una técnica de esculpir que utiliza periódicos y pegamento líquido. (Capítulo 9–4)

Perceive/Percibir   Darse cuenta de la naturaleza particular de los objetos por medio de los sentidos. (Capítulo 5–1)

Perceiving/Percibir   Observar detenidamente y profundizar sobre lo que uno ve.

Petroglyphs/Petroglifos   Piedras grabadas y pintadas. (Capítulo 13–1)

Pietà/Piedad   Una obra que representa a María llorando la muerte de Cristo que está en sus brazos. (Capítulo 11–1)

Pigment/Pigmento   El polvo fino que le da color a la pintura. (Capítulo 2–1)

Pixels/Pixeles   Cuadrados individuales en la pantalla de un computador. (Capítulo 2–1)

Pointed arch/Arco ojival   Una construcción de piedra en forma de curva con un pico central. (Capítulo 10–3)

Pointillism/Puntillismo   Una técnica en la que se pintan pequeños puntos de color para crear figuras. (Capítulo 15–2)

Polychrome/Policromo   Que tiene muchos colores. (Capítulo 13–3)

Porcelain/Porcelana   Un tipo de cerámica de grano fino de alta calidad. (Capítulo 5–1)

Portrait/Retrato   Una pintura que representa a una persona. (Capítulo 12–1)

Portfolio/Carpeta de trabajos   Una colección de obras de arte que un estudiante o artista profesional selecciona con cuidado y conserva.

Post and lintel system/Sistema de puntal y dintel   Una manera de construir en la que un madero horizontal se coloca encima de dos postes. (Capítulo 4–3)

Post-Impressionism/Postimpresionismo   Un movimiento artístico que surgió después del impresionismo. (Capítulo 15–1)

Printing plate/Placa de imprimir   Una superficie en la cual se coloca o talla la imagen. (Capítulo 2–1)

Printmaking/Grabar   Una técnica en la que se entinta una imagen en una superficie preparada y se traslada a otra superficie. (Capítulo 2–1)

Proportion/Proporción   El principio artístico que trata de la relación de una parte con otra y con el todo. (Capítulo 1–3)

Pueblos/Pueblos   Los poblados de los indios pueblo que comprendían viviendas de adobe para muchas familias, apiladas una sobre otra. (Capítulo 13–1)

R

Realism/Realismo   Un estilo artístico en el que las escenas y eventos de la vida diaria se pintan tal y como son. (Capítulo 15–3)

Regionalism/Regionalismo   Un estilo artístico que documenta escenas y eventos locales del área o región donde vive el artista. (Capítulo 16–3)

Relief Sculpture/Escultura en relieve   Una escultura que está sólo parcialmente rodeada por espacio vacío. (Capítulo 2–3)

Renaissance/Renacimiento   Un período de gran actividad intelectual y artística. (Capítulo 11–1)

Rhythm/Ritmo   El principio artístico que trata de la repetición de un elemento para hacer parecer que hay actividad o vibración en una obra. (Capítulo 1–3)

Rococo/Rococó   Un estilo artístico que enfatiza el movimiento libre y lleno de gracia, los colores vivos y el contenido alegre. (Capítulo 12–3)

Romanticism/Romanticismo   Un estilo artístico que utiliza lo dramático y exótico como sujetos. (Capítulo 14–1)

Round arch/Arco de medio punto   Una construcción de piedra en forma de curva sobre un espacio vacío. (Capítulo 7–3)

S

Salon/Salón   Una exposición de arte anual. (Capítulo 14–3)

Sand painting/Pintar en la arena   El verter polvo de piedras de distintos colores sobre una sección plana de tierra para crear una imagen o diseño. (Capítulo 13–3)

Screen/Mampara   Un separador movible que se usa como pared para dividir una habitación. (Capítulo 5–3)

Scroll/Rollo   Un carrete largo de pergamino o seda ilustrado. (Capítulo 5–1)

Shape/Contorno   El elemento del arte que se refiere a una imagen de dos dimensiones, destacada por uno o más de los otros elementos visuales del arte. (Capítulo 1–1)

Shoulder masks/Máscaras de hombros   Grandes caretas talladas que descansan en los hombros de los que las llevan puestas. (Capítulo 9–3)

Sketchbook/Cuaderno de bocetos   Un bloc en el que un artista dibuja, toma notas y perfecciona sus ideas para una obra. (Capítulo 2–1)

Social protest painting/Pintura de protesta social
Un estilo artístico que ataca los males de la vida en las grandes ciudades. (Capítulo 17–3)

Solvent/Solvente Un material que se usa para diluir el aglutinante de una pintura. (Capítulo 2–1)

Space/Espacio El elemento del arte que se refiere al área entre, alrededor, arriba, debajo y dentro de las cosas. (Capítulo 1–1)

Stained glass/Vidrio de colores Pedazos de cristal de colores que se sostienen en su sitio con tiras de plomo. (Capítulo 10–3)

Stele/Estela Un monumento hecho de un pedazo de piedra tallada. (Capítulo 4–3)

Stupas/Stupas Templos con cúpulas en forma de colmena. (Capítulo 8–1)

Style/Estilo La manera particular que tiene un artista de utilizar los principios y elementos artísticos y de expresar sus sentimientos e ideas. (Capítulo 3–3)

Stylized/Estilizado Simplificado o exagerado para hacer que se conforme con las reglas de un tipo de diseño. (Capítulo 6–3)

Subject/Sujeto La imagen que un observador puede identificar con facilidad en una obra. (Capítulo 3–1)

Surrealism/Surrealismo El movimiento artístico que exploró el inconsciente y el mundo de los sueños. (Capítulo 17–1)

Symbolism/Simbolismo El uso de imágenes para representar una cualidad o idea. (Capítulo 11–3)

Tempera/Al temple Un medio de pintar en el que se mezcla el pigmento con yemas de huevo y agua, y se pinta con pinceladas muy pequeñas. (Capítulo 10–1)

Tepee/Tipi Una casa portátil. (Capítulo 13–1)

Texture/Textura El elemento del arte que se refiere a la manera en que las cosas se sienten o parece que deben sentirse al tocarlas. (Capítulo 1–1)

Totem pole/Tótem Un tronco tallado con las historias de una familia o clan. (Capítulo 13–1)

Triumphal arch/Arco de triunfo Un monumento construido para celebrar grandes victorias militares. (Capítulo 7–3)

Ukiyo-e/Grabado en madera El nombre japonés de un estilo artístico que significa "ilustraciones de un mundo flotante." (Capítulo 5–3)

Unity/Unidad La manera en que los elementos se arreglan en el medio de expresión, de acuerdo con los principios artísticos, para crear la noción de que la obra está terminada o entera. (Capítulo 1–3)

Urban planning/Planificación urbana Organizar la construcción y servicios de una ciudad para mejor proporcionar lo que el pueblo necesita. (Capítulo 4–4)

Variety/Variedad El principio artístico que trata de la combinación de elementos para crear interés a través de pequeños cambios. (Capítulo 1–3)

Warp/Urdimbre Los hilos verticales que sujeta el telar. (Capítulo 13–2)

Weaving/Tejer Una artesanía en la que se entrelazan hilos para hacer tela u objetos. (Capítulo 13–1)

Weft/Trama Los hilos horizontales que se pasan por arriba y por debajo de los de la urdimbre. (Capítulo 13–2)

Woodblock printing/Grabado en madera Tallar imágenes en bloques de madera para hacer grabados. (Capítulo 5–3)

Yamato-e/Estilo japonés El nombre japonés de un estilo artístico que significa "a la japonesa." (Capítulo 5–3)

Ziggurat/Zigurat Una montaña escalonada hecha de tierra cubierta de ladrillos. (Capítulo 4–4)

Bibliography and Resource List

The following resources provide information in various areas of art and education. The entries are organized by subject and each title is followed by a brief description to help you choose the subjects you wish to read about.

Art History

Anderson, Bjork. *Linnea in Monet's Garden*. New York: R and S Books, 1985. When Linnea visits Claude Monet's garden in Giverny, she gets to stand on the bridge over his lily pond and walk through his house. Later, when she sees his paintings in Paris, she understands what it means for a painter to be called an Impressionist. This delightful book contains photographs of Monet's paintings as well as old family snapshots.

Avi-Yonah, Michael. *Piece by Piece! Mosaics of the Ancient World*. Minneapolis, Minn.: Lerner, 1993. This book describes ancient and modern techniques as well as early Greek, Roman, and Byzantine mosaics.

Barnicoat, John. *Posters: A Concise History*. New York: Thames and Hudson, 1985. The importance of the poster, including its role in various artistic movements.

Capek, Michael. *Artistic Trickery: The Tradition of Trompe L'Oeil Art*. Minneapolis, Minn.: Lerner, 1995. From the ancient Greeks to contemporary designers, artists have long been inspired to play visual jokes. This book lets the reader in on some of the gags.

Davidson, Rosemary. *Take a Look: An Introduction to the Experience of Art*. New York: Penguin, 1993. This book introduces the history, techniques, and functions of art through discussion and reproductions of paintings, photographs, drawings, and design elements. It also includes valuable diagrams and information about seeing and looking at art.

"Introduction to the Renaissance," *Calliope: World History for Young People*. Peterborough, N.H.: Cobblestone Publishing, May/June 1994. This issue of *Calliope* deals with many aspects of the arts and sciences during the Italian Renaissance. It features articles on artists such as Michelangelo and Leonardo da Vinci, rulers such as Isabella d'Este, and composers such as Monteverdi.

Biography

Gilow, Louise. *Meet Jim Henson*. New York: Random House, 1993. The creator of the Muppets, puppet stars of television and the movies, is the subject of this biography.

Greene, Katherine, and Richard Greene. *The Man Behind the Magic: The Story of Walt Disney*. New York: Viking, 1991. This biography of Walt Disney discusses his boyhood on a Missouri farm, his struggles as a young animator, and his building of a motion picture and amusement park empire.

Heslewood, Juliet. *Introducing Picasso: Painter, Sculptor*. Boston: Little, Brown, 1993. By examining the life of the well-known modern painter and the historical and artistic influences on his work, this book gives young readers a sense of who Picasso was and how his art developed. Photographs illustrate his work and his life.

Kastner, Joseph. *John James Audubon*. New York: Harry N. Abrams, 1992. This biography chronicles the life of Audubon from his childhood in France to his adventures in the New World, and shows how he captured these adventures in his artwork.

Neimark, Ann E. *Diego Rivera: Artist of the People*. New York: HarperCollins, 1992. Diego Rivera is brought to life in this comprehensive biography. It is illustrated with reproductions of Rivera's artwork.

Newlands, Anne. *Meet Edgar Degas*. New York: Lippincott, 1988. Degas talks to the reader about 13 of his paintings, describing what it's like to be a young artist in Paris.

Careers

Gordon, Barbara. *Careers in Art: Graphic Design*. VGM Career Horizons, 1992. Provides descriptions of careers in the graphic design field including art directors, book and magazine publishers, industrial designers and production artists. Information on courses and training requirements, job opportunities, and portfolio preparation.

Kaplan, Andrew. *Careers for Artistic Types*. Brookfield, Conn.: Millbrook, 1991. The author interviews 14 people who work in careers that are of interest to young people who like art.

Media and Techniques

James, Jane H. *Perspective Drawing: A Point of View.* 2d ed. Englewood Cliffs, N.J.: Prentice Hall, 1988. For students who want to learn more about perspective.

Kehoe, Michael. *A Book Takes Root: The Making of a Picture Book.* Minneapolis, Minn.: Carolrhoda, 1993. This book traces the process of making a picture book from idea to manuscript to final production. Color photographs accompany the text and make this a fun-to-read and informative book.

Lauer, David A. *Design Basics.* 2d ed. New York: Holt, Rinehart and Winston, 1985. A resource for design students.

Mayer, Ralph. *The Artist's Handbook of Materials and Techniques.* 5th ed., rev. and updated. New York: Viking-Penguin, 1991. An up-to-date reference on art materials and techniques.

Meilach, Dona Z., Jay Hinz, and Bill Hinz. *How to Create Your Own Designs: An Introduction to Color, Form and Composition.* New York: Doubleday and Co., 1975. An excellent introduction to the elements of design.

Patterson, Freeman. *Photography and the Art of Seeing.* Rev. ed. San Francisco: Sierra Club Books, 1990. This book offers good advice on creative photography and is of particular interest to the beginning photographer.

Porter, Albert W. *Expressive Watercolor Techniques.* Worcester, Mass.: Davis Publications, 1982. A useful resource with valuable information on techniques and processes.

Sheaks, Barclay. *Drawing Figures and Faces.* Worcester, Mass.: Davis Publications, 1987. A helpful resource for students who wish to expand their drawing techniques.

Weldon, Jude. *Drawing: A Young Artist's Guide.* London: Dorling Kindersley, 1994. This well-designed and beautifully illustrated book guides the young artist through a wide variety of artistic experiences. Each idea is illustrated with master drawings and paintings. Topics include light and shade, color, imagination, and storytelling.

Multimedia Resources
Laserdiscs

American Art from the National Gallery A collection of 2,600 paintings and sculpture by American artists spanning three centuries.

Louvre Compendium Includes more than 5,000 works of art and 35,000 detailed images in a three-volume series.

Videodisc Volume I: Painting and Drawings

Videodisc Volume II: Sculpture and Objets d'Art

Videodisc Volume III: Antiquities

The National Gallery of Art A guided tour of the National Gallery featuring more than 1,600 masterpieces. A printed catalog and on-screen captions identifying each work are included.

The National Gallery of Art Laserstack Use this laserstack to create your own notes or slide lists for presentations. Works may be arranged by artist, nationality, period, style, date, medium, or subject.

Regard for the Planet A resource for 50,000 photographs documenting world cultures, places, and events of the last 40 years.

CD-ROMs

Art and Music Series Focuses on art and music from medieval times to Surrealism, with text linked to 24-volume student encyclopedia and glossary. Events, challenges, and achievements of each time period are highlighted. (lab packs available) WIN & MAC

National Museum of Women in the Arts Access to 200 artworks from the collection. Available on CD-ROM or videodisc.

With Open Eyes Access to images through time line, geographical location, and close-ups. View 200 multimedia and multicultural artworks from the collection of the Art Institute of Chicago. View any object in a virtual-reality gallery to get a sense of scale. Includes games, music, poetry, and sound effects. WIN & MAC

Index

R

Radial balance, 9, 10, *Fig.* 1–9
Raphael, 164
The Small Cowper Madonna, 164, *Fig.* 11–5
Realism
American, 232–237, *Figs.* 15–6, 15–7, 15–8, 15–9, 15–10
Ashcan school, 248–249
defined, 233
New Realism, 265–266, *Fig.* 17–12
sculpture, 266–267, *Fig.* 17–5
Red/White, 264, 265, 268, *Fig.* 17–10
Reformation, Protestant, 178
Regionalism, 250, *Fig.* 16–10
defined, 250
Relief printing, 21
Relief sculpture, 24, 25, *Fig.* 2–9
African, 132–133, *Fig.* 9–4
ancient Indian, 59, *Fig.* 4–15
ancient Roman, 106, 107, *Fig.* 7–15
defined, 24
frieze, 25, 99, *Fig.* 2–9
Mayan, 84, *Fig.* 6–5
plaster relief, 282
studio lesson, 150–151
technique tips
clay mold for plaster relief, 282
mixing plaster, 282
Rembrandt van Rijn, 182
Portrait of a Lady with an Ostrich Feather Fan, 182, *Fig.* 12–6
Renaissance period, 160–175
defined, 162
in Italy, 162–167
in Northern Europe, 168–173
painting
in Italy, 162–164, *Figs.* 11–2, 11–4, 11–5
in Northern Europe, 168–173, *Figs.* 11–11, 11–12, 11–14
sculpture, in Italy, 164–165, *Figs.* 11–6, 11–7
studio lessons
still life, 166–167
visual symbols, 172–173
Renoir, Pierre Auguste, 9, 208–209, 217, 292
Madame Henriot, 217, *Fig.* 14–6
The Dance at Bougival, 208–209, Chapter 14 Opener
Young Spanish Woman with a Guitar, 9, *Fig.* 1–8

Returning from a Visit, 70, *Fig.* 5–3
Revenge of the Goldfish, 270, *Fig.* 17–18
Rhythm, 11
Rio Isla, castle on, 150, *Fig.* 10–8
Rivera, Diego, 250, 251, 294
artist profile, 294
Liberation of the Peon, 250, 251, 294, *Fig.* 16–11
Rock carvings and paintings. *See* Cave art; Petroglyphs
Rock-Rock, 8, 9, *Fig.* 1–7
Rococo style, 184–189
architecture, 184, 185, *Fig.* 12–9
defined, 184
painting
in France, 184–186, 188, *Figs.* 12–10, 12–11, 12–13, 12–14
in Spain, 187
studio activity, 187
studio lesson, 188–189
Rodin, Auguste, 218, 219
Claude Lorrain, 218, 219, *Fig.* 14–8
Roman art. *See* Ancient Roman art
Romanesque period, 146–151
architecture, 146–147, *Figs.* 10–1, 10–2, 10–3, 10–4
castles, 146–147, *Fig.* 10–1
churches, 147, *Figs.* 10–3, 10–4
studio lesson, 150–151
walled cities, 147, *Fig.* 10–2
illuminations, 144, 149, *Fig.* 10–6
painting, 149, *Fig.* 10–6
sculpture, 148, *Fig.* 10–5
Romanticism, 211–213
Room in New York, 40, 41, *Fig.* 3–6
Roses, Bonvolvulus, Poppies, and Other Flowers in an Urn on a Stone Ledge, 181, *Fig.* 12–5b
Round arches
ancient Roman, 104
defined, 104
Roshu, Fakaya, 74,
Tsuta-no-hosomìchi (The Ivy Lane), 74, *Fig.* 5–9
Rousseau, Henri
The Equatorial Jungle, xviii
Rubbing, technique tips, 286
Rubens, Peter Paul, 180–181
The Assumption of the Virgin, 180–181, *Fig.* 12–4
Rugs
Persian or knotted-pile, 123, *Fig.* 8–13
studio activity, 123

Runners in a Race, 100, 101, *Fig.* 7–5
Ruler Dressed as Chac-Xib-Chac and the Holmul Dancer, 84, *Fig.* 6–5
Ruysch, Rachel
Roses, Bonvolvulus, Poppies…, 181, *Fig.* 12–5b
Ryder, Albert Pinkham, 234, 235, 294
artist profile, 294
Moonlight Marine (Toilers of the Sea), 234, 235, 294, *Fig.* 15–8

S

Sacred Rain Arrow, 192–193, Chapter 13 Opener
Safety tips
chalk, 247
cutting tools, 109
markers, 71
paints, 13, 102, 230
Sage, Kay, 256, 257
I Saw Three Cities, 256, Chapter 17 Opener
Saint Gerome in His Study, 169, *Fig.* 11–11
Salon
defined, 216
Impressionism and, 216–217
San Carlo alle Quattro Fontane, 178, *Fig.* 12–1
Sanchi, Great Stupa at, 114, *Fig.* 8–1
Santa Maria la Real Church, 148, *Fig.* 10–5
Sarcophagus of Tutankhamun, 64, *Connections*
Scenes from the Life of King David, 145, *Chapter 10 Opener*
School tempera. *See* Poster paint
School's Out, 254, *Connections*
Science connections, 14, 15, 31, 64, 143, 207, 222
Scissors, safety tip for, 109
Scoring paper, 284, 286
Screen printing, 21, 308–309
Scroll
Chinese scroll painting, 68, 70, *Fig.* 5–3
defined, 68
Japanese scroll painting, 74, *Fig.* 5–9
Sculpture, 24–25
abstract, 261, *Fig.* 17–6
African
figure sculptures, 130–135, *Figs.* 9–2, 9–3, 9–4, 9–5, 9–6

Index

Credits

Student Art Contributors

The following students contributed exemplary works for Studio Activities and Studio Lessons.

Figure 1-12 **Julie Brown**, El Modena High School, Orange, CA; Figure 2-15 **Leanne Bellar**, Medina Elementary, Bothell, WA; Figure 4-8 **Brenna Sullivan**, St. Athanasius School, Evanston, IL; Figure 5-4 **Cathleen Cramer**, St. Athanasius School, Evanston, IL; Figure 5-13 **Allison Hengemuhle**, Junction Middle School, Palo Cedro, CA; Figure 5-13 **Rachel Simon**, Junction Middle School, Palo Cedro, CA; Figure 5-13 **Jenny Spencer**, Junction Middle School, Palo Cedro, CA; Figure 6-9 **Kayci Mackey**, Junction Middle School, Palo Cedro, CA; Figure 6-19 **Eric Sargeant**, El Modena High School, Orange, CA Figure 6-19 **Shelly Eaddy**, South Florence High School, Florence, SC; Figure 8-16 **Annie Medina**, El Modena High School, Orange, CA; Figure 8-7 **Emilia Hofmeister**, St. Athanasius School, Evanston, IL; Figure 8-7 **Catherine Harr**, St. Athanasius School, Evanston, IL; Figure 8-7 **Iwona Klapa**, Akron Central School, Akron, NY; Figure 8-7 **Andrea Hallbach**, Akron Central School, Akron, NY; Figure 8-7 **Jamie Jacobs**, Akron Central School, Akron, NY; Figure 9-11 **Chris DeNardo**, St. Athanasius School, Evanston, IL; Figure 9-13 **Crystal Crain**, Juncton Middle School, Palo Cedro, CA; Figure 10-9 **Anthony Kaster**, Junction Middle School, Palo Cedro, CA; Figure 10-15 **Jason Markus**, Valleywood School, Kentwood, MI; Figure 11-9 **Michael Morel**, St. Athanasius School, Evanston, IL; Figure 12-7 **Pedro Arcos**, El Modena High School, Orange, CA ; Figure 14-9 **Jack Nondorf**, St. Athanasius School, Evanston, IL; Figure 14-11 **Tim Zazynski**, Akron Central School, Akron, NY; Figure 15-5 **Paul Sargeant**, El Modena High School, Orange, CA; Figure 15-11 **Andrea Sagerman**, Akron Central School, Akron, NY; Figure 16-6 **Annie Medina**, El Modena High School, Orange, CA; Figure 16-13 **Patrick Kennelly**, St. Athanasius School, Evanston, IL; Figure 17-17 **Susan Ramsden**, El Modena High School, Orange, CA; Figure S-2 **Ben Scannell**, Skyview Junior High, Bothell, WA; Figure S-4 **Cassie Armstrong**, El Modena High School, Orange, CA; Figure S-7 **Sean Kebely**, Medina Elementary, Bothell, WA;

Artists Rights Society (ARS)
Georges Braque, *Still Life: Le Jour*, 1929, 246, Fig. 16-5 ©1997 Artists Rights Society (ARS), New York/ADAGP, Paris; **Alexander Calder**, *Zarabanda (Un Disco Blanco)*, 266, Fig. 17-3 ©1997 Artists Rights Society (ARS), New York/ADAGP, Paris; **Marc Chagall**, *Green Violinist*, 1923-24, 4, Fig. 1-3 ©1997 Artists Rights Society (ARS), New York/ADAGP, Paris; **Willem de Kooning**, *Merritt Parkway*, 34, Fig. 3-1 ©1997 Willem de Kooning Revocable Trust/Artists Rights Society (ARS), New York; **Arshile Gorky**, *Golden Brown*, 264, Fig. 17-9 ©1997 Estate of Arshile Gorky/Artists Rights Society (ARS), New York; **Luis Jiménez**, *Vaquero*, 16, Chapter 2 Opener ©1997 Luis Jimenez/Artists Rights Society (ARS), New York; **Käthe Kollwitz**, *The Mothers*, 244, Fig. 16-3 ©1997 Artists Rights Society (ARS), New York/VG Bild-Kunst, Bonn; **Richard Lindner**, *Rock-Rock*, 8, Fig. 1-7 ©1997 Artists Rights Society (ARS), New York/ADAGP, Paris; **René Magritte**, *Time Transfixed*, 262, Fig. 17-7 ©1997 C. Herscovici, Brussels/Artists Rights Society (ARS), New York; **Henri Matisse**, *Pianist and Checker Players*, 242, Fig. 16-1 ©1997 Succession H. Matisse, Paris/Artists Rights Society (ARS), New York; **Joan Miró**, *Dutch Interior*, 259, Fig. 17-2 ©1997 Artists Rights Society (ARS), New York/ADAGP, Paris; **Joan Miró**, *Femme*, 27, Fig. 2-13 ©1997 Artists Rights Society (ARS), New York/ADAGP, Paris; **Pablo Picasso**, *Mandolin and Guitar*, 42, Fig. 3-7 ©1997 Estate of Pablo Picasso/Artists Rights Society (ARS), New York

Photography: **R. A. Acharya/Dinodia** 114; **Art Resource**, New York 25T, 96, 152, 178; **Bill Ballenberg** 89L; **Gary Braash** 73(3); **Jack Breed** 201R; **Digital Art**/Westlight 304; **Laima Druskis** 299L; **Robert Frerck**/Odyssey, Chicago 55B, 83T, 84T, 90, 105(2), 115B, 122(3), 146, 147T, 148, 150R; **Ann Garvin** 297(2), 298(2), 299(2), 301(2), 302(2), 303L; **Giraudon**/Art Resource, New York 49T, 149, 187, 190; **Jack Stein Grove**/Photo Edit 91T; Erich Lessing/Art Resource, New York 64, 163, 176, 182; Erich Lessing/Photo Edit 106L; **Ray Lutz** 196L; **Bruno Maso/Bill Roberts**/Photo Edit 185T; **Douglas Mazonowica** 52; **Stephen McBrady**/Photo Edit 300R; **National Museum of American Art**, DC/Art Resource 254; **Henry Nelson** 20T; **Nimatallah**/Art Resource 100R, 174; **Dennis O'Clair**/Tony Stone Images 296; **Odyssey** 115B; **RIL**/Westlight 299; **M. Richards** 303R; **Bill Roberts**/Photo Edit 150L, 153B; **Scala**/Art Resource, New York 61, 85T, 100L, 101, 107T, 154B, 165T, 172, 179L, 185; **Tektronix** 300L; **Susan Van Etten**/Photo Edit 73R; **Westlight**/Comnet 50B; **Nick Wheeler**/Black Star 60; **R. White** 49B; **Lee White**, selected student works.

Maps: Eureka Cartography, Berkeley, California